To Bind Up the Wounds

To Bind Up the Wounds

CATHOLIC SISTER NURSES
IN THE U.S. CIVIL WAR

Sister Mary Denis Maher

Louisiana State University Press

BATON ROUGE

Louisiana Paperback Edition, 1999
08 07 06 05 04 03 02 01 00 99
5   4   3   2   1

Library of Congress Cataloging-in-Publication Data

Maher, Mary Denis.
    To bind up the wounds: Catholic sister nurses in the
U.S. Civil War / Mary Denis Maher. —Louisiana pbk. ed.
        p.   cm.
    Originally published: New York: Greenwood Press, 1989.
    Includes bibliographical references and index.
    ISBN 0-8071-2439-7 (pbk. : alk. paper)
    1. United States—History—Civil War, 1861–1865—
Medical care. 2. United States—History—Civil War,
1861–1865—War work—Catholic Church. 3. United
States—History—Civil War, 1861–1865—Women.
4. Monasticism and religious orders for women—
United States—History—19th century. 5. Nursing—
United States—History—19th century. I. Title
E621.M34 1999   99-33889
973.7'75—dc21   CIP

The paper in this book meets the guidelines for
permanence and durability of the Committee on
Production Guidelines for Book Longevity of
the Council on Library Resources. ∞

Contents

Acknowledgments

To the Sisters of Charity of St. Augustine for personal and financial support in this as in many other projects in my life, my prayerful gratitude.

To the archivists of all the religious communities for generous and easy access to their archives, my overwhelming appreciation. Special thanks to Sr. Romauld Burns of the St. Louis Sisters of Mercy for arranging her schedule for me to use material in Vicksburg, Mississippi; to Sr. Campion Kuhn of the Holy Cross Sisters, Saint Mary's, Notre Dame, Indiana; to Sr. Aloysia Dugan of the Daughters of Charity, Emmitsburg, Maryland; to Sisters Alberta and Anne Francis of the Sisters of Charity of Our Lady of Mercy, Charleston, South Carolina; and to Sr. Laura Marie Watson of the Sisters of Charity of Cincinnati, Ohio. They all shared both their extensive archives and their community life with me during the process of this work.

To the personnel of the Cleveland Public Library, especially in the History Department, who assisted me in utilizing the vast resources of its holdings; and to the staff of the medical library at St. Vincent Charity Hospital, Cleveland, who quickly secured copies of many difficult-to-find nursing and medical journal articles, my special gratitude.

To Fr. William Burn, archivist of the Diocese of Charleston, South Carolina, for the opportunity to leisurely and comfortably research the papers of Bishop Patrick Lynch, my deep appreciation.

To Roberta Wollons at Case Western Reserve University, Cleveland, Ohio, for her genuine interest and persistent questions on earlier versions of this book, my gratitude. To Case Western Reserve University for a Graduate Alumni Award which funded a research trip to Charleston, South Carolina, my thanks.

To Sr. Michael Francis, OSU, and Ann Trivisonno, friends and colleagues at Ursuline College, Pepper Pike, Ohio, and Terry Peck Maher, my sister-in-law, for their kindly but perceptive comments and judicious editing, especially when my own interest and energy flagged, my continued pledge of mutual support.

To Teddi Denk, who first deciphered my innumerable drafts and put everything on the word processor, to Sr. Allan Kenzig, CSA, who later assisted me in making the revisions, and to Sr. Mary Patricia Barrett, CSA, for the generous use of the facilities of CSA Health and Human Services, Richfield, Ohio, my utmost admiration and personal thanks.

And as always, to my parents, William and Iola Maher, for their love and belief in me, my love and prayers.

To Bind Up the Wounds

Introduction

"It seems strange that [the sisters] can do with honor what is wrong for other Christian women to do," mused Confederate nurse Kate Cumming, struggling to understand why she could not obtain enough women to help nurse the wounded Southern soldiers.[1] Not everyone had the same perceptions about the work of the sisters. A Vermont senator in 1871 sought to disallow funds to rebuild a war-ravaged orphanage for the Sisters of Charity of Our Lady of Mercy. Their cause had been advanced because of their unwavering care of both Union and Confederate soldiers in Charleston, South Carolina, but he dismissed the claim by saying, "They have done no more than their duty"—any patriotic citizen would have done as much, he felt.[2]

Nevertheless, almost fifty years later, in 1921, another Congressman, Rhode Island Representative Ambrose Kennedy, would speak on behalf of establishing a monument in Washington, D.C., for the "Nuns of the Battlefield,"[3] whose "services were not only conspicuously national; they were also singular and unique."[4] These nuns were part of the almost 600 Roman Catholic sisters of twenty-one separate religious communities of twelve different orders who nursed sick and wounded soldiers during the US Civil War, 1861–1865.[5]

Were the sisters pathbreakers for women's activities, as Cumming suggested, and thus deserving of honor and respect? Were they just ordinary citizens with special skills doing their patriotic duty as the senator implied, and thus not worthy of any special consideration? Or were their services singular and unique, as Representative Kennedy testified, qualifying them for a national monument?

Together, these three comments by outside observers—one a nurse who had direct contact with the sisters, one a Northern senator who opposed a Southern state's petition for restitution, and one far removed from the battles or the politics of the Civil War who was impressed by the historical data—identify three major aspects of the sisters' services: commitment to religious duty, skilled service, and their singular and unique example for other women.

The mission of the sisters in nineteenth-century America was to carry out works of Christian charity by teaching, caring for orphans, nursing the sick, and providing spiritual assistance for the dying. Particularly in their mission to serve the sick, the sisters could be considered pathbreakers. Even though nursing one's own family members was an acceptable and expected occupation, nursing as a profession or lifelong commitment was almost unknown, except among Catholic women's religious communities. However, in a sense, they could also be merely doing their duty. For example, some sisters had nursed wounded soldiers in the Revolutionary War and the War of 1812, as well as in the cholera epidemics between 1830 and 1860. In addition, they had established some twenty-eight hospitals by 1860.[6] Yet the sisters were indeed unique and singular among the few thousand women who cared for the sick during the Civil War. They demonstrated not only a strong religious commitment in their work on the battlefield, in the government hospitals, and on military transports, but also very practical skills, which enhanced this service.

Thus, in order to understand the unique role and special function of the sisters in the Civil War, four fundamental questions must be answered:

Who were the religious communities of sisters who served in the war and how did they become involved?

Where did the sisters nurse and what did "nursing" consist of during the Civil War era?

How were the sisters and their work regarded by the doctors, other female nurses, the military, and governmental officials and the soldiers themselves?

Why were the sisters willing to serve and how did they view their services?

Answering these questions is difficult since little has been written about these sisters and their service. In spite of the qualifications the sisters brought to their Civil War work, neither the history of religion in America,[7] (including the history of American Catholicism),[8] nor the history of nineteenth-century American women[9] give more than scant reference to Catholic sisters prior to or during the war.[10] Catholic hospitals or other health-care institutions do not receive even a heading in the index of such works. Neither is there a single volume covering the history of

Catholic health care in the United States,[11] as there is for education or Catholic social service. While the history of nursing[12] and of Civil War medical history[13] offers some brief mention of the sisters' services rendered during the war, the pages generally are as mute as the cannons now in the Civil War parks.[14]

Similarly, literature on other women in the Civil War is also limited. Writing shortly after the war, historian Frank Moore remarked, "The story of the war will never be fully or fairly written if the achievements of women in it are untold. They do not figure in the official reports; they are not gazetted for deeds as gallant as were ever done; the names of thousands are unknown beyond the neighborhood where they live or the hospitals where they loved to labor; yet there is no feature in our war more credible to us as a nation, none from its positive newness so well worthy of record."[15]

Even though more than a hundred articles based on women's experiences were published between 1865–1914, mostly firsthand accounts by female nurses, teachers of freedmen, U.S. Sanitary Commission workers and others,[16] a twentieth-century women's historian could still lament that while "the Civil War has produced tons of literature, there are few studies of the contributions of women."[17]

Unlike their more prolific female nurse counterparts, the sisters left little written material concerning their experiences in the Civil War. Fires, lack of awareness of the historical value of such documents, little desire or incentive for the sisters to record their experiences, and an overriding sense that they were simply extending their works of charity by caring for the sick and providing assistance for the dying left little material from which to study and evaluate the experiences of these women.[18] Sufficient material does exist, however, in primary and selected secondary sources relating to the official records of the Civil War and in the official medical and surgical history of the war. In addition, secondary sources relating to medical history, nursing accounts, and other memoirs do exist. These sources provide sufficient evidence to construct a composite picture of the Roman Catholic sister nurse during the Civil War.

NOTES

1. Kate Cumming, *Kate: The Journal of a Confederate Nurse*, ed. Richard B. Harwell (Baton Rouge: Louisiana State University Press, 1959), p. 178.

2. *Congressional Globe*, Third Session of the Forty-first Congress, Mar. 3, 1871, pp. 2008–2009.

3. The monument was erected at the corner of Rhode Island and Connecticut Avenues in 1924 and depicted, in bas-relief, sisters from the twelve different orders of the twenty-one separate communities who nursed in the war.

The efforts of Mrs. Mary Ryan Jolly, supported by the Ladies Auxiliary of the Ancient Order of Hibernians, had made the research and monument possible.

4. Hon. Ambrose Kennedy, "Speech of Hon. Ambrose Kennedy of Rhode Island in the House of Representatives, Mon., Mar. 18, 1918," *Federal Register*, Mar. 18, 1918, Washington, D.C.: U.S. Government Publications, 1918, p. 4.

5. The term "nun" and "sister" are both encompassed by the term "women religious." Until 1983 the former terms had precise and distinct meaning in canon law: "nuns" were those with solemn vows of poverty, chastity, and obedience with strict rules of enclosure and devoted completely to lives of prayer; "sisters" had simple vows, modified rules of enclosure, and were engaged in charitable works in addition to their focus on prayer. "Order" was the term applied to a group with solemn vows, and "community" was used for sisters in simple vows, as well as for a smaller unit of sisters within an order or a larger community. However, in common speech, the terms, "sister," "nun," and "woman religious" were and are used interchangeably and will be so used here unless their canonical meaning is intended and specifically noted.

6. Ann Doyle, "Nursing by Religious Orders in the United States," *American Journal of Nursing* 29 (July-Dec. 1929): 775–786, 959–969, 1085–1095, 1197–1207, 1331–1343, 1466–1484.

7. See Sydney Ahlstrom, *A Religious History of the American People* (New Haven: Yale University Press, 1972); Edwin Gaustad, ed., *A Documentary History of Religion in America*, 2 vols. (Grand Rapids: William B. Eerdmans, 1982); Robert Handy, *A History of the Churches in the United States and Canada* (New York: Oxford University Press, 1977); Winthrop Hudson, *Religion in America: An Historical Account of the Development of American Religious Life*, 3rd ed. (New York: Charles Scribner's Sons, 1981); Martin E. Marty, *Pilgrims in Their Own Land: 500 Years of Religion in America* (New York: Penguin Books, 1984); Mark Noll et al., eds., *Eerdman's Handbook to Christianity in America* (Grand Rapids: William B. Eerdmans, 1983).

8. See Jay P. Dolan, *The American Catholic Experience: A History from Colonial Times to the Present* (Garden City, NY: Doubleday, 1985); John Tracy Ellis, *American Catholicism*, 2nd ed. (Chicago: University of Chicago Press, 1969), p. 293; James Hennesey, *American Catholics: A History of the Roman Catholic Community in the United States* (New York: Oxford University Press, 1981); John Gilmary Shea, *History of the Catholic Church in the United States*, 4 vols., (New York: John G. Shea) 1886–92.

Dolan and Hennesey do give some attention to women, as do other recent works, such as John Tracy Ellis and Robert Trisco, eds. rev. ed., *A Guide to American Catholic History* (Milwaukee: Bruce Publishing Co., 1982); James Hennesey, *American Catholic Bibliography, 1970–1982* (Notre Dame: Cushwa Center Working Papers, Series 12, No. 1, Fall, 1982) and the *Supplement to American Catholic Bibliography*, Series 14, No. 1, Fall, 1983.

9. In general, little is written on women in religion. For exceptions to this, see Janet Wilson James, ed., *Women in American Religion* (Philadelphia: University of Pennsylvania Press, 1980). Several of the twelve articles in this book originally appeared in *American Quarterly*. See also Rosemary Radford Ruether and Rosemary Skinner, eds., *Women and Religion in America: A Documentary History*, 3 vols. (San Francisco: Harper and Row, 1981, 1983, 1986). Volume I deals with the

nineteenth century, Volume II with the colonial and revolutionary periods, and Volume III with the twentieth century. The volumes have excellent footnotes, an index, and illustrations. There are, of course, some individual volumes on women in various religious organizations in the nineteenth century. See R. Pierce Beaver, *All Loves Excelling* (now published under the title *American Protestant Women in World Missions: History of the First Feminist Movement in North America*) (Grand Rapids: Eerdmans, 1968), rev. ed. 1980. Amanda Porterfield, *Feminine Spirituality in America* (Philadelphia: Temple University Press, 1980).

10. For notable attempts to address the void, see Sr. Mary Ewens, *The Role of the Nun in Nineteenth-Century America* (New York: Arno, 1978); Sr. Barbara Misner, "A Comparative Social Study of the Members and Apostolates of the First Eight Permanent Communities of Women Religious within the Boundaries of the United States, 1790–1850." Ph. D. Diss., Catholic University of America, 1981; Margaret Susan Thompson, in "Discovering Foremothers: Sisters, Society and the American Catholic Experience," *U.S. Catholic Historian* 5 (Summer/Fall 1986): 273–290, indicates that she is working on an integrated history to be published by Oxford University Press, entitled *The Yoke of Grace: American Nuns and Social Change, 1808–1917.*

11. See Ursula Stepsis, CSA, and Dolores Liptak, RSM, eds., *Pioneer Healers: The History of Women Religious in American Health Care* (New York: Continuum-Crossroad, 1989). The most extensive treatment of Catholic hospitals is contained in the dated John O'Grady, *Catholic Charities in the United States* (Washington, D.C. 1930, rpt. Arno, 1971), pp. 183–212.

12. The classic history of nursing is Mary Adelaide Nutting and Livinia Dock, *A History of Nursing*, 2 vols. (New York: G.P. Putnam's Sons, 1907–1912). See also Anne Austin, *History of Nursing Source Book* (New York: G. P. Putnam's Sons, 1957); Vern and Bonnie Bullough, *The Care of the Sick: The Emergence of Modern Nursing* (New York: Prodest, 1978); Josephine A. Dolan, *Nursing in Society: A Historical Perspective* (Philadelphia: W. B. Saunders, 1978); Philip and Beatrice Kalish, *The Advance of American Nursing* (Boston: Little Brown, 1978).

13. George W. Adams, *Doctors in Blue: The Medical History of the Union Army in the Civil War* (New York: Henry Schuman, 1952); Horace H. Cunningham, *Doctors in Grey: The Confederate Medical Service* (Baton Rouge: Louisiana State University Press, 1958).

14. Ellen Ryan Jolly, *Nuns of the Battlefield* (Providence, RI: Providence Visitor, 1929). However, the work, though using archival material and personal interviews, has no footnotes and reflects Jolly's uncritical admiration and praise for those who nursed.

15. Frank Moore, *Women of the War: Their Heroism and Self-Sacrifice* (Hartford, CT: S. S. Scranton, 1867), pp. v-vi.

16. Mary Elizabeth Massey, *Bonnet Brigades* (New York: Alfred A. Knopf, 1966), p. 187.

17. Catherine Clinton, *The Other Civil War: American Women in the Nineteenth Century* (New York: Hill and Wang, 1984), p. 219.

18. See letter to the author, dated Nov. 29, 1985, from archivist Sr. Mary Hyacinth Breaux, O. Carm., for a typical response to a request for archival materials. She wrote, "We know that a great deal of Archival material was destroyed in Thibodaux [Louisiana], because people did not know the value of

such things." See also letter dated Nov. 15, 1985, from archivist Sr. Constance Golden, RSM, stating, "The nightmare of every archivist apparently occurred. Some well-intentioned person typed from the original and then disposed (!!!) of it."

Nuns of the Battlefield Monument, Washington, D.C. Columbia Historical Society, David Blume, photographer; Ms. 367, James M. Goode *Outdoor Sculpture of Washington* Papers.

Daughters of Charity with doctors and soldiers. Satterlee Hospital, Philadelphia. Courtesy, St. Joseph's Provincial House Archives.

Daughters of Charity in the kitchen. Satterlee Hospital, Philadelphia. Courtesy, St. Joseph's Provincial House Archives.

Daughters of Charity outside the kitchen and storeroom. Satterlee Hospital, Philadelphia. Courtesy, St. Joseph's Provincial House Archives.

Holy Cross Sisters on the Red Rover hospital ship. *Harper's Weekly*, May 9, 1863.

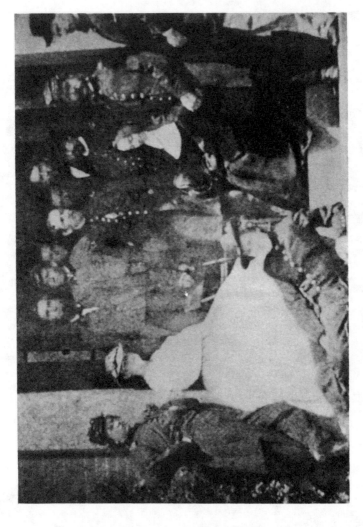

Sister Colette O'Connor, RSM, with doctors and soldiers. Douglas Military Hospital, Washington D.C. Courtesy, Archives, Sisters of Mercy, Province of Baltimore.

1

Catholic Sisters in Mid-Nineteenth Century America

"What or *who* are they?" queried a curious group of onlookers surrounding five Daughters of Charity coming to Marietta, Georgia, to nurse Confederate soldiers in 1863. "Are they men or women?" the bystanders continued, wondering what kind of strange uniform the country had adopted. "Surely, the enemy will run from them," another responded. Finally, when one sister spoke, many of the people clapped their hands, shouting, "She spoke! She spoke!"[1]

This Civil War incident reflects the fact that Catholic nuns in the United States at mid-nineteenth century were little known and less understood by most Protestant and even Catholic Americans. However, the truth is that in the 1850s, just prior to the war, Catholic sisters did belong to the worlds of the immigrant Roman Catholic and of nineteenth-century American women, sharing some of the qualities and characteristics of each. They were organizers of educational, health, and social-service institutions in a period when some of their female Protestant counterparts were going to foreign lands as missionaries. In addition, they were women possessed of the qualities of piety, purity, submissiveness, and domesticity in a time when those qualities were set as a feminine ideal by male and female alike. Yet, unlike their Protestant contemporaries, these sisters had lifelong vows of poverty, celibacy, and obedience, were dedicated to a life of service to others, and lived in community with like-minded women. Thus, they were a striking alternative to women in the socially expected and approved married state. However, the sisters were generally abhorred, misunderstood, or criticized as aberrations of foreign devils because of the apparent constrictions of their lifestyle, as symbolized by their strange garb, their structured life, and the convent walls. Thus, the real values of sisterhood, and the sisters' special opportunities for service, which were unavailable to other nineteenth-century women, were unknown or overlooked. Only through the experiences of the Civil War would the sisters' qualities of committed service, experience in caring for the sick and educating others, and the ability to organize and move on quick notice become visible to many Americans.

To understand the change that the Civil War made in the public's experience and understanding of the sisters, the larger context of American Catholicism must be examined. The Roman Catholic Church in America to which these sisters belonged might best be characterized by Alexis de Tocqueville, himself of French Catholic background. Struck by the religious atmosphere of the country, de Tocqueville, in his visit to the United States in 1830, characterized the more than one million American Catholics he found as "very submissive and very sincere . . . loyal in the practice of their worship and full of zeal and ardor for their beliefs."[2] Catholics were found by the observant Frenchman to "form the most republican and democratic of all classes in the United States." Explaining this phenomenon, de Tocqueville said Protestantism promoted independence, while Catholicism emphasized human equality. "It mingles all classes of society at the foot of the same altar, just as they are mingled in the sight of God," he wrote.[3] Poverty, social inferiority, and minority status all contributed, de Tocqueville concluded, to the development of the democratic spirit among American Catholics, even if the nature of their beliefs may not have given them "any strong impulsion toward democratic and republican opinions."[4]

Between 1785 and the beginning of the Civil War, these Catholics grew from a group of twenty-five thousand to a church of over one million, with nearly a third coming to the United States in the decade before the attack on Fort Sumter.[5] Church historian John Tracy Ellis characterized American Catholicism at mid-century as the religious faith of a minority who suffered from traditional prejudice. Furthermore, their predominantly foreign cast caused increased attacks, which accentuated the differences of Catholics from their fellow citizens. Politically, Catholics were usually Democratic, since that party was friendliest to their interests. Generally, they belonged to the poorer class and lived in the rising industrial towns of the East and Midwest. Nevertheless, they enjoyed America's religious freedom, which enabled Catholicism to expand without interference from government.[6]

To serve this church, priests and nuns from European countries were recruited and supported until enough Americans could join or start their own seminaries and communities.[7] While the clergy largely organized and serviced parishes, the women religious, who numbered over 1,500 by mid-century, had established forty-one communities of twenty-three orders, whose main purpose was to establish and staff institutions of education, health, and social welfare.[8]

The first community in the United States was the French Ursulines, who in 1727 pioneered education for women with a female academy for ages seven to fifteen in New Orleans.[9] They were followed in 1790 by cloistered Carmelites at Port Tobacco, Maryland, but the majority of the early communities were active religious of simple vows devoted to works of education and charity, such as care of orphans and the sick poor. Though many of the early communities were European in origin, primarily French and Irish, and later German, American women soon joined or started their own communities. The commitment of women's religious communities, both those founded by American women and those of mixed immigrant and American women,[10] was strong from the beginning in responding to needs of the evolving American Church. For example, Saint Elizabeth Bayley Seton, a wife, mother, and convert from the Episcopal Church, began the first American community—the Sisters of Charity—in 1809, the first free parochial school in 1810, and the first Catholic orphanage in 1810 in Emmitsburg, Maryland. The community later established the first Catholic hospital in St. Louis in 1828.[11]

By 1812, two other American communities, the Sisters of Loretto and the Sisters of Charity of Nazareth, were established in the Kentucky wilderness. They were followed ten years later by Dominican Sisters at Saint Catharine, Kentucky. Completing the roster of active communities founded by American-born women or women who had been assimilated into American life were the Baltimore-based Oblate Sisters of Providence, a community of Black sisters formed to work among their own people, and the Sisters of Charity of Our Lady of Mercy, located in Charleston, South Carolina, both begun in 1829.[12] Seton's Sisters of Charity (later called Daughters of Charity), the Sisters of Charity of Nazareth, and the Sisters of Charity of Our Lady of Mercy were involved in education, health care, and social service; the Sisters of Loretto and the Dominicans were primarily teachers of young women.[13]

Charitable institutions staffed largely by these active sisters' orders, as well as by their independent branches, and other communities that started before the war preserved the religious faith of the immigrants and assisted them in adapting to their new environment, thus partially insulating them from prejudice.[14] For example, increasing immigration and periodic epidemics demonstrated the need for Catholic hospitals. Thus, St. Vincent's Hospital was established in New York City in 1836 so that poor immigrants could have spiritual comfort and relief from the conditions that Catholics often faced in Protestant hospitals.[15] Medical historian Charles Rosenberg described some of these conditions and underscored the reasons that prompted Catholics to build their own institutions and find sisters dedicated to the corporal works of mercy to staff them. He cited, as an example, a lay Boston trustee at Massachusetts General Hospital in 1851 who, alarmed at the number of Irish-Catholic laborers treated there, suggested that it might be advisable to build a "cheap building" or rent one in the vicinity of the hospital in order to care for these "ignorant immigrants." "They cannot appreciate," he explained, "and do not really want some of those conveniences which would be deemed essential by most of our native citizens."[16]

The famous preacher Reverend Lyman Beecher epitomized many views about Catholics when he said, in 1834: "The Catholic Church holds now in darkness and bondage nearly half the civilized world ... It is the most skillful, powerful, dreadful system of corruption to those who wield it, and of slavery and debasement to those who live under it."[17]

Anti-Catholic lectures, tracts, newspapers, riots, and burnings were often the result of the antagonism.[18] Among the more popular of anti-Catholic writings were the titillating tales of convent horrors, promoted by the lecture-circuit authors of two of the most famous novels. Rebecca Reed's *Six Months in a Convent* (1835)[19] offered tales of austere practices, and Maria Monk's *Awful Disclosures of the Hotel Dieu Nunnery in Montreal* (1836)[20] graphically described fables of infants, born of priest-nun relationships, murdered and buried in convent basements.

As Mary Ewens has demonstrated in her study of this literature, sisters, especially in the three decades preceding the Civil War, were generally depicted as "mournful prisoners doomed by unhappy love affairs to lives of sinful indolence."[21] The purpose of these publications, from the Protestants' point of view, was well stated in the preface to Reed's novel, which said that if the book has:

this blessed effect in guarding the young women of our land against the dangers of early impressions imbibed at convents in favor of a form of religion which is to be *tolerated* but never to be *encouraged* in a free country, it will do more even than the laws can do in suppressing such outrages as the riot at Charleston; for if Protestant parents will resolve to educate their daughters at Protestant schools and patronize no more Nunneries, then no more Nunneries will be established in this country and there will be none for reckless mobs to destroy.[22]

In spite of the charitable works of Catholic sisters, much of the knowledge about them was derived from this popular literature, largely the work of anti-Catholic writers or self-styled "escaped nuns," rather than from personal experience. While anti-Catholic incidents and literature of the period disclosed a fear of Catholicism far out of proportion to the actual power and motivations of American Catholics, historian Amanda Porterfield has suggested that the fear was often linked to an obsession with Catholic "perversions of womanhood." Because of the convent exposés,

Porterfield concluded, "imaginative Protestants perceived convent chastity as an escape from the Christian responsibilities of marriage and as an excuse for sexual promiscuity between monks and nuns."[23]

The emotionalism engendered by these tales, coupled with public anti-Catholic sentiment, was perhaps epitomized in the burning of the Ursuline Convent in Charlestown, Massachusetts, on August 11, 1834. The incident was apparently inspired by misinformation circulated in the Boston area by Rebecca Reed, who had been dismissed as unsuited for religious life after a six-month period. In addition, it was incorrectly rumored that Elizabeth Harrison, a sister who had left briefly because of a nervous breakdown and then re-entered, was being held by force against her will. A mob of about fifty men, who first looted the building, proceeded to desecrate the chapel and frighten the sisters and pupils who got out; they ultimately burned the four-story academy and convent. Subsequent trials were considered farcical, the legislature refused to compensate the diocese, and the Ursulines were forced to return to Canada.[24]

The austere practices of early rising, hours of prayer, rules of enclosure within the convent, and withdrawal from society, family, and friends that were portrayed in the popular novels did have some basis in the lifestyle of the sisters. Nevertheless, the reality of the lives of the sisters, who largely ran the alternative social institutions for the immigrant church, was far different from the stereotype of the nun as sex-crazed or unwillingly constrained. A young woman in nineteenth-century America joined a community in her twenties or early thirties, went through a period of trial of several months to a year as a postulant, then received the habit of the order with a white veil or bonnet for a one- to two-year term as a novice. Temporary vows of poverty, chastity, and obedience and promises to live according to the constitutions of the community were made for one to three years, and a black veil or bonnet replaced the white as a sign of the professed sister. After the temporary period was over, the sister would make final vows for life.[25]

During these years of probation, a sister, with the guidance of more experienced sisters, learned the spirit of the community and the prayers and practices of the group and was trained in the work that the community undertook. During all these times, assisting with the "common" work of cooking, cleaning, mending, and making habits was generally part of a sister's life. Those communities of European origin with strong enclosure rules and solemn vows might have lay sisters do the manual labor while the "choir" sisters engaged in the teaching. In these periods of gradual assimilation into the religious lifestyle, the sister could leave the community, or be dismissed or encouraged to leave if she did not seem fitted for the life.

The community itself would have a mother superior ruling the group with the aid of a council of senior sisters, varying according to community, but an ecclesiastical superior—the bishop or some priest designated by him—exercised extensive powers over the life of a community. These powers might include confirming the election of a superior, sometimes appointing or removing the superior, and imposing corrections on sisters.[26] Church or canon law governed much of what was part of religious life: types of vows, rules regarding how the superior was to govern, religious practices, and the habit.

However, as Mary Ewens has demonstrated, the Church's formal role definition for nuns was generally based on a twelfth-century view of a woman as immature, inferior, evil, incapable of directing her own life, and requiring constant surveillance lest she fall.[27] Thus, this type of life, "frozen into Canon law regulations," Ewens concluded, was the result of a medieval society with an economic system in which fathers sometimes sent their daughters to convents for financial rather than religious motives.[28]

Communities differed in their own internal rules and practices. For example, those communities with European origins, such as the Sisters of Mercy or the Sisters of Charity (who amalgamated with the French Daughters of Charity in 1850) or the Sisters of St. Joseph of Carondolet (who separated from France) often had years of tradition and written rules and customs. American communities, often formed or encouraged by bishops desperately in need of someone to begin schools and services for the poor, did not have written documents. However, the sisters were often encouraged to utilize sections from the rules of other, more established communities, thus creating similar practices among many groups of women religious.

In spite of the Church's often archaic view of women religious, the needs of the American wilderness and the developing country certainly did not allow for well-built European convents with walls, for adherence to a rigid schedule of the day, or for rules of strict seclusion from the public. Not surprisingly, sometimes there were tensions between the sisters and some bishops, between the bishops with Rome, or between the American sisters and their European motherhouses over understanding or carrying out various regulations.

Nevertheless, the nuns often came from European communities for whom America was missionary territory. This was in contrast to the sisters' Protestant counterparts in the American women's benevolent and missionary societies, who frequently turned their attention to foreign mission lands.[29] Indeed, the U.S. Church was officially considered "mission country" by the Vatican until June 29, 1908.[30] The struggles to meet the demands of this mission and frontier country are recounted in the early histories of most communities. For example, Sr. Frances Jerome Woods, in chronicling the work of congregations of women in the South, recounted stories of sisters planting and harvesting fields, chopping wood, struggling with snakes and other animals, being flooded out, and doing other manual work to fix up buildings for their early convents, schools, and hospitals. Those sisters who came from European countries to start American branches often saw themselves as coming to convert the savage Indians.[31] The American women who joined the communities might be aware they were probably not going to be converting Indians, at least not in the East and Midwest of the country. Nevertheless, the frontier experiences, the long distances from other Catholic settlements, and the physical hardships of establishing themselves and their schools caused the sisters to be clearly aware that this was pioneer mission territory as far as Catholics were concerned.

Cognizant of these conditions, the six archbishops and twenty-six bishops gathered together in 1852 for the First Plenary Council of Baltimore declared in their pastoral letter: "The wants of the Church in this vast country, so rapidly advancing in population and prosperity, impose on us, your pastors, and on you, our children in Christ, peculiar and arduous duties." After delineating the need for churches, more clergy, and Catholic education for youth, the letter stated, "Not only have we to erect and maintain the Church, the Seminary, and the School-house, but we have to found Hospitals, establish orphanages and provide for every want of suffering humanity, which Religion forbids us to neglect."[32] The sisters were the major contributors to this plea for health, education, and social-service institutions.

Renouncing marriage, motherhood, and home, the nuns lived an alternative life in a communal, single-sex setting and worked in these educational, health, and social-welfare institutions, where they held responsible, powerful, and influential positions. As Ewens has demonstrated, entrance into convent life, even in a hierarchical, patriarchal church, often gave these women leadership opportunities not available to many other women in mid-nineteenth-century America.[33]

Joseph Mannard, studying the relationship of these pioneer nuns to the antebellum ideology of domesticity, concluded that such divergence from traditional behavior of the "true women" did not reflect or foster changes in the sisters' value system. Little evidence exists, he determined, to suggest that the nuns challenged their continued subordination to males within church and society or criticized the male exclusiveness of the Catholic clergy and hierarchy.[34] Basically, Mannard believed they accepted the gender distinctions and accompanying sex roles as defined by the ideology of domesticity, and that they attempted to pass these ideals on to other women. "If nuns helped pioneer new variations on traditional roles and greater participation for women beyond the immediate family circle," he concluded, "the effect was only to broaden the meaning of the female sphere without questioning the validity of that concept."[35] Mannard's research suggests, rather, that nuns, by practicing "maternity of the spirit," fulfilled the functions of domesticity and conformed to its assumptions about the female nature.[36]

This women's sphere of domesticity, as reflected in letters, in diaries of white Protestant New England women, in the sermons preached in the late eighteenth and early nineteenth centuries, and as popularized in women's magazines, was in that place of salvation: the home. Separated from the arena of the world in which men labored in an arduous but energizing fashion, women were supposed to find satisfaction, happiness, and salvation in domestic occupations, spiritual care, and maternal destiny; their vocation was "to stablize society by generating and regenerating moral character."[37] Middle- and upper-class women especially, between 1820 and 1860, were merely "female appendages" to male activity in labor, business, politics, and the professions.[38]

James Kenneally suggested that to many American Catholics, the broad concept of true womanhood was an acceptable and familiar model. The concept rested in part on a Christian tradition that held that such a pattern was designed by God, exemplified by the Virgin Mary, and revealed by a Pauline interpretation of scripture and natural law. Furthermore, Kenneally noted that the belief was reinforced by biological differences and supported by a historical tradition proclaiming the supremacy of man. Consequently, numerous Catholics believed in distinct spheres of activity for each sex. Woman's sphere, of course, centered around her position as perpetuator of the race and nucleus of the family.[39] However, the extent to which American Catholic women, North or South, were influenced by these concepts of domesticity through sermons in their own churches, general popular magazines, and other forces, such as lectures, newspaper articles, or contact with Protestant women, remains to be examined in extensive detail by studying their letters, diaries, or journals.[40]

Education, religion, and sisterhood, as described by Nancy Cott, were all key concepts in developing the ideology of domesticity, regardless of the apparent lack of written evidence linking Roman Catholic women and nuns to the ideology of true womanhood.[41] It is reasonable to presume that Roman Catholic nuns themselves might have easily identified with many of these concepts. The two studies of Roman Catholic sisters, by Misner and by Ewens, when placed in the context of other studies on women and religion in the early nineteenth century,[42] suggest that the American women religious were not anomalies, even though they appeared suspect because of the different manner in which they expressed their ideals of womanhood.[43]

Education, for example, though seen as a responsibility of the mother in the nineteenth-century American family, was not a lifelong career. However, most religious communities were engaged in teaching, provided in-service training for their members, and saw their role as educators of future wives and of their families. Furthermore, the permanent vows the sisters took committed them for life to these educational activities.

Similarly, religion and piety, the signs of the nineteenth-century woman's virtue and the source of her strength, were prized because they did not take her away from her "proper sphere," her home.[44] Religion as practiced by the sisters, however, was seen by Catholics, at least, as a "higher calling" than marriage and the family. Sisters, therefore, were considered generous and self-sacrificing in giving up the pleasures and comforts of home, not as selfishly denigrating the ideas of true womanhood by their lifestyle. Some communities even used the title "Mother" for each of the sisters, and all communities had an understanding that sisters were the "brides of Christ."

Further, women, viewed by both Church and State as weak and ill-prepared to make important decisions, often looked to sisterhood with other women as a means of companionship and of exercising some influence on society. Most of the benevolent and missionary societies of the period, which were part of the Protestant revival movement, developed out of this model. Even though sisterhood, as practiced in Catholic religious communities, was otherwise unknown in the United States, some of its values often appealed to some Protestant women, like Catharine Beecher, who were intent upon social and educational reform.[45] In this model, they found an alternative to the primary calling of a woman to marriage and a family. Perhaps a major difference between the Protestant social reformers[46] and Roman Catholic sisters, however, was that the Protestant women were just beginning to form or join voluntary, benevolent, missionary, or reform organizations.[47] Developing institutions would come later. The sisters, on the other hand, already lived in an organized and structured form of benevolent and missionary association. Thus, they could devote themselves to building, developing, and administering social reform institutions, establishing places of salvation in the world. Thus, education, religion, and sisterhood reflected values of domesticity the sisters shared, though expressed differently, with Protestant women.

Nevertheless, the nineteenth-century American Catholic Church, like the rest of society, did not expect women to act independently. Thus, major decisions in religious communities usually required at least the approval of the bishop or his representative. The question of the authority of the community versus that of a local bishop was, perhaps, the single most important factor in the difficulties that arose as the sisters within each community moved from pioneer groupings to more structured institutions.[48] Despite this, the women religious did hold most of the responsibility for their own finances, for the day-to-day management of their institutions, which grew from one-room cabins to brick buildings, and for the future expansion of their works of education, health care, and social services. Further, sisters had opportunities for education and on-the-job training, "careers," administration, and a relative independence in their work, all of which were rarely achieved by other nineteenth-century women.[49]

As a result of the interaction of the nuns with their milieu, both European and American attitudes toward nuns were gradually modified. The American view eventually changed from one of hostility to one of acceptance and respect, and the Catholic church slowly became aware that some of its obsolete European role definitions for nuns had to be changed if sisters were to work effectively in a different cultural setting.[50]

Many of the role conflicts that developed were actually the result of cultural clashes between European and American values that were apparent in other aspects of American Catholic life.[51] The European values were codified in the canon law for religious, which governed every aspect of their lives: daily schedule, clothing, work, rules on enclosure. The prevailing European concept of a sister as one who had solemn vows and hence was cloistered was somewhat clarified by the decision in 1864, that, with few exceptions, all sisters in America should take simple vows, thus modifying the regulations regarding the cloister.[52]

Ewens points out that in the decade of the 1860s, sisters generally continued to play the same roles they had earlier. The American foundations of European motherhouses begun during the earlier period gradually became Americanized as adaptions, such as the addition of American members, the pressure of bishops, and other factors worked to lessen their foreign characteristics.[53] The Civil War, of course, hastened this change. With approximately one-fifth of the sisters in the United States involved at some point in nursing,[54] their schedules were disrupted, and they were exposed to a greater cross-section of Americans.[55]

As part of the largely immigrant Catholic Church, Roman Catholic sisters belonged to a minority group, and were misunderstood and even hated because of foreign or strange ways. Though not part of the culture of nineteenth-century Protestant, middle-class, married women, whose life and values set the standards for domesticity, the American sisters did reflect qualities of purity, piety, service, and submissiveness in their lives. The sisters' nineteenth-century feminine, domestic qualities were strikingly enhanced by their life in a female religious community, with values of a common goal of service to all those in need, organization for that purpose, and mutual support. Above all, the sisters' training and experience in nursing and other social services, done out of a missionary purpose rather than a reforming, professional zeal, made them generally admired, though sometimes envied, by Protestant women. However, the essence of the mission and the purpose of all Catholic women religious was the desire to make the Catholic religion better understood and known through continuing charitable works of education, social service, and health, especially for the immigrant Catholic Church and for the poor. Thus, on the eve of the Civil War, the sisters possessed those qualities that would ultimately set a standard for skilled nursing care, modify decades of negative attitudes about their lives, and win understanding and appreciation for themselves and for their Church.

NOTES

1. Archives of the Daughters of Charity, Emmitsburg, MD, (ADC), *Annals of the Civil War*, Vol. I, p. 13.

2. Alexis de Tocqueville, *Democracy in America*, eds. J. P. Mayer and Max Lerner (New York: Harper, 1966), p. 414.

3. de Tocqueville, p. 265.

4. de Tocqueville, p. 266.

5. Edwin Gaustad, *Historical Atlas of American Religion* (New York: Harper and Row, 1975), pp. 36, 42, 111.

6. John Tracy Ellis, *American Catholicism*, rev. ed. (Chicago: University of Chicago Press, 1956), pp. 82–83.

7. Sr. Mary Christine Sullivan notes in her study, "Some Non-Permanent Foundations of Religious Orders and Congregations," *U.S. Catholic Historical Society Records and Studies* 31 (Jan. 1940), 7–118, that in these approximately seven communities, which did not survive due to "fire, floods, lack of subjects, misunderstanding, calumny, and even persecution," the foundresses (except for the Visitandine Nuns at Georgetown, District of Columbia), were of European origin (pp. 8–11). See also Barbara Misner, "A Comparative Social Study of the Members and Apostolates of the First Eight Permanent Communities of Women Religious within the Boundaries of the United States, 1790–1850," Ph.D. Diss., Catholic University of America, 1981. Misner indicates that by 1830, the eight permanent communities, which included two cloistered communities (the Carmelites and the Visitandines), totaled 1,441 members (Misner, p. viii).

8. Elinor Dehey, *Religious Orders of Women in the United States* (Hammond, IN: W. B. Conkey, 1930). My own examination of the official Catholic directories for 1850 indicates the impossibility of getting accurate figures, as each diocese reported statistics in different ways, and total numbers of sisters were not given, though some dioceses did list the number of sisters at given institutions. The best method to ascertain the number might be to request the figures from each individual community still in existence that kept a register, if the record has not been destroyed by fire or other calamity.

9. John Tracy Ellis, *Catholics in Colonial America* (Baltimore: Helicon Press, 1965), p. 249.

10. Though a sociological profile of these sisters in antebellum America would be valuable to have, the data remain fragmentary or nonexistent. Misner, as a part of her dissertation, did a computer analysis on what information was available on the first eight permanent communities of women religious; she acknowl-

edges that while more information can be found about these women than for any other group of women of similar size (1,441) during the early nineteenth century, "Much of the data was not available." Misner, pp. vii-viii.

11. Ellis, *American Catholicism*, pp. 54–56.

12. Misner, pp. vi-vii.

13. Misner, pp. vi-vii. See also Dehey for specific information on each community.

14. See Dehey for dates and names of these communities. These data are also summarized in a table in Sr. Evangeline Thomas, *Women Religious History Sources: A Guide to Repositories in the United States* (New York: R. R. Bowker, 1983).

15. Jay Dolan, *The Immigrant Church*, p. 130.

16. Charles Rosenberg, "And Heal the Sick: The Hospital and the Patient in Nineteenth Century America," *Journal of Social History* 10 (Summer 1977): 438.

17. Lyman Beecher, quoted in Hennesey, p. 119.

18. Hennesey, pp. 116–127.

19. Rebecca Reed, *Six Months in a Convent* (Boston: Russell, Odeorne and Metcalf, 1835).

20. Maria Monk, *Awful Disclosures of the Hotel Dieu Nunnery in Montreal* (New York: Howe and Bates, 1836).

21. Sr. Mary Ewens, *The Role of the Nun in Nineteenth-Century America* (New York: Arno, 1978) p. 250.

22. Reed, p. 13.

23. Amanda Porterfield, *Feminine Spirituality in America* (Philadelphia: Temple University Press, 1980), p. 122.

24. "Destruction of Charleston Convent from Contemporary Newspaper Accounts," *U.S. Catholic Historical Records and Studies* 13 (May 1919): 106–119. For another view see James Kenneally, "The Burning of the Ursuline Convent: A Different View," *Records of the American Catholic Historical Society* 90 (Mar.-Dec. 1979): 15–22.

25. The general information in this and the following paragraphs is drawn largely from Ewens, pp. 105–122.

26. See Sr. Patricia Byrne, "Sisters of St. Joseph: The Americanization of a French Tradition," *U.S. Catholic Historian* 5 (1986): 256.

27. Ewens, p. 326.

28. Ewens, p. 326.

29. See Keith Melder, "Ladies Bountiful: Organized Women's Benevolence in Early Nineteenth Century America," *New York History* 48 (July 1967), 231–254. Mary B. Treudly "The Benevolent Pair: A Study of Charitable Organization Among Women in the First Third of the Nineteenth Century," *Social Service Review* 19 (Dec. 1940): 509–522.

30. Ellis, *American Catholicism*, p. 124.

31. Woods, pp. 104–105.

32. Peter Guilday, ed. *The National Pastoral Letters of the American Hierarchy (1792–1919)* (Maryland: The Newman Press, 1954), p. 187.

33. Ewens, especially conclusion, pp. 326–331.

34. Joseph Mannard, "Maternity of the Spirit: Nuns and Domesticity in Antebellum America," *U.S. Catholic Historian* 5 (Summer/Fall 1986): 322.

35. Mannard, p. 324.

36. For another view, see James Kenneally, "Eve, Mary, and the Historians: American Catholicism and Women," in Janet W. James, ed., *Women in American Religion* (Philadelphia: University of Pennsylvania Press, 1980). He says that ladylike qualities, nurtured and fostered by the institutional Church, made nuns ideal for teaching children, Blacks, and Indians, and for running orphanages and nursing the infirm and aged. On the other hand (p. 197), these activities, wherein sisters performed as administrators and superiors, or natural "male roles," sometimes led to clashes with the hierarchy. Of the twelve nuns listed in *Notable American Women*, six had difficulties with male superiors (pp. 197–198).

37. Nancy Cott, *The Bonds of True Womanhood* (New Haven: Yale University Press, 1977), p. 92.

38. Ronald Hogeland, "The Female Appendage: Feminine Life Styles in America, 1820–1860," *Civil War History* 27 (1971): 104–114.

39. Kenneally, p. 191.

40. Colleen McDannell, *The Christian Home in Victorian America, 1840–1900* (Philadelphia: Temple University Press, 1986). She compares Protestant and Catholic homes and devotes one chapter to Catholic domesticity (pp. 52–76). McDannell noted that it took almost fifty years before Irish Catholic immigrants developed a Victorian domesticity similar to Protestant sensibilities, mainly due to their social and economic situation. Thus, the time lag precludes any definitive comparisons being made between Catholic and Protestant concepts of domesticity in the antebellum period.

41. Cott cites the current uses of the term "domesticity," p. 1. All uses apply only to the Puritan Protestants.

42. See those by Welter, Cott, and Porterfield.

43. Misner, p. 287.

44. Welter, pp. 152–153.

45. Catharine Beecher, *The American Woman's Home* (New York: J. B. Ford, 1870), p. 451. See also Kathryn Sklar, *Catharine Beecher: A Study in American Domesticity* (New Haven: Yale University Press, 1973), pp. 171–172.

46. As Rosemary Reuther and Rosemary Keller in *Women and Religion in America: The Nineteenth Century: A Documentary History* (San Francisco: Harper and Row, 1981) point out, there was no uniformity within the ranks of Protestant reformers. Tension existed between conservative and radical, educational and abolitionist reformers, debating whether woman's sphere was to be exercised within the home and church—the extension of the private, domestic world—or within their own moral judgment and reason in the larger world beyond the home (p. 300).

47. See Carolyn Gifford, "Sisterhoods of Service and Reform: Organized Methodist Women in the Late Nineteenth Century: An Essay on the State of the Research," *Methodist History* 24 (Oct. 1985): 15–30.

48. Misner, p. 253.

49. Mannard, p. 322. For a view of late-nineteenth-century reformers who did develop institutions, see Estelle Freedman, "Separation as Strategy: Female Institution Building and American Feminism, 1870–1930," *Feminist Studies* 5, No. 3 (Fall 1979): 513–529.

50. Ewens, p. 12.

51. Ewens, p. 12.

52. Ewens, pp. 204–217.

53. Ewens, p. 217.

54. The one-fifth figure is derived from the available statistics of the communities that served in the Civil War.

55. Ewens, pp. 250–251. See also Dolan, *The American Catholic Experience*, pp. 121–124.

Backgrounds of Catholic Nursing in the United States in the Nineteenth Century

Roman Catholic sisters, in spite of their minority status and misunderstood life, offered the only source of trained nurses for the Civil War, especially in its chaotic beginnings. The significance of their contribution becomes clearer when it is viewed in the context of early efforts to develop almshouses and private hospitals, to provide nursing care, and, (a movement led by Florence Nightingale) to reform nursing. Those on both sides of the Atlantic who decried the conditions of these early health-care institutions turned to the model of the religious sisterhoods, especially the Roman Catholic nursing communities, as examples of how single Protestant women might be religiously motivated and organized to carry out this nursing care. An examination of this nursing history and the care that was given by the sisters in Catholic and other early hospitals in the three decades before the war will demonstrate that sisters were uniquely positioned by their traditions, their experience, and their community constitutions to provide nursing care when the Civil War began.

Although the first hospital in the continental United States was established in 1658 by the Dutch West India Company in Massachusetts for sick employees,[1] the sick were ordinarily cared for within the family by mothers, sisters, and wives. Strangers and travelers who fell ill were generally taken in by benevolent families and nursed back to health or buried. However, epidemics of cholera, typhoid, and smallpox, along with immigration and emigration patterns, changed this system of home or even company nursing care. Two types of hospitals gradually developed: the voluntary hospital, supported by private philanthropy, such as general hospitals in Pennsylvania (1751), New York (1775), and Massachusetts (1821), and the almshouse hospital established by cities, beginning with Philadelphia in 1713, where William Penn provided the necessary leadership. Some, like Charity Hospital in New Orleans, which was established in 1737 by a private gift of a sailor, took both poor and paying patients.[2] By 1840, most of the major American cities had almshouses, which included infirmaries for the sick and poor and pest houses for the isolation of contagious diseases. Social medical historian Paul Starr stated that these early hospitals were considered, at best, unhappy necessities, filthy, overcrowded, and used as combinations of prisons, poorhouses, pest houses, and homes for the aged. Contagious diseases spread rapidly in them, and the mortality rates were high.[3]

In the almshouses, most of the care was given by the other inmates. In the hospitals, nursing, done by women of the lower classes who were sometimes recruited from the almshouses or penitentiary, was classed with scrubbing the floors; no special training was expected or desired.[4] Even at its best, nursing was considered a domestic art and, as such, was passed from person to person by word of mouth and by demonstration. Keeping the patients clean and giving them nourishment was the major responsibility, and there were no nurses at night except in emergencies. Regular inspection of hospitals or nursing care was not done.[5]

The early hospitals kept very few medical records, usually just admissions and discharges, summaries of age and nationality, and a statement of the disease and condition on discharge.[6] Thus, other than a general awareness of deplorable conditions surrounding these early institutions, little is actually recorded about the hospitals or the specifics of the care of patients in them. For example, in trying to reconstruct the early history of city hospitals, historian Harry Dowling said that historians know much more about when and where these almshouses were built than about the care given the patients. Even so, the data consist of a date and a geographical location.[7] Nursing historians Adelaide Nutting and Lavinia Dock, using an 1854 article describing Bellevue Hospital in New York as an example of the fragmentary information about early nursing, noted that "not a word was said about the nursing or the care of the patients."[8]

In the decade before the Civil War, a few doctors, notably Dr. Joseph Warrington of Philadelphia and Dr. Marie Zakrzewska of the New England Hospital for Women in Boston, provided some basic lectures and instruction in cleanliness for female nurses on the maternity cases. In spite of these efforts, however, there were only fifty women trained by Dr. Warrington between 1839 and 1850, and Dr. Zakrzewska had only one applicant in 1859.[9] There were some printed materials, like Warrington's *The Nurses Guide* (1839), on the nursing of women and children, and a few on general nursing.[10] While they were intended, for the most part, for home nursing, these materials were used by some of the early hospital nurses, religious as well as secular.[11]

In the United States, where ties with England had always been close, the English example of Florence Nightingale and her nursing reforms was influential even though there was also an independent American reform movement.[12] However, even in 1844, when Nightingale first knew with certainty that her vocation lay among the sick in hospitals, she did not have the actual practice of nursing in her mind. She had spoken to Dr. Samuel Howe, husband of Julia Ward, of "devoting herself to works of charity in hospitals," thinking that the qualities needed to relieve the misery of the sick were tenderness, sympathy, goodness, and patience. But after a brief experience of nursing some family members, she realized that only knowledge and expert skill could bring relief, even though it was universally assumed that being a woman was the only qualification needed for taking care of the sick.[13]

Concurrent with Nightingale's interest in devoting herself to the sick, nursing reform in England was developing out of the high-church religious revival of the 1840s and 1850s. The new Anglican sisterhoods, as women's historian Martha Vicinus has demonstrated, saw nursing the sick poor as one of their prime objectives, reviving the ancient tradition of the religious vocation of nursing. Similar reforms, she pointed out, were also being undertaken by Roman Catholic nuns in France and Lutheran deaconesses in Germany. Although all these religious orders, both in England and on the Continent, put little emphasis upon formal training, Vicinus concluded they set "new standards of cleanliness and conscientiousness."[14]

Thus, when Nightingale went to the Crimean Peninsula in 1853, during the war between Russia and the allied powers, which included England, twenty-four of her thirty-eight nurses were from Anglican and Roman Catholic religious orders. In fact, as Mary McAuley Gilgannon has demonstrated, it was the Sisters of Mercy from Ireland and from England who gave Nightingale's Female Nursing Establishment "whatever semblance it possessed of being a cohesive body."[15] The women's success in the Crimea brought fame to Nightingale's nurses and a heightened public interest in nursing as a vocation. Both Nightingale and her nursing reformers and the religious orders benefited from these achievements.[16]

The specific example of the Roman Catholic sisters in Europe and England was laid before the English people by another advocate of nursing reform: author, art historian, and lecturer Mrs. Anna Jameson. She followed the lead of physician and philanthropist Dr. Robert Gooch in publicly advocating a Protestant nursing order. An 1855 lecture, entitled "Sisters of Charity Abroad and at Home," cited example after example of what Roman Catholic sisters had done throughout Europe as inspiration for her challenge to the British,[17] even though she was "not a friend of nunneries [sic]...[or] even of Protestant nunneries."[18] The lecture was so well received that it was later published in England and America.

She acknowledged that while some concepts of Catholicism were repugnant, such as images of "forced celibacy and seclusion," and other traditions Protestants regarded "with terror, disgust, and derision," Jameson suggested that just as the British used old cathedrals and colleges for pious ends and social benefits, Protestant women could dispense with some of the ornaments and appendages of Catholicism and retain the basic concept of nursing.[19]

As American reformers such as Catharine Beecher, Jane Woolsey, and Mary Livermore were to do in the United States, Jameson concluded with a resounding plea for Protestant women to follow the example of the "well-trained" Roman Catholic sisters in the Crimea who "held on with unflagging spirit and energy ... meeting all difficulties with a cheerful spirit and a superiority which they owed to their previous training and experience, not certainly to any want of zeal, benevolence, or intelligence in their Protestant sisters of the better class."[20]

Jameson acknowledged that British doctors in the Crimean War, who felt that any experiment with volunteer nurses "*must* end in total failure" in spite of Nightingale's sometimes controversial efforts to win their confidence and support, were "loud and emphatic" in their admiration of the Catholic sisters.[21] Reasoning, then, that men did not object to women as nurses but only to Protestant women as nurses, she brought her argument to a logically ordered conclusion: "Now, do they mean to say that there is anything in the Roman Catholic religion which produces these efficient women? or that it is impossible to train any other women to perform the same duties with the same calm and quiet efficiency, the same zeal and devotion? Really I do not see that feminine energy and efficiency belong to any one section of the great Christian community."[22]

Vicinus concluded that nursing and religious commitment were closely linked in the minds of the educated British public because no one believed that anyone but a sister would be willing to do the work.[23] Even the advocates of reformed nursing from Evangelical or nonconformist backgrounds, who wished to move leadership out of the hands of High Anglicans and wanted "commitment without incense," unanimously agreed that religious inspiration was essential if gentlewomen were to consent to a lifetime of unpleasant work.[24]

These views were similarly applied in America, though in the United States anti-Catholic sentiment made women of any religious grouping somewhat suspect. Thus, according to the Bulloughs, Protestant reformers in America who, as in England and Europe, greatly admired the work of the Catholic nursing orders, sought to mobilize Protestant women for works of charity without establishing convents.[25]

On a smaller scale than Catholics, Protestant churches also trained nurses, usually called deaconesses.[26] Four Lutheran deaconesses were first brought by Pastor Theodore Fliedner in 1849 to Pittsburgh from Kaiserswerth, Germany, where the movement had begun and flourished. The Pittsburgh Infirmary, founded by Rev. Dr. William A. Passavant, was one of four Lutheran hospitals started by him before the Civil War. When the war broke out, Dr. Passavant offered the deaconesses' services to Miss Dorothea Dix, Superintendent of the Union army female nurses, who received them graciously.[27] The Episcopal Church also began a deaconess movement, organized in 1855 by the Reverend Horace Springfellow in Baltimore. Though short-lived as a group, they did staff St. Andrews's Infirmary there.[28] The first Episcopal sisters, distinguished from deaconesses by vows and enclosure, were loosely organized in 1845 and formally established in 1852 by Rev. William A. Muhlenberg, who started a dispensary in New York City which later became St. Luke's Hospital.[29]

In spite of these efforts by Protestant sisterhoods to provide better nursing care, two factors, according to the Bulloughs, limited their expansion. First, the communities lacked sufficient recruits to adequately staff expanding numbers of hospitals. More seriously, there was antagonism from Protestants who saw such groups as havens for secret Catholics, causing even Muhlenberg to dissolve his sisterhood for a time.[30]

In addition to these religiously organized groups, in 1813 the Ladies' Benevolent Society of Charleston, South Carolina, began nursing the sick at home in the first known example of organized, untrained, lay nursing in America.[31] Furthermore, women who were thwarted in their attempts to be part of the larger medical field in antebellum America—often a difficult task—sometimes were forced to undertake nursing as an alternative, at least during the Civil War.[32] For example, Dr. Mary Walker was the only woman who officially practiced medicine during the Civil War; it is believed that others, like Esther Hill Hawkes, who was denied the opportunity to serve as a doctor, turned to nursing.[33]

Thus, in spite of some reform efforts, neither in nursing nor in medicine was there a strong background, tradition, or experience in caring for patients among women in the United States. On the other hand, although there were no doctors among them, the Roman Catholic sisters who served in the Civil War, regardless of whether they came from European or American communities or whether their community was devoted primarily to nursing care or to other forms of charity, came from a long tradition in which care of the sick was done from religious motivation.

That tradition had its beginning in the Middle Ages, where devotion to the sick for religious reasons caused an important forward step in nursing. To assist in carrying out the religious ideal, medieval men and women developed various Catholic institutions, especially hospitals and nursing orders devoted to relieving pain and suffering.[34] Unfortunately, many of these institutions were closed, the lay groups disbanded, and religious orders dissolved during the Protestant Reformation.[35] Though male nurses, many of whom were part of the monastic orders or lay groups, largely disappeared, Catholic nursing orders organized after 1500 were for women.[36] Whatever may have been the detrimental effects of the Protestant Reformation on Catholics, one result was to put the care of the sick in the hands of female religious communities, who devoted their lives to this work by serving in institutions that were closely connected to, as well as controlled by, the Catholic hierarchy. This single-minded devotion to the sick, which was supported by visible institutional structures as well as regulated by some of the constricting rules of religious life, would eventually be brought to the United States or adapted in some way by the communities that would come or be started two centuries later.[37]

Aware of the value of dedicated people serving others, but also aware of the constrictions of cloistered female religious life, St. Vincent De Paul initiated the most important development in nursing in Catholic countries by founding the Sisters (later called Daughters) of Charity in seventeenth-century France. In his work with convicts and galley slaves in France, he first founded the Congregation of Priests of the Missions. During his work, he became acquainted with two noblewomen, Madame de la Chassaigne and Madame de Brie, who spent most of their time aiding the poor or nursing the sick. In the beginning he simply organized a society of ladies to help in better distributing food and services for the needy. Later, a community was established under the direction of Louise de Marillac. As the community developed, it underwent various modifications in theme and purpose; however, by 1634, de Marillac assumed leadership of what was by then called Sisters of Charity. Vincent De Paul was opposed, though, to either the earlier ladies of charity or the sisters becoming nuns since he felt there was a real need for women who could visit with the sick in their homes. This visiting would have been almost impossible for nuns, who were bound under strict, cloistered rules, which kept them within the confines of their convents.[38] He wrote: "It is true [there were] religious [orders] and hospitals for the assistance of the sick, but before your establishment there was never a community destined to go and serve the sick in their houses. If, in some poor family, anyone fell sick, he was sent to the hospital, and this separated the husband from his wife, and the children from their parents."[39]

Other communities of sisters, focusing on similarly active ministries, rather than the contemplative prayer ministries of nuns, soon followed.

Some were based on ideas of Vincent De Paul and emphasized care of the sick, along with education and other works of charity. For example, by 1816, Mary Aikenhead of Cork founded the Irish Sisters of Charity; she later was in charge of Dublin's St. Vincent's Hospital, the first hospital in Ireland to be served by nuns. The Sisters of Mercy, several branches of which came to the United States, were founded in 1827 by Catharine McAuley in Dublin. Though these communities and others were distinct in name, purpose, regulations, and dress, the differences were often indistinguishable in the view of the ordinary person, and all sisters were often called Sisters of Charity or Sisters of Mercy after these early communities, which focused on charitable works.

Concurrent with the developments in Europe, the medieval legacy of care of the sick done by religious orders, as revitalized by Vincent De Paul and Louise de Marillac and as carried out by the formation of apostolic communities of women religious, was being developed in North America. The first attempt to train nurses on the North American continent was made by the Ursuline nuns of Quebec, who, about 1610, taught the Indian women to care for their sick.[40] In 1639, three Augustinians from Dieppe, France, whose community had been established in 1155 as hospital sisters, also came to Quebec to nurse Indian smallpox victims in a New World Hotel Dieu.[41] The first whites to be nursed by sisters were soldiers of the Revolutionary Army suffering from smallpox and scarlet fever contracted during the siege of Quebec. They were taken to Hotel Dieu and cared for by the Augustinians, as were both Americans and French in the Battle of Three Rivers in 1776.[42]

Although there were these examples of French Canadian sisters nursing in North America, hospital care in the continental United States was started primarily by American-founded communities. Particularly influential in forming American concepts of nursing was the work of Elizabeth Ann Bayley Seton: wife, mother, and widow, and the first native-born American to be canonized a Roman Catholic saint.[43] After her conversion to Catholicism, she organized the St. Joseph's sisterhood at Emmitsburg, Maryland, in 1809. The group soon adopted the rule of the Sisters of Charity of St. Vincent De Paul, and a union with the French society was effected in 1850. From the beginning, care of the sick was a major work of this community. Between 1828 and 1860, these Sisters of Charity (later called Daughters of Charity) opened eighteen hospitals in ten different states and the District of Columbia;[44] these constituted more than half the twenty-eight Catholic hospitals established before the Civil War.[45] Other communities soon followed the Sisters of Charity in establishing hospitals for the sick and diseased.

Similar to the findings of the medical and nursing historians cited earlier, facts on the establishment of these Catholic institutions and the care provided by them are also sparse. Ann Doyle, in her research on nursing by religious orders in the United States, first points out the difficulty of compiling any comprehensive or complete history of the contributions made by various religious groups, Catholic or Protestant. Even the words "hospital" and "nursing," she found, were not used in early books. Citing both the "limitations and difficulties of the times" and the "extreme modesty and self-effacement" of the various sisters, Doyle further suggests that even when brief accounts of the beginnings of the religious communities were done, the sister historians were largely teachers and thus often neglected research into the beginnings of hospitals, focusing rather on educational endeavors and the internal history of the community.[46]

Nonetheless, from the data that do exist, it can be determined that sisters took care of patients in at least seven hospitals, often called infirmaries, asylums, or retreats, in the period before 1840.[47] The Baltimore Infirmary, Maryland, begun in 1823, had four wards, one of which handled eye cases, was attended by doctors and students from the University of Maryland, and had seven or eight Sisters of Charity by 1827.[48] Four Sisters of Charity in St. Louis started the St. Louis Mullanphy Hospital in 1828 in a three-room log house until a brick building was constructed in 1831. The Baltimore Infirmary is considered the first instance of women religious in active hospital work in the United States,[49] and Mullanphy Hospital, the first permanent Catholic hospital.[50] During the years 1830 to 1840, when yellow fever and cholera scourged Charleston, South Carolina, the Brotherhood of Saint Marino, an association of mechanics and laborers, rented a house, furnished it with beds, linens, and other supplies, and then put it under the direction of the Sisters of Our Lady of Mercy (now called Sisters of Charity of Our Lady of Mercy), an American community founded by Bishop John England to serve the poor in his diocese of Charleston, South Carolina.[51] Similarly, the origins of the St. Vincent Infirmary of the Sisters of Charity of Nazareth, established about 1836, for the sick of Louisville, Kentucky, were in a few spare rooms of an orphanage built after the cholera epidemics of the 1830s.

As Charles Rosenberg points out in his history of the United States' cholera epidemics of 1832 and 1849, hospitals were the most immediate need in cholera-stricken communities, but the need was not easily filled.[52] Only in a few cities, such as Philadelphia, Baltimore, Louisville, St. Louis, and Cincinnati in 1832, and in Buffalo, Boston, and St. Louis in 1849, where various communities of Sisters of Charity allowed their hospitals to be used for treating cholera patients, could health authorities turn to hospitals already staffed and functioning.[53]

During these epidemics, sisters were also asked sometimes to staff other hospitals. For example, Blockley, the municipal almshouse of Philadelphia, was managed briefly by the Sisters of Charity during the cholera epidemic of 1832.[54] Admiration was earned by the sisters, Rosenberg concludes, for their practical benevolence, which demonstrated that their lives were "not idled away in the convent living tomb."[55]

The Daughters of Charity were asked to take charge of Charity Hospital in New Orleans in 1834,[56] served at Maryland Hospital in Baltimore from 1834 to 1840, and opened the Richmond Infirmary in 1838. Some of these early beginnings, like Charity Hospital, Mullanphy Hospital (which became St. Louis Hospital in 1930), and St. Vincent Infirmary (which became St. Joseph Infirmary) lasted into the twentieth century. All of them set the pattern of sisters both initiating their own institutions and being asked to staff other public and private institutions.[57]

Although it is not clear what precise tasks were performed by the sisters in these early hospitals, it is presumed the duties involved dressing wounds, bathing the patients, keeping the bedding and rooms clean and aired, preparing and serving food, and providing spiritual support for the suffering and dying.[58] A letter from a priest in Baltimore to Bishop Benedict Flaget in Kentucky stated that the sisters at the Baltimore Infirmary in 1829 received $42 a year each, and that their duties included dressing "sore legs and blisters" and "all the wounds of the women, unless from an operation," and "administering all the medicine."[59]

The Daughters of Charity, the Sisters of Charity of Nazareth, the Sisters of Charity of Our Lady of Mercy, all American-founded communities, were the three communities with sisters in these early hospitals. Numbers are difficult to determine, but generally three or four sisters began in these places, with their number perhaps doubling as needs demanded.[60]

In the period from 1840 to 1860, the Daughters of Charity started additional hospitals. Other women came from Europe to begin communities for visiting the sick in their homes and to start hospitals, as well as to engage in education and other works of charity. Sisters of Mercy, arriving from Ireland in 1843, came with a tradition of visiting the sick in their homes. In the United States, they established their first hospital in Pittsburgh in 1847, another one in Chicago in 1851, and St. Mary's Hospital in San Francisco in 1857. A hospital in Wheeling, Virginia (now West Virginia) in 1853 and in St. Paul, Minnesota, in 1854, were established by the Sisters of St. Joseph of Carondelet, who had come from France in 1836. Sisters of the Poor of St. Francis, coming from Germany to America in 1850, established St. Mary's Hospital in Cincinnati in 1859 and St. Elizabeth's Hospital in Covington, Kentucky, in 1860. Another Franciscan community, the Sisters of the Third Order of St. Francis, founded St. Mary's Hospital in Philadelphia in 1860. In addition, the Sisters of Charity of St. Augustine, brought to Cleveland by Bishop Amadeus Rappe for the express purpose of establishing a Catholic hospital, started St. Joseph Hospital in 1852, which closed in 1856 but was later reestablished as St. Vincent Charity Hospital in 1865. This work is similar to the activities of other religious communities who staffed hospitals for only a period of time, particularly during the various cholera epidemics in the 1840s and 1860s.[61]

Typical of the beginnings of these hospitals between 1840 and 1860 were the three dilapidated log buildings in Detroit that were the start, in 1844, of St. Mary Hospital. Two stables in Rochester, New York, were the beginnings in 1857 for St. Mary's Hospital there. The old ballroom of the Sisters of Mercy residence in Pittsburgh became Mercy Hospital in 1849 to care for men suffering from ship fever aboard boats on the Ohio River. A temporary building was the origin of Wheeling Hospital, Virginia, begun in 1853 by the Sisters of St. Joseph. In contrast to these usual beginnings was St. Joseph Hospital in St. Paul, Minnesota, built in 1854, which was made of stone and was four stories high. Generally, the approximately twenty hospitals established during this period by the sisters, sometimes with the support of the bishop or doctors, were begun in response to acute needs, such as cholera or smallpox.[62]

In addition to the above communities, all of whom were later involved in the Civil War nursing effort, there were several other communities devoted to nursing established prior to the war, such as the Sisters of the Incarnate Word in Texas and the Sisters of Charity of Providence in Washington state. Probably because of geographic location, these communities were not involved in the war.[63] Also, the Sisters of Providence of St. Mary of the Woods, Indiana, who came from France in 1840, and the Sisters of the Holy Cross of South Bend, Indiana, who came in 1843, later established hospitals as a result of their Civil War experience, although they had not been involved with health care before the war.

These early hospitals, opened primarily to meet acute needs and to help the influx of poor immigrants, [64] were small. Perhaps largest was the forty-bed St. Vincent Hospital in New York City; all were greatly handicapped by lack of resources and personnel. The major reason for this was that the people on whom the sisters had to depend for support were mostly newly arrived immigrants, who were hard pressed in obtaining even the necessities of life.[65] For example, the Daughters of Charity reported that Detroit Bishop Paul Lefevre was anxious to tell the people that the sisters would open a hospital in 1845 and that they should support it by bringing bedding and articles to furnish the wards. Nevertheless, the sisters recounted that they only got "a few bed ticks, somewhat longer than pillow-ticks, with a little straw in them."[66]

While by modern standards the sisters had little special preparation when they opened their first hospitals, they were reported to have "zeal, self-sacrifice and sympathy for the suffering that made them an inspiring challenge to Protestant institutions."[67] Although some doctors and various reformers decried the lack of adequate medical care in most public institutions, most nursing historians state that methodical attendance of the sick was probably undertaken until well into the nineteenth century only by the Catholic religious orders in both the United States and England.[68] For example, Robin O'Connor has found that in contrast to lay nurses, "The Catholic sisterhoods trained their own members well, creating educated and disciplined nurses." He noted that New York City, Baltimore, and Philadelphia often hired the Daughters of Charity for emergency nursing service, and a few cities, such as Mobile, Alabama, in 1830, and Augusta, Georgia, in 1834, established hospitals with the intent of having Catholic sisterhoods manage them.[69]

There are few written records of the nursing practice even during these years just before the war. Judging from the practice of medicine at the time, it is reasonable to suppose, as Doyle believes, that it was very simple and probably confined to procuring cleanliness, nourishment, and safety for the sick, and to the administration of simple medicine. In addition, the work of the sisters was extended to the kitchen, the laundry, supervision of the wards, and care of the spiritual welfare of the patients.[70]

Although written documents concerning the actual training and nursing practice in Catholic hospitals may seem sparse to most nursing and medical historians, an extemely important set of documents has been overlooked by them. The rules and constitutions of communities with European origins, like the Sisters of Mercy, or with European affiliations, like the Daughters of Charity, were used as models by American communities. These contained sections that served as a practical guide to nursing care for the sisters. The constitutions clearly spelled out how the sick were to be regarded and treated, what kind of food should be served, how the linens and rooms should be cleaned, what the schedule of the day should be, how doctors should be regarded, and above all, how the dying should be prepared for death.[71] The reading and studying of these basic documents, which covered all phases of a sister's life, including the specific rules for care of sick sisters as well as directives for sisters visiting the sick or working in hospitals, were a part of the early training and life long experience of the sisters. In addition, the apprenticeship of these beginning religious with an experienced sister served as formal training in the many aspects of living and working.

These same constitutions and commentaries of both Sisters of Charity and Sisters of Mercy also provided conventional wisdom and nursing training. These regulations exhorted the sisters not to warm the broth for the infirm more than an hour, lest it become too salty,[72] to make sure that those who are very weak "occasionally have something nice to eat and drink,"[73] and to cleanse frequently the mouths of the sick, as well as their bodies, for fear of canker sores. In addition, the sisters were reminded that complete ventilation, without permitting draughts of air to flow on the patient, was essential, and that with doctors, the "sisters' manners should be ever reserved, polite, and self-possessed, attentive to take directions, vigilant and exact in fulfilling them."[74] Further, sister pharmacists should take great care to keep the drugs in a good state.

These simple and practical attempts to regard the patients with dignity and keep them clean and well-fed seem almost insignificant by modern standards. However, in contrast to the general conditions of care in the almshouses and city hospitals, these measures were extremely important for the health and well-being of the patients. The generally small houses, called hospitals, cleaned and fitted up by the sisters to care for the sick, were primitive compared to twentieth-century institutions, yet these beginning hospitals were exactly the type of structures that would be used to house the wounded in the early years of the war.

Furthermore, the overall spiritual context in which the care of the sick was carried out by all communities was clearly and similarly expressed. The Daughters of Charity, for example, gave as the first rule in the section on sisters in hospitals:

The end for which the Daughters of Charity are sent to a Hotel-Dieu or hospital is to honor Our Lord Jesus Christ, the Father of the sick poor, both corporally and spiritually; corporally, by serving them and giving them food and medicine, and spiritually, by instructing the sick in what is necessary for their salvation; advising them to make a good general confession of their past life, that by this means those who die may depart hence in the state of grace, and they who recover may take the resolution never more with the help of God's grace, to offend Him.[75]

The Sisters of Mercy in their constitutions reminded the sisters that in visiting and caring for the sick they were part of a long line of saints, both men and women following Jesus Christ, who performed many miraculous cures, had great tenderness for the sick, and gave His powers of healing to His Apostles and followers.[76] Though this spiritual motivation was the primary cause of the commitment of the sisters before, during, and after the Civil War, nonetheless, it was the practical focus of their training that ultimately earned them the respect of doctors and soldiers alike. As the commentary on the Mercy constitutions stated: "The sisters should not only evidence compassion, but a practical desire to relieve and promote the temporal comfort of the sufferer as much as they can."[77]

On the eve of the Civil War, then, the only source of any kind of trained nurses—male or female—existed primarily in the twenty-eight Catholic hospitals, which were run by several different women's religious communities. Additional communities, though not primarily nursing orders, would join these communities and demonstrate that caring and

compassion, especially when combined with a tradition of trained experience or willingness to learn on the part of those sisters with no
experience, could make a significant difference in the quality of care
given to the wounded and dying Union and Confederate soldiers.

Some twenty years after the war, Sanitary Commission worker and
later women's rights leader, Mary Livermore, set the sisters' work in the
context of the nursing issues of the period:

I am neither a Catholic, nor an advocate of the monastic institutions of that
church. Similar organizations established on the basis of the Protestant religion,
and in harmony with republican principles, might be made very helpful to
modern society, and would furnish occupation and give position to large numbers of unmarried women, whose hearts go out to the world in charitable intent.
But I can never forget my experience during the War of the Rebellion. Never
did I meet these Catholic sisters in hospitals, on transports, or hospital steamers,
without observing their devotion, faithfulness, and unobtrusiveness. They gave
themselves no airs of superiority or holiness, shirked no duty, sought no easy
place, bred no mischiefs. Sick and wounded men watched for their entrance
into the wards at morning, and looked a regretful farewell when they departed
at night. They broke down in exhaustion from overwork, as did the Protestant
nurses: like them, they succumbed to the fatal prison-fever, which our exchanged
prisoners brought from the fearful pens of the South.[78]

Thus, the sisters in the United States, whether of American or European origin, brought to the Civil War four major contributions. First,
they brought a tradition and history of commitment to nursing derived
from centuries of European sisters being involved in care of the sick.
Second, they earned the recognition on both sides of the Atlantic, from
Nightingale and others who desired to initiate reforms for the better-
ment of the sick, that the sisters with their two-fold combination of
nursing skills and religious commitment offered a model for certain
aspects of care of the sick. Third, the communities running the Catholic
hospitals, which had been started to meet emergencies of diseases and
epidemics, showed a willingness to consider service in other hospitals
when the need arose. Fourth and foremost, the written regulations of
their community life served as a training manual for how patients should
be treated, and their religious community life itself provided the daily
living experience and personal example for other women religious in
the practice of these regulations.

While the restrictiveness of many of the regulations surrounding the
sisters' lives perplexed and puzzled many Americans, the practical nature
of their nursing work, learned in a community setting where the written
regulations were demonstrated, passed down to newer members, and
inculcated in the beginnings of their hospitals, made these sisters unique
as a group of women when they served the sick and wounded in the

Civil War. No other group of women had the tradition, organization, commitment, or hospital and nursing experience to bring to the desperate needs of the war. The Civil War would provide the sisters with the opportunity to put these practical skills, so admired by the doctors, and their religious commitment, so appreciated by the soldiers, to work in a larger setting. Thus, in spite of the anti-Catholicism of the antebellum period, there was a recognition that the sisters had a contribution to make in the care of the sick, that they had a history of coming to aid in other crises, and that they could work with medical and governmental authorities in these situations.

NOTES

1. Anne Austin, *History of Nursing Source Book* (New York: G. P. Putnam's Sons, 1957), p. 304.

2. Charles Rosenberg, "The Origins of the American Hospital System," *Bulletin of New York Academy of Medicine* 55 (Jan. 1979): 13. See also Harry Dowling, *City Hospitals: The Undercare of the Underprivileged* (Cambridge: Harvard University Press, 1982), pp. 16–21; Vern L. and Bonnie Bullough, *The Care of the Sick: The Emergence of Modern Nursing* (New York: Prodist, 1978), p. 63.

3. Paul Starr, *The Social Transformation of American Medicine* (New York: Basic Books, 1982), p. 155.

4. Bullough, p. 104.

5. John O'Grady, *Catholic Charities in the United States* (Washington, D.C. National Conference of Catholic Bishops, 1930; rpt. New York: Arno, 1971), p. 193.

6. Ann Doyle, "Nursing by Religious Orders in the United States," *American Journal of Nursing* 29 (Aug. 1929): 966.

7. Dowling, p. 14.

8. Mary Adelaide Nutting and Lavinia Dock, *A History of Nursing*, vol. 2 (New York: G.P. Putnam's Sons, 1907–12), p. 331.

9. Nutting and Dock, p. 342; 347.

10. Austin, pp. 330–331.

11. Doyle, p. 966.

12. Bullough, p. 105.

13. Cecil Woodham-Smith, *Florence Nightingale* (New York: McGraw-Hill, 1951), pp. 34, 38.

14. Martha Vicinus, *Independent Women: Work and Community for Single Women, 1850–1920* (Chicago: University of Chicago Press, 1985), pp. 88–89.

15. Mary McAuley Gilgannon, RSM, "The Sisters of Mercy as Crimean War Nurses," Ph.D. Diss. University of Notre Dame, 1962, p. 2.

16. Vicinus, p. 89.

17. Anna Jameson, *"Sisters of Charity" and "The Communion of Labour": Two Lectures on the Social Employment of Women* (London: Longman, 1859), pp. 20–23.

18. Jameson, p. 34.

19. Jameson, p. 18.

20. Jameson, p. 142.

21. Gilgannon, pp. 94–95.

22. Jameson, p. 132.

23. Vicinus, p. 89.

24. Vicinus, p. 89. See also Richard Shyrock, *The History of Nursing: An Interpretation of the Social and Medical Factors Involved* (Philadelphia: W. B. Saunders, 1959), p. 287.

25. Bullough, p. 105.

26. While there were Methodist, Evangelical, and Mennonite deaconesses at a later period, none was organized at the time of the Civil War.

27. Doyle, "Nursing by Religious Orders in the United States," *American Journal of Nursing* 29 (Oct. 1929): 1200.

28. Doyle, "Nursing by Religious Orders in the United States" *American Journal of Nursing* 29 (Nov. 1929): 1331–1334.

29. Doyle, "Nursing by Religious Orders in the United States," *American Journal of Nursing* 29 (Oct., Nov., Dec. 1929): 1197–1207; 1331–1143; 1466–1484.

30. Bullough, p. 33.

31. Victor Robinson, *White Caps: The Story of Nursing* (Philadelphia: J. B. Lippincott, 1946), p. 373–374.

32. See John B. Blake, "Women and Medicine in Antebellum America," *Bulletin of the History of Medicine* 39 (March-April 1965): 106–111. See also Mary Walsh, *Doctors Wanted: No Women Need Apply* (New Haven: Yale University Press, 1977). Walsh credits Harriot Hunt with being the first woman to practice medicine successfully in America, p. 1. Elizabeth Blackwell is the first woman doctor to receive an M. D. degree.

33. See Gerald Schwartz, ed., *A Woman Doctor's Civil War: Esther Hill Hawks' Diary* (Columbus, SC: University of South Carolina Press, 1984). Esther Hawks actually spent most of her time teaching in a school for freedmen, rather than as doctor or even nurse.

34. See Robinson, p. 372.

35. Bullough, p. 53.

36. Bullough, p. 54.

37. Bullough, p. 54.

38. Bullough, p. 62.

39. St. Vincent De Paul, quoted in Bullough, p. 62.

40. Josephine Dolan, *Nursing in Society: A Historical Perspective* (Philadelphia: W. B. Saunders, 1978), p. 193.

41. Robinson, pp. 372–373.

42. Doyle (July 1929), 775.

43. Bullough, pp. 104–105.

44. William Cavanaugh, "The Hospital Activities of the Sisters During the Civil War and Their Influence on the Catholic Hospital System Movement up to 1875," Masters Thesis, Catholic University of America, 1931, p. 13.

45. It is difficult to establish the exact number. The Cavanaugh thesis gives twenty-eight (pp. 13 and 14), yet one hospital listed simply changed hands from the Mercy Sisters to the Daughters of Charity. O'Grady implies twenty-five (p. 185–188), yet doesn't give the names of all of them. Doyle lists two "infirmaries" not included in Cavanaugh. Lack of records and some hospitals started that did

not continue also contribute to the difficulty in gathering exact numbers. General hospitals, hospitals for the insane, maternity, and infant-care hospitals sometimes were listed and sometimes not. Some institutions were also part hospital and part orphanage. Terms like "infirmary," "asylum," and "retreat" were often used synonymously. The official Catholic almanacs of the time did not have consistent data, as they were dependent on each individual diocese sending in information somewhat in the fashion each chose. *The Metropolitan Catholic Almanac* (Baltimore: John Murphy & Co., 1861) lists twenty-eight, and that may have been the source for Cavanaugh.

46. Doyle (July 1929): 779. See Barbara Misner, "A Comparative Social Study of the Members and Apostolates of the First Eight Permanent Communities of Women Religious within the Boundaries of the United States, 1790–1850," Ph.D. Diss. Catholic University of America, 1981, pp. 211–234, for some recent archival research on the sisters' care of the sick between 1830–1850.

47. Doyle (Aug. 1929): 962

48. O'Grady, p. 183.

49. Doyle (July 1929): 775.

50. O'Grady, p. 183.

51. Doyle (July 1929): 783.

52. Charles Rosenberg, *The Cholera Years: The United States in 1822, 1849, and 1866* (Chicago: The University of Chicago Press, 1962), p. 119.

53. Rosenberg, pp. 95, 119.

54. O'Grady, p. 191.

55. Rosenberg, p. 139.

56. See Stella O'Connor, "Charity Hospital at New Orleans: An Administrative and Financial History," *Louisiana Historical Quarterly* 31 (Jan. 1948), 6–109.

57. Doyle (July 1929): 783–84.

58. Doyle (July 1929): 782–83.

59. Misner, pp. 278–79.

60. Misner, p. 212.

61. Data on the names and dates of the communities and hospitals are taken from Doyle (July and Aug. 1929): 775–785, 959–969.

62. Doyle (Aug. 1929): 961–62. In Doyle, some information on Wheeling Hospital may be innacurate.

63. Doyle (Aug. 1929): 960.

64. O'Grady, p. 192.

65. O'Grady, p. 185.

66. Misner, p. 218.

67. O'Grady, p. 191.

68. Bullough, p. 104.

69. Robin O'Connor, "American Hospitals: The First 200 Years," *Hospitals* 50 (Jan. 1, 1976): 67.

70. Doyle (July 1929): 781.

71. Archives of the Sisters of Mercy of Vicksburg, Mississippi, (ARSMV), Handwritten copy of Mother M. de Sales Browne's *Constitution of the Sisters of Mercy* and *A Guide for the Religious Called Sisters of Mercy, Part I and II*. Although the *Guide*, compiled by Mother Mary Francis Bridgeman, who was with Night-ingale in the Crimea, was not published until 1866, it grew out of a series of

discussions designed to establish some conformity among the practices of the Irish Mercy sisters. Presumably, though, the oral tradition of these directions for care of the sick would have been handed down to the Sisters of Mercy in the United States from those who came from these foundations in Ireland. See Gilgannon, pp. 371–372. Further, there was a written commentary on the Rule and Constitution, written by the founder Mother Catharine McAuley (Gilgannon, 378–383). See also Archives of the Daughters of Charity, Emmitsburg, Maryland (ADC), *Constitution of the Daughters of Charity of St. Vincent de Paul* (Paris: Motherhouse, 1954), and Sister Louise Sullivan, trans., *Spiritual Writings of St. Louise de Marillac* (Albany, NY : De Paul Provincial House, 1984).

72. ADC, *Constitutions*, p. 141.

73. ADC, *Constitutions*, pp. 142–43.

74. ARSMV, *A Guide for the Religious Called Sisters of Mercy*, Part I and II, p. 41.

75. ADC, *Constitutions*, p. 136.

76. ARSMV, handwritten copy of *Constitution of the Sisters of Mercy*, n.p.

77. ARSMV, *A Guide*, p. 29.

78. Mary Livermore, *What Shall We Tell Our Daughters: Superfluous Women and Other Lectures* (Boston: Lee and Shepard, 1883), pp. 177–178.

Medical Care and Lay Female Nursing During the Civil War

As the Civil War began, armies of soldiers and officers, supplies of weapons and ammunition, military strategies on land and sea, and support of politicians and citizens alike were the major governmental and military issues. Almost overlooked in the early planning on either Union or Confederate side was the need for medical and nursing personnel to care for the thousands of men who would become sick or wounded during the course of the war. Disorganization and chaos characterized the early efforts of medical personnel as the casualties of the war overwhelmed their inadequate staff, makeshift facilities, untrained assistants, and limited medical knowledge. Even when these limitations were addressed during the course of the war, wounded and sick men needed more care than the doctors and hospitals could provide. Nurses were desperately needed to dress wounds, distribute medicine and supplies, keep patients clean and fed, offer support when nothing more could be done, and coordinate all these tasks. Disabled soldiers pressed into service for these duties simply did not suffice.

However, women of the North and South, willing to extend their maternal care, domestic skills, and moral values to the larger home of their country, eagerly stepped forward to offer their services when the governments were pleading for male volunteers to fight. Whether providing general support for the soldiers by sewing, making bandages, sending food packages, raising money, or specifically rushing to temporary hospitals to nurse, the women found a new role outside their homes. While attempts were made in the North by reformer Dorothea Dix and by the US Sanitary Commission to coordinate these efforts, the suddenness of the war, the lack of experience, and the disorganization surrounding the volunteer efforts added to the general consternation of male doctors faced with a mass of women moving into their domain.

The patriotic women, anxious to do what they believed they could do best—care for the sick—did expand the public's awareness of what women could do in improving the care given to the wounded and ill. However, prejudices against females caring for strange men, particularly when good will and not skill was the women's main contribution, were only partly overcome in the four years of the war. Nevertheless, what many doctors were willing to accept, and what some did get, were Roman Catholic sisters who were trained and organized, had experience, and would care for the sick with dedication and quiet good order. To understand why the sisters became the preferred nurses and were able to change attitudes about the place of women in nursing, and to highlight the value of training for those who would care for the sick, three aspects of Civil War medical care must be examined: first, the chaotic state of medical knowledge, practice, and facilities at the beginning of the war; second, the absence of any nursing care, and the women's efforts to express their patriotism and concern by rushing to fill this gap; and third, the resulting attitudes toward what these women did, and how they were regarded by doctors and soldiers. These issues provide the context in which the unique role of the sister nurse can be understood.

The catastrophic nature of the war was grasped by wound dresser and poet Walt Whitman, who observed, "So much of a race depends on what it thinks of death, and how it stands personal anguish and sickness." He found the main interest of the Civil War and its significance to be in the "two or three millions of American young and middle-aged men, North and South, . . . especially the one-third or one-fourth of their number stricken by wounds or disease" rather than in the "political interests involved."[1] The impact of the war is best revealed in the mortality statistics, which directly reflected the medical aspects of the conflict.

In the 2,196 battles fought, in which 67,000 Union soldiers were killed, 43,000 died of wounds; 250,000 died from disease; and some 130,000 were left with scars, amputations, and other lifetime reminders of the common people's war. Among the Confederates, approximately 94,000 died of wounds, and 164,000 of disease.[2] Though pictorial representations often show Civil War soldiers with bayonets and sabres, only 56 of the 922 Union wounds caused by these weapons were fatal. However, the small leaden Minié ball caused 94 percent of the wounds and the canister (a metal cylinder packed with small shot and fired from a cannon) about 6 percent for both Confederate and Union soldiers.[3]

The diseases, such as typhoid, dysentery, diarrhea, measles, smallpox, and fevers, such as erysipelas, caused the greatest death toll on both sides, with Confederate soldiers having a disproportionate share of respiratory-pulmonary diseases in the first year-and-a-half of the war.[4]

Medical historian Richard Shryock has estimated that the average soldier was ill between two and three times each year, with the annual mortality rate from sickness more than 5 percent. Compared with male civilians of military age, servicemen were five times as likely to become ill, and they experienced a mortality rate that was five times as high as that of those who remained at home.[5]

The inital belief of both sides that the conflict would be short caught everyone, including the Federal Army Medical Department, unprepared for many aspects of a prolonged and decimating war. There was no general military hospital and only one army-post hospital; it had forty-one beds in Fort Leavenworth, Kansas.[6] A medical staff of ninety-eight officers, but little support staff, no ambulances, and no nursing corps composed the rest of the Medical Department.[7] Though some surgeons resigned to aid the Southern states, the Confederacy was even less prepared.

While modern practice would judge Civil War surgeons as "deplorably ignorant and badly trained," they actually were better trained than the generation of physicians preceding them.[8] As Confederate medical historian Horace H. Cunningham and Union historian George W. Adams both pointed out, the rise of American nationalism during the second and third decades of the nineteenth century had contributed to the increasing number of native medical schools. Most of these were in the North, so that the South experienced a "medical dependence on the North as marked as [its] economic dependence,"[9] according to Cunningham. Nevertheless, in spite of schools, students still continued in the traditional mode of obtaining their training in the offices of older practitioners, who served as preceptors.[10]

By the antebellum period, opportunities for medical education had improved somewhat in both the North and South. For example, medical journals and professional societies existed to support the doctor in his practice.[11] Furthermore, Southern medical institutions increased in number, and their faculties compared favorably with those in the North from both a quantitative and a qualitative standpoint. In spite of some doctors with lack of experience, Cunningham credited the South with having some of the most competent medical men in the nation on the faculties of growing medical schools with relatively high standards. In spite of these growing opportunities for medical education, many young doctors in both the North and the South still began their careers without having had the opportunity to observe an operation closely, let alone perform one.[12]

While some Civil War doctors were often accused by coworkers of a lack of training or knowledge, general ineptitude, disregard for the patients, and drunkenness,[13] many were competent and concerned for their patients. For example, Walt Whitman, who worked as a wound dresser in various Washington hospitals and had seen "many hundreds of them [doctors]," said:

I must bear my most emphatic testimony to the zeal, manliness, and professional spirit and capacity, generally prevailing among the surgeons, many of them young men, in the Hospitals and the army. I will not say much about the exceptions, for they are few; (but I have met some of those few, and very incompetent and airish they were) I never ceas'd to find the best young men, and the hardest and most disinterested workers, among these Surgeons, in the Hospitals. They are full of genius, too.[14]

However, the difficulties and strains of practicing medicine under inadequate and crowded conditions, with erratic supplies and often meager food, were overwhelming burdens for many doctors who had to assume leadership of military hospitals. As a consequence, Medical Director Dr. John Brinton, cousin of General George McClellen, was grateful for money sent by Northern men and for food and supply boxes sent by women. He recalled:

During my short stay at Mound City Hospital [Illinois], I first learned what it really was to be in authority. The responsibility which to me was always commensurate with the authority, weighed heavily upon me. I did my best to get for the patients in the hospitals all the comforts I could not only from the government supplies but also with the aid societies which at that time were springing up everywhere in the west and the east.[15]

In addition, Brinton also had to perform rites for the dead when he was left without a chaplain.

Basic medical knowledge taken for granted today was unknown to Brinton and other doctors. While anesthesia was used just prior to the Civil War (1846) and chloroform was administered by some surgeons,[16] whiskey forced down a man's throat by attendants holding him prone for the surgery (often amputation) was common on the battlefields of the North and South. More significantly, Joseph Lister's first paper on antiseptic surgery was not published until 1867, and Louis Pasteur's discoveries on the germ theory of infection were not known in America.

Consequently, while Civil War surgeons knew that carbolic acid would clean out infected wounds, they did not think to use it to sterilize instruments. In spite of their practical wartime experience with wounds, surgeons still believed that infections were caused by "noxious effluvia" arising from filth and carried through the air. Thus, while ordinary cleanliness in hospitals and fresh air was known to be important and later incorporated in the designs of government-built hospitals in the latter half of the war,[17] "laudable pus" in a wound was seen as desirable, and a surgeon's hands seemingly had nothing to do with the spread of disease.[18]

Dr. William Keen, who utilized his wartime experience in writing extensive scientific monographs after the war, graphically described the conditions:

We operated in our old blood-stained and often pus-stained coats.... We used undisinfected instruments from undisinfected plush cases, and still worse, used marine sponges which had been used in prior pus cases and had been only washed in tap water. If a sponge or an instrument fell on the floor it was washed and squeezed in a basin of tap water and used as if it were clean.... The silk with which we sewed up all our wounds was undisinfected. If there was any difficulty in threading the needle we moistened it with (as we now know) bacteria-laden saliva, and rolled it between bacteria-infected fingers.... In opening wounds...maggots as large as chestnut worms abounded in the Summer. While disgusting they did little or no harm....[19] We were wholly ignorant of the fact that the mosquito, and only the mosquito, spreads yellow fever and malaria.... We did not even suspect that the flea and rat conspired to spread the bubonic plague and that the louse was responsible for the deadly typhus.[20]

While innumerable doctors on both sides kept careful diaries and journals, in which they described and often illustrated the illnesses and surgical procedures they were doing,[21] these were not available for circulation during the war. In any case, the exigencies of the battlefields, the demands in the field and general hospitals, and the hazards of the blockades, especially for the Southerners, left little time to study new techniques and methods. Thus, the same general medical knowledge, surgical techniques, and beliefs about disease and sanitation prevailed among both Union and Confederate doctors.

Physical facilities for the sick were also woefully lacking throughout most of the war in the South and in its early stages in the North. At first, schools, churches, warehouses, private residences, and public buildings on both sides were all hurriedly pressed into service as general hospitals, but most were poorly furnished and badly managed. As the war proceeded, private hospitals sometimes had contracts with the government, and soldiers went to them, hoping the government would pay their bills for what they believed would be better care.[22]

The usual procedure on both sides was to transfer a seriously sick soldier from the field or regimental hospital, usually located in a canvas tent, to a "general" hospital, which was not restricted to men of any particular military unit.[23] However, even the facilities for transporting the wounded to these hospitals were inadequate. The war began with no ambulance system for either army. The Union army, after the devastating campaigns of 1862, finally had ambulances taken from the authority of the Quartermaster Corps and placed under Dr. Jonathan

Letterman, medical director of the Army of the Potomac, who gradually developed a system of adequate, better designed ambulances.[24]

On the Confederate side, early battles around the capital of Richmond, Virginia, all filled to overflowing the buildings of Richmond and the surrounding areas held by the Confederates. As a result, in late 1862, Surgeon-General Samuel P. Moore, with the assistance of hospital directors William S. Carrington, Samuel H. Stout, and James McCaw, and with monies from the Confederate Congress, finally organized a Confederate hospital system and began building military hospitals.

Many efforts were made to address the problems. The widespread belief about poisons circulating in the air and the recommendations from the Crimean War doctors in regard to the value of fresh air had three effects: tent hospitals in the field were in use until the end of 1865; general hospitals of canvas were erected in 1862; and the design of the pavilion hospitals, initially built under Union Surgeon William A. Hammond's direction in 1862, provided excellent ventilation. By the end of the war, the Union claimed 204 hospitals and 136,894 beds, ranging in size from Satterlee Hospital in Philadelphia, with 3,500 beds, to Hospital #20 in Tullahoma, Tennessee, with 100.[25] Ultimately, the Confederates had about 150 general hospitals, with about 50 located around or in Richmond. The 8,000-bed Chimborazo Hospital, near Richmond, was believed at the time to be the largest ever built in the world.[26]

As a result of these building efforts, Joseph J. Woodward, Assistant Surgeon General, could claim that "never before in the history of the world, was so vast a system of hospitals brought into existence in so short a time." He further cited the Union's practice of putting these hospitals under medical directors rather than ordinary officers, which had been the practice in the Crimean War. A consequence of this action, he felt, was a very low mortality rate and little spread of disease in these hospitals.[27]

Walt Whitman's comment, though, may have been closer to the truth experienced by those who worked day in and day out with the "system," especially in the first two years of the war:

There are, however, serious deficiencies, wastes, sad want of system, etc., in the Commissions, contributions, and in all the Voluntary, and a great part of the Governmental, nursing, edibles, medicines, stores, etc. . . . Whatever puffing accounts there may be in the papers of the North, this is the actual fact. No thorough previous preparation, no system, no foresight, no genius. Always plenty of stores, no doubt, but always miles away; never where they are needed, and never the proper application. Of all the harrowing experiences, none is greater than that of the days following a heavy battle. Scores, hundreds of the noblest young men on earth, uncomplaining, lie, helpless, mangled, faint, alone, and so bleed to death, or die from exhaustion, either actually untouch'd at all, or merely the laying of them down and leaving them, when there ought to be means provided to save them.[28]

Although from a later perspective the disease mortality rate was appalling, army leaders thought their record was quite satisfactory compared with that of previous wars.[29] Yet much unnecessary illness was caused by the utter lack of preparation and subsequent inefficiency of the medical services. Shryock notes, though, that this inefficiency was not the fault of any one group. Sharing in responsibility, he concludes, were "the original medical officers, indifferent generals, and politicians, a mediocre profession, and rural regiments hitherto unexposed to infections and unfamiliar with the rudiments of hygiene."[30]

In this quagmire of medical inefficiency, nurses to assist these doctors, especially in the field hospitals, were more likely to be disabled soldiers than females. Though mistaken notions of Clara Barton and her work often fostered the legend that women nurses played an important role on Civil War battlefields, the number who functioned in field hospitals, probably one in five, was actually never large, according to Adams.[31] Nevertheless, George Augustus Sala, a British journalist, described the Civil War as "a woman's war,"[32] a war that utilized women's talents and capitalized on their patriotism and domesticity.

Most women worked for the multitudinous and successful aid societies, especially the US Sanitary Commission and the Christian Commission in the North, by sewing, scraping lint for bandages, preparing food packages, and raising money. However, about 9,000 did serve specifically as Union nurses and 1,000 as Confederate nurses. In 1890, after bills had been proposed in Congress for back pay and pensions for female US Army nurses, Samuel Ramsey, chief clerk in the Surgeon-General's office, attempted to clarify various issues surrounding the legislation and, in estimating these numbers, distinguished seven classes of women employed in nursing. The first class included the approximately 3,214 nurses appointed partly by Dorothea Dix and partly by other officials, hired under the Act of August 3, 1861, and receiving salaries of 40 cents and one ration in kind each day. Paid out of Army funds, these nurses had a legal status as employees of the Union.[33]

The second group Ramsey described as "Sisters of Charity [generic name] who received forty cents a day, when paid at all—number uncertain but certainly smaller than the previous class."[34] The third category, estimated at 4,500, were women of all classes who did a variety of domestic chores, such as cooking, scrubbing floors, and washing dishes and were paid "anything that might be agreed on" from "anyone who would take the risk of paying them." "Colored women hired under General Orders in 1863 and 1864 at $10 a month" comprised the fourth class.[35]

A fifth group was composed of those that gave their services without compensation, and a sixth classification were those women "who accompanied regiments," generally called camp followers.[36] Women volunteering through various relief organizations, particularly those of the US Sanitary Commission, the Western Sanitary Commission, and the US Christian Commission, comprised the final group of nurses.

"Was the system of women-nurses in the hospitals a failure?" Union nurse Jane Woolsey, one of a family of seven sisters who served in the war, rhetorically asked. Cognizant of the power of the women and citing examples of the myriad ways in which women came to "nurse" during the war, she concluded, "that the presence of hundreds of individual women as nurses in hospitals was neither an intrusion nor a blunder, let the multitude of their unsystematized labors and achievements testify."[37]

Nevertheless, few of these women possessed actual hospital experience or other qualifications beyond a patriotic desire to serve, or perhaps, in some cases, physical strength to do the chores connected with nursing. As Woolsey explained, these women, usually eight to twenty of them, only slightly educated and without training or discipline, were set adrift in a hospital with no organization or officer to whom to report.[38]

One woman, though, did attempt to provide some organization and structure for these nurses. On the day after Lincoln's call for volunteer soldiers, Dorothea L. Dix, a Boston schoolteacher who had earned a national reputation for two years of work in improving the conditions of the mentally ill, went straight from Trenton, New Jersey, to the War Department in Washington to offer her services to care for the wounded and sick soldiers.[39] She was appointed superintendent of United States Army Nurses on April 23, 1861, by the following order from Simon Cameron, Secretary of War:

The free services of Miss D. L. Dix are accepted by the War Department and that she will give at all times all necessary aid in organizing military hospitals for the cure of all sick and wounded soldiers, aiding the chief surgeon by supplying nurses and substantial means for the comfort and relief of the suffering; also that she is fully authorized to receive, control, and disburse special supplies bestowed by individuals or associations for the comfort of their friends or the citizen soldiers from all parts of the limited states; as also, under action of the Acting Surgeon-General, to draw from the army stores.[40]

Scarcely a week later, floods of women wishing to serve often moved ahead to hospitals without any authorization, compelling Acting Surgeon-General Robert C. Wood to issue a notice telling the women they first needed to contact Dix before starting to work. He further added that the ladies should: "exert themselves to their fullest extent in preparing or supplying hospital shirts for the sick; also articles of diet, as delicacies may be needed for individual cases, and such important articles as eggs, milk, chickens, etc."[41]

In a later attempt to handle the women volunteers, General Order No. 31 came on June 9, 1861, indicating that women nurses were not to reside in the camps nor accompany regiments on a march, and those who applied for service had to have certificates from two physicians and two clergymen of good standing.[42]

Although Secretary of War Cameron reported to Lincoln on July 1, 1861, that the nursing services of patriotic women were entrusted to Dix,[43] the role and duties assigned by the general orders and assumed by Dix as she went about her tasks were not clearly delineated from the beginning. The result was often confusion and misunderstanding on the part of many who dealt with Dix and her nurses throughout the war.

In addition to selecting nurses, Dix was almost immediately called on, because of her prior experience in inspecting hospitals, to give advice and direction in matters of hospital supplies, equipment, and a thousand other details so that her position took on huge but unclear proportions. As her biographer, Helen Marshall, has pointed out, Dix found it hard to realize that no system could be organized overnight and be perfect. "For twenty years, she had been inspecting hospitals, pointing out mistakes, and remedying abuses," Marshall explains, "and it came to her as second nature to ferret out inefficient management, carelessness in attendants, shirking and indifferent physicians," causing antagonism and frustration on the part of many doctors.[44]

Although not a nurse herself, Dix was determined to create admission requirements for the Army Nursing Corps that would screen out women whose conduct might undermine the fragile reputation of the female nurses. Thus, her bulletin stated: "No woman under thirty need apply to serve in the government hospitals. All nurses are required to be plain looking women. Their dresses must be brown or black with no bows, no curls, no jewelry, and no hoop skirts."[45] Her second goal was to bring all unregulated nursing activities everywhere under her control.[46]

In the early days, she had the support of Surgeon-General Wood, who on May 20, 1861, "recommended to all commanding officers and enjoined on all medical officers of the regular and volunteer forces to aid her in her benevolent views."[47] He further ordered:

In reference to the national reputation of Miss Dix as connected with objects of philanthropy and usefulness, she is authorized to exercise a general supervision of the assignment of nurses to the hospitals, general and regimental, occupied by the troops at Washington, and its vicinity, subject to the advisement and control of the Surgeon General's Office in matters of detail, numbers, etc., and excepting such hospitals as already have a permanent organization of nurses.[48]

By October 1863, General Order 351 was issued through the Surgeon-General's office by order of Secretary of War Edwin Stanton in an attempt to clarify the differences existing between the medical staff and Dix. However, the result of the order, which gave the Surgeon-General the right to appoint nurses, undercut most of Dix's authority during the remainder of the war.[49] Doctors who did not want her nurses or preferred other female nurses simply went to the Surgeon-General.

Even before this order, there were ways around the requirements for women who wanted to nurse if Dix rejected the eager volunteers. Cornelia Hancock recalled her experience of going to Baltimore hoping to get to Gettysburg to help the wounded after the battle:

Dorothea Dix appeared on the scene. She looked the nurses over and pronounced them all suitable except me. She immediately objected to my going on the score of my youth and rosy cheeks. I was then just twenty-three years of age. In those days it was considered indecorous for angels of mercy to appear otherwise than gray-haired and spectacled. Such a thing as a hospital corps of comely young maiden nurses, possessing grace and good looks, was then unknown. Miss Farnham [Eliza—a public-spirited woman who also had a pass as a volunteer nurse] explained that she was under obligation to my friends who had helped her get proper credentials. The discussion waxed warm and I have no idea what conclusion they came to, for I settled the question myself by getting on the car and staying in my seat until the train pulled out of the city of Baltimore. They had not forcibly taken me from the train, so I got into Gettysburg the night of July sixth [1863] where the need was so great that there was no further cavil about age.[50]

In addition to Dix's strict view on nurses, many found her personally difficult to get along with. For example, Hancock later wrote to her niece, quoting pioneer woman-journalist Mrs. Jane Swisshelm's comment upon Dix: "[She] is a self-sealing can of horror tied up with red tape." Hancock qualified her judgment somewhat by adding that "Miss Dix's nurses are like all others in my estimation, some excellent, some good, some positively bad. So it would be, let who *would* have charge."[51] Later Louisa May Alcott, whose descriptive account of her service became well known in spite of her brief, six-month length of duty, wrote that Dix was "a kind, old soul, but very queer and arbitrary."[52]

While Dix's reformer reputation and spontaneous offer to coordinate the nursing service gained her an immediate welcome, the difficulties engendered by overwhelming numbers of volunteers and her desire to control all nursing activities herself caused clashes with nurses and doctors. How much of this conflict was due to her personality, how much to the general disorganization of the medical and nursing aspects of the war, and how much was due to general attitudes about women is difficult to determine. These trying circumstances may be some of the reasons why Dix herself said that her Civil War efforts were not the experiences by which she wished to be remembered.[53]

In addition to Dix's nurses and others engaged in direct care of the sick, additional women offered support to the sick and wounded. On April 15, 1861, when Lincoln called for volunteers, some women in Northern cities immediately started organizing relief societies or mobilizing already existing groups to collect supplies, food, clothing, and blankets, and to sew for the men and furnish nurses for the wounded. The first Northern relief society was started at Bridgeport, Connecticut, on April 15, 1861.

Within two weeks after the outbreak of war, there were more than twenty thousand aid societies at work in the Union and Confederacy, but not all were able to continue throughout the conflict, and many in the South were compelled to disband because of invasion, civilian displacement, and scarcity of supplies.[54] Early in the war, these local societies supplied items only for men from their own community or state, and in the Confederacy this generally continued to be the situation throughout the war. In the North, however, many local groups were coordinated under the supervision of the US Sanitary Commission.

In reflecting on the background of the US Sanitary Commission, Dr. Elizabeth Blackwell recalled that at the outbreak of the war, an informal meeting of the lady managers of the New York Infirmary for Women and Children was called on April 25, 1861, to "see what could be done towards supplying the want of trained nurses felt after the first battles." Out of that meeting, the National Sanitary Aid Association and the Ladies' Sanitary Aid Association were formed. The associations worked during the entire war, receiving and forwarding contributions and comforts for the soldiers, but their special work was the forwarding of nurses to the battlefront. Blackwell noted, however, that because of the extreme urgency of the needs, all that could be done was to sift out the most promising women from the multitudes that applied as nurses, to put them in training for a month at New York's Bellevue Hospital, which consented to receive relays of volunteers and send them on for assignment to Dix.[55]

From that meeting, too, came a delegation headed by Reverend Dr. Henry Bellows, pastor of the First Unitarian Church of New York, which discussed with Lincoln and Acting Surgeon-General Wood a proposal for creating a government-approved sanitary association that would "consider the general subject of the prevention of sickness and suffering among the troops."[56] The proposed organization was to operate separately from the Medical Bureau. Lincoln dismissed the plan calling it "the fifth wheel to the coach."[57] However, a new plan was drawn up that resulted in an order, signed by Lincoln on June 13, 1861, creating the US Sanitary Commission, whose purpose was to care for the wounded without duplicating government activities.[58] These early efforts of the Sanitary Commission were strongly influenced by the experiences of Florence Nightingale, who noted that the great loss of life in the Crimean War was due to lack of cleanliness, proper nourishment, and nursing care.

Summarizing these endeavors of the Sanitary Commission, William Maxwell, a twentieth-century historian, concludes that in spite of Elizabeth Blackwell's influence, she found herself hampered by traditional prejudices. Under Sanitary Commission auspices, only a limited number of women received instruction for a period of weeks before turning to help the army. Further, dislike of this assistance was reportedly more pronounced in the medical corps of the East than in the West. Finally, in October 1862, the Sanitary Commission dropped its training program, though it continued to supply nurses.[59]

Unlike the North, the Confederacy, unfortunately, did not have a similar organizer or agency to coordinate the nursing or aid work. However, through real sacrifice and effort on the part of individuals, particularly when their cities were overrun and transportation systems ruined, Southern groups were quite successful in providing some assistance. That the Southern women's efforts were not coordinated as they were in the North was not so much the fault of the women as of the state and of the Confederate officials who often refused to cooperate for the common good.[60]

The Confederate States set up an act in September 1862 to "better provide for the sick and wounded of the Army in hospitals."[61] However, prior to that time, there was notable civilian relief work on a large scale in which Southern women played a major role.[62] Many Southerners were wounded in the first battles, and many more became ill with measles, typhoid fever, dysentery, camp fever, and the other diseases that usually developed among soldiers experiencing the close quarters of camp life for the first time. Even less equipped than the Union government for dealing with the large masses of casualties, the Confederate government had to rely on these various women's relief societies then springing into existence. Food (both luxuries and staples), drugs smuggled in the folds of their gowns, bandages, and bedding were all collected and distributed by these groups.

The founding of hospitals to care for the wounded was also undertaken by groups such as the Southern Mothers' Society. However, the resources of the women were soon inadequate to handle the treatment of all the disabled of the Confederate armies. There were no trained nurses among the Southern women, and the hospitals needed the discipline of skilled experts with the authority of the government behind them. During the last months of 1861 and the first months of the following year, therefore, the Confederate government assumed the control and partial support of all soldiers' hospitals in the South. The change from voluntary to official management did not result, however, in women disappearing from the hospital scene. The hospital relief societies continued to supply these institutions with food and clothing. An important and able group of lay women found work as matrons, and a few women of exceptional ability, such as Sallie Tompkins and Ella King Newsome, remained as managers. In fact, Southern historians Francis Simkins and James Patton conclude that the services of women continued to be so varied and extensive that the significance of their efforts was in "no sense lessened by the fact that the managerial phases of hospital work largely passed into masculine hands."[63]

The September 1862 act concerning the hospitalized sick and wounded of the Confederate army also provided for a financial allotment to each hospital, for pay with rations based on responsibility, and for suitable places of lodging for those caring for the sick. Two matrons, two assistant matrons, other nurses and cooks as might be needed, and a ward master for each ward were specifically designated. In all cases, preference was given to "females where their services may best subserve the purposes."[64]

Confederate medical historian Cunningham, citing the low mortality rates in many of the hospitals set up by Southern women, points out that this convincing proof of feminine superiority in nursing caused the Confederate government to believe that many women would now come forward as hospital attendants. However, Cunningham concludes that the prevailing belief that full-time service in the hospitals was not respectable work for women acted as a deterrent in keeping many from taking up this needed work.[65]

In the South, it was generally held that nursing, which involved such intimate contacts with strange men, was unfit for self-respecting women to pursue, especially for young and unmarried women. The majority of surgeons shared this contemporary prejudice against the service of women in the hospitals. The effects of this belief were to reduce the number of women who were willing to ignore or flout public opinion to a level far below the actual needs of the hospital service, and it tended to drive the "better class" of women away from the hospitals and throw the positions open to women of "indifferent" character and training.[66]

Not every Southerner held these views, however. In response to the argument concerning a lady's modesty, Confederate nurse Kate Cumming responded:

As far as my judgment goes, a lady who feels that her modesty would be compromised by going into a hospital, and ministering to the wants of her suffering countrymen, who have braved all in her defense, could not rightly lay claim to a very large share of that excellent virtue—modesty—which the wise tell us is ever the companion of sense. . . . There is scarcely a day passes that I do not hear some derogatory remarks about the ladies who are in the hospitals, until I think, if there is any credit due them at all, it is for the moral courage they have in braving public opinion.[67]

But the presence of women in crowded conditions with strange male patients and primarily male nurses, doctors, and other assistants did continue to raise issues of motivation and propriety. A typical situation involving all these concerns was described by Confederate diarist Mary Boykin Chestnut. In her diary, Chestnut recounted the struggles of a Mrs. Louisa Susanna McCord, an author who also ran a military hospital. Though McCord "gave her whole soul to the hospital," there was insufficient medical aid; good nurses were needed, as those she hired ate and drank the food provided for the sick and wounded.[68] Chestnut sympathized with McCord's troubles, saying "a nurse who is also a beauty had better leave her beauty with her cloak and hat at the door." After hearing about a "lovely lady nurse" who had asked a "rough old soldier" what she could do for him," she received the reply, "Kiss Me." The nurse, who apparently did not kiss him, but told the story, was the cause of McCord's fury since she brought the "hospital in disrepute," "and very properly," as Chestnut concluded. Chestnut said that McCord wanted nurses to come dressed as nurses—as Sisters of Charity—not as fine ladies. If they did, there would be no trouble. When McCord saw women coming in angel sleeves, "displaying all of their white arms, and in their muslin, showing all of their beautiful white shoulders and throats," she felt disposed to order them off the premises: that was no proper costume for a nurse. On the other hand, one woman who was praised by McCord was a Mrs. Bartow, who came in her "widow's weeds."[69]

The attitude that a woman must sacrifice her modesty, if not her virtue in order to care for the sick, though more dominant in the South, was hardly confined to the Confederate states. Dr. Samuel Howe, husband of Julia Ward Howe, refused to let his wife do any war work more unconventional than the making of lint and bandages and, toward the end, some hospital visiting, even though it was he who, many years before, had encouraged the young Nightingale to take up a nursing career. When charged with this inconsistency, he justified his stand by saying that it was Nightingale's not being married that made all the difference. He told his wife that "if he had been engaged to Florence Nightingale, and had loved her ever so dearly, he would have given her up as soon as she commenced her career as a 'public woman.' " By "public woman," Dr. Howe seems to have meant any female who had any activities outside home and church.[70]

Because of these attitudes expressed by many doctors and other male medical assistants, such as male nurses and ward masters, Dix and other women who tried to run hospitals generally had to set rigid standards if they expected to overcome the prejudice against them. Even those who saw some value in female nurses had differing views on who should care for the sick.

But the women themselves, although untrained and motivated by a variety of intentions, came with a combination of ideas about women's maternal calling, their mission as homemakers, and their responsibility for bringing refinement, tenderness, and gentility to a male-dominated society. Because of these qualities, the patients usually appreciated the nurses, even if the doctors often disliked them. The soldiers were often young men who were homesick and grateful for motherly ministrations. Thus, the women's attitudes were normally reinforced, rather than refused. Indeed, the titles of many of the famous nurses were "Mother," "Sister," or "Angel."

Louisa Alcott, describing her care of a soldier, explained, "And now I knew that to him, as to so many, I was the poor substitute for mother, wife, or sister, and in his eyes no stranger, but a friend who hitherto had seemed neglectful."[71] "The soldiers talk much of their mothers and sisters, as all men do now," recalled Cumming, alluding to the same attitudes. " 'Home, Sweet Home,' is the dearest spot on earth to them, since they are deprived of its comforts, and mother, wife, and sister seem to be sweeter to them than any words in the English language," she added.[72]

In caring for their patients in the wards, then, women emphasized the familiar domestic virtues, including religious observance, abstinence from alcohol, and familial concern. Yet, while anxious to alleviate the soldiers' suffering, they sometimes grew overly enthusiastic about their maternal role. "The doctors do not like the wives of the men to come and nurse them; they say they invariably kill them with kindness," remarked Cumming. But she added, "There are some ladies who come to take care of their relatives, who seem to understand nursing, and are a great help, not only to their own folks, but to others around them; those the doctors do not object to."[73]

Among the duties assumed by these women, concern for the quantity and quality of the food for the men was paramount. Jane Woolsey wrote from a general hospital in the North:

I have one hundred men in my ward, all in bed. The surgeons appear to give very little care to the diet, but are down on any one else who does. The food is very poor and insufficient. The cooks [male] seem to have it all their own way. The ladies are not allowed to superintend in the kitchen or have anything to do with it. For thirty-eight of my men the ward surgeon orders, in general terms, milk and eggs. It is grimly amusing to hear him say day after day, 'milk and eggs for thirty-eight.' One egg apiece, each meal is all I can ever get from the.

cooks, and for two days there have been no eggs at all. The milk rations are always short.... All this wears upon one infinitely more than the hard work.[74]

Appalled at the sidetracking of food supplies for the men,[75] Annie Wittenmyer, who became famous for the development of special Union diet kitchens, found that "no part of the army service was so defective, during the first two years of the war, as its cooking department in the U.S. government hospitals."[76]

Ordinarily, conditions in the South for patient and nurse were worse. Cumming, though usually complaining about the "sameness of the diet," does recount that sometimes things "improved" temporarily. An improvement for the nurses consisted of "batter-cakes made of the mush left over from the previous meal, rice, and stale bread, (I do not mean what the men leave as nothing is used which has been in the wards,) hash made out of soupmeat, toast, mush, milk, tea, coffee, and beefsteak. Our batter-cakes never have eggs in them; they have a little flour and soda and are very nice."[77]

Besides concern for the food, the other duties of the nurses varied depending on the particular hospital, the attitude of the surgeon in charge, or battle conditions. For example, Alcott, responding to someone who wondered if nurses were obliged to witness amputations as part of their duty, said,

I think not, unless they wish; for the patient is under the effects of ether, and needs no care but such as the surgeon can best give. Our work begins afterward when the poor soul comes to himself, sick, faint and wandering; full of strange pains and confused visions, of disagreeable sensations and sights. Then we must sooth and sustain, tend and watch; preaching and practicing patience, till sleep and time have restored courage and self-control.[78]

In spite of her limited length of service, Alcott, unlike many women, did witness several operations because, as she explained: "The height of my ambition was to go to the front after a battle, and feeling that the sooner I inured myself to trying sights, the more useful I should be." Echoing what was often a criticism of the female nurses, Alcott remarked that some of her friends avoided such sights, "for though the spirit was wholly willing, the flesh was inconveniently weak."[79] She went on to describe "one funereal lady" who said she fainted at the sight of blood, was nervous about infections, couldn't take care of delirious persons, and so was dismissed. "I hope she found her sphere," Alcott concluded, "but [I] fancy a comfortable bandbox on a high shelf would best meet the requirements of her case."[80]

In contrast to this woman, Union nurse Woolsey devoted a chapter in *Hospital Days*, her detailed and insightful account of wartime experiences, to the duties of being a superintendent. Requisitioning and deploying supplies for the wards; supervising the preparation of the food in the kitchen; overseeing the "wittles train";[81] listening to and responding to complaints about the food; handling paperwork related to obtaining supplies; receiving reports from the women nurses; taking care of visitors; talking with the men as they came for their supplies and tobacco—all these activities made up the "Superintendent's day—with its digressions," as Woolsey described her demanding work.[82] All matrons did not necessarily have her abilities, her concern, nor her access to the resources of the Sanitary Commission; nonetheless, the duties of a matron or superintendent were similar and the frustrations uniformly the same.

Southern conditions were more spartan, and Confederate nurse Cumming, who performed duties similar to Woolsey's, recalled her typical day's work:

Mrs. Williamson and I live like Sisters of Charity; we get up in the morning about 4 o'clock, and breakfast by candle-light, which meal consists of real coffee without milk, but sugar, hash, and bread; we eat it in our room. Unless we get up early, we find it impossible to get through with our duties. Mrs. Williamson prepares toddies and egg-nogs; I see that the delicacies for the sick are properly prepared. After the duties of the day are over, we then write letters for the men, telling their relatives they are here, or informing them of their decease; other times mending some little articles for them. Mrs. Williamson is up many a night till 12 o'clock, working for her "dear boys," as she calls them.[83]

The female nurses, whether cook, nurse, or superintendent, often felt they knew how to run the hospital better than the military or medical administrators, and saw many regulations, which were standard military procedure, as tedious or obstructive, to be ignored if possible rather than obeyed. Accordingly, whether out of maternal solicitude or moral superiority, nurses were usually not hesitant to openly criticize medical officers, characterize their treatment of patients as cold and unfeeling, and view the hospital system as in need of women's guidance. Drunkenness was the commonest charge against the surgeons, and the women especially noted "drunken carousals" and resulting neglect and mistreatment of patients, though the major complaints concerned rough handling and the dressing of wounds.[84]

Thus, their understanding of their position and tasks sometimes brought the female nurses into conflict with the hospital authorities. It was unthinkable to the majority of these women that professional medical men could exert the kind of benevolent and healing effect upon the sick and wounded that they, with womanly understanding and gentleness, could. As John Brumgardt explains, these beliefs came from the fact that, first, they were women, and second, they believed that the doctor's work proceeded either from obedience to military duty or a contract for pay, not from real concern for their patients.[85]

The nurses' perception that surgeons were unfeeling toward their patients was not without some foundation. However, as Brumgardt concludes, objective, scientific regard for the patients could hardly be personal, and this tendency of the doctors to have a clinical perspective was reinforced by an order from the surgeon-general that all doctors had to file reports on cases treated as part of the project to compile a medical history of the war.[86]

Assessing the activities of these women and the attitudes displayed toward them has resulted in two twentieth-century views. Nina Bennet Smith, in her dissertation on the Union Army nurse, has suggested that the women who went to war were not seeking to establish careers in nursing, nor were renouncing relations with men, since most were married or expected to be. Neither were they feminists, however that word is defined, but rather saw their nursing as a local and charitable extension of their home duties; thus, they saw themselves as morally and practically superior to men. Smith argues that the doctors who found fault with them were objecting to a challenge to their authority rather than to the idea of female medical assistants, since the doctors approved of Catholic nursing orders.[87]

On the other hand is a view of women's participation that is more confrontational to male medical authority. Ann Douglas Wood, in an article on Union nurses, proposed that:

Basic to these women's complicated urge to make the front truly a home-front, to replace the captain with the mother, the doctor with the nurse, and even to out-soldier the soldiers, was their sense that they were being kept out of medicine, of war, of *life itself*, by a complicated professional code that simply boiled down to men's unwillingness to let anyone—including themselves—know what a mess they had made. . . . In bringing home virtues to witness against "professional" methods, they did not so much make the world a home, as they helped to make themselves at home *in the world*. Nursing the troops in the Civil War had not only offered them a chance to criticize the imprisoning professional code of the military medical corps from the perspective of their maternal natures; it had also given them the opportunity to make a profession, and a competitive one, out of their maternity.[88]

While Smith's conclusions are based on a larger study of sources than Wood's, the truth may be less definitive than either writer holds. The sources for both positions come largely from more than one hundred volumes and many more articles published between 1865 and 1914, based on women's own experiences as nurses, as Sanitary Commission workers, as teachers of freedmen, and on other adventures such as soldiering and spying. These largely white, middle-class or upper-class women often kept both journals and published memoirs. They went to war primarily out of patriotism, and in their accounts spoke largely of their duties, their difficulties with the system, and their often romanticized concern for the soldiers "who had been reared as tenderly as girls, and who were just from under their mothers' wing...silent heroes, whose gentle patience and uncomplaining fortitude glorified the rough wards."[89] Nonetheless, in spite of some similarities, these accounts are individual views, expressed in nineteenth-century ideology, and not a collective experience of women with twentieth-century perspectives. Thus, Smith's less definitive but more comprehensive view is more valuable in understanding these women than Woods'.

In spite of their efforts in the hospitals and in a multitude of other situations, female nurses did not receive much public praise and recognition during the Civil War itself. Massey suggests the causes for this lack of recognition are complex, but underlying other reasons was the nurses' "inability to overcome in only four years the long-standing, deep-seated prejudice of the general public and the military officials."[90]

Four years was a short time in which to change many of the general medical and surgical understandings, practices, and facilities, let alone specific ideas about the place of female nurses. By the end of the war, the Union army did have twelve thousand doctors, organized into seven ranks, and a system of over two hundred hospitals.[91] Further, knowledge about disease, infection, and surgical procedures learned in crisis situations was in the process of being gathered into written reports that would educate doctors in the future. Clearly, the energies of the doctors and officers, besides dealing daily with the wounded men, were devoted to increasing their medical corps, constructing hospitals, and developing information on the medical and surgical situations with which they were faced. The lack of medical knowledge and the limited number of doctors and hospitals that characterized the early years of the war understandably made these concerns top priority.

In addition, recognition of the value of trained women as nurses was complicated by their lack of training, frequent disorganization, relatively small numbers, and the traditional prejudices against them. Patriotic good will simply did not overcome the lack of experience and skills on the part of many women, even when they fed patients, dressed wounds, and sometimes organized whole hospitals. Individual dedicated and efficient female nurses, such as Cumming and Woolsey, were sometimes appreciated. Nevertheless, even the efforts of Dorothea Dix and of the US Sanitary Commission in the first years of the war were insufficient to mobilize individual women into some kind of trained nurse corps, whose concerted strength might serve to break down the doctors' prejudices.

However, by the war's end, one group of female nurses did gain recognition and earned praise: the Catholic sisters. They, too, were initially viewed with suspicion and suffered the additional prejudices associated with their religion and lifestyle. Unlike other female nurses, however, their services were in demand because they offered nursing skills, hospital experience, and predictable, orderly service arising from their religious commitment and community purposes. Against a background of weak medical staffs, confusion of nursing efforts, and the often negative attitudes of doctors about women, the multitude of requests for sisters to serve in the war can be readily comprehended.

NOTES

1. Walt Whitman, *Memoranda During the War*, (n.d., rpt. Bloomington: Indiana University Press, 1962), pp. 4–5.

2. Thomas L. Livermore, *Numbers and Loses in the Civil War in America* (Boston: Houghton, Mifflin, 1901), pp. 5–8.

3. Stewart Brooks, *Civil War Medicine* (Springfield, IL: C. C. Thomas, 1966), p. 76.

4. George W. Adams, *Doctors in Blue: The Medical History of the Union Army in the Civil War* (New York: Henry Schuman, 1952), p. 14.

5. Richard Shryock, "A Medical Perspective in the Civil War," in Shryock, *Medicine in America: Historical Essays* (Baltimore: Johns Hopkins University Press, 1966), pp. 94–95.

6. Brooks, p. 41.

7. Adams, p. 4.

8. Adams, p. 49.

9. Horace H. Cunningham, *Doctors in Gray: The Confederate Medical Service* (Baton Rouge: Louisiana State University Press, 1958), p. 10.

10. See Adams and Cunningham.

11. Cunningham. p. 20.

12. Cunningham, pp. 11–13.

13. Adams, pp. 54–55.

14. Whitman, pp. 37–38.

15. John Hill Brinton, *Personal Memoirs of John H. Brinton, Major and Surgeon USV 1861–1865* (New York: The Neale Publishing Co., 1914), p. 47.

16. Stevenson, p. 910.

17. Adams, p. 151.

18. Shryock, pp. 92–93.

19. See Adams. The accidental discovery that maggots cleaned out the wounds was made by Confederate doctors who were prisoners and were denied medical supplies to treat their men (p. 129).

20. Isabel Stevenson, "Medical Literature of the Civil War," *CIBA Symposia* 3 (July 1941): 918.

21. See National Archives (NA), John Brinton papers. Brinton kept innumerable small notebooks, in which he drew sketches of various surgical wounds and wrote descriptions and statistics for medical and surgical cases. His material

was used in the official *Medical and Surgical History of the War of the Rebellion.* 1875.

22. Adams, p. 150.

23. John Billings, *Hardtack and Coffee or the Unwritten Story of Army Life* (Boston: George M. Smith, 1887), pp. 300–302.

24. Billings, pp. 304–315; Adams, pp. 59–83.

25. Adams, p. 153.

26. Brooks, p. 48.

27. *Circular No. 4. Reports on the Extent and Nature of the Materials Available for the Preparation of a Medical and Surgical History of the Rebellion* (Philadelphia: J. B. Lippincott, 1865), p. 152.

28. Whitman, pp. 37–38.

29. Shryock, p. 95.

30. Shryock, pp. 95–96.

31. Adams, p. 69. See also Brooks, p. 31.

32. George Augustus Sala, as quoted in Massey, p. 25.

33. Samuel Ramsey, quoted in Julia Stimson and Ethel Thompson, "Women Nurses with the Union Forces During the Civil War," *Military Surgeon* 62 (Feb. 1928): 222.

34. Ramsey in Stimson and Thomas, 222.

35. Ramsey in Stimson and Thomas, 222.

36. Ramsey in Stimson and Thomas, 222.

37. Jane Woolsey, *Hospital Days* (New York: D. Van Nostrand, 1868), p. 41.

38. Woolsey, pp. 41–42.

39. Helen Marshall, *Dorothea Dix: Forgotten Samaritan* (New York: Russell and Russell, 1967), p. 202.

40. US War Dept., *The War of the Rebellion: A Compilation of the Official Records of the Union and Confederate Armies* (Washington, D.C.: U.S. Government Printing Office, 1880–1901), Series III, Part I, p. 107. Hereafter cited as *Official Records.*

41. Joseph K. Barnes et al., *The Medical and Surgical History of the War of the Rebellion, 1861–65*, vol. 1 (Washington, D.C.: Government Printing Office, 1875), pp. 139–140.

42. Barnes, p. 262.

43. Barnes, p. 308.

44. Marshall, p. 219.

45. Marshall, p. 206.

46. Agatha Young, *The Women and the Crisis: Women of the North in the Civil War* (New York: McDowell, Obolensky, 1959), p. 98.

47. Barnes, p. 217.

48. Barnes, p. 217.

49. Marshall, pp. 225–226.

50. Cornelia Hancock, *The South after the Civil War* (New York: Thomas Y. Crowell, 1956), p. 6.

51. Hancock, p. 131.

52. Louisa May Alcott, quoted in Ernest Earnest, *The American Eve in Fact and Fiction, 1775–1914* (Urbana: University of Illinois Press, 1974), p. 170.

53. Marshall, p. 207.

54. Mary Massey, *Bonnet Brigades: American Women and the Civil War* (New York: Knopf, 1966), p. 32.

55. Elizabeth Blackwell, *Pioneer Work in Opening the Medical Profession to Women* (London: Longmans, 1895), pp. 235–236.

56. Charles Stille, *History of the United States Sanitary Commission, Being the General Report of its Work During the War of the Rebellion* (Philadelphia: J. B. Lippincott, 1866), pp. 528–530.

57. William Maxwell, *Lincoln's Fifth Wheel: The Political History of the United States Sanitary Commission* (New York: Longmans, Green, 1956), pp. 1–30.

58. Stille, p. 529.

59. Maxwell, p. 63.

60. Massey, p. 33.

61. *Official Records*, Series VI, Part 2, p. 199.

62. Francis Simkins and James Patton, "The Work of Southern Women Among the Sick and Wounded of the Confederate Armies," *Journal of Southern History* 1 (Nov. 1935): 475.

63. Simkins and Patton, p. 479.

64. *Official Records*, Series IV, Part 2, pp. 199–200.

65. Cunningham, p. 73.

66. Simkins and Patton, pp. 484–85.

67. Kate Cumming, *Kate: The Journal of a Confederate Nurse* (Baton Rouge: Louisiana State University Press, 1959), p. 178.

68. C. Vann Woodward, ed. *Mary Chestnut's Civil War* (New Haven: Yale University Press, 1981), p. 386.

69. Woodward, p. 414.

70. Young, p. 61.

71. Louisa May Alcott, *Hospital Sketches* (Cambridge: Harvard University Press, 1960), p. 52.

72. Cumming, p. 18.

73. Cumming, p. 93.

74. Woolsey, pp. 154–155.

75. Annie Wittenmyer, *Under the Guns* (Boston: E. B. Stillings, 1895), pp. 193–201.

76. Wittenmyer, pp. 259–267.

77. Cumming, pp. 94–95.

78. Alcott, p. 86.

79. Alcott, pp. 86–87.

80. Alcott, pp. 86–87.

81. Woolsey, p. 29.

82. Woolsey, p. 37.

83. Cumming, p. 94.

84. Adams, pp. 54–55.

85. John Brumgardt, ed. *Civil War Nurse: The Diary and Letters of Hannah Ropes* (Knoxville: University of Tennessee Press, 1980), p. 33.

86. Brumgardt, p. 35.

87. Nina Smith, "The Women Who Went to the War: The Union Army Nurse in the Civil War," Ph.D. Diss., Northwestern University, 1981.

88. Ann Wood, "The War within a War: Women Nurses in the Union Army," *Civil War History* 18 (Sept. 1972): 197–212.

89. Mary Livermore, *My Story of the War* (Hartford, CT: A. D. Worthington, 1887), p. 325.

90. Massey, p. 64.

91. Brooks, p. 43.

Catholic Sisters Respond to Requests for Nursing in the Civil War

"All the country was hospital, save space for cemetery," a Daughter of Charity concluded, surveying the battlefield the day after the Gettysburg massacre on July 1–3, 1863.[1] This observation accurately described most of the battle-blighted country during the Civil War as public and private hospitals, churches, schools, public buildings, warehouses, homes, and barns near the sites of the battles were quickly converted into service as military hospitals.

A major result of turning much of the country into an extended hospital was the emergence of thousands of women offering to care for the soldiers in these various buildings. However, in contrast to the numerous Union and Confederate women who individually volunteered their services for nursing, generally the Catholic sisters as communities were specifically requested by various authorities to assist the sick and wounded. To understand the unique work of the sisters in the war, it is important to focus first on the communities that became involved in the war, then on the various categories of authorities who requested them, and finally on the arrangements under which they served.

In the course of the war, at least 617 sisters from twenty-one different communities, representing twelve separate orders, nursed both Union and Confederate soldiers. The largest number of sisters, estimated at 232 serving in approximately thirty geographic areas throughout the course of the war, was the Daughters of Charity, whose headquarters was in Emmitsburg, Maryland.

Next to the Daughters, the Holy Cross Sisters from South Bend, Indiana, whose works had not included nursing prior to the war, formed the second largest group of sisters, with sixty-three, serving in at least ten different institutions. In the South, at least eighteen Sisters of Charity of Our Lady of Mercy (then called Sisters of Mercy) in Charleston, South Carolina, and eighteen Sisters of Mercy of Vicksburg, Mississippi, provided sisters throughout the course of the war.

Of other communities of Sisters of Charity, thirty-six Sisters of Charity of Cincinnati, thirteen Sisters of Charity of New York City, and thirty-seven Sisters of Charity of Nazareth, Kentucky—all separate orders—provided nursing care for extended periods. The Sisters of Mercy also were represented with eleven sisters from Cincinnati, twenty-two from Baltimore, fifteen from New York, thirty-four from Pittsburgh, and ten from Chicago. While the city of origin of these sisters identifies the community, often their geographic place of service during the war was elsewhere. The actual locations are not easily identifiable as the temporary hospitals often moved from place to place with the soldiers, or the sisters only served a limited period of time.

Several other communities, with both nursing and teaching backgrounds, also nursed. Of the nursing groups, the Sisters of St. Joseph had ten sisters throughout the war in their own hospital in Wheeling, (West) Virginia, while the Sisters of St. Joseph of Philadelphia had fourteen who nursed in the area around that city. Ten Sisters of the Poor of St. Francis from Cincinnati served in hospitals there and in Columbus. In addition, at least eleven Sisters of Providence, whose motherhouse was in St. Mary of the Woods, Indiana, served in two hospitals in that state for most of the war. Sixteen Dominican Sisters nursed in hospitals in Memphis, Tennessee.[2] These latter communities were not engaged in hospital work before the war, though they, like the Holy Cross Sisters, have remained in hospital work to this day.

Some communities provided only limited help. The smallest group encompassed six Ursuline Nuns in Galveston, Texas, who served in their own convent, which was twice turned into a hospital. Nine Sisters of Our Lady of Mt. Carmel in New Orleans, twenty-four Dominican Sisters in Perrysville, Kentucky, and eight Sisters of Mercy in Little Rock, Arkansas, responded to immediate and short-term battle needs in their own geographic area. These latter three were actually teaching communities that served in the war for only a matter of weeks.

Though statistics are difficult to reconstruct, these sisters probably represented about one-fifth of all the sisters in the United States at the outbreak of the war. In regard to nationality, 320 have been identified as Irish-born or of Irish descent; approximately 200 were American-born, and the rest were mainly French- or German-born.[3]

In general, requests for the use of buildings and institutions under the control of these women's religious communities, and especially for the services of sisters, who often were all called "Sisters of Charity" or "Sisters of Mercy," regardless of the specific name of the religious community, came first from the governmental and political leaders of the Union and Confederacy at national, state, and local levels. Shortly after the start of the war, Surgeon Generals of the various states or of specific hospitals requested sisters, as did various citizens' groups or other organizations. Often, there is no clear record of who actually made the request, and seemingly, oral requests were passed through some combination of the above sources. In a few cases, as will be seen, the requests were more a demand for the use of a building to which the sisters often willingly complied while also offering services where and when they could. Sometimes the requests went to the primary administrators of the religious community and sometimes to the local unit of the community in charge of a specific hospital or usable building. In addition, the requests frequently came through the bishop of the diocese in which the sisters were located, or the bishop offered the services of the sisters under his jurisdiction.

In many cases, documentation on the specific reasons for requesting the sisters does not exist; nevertheless, the availability of sisters in a hospital in a given area, or their willingness to take on the work, must have been a strong determining factor. The general attitudes of those requesting the sisters can be illustrated by part of a letter of Brigadier General John F. Rathbone of Albany, New York. He wrote to Bishop John McCloskey on June 1, 1861, from the military depot there requesting the services of the Sisters of Charity:

Nevertheless, there are now over one hundred men in our Hospital, and the number of nurses employed is quite insufficient to ensure their comfort and proper treatment. The superiority of the Sisters of Charity as nurses is known wherever the names of Florence Nightingale and the Sisters who accompanied her to the Crimea have been repeated, and these soldiers, most of whom have had woman's tender hands to minister to their want before leaving home to engage in their country's battles, would feel encouraged by their kindness and care. I should esteem it a personal favor, should they be able to comply with my request.[4]

One sister did go to the depot from St. Mary's Hospital.[5]

The early requests for sisters followed a pattern that continued throughout the war. The first such request came to the community of the Daughters of Charity, which had a hospital in Norfolk, Virginia. When the Norfolk Navy Yard was destroyed by Confederates on April 20, 1861, the hospital was emptied and the Marine Hospital, in nearby Portsmouth, was prepared for the Union sick. According to the sisters' annals, the "northern authorities" asked for sisters to attend the soldiers, which they promptly did.[6]

The second request involved the recently built City Hospital in Indianapolis, which had been offered and accepted by the medical authorities for sick soldiers in April 1861. Records indicate that management was unsuccessful due to a lack of proper help and organization, which distressed the doctors and authorities. Thus, they turned to the nearby Sisters of Providence, who had no previous nursing experience but had visited sick in their homes. The sisters, known mainly for their schools, quickly took charge by the end of April.[7]

Due to an epidemic, the next request came from Cincinnati. Sr. Anthony O'Connell, a Sister of Charity of Cincinnati at that city's St. John Hospital, recounted that on May 1, 1861: "The most Rev. Archbishop [John] Purcell and Mayor [George] Hatch called upon me at the desire of Governor [William] Dennison, and requested that a colony of the Sisters be sent to Camp Dennison to attend the sick soldiers, the worst form of measles had broken out among them and they needed immediate attention."[8]

By May 16, 1861, the Confederate medical authorities at their headquarters in Richmond, Virginia, had asked the Daughters of Charity to admit sick soldiers to the Infirmary of St. Francis De Sales, which they ran.[9] Within a month, this was too crowded, and the government took over several houses in the city, intending that male nurses would care for the wounded. However, the sisters' annals record: "Within a few days, the Surgeon and Officers, in charge, came to the Sisters of the Infirmary and [orphan] Asylum begging them to come to their assistance as the poor men were in much need of them."[10] Thus, throughout the war, variety characterized the kinds of requestors, and spontaneity generally typified the sisters' responses to the requests. Even in these first four requests at the beginning of the war, a predictable pattern was already apparent: three religious communities that already had hospitals were asked to take in the wounded, though one was asked by the Union government to serve in a hospital other than its own Catholic institution; a mayor requested one community to serve in a camp where an epidemic had broken out; another group of sisters, responding to a general's request, took soldiers into its own hospital; the fourth community had never nursed, except perhaps its own sisters, and yet was asked by civil and medical authorities to take over a city hospital. To these early requests, the response of all these sisters was immediate, and no particular conditions of service were negotiated by the sisters or those asking their services. Throughout the war, requests for sisters would follow a similar pattern of some official aware of critical war needs initiating a call for sisters. Only as the war continued were any kinds of specific agreements sometimes worked out between the sisters and those who asked for them.

While the requests came from a variety of categories of people and groups, the absence of detailed documented reasons given for requesting the sisters probably implies that most people took it for granted that the sisters would and could help. The question was simply whether or not they would be able to take on a specific hospital or nursing task. For example, Dr. John Brinton, well-known for his outspoken attitude against the "terrible, irritable, and unhappy"[11] women generally plaguing the office of the medical director, typified the attitude of most doctors who had experience with any order of sisters. Disgusted with the lay "female nurse business," which "was a great trial to all the men concerned" and to himself, he determined to try to get rid of them from the Mound City, Illinois, Hospital. He explained:

In answer to my request to the Catholic authorities of, I think, North and South Bend, Indiana, a number of Sisters were sent down to act as nurses in the hospital. Those sent were from a teaching and not from a nursing order, but, in a short time they adapted themselves admirably to their new duties. I have forgotten the exact title of the Order. . . . I remember their black and white dresses, and I remember also, that when I asked the Mother, who accompanied them, what accommodations they required, the answer was 'one room, Doctor,' and there were in all, I think fourteen or fifteen of them. So I procured good nurses for my sick and the whole tribe of sanitary "Mrs. Brundages" passed away. The sick patients gained by the change, but for a few days, I was the most abused man in that department, for the newspapers gave me no mercy.[12]

To determine exactly who specifically called for the sisters' services in any instance is difficult. The phrase "the Union government in Washington" or the "Confederate governmental officials" might imply that Abraham Lincoln or Jefferson Davis requested the sisters. However, there is no direct evidence that either man personally requested the sisters' services, though both later graciously acknowledged their efforts. However, South Carolina Bishop Patrick Lynch, in writing to New York Bishop John Hughes on December 15, 1861, said that Davis did invite the Sisters of Charity of Our Lady of Mercy to go to Greenbrier White Sulphur Springs, which they did.[13] This may have reflected the fact that Lynch was a strong Confederate supporter who was often in contact with Davis, especially when arrangements were being made for Lynch to represent the Confederacy at the Vatican.

On the Union side, the highest ranking official to request sisters was Secretary of War Edwin Stanton. He made several requests, perhaps prompted by other people, for at least two Sisters of Mercy communities and for the Daughters of Charity. The request for Sisters of Mercy in New York was made by Major General Ambrose Burnside through the Vicar General of the New York diocese in 1862. Brigadier General John G. Foster reported to Stanton, who facilitated the request, on July 21, 1862: "At the request of Major General Burnside, nine Sisters of Mercy have arrived from New York to take charge of the hospital at Beaufort [North Carolina] and under their kind and educated care I hope for a rapid improvement in the health of patients."[14] The Sisters of Mercy in

Pittsburgh, in charge of Mercy Hospital since 1847, also received a request from Stanton in November 1862 through Bishop Michael Domenec.[15]

Although requests sometimes originated at the top levels of government, the battles were local, and governors and mayors, faced with their local needs and sometimes more familiar with the religious communities, also asked for sisters. For example, a Daughter of Charity in charge of City Hospital in Mobile, Alabama, recounted, "During the first year of the war, the Confederate Governor asked for sisters to take charge of their sick and wounded. About the second year of the war, we had to take in our Hospital the Confederate sick besides the city patients and occasionally Federal Prisoners were sent to us."

The willingness of these sisters to serve was attested to by the superior who remarked that she only had two sisters to give, leaving only herself and two remaining sisters to continue their own hospital. Yet, she concluded, "I gave them freely knowing our Lord would help us in time of need which He did most amply."[16]

Union officials also took care of local needs. For example, after the battle of Shiloh on April 6–7, 1862, Cincinnati Mayor George Hatch, aware of the earlier response of the Sisters of Charity of Cincinnati to help at Camp Dennison, appealed to Archbishop John Purcell for more nursing sisters to look after the Ohio wounded. Cincinnati philanthropist Mrs. Sarah Peter had already taken the Sisters of the Poor of St. Francis on a transport boat to get the wounded from the battlefield. The Mercies also responded with three sisters, one-third of their community. Fortunately, two of the three had nursing experience in Ireland during the plague, and all were connected with the Mercy Sisters who had gone to Crimea and thus were acquainted with the practical nursing methods employed there.[17]

Unlike the Mayor of Cincinnati, the Mayor of New York, though not opposed to sisters, was reluctant to initiate any care for the wounded in his city. In September 1862, the Central Park Commissioners had offered old Mt. St. Vincent's school to be used for a hospital. The building was on property that had been purchased for the park from the Sisters of Charity of New York prior to the war. Mayor Fernando Wood, however, did not want a hospital started because he felt the city would have to pay for it; he believed the federal government or the state should pay.[18] Nevertheless, after Edward Pierpont made a specific request to Secretary of War Stanton, a hospital was finally established there and the Sisters of Charity served until 1866.[19]

In addition to governmental authorities, generals or other top officers concerned for their men frequently made requests for the sisters, often through circuitous channels. For example, General Lew Wallace made a special request for twelve Sisters of the Holy Cross through Governor

Oliver P. Morton of Indiana, who relayed it to Fr. Edward Sorin, founder of Notre Dame. Sorin then rode across the road to the sisters at South Bend, on October 21, 1861. Though not a nursing community, the Holy Cross sisters eventually served in several military hospitals, and finally on the hospital boat "Red Rover" as the first Navy nurses.[20]

The Daughters of Charity were likewise requested by military authorities. A Daughter of Charity, who served the Military Hospital House of Refuge in St. Louis, recounts that the sisters went there on August 12, 1861, at the request of Major General John C. Fremont, commander of the West. She recalled that he "desired that every attention be paid to soldiers who had exposed their lives for their country, visited them frequently, and perceiving that there was much neglect on the part of the attendants, applied to the Sisters at St. Philomena's School for a sufficient number of sisters to take charge of the hospital, promising to leave everything to their management."[21] Since their ecclesiastical superior, Father J. Francis Burlando, had foreseen the possibility of this request a few months earlier, the sisters were aware of the conditions under which they would and could curtail their educational efforts and take on hospital work.[22]

Similar requests by military officials were made to the Daughters of Charity in Mobile, Alabama, and to the Sisters of Mercy of Chicago. The former went to take care of the Floridians and Alabamians with fever, measles, and other diseases.[23] The situations these sisters faced were sometimes perilous. For instance, the Sisters of Mercy of Chicago, were originally requested by Col. James A. Mulligan of the Illinois Irish Brigade, who in 1861 asked them to go to Lexington City, Missouri, to care for the wounded. The sisters, however, were forced by Confederate fire on the ship "Sioux City" to return to Jefferson City, Missouri. Once there, Mother Mary Francis Monholland and several of her sisters were invited by the US Sanitary Commission to take charge of the Jefferson City Hospital, where they stayed until it closed in April 1862.[24]

A more difficult experience comes from an account from the Daughters of Charity. Three days after the bombardment of Natchez, Mississippi, in 1861, three Daughters of Charity were to be sent from St. Mary's Asylum in Natchez to Monroe, Louisiana, at the request of Confederate General Albert Blanchard. According to the sisters' account, Blanchard, commander of the military in Monroe, was "a good Catholic who wished his soldiers to be treated with every care and attention."[25] He had a matron and nurses employed in the hospital; however, he discharged the former and made arrangements for the sisters to take charge the day after their arrival.

The sisters left Natchez immediately because of a report of the imminent arrival of the Federal gunboat, the "Essex," which would have prevented their departure the next day. Accompanied by the Bishop of

Natchez, William Elder, who was concerned for their safety, they crossed the Mississippi River in a small skiff in the middle of the night. After landing, they traveled two days over "a very rough and dangerous road," to get to their destination. [26]

Others faced danger closer to home. The Sisters of Mercy of Vicksburg, Mississippi, and the Dominican Sisters in Kentucky, facing battles in their own towns, offered their services for the wounded. In Vicksburg, the inhabitants fled into the surrounding country. Those who could not find houses camped out in the woods and lived in caves, which they dug in the sides of hills during the siege of the city in 1862. With the town under siege, the Sisters of Mercy were "solicited to preside" at a hospital in Mississippi Springs.[27] They were originally all teachers, but their school of one hundred pupils had gradually broken up as the war progressed and the city was shelled. Thus, the sisters took up nursing, moving with the Confederate army as it retreated along the railroad line into Alabama. At one point, the sisters, anxious about whether they would be able to continue their nursing work, were invited by Dr. Warren Buckell, through their ecclesiastical superior, Father Francis Xavier Leray, to take a house hospital in Jackson, Mississippi.[28]

Similar to the Mercy sisters in Vicksburg, the Dominican sisters found themselves in the middle of the battle at Perrysville, Kentucky, on October 8–9, 1862. Immediately, they offered their convent to care for the wounded. The sisters' annals record:

St. Catharine's Convent was hastily transformed into a military hospital. The dormitories with their rows of snowy white beds and long corridors, the class rooms, the recreation room were all filled with men who had been carried from the field of strife in every kind of available farm vehicle, which served as crude ambulances. Long after midnight of that memorable October 8 and 9, 1862, wagon loads of bruised and shattered heroes were still being brought to St. Catharine. There some Sisters were on duty receiving the soldiers, while others remained for additional service on the battlefield, helping to lift the sick and wounded onto the wagons. When each rumbling cart had its full quota, it started out for the convent hospital. The last seat was reserved for a Dominican Sister who sat there, the embodiment of mercy.[29]

The major battles of 1862, including the Seven Days' Battle, Second Bull Run, Harper's Ferry, Antietam, and Fredericksburg, increased the number of patients and strained the already overcrowded medical facilities and the overworked personnel. Thus, as the reputation of the sisters spread, requests for their services increased, especially from doctors. For example, on June 14, 1862, Surgeon General William A. Hammond at Washington asked for one hundred Daughters of Charity to be sent to the "White House," General Lee's former home in Virginia, which was now in the possession of Union troops. The sisters related that "too many were already among the war-stricken soldiers to admit of that number being sent, but sixty sailed from Baltimore for this place."[30] After some difficulties getting settled there, however, the sisters received another request from Hammond asking them to go on to Fortress Monroe, Virginia, where there was a greater need.[31]

In the spring of 1862, efforts were made to bring the Union wounded and sick from the southern battlefields to the larger northern cities. The medical authorities felt better care could be provided for the men in specially built hospitals, rather than in the field tent hospitals or makeshift facilities. This necessitated frequent trips on hospital transport ships, which were basically river boats fitted up with supplies and personnel and operated by various military and governmental groups.[32]

Sisters, as well as female nurses of the US Sanitary Commission, worked on these boats at various times throughout the war. In one case, several doctors, including Dr. George Blackman, a surgeon at St. Mary's Hospital, Cincinnati, requested the help of the Sisters of the Poor of St. Francis. With the encouragement of Mrs. Sarah Peter, who accompanied them, five sisters set sail for Pittsburgh Landing on the steamer "Superior," which towed several large barges that were really three-story barracks. During the trip the sisters and Mrs. Peter prepared bandages, lint, and straw mattresses.[33]

Requesting six, but getting five sisters for the "Commodore" and the "Whillden" boats operating from Fortress Monroe, Surgeon General Smith of Philadelphia again requested six more Sisters of St. Joseph to take with him on boats going to Richmond. Smith promised the trip would be "pleasanter" than a previous trip to Yorktown. Despite his promise, when a southern gunboat was about to open fire, the officers had the sisters appear on deck to prove that their errand was peaceful; nonetheless, a flying bullet just missed Mother Monica.[34]

Once the sick were in the northern cities, the sisters were then requested to work in these hospitals as well. For example, on May 28, 1862, a requisition was made by Surgeon General William Hammond through Dr. I. J. Hayes for twenty-five Daughters of Charity to nurse the sick and wounded soldiers in the West Philadelphia Hospital, afterwards known as the Satterlee Hospital. The hospital, ultimately to have 3,500 beds and become the largest Union hospital, was not quite finished. However, Dr. Hayes wanted the sisters "on the spot to make preparation" and set the date for the 9th of June. Accordingly, twenty-two sisters arrived at 10 A.M.[35] By the war's end, about ninety Daughters of Charity had worked there.

Geographic proximity to the battlefields was the reason Washington, D.C., with its sixteen hospitals and others in the nearby areas, led all other cities in bed capacity.[36] By 1862, the city of Washington had been turned into a huge hospital, with every building substituting for a medical facility; tents also were erected. Thus, both the Daughters of Charity and the Sisters of Mercy were asked by Hammond to attend the sick and wounded in Washington. The Daughters of Charity, in addition to serving at Providence, Eckington, and Cliffburn Hospitals, also went to Lincoln Hospital in 1862,[37] and the Sisters of Mercy of Pittsburgh went to Stanton Hospital in 1862.[38]

In addition to these many hospitals previously established or erected by the Union medical authorities, the sisters' own institutions were asked to become official government hospitals. A typical instance of this occurred at Wheeling Hospital in Virginia (West Virginia after 1863). The hospital, in existence since 1850, had been run by the Sisters of St. Joseph since 1856. When the battle of Harper's Ferry in September 1862 brought two hundred wounded soldiers into Wheeling, Mother De Chantel, faced with a military request to turn over her entire hospital, sent the orphans housed in the north wing of the building to a farmhouse. Beds or pallets of blankets were set up there within a few hours' time.[39] On April 23, 1864, the Federal government took over the hospital as a post hospital, added field tents on the grounds when the situation demanded, rented the hospital for $600 a year from the sisters, and hired five of them at government pay as nurses.[40] The sisters were supported in this cooperative action by Bishop Richard Whelan of Wheeling.

While the previous examples have illustrated primarily situations in which requests came from official governmental, military, or medical authorities, doctors who had previously worked with the sisters sometimes made their own requests either directly or indirectly through others. For example, Dr. E. Burke Haywood, in charge of the State Hospital at the Fairgrounds, Raleigh, North Carolina, called on Father Thomas Quigley, to find out how he could get three Sisters of Mercy to aid him in nursing the sick. He promised them a large room in a house, where, he said, they would be free from all intrusion and from insult, since the place was guarded by military law and there was a chaplain there.[41] Unfortunately, there were no sisters available to go, even after Father Quigley wrote to Bishop Lynch.

Dr. Henry Smith, Surgeon General of Pennsylvania troops, had more leverage. He was the personal physician of Mother Monica, of the Philadelphia Sisters of St. Joseph. She had also been superior of St. Joseph's Hospital. Thus, he could make his request for Sisters of St. Joseph directly to the superior of the community, Mother St. John Fournier, who consulted with Bishop James Wood. Smith himself explained that though he was "beset by applicants," he had "refused every female applicant being unwilling to trust any but his old friends, the Sisters of St. Joseph."[42] Hoping the sisters would not disappoint him in his requests for their services at Camp Curtin, outside Harrisburg, Pennsylvania, and at Church [Methodist] Hospital in the city, Dr. Smith promised, "There is waiting ... a large field of usefulness, but it is to be properly cultivated only by those whose sense of duty will induce them to sacrifice personal comfort. The living is rough, the pay poor, and ... nothing but the sentiments of religion could render any nurses contented."[43] The Sisters of St. Joseph went in early 1862. When the camp closed several months later, Surgeon General Smith again requested sisters for the floating ships going to Fortress Monroe and to Philadelphia. The sisters ministered on these hospital ships for several months until Camp Curtin opened again.[44]

The fact that so many doctors, ranging from Union Surgeon General Hammond to an ordinary doctor in charge of a small general hospital, asked for the sisters is of greater significance than the status of the other requesters. The national and local governmental officials and heads of citizens groups, who often felt the need to do something quickly about frequent crisis situations, might understandably overlook any specific concerns about quality of care and just request any available nursing help. However, the doctors, though equally hard-pressed for assistance, were often prejudiced against women nurses, most of whom they found more of a hindrance than help. Thus, the doctors were probably more careful in seeking out those they considered suitable helpers. Thus, previous personal experience with the sisters, as in the case of Dr. Smith, or awareness of their reputation played a significant part in the doctors' decision to request the sisters.

Perhaps a more predictable source of requests were the petitions for the sisters' service that came through the Catholic bishops. In 1861, there were seven archbishops and thirty-seven bishops, three-fourths of whom were located in dioceses in Union territory, and some of whom were far from the actual battlefront. The eleven Confederate states comprised eleven dioceses. Though there were some Southern-born bishops serving in Union territory, none of the bishops in the Confederate territory was born in the seceded states; many had been born in Ireland or France.[45]

In spite of varying political differences of the bishops and of the general strain among Catholics in the various territories, the Catholic church took no official position on the war and thus was saved from splintering.[46] Whatever the political opinions of the bishops, though, all were concerned mainly with supplying chaplains for the soldiers and generally were supportive of sisters from their various dioceses being involved in the war. Both actions reflected their concerns for the spiritual needs of the men. The bishops of the dioceses in which sisters had hospitals or other institutions, including their central headquarters (motherhouse), were often involved in facilitating the requests for services. However, an atypical reaction was that of a strong Union sympathizer, New York Archbishop John Hughes. In a May 1861 letter to Archbishop Francis Patrick Kenrick of Baltimore, he said that although

the Sisters of Charity of his diocese were willing to volunteer from fifty
to one hundred nurses, he strongly objected, saying, "They have as much
on hand as they can accomplish."[47] Hughes may have been referring to
the needed work of education and care of the orphans in his immigrant-
crowded New York diocese. In any case, as the war went on, sisters from
his diocese became actively involved in nursing, and he apparently did
not object.

On the other hand, Bishop Martin John Spalding, from border state
Kentucky, had offered the services of the Sisters of Charity of Nazareth,
Kentucky, to Federal General Robert Anderson. This offer was made
without any reference to the political questions—to nurse all sick or
wounded "on both sides." Spalding recorded in his diary that "now in
December [1861] three hospitals are graciously attended by 18 Sisters,
six in each. Few of the sick, more than a thousand in number, are
Catholics but many who were dying were baptized and sent to heaven.
The Sisters are very devoted and zealous and are doing much good."[48]

Following the Confederate victory at Manassas, July 21, 1861, Bishop
James Whelan of Nashville, Tennessee, offered his cathedral for hospital
purposes and the services of the Sisters of St. Dominic of Memphis. By
August of 1861, he wrote to South Carolina Bishop Patrick Lynch requesting sisters for Tennessee,[49] which had seceded on June 8, 1861.
Sixteen Sisters of St. Dominic of St. Agnes Convent, Memphis, accepted
his request to visit hospital homes in Memphis and to take over the City
Hospital there.[50] When Sherman took over the city on July 24, 1862, he
pitched his tents on their convent grounds, but promised the sisters safety
and allowed them to visit the Federal hospital.[51]

Like Bishops Spalding and Whelan, Bishop Maurice de St. Palais of
the Vincennes, Indiana, diocese took the initiative in offering buildings
and the services of the sisters. The Sisters of Providence related that at
the camp formed to receive recruits near Vincennes, some of the men
fell sick of a "virulent disease," which made it necessary to care for them
apart. Bishop de St. Palais offered a college building and asked for two
sisters to take charge of the stricken soldiers. Community records indicate that there were no sisters at Saint Mary-of-the-Woods, Indiana,
who could be spared for that purpose. So, in order to respond to the
request, Sisters Saint Felix and Sophy were called from their respective
establishments to Vincennes to be employed.[52] This emergency hospital
opened about the middle of April 1861 and closed the end of July. One
sister wrote that while the time of service was brief:

Those three months of service . . . were equal to as many years, or more, of
ordinary hospital work, on account of the hardships endured. An epidemic had
broken out; the contagion created a panic, and it was only with greatest difficulty
that supplies could be obtained. . . . The hired help fled at the approach of dan-

ger, leaving the Sisters alone to care for the stricken. The lives of the Sisters were often in danger from delirious fever patients, as well as from the epidemic. Defenseless and isolated, the Sisters still remained at their post; even washing the linen at night, and cutting wood for the fires.[53]

After the battle of Fort Donelson, in February 1862, Indiana soldiers, according to the policy of Governor Morton, were brought home to be cared for. This time the bishop of Vincennes offered the use of the Catholic seminary for the sick, and again he offered the assistance of Sisters of Providence in caring for them, thus demonstrating the co-operation of the church authorities and the willing service of its sisters for war needs.[54]

In early 1864, the Sisters of the Poor of St. Francis at St. Francis Hospital in Cincinnati, Ohio, were requested by Cincinnati Archbishop John Purcell to visit the soldiers at Camp Chase to provide both spiritual and material support to the men. Apparently, due to a prejudice against Catholic clergy on the part of some of the officers, priests were not allowed to visit the camp. This made the archbishop concerned about the spiritual needs of the soldiers; he felt, however, that the sisters might be accepted since they were women and by now were known for their generous and impartial service to the soldiers.[55]

Certainly, by war's end, the bishops were cognizant of the value and impact of the sisters' visible service, which contributed to a favorable view of Catholicism. Since the communities ordinarily were directly under their bishop or his representative, especially in the dioceses in which the motherhouses or main administrative headquarters were located, some contact between the sisters and the bishops over their service in the war is presumed, though there is little remaining documentation detailing that contact.

While generally the sisters were involved in some kind of discussion with ecclesiastical authorities, or at least with their own religious communities, sometimes time and circumstances did not allow the sisters to check with various community and church authorities before accepting requests for service. For example, Sisters of Charity of Nazareth from St. Mary Academy, Paducah, Kentucky, closed their academy and nursed both Union and Confederate soldiers in the early winter of 1861. In September of that year, Confederate General Leonidas Polk had moved from Tennessee and had occupied Columbus, Kentucky. Federal forces under General Ulysses S. Grant responded immediately by occupying Paducah and building Fort Anderson to protect their position. Thus, before the end of the year, many wounded and sick soldiers were brought to Kentucky, and Union General C. F. Smith requested that the Sisters of Charity nurse these men. Communication with the Nazareth motherhouse was impossible; hence, Sister Martha Drury, the superior of the

academy, acted on her own responsibility in closing the school and com-
plying with the request.[56]

Often, the sisters initiated offers of service themselves as they saw the
needs. After the Infirmary in Washington burned to the ground, for
instance, the "Sisters [of Mercy of Baltimore] barely escaped with their
lives having risked them in trying to save the patients." Immediately,
Mother Alphonsus "hastened to Washington to bring the sisters supplies." Responding to the continued need for medical facilities, the War
Department shortly took possession of three senatorial residences near
the Capital and transformed them into a military hospital known as the
Douglas, after Senator Stephen Douglas. The sisters immediately responded, as their annals record:

Not being satisfied with the good being done in the "Old Armory" [where the
patients had been taken after the fire] Mother Alphonsus wrote the government
officials offering the Services of the sisters to nurse in the military hospital where
the wounded had been arriving daily. The offer was gratefully accepted . . . and
at once the sisters took up their residence at the Douglas, full charge being
assigned them by the Government.[57]

Another offer on the part of the sisters was that of the Holy Cross
Sisters. In June 1862, Mother Angela offered the services of the sisters
for a "hospital boat" and Flag Officer Charles H. Davis, commanding
the Western Flotilla, wrote to Fleet Officer A. M. Pennock to make
arrangements for their coming. While Navy records indicate no conclu-
sive evidence that women served as nurses on the "Red Rover" prior to
the time that she was fitted out and commissioned as a US Navy hospital
ship at the end of the year,[58] the Holy Cross archives do indicate that
these sisters had earlier been on board "Red Rover." [59] While at this
point in the war, the Holy Cross Sisters, originally all teachers, had
become experienced in nursing, the discrepancy might be explained by
the fact that the boat was first an army vessel after it was captured by
the Union authorities. Thus, the sisters may have been on it under army
auspices.

On occasion, the sisters' generous offer to nurse caused them difficulty
once the town was captured by opposing forces. For example, in Arkansas, the only sisters were Sisters of Mercy, who were teachers. However, when the Confederate hospitals became overcrowded, they freely
opened a building in Little Rock to serve the wounded. In spite of their
generosity, after the capture of the city by General Frederick Steele on
September 10, 1863, a local Arkansas historian recounted that the "position of the sisters became almost unbearable, on account of the rude
behavior of federal officers, who resented the kind treatment which the
sisters were giving the Confederate sick."[60] The sisters, however, con-

tinued their same impartial treatment by opening their school building in Helena, Arkansas, to care for both Union and Confederate soldiers.[61]

However, government officials did not always look kindly on offers of assistance. The Cincinnati Sisters of Mercy had their offer to serve refused by the government. When the local military was looking over every building for possible use, they asked for the Sisters' House of Mercy in October 1861. The sisters rented the building to the government, which officially rechristened it "McLean Barracks" and reopened it as a "receiving depot for prisoners of war and state prisoners, deserters, and stragglers."[62] The House of Mercy was compressed into the convent above it. The first impulse of the sisters was to come to the assistance of the men being moved into the sealed-off House of Mercy, but when they offered nursing services to the "wretched" inhabitants, the officials, for unknown reasons, were not interested. Finally, under the influence of Mrs. Sarah Peter, sisters were permitted to at least visit the unfortunate soldiers, many of whom were prisoners from the Southern army, even though the military persisted in refusing nursing privileges. The sisters visited the men regularly until the last prisoner was freed or removed, some time around November 1, 1865.[63]

In addition to requests from specific, individual authorities, petitions for the sisters' services also came from various combinations of aid groups, officials, donors, or involved citizens. Because the aid societies largely confined their work to providing clothing, bandages, and small comforts for the soldiers, which they often distributed themselves, they sometimes saw other needs, which they directed to the sisters. For instance, on March 4, 1864, Mother De Chantal of the Sisters of St. Joseph in Wheeling was requested by the Soldiers' Aid Society to take care of all the military patients in the Athenaeum, the city jail. The sisters had been visiting the jail, in addition to their work at Wheeling Hospital, so they were acquainted with the men. However, this added forty-seven ill and disabled soldiers immediately to the already filled hospital, though the sisters willingly took them in.[64]

Though most of the requests for sisters' services came in the first year of the war, and some terms of service were only of a few months, the changing nature of the war created new demands, especially in the South. As the Daughters of Charity in Richmond reported near the end of the war, "The Southern Confederacy seeing their cause likely to fail resolved to concentrate their hospital facilities in or near Richmond. Upon arrival there we were immediately called upon, they begging us to take the hospital under our care and charge."[65]

The existing data on requests indicate that the sisters were asked to serve primarily in the first two years of the war. However, lack of documentation for the last two years does not indicate that the sisters were no longer wanted; rather, it reflects the fact that most of these sisters or their communities were still serving and thus had no more sisters to send. Too, in the North, the men were moved to large governmental or other stable hospitals, and those sisters who could be spared were in such places as Satterlee or Point Lookout, as well as working on the transport boats bringing soldiers to these and similar places.

On at least one occasion, requests for service or the sisters' desire to serve caused difficulties within the sisters' own communities and among church or governmental authorities because their privacy or cloistered protection would be invaded. In August 1861, Ursuline Mother St. Pierre offered the new convent building in Galveston, Texas, to the Confederates for a base hospital. The sisters' own annals record, "This act, prompted by the generosity of the nun's heart, opened the flood gates of much criticism. Reverend Father Chambodut, [ecclesiastical superior at the time] an impetuous man himself and the only priest who is thought to have pulled the lanyard of a cannon on the side of the Confederacy, reprimanded Mother Saint Pierre severely."[66]

The action was criticized by some of the sisters, as well as the chaplain, all of whom wrote to Bishop John Odin about her. Others, however, supported her. One priest wrote, "The Sisters seem fearless with the yellow flag flying above their convent."[67] Mother St. Pierre herself was aware of the controversy surrounding her actions and recorded in the annals: "Unfortunately, this act—the offering of the house as a hospital—seemingly good, was praised by some and blamed by others. Dearly did my heart pay for having been too hasty in following my natural disposition on this occasion."[68] She had to contend with the sisters in her community. Some complained about the "invasion of their privacy," saying, "The Chapter should have been consulted before the offer was made; not afterwards. If seculars are admitted into our house, what becomes of the cloister?"[69]

Nevertheless, Dr. Oaks, the surgeon, took possession of the convent building in the name of the Confederacy and designated the place as a "Confederate Hospital." Perhaps in an effort to recognize the concerns of some of the sisters, Father Anstaedt obtained permission for only older nuns to act as nurses in order that the entire convent life and the younger sisters would be protected.[70]

While there may have been controversy among the Ursulines, they did use their buildings for the wounded. One community of sisters, though, was not willing to give up their buildings for use as a hospital. Archbishop Francis Kenrick of Baltimore recounted to Bishop Patrick Lynch that "the Sisters of Georgetown (Visitation) were called on by Dr. Lamb in the name of the public purveyor to give a portion of their buildings for an hospital for soldiers, but were excused on appealing to General Winfield Scott, whose daughter died within their convent, though the Jesuit fathers next door had a regiment quartered in their college."[71] This refusal can probably be explained by the fact that the sisters were a cloistered, rather than an active order.

Although some active communities did have hospital experience, or at least experience in caring for the infirm members of their own communities, many sisters were teachers or in charge of orphans. Nonetheless, the spirit and attitude in which they, the superiors, and the bishops engaged in the work is well summed up by the ecclesiastical superior of the Daughters of Charity, who wrote the following to the Paris motherhouse shortly after the war ended:

Called for the first time to exercise their services on the field of battle, our Sisters were without practical experience; for this reason I did not hasten to acquiesce to the desires and solitations of many, who pressed me to offer to the Government the assistance of the Sisters for the work of the ambulances. It was to be feared moreover that they were apt at this kind of services, might they not stray from the spirit of regularity which seems incompatible with camp life. However, the will of God was manifested through the medium of superiors, and I cast aside these fears to count more assuredly upon the succor of God as we confronted the designs of his Providence.[72]

In addition, this opportunity to serve in the war was seen by at least one nonteaching community as a real opportunity to expand services. As the Sisters of Providence remarked, "To have a hospital has long been desired; a choice has come at last to have one. We have a fine opening to commence that branch of our vocation."[73]

Although care of the sick and wounded was the major service that the sisters were asked to do, visiting prisoners was also a requested service, or a service they took on voluntarily. The route was often circuitous; governmental officials, eager for sisters of any community, usually went to the bishop of the area, who then went through the religious community. For instance, Colonel Ware, in charge of Illinois prisons, applied to the Bishop of Alton, Illinois, Reverend Henry Juncker, for some Daughters of Charity. He, in turn, applied to the superior of St. Philomena's School, who secured permission from Father Francis Burlando, who was actual superior of the sisters' community.[74]

With less complication, other communities visited prisoners in both the South and North. For example, the Sisters of Charity of Our Lady of Mercy in Charleston, South Carolina, visited prisoners of war at four locations there: the jail yard, the work house, Roper Marine Hospital, and the Race Course (Fair Grounds Prison).[75] After caring for the seriously ill prisoners in the Union Military Hospital in Indianapolis, Providence Sister Athanasius Fogerty was allowed by military authorities to visit the men when they were transferred to Camps Morton and Carrington.[76] Generally these sisters became involved in visiting prisoners either because the soldiers had been first their patients or because the sisters were viewed as "neutral" or equally attentive to both Union and Confederate men in need.

Responding readily to the myriad requests for serving the sick and wounded of both Union and Confederate forces, the sisters did not generally seem to draw up formal agreements, except in the case of the Daughters of Charity and of the Sisters of Charity of Nazareth. However, the sisters did have specific, nonnegotiable needs of a religious nature. For example, the opportunity for church services on Sunday and sometimes throughout the week, an obligation and practice all communities of sisters observed, was generally a stated expectation on the part of all the sisters or their male ecclesiastical superior or bishop who was serving as an intermediary. However, chaplains of any denomination were often scarce during the war,[77] even though efforts were made by the governmental and military authorities, individual denominations, or through the efforts in the North of the US Christian Commission, to supply them to the troops.[78]

Among Catholic chaplains, it has been estimated that only thirteen priests were appointed hospital chaplain by Lincoln on May 20, 1862; there were only forty chaplains in the volunteer regiments of the Union Army; only about twenty took care of the spiritual needs of the soldiers in their geographic area; and only about twenty-eight who were Confederate chaplains in hospitals and in regiments.[79] Thus, obtaining priests for soldiers or sisters was not an easy task.

The records sometimes reveal attempts to place a chaplain or make provisions for one. Lincoln himself wrote a memo in September 1862, after a visit from a Daughter of Charity working in a Washington hospital, asking that Father Joseph O'Hagan, a regimental chaplain, become a hospital chaplain. The Catholic chaplain already appointed, she explained, could not handle all the Catholic soldiers.[80]

This scarcity of chaplains was similarly noted by some bishops. Baltimore Archbishop Francis Patrick Kenrick wrote to New York Archbishop John Hughes in 1862 asking for sisters from the New York diocese and explaining that, though the Surgeon General wanted more sisters, the Daughters of Charity could not provide any more. Kenrick pointed out the difficulties in getting chaplains appointed:

The Sisters may experience difficulty in regard to their spiritual duties unless some arrangement be made for chaplains. These are generally Preachers [Dominicans?]. It is hard for the Sisters to hear Mass even on Sundays. The Surgeon General asked me some months ago to designate a priest for them, and took no notice of my request to have him appointed and provided for. The Jesuits will no doubt look to those who will be in charge of the St. Aloysius' Hospital in Washington. Public notice has been given that no new chaplains will be appointed. If a moderate addition were made to the allowance for the Sisters, it might be the least invidious mode of providing for the priest in attendance.[81]

In a similar vein, Bishop McGill of Richmond, Virginia, writing in 1862 to Bishop Patrick Lynch of Charleston, South Carolina, said he could have any sisters from his diocese provided he could "either fund or furnish a chaplain for them."[82]

If there were no chance of having a chaplain for services for both the sisters and the Catholic soldiers, this sometimes was a reason for sisters not going to a specific location or for pulling out. For example, Father Francis Burlando ordered the Daughters of Charity to leave shortly after they had begun working on hospital transport boats. As Burlando explained to his superiors in France:

Those floating hospitals were, however, very frightful: more than four or five hundred sick and wounded lay heaped on one another; the bottom, middle and hold of the ships were filled with sufferers. Willingly would we have continued our services, but our Sisters were deprived of all spiritual assistance; no mass or communion even when they entered the port, it was hard for them to go to church, either because they did not know where there was one, or because the distance would not allow them. We were therefore obliged to remove and place them in the organized hospitals on land, where they can at least rely on the assistance of a priest. It is true, some were promised me, but their number is too small.[83]

Other communities, though, who worked on the transport ships seemed to adjust to the situation in other ways. For instance, the Sisters of Charity of Cincinnati served on the transports and at least did not record any particular concerns about participating in services on Sunday. They may have been able to dock along the way, as the Holy Cross Sisters seem to have done on two occasions at Natchez, Mississippi, as recorded by Archbishop Elder in his diary.[84]

Similarly, St. Joseph superior Mother St. John anticipated the possible difficulties of fulfilling religious duties and made arrangements before the sisters went. Writing to her sisters who were about to set out on floating boats, she commented:

The Bishop [James F. Wood] has already given the necessary dispensations. . . . Go to Holy Communion when you have that favor. . . . Make your Meditation in the morning after your prayers and be not troubled if you can say no other prayers of the community, not even if you are deprived of Mass on Sundays. In the meantime, I recommend you all to unite yourselves to the prayers of the community, and often times through the day to make short ejaculations and never give a short answer to a Sister or any one else.[85]

Perhaps aware that there were possible difficulties, Holy Cross Superior Mother Angela in corresponding with Mississippi Fleet Surgeon Ninian A. Pinkney, said:

I hasten to inform you that I have not the slightest inclination to remove our Sisters from the Red Rover [Navy Ship]—provided they are enabled to attend Mass (as they do at present).... It was a deep source of regret to me when I feared we might have to do it—mainly because the nature of the boat's movement would continue to prevent the fulfillment of one of our essential duties. But as this obstacle is removed I am rejoiced to have them stay as long as their services are needed.[86]

While working on the transport ships understandably posed problems for obtaining the services of a chaplain, there were other kinds of service which also had to be refused on religious grounds. For instance, after work among measles patients at Camp Denison was finished, the Sisters of Charity of Cincinnati planned to return to St. John's Hospital in the city. Some of the Ohio regiments, however, desired the sisters to continue their services with the army as it marched southward. The Mother Superior granted the permission, but she withdrew it when she learned that a Baptist minister, and not a Catholic priest, was to accompany the troops from Camp Denison.[87]

In spite of these requirements for spiritual services, as well as the desires of the sisters, the realities of the war and the urgency of caring for the wounded often took precedence over the kind of regularity of religious exercise observed in the quiet of the prewar convent days. A Daughter of Charity reported that on their return to Richmond:

We had at once a pious chaplain and the Holy Mass four days in the week. For the first three years of the war, we had Mass only on Sunday and very, very often had only time for vocal prayers, then read meditation, and hurried to the dying men. Thus passed the day and after heavy battles, we could not retire until ten or eleven o'clock. We were called during the night short as it was; but we always rose at four o'clock. When the condition of our sick would admit it, our blessed exercises were resumed with renewed fervor.[88]

The difficulties surrounding Mass attendance were specifically noted by two communities working in the South. A Daughter of Charity working in Marietta, Georgia, recounts, "Five weeks without Mass. At last, two sisters went to Atlanta where there were two priests—did get one to come for Mass on Easter."[89] The Sisters of Charity of Our Lady of Mercy from Charleston, serving at the Confederate hospital in Montgomery White Sulphur Springs, Virginia, were without a chaplain for six weeks while Bishop Lynch attempted to find a replacement and get him commissioned.[90]

Concern for the sisters' inability to perform their religious duties was also expressed by others besides the bishops and the communities. A letter appeared in the Indianapolis *Sentinel* on February 25, 1862, in which the writer called for public attention to the problem.

I consider it as fact worthy of notice that the Sisters of Providence who have charge of the Military Hospital, are not furnished with a conveyance to and from the city, but are obliged to wade through mud and mire on foot. A carriage is furnished them on Sundays, it is true, but the religious duties of the Sisters make it necessary that they should come in town every day, and it is a crying shame that they should be allowed to walk. I can safely say that the greater part of the way to the Hospital the mud is knee deep. A small one-horse spring wagon would be of infinite use; and where so much money is spent, why not a little be invested to this good purpose? The Sisters are uncomplaining, and for that reason, their comfort should be more carefully looked after.[91]

In a few cases, the sisters recalled being able to perform all their religious exercises as well as attend Mass, much the same as they had been in their convents in prewar times. For example, the Galveston Ursulines, not a nursing community, remarked, "Our new vocation, which sad circumstances forced on us, won for us the sweet title of 'Sisters of Charity,' whose vocation we so awkwardly fulfilled. Having charge of the hospital did not interfere in the least with our religious observances; neither did the war prevent us from giving the holy habit to our two postulants."[92]

In addition to the requirement of a chaplain for fulfillment of spiritual duties, the Daughters of Charity, probably under Father Burlando's specific direction, laid down the following conditions under which they would nurse:

1. In the first place that no *Lady Volunteers* be associated with the Sisters in their duties as such an association would be rather an encumbrance than a help;

2. That the Sisters should have entire charge of the Hospitals and ambulances;

3. That the Government pay the traveling expenses of the Sisters and furnish them board and other actual necessities during the war. Clothing also in case it [the war] should be protracted.[93]

The Sisters of Charity of Nazareth, Kentucky, had a similar arrangement, though worded somewhat more tactfully, which they worked out with General Robert Anderson. A copy went to Bishop Martin Spalding of Kentucky, who later sent a copy to Bishop Purcell.[94]

1. The Sisters of Charity will nurse the wounded under the direction of army surgeon without any interference whatsoever;

2. Everything necessary for the lodging and nursing of the wounded and sick will be supplied to them without putting them to expense; they will give their services gratuitously;

3. So far as circumstances will allow they shall have every facility for attending
   to their religious devotional exercises.[95]

The only other formal arrangements were made by the Sisters of
Mercy of New York when they took charge of the military hospital at
Beaufort, North Carolina. They required that a chaplain was to be appointed, paid, and maintained; private apartments allotted to the use of
the sisters; and provisions, medicines, and utensils supplied for the patients and themselves.[96] Records indicate the chaplain was so appointed.[97]

Precise reasons why some communities had written regulations and
some did not is difficult to determine because of limited evidence. Because the Daughters of Charity were the largest group of sisters serving
in the war, and their ecclesiastical director, Father Burlando, was active
in most of the arrangements for the sisters to nurse, it is understandable
that they would develop these regulations at some point in the war.
However, exactly when and where the Daughters' requirements were
developed, implemented, or even whether they were always written
down is not known. The one extant penciled copy may just be a written
version of oral agreements.

Nevertheless, Bishop Martin Spalding, writing to Archbishop John
Purcell of Cincinnati, probably summarized the prevailing cooperative
attitude of the authorities toward the regulations of the communities
who had them. Spalding said, "We have the Sisters here at the Military
Hospital, and they are not annoyed but treated as well as could be
expected. The spirit of my agreement with General Anderson seems to
have been at least substantially carried out, and I apprehend but little
difficulty in the future."[98]

The reasons behind these stipulations, particularly on the part of the
sisters, included the need of the sisters, especially those who had hospital
and nursing experience, to control those conditions that would make
for good nursing care as well as the primacy with which they and their
advisers saw the need and importance of fulfilling spiritual desires and
obligations. For example, ability to enforce standards of cleanliness,
proper nutrition, and suitable order in the wards for the comfort of
those recovering or dying were all aspects of proper care. In addition,
disabled soldiers put to work nursing other soldiers, completely untrained ward masters and medical assistants in the field and general
hospitals, hordes of well-meaning but often interfering women visitors,
and other untrained female nurses were all sources of complaints by
many doctors and by the other more experienced and organized female
nurses. Thus, the sisters' need to be in complete charge, as they were in
their own institutions, without being hampered by female volunteers,
can be understood. The requirements, then, though seemingly stringent,
were probably appropriate at the time, even if some of the stipulations

were occasionally met with strained relations within the hospital setting or became the source of critical attitudes from others.

Whether communities had formal agreements or not, other issues, particularly remuneration, were handled in a number of ways. The standard pay for female nurses hired by the Union through Dorothea Dix was forty cents a day plus rations; however, the sisters were not under her jurisdiction. Thus, they generally were not listed on the official records and rolls of the army records, so determining their actual pay is almost impossible. Payment policies for the sisters serving the Confederacy are equally unclear.

For example, internal evidence from the Sisters of Charity of Our Lady of Mercy in Charleston shows that they received no remuneration from the Confederate army. As proof, a letter from Sister De Sales to Bishop Lynch comments on a visit from a Dr. Archer, who said that the Daughters of Charity at the Alms House Hospital in Richmond received $330,000 from the Surgeon General in charge. The doctor was surprised to learn from the Sisters of Mercy that they received no remuneration.[99] However, the $330,000 in Confederate money may well have been the food and clothing allowance stipulated in the Daughters of Charity written agreement. Similarly, Sister M. Ignatius Sumner, a Vicksburg Mercy Sister describing conditions as they traveled with the fleeing Confederate army eastward through Mississippi to Alabama, said, "From the beginning we had refused all compensation, but fortunately we had a little money left to buy what provisions we could find.[100] These same sisters did receive in 1862 "in recompense for their services [in Oxford, Mississippi] . . . sufficient means from the Confederate government to rent a small cottage of four rooms which they formed into something like a convent home complete with chapel."[101]

The Holy Cross Sisters who served on the Navy boat "Red Rover" received fifty cents a day, ten cents more than army nurses, though no actual total of monies earned can be determined.[102] Even if records had been kept, the frequency of payment may have been erratic. For example, Mother Angela of the same community noted on January 1, 1862, in the fragment of what appears to be the Mound City Hospital account book: "The paymaster is generally very tardy, leaving an interval of several months between his appearances."[103]

Though the Daughters of Charity may have asked for "no remuneration," certainly the "provisions" would have been in keeping with the regular female nurse pay. Since only the Satterlee Hospital account book remains from any of the places where the Daughters served and the actual sources of income are not clear, the various expenditures for the sisters' clothing items may or may not have been paid for by the government. On the other hand, in Lynchburg, each Daughter of Charity was paid $18.50 per month for nursing at General Hospital #3, which incorporated the college building, Division #1, and Fergusan's (Tobacco) Factory, Division #2.[104]

Of particular interest is the fact that in December 1864, Sister Ann Simeon Norris, the head of the Daughters of Charity, made a petition to the Congress of the United States, at the recommendation of Lincoln, that the material for the habit worn by the sisters, which was manufactured only in France, be admitted duty free. In her petition, she referred to her contact with Lincoln, saying, "His Excellency, the President kindly replied: that in consideration of the Services the Sisters had rendered the Union soldiers in the different Hospitals of the United States, he would most willingly grant this favor, but that the law required an act of Congress."[105] However, the Daughters have no record this was ever done. Records of Congress indicate only that a bill was introduced in 1864 and then referred to the finance committee.[106]

This last example underscores the fact that the written or oral agreements for the sisters' services that still exist relate not to any demands or requirements of the requestors, but rather to issues the sisters or their ecclesiastical authorities wanted clarified. Because few of these agreements are in existence, only tentative conclusions can be drawn.

These stipulations, dealing primarily with the fulfillment of religious obligations or clarification of authority lines in the hospital setting, seem to originate directly from the male ecclesiastical authority over the community, rather than from the sisters themselves. While this is probably a reflection of the nineteenth-century dependency of women religious on male hierarchical structure or of the practices of certain communities, some of the issues seem to represent the sisters' desire to have necessary control over certain areas of the hospital or the care in order to do a good job.

While not all nursing communities had such regulations, those agreements that still exist are only from nursing communities. It might be concluded that experiences in dealing with issues of control of the hospital or the nursing setting, as well as the anticipated difficulty of fulfilling their religious duties in a non-Catholic setting, may have caused these communities to develop such "conditions of services" as the war went on.

That over six hundred sisters from twenty-one different communities of twelve orders responded in some way to the many requests underscores two important points. First, in responding, the sisters demonstrated a willingness to adjust their lifestyle to the needs of their country and its wounded. Second, they had a flexibility that enabled them to exercise their nursing skills in new and difficult situations or to learn nursing skills quickly on the job. Only the lack of sisters in the many small religious communities, or in a few cases the inability to fulfill their religious duties, caused a difficulty in the sisters' response. Rather, in cases where the sick and wounded were in the immediate geographic vicinity, sisters responded with whatever services, buildings, and supplies they could offer. Those communities who had the largest number of sisters and the most experience, like the Daughters of Charity, who supplied over one-half of the sisters who served in the war, were in the greatest demand. Nevertheless, even though ten of the twenty-one communities who served were teaching orders, they willingly took up the tasks of nursing.

Thus, prior reputation and experience, as the Civil War began, and visibility, respectability, willingness to serve, and flexibility in adjusting to new situations as the war continued were the key strengths of the sisters. Yet, primary to the sisters as they exhibited these qualities in their specific nursing duties on battlefields, transport boats, and in hospitals, was the opportunity to continue their own religious commitment and to extend the values of religion to those they worked with and cared for, especially the wounded and dying. Significant, too, was the fact that those who requested the sisters were willing to permit the sisters to carry out the religious duties that sustained their own commitment and service during the Civil War.

NOTES

1. Archives of the Daughters of Charity, Emmitsburg, Maryland (ADC), *Annals of the Civil War*, vol. I, p. 47.

2. Statistics taken from Ellen Jolly Ryan, *Nuns of the Battlefield* (Providence, RI: The Providence Visitor Press, 1927). She cites twenty communities; however, the Sisters of Mercy in Arkansas appeared to have served for a limited time. Jolly's statistics for the number of sisters from each community came from figures supplied to her. In some cases, the figures now seem slightly different, perhaps reflecting increased attention to records in these intervening years. Jolly also indentified the nationality of sisters.

3. The figure of one-fifth is an estimate based on figures supplied by those communities that had data and extrapolating for those that did not have data. There is no way to accurately determine the figure for the historical period. For additional figures, see Eileen Mary Brewer, *Nuns and the Education of American Catholic Women, 1860–1920* (Chicago: Loyola University Press, 1987), p. 15.

4. Archives of the Daughters of Charity, Albany, New York (ADC-Albany), Letter of Brig. General John Rathbone to Bishop McCloskey, June 1, 1861.

5. ADC-Albany, "St. Mary's Hospital and the Civil War," p. 5.

6. ADC, *Annals of the Civil War*, vol. I, p. 14.

7. Sr. Mary Theodosia Mug, *Lest We Forget: The Sisters of Providence of St. Mary of the Woods in Civil War Services* (St. Mary of the Woods, IN: Providence Press, 1931), p. 17.

8. Archives of the Sisters of Charity of Cincinnati (ASCC), "Memoirs of Sr. Anthony O'Connell," n.p.

9. ADC, *Annals of the Civil War*, vol. II, p. 58.

10. ADC, *Annals of the Civil War*, vol. II, p. 58.

11. John Brinton, *Personal Memoirs of John H. Brinton* (New York: The Neale Publishing Co., 1914), p. 294.

12. Brinton, p. 199.

13. Charleston Diocesan Archives (CDA), H361 (old numbering), Letter of Patrick Lynch to John Hughes, n.d.

14. US War Department, *The Wars of the Rebellion: A Compilation of the Official Records of the Union and Confederate Armies* (Washington: Government Printing Office, 1880–1901), Part I, Vol. IX, p. 411 (hereafter cited as *Official Records*).

15. *Official Records*, Part I, Vol. IX, p. 411.

16. ADC, *Annals of the Civil War* (handwritten copy), pp. 478–481.

17. Mary Ellen Evans, *The Spirit Is Mercy* (Westminster, MD: The Newman Press, 1959), p. 90.

18. Sr. Marjorie Walsh, *The Sisters of Charity of New York, 1809–1959*, vol. I (New York: Fordham University Press, 1960), p. 198.

19. Archives of the Sisters of Charity of New York City (ASCNYC).

20. Congregational Archives of the Sisters of the Holy Cross, Saint Mary's, Notre Dame, IN (ACSC), Civil War, "Red Rover" file.

21. ADC, *Annals of the Civil War*, vol. II, p. 111.

22. ADC, *Annals of the Civil War*, vol. II, p. 111.

23. Michael Gannon, *Cross in the Sand: The Early Catholic Church in Florida* (Gainsville: University of Florida Press, 1967), pp. 175–176.

24. Jolly, pp. 231–233.

25. ADC, *Annals of the Civil War*, vol. II, p. 105.

26. ADC, *Annals of the Civil War*, vol. II, p. 105.

27. Archives of Sisters of Mercy, Vicksburg (ARSMV), Sr. M. Ignatius Sumner, "Register of the Events from the Foundation of the Convent of the Sisters of Mercy, Vicksburg, Miss.," pp. 6–7.

28. ARSMV, Sumner, p. 10.

29. Archives of the Sisters of St. Dominic, St. Catharine, KY, (AOPK), Sr. Margaret Hamilton, "In My Times," typescript, pp. 53–55.

30. ADC, *Annals of the Civil War*, vol. I, p. 19.

31. ADC, Letter of Fr. Francis Burlando to Mother Ann Simeon Norris, June 23, 1862. For another point of view on the difficulties of the sisters' getting settled, see Frederic Law Olmsted, *Hospital Transports* (Boston: Ticknor, 1863), pp. 113–114, 134. See also Anne Austin, *The Woolsey Sisters of New York* (Philadelphia: American Philosophical Society, 1971), p. 57.

32. George W. Adams, *Doctors in Blue: The Medical History of the Union Army in the Civil War* (New York: Henry Schuman, 1952), p. 82.

33. Betty Perkins, "The Work of the Catholic Sister in the Civil War," Masters thesis, University of Dayton, 1969, p. 89.

34. Sr. Maria Kostka Logue, *Sisters of St. Joseph of Philadelphia* (Westminster, MD: The Newman Press, 1950), p. 128.

35. ADC, *Annals of the Civil War*, vol. I, pp. 19–20.

36. Adams, p. 152.

37. ADC, *Annals of the Civil War*, vol. I, p. 11.

38. Sr. Jerome McHale, *On the Wing: The Story of the Pittsburgh Sisters of Mercy, 1843–1968* (New York: The Seaburg Press, 1980), p. 111.

39. Sr. Rose Anita Kelly, *Song of the Hills: The Story of the Sisters of St. Joseph of Wheeling* (Wheeling, WV: Sisters of St. Joseph, 1962), pp. 216–217.

40. Kelly, p. 215.

41. CDA, 27D4, Father Thomas Quigley to Bishop Lynch, May 10, 1862.

42. Logue, p. 121.

43. Logue, p. 121.

44. Logue, pp. 125–129.

45. Benjamin J. Blield, *Catholics and the Civil War* (Milwaukee: Bruce, 1945), pp. 36–52, surveys the bishops of the Northern states; pp. 53–69, surveys the bishops of the Southern states.

46. See Willard Wight, "War Letters of the Bishop of Richmond," *The Virginia Magazine* 67 (July 1959): 259–270; Wight, "Bishop Verot and the Civil War," *Catholic Historical Review* 47 (May 1961): 153–163; Wight, "Bishop Elder and the Civil War," *Catholic Historical Review* 44 (Oct. 1958): 290–306; Wight, ed., "Some Wartime Letters of Bishop Lynch," *Catholic Historical Review* 43 (April, 1957): 20–37.

47. Archbishop John Hughes quoted in Walsh, p. 198. For a life of Hughes see Richard Shaw, *Dagger John* (New York: Paulist Press, 1977). For Hughes's relationships with the Daughters of Charity, see Joseph Code, *Bishop John Hughes and the Sisters of Charity* (n.c.: Miscellaneous Historical reprint, 1949).

48. Archives of Sisters of Charity of Nazareth, KY (ASCN), reference taken from Diary of Martin Spalding, n.p.

49. CDA, 26 H4. Letter of Bishop James Whelan to Bishop Lynch, Aug. 22, 1861.

50. AOPK, "Activities of St. Agnes," manuscript, p. 9.

51. Jolly, p. 97.

52. Archives of Sisters of Providence, St. Mary of the Woods, IN (ASP), "Extracts from the Annals of the Sisters of Providence re: Civil War," typed sheet.

53. Mug, pp. 64–65.

54. Sr. Eugenia Logan, *History of the Sisters of Providence of St. Mary of the Woods*, vol. II (Terre Haute, IN: Moore-Langen, 1978), p. 73.

55. Perkins, p. 91.

56. Sr. Mary Agnes McGann, *The History of Mother Seton's Daughters: The Sisters of Charity of Cincinnati*, vol. III (New York: Longmans, Green, 1917), p. 47.

57. Archives of Sisters of Mercy, Baltimore (ARSMB), "Baltimore Interests," p. 2.

58. E. Kent Loomis, "History of the U.S. Navy Hospital Ship *Red Rover*," typescript, 1961, p. 3.

59. ACSC, Civil War, "Red Rover" file.

60. J. M. Lucey, "Arkansas Sisters of Mercy in the War," in *Confederate Women of Arkansas in the Civil War* (Little Rock: J. Kellogg, 1907), pp. 135–136.

61. Lucey, pp. 135–136.

62. Evans, p. 87.

63. Perkins, p. 88.

64. Kelly, p. 214.

65. ADC, *Annals of the Civil War*, vol. I, p. 51.

66. Archives of Ursuline Nuns of Galveston, TX (AUNG) "Account taken

from the Annals of the Ursuline Community of Galveston, Texas," typescript, p. 1. See also the Archives of the University of Notre Dame, South Bend, IN (ANDU), papers of Bishop John Odin, New Orleans, VI–2-e. Letters of Louis Chambodut to Odin; Mother St. Pierre Harrington to Odin; Joseph Anstrett to Odin; Napoleon Perché to Odin; Mother St. Pierre Harrington to Stephen Rousselon.

67. ANDU, VI–2-e, Letter of Father Louis Chambodut to Bishop John Odin, October 8, 1861.

68. AUNG, "Account taken from Annals," p. 1.

69. AUNG, "Account taken from Annals," p. 1.

70. AUNG, "Account taken from Annals," pp. 1–2.

71. CDA, 26D3, Bishop Kenrick to Bishop Lynch, May 12, 1861.

72. ADC, "Annals of the Civil War," manuscript, Letter of Fr. Francis Burlando to Fr. Etienne, April 10, 1868, preface, n.p.

73. ASP, "Journal of Mother Cecilia," typescript, n.p.

74. ADC, *Annals of the Civil War*, vol. I, pp. 3–4.

75. Perkins, p. 131.

76. Logan, p. 68.

77. See Rollin Quimby, "The Chaplain's Predicament," *Civil War History* 8 (Mar. 1962): 25–37.

78. The Christian Commission was formed Nov. 15, 1861, by the Young Men's Christian Association, to publish religious tracts, supply nurses, and aid the soldiers.

79. Blield, pp. 107–116; 122–23; see also Aidan H. Germain, "Catholic Military and Naval Chaplains, 1776–1917," *Catholic Historical Review* 15 (July 1929): 172–174.

80. ADC, photocopy of original memo of Abraham Lincoln, Sept. 22, 1862.

81. "Notes and Comments," *Catholic Historical Review* 4 (1918): 387.

82. CDA, 27R4, Letter of Bishop McGill to Bishop Lynch, Sept. 2, 1862.

83. ADC, *Lives of Our Deceased Sisters, Reports of 1862*, p. 29.

84. Elder, pp. 110, 120.

85. Logue, p. 126.

86. ACSC, Civil War, Letter of Mother Angela to Surgeon Pinkney, typescript, Aug. 11, 1863.

87. ASCC, "Memoirs of Sr. Anthony O'Connell," n.p.

88. ADC, *Annals of the Civil War*, vol. I, p. 51.

89. ADC, *Annals of the Civil War*, vol. I, p. 49.

90. Sr. Anne Francis Campbell, "Bishop England's Sisterhood, 1829–1929," Ph.D. Diss., St. Louis University, 1968, pp. 122–123.

91. ASP, Copy of letter of Feb. 25, 1862, in *Indianapolis Sentinel*, n.p.

92. AUNG, "Account Taken from Annals, p. 2.

93. ADC, in *Annals of the Civil War*, manuscript, p. 503. Penciled note, no date, no sender/receiver given.

94. ASCN. See also ANDU, Purcell papers, II–5-a, Letter of Bishop Spalding to Bishop Purcell, Oct. 29, 1861.

95. ASCN. See also ANDU, Spalding to Purcell, Oct. 29, 1861, enclosure of copy of memo of General Robert Anderson to Martin Spalding, Sept. 24, 1861.

96. Archives of the Sisters of Mercy of New York (ARSMNYC), "From the Annals," n.p.

97. *Official Records*, Series I, Vol. IX, pp. 410–411.

98. ANDU, Letter of Bishop Martin Spalding to Bishop John Purcell, Oct. 29, 1861.

99. CDA, 28S2, Letter of Sr. De Sales to Bishop Lynch, Mar. 12, 1863.

100. Mother Bernard McGuire, *The Story of the Sisters of Mercy in Mississippi* (New York: P. J. Kennedy, 1931), p. 20.

101. McGuire, p. 17.

102. ACSC, Civil War, "Red Rover" file.

103. ACSC, Civil War, Mound City account book, manuscript.

104. Cornelius Buckley, *A Frenchman, a Chaplain, a Rebel: The War Letters of Père Louis-Hippolyte Gauché, SJ* (Chicago: Loyola University Press, 1981), p. 166.

105. ADC, Letter of Mother Ann Simeon Norris to the Senate and the House of Representatives, Dec. 8, 1864.

106. *Congressional Globe* Dec. 21, 1864, p. 95; Jan. 5, 1865, p. 127.

5

Catholic Sister Nurses in the Civil War

The key to understanding why military and medical authorities so desired the values brought by the sisters to the Civil War health-care needs lies in the very nature of religious life with its emphasis on community life and charitable service to others as expressed by public, lifelong vows of poverty, obedience, and chastity.

For the sisters, there was an underlying religious and theological basis for a life of service to others. As Jesus Christ gathered apostles and disciples around him, gave them a commandment to love all people, and sent them out to teach, preach, and heal, so did Roman Catholic sisters live in community and engage in various services in order to be faithful to Christ's example. The three vows, which were customarily pronounced for life, were simply a public declaration of the sister's commitment to this life. Thus, a willing sacrifice of one's will, one's material possessions, and one's desire to marry and have children was done in imitation of Christ, who was obedient to God's will, poor in order to share His life with all, and chaste so that His love might be given to all. Admittedly, the authorities generally did not understand the religious lifestyle nor consciously refer to the structure of religious life in requesting the sisters. Rather, they focused on the sisters' nursing experience or on a general impression that the sisters could and would learn to do what was needed. Nevertheless, it was these inherent, underlying qualities of religious life that caused the sisters to be able and willing to respond quickly to the requests, to move to a variety of locations and situations, and to assume the multitude of duties loosely classed as "nursing."

Living out the vow of obedience meant being willing to mobilize oneself or the community to respond to needs of others as articulated through the requests of legitimate religious authority, usually the superior or bishop. Poverty was expressed by a simple life style, the sharing of goods in common, and often, in the mid-nineteenth century, rigorous physical and material hardships. Chastity, though largely understood in the negative sense of not being married, also implied an attitude of inclusiveness of all people in a sister's or a community's love and service. In addition, the constitutions and regulations of the various communities, which provided commonsense wisdom and basic rules for caring for the sick, enabled the sisters to know what to do or to easily learn from one another once they arrived at the various medical facilities.

Thus, while other female nurses sometimes did serve in comparable battlefield, transport ship, and hospital situations and performed similar duties, the sisters were often preferred as nurses because the special characteristics of their lives enabled them to function as a cohesive group, to accept difficult physical and material circumstances, and to relate to the soldiers in a nonsexual, even-handed manner. From the sisters' perspective, the hardships of the Civil War experiences were not minimized. However, they willingly took on the different situations and duties as an expansion of their main purpose, which had always been to instruct, to care for the homeless, and to comfort the sick and dying in imitation of Jesus Christ, "Amen, I say to you as long as you did it to one of my least brethren, you did it to me."[1]

While no sisters or lay women are recorded as having been assigned as nurses to any regiments, sisters did serve in every other place where there were wounded and sick soldiers. Battlefields, hospital transport ships, field hospitals, hastily established hospitals in various buildings, tent hospitals, and their own or other private, already established hospitals were all scenes of the sisters' services, especially in the first two years of the war. During the last two years, they served in general hospitals specifically built by the Union. These locations varied, but conditions for the soldiers and for themselves were invariably depressing, dirty, and demoralizing.

Just as the general experiences and functions of the few thousand female nurses in the Civil War constitute a relatively unknown chapter in the history of the rebellion, so too, the variety of places the sisters served and the duties they performed comprise a similar, obscure historical record. Yet, careful examination of extant archival sources shows that sisters were hardly confined to Catholic hospitals, caring only for religious needs of soldiers, as might be presumed. Rather, they were engaged in an amazing number of situations accomplishing a wide variety of duties. The cumulative effect of these accounts shows not only the sisters' willingness to respond, but also their ability to nurse or quickly learn to nurse under trying circumstances; their flexibility in adjusting to constantly changing conditions; and, above all, the underlying religious commitment that enabled them to respond to these many environments and duties.

The display of these qualities and the typical response they elicited in others is illustrated by the experience of Cincinnati Sister of Charity Anthony O'Connell. On a transport boat holding 700 men, that was caught on the shoals at Louisville after the battle of Shiloh in 1862, the captain told the sisters they would have to leave the ship if they wished to live. However, Sister Anthony explained, "None would think of doing so. All expressed their willingness, their determination to remain." The doctor, seeing the sisters' firm resolve, said, "Since you weak women display such courage, I, too, will remain."[2]

In their obedient response to requests, sisters were to be found following the movement of men from battlefield to transport ship, to field and general hospital, and eventually to permanent hospital. A common practice in the North was to go to the battlefield in order to bring the men back on Army or US Sanitary Commission transport ships to general hospitals. At least six communities recorded the horrors of the battlefield and of the transport ships and of the heroics of the sisters' work. In almost every instance, the evidence documenting the sisters' activities, directly or indirectly, includes an awareness of the values of religious life that initiated and animated their work.

For example, the annals of the Holy Cross Sisters of South Bend, Indiana, indicate that the sisters' custom was to go out on the battlefield to "succor the wounded and dying" after the battles, but it was not an easy task. The "sight of a macerated face and stench of his wounds dreadful" caused one of the doctors' wives, who traveled with the sisters, to suggest they "turn to other soldiers." Yet one sister, conscious of the religious motivation that enabled her to endure the situation, gently reminded the woman of the Scriptural passage, "Whatsoever you do to the least of mine, you do to Me." The willingness of the sister to share her own motivation helped the doctor's wife. The annals record that the wife remained, and, after that, "could never do enough for wounded soldiers."[3]

Another battlefield experience attesting to the sisters' willing response and quick mobility was that of the Daughters of Charity after the Battle of Gettysburg. The property of the Daughters of Charity in Emmitsburg, Maryland, a scant ten miles south of Gettysburg, had been the scene of a Union encampment and General George Meade's headquarters days before the tragic battle. Confederate scouts moved in as the Union troops marched toward Gettysburg. Though spared the fighting on their own land and property, several Daughters of Charity and their priest superior traveled under a flag of truce to the battleground, reaching it on the morning of July 5, 1863. They tended some wounded on the field and then were directed into the town, where all available buildings had been

turned into makeshift hospitals. St. Francis Xavier Catholic Church and
the Methodist church, hastily set up with boards across the pews for
operating tables, were among the sites of the sisters' work during the
next several days as all of Gettysburg turned out to tend the wounded.[4]

A major task after battles was moving the wounded and dying men
from the battlefield onto transport boats of the US Sanitary Commission,
which went up and down the Ohio, Mississippi, and other rivers. According to eyewitness reports, the horrors of the screams and the sights
on the transport ships were compounded by the overcrowding. One of
the most graphic descriptions of this experience was that of a Daughter
of Charity:

When men, sisters, provisions, horses, etc. were all on board, we were more like
sinking than sailing. . . . Here misery was in her fullness and her victims testified
to her power by the thousand-toned moans of bitter waves. . . . Here our sisters
shared with their poor patients every horror except that of feeling their bodily
pains. They were in the lower cabins; the ceiling low, and lighted all day by
hanging lamps or candles; the men dying on the floor with only space to stand
or kneel between them.[5]

Obviously, most of the wounded, who already may have waited for
days on the battlefield, needed attention long before the boats reached an
established hospital. "At one time our boat deck looked like a slaughter-
house, wounded everywhere," described Cincinnati Charity Sister Theodosia. "I have seen Dr. Blackman cut off arms and limbs by the dozens
and consign them to a watery grave. Accompanied by Miss Hatch
[Daughter of Mayor Hatch of Cincinnati] or a Sister I would pick my
steps among the wounded bodies to follow the doctor, dressing the
wounds of those brave boys. . . . The groans of those poor boys as they
lay on deck in that pool of blood would rend the stoutest heart."[6]

Of unique interest among sisters serving on transport boats were the
four Sisters of the Holy Cross who served on the "Red Rover," a captured
Confederate ship, after it was refitted by the Federal Army.[7] Along with
five Black female nurses working under their direction, they are considered the pioneers or forerunners of the US Navy Nurse Corps because
the "Red Rover" eventually became a Navy vessel in late 1862, carrying
over 200 patients.[8] While accounts by the sisters on board the ship are
rare, *Harper's Weekly* in May 1863 carried three drawings by Civil War
artist Theodore R. Davis, one depicting the "Red Rover" and two showing sisters in the wards moving from soldier to soldier. Part of the caption
reads, "The sister is one of those good women whose angelic services
have been sung by poets and breathed by grateful convalescents all the
world over."[9]

Though not equally eulogized, the Sisters of the Poor of St. Francis of Cincinnati also served on a transport, the "Superior," gathering the wounded Union soldiers from southern battlefields.[10] In addition, the Sisters of Mercy of Cincinnati and the Sisters of St. Joseph of Philadelphia spent time on the hospital transport boats,[11] the former spending the time on the way to Pittsburgh Landing "sewing ticks, folding bandages and preparing supplies."[12]

This battlefield and transport work offered perhaps the greatest challenge to the sisters. The immediacy with which they had to respond when battle occurred, the difficulties of attending to the sick because of the cramped and crowded quarters, the uncertain length of the trip, and the probable lack of any privacy all reflected the sisters' commitment to being flexible.

While battlefield and transport ship conditions were grim, work in the hospitals was almost as difficult since many were makeshift facilities. Even if there was a building, the situation was almost always primitive. For example, in the Cumberland, the Sisters of Charity of Cincinnati recalled that accommodations were poor because hotels and warehouses had been converted into temporary hospitals. In addition, the weather was cold, and the twelve hospitals were some distance from one another, which made it impossible for the sisters to give proper attention to the sufferers. One of the sisters pointed out that crowded into these hospitals at one time were 2,200 soldiers suffering from typhoid fever, pneumonia, scurvy, erysipelas, and other diseases.[13]

The Southern experiences were even more difficult, and sisters laboring there rarely had a chance to stay long even in a makeshift hospital. This situation undoubtedly added to the sisters' work as well as to their frustrations. For example, arriving at Mississippi Springs, Mississippi, to hastily set up a hospital for the sick soldiers being hurried out of Vicksburg, the Sisters of Mercy found that the assigned house was dirty, neglected, and entirely unfurnished. Further, the mattresses had been burned on the railroad cars coming out because they were contaminated, and the sisters lacked the necessary equipment or supplies for cooking. After describing their plight, the sister recorder added, with the characteristic compassion of all sisters, that "the sisters suffered much in seeing the sick suffer."[14]

These primitive conditions taxed the sisters' energies. Nevertheless, previous experience in preparing old houses for schools and hospitals, and working long hours cleaning and scrubbing their own institutions and convents, were familiar tasks for the sisters. Thus, their particular attention to cleaning was a needed and valued skill that contributed to the overall care of the wounded.

Even though the sisters may have been able to restore some cleanliness and order to the temporary medical facilities, the constantly changing nature of the battles brought new challenges to their compassion and

ingenuity. Frequently, seriously wounded men were brought hastily to
the hospitals on the boats and in ambulances, leaving the sisters no time
to get beds and supplies ready. For example, Sister of Charity of Our
Lady of Mercy Agatha wrote to South Carolina Bishop Patrick Lynch
about the sisters' exhaustion caused by a large crowd of badly wounded
men brought in without "one moment's warning." The wounded were
carried in on litters, she wrote, and "left before my ward until my heart
grew sick and I was compelled to whisper to myself again and again
during the day your salutary advice, 'Take it easy.' "[15] She added that
these men with broken legs and arms and other dreadful wounds had
not tasted a morsel for fifty-two hours and were nearly exhausted.[16]

Writing after the Battle of Fort Donelson, February 16, 1862, Holy
Cross Sister Calista recorded one of the more graphic descriptions of
the condition of the wounded men. "Many had to be neglected on the
field; frozen fingers, ears and feet were the result, but the cooling of
the blood must have saved many from bleeding to death. Sometimes
men were brought in with worms actually crawling in the wounds. Some
were blind, their eyes being shot out."[17]

The difficulties of handling horribly wounded men brought on short
notice after the battles was compounded by the fact that there was a
limited number of sisters to nurse hundreds of men. As one sister explained, "After one battle there were seven hundred in the hospital and
only four sisters to wait on them. It was a heartrending sight to see the
poor men holding out their hands to the sisters to attract their attention
for many were not able to speak."[18]

No Union hospital had more men crowded in it than the Satterlee
Hospital in Philadelphia. A unique handwritten journal kept by the
Daughters of Charity at Satterlee Hospital had entries for July 5, 7, 8,
1863. The account indicates that a "great commotion was created
throughout the hospital by the arrival of several hundred of the
wounded" after the Battle of Gettysburg. This continued for several
days until "the hospital [was] filled in every hole and corner with those
who have been wounded . . . and nearly all are from Pennsylvania." The
sisters recorded that those who came in on July 7th had been wounded
since the 1st. These soldiers told them that other men who were more
dangerously wounded were still on the battlefield, since there was no
means of removing them. The sisters received orders, then, to "prepare
for two thousand more which will make nearly five thousand patients."
By July 8, the sisters explained that four rows of beds were in each ward,
with the two rows in the center pushed together. Again, demonstrating
their willingness to serve where needed and to be attentive to the most
critical soldiers, the sisters assisted as much as possible in dressing the
wounds since there were few attendants in the wards, and watched the

most dangerous cases as many of the soldiers' wounds would frequently bleed during the night, causing death.[19]

Often the sheer numbers of sick and wounded required tents to be set up on the grounds of a general hospital. This was the situation for the Sisters of Mercy from Pittsburgh who, besides being at Stanton Hospital in Washington, also served at West Penn Hospital, Pittsburgh. There, the increased number of wounded and convalescent soldiers caused the erection of the "City of Tents," which one sister said sheltered thousands who had been brought to Pittsburgh from the battlefield, encampments, and prisons.[20] The Sisters of Saint Joseph of Philadelphia also served briefly at two different times at the tent hospitals at Camp Curtin in Pennsylvania, which were opened and closed as the needs dictated.[21]

What is clear from the cumulative archival accounts of the sisters is that their nursing was hardly confined to one place or even to one type of medical facility. While the sisters certainly took the wounded into their own hospitals, in most cases, these were not near the battlesites, and so they went wherever they were asked for, primarily places of immediate need. Nothing in their previous experience, though, could have prepared them for the thousands of men, seriously wounded and ill, who crowded into the hastily converted building or huge government hospitals. Even those communities which had hospitals had never dealt with the numbers of sick and wounded brought in by the war. In addition to the unpredictability of the numbers, the sisters had to face the problems related to evacuating the men when opposing forces moved in. This, too, required both flexibility and ingenuity.

The ingenuity is illustrated well by three Sisters of Mercy, who were with a group of seriously ill Confederates who had been evacuated to several sites at the rear of the line near Pensacola Bay, Florida, in 1861. Faced with the possibility that Union soldiers from Fort Pickens would believe the hospital was deserted and shell it, the sisters paraded back and forth all day in front of it.[22] When the expected Union attack failed to materialize, the evacuees were quickly moved back to the hospital from the hastily constructed open shed in which they had been placed. By then, many of the men had already died from exposure, and the sisters were anxious to get the living back into the hospital. However, as one of the returning sisters wrote, "We were merely settled when too [sic] our astonishment they [Union troops] opened fire on the hospital without the least warning." Frantically, the sisters worked to remove the patients while three shells crashed into the building, one nearly killing a sister.[23]

Another group of sisters who risked the possibility of being shelled was the Ursuline Sisters in Galveston, Texas, after the Battle of Galveston on January 1, 1863. Shells were falling around the convent-turned-hospital when a Confederate courier, dispatched by General John Magruder, came dashing up, yelling for a yellow flag to be immediately put up to keep the building from being hit. As the sisters' annals record, "A search for the desired article was immediately begun, but yellow flags are not easily come by at anytime. Finally, after what seemed an eternity of bursting shells and shuddering earth, someone produced a bit of cream-colored flannel, in reality a sister's old and well-washed winter petticoat."[24]

Even if the evacuation efforts as a result of enemy occupations did not threaten the lives of the sisters or their charges, the confusions and hardships involved in moving with the men were traumatic enough. A typical experience was that of the Vicksburg Sisters of Mercy. They, along with a doctor and wounded Confederate soldiers, moved in boxcars from Meridian to Demopolis to Selma in Mississippi, and then finally to Shelby Springs, Alabama, "boiling coffee by the side of the road." Settling at Shelby Springs in what had once been a resort, the sisters quickly converted the ballroom into a surgical ward. "We had found," Sister M. Ignatius Sumner recalled, "whole rations not too much, we were now put on half rations, until the sick came. The dirt as usual [was] in melancholy ascendancy, and one of the sisters not yet recovered from the jaundice, [and] from exposure."[25] Nonetheless, they made do with limited food, cleaned the building, and readily began the nursing tasks again.

Though the living quarters of the sisters, at least in the North, were improved after the hospital complexes were built, the sisters' personal living conditions in the early years mirrored conditions of the buildings used for hospitals. From Frederick, Maryland, a sister wrote,

When we reached the hospital, we were received by an orderly who showed us our room in an old stone barrack.... On entering, the sisters looked at each other and smiled, for it seemed quite too small for the number of occupants. There were ten beds jammed together, at the end of which was an old table and two or three chairs, the only furniture in the room with the exception of an old rickety wash stand and two affairs that seemed to be fixed up to ornament the place. [Yet], ... we had enough when we saw the condition of the poor wounded soldiers who were without food and nourishment enough, and even that was ill-prepared.[26]

A similar experience is recorded by the Holy Cross Sisters who, arriving in Mound City, Illinois, found Mother Angela "scrubbing the floor ... and a very miserable barracks of a place, an unfinished warehouse with out even the common necessities of life. One bed and one chair had to do service for five sisters. Mother Angela and I slept on a table on some clothes which had been sent to be washed."[27]

The willingness of the sisters to put up with these difficult physical conditions in their own living quarters stemmed from their general orientation toward simple living and enduring hardship without complaint, as well as from a certain recognition that whatever their own personal hardships, the men they were caring for were in worse condition. This contrasted with the attitude of many of the lay female nurses, who, as Dr. John Brinton remarked, wanted a room and a looking-glass for themselves.[28] Whatever the legitimacy of such requests by the women might have been, the demands were impossible, and even ludicrous, in wartime. Thus, the sisters' demonstrated ability to adjust to the ebb and flow of wounded men, to the physical constraints of the boats and hospital buildings, and to the dangers of the shelling during occupation, combined with their uncomplaining acceptance of cramped and uncomfortable physical quarters for themselves, all caused them to be preferred to other female nurses. Clearly, the qualities inherent in their religious commitment enabled them to make these adjustments.

As has been seen, battlefields, transport boats, tent hospitals, and other temporary facilities were the sites for service by nearly half the communities of sisters. A greater number of sisters, however, nursed in the various buildings designated as hospitals by the Union and Confederate governments. Some, like the Sisters of St. Joseph in Wheeling, West Virginia, nursed in their own hospital when it was leased to the Union government for a military hospital.[29] The Daughters of Charity in New Orleans and Richmond continued to use their own institutions. The same was true for the Daughters of Charity at St. Mary's Hospital in Albany, New York, which had a government contract from March 1863 to the end of the war.[30]

Later, as the Federal Government built huge army hospitals on the "Pavilion" plan,[31] the Daughters of Charity served at hospitals at Point Lookout, Maryland; Lincoln General Hospital in Washington; and Satterlee Hospital in Philadelphia. The sisters' service in some of these newly built government hospitals is clear not only from their own archival sources, but, more significantly, from several official descriptions of the physical layouts of the buildings, which made special provisions for female nurses in general and sisters in particular.

Under Stanton's order of July 20, 1864, instructions for building all general hospitals were to include "quarters for female nurses" and a "chapel."[32] The standard plan provided quarters that were to be a "detached building containing lodging-rooms, dining room, and kitchen for the female nurses."[33] The chapel was to be a "detached building, fitted for the purpose of religious services, so arranged as to be used also as a library and reading room."[34] While this multipurpose room was constructed primarily for the soldiers' use, the fact that it was required presumably made it easier for the sisters to participate in religious services. Thus, the sisters' ability to serve in these permanent army hospitals was enhanced.

As the Union government began to construct various hospitals according to these instructions, some plans made specific provisions for sisters' quarters, notably at Point Lookout, Maryland, and Lincoln General Hospital in Washington (two types of pavilion-constructed hospitals) and also at Satterlee Hospital in Philadelphia. The hospital at Point Lookout, Maryland, was described as arranged like the spokes in a wheel, with about 1,400 beds serving large numbers of Confederate prisoners as well as Union soldiers.[35] Corporal Bishop Crumrine, in his letters, gave a description and map of Point Lookout, corroborating the sisters' presence both in the location of their living quarters and in their work in the kitchen and storerooms.[36] In addition, in circular #4 of the Surgeon General concerning hospital organization and construction, Surgeon J. J. Woodward described the sisters' quarters at Lincoln General Hospital as follows, adding a personal note that was atypical of the rest of his precise description of every other part of the hospital:

The building is 23 by 51 feet, with a wing 16 by 28, forming a letter "L." It is divided into chapel, sitting room, kitchen, etc. Twenty-eight Sisters of Charity were on duty, and I must bear evidence to their efficiency and superiority as nurses. The extra-diet kitchen is under the care of a sister and one is detailed by the superior for each ward. They administer medicine, diet, and stimulants, are under the orders of the ward surgeon, and are responsible to him alone. They have been beloved and respected by the men.[37]

A similar description and personal comment is also provided in the official *Medical and Surgical History of the War of the Rebellion*. Surgeon I. I. Hayes, in charge of Satterlee Hospital, West Philadelphia, said he was "fortunate in being able to engage, as directed when the hospital was first opened, forty Sisters of Charity whose labors have been unceasing and valuable."[38] In describing the elaborate building, he said, "These corridors terminate at the eastern end each in a storehouse, which is two stories high; the second story furnishes quarters for the Sisters of Charity.... At the end of the ward which joins the corridor are two rooms, one on either side, ten by eight feet, one of which is used for a wardmaster, the other for a female nurse (Sister of Charity)."[39]

These unusual personal testimonies included in official reports add two important facts to the history of sisters serving in the Civil War. First, through official governmental documentation, the statements establish the accuracy of the record of the sisters' presence. More importantly, the highly unusual nature of words of praise and gratitude inserted in the otherwise very factual accounts supports the view that the sisters were very highly regarded. Thus, the medical authorities wished to make special note of their contribution in official records. No similar comments exist in regard to any other personnel, let alone other female nurses.

Whether on battlefields, transport ships, or in temporary or permanent hospitals, whether serving Union or Confederate soldiers, the sisters took on a multitude of duties subsumed under the title "nurse." During the Civil War, the word "nurse" for both the lay woman and the sister encompassed different activities than the common understanding of the word does today. In general, the sisters, like their lay counterparts, provided services in the areas of administration, direct nursing, housekeeping, cooking, and other support staff functions. For example, sometimes sisters were in charge of the whole hospital, with the sisters' superior assigning sisters and others to various duties within the hospitals, including wards, kitchens, and laundry facilities. More often, however, the sisters nursed in the wards with a doctor or, occasionally, a matron in charge of the hospital. In their nursing duties, the sisters dressed wounds, gave medicines, often tended contagious diseases, and sometimes even assisted with surgery. Cleanliness and nutrition were key elements in preventing disease, keeping infection from spreading, and helping the soldiers regain their strength, so sisters also functioned as housekeepers, laundresses, dietitians, and cooks.

Among documented miscellaneous duties assumed by sisters during the war were obtaining and dispensing the supplies that came from friends, the US Sanitary Commission, and other aid groups. In addition, mediating quarrels among the soldiers, staff, and other personnel, handling special cases such as the female soldiers (usually discovered when they were wounded or sick), and preparing corpses for burial were all tasks that sisters were engaged in. Since the wounded sometimes were prisoners of war, the sisters also cared for them and even visited them later when they were transferred from hospital to prison. Though other female nurses may have assumed most of these same duties, the sisters had a different underlying motivation that sustained them. More importantly, the sisters assumed another major duty consonant with that motivation. Primary in the sisters' view was their desire to be with the dying soldiers, baptizing those who wished it, and encouraging repentance and providing a peaceful atmosphere for all.

A key benefit in having sisters rather than other women work in a hospital was that sisters, because of their religious training, were used to being assigned demanding tasks within the convent and institutional structures, and working and learning easily from each other. Thus, it is valuable to look at the variety and multiplicity of all these tasks in greater detail, especially the sisters' religious duties on behalf of the men.

A typical situation was described by Father Neal Gillespie, brother of Mother Angela of the Holy Cross Sisters, after he had visited Mound

City Hospital, Illinois, where she was in charge, with ten sisters working with her. He explained that each sister had one or two wards for her special care. To assist her was a wardmaster for each ward and a certain number of soldier-nurses from the different regiments. However, in addition to supervising all these, Mother Angela was also the cook for some of the sick as well as the correspondant with various aid societies to get little comforts for the soldiers.[40] In spite of these many tasks, Fr. Gillespie, as a concerned brother, was pleased to say that the doctor in charge tried to provide everything for the sick that the sisters wanted.[41]

Another hospital administrator with a multitude of duties was Charleston Sister De Sales Brennan, matron of the Confederate hospital in White Sulphur Springs, Virginia. Her letters give the most complete account of the sisters' duties in the war. In 1862, for instance, she wrote to Bishop Lynch that they were very much in need of another sister, as the number of patients had increased very rapidly during the previous eight or ten days. She also indicated that she had taken on the duty of staying up with a patient until midnight in order to dispense a special life-sustaining medicine because the doctor needed someone he could count on. She closed the letter by saying that it was late and she still had some eight or ten blisters to dress. In that hospital, as well as in others, the distribution of the medicines was turned over to the sisters because they could be counted on to be conscientious. Willingly, the sisters took on the task, even though they were then almost constantly confined to the wards, barely able to care for all the men they already had.[42]

Since so many more men were sick from disease than from wounds, much of the sisters' work involved nursing men suffering from a variety of diseases. Typhoid, pneumonia, erysipelas (a streptococcal infection), measles, and smallpox were among the contagious diseases frequently encountered. Smallpox was especially dreaded; the Sisters of Mercy of Cincinnati recount that they had the assistance of lay women in getting the wounded on the transport ships "until smallpox broke out. . . . The ladies then fled in dismay, leaving the sisters to continue alone their labor of love and danger."[43]

From November 1862 through the spring of 1863, Sister De Sales was concerned with smallpox, which was first brought in by one wounded soldier and later reappeared among other soldiers in the Confederate hospital in West Virginia. "Employees, patients, and Negroes are all panic stricken," she wrote, as she described the various measures taken to prevent the spread of the disease.[44] The sister, who was to visit a man in the small house in which he was isolated, was told by the doctors "not to protract her visits lest she might take the contagion in her habit to the other patients."[45] For a time, Sister De Sales did assign a sister to the smallpox hospital, but later quarantine regulations caused her to withdraw the sister because there was not a separate room she could occupy.[46]

While the majority of the sister nurses dealt with diseases similar to those described by Sister De Sales, they might also be asked to assume other tasks, especially if there was a shortage of doctors. However, the only recorded instance of a sister assisting with surgery was that of Sister Anthony O'Connell. She did not specifically explain what her responsibilities were, but judging from the surgical practice of the time, she probably assisted by providing surgical instruments and dressings, perhaps administering the chloroform or ether, or holding limbs as the doctors amputated.

She reminisced,

The Sisters of Charity of Cincinnati went to the war, as nurses, but it sometimes fell to their lot to be assistant surgeons. After the battle of Shiloh the young surgeons were off on a kind of lark as they called it, to prevent blue mal. I became Dr. Blackman's assistant in the surgical operations. He expressed himself well pleased with the manner in which I performed this duty and indeed I was well pleased to be able to alleviate in any degree the sufferings of these heroic souls.[47]

Consistently permeating the duties that the sisters performed was an awareness of the soldiers' sufferings and a desire to alleviate them. Though the tasks of administering the wards, dressing wounds, giving medicines, treating diseases, and even assisting surgeons were all duties that even today come under the heading of nursing, cleaning and cooking were also key responsibilities of the sisters. Again, the constitutions of many of the orders spelled out the importance of cleanliness and good food as a major part of proper care of the sick. Thus, the sisters came to their wartime duties with a clear understanding and knowledge of all the needed basic nursing skills.

Whether or not the sisters were officially in charge of housekeeping, generally their first task upon coming to any building designated as a "general" hospital was to make the place habitable. The Sisters of Mercy from Vicksburg recalled going to take charge of Mississippi Springs Hospital, at the time a "fashionable watering place" about forty miles from Vicksburg. The steward had had to whisper something about "smallpox" to get the guests to leave. The frightened inhabitants took flight precipitously, leaving the sisters "such an accumulation of dirt to clean up as they had never beheld."[18]

The Sisters of Providence took charge of the cooking, cleaning, washing, and general housekeeping of the military hospital in Indianapolis, reported the *Indianapolis Daily Journal* in 1861, praising their "unpleasant but noble duty."[49] Clearly, the sisters made a significant improvement, for in 1864, the same newspaper reported that the laundry, under the sisters' direction, was washing and ironing a thousand pieces of clothing and five hundred sheets every week.[50]

At the Satterlee Hospital in Philadelphia, housing 7,000 men after the battle of Gettysburg, Sister Angela, a Daughter of Charity, was in charge of thirty women who did the laundry. A major responsibility was to count and sort the clothes from the various patients and departments and return them when clean. Due to the great influx of patients, Sister Angela had to be reassigned by the sister superior to one of the wards and the surgeon assigned a "reliable gentleman" and several male assistants to do the heavy laundry work, presuming that the work would be done even better with the extra help. However, as the sisters' journal records, "It became in a few days a kind of Bedlam, dancing, singing, quarreling, and fighting constituted a large part of each day's work and at the end of the first week, doctors, druggists, clerks, Ward Masters looked for their clothes in vain. All were mixed together and everything in confusion."[51] After one more week's trial, Sister Angela went back to the laundry, where order was restored. The return to normality attested not only to her ability to keep things clean, but also to her ability to organize things and keep peace.[52]

Besides actually doing the laundry or supervising those who did it, sisters, especially in smaller hospitals, often distributed it, thus ensuring that supplies were equitably distributed and clothing given to the right people. This task was not equally demanding in all hospitals, probably due to the fluctuations in occupancy. For example, just distributing the linen was an "arduous task" for Sister Stanislaus, a Sister of Charity of Our Lady of Mercy, in the Confederate hospital in West Virginia.[53] On the other hand, at Mound City, Illinois, a Holy Cross Sister was placed in the linen room so she would have time to visit the sick and poor in the neighborhood.[54] Clearly, time was not wasted.

In addition to making sure the hospital and the linen and clothing were clean, the sisters were concerned with providing the basic dietary necessities for the soldiers, as well as preparing special meals. An example of this can be inferred from a letter of Frank Hamilton, the surgeon in charge of St. Joseph's Government Hospital, Central Park, New York, to Sister Ulrica, the superior. The sisters must have requested a special dinner for the soldiers because Hamilton wrote that it would give him great pleasure to grant the sisters' request for a Thanksgiving dinner for the men.[55] At the same hospital, the sisters also had been looking for a resident baker so that they might directly supervise the making of special delicacies for the men. Hamilton granted this request as well.[56]

Those outside the hospitals also confirmed the special attention sisters gave to the dietary needs of the soldiers. An article in the *Indianapolis*

Daily Journal, March 8, 1864, reported on its investigative tour of City Hospital. The editors commented favorably on everything; however, the cooking and the Sisters of Providence were singled out for special mention. The sisters superintended and directed all the domestic arrangements and, the paper noted, "give comfort and cheer to the sick in a thousand kind attentions."[57]

Part of the reason the sisters' efforts were often called "excellent" was due to their ability to assess difficult situations and make appropriate changes. This was as true in dietary areas as it was in the laundry. For example, Sister De Sales, a Sister of Charity of Our Lady of Mercy, recalled that complaints in the dining room caused her to go into there, although it wasn't her area of responsibility, and attend to the men's concerns. She humorously recalled that before opening the dining-room doors for the first meal, the crush of people at the door was indescribable because the men didn't know she was there. She wrote:

The man who opened the door was compelled to close it again per force—as soon as they became quiet, I went to the door. As soon as they saw me, one man called out "boys, it is a lady that is here—fall back." Every man fell back to his place and they walked in two by two in perfect order. When the next meal came round, every man stood in rank at the door, and walked in perfect silence, taking off hats and saying good morning Sister. As one came in he said, "There is no 'storming the battery now' Sister."[58]

Realizing that a shortage of dishes and lack of organization were causes of the complaints, she got permission from the doctors to buy cups and spoons and directed that the ward masters march their men in two by two. No doubt, previous experience with schoolchildren helped her considerably.

Thus, part of the sisters' responsibility in most hospitals was obtaining and distributing food, clothing, and other supplies. These tasks were handled by the sisters partly because provisions and supplies were often connected with particular dietary or housekeeping duties and partly because the sisters sometimes had ingenious ways of obtaining supplies for the hospital and themselves when no one else could. More importantly, the sisters could be trusted with the equitable distribution of the food and medical supplies.

Generally, food and other supplies were scarce, though the sisters did recount provisions' coming from the US Sanitary Commission, various aid societies, and friends. These donations were welcome as conditions were often destitute, especially in the South. For example, in Frederick, Maryland, a Daughter of Charity recalled, "Our food consisted of the soldiers' rations, and not enough of them. It was served . . . on broken dishes, with old knives and forks, red with rust. The patients often amused us at mealtime by saying, 'Sisters, there is no need for the doctor to order us the tincture of iron, three times a day; don't you think we get enough off our table service.' "[59]

A more critical experience was that of the Vicksburg Mercy Sisters, who followed the Confederate sick from hospital to hospital as the Union lines closed in on them. Typical of the sisters' generosity and foresight, they brought their own provisions with them. As Sister M. Ignatius Sumner recalled later, "It was well we did because though there were provisions in the country, little experience and forethought in collecting and distributing them and officers who were 'busy making themselves friends of the mammon of iniquity,' distributing supplies to their friends, left the Sisters trying to meet the needs of the sick."[60]

Although the South did not have a Sanitary Commission, individual benefactors, as well as groups, were organized to assist. For example, Sister De Sales reported that the South Carolina Association sent to the Montgomery Sulphur Springs Hospital, probably in 1864, another large box of clothing; five gallons of brandy, port, and cherry wine; sugar; tea; coffee; and a variety of other staples.[61] Of particular note are the recollections of the Daughters of Charity in Richmond, who reported that Mrs. Jefferson Davis often came to the hospital to see the sick Union soldiers and supplied them with tobacco, cigars, soap, razors, and anything they asked for. She requested the sisters not to let patients know who she was, commenting that the Confederates would be well supplied by the Southerners but that the Union soldiers needed things.[62]

In addition, the sisters often used their own ingenuity in securing provisions. In the fall of 1863, Sister De Sales wrote to Bishop Lynch several times requesting his permission to go to Baltimore to get needed supplies. One of her arguments was that "the Sisters of Charity cross continually and bring over any amount of things"[63] to the sisters in Lynchburg. She promised that since there were two flags of truce each month, she would not be gone longer than two weeks.

Besides getting supplies for the hospital, the sisters, especially in the South, had to devise ways of getting clothing for themselves. For example, the Sisters of Mercy of Vicksburg described the rabbit-skin shoes that Father Francis X. Leray, their chaplain, constructed for all of them, and added, "We sewed our own clothes [black] with white thread, and we made him [Leray] trousers out of a shawl, and a brown delaine shirt from a dress. A calico [dress] for our postulant cost $113, and she was much afraid the Father would covet it as a homespun dress had gone for a shirt."[64]

The experience of these limited supplies and donations had its humorous side. A Sister of Charity recounted a story of the sisters trying to get eggs for their sick Union soldiers from various benefactors. Finally, a large box arrived from the North, and everyone eagerly crowded around to see the opening of the box. Unfortunately, the eggs, long in transit and short in freshness, burst over the spectators when the lid was opened.[65]

The supplies that the sisters received from others or procured themselves had to be carefully distributed, a task that was often entrusted to the sisters. Special placards were printed with words such as, "All articles, donations, etc., for the use of the soldiers here, are to be placed under the care of the Sisters, as also, paper, books, clothing, money and delicacies."[66] Clothing, food, and other supplies intended for the patients, but taken by others or diverted to officers, seemed to be a common difficulty. For example, on November 16, 1862, Surgeon Frank Hamilton, at St. Joseph Hospital, Central Park, reminded the hospital staff that whatever was received as private or public contributions intended for the soldiers must be held sacred for that purpose. No officer or attendant was permitted, under any circumstances, to appropriate them to his own use. Supported by this order, the Sisters of Charity of New York, serving at the hospital, were designated to oversee the contributions. Hamilton believed in their integrity and in their impartial distribution of goods.[67]

The sisters' tasks of nursing, supervision, housekeeping, cooking, and procuring and distributing supplies flowed from the general nature of serving the direct needs of the wounded soldiers and caring for them in some kind of institutional setting. Often these duties were carried out by other female or male nurses and assistants as well. Those working with the sisters, however, generally turned to them for assistance because of the sisters' training and experience, their general religious commitment, or their reputation as women who would be honest and impartial toward all. These qualities, of course, were the direct result of the lifestyle and purpose of the sisters.

In addition to these duties, which might be considered normal "nursing" tasks for the Civil War period, sisters sometimes were called on to engage in two other activities. Their reputation as dedicated women enabled them to respond to specific situations of peacemaking and of attention to female soldiers. Two situations where sisters were called on to resolve arguments illustrated the respect that the men had for the sisters, both as women and as sisters.

One instance was at a hospital in Winchester, Virginia. The Daughters of Charity recounted that after hearing "loud threats and angry jargon" coming from the kitchen, two sisters hurried there and found two "colored men," a cook and a nurse, fighting. The sisters forced them apart by stepping between them and mildly requested each man to calm himself. Acknowledging the sisters' request, the men stopped with no further incident.[68] In a slightly different situation, at Antietam, a Northern steward and a Southern surgeon had a disagreement, and one challenged the other to meet him in a quiet spot. With loud, angry threats, both withdrew to an old shed. At first, no one was willing to interfere; then, one of the Daughters of Charity followed them and after "speaking to them firmly and reproachingly," she persuaded them to separate. Like docile children they returned to their posts.[69]

Quarreling and fighting certainly were expected events among men in the camps and hospitals; however, a much more unusual situation for the sisters was that of caring for women dressing as men. Though female soldiers were not common in the Civil War, over 400 women disguised themselves as men in order to serve in the army, to be with a husband or lover, or to serve as a spy.[70] That women served at all illustrates the inadequacies of the recruitment techniques and physical exams given to any Union or Confederate soldier. Often, the females were not discovered until they were wounded or sick. Thus, in hospitals where there were sisters, such cases were assigned to them and several different communities of sisters noted their care of such women. The records of the Holy Cross Sisters record an incident of a young girl who enlisted with the express purpose of shooting her stepfather. When she became ill, a doctor discovered her sex and her pregnant condition; the sisters cared for her, and their kindness and concern caused the girl to become a Catholic convert.[71] Because of the sisters' experience in the education of young women, a female soldier was brought to the Daughters of Charity in Richmond, Virginia, so that she might be "taught to know her place and character in life."[72]

In another situation in Memphis, a Holy Cross sister wrote about a young orderly, pretty and small, who became very ill and was sent to her ward, wrapped in a shawl. The surgeon in charge sent word to the sister to keep the patient separate and not to have the men wait on "him." The sisters recalled that "he" seemed a "pretty hard case who would curse and swear and scream." The screaming finally gave the soldier away. The sisters cared for her for three weeks until she died and also baptized her before her death.[73] In most situations, if the sick female lived, she was usually sent home immediately, so the sisters' contact with these women was limited. Apparently, however, it was strong enough for the sisters to have the opportunity to discuss religious values with the women.[74]

The opportunity to relate to the soldiers, and sometimes other doctors and staff, in a religious way was the most unique aspect of the sisters' work. This religious dimension was also the quality that motivated and enabled them to carry out the other nursing duties that were often demanding and difficult, even for those sisters who had previous nursing experience. Cincinnati Charity Sister Ambrosia said of her arduous tasks in the Cumberland, "Our duties [were] fatiguing and often disgusting to flesh and blood, but we were amply repaid by conversions, repentances, and the removal to a great extent of certain prejudices to our Holy Faith."[75] Her attitude succinctly expresses the nursing experience of all the Civil War sisters.

Regardless of how the sisters became involved in the war, where they worked, or what activities they engaged in, the written accounts that remain all stress the sisters' overwhelming desire and need to offer spiritual support to the wounded and dying, and often to the doctors and officers as well. Typical of the hagiographic writing of the period, the sisters' archival accounts and the two published accounts that exist recount primarily the conversion experiences and deathbed religious conversations.[76] In retrospect, much of the seeming emphasis on this aspect of the sisters' experience may be due to the fact that most extant material written by the sisters was completed shortly after the war, and they may have wished to emphasize the religious focus of their work. Further, specific questions such as the number of baptisms were asked for in some written accounts.[77] However, given the facts of the sisters' life of religious commitment, the major purposes of their communities, the mid-nineteenth-century Protestant-Catholic tension, and the desire of the minority, immigrant Catholic church for an increase in numbers, the emphasis on conversion stories is probably not just a fact of skewed records.

Even tasks as simple as writing letters for soldiers, a common occupation of women who visited soldiers, was done for a different motive by the sisters. One sister, trying to give examples of difficult situations the sisters sometimes found themselves in, wrote of a dying young man who seemed impervious to the sister's attempts to speak to him about his soul. Finally, he asked her to write a letter to his fiancée, promising that he would then listen to her. The sisters' account records: "The poor sister thinking that the soul was worth too much to stop at any terms asked him what she should say, and wrote accordingly. All the ward was attentive to hear it. When done, it was read to him. He was satisfied now to do as she advised, and being prepared for baptism died with very pious disposition."[78]

Among the corporal works of mercy articulated in the Catholic tradition are the admonitions to heal the sick and to bury the dead; the spiritual works include praying for the living and the dead. Thus, the sisters, in a blend of practical action and spiritual wisdom, often combined religion and the care of the sick and wounded. As a consequence, they frequently had a closer relationship with the men than some visiting clergyman.

For example, in a Washington hospital, a man called out, "I want a clergyman . . . a white bonnet [referring to the head dress of the sisters] clergyman, such as you ladies have." He was not a Catholic but continued to ask for a catechism or any book that would instruct him on the "White

Bonnet Religion"[79] Another instance where the men preferred the sisters to the clergy was at the prison in Alton, Illinois, which was frequently visited by a Catholic priest. While he was there, a sick man asked for baptism, but when approached by a priest, cried out, "No, I want Sister to baptize me!" In an unusual gesture, the priest told the sister, a Daughter of Charity, to baptize the soldier while he stood looking on.[80]

The baptisms, while extremely important to the sisters, were not universally appreciated by others with whom the sisters worked. One sister wrote to Charleston, South Carolina, Bishop Lynch saying that some of the doctors "are frantic at the influence we have over the men and at the number that have been baptized." She recounted that, largely because of the admiration the men came to have for the sisters' work, they were receptive to being baptized Catholics when they were dying. Though the fear of dying may have also contributed to the soldiers' requests for baptism, the sister also recorded at least three other men, not in danger of death, who studied the Catechism and asked for baptism.[81]

Though all communities ministered to the sick and assisted the dying, it is specifically recorded that the Sisters of St. Joseph, Wheeling, also prepared the corpses for burial and made the shrouds.[82] Further, the Indianapolis *Daily Journal* noted that at the City Hospital there, the Sisters of Providence beautifully arranged the dead rooms, hanging them with "white muslin, festooned with crepe, and at the head of each room are the Stars and Stripes also draped in mourning."[83] This special attention to concern for the dead came from the spiritual injunction of the corporal work of mercy that enjoined them to bury the dead.

In spite of the demands of both their physical and spiritual duties, the sisters had occasional moments of respite. For example, from White Sulphur Springs in March 1862, Sister De Sales wrote to her sisters about the beautiful rosebuds and the japonicas given for their altar by a storekeeper in town. After she explored the mountains "before the hospital fills in," she described the scenery as "truly beautiful" even though the sulphur water was "horrid."[84]

More often, however, the sisters' labors caused them fatigue, disease, and sometimes death. A Daughter of Charity recalled that the sisters, hoping for a little rest after the exhaustion of caring for the Confederate wounded, were startled by a terrible noise just as they were settling down in chapel. Running out, they momentarily thought it was the day of judgment as they saw bodies of men and the heavens on fire. The powder magazine had exploded, so: "With a right good will we went to work and we took good care not to console ourselves again with the thought of rest, fearing another catastrophe."[85]

Exhaustion was one consequence of Civil War nursing for the sisters, but sickness had more serious consequences. Confederate nurse Kate Cumming recalled a meeting with her old friend, Mrs. Ella King New-some, whose health had been ruined by extensive nursing duties in Atlanta. This was the same tent hospital, Cumming recalled, which the Daughters of Charity had left because they, too, could not stand the work or exposure to the weather.[86]

Sisters, too, sometimes fell victim to the diseases to which they were exposed. For example, Sister De Sales wrote to her sisters back in Charleston, South Carolina, in September 1862, saying, "I can scarcely write my little finger is exceedingly sore. I am fearful that I have contracted erisipelas as I have three cases of it in my ward."[87] Clearly, as the records show, the sisters were not sheltered or protected. They were not only fully engaged in various nursing tasks, but also suffered the consequences inherent in those tasks. Some sisters lived to see the monument to the "Nuns of the Battlefield" erected in Washington, D.C., in 1914, but several sisters died in the course of their labors in the Civil War.[88] Sister of Charity of Nazareth Sister Lucy Dosh was given a military funeral as the first sister to die while on duty. Assigned to nurse typhoid fever patients, she died at the Central Hospital in Paducah, Kentucky, on December 29, 1861. Her remains were taken to Uniontown, Kentucky, by gunboat under a flag of truce and then overland to the cemetery near St. Vincent Academy in Union County.[89]

While Mary Ryan Jolly in her research indicates that the only Daughter of Charity who died was Sister Consolata Conlon, who was buried with military honors on the banks of the Potomac,[90] a search of the records at the Motherhouse at Emmitsburg, Maryland, indicates that at least two other sisters also died. The sisters' handwritten account book of their experiences at Satterlee Hospital in Philadelphia indicates that two sisters had died during the time they were there,[91] although the official community records list only a Sister Xavier Lucot.[92] Jolly, on the other hand, does not list this sister at all for Satterlee, but lists a Sister Xavier Van Drome as serving at Satterlee during the war.[93] This is an apparent error, perhaps in last names, because the religious name of the sister—"Xavier" in this case—was not given out until after a sister died. Jolly also lists a Sister Catherine Chrismer as having served at Gettysburg,[94] but the community records list her as dying in 1862 at Mt. Hope Infirmary in Baltimore, an institution not otherwise known to have Civil War soldiers.[95]

The Holy Cross Sisters record the death in 1862 of Sister Elise O'Brien, whose body was given a military escort, at the general hospital in Cairo, Illinois,[96] and of Sister Fidelis Lawler, at Mound City Hospital, Illinois, whose body had to be taken by boat due to flooding at the Ohio River.[97] Sister Gerard Ryan of the Mercy Sisters of New York, serving in North

Carolina, died in 1864 "as a result of hardships."[98] At the Douglas Hospital in Washington, Sister Coletta O'Connor of the Baltimore Mercy Sisters died in 1864 and was buried with the military honors of a major.[99]

Whether death, disease, or exhaustion was the consequence of the sisters' many services, a Daughter of Charity in Richmond eloquently summarized the sisters' approach to their nursing:

Day and night our Sisters constantly administered by turns to soul and body; nourishment, remedies and drinks to the body and as best they could "living waters to the soul." Indeed, as far as possible, our dear Sisters subtracted from food and rest, the dying and suffering state of these poor men, causing them to make all sacrifices to them even joyfully, regarding such sacrifices as only a drop or cipher compared to the crying duties before them. While they were attending to some, others would be calling to them most piteously to give their wounds some relief.[100]

Clearly, the sisters were not the only women nurses functioning on battlefield, ships, and in hospitals, carrying out a multitude of duties, and often suffering from the consequences of hard work. They were but a sixth of such women, who themselves were but a small part of those who cared for the sick and wounded during the Civil War. What set them apart was the entire context of religious life, which consciously and unconsciously shaped the sisters and their actions. The result of this shaping produced a group of women like no other, willing to serve in a variety of places and doing a multitude of jobs in a manner that exhibited dedication and organization. But no matter what others saw as the value of their nursing services, the sisters saw themselves as missionaries promoting religion, not nursing pioneers opening up new areas for themselves or other women. To them the fundamental purpose for serving was to care for the sick and suffering as Jesus Christ would, bringing sick and dying men to think of God in their suffering and to be baptized if they were not. Often, in their memoirs and letters, the sisters seemed cognizant of the hard work needed to accomplish their job, but, they seemed to have no particular awareness that they had a skill that could or should be promoted among other women. Basically, whether the sisters came from hospital service or from teaching, care of children, or some other ministry, the areas in which they served in the Civil War and the duties which they performed simply were viewed as an extension of their ministry of doing good for those in need. As one Holy Cross sister succinctly stated, "We were not prepared as nurses, but kind hearts lent willing hands and ready sympathy and with God's help, we did much toward alleviating suffering."[101]

NOTES

1. Archives of the Sisters of Mercy of Vicksburg, Mississippi, (ARSMV), Handwritten copy of Mother M. de Sales Browne's *Constitution* of *the Sisters of Mercy*, Chapter II, Section 1, n.p.

2. Archives of Sisters of Charity of Cincinnati (ASCC), "Memoirs of Sr. Anthony O'Connell," n.p.

3. Congregational Archives of the Sisters of the Holy Cross, Saint Mary's, Notre Dame, IN (ACSC), Civil War, "Civil War narrative about Mother Angela," n.p.

4. Archives of the Daughters of Charity, Emmitsburg, MD (ADC), *Annals of the Civil War*, vol. I, pp. 40–47.

5. ADC, *Annals of the Civil War*, vol. I, pp. 19–20.

6. ASCC, "Memoirs of Sr. Theodosia," n.p.

7. Records in the Archives of the Sisters of the Holy Cross seem to indicate some sisters may have been on board the ship earlier than the records of the US Navy indicate (see Loomis below); however, the discrepancy might be explained by the fact that the "Red Rover" was an Army ship for a period of time after it was captured, and the Sisters may have been serving for the Union Army.

8. E. Kent Loomis, "History of the U.S. Navy Hospital Ship *Red Rover*," typescript, 1961, p. 7.

9. *Harper's Weekly* 7, No. 332 (May 9, 1863): 300–301.

10. Ellen Ryan Jolly, *Nuns of the Battlefield* (Providence, RI: Providence Visitor, 1927), p. 118.

11. Sr. Marie Kostka Logue, *Sisters of St. Joseph of Philadelphia: A Century of Growth and Development* (Westminster, MD: The Newman Press, 1950), pp. 127–129.

12. Mary Ellen Evans, *The Spirit Is Mercy: The Sisters of Mercy in the Archdiocese of Cincinnati, 1858–1958* (Westminster, MD: The Newman Press, 1959), pp. 90–91.

13. ASCC, "Memoirs of Sr. Ambrosia," n.p.

14. Archives of Sisters of Mercy, Vicksburg (ARSMV), Sr. M. Ignatius Sumner, "Register of the Events from the Foundation of the Convent of the Sisters of Mercy, Vicksburg, Miss.," p. 7.

15. CDA, 29W6, Sister Agatha to Bishop Patrick Lynch, Nov. 10, 1863.

16. CDA, 29W6.

17. ACSC, Civil War, Archives Narrative, Saint Mary's Convent, Vol. 1, "Memoirs of Sr. Calista," pp. 211–212.

18. ACSC, "Memoirs of Sr. Calista," pp. 211–212.

19. ADC, Satterlee notebook, manuscript, pp. 50–51.

20. Archives of Sisters of Mercy of Pittsburgh (ARSMP).

21. Logue, p. 129.

22. Michael Gannon, *Cross in the Sand: The Early Catholic Church in Florida* (Gainsville: University of Florida Press, 1967), p. 176.

23. Gannon, p. 176.

24. Archives of Ursuline Nuns, Galveston Texas (AUNG), "Annals," p. 4. See also Archives Notre Dame University (ANDU), VI–2-e, Letter of Chambodut to Bishop Odin, Oct. 8, 1861.

25. ARSMV, Sr. M. Ignatius Sumner, p. 18.

26. ADC, *Annals of the Civil War*, vol. I, p. 28.

27. ACSC, "Memoirs of Sr. Calista," pp. 211–212.

28. John Brinton, *Personal Memoirs of John H. Brinton* (New York: The Neale Publishing Co., 1914), p. 294.

29. Archives of the Sisters of St. Joseph, Wheeling, West Virginia (ACSJW).

30. ADC, Albany, "St. Mary's Hospital," p. 11.

31. U.S. Surgeon General's Office, *Reports on the Extent and Nature of the Materials Available for the Preparation of a Medical and Surgical History of the Rebellion*, Circular No. 6 (Philadelpia: J.B. Lippincott, 1865), p. 153.

32. Joseph K. Barnes, et al., *The Medical and Surgical History of the War of the Rebellion, 1861–65*, vol. III (Washington: Government Printing Office, 1875), pp. 942–45.

33. Barnes, vol. I, p. 154.

34. Barnes, vol. I, p. 154.

35. Edwin Beitzell, *Point Lookout Prison Camp for Confederates* (Abell, MD: E. W. Beitzell, 1972), p. 22.

36. Beitzell, p. 104.

37. The quoted description by Woodward is from a description furnished by Brevet Lieutenant Colonel J.C. McKeen, Surgeon, USA, surgeon in charge. The hospital was constructed in 1862 and first occupied in January 1863, with twenty pavilion wards and support-services buildings covering thirty acres; it closed August 22, 1865, after handling almost 25,000 patients. Circular No. 6, pp. 157–158.

38. Barnes, vol. III, p. 926.

39. Barnes, vol. III, p. 928.

40. ACSC, Civil War, Letter of Fr. Neal Gillespie to Mrs. Gillespie, Jan. 6, 1862.

41. ACSC, Civil War, Letter of Fr. Gillespie to Mrs. Gillespie, Jan. 6, 1862.

42. CDA, 27C6, Letter of Sr. De Sales to Bishop Lynch, April 15, 1862.

43. Evans, p. 91.

44. CDA, 28C7, Letter of Sr. De Sales to Bishop Lynch, Nov. 14, 1862.

45. CDA, 28C7.

46. CDA, 28Sl, Letter of Sr. De Sales to Dr. Woodville, Mar. 7, 1863.

47. ASCC, "Memoirs of Sr. Anthony O'Connell," n.p.

48. ARSMV, Sr. M. Ignatius Sumner, p. 36.

49. Archives of Sisters of Providence, St. Mary of the Woods IN (ASP), *Indianapolis Daily Journal*, June 18, 1861, typed copy.

50. ASP, *Indianapolis Daily Journal*, June 11, 1864, typed copy.

51. ADC, Satterlee notebook, manuscript, pp. 27–29.

52. ADC, Satterlee notebook, manuscript, p. 29.

53. CDA, 27T4, Letter of Bishop Augustine Verot to Bishop Lynch, Sept. 19, 1862.

54. ACSC, "Civil War narrative about Mother Angela," n.p.

55. Archives of the Sisters of Charity of New York City, (ASCNYC), item 243. Letter of Surgeon Frank Hamilton to Sister Ulrica, Nov. 19, 1862.

56. ASCNYC, item 240, Letter of Charles Devlin to Dr. McDougal, Oct. 30, 1862.

57. ASP, *Indianapolis Daily Journal,* Mar. 8, 1864, typed copy.

58. CDA, 28E1, Letter of Sr. De Sales to Bishop Lynch, Nov. 25, 1862.

59. ADC, *Annals of the Civil War,* vol. I, p. 28.

60. ARSMV, Sr. M. Ignatius Sumner, p. 36.

61. CDA, 30K7, Letter of Sr. De Sales to Bishop Lynch, Mar. 18, 1864.

62. ADC, *Annals of the Civil War,* vol. II, pp. 64.

63. CDA, 29N5, Letter of Sr. De Sales to Bishop Lynch, Sept. 14, 1863.

64. ARSMV, Sr. M. Ignatius Sumner p. 19.

65. ASCC, "Memoirs of Sr. Anthony O'Connell," n.p.

66. ADC, *Annals of the Civil War,* vol. I, p. 10.

67. ASCNYC, Memo from Surgeon Frank Hamilton to "Those in charge," Nov. 16, 1862.

68. ADC, *Annals of the Civil War,* vol. II, p. 57.

69. ADC, *Annals of the Civil War,* vol. II, p. 71.

70. Mary E. Massey, *Bonnet Brigades: American Women and the Civil War* (New York: Alfred Knopf, 1966), p. 17.

71. ACSC, Civil War, Archives Narrative, Saint Mary's Convent, vol. I, "Memoirs of Sr. Placides," p. 226.

72. ADC, *Annals of the Civil War,* vol. I, p. 62. See another example in Mary A. Holland, *Our Army Nurses* (Boston: B. Wilkens, 1895), p. 341.

73. ACSC, Civil War, Archives Narrative, Saint Mary's Convent, vol. I, "Memoirs of Sr. Matilda," p. 227.

74. See ACSC, "Memoirs of Sr. Matilda," p. 227, for another instance at Mound City Hospital, Illinois, where a female soldier was sent home from the cavalry after she became ill.

75. ASCC, "Memoirs of Sr. Ambrosia," n.p.

76. See Jolly; see also George Barton, *Angels of the Battlefield* (Philadelphia: Catholic Art Publishing Co., 1898).

77. ADC, Burlando's outline for writing the accounts of the war.

78. ADC, *Annals of the Civil War,* vol. I, p. 10.

79. ADC, *Annals of the Civil War,* vol. I, pp. 7–8.

80. ADC, *Annals of the Civil War,* vol. I, p. 5.

81. CDA, 27P5, Sr. De Sales to Bishop Lynch, Aug. 27, 1862.

82. Sr. Rose Anita Kelly, *Song of the Hills: The Story of the Sisters of St. Joseph of Wheeling* (Wheeling, WV: Sisters of St. Joseph, 1962), p. 220.

83. ASP, *Indianapolis Daily Journal,* June 11, 1864, typed copy.

84. CDA, 27B3, Letter of Sr. De Sales to Sr. Agatha, Mar. 11, 1862.

85. ADC, *Annals of the Civil War,* manuscript, Account of Sr. Gabriella, pp. 478–481.

86. Kate Cumming, *Kate: The Journal of a Confederate Nurse* (Baton Rouge: Louisiana State University Press, 1959), p. 262.

87. CDA, 27S4, Letter of Sr. de Sales to "My Beloved Sisters [Sister?]," Sept. 14, 1862.

88. See Jolly's introduction in *Nuns of the Battlefield,* pp. viii-ix, and references throughout the text.

89. Sr. Mary Agnes McGann, *The History of Mother Seton's Daughters: The Sisters of Charity of Cincinnati, vol. III* (New York: Longmans, Green, 1917), p. 47.

90. Jolly, pp. 73–74.

91. ADC, Satterlee Record Book, n.p.

92. ADC, Record sheet of Sr. Xavier Lucot.

93. Jolly, p. 83.

94. Jolly, p. 78.

95. ADC, Record sheet of Sr. Catherine Chrismer.

96. Jolly, p. 141.

97. ACSC, Civil War, Notebook of Sister Paula, typescript, "Civil War Narrative," pp. 1–7.

98. Jolly, p. 219.

99. Sr. Mary Loretto Costello, *The Sisters of Mercy of Maryland, 1855–1930* (St. Louis, MO: B. Herder, 1931), p. 48.

100. ADC, *Annals of the Civil War*, vol. I, p. 15.

101. ACSC, Civil War, Archives Narrative, Saint Mary's Convent, Vol. I, "Memoirs of Mother Augusta," p. 216.

Contemporaneous Attitudes about the Catholic Sisters in the Civil War

Regardless of how the sisters themselves regarded the inner religious purpose for their external work, what other people actually thought about sisters' nursing in the war clearly served both to define the sisters and to set them apart from other lay women nurses. The range of recorded perceptions and attitudes about them demonstrate that the sisters were definitely not invisible women. In the midst of the chaos of the war, people were aware of their presence and commented on them. These attitudes form the basis for comparing the sisters to other female nurses, for comprehending why the sisters were chosen for the work, and for understanding why the sisters were better known and understood after the war than before. More importantly, a study of the various attitudes toward the sisters reveals whether the religious values motivating the sisters' work were discernible to others.

Praise for the sisters was the typical, though not completely universal, response of those who came in contact with them during the Civil War. The attitudes, as expressed in writing by doctors, other women with whom the sisters worked or interacted, the soldiers themselves, and other military and governmental authorities ranged from apprehension or mistrust—stemming from ignorance about sisters or from religious prejudice—to acceptance, support, and warm appreciation. Though each of these categories of people generally responded in a variety of ways depending on the situation and length of interaction, the responses from each group were fairly consistent, except for those of the female lay nurses.

As has been previously pointed out, doctors, especially in the North, generally did not favor female volunteer nurses because they felt the

women had little or no experience, were disorganized, or were too regulated by Dorothea Dix. Thus, doctors felt that female nurses tended
to mother the men and disregard orders regarding diet and medicine.
In the South, a prevalent view among doctors was that women did not
belong at the bedside of strange men.

However, because doctors worked directly with the sisters, whose assistance in caring for the patients and directing various support areas
of the hospitals was beneficial, their attitudes toward the sisters were
generally positive. The most famous comments came from Dr. John
Brinton, whose attitude toward most female lay nurses was direct and
negative because of their "inexperienced and troublesome presence."[1]
Yet, he decided to replace female lay nurses in his Mound City, Illinois,
hospital with the Sisters of the Holy Cross, who were not even nurses,
because he believed they would be better nurses for his sick men. These
men, he reported, not only improved under the sisters' care,[2] but they
grew to love and respect the sisters.[3]

The doctors' attitudes toward the sisters can sometimes be determined
through the sisters' correspondence. For instance, at a West Virginia
Confederate hospital, the sister superior wrote that everything was getting on quietly and satisfactorily, once a Dr. Woodville "rightly took
charge" of the post, because he was always satisfied at any arrangements
the sisters made. She added that the doctors and other nurses preferred
the sisters to be in charge of the wards since they could "handle the men
better," thus ensuring cooperation and good order.[4] She later recounted
a visit from the Confederate examining physician from General Jones'
staff, who examined the hospital very thoroughly and pronounced it the
best kept and the best organized in the Confederacy.[5] Further, the examination indicated that Jones was very fearful of losing the sisters'
services and was "determined to do all in his power to retain them."[6]

This positive attitude and desire to retain the sisters was found equally
among Union doctors. One example of this occurred toward the end of
the war, when the Daughters of Charity at a Washington hospital were
completing the inventory of all hospital goods prior to the hospital's
closing. As they finished, the sisters recorded that the surgeons and
officers in charge expressed much gratitude and confidence in what
had been done by the sisters. The first surgeon, wrote one sister, especially was at a loss to put his satisfaction into words, saying, "The Sisters
of Charity were able to lessen the cares and labors of the physicians and
surgeons in any hospital they might be placed."[7]

Typifying the attitude of most doctors, Surgeon-General Isaac J. Hayes
wrote to the superior of the Daughters of Charity as they terminated
their services at the Satterlee Hospital, Philadelphia. Aware that almost
ninety sisters had served there during the war, he said:

My most sincere and hearty thanks for the faithful and efficient manner in which you have performed your duties. Joining it [Satterlee] at its foundation under an impulse of true Christian charity you have remained true and stedfast [sic] to the end; suffering discomfort, working early and late, never murmuring. You have won my gratitude and the gratitude of every true soldier, and have confirmed me in the profound esteem which I have always entertained for your noble order.... May the knowledge of the good which you have done to the sick and wounded and weary soldiers of our common country be to you a satisfaction and reward.[8]

The generally positive and supportive attitude of doctors was appreciated by the sisters, especially when it lessened the prejudice of their patients. For instance, the Daughters of Charity in their *Annals of the Civil War* remarked, "Fortunately the corps of doctors then employed in the hospital were in our favor, and occasionally through their means we would be enabled to soften the prejudice of the patients who saw the respect the doctors showed us by the attention they would give to any remarks it was necessary to make; and by degrees we gradually gained their confidence."[9] Besides the doctors, in the actual day-to-day activities of the wartime hospitals, other men, such as orderlies, male nurses, and ward masters probably had direct experience with the sisters. However, because these hospital workers did not generally leave written accounts, their views of the sisters are not known. Thus, in terms of people with whom the sisters worked, the other major group was other women. These women fell into three broad categories: other female nurses, including those selected and appointed by Dorothea Dix; members of various ladies' aid societies and church groups, which visited patients and brought supplies; and members of the US Sanitary Commission, who inspected the hospitals as well as supplied various clothing and food items. Within these categories, there were wives of doctors and officers, who remained with their husbands and sometimes assisted the sisters in the hospital in some capacity; auxiliary helpers in the hospitals, such as laundry, dietary, housekeeping; and nurse's "aides."

Attitudes of other women toward the sisters varied considerably, from that of a nurse "who had registered a vow not to serve with any sisters— or with members of any secret society"[10] to that of Sanitary Commission leader Mary Livermore, who said, "The world has known no nobler and no more heroic women than those found in the ranks of the Catholic Sisterhoods."[11]

The largest group of women with whom the sisters worked were other female nurses. Not all religious communities had a written stipulation in their agreement that they would not serve under a female matron (nurse superintendent) or with other female nurses, but that generally seemed to be the case, and the two groups apparently did not work well together. The issue seemed to be one of control of the hospital facilities and services. For instance, from the beginning the Sisters of Charity of Our Lady of Mercy, Charleston, had difficulty with Miss Emily Mason, a woman encouraged by Bishop Patrick Lynch to start the Confederate hospital in White Sulphur Springs, West Virginia, where the sisters went. In offering one viewpoint for the cause of the difficulty, the chaplain, Father L. P. O'Connell, wrote confidentially in January 1862 to Bishop Lynch that the sisters, though justifiably dissatisfied, should be patient for a time. He concluded that "the bone of discontent consists in their not having supreme government over the hospitals and the stores connected therewith."[12] Certainly, the sisters were used to being in charge of their own institutions, and there may have been an initial misunderstanding in this particular situation.

The greatest clashes between sisters and female nurses, however, involved Dorothea Dix and her nurses. It might be thought that Dorothea Dix, whose nurses were expected to be over thirty, plain-looking, and wearing black or brown with no jewelry or hoop skirts, might appreciate or, at least, respect the sisters. However, as Civil War medical historian George Adams has noted, one of Dorothea Dix's "oddities was the resolute anti-Catholic feeling which made her refuse appointment to a Catholic woman."[13] She discriminated against Catholic nurses, lay or religious, despite the fact that the doctors preferred the nuns.

The sisters were never under Dix's jurisdiction, and this fact became even clearer and perhaps more irritating to Dix as the war went on. Finally, in 1863, attempts were made to respond to some of the doctors' complaints against female nurses by General Order 351, which limited Dix's authority. The general order, issued by Secretary of War Stanton, required that "certificates of approval" be given by Dix to each nurse approved by her and countersigned by the medical director in whose department the nurse was to serve. Further, assignment of women nurses was to be made only by the surgeon in charge through the medical director to Dix. The final provision stated that the women nurses, while on duty, were under the exclusive control of the senior medical officer, who could discharge them when they were considered "supernumerary" (only one female nurse per thirty beds was allowed), or for incompetence, insubordination, or violation of his orders. There was one exception: while no female nurse could serve without a certificate, Surgeon-General William Hammond could specifically appoint any nurse he wished. On the reverse side of the copy of the order in the possession of the Holy Cross Sisters, it was specifically written on Hammond's authority that "Sisters of Charity" [generic] were not part of the order.[14]

The situations in which this Order was enforced sometimes added to the conflicts between the sisters and the female nurses. For instance, at Point Lookout, Maryland, the Daughters of Charity remarked on "a band of philanthropic lady nurses" who arrived in 1863 and who showed surprise that the sisters were there before them. The sisters, who were the only nurses allowed to attend the newly arrived Confederate prisoners, noted that "the women would have greatly annoyed us, but their duties were sufficiently apart from ours. They were as hostile to Catholicity as was the North and South to each other."[15] When General Order 351 came from Washington stating that no female nurses were to remain at the Point, the sisters made preparations to leave. However, the doctor said, "Remain, sisters, until I hear from Washington for we *cannot* dispense with the services of the sisters." He telegraphed and received the reply, "The Sisters of Charity are not included in our orders; they may serve all . . . at the Point, prisoners and others, but all other ladies are to leave the place."[16] While this response did not endear the sisters to the other female nurses, it certainly demonstrated that the skills and experience of the sisters were in great demand.

Another conflict over this same general order involved the Sisters of Charity of Cincinnati. Vowing not to leave Hospital #14 in Nashville, Tennessee, when General Order 351 was first received, Sister Anthony O'Connell wrote in October 1863 to Cincinnati Bishop John Purcell. "This day I received a copy or certificate which places us under the special direction of Miss Dix. I thought it best to send you mine, which you will pleas[e] return as I could not draw anny [sic] pay without it. I hardly thought you would be willing to leave us subject to Miss Dix's whims."[17] Bishop Purcell apparently encouraged them to stay, for a few weeks later, Sister Anthony again corresponded with the bishop, saying:

I received your letter yesterday and also the one previous both approving my remaining longer with the sisters to care for the sick and wounded Soldiers. I send you a letter, Mr. Read Sanitary Inspector sent me, and also an apiel [sic] from the soldiers. I would not like to lieve [sic] now it would be gratifying to the Presbetarian [sic] Minister and Miss Dix's Delegates for us to get out of the way. We are now so independent, we can stay as long as we plies [sic], there is anny ammount [sic] or rather number, of sick brought in whilst I am writing to you, they appear more like cacis [sic] of starvation than anny [sic] I have ever nursed before.[18]

The *Catholic Telegraph*, diocesan newspaper of Cincinnati, two days later quoted a letter in the Nashville *Daily Commercial*, which took up the sisters' cause:

The thousands of sick and wounded soldiers in the hospitals here, whose wants have been ministered to and whose beds of pain have been smoothed by those devoted women, Sisters of Charity, regret to learn that Sister Anthony and her co-laborers of your city have been recalled from Nashville for other fields of labor. I do not understand the cause of their withdrawal, but it is stated that some rules of restrictions instituted by Miss Dix at Washington, conflicted with, or were unacceptable to the rules of the Sisters, and their recall from this field of labor followed. No humane system during the war has been so successfully and usefully carried out as that of the Sisters of Charity, and whether their labors are recognized and appreciated by the rulers or not, certain it is the soldiers, who are most interested, will miss their kind ministrations and never cease to regret their absence from the hospital.[19]

Whether it was the determination of the sisters, the desire of the doctors, the influence of the bishop, the pleading of the patients, the support of the publicity or a combination of all these influences, the sisters did remain at Nashville.

Others of Dorothea Dix's nurses also remarked with criticism, curiosity, praise, or envy, about additional aspects of the sisters that they observed. One critic was a Mrs. Pomeroy, who recounted her visit to "St. Alyosus [sic] Hospital, under the control of the Sisters of the Sacred Heart." (Actually, St. Aloysius Hospital in Washington, D.C., was under the Sisters of the Holy Cross.) Commenting first on the sisters' clothing and what she perceived was its negative effect on the soldiers, she said, "This order wears black woolen dresses and capes, white muslin caps or bonnets, with black woolen veils hanging negligently graceful over the back; thick boots and checked aprons. A heavy leaden cross, and quite a large leaden heart, are suspended from the neck. What looking objects to wait upon our sick and dying boys!"[20] In addition, Pomeroy, acknowledging that Dix was equally disturbed about the sisters, noted with shame that the surgeons generally preferred Catholic sister nurses to Protestants. Pomeroy did concede, however, that a reason for this preference was the fact that many of the Protestant nurses got married and left. In contrast, with the sisters' vow of celibacy, which publicly acknowledged that they would not marry, and their vow of obedience, which assured their service to the hospital where they had been sent by the community, the sisters were understandably more dependable than female nurses.

A different view was presented by Dix-appointed nurse Sophia Bucklin. She mingled admiration for the sisters with an envy for their working conditions, as well as an observation on their humanness. In her memoirs she told of twenty-five Sisters of Charity at Point Lookout, Maryland, who cared for the freshly wounded from Fredericksburg in newly built quarters. Dix's nurses were in an older section, where, Bucklin recalled, the sisters had charge of the linen room. There she sometimes caught a glimpse of "a sweet placid face from under the long white bonnets which they wore," and she noted that the sisters were ceaseless in the work of mercy amongst those poor suffering soldiers." Yet, as she observed, they did not prove "entirely impervious to the wiles of those passions which belong to this earthly state, for by-and-by one of them was wooed by, and fell in love with a Union officer." Bucklin reported that the sister denounced her faith, went to Seven Pines, Maryland, and was married to the officer.[21]

Since Dix's biographer Helen Marshall offers no particular reason for Dorothea's anti-Catholicism, the conflict between Dix, some of her nurses, and the sisters may have been due more to issues of control of the hospital and approval by the doctors than to anti-religious feelings, even though the conflicts were often stated in those terms by both parties. Certainly, the earlier anti-Catholic feelings continued during Civil War times. The sisters, many of them immigrants and conscious of such sentiments, understandably would generally not be supportive of efforts by Protestants to move them out of areas where they were. Too, the sisters were used to being in charge of their own schools and hospitals, even though other women may also have worked with them, and probably the sisters did not want to be told what to do by outsiders.

Thus, the conflict may have stemmed more from a power struggle between the doctors and Dix, who (as even her admirers admitted) was a difficult person to work with, than from a problem between the sisters and the nurses. Mary Livermore assessed the multiple aspects of the situation by noting:

Unfortunately many of the surgeons in the hospitals did not work harmoniously with Miss Dix. They were jealous of her power, impatient of her authority, condemned her nurses, and accused her of being arbitrary, opinionated, severe, and capricious. Many, to rid themselves of her entirely, obtained permission of Surgeon-General Hammond, to employ Sisters of Charity only in their hospital, a proceeding not at all to Miss Dix's liking. I knew by observation that many of the surgeons were unfit for their office; that too often they failed to carry skill, morality, or humanity to their work; and I understood how this single-minded friend of the sick and wounded soldier would come in collision with these laggards.[22]

Another reason for the clash between some of the female nurses, especially in the North, and the sisters may have been a strong desire on the part of some female nurses to have the same spirit and prestige that came with an organized group of women working for the public good. For example, reflecting the views of many of these Protestant nurses, Union nurse Jane Woolsey wrote after the war, "The Roman Catholic system had features which commended it to medical officers of a certain cast of mind. The order and discipline were almost always good. The neatness, etc., were sometimes illusory." Though Woolsey offered no specifics, she added that there were great objections to the general introduction of such a system among American volunteer soldiers. Further, she concluded with a desire that Catharine Beecher, Kate Cumming, Mary Livermore and other American and English women had expressed elsewhere, "There was nothing good in it that we also might not have had; and taking the good, leaving the bad, and adapting the result to the uses of the country and the spirit of the time, we might have had an order of Protestant women better than the Romish sisterhoods, by so much as heart and intelligence are better than machinery."[23]

Nevertheless, as Mrs. Lew Wallace, wife of the Union general, explained in a letter to her mother in December 1861, "Nothing in our churches equals the devotion of these women. When Protestant Sisters [nurses] get tired they go home, but the Sisters of the Holy Cross live among the patients without thought of deserting infected places or avoiding contagion by flight." About Mother Angela of St. Mary's Academy, who had come to Mound City, Illinois, with thirty nuns, Mrs. Wallace said, "A flock of white doves—to nurse in the hospitals, where the stillness is like the silence of death."[24]

Since there were only about one thousand women nurses, and perhaps one hundred sisters in the Confederate states, recorded attitudes there about the sisters were generally positive and did not seem to reflect strong conflicts. This was partly due to the fact that there was no issue of control in the South, because female nurses were not mobilized under any government agency. For example, experienced Confederate nurse Kate Cumming praised the Sisters [Daughters] of Charity, who were at the Cantey Hospital, Mobile, Alabama, saying, "The Sisters of Charity are its matrons, and we all know what they are in hospitals. And, by the way, why can we not imitate them in this respect, during these war times? Here one of them is a druggist; another acts the part of steward; and, in fact, they could take charge of the whole hospital, with the exception of the medical staff."[25]

Perhaps frustrated herself by untrained female nurses, who were often more hindrance than help, Cumming frequently spoke of her desire and that of others that there be a Protestant sisterhood. One time when Cumming and her nurse were at church, the minister

adverted to our having an order of sisterhood in the church; this he seems to have very much at heart. We had our sunbonnets with us, and he wished to know if they were our uniform; we have never worn any, as we cannot afford any clothes but what we may have. We have always made it a rule of wearing the simplest kind of dress, as we think of any other kind sadly out of place in a hospital; calico or homespun is the only dress fit to wear; but to get the former is a real treat.[26]

Previously, the minister had suggested to her that he thought another hospital, started by a clergyman and some Mobile ladies, had been a failure. This, he said, was because the ladies had not been educated in nursing, as were the Sisters of Charity. The minister hoped that some day there would be a sisterhood in the church as there was in the day of the apostles and in many parts of the old country.

Besides Dix's nurses and the other nurses of the North and South, the other large organized group of females often in contact with the sisters was the US Sanitary Commission. Though he gives no specific examples, historian William Maxwell, in his work on the US Sanitary Commission, commented on the rivalry that sprang up between Protestant nurses and Catholic sisters. According to Maxwell, complaints reached the Sanitary Commission that army officers preferred nuns because they were docile and obedient workers who took no notice of the evils denounced by Protestants. In addition, Maxwell said that critics accused the sisters of showing partiality to Catholic soldiers and withholding the consolation of the Bible from men of other faiths. Further, the sisters supposedly lacked warmth, exercised formal discipline, and turned a hospital into a house of reform. However, Maxwell stated that when the champion of Catholic nurses, the non-Catholic Surgeon-General Hammond, was asked why the sisters were numerous in the army hospitals, he replied that the sisters were there because they were good nurses. Hammond further asked where one could find Protestant nurses comparable to the Sisters of Charity in efficiency and faithfulness. Nevertheless, though Hammond deplored any attempt to discharge loyal servants on the basis of religious difference, he agreed to increase the number of Protestant nurses, according to Maxwell.[27]

Both Mary Ann Hoge and Mary Livermore, US Sanitary Commission leaders who inspected the Union hospitals and transport boats serviced by the commission, referred to the prejudice against the "Protestant" nurses and the preference for the Catholic sisters. Hoge found everywhere the greatest prejudice against Protestant women nurses: medical directors, surgeons, and even ward masters, she explained, openly declared they would not have them in the service and that only the "Sisters" of the Catholic church should receive appointments. In trying to find the cause of this attitude, Hoge quoted a surgeon who said:

Your Protestant nurses are always finding some mare's-nest or other, that they can't let alone. They all write for the papers, and the story finds its way into print, and directly we are in hot water. Now the "Sisters" never see anything they ought not to see, nor hear anything they ought not to hear, and they don't write for the papers and the result is we get along very comfortably with them.[28]

Hoge, herself, felt it was futile to combat the prejudice of the doctors. She decided to content herself with refusing to fill the hospitals and boats with Catholic sisters, as she had been entreated, or consenting to do anything to discourage the detailment of Protestant nurses.

Later, Hoge's coworker Mary Livermore met a group of Protestant nurses, all "women of experience, carefully examined, and properly detailed" by Dix. The Protestant nurses were determined to appeal to Secretary of War Edwin Stanton if the medical authorities employed Catholic sisters instead of them. "The Protestant nurses," Livermore reported, "carried the day, chiefly because of their good sense and worth, and hundreds went to the front before the end of the war, welcome by both surgeons and patients, and rendering invaluable service."[29]

Nevertheless, she and Hoge were both lavish in their praise of the Holy Cross Sisters in the general hospital in Cairo, Illinois,[30] and Mound City, Illinois.[31] "It is not necessary here to say more than that we were satisfied that the sanitary stores were wisely appropriated, under the supervision of Mother Angela, at Mound City," wrote Hoge.[32] Livermore praised Mother Angela as "a gifted lady, of rare cultivation and executive ability, with winning sweetness and of manner." Further, Livermore noted that the sisters had nearly broken up their famous schools at South Bend, Indiana, to answer the demand for nurses. She concluded, "If I had ever felt prejudice against these sisters as nurses, my experience with them during the war would have dissipated it entirely."[33]

Later, Hoge and Livermore's excellent report on the "Brick Hospital" in Cairo, Illinois, noted:

Here the "Sisters of the Holy Cross" were employed as nurses, one or more to each ward. Here were order, comfort, cleanliness, and good nursing. The food was cooked in a kitchen outside the hospital. Surgeons were detailed to every ward, who visited their patients twice daily, and more frequently if necessary. The apothecary's room was supplied with an ample store of medicines and surgical appliances and the store-room possessed an abundance of clothing and delicacies for the sick.[34]

The recorded reaction of female nurses and Sanitary Commission workers fell into three consistent patterns. They respected the sisters completely, or they admired their work without necessarily favoring the aspects of Roman Catholic religious life that permeated the sisters' services, or they resented them. However, other women also came in contact with the sisters, and there are scattered reactions and comments from them.

Accounts, both positive and negative, from various women's church and aid societies differed, but not necessarily because of any religious affiliation of the women. Sometimes women praised the sisters because they were Catholics or conversely felt they were suspect because of their religion. Some thought it admirable that the sisters took care of Union or Confederate soldiers and prisoners; others saw this action as the sisters treating the "enemy." Further, sisters were both praised and criticized because they established a certain order and atmosphere or enforced various visiting and food distribution regulations for the good of the hospital and patient. In other words, they praised or blamed the sisters because of what they did or did not do, not because of religion. Nevertheless, the sisters and the hospitals they served in were often the grateful recipients of food and supplies from various religious aid groups, even if comment or criticisms came along with the supplies.

For example, the Daughters of Charity in St. Louis Military Hospital recounted that the Ladies of the Union Aid Society, who visited the hospital twice a week, became jealous of the good that the sisters were doing. The women feared, the sisters said, that everyone would become a Catholic. The ladies even tried to make the patients call them sisters, telling the soldiers they were charitable ladies who went about doing good. However, as the sisters noted, the women could not succeed because "the poor patients knew how to distinguish between real merit and big talk." In spite of the fact that the ladies could not see or understand how the sisters could have so much influence over the patients, they showed the sisters the greatest respect. The sisters recalled the women would often say, "How happy the sisters look! and they make all around them happy, too, I wish my presence could be a sunshine somewhere."[35]

Although the ladies in St. Louis may have been irritated by the sisters' attempts to keep good order and provide care to all, diarist Mary Boykin Chestnut, who often visited Confederate hospitals, appreciated the sisters' efforts. In discussing the care given to officers of both sides, she recorded in her diary that in the hospitals with the Sisters of Charity, the Union prisoner officers were better off than the Confederate men at other hospitals without sisters as nurses. That care, she said, she "saw with her own eyes."[36]

Sometimes the women visiting the soldiers became themselves the subject of amusing stories. For example, a Vicksburg Sister of Mercy remarked, "Many persons from the country round visited the hospital; at first from curiosity or prejudice, but after some time, with better feeling, often bringing food to the patients."[37] Nonetheless, she noted, they generally selected the "handsome fellows" for the distribution of favors. The sisters humorously observed that this caused the male nurses to sometimes jump in bed with their boots on, so that some sentimental lady would bestow upon them preserves and the gentle motion of the fan.[38]

In contrast, those soldiers who were too sick or too repulsive to attract "a dainty notice received the tenderest care of the sisters in charge." Because of this, one time, a soldier not ill enough to require much attention, "complained to some bigoted women that he was not treated well." The women then went to the sister, took her by the arm and shook her saying, "Woman, how dare you treat a sick man so." The memoirs of these Vicksburg Sisters of Mercy observed that the actions were noted

by the soldiers who were there day in and day out. A truly ill man,
appreciative of the sister's efforts, said, "Never mind, sister, you do the
best for all."[39]

This was the usual reaction once the soldiers got to know the sisters.
However, the soldiers were initially perplexed or frightened by the sisters, either because of the sisters' strange garb or by what they had heard
about Catholics. "Great heavens!" shrieked one suffering soldier to the
Sister of Mercy that bent over him, "are you a man or a woman? But
your hand is a woman's hand; its touch is soft, and your voice is gentle—
what *are* you?."[40] Some soldiers called them "holy Marias,"[41] and another
group thought that the nine black-robed sisters making their way along
a narrow wharf to a hospital in Beaufort, North Carolina, were "lone
widows" coming for their husbands' bodies.[42] Someone thought they
might be Freemasons.[43]

The sisters themselves recounted many stories that amused them about
the reaction provoked by their strange garb, especially the various head-
dresses. Cincinnati Charity Sister Ann Cecilia recalled:

We were frequently asked why we dressed so different from other ladies. One
boy told us that the girls up at his place, wore low necks and short sleeves—
adding—"you know them dresses make you look so funny." Another—quite
young and innocent desired to play with my beads—thought they would make
a pretty watch chain; but how different were his ideas regarding my "Rosary"
after he was instructed and baptized in our holy religion. Oh! with how much
ignorance did we not meet.[44]

Once the soldiers got used to the sisters, they sometimes tried to show
their appreciation for their care by trying to buy clothing for the sisters,
not realizing their garb was made by them and not available in stores.
At the Satterlee Hospital in Philadelphia, one soldier asked if the government provided the sisters' "uniforms" while they were in service.
Another proposed to buy a silk dress for a sister after pay day,[45] and a
third wandered the streets of Washington all day "to buy one of your
white bonnets but did not find a single one for sale."[46]

The amusement, perplexity, and curiosity that the sisters' clothing
caused was not confined just to the soldiers. The Sisters of Charity of
Cincinnati, going to the Cumberland, recalled that as they marched in
procession through the streets to the hotel where they were to lodge one
night, the streets were crowded with men, women, and children wanting
to see the sisters. Later, while the sisters were waiting for supper, "The
windows were besieged from without by children, white and black, peep-
ing in to see the curiosity."[47]

The headdress, especially, was strange and often terrifying, particularly the spread-eagled, white cornette of the seventeenth-century

French peasant worn by the hundreds of Daughters of Charity. US Sanitary Commission leader Mary Livermore said she often sympathized with some of the sick men who frequently expressed a wish for a reform in the "headgear" of the sisters. " 'Why can't they take off those white-winged sun-bonnets in the ward?' " asked one man. " 'Sun-bonnets!' " sneered another of the irreverent critics, Livermore reported, " 'they're a cross between a white sun-bonnet and a broken-down umbrella and there's no name that describes them.' "[48]

Some other sisters remembered that new patients continued to cover their heads with blankets while the sisters were in the wards. The soldiers were frightened—or "skerte," as they used to say—by the sisters' appearance. The Confederate soldiers were anxious to know to what regiment the sisters belonged or if they had been engaged in any battles. They thought the sisters should go to battle because the Yankees would be more afraid of them than any gun the boys could show them.[49] Though a soldier who had never seen a sister before might say, "I do not want to stay in this ward for I do not like the looks of that woman who wears that Bonnet," he would usually be answered by another who said there was nothing to fear, for she was a Sister of Charity.[50]

"The general prejudice toward Catholics was, at least initially, displayed toward the sisters though this often changed after the soldiers watched the sisters," recalled a Daughter of Charity. "Many of our·sick, who seemed to fear and hate us on their arrival, soon showed they had been mistaken and would even place money in our hands when they received it, and would try to find out what we would like to have, that they might get it for us."[51]

In a Norfolk, Virginia, hospital after a Union takeover, the sisters remembered in particular one very sick man who seemed to hate them. He refused his medicine, and tried to strike the sisters and spit upon them when they would offer it to him. After often acting in this manner and finding that the sister still hoped he would take it, for his life depended on it, the man said: *Who* or *what* are you anyway?" The Annals record that the sister said, "'I am a Sister of Charity.' 'Where is your husband?' he said. 'I have none,' said the sister, 'and I am glad that I have none.' 'Why are you glad?' he asked, still very angry. 'Because,' she replied, 'if I had a husband, I would have to be employed in his affairs, and consequently could not be here to wait on you.' As if by magic, in a subdued tone he said, 'that will do,' and turning his face from her, he remained silent."[52] Later, he took his medicine and asked about instructions in religion. "He was very soon a true friend of the sisters, but so ignorant of religion in every way that he hardly knew he had a soul,"[53] the sisters recalled.

Generally, then, the sisters had to overcome initial prejudice related to their clothing or to their religion. Nevertheless, their care and concern almost always disarmed those who were in close contact with them. For example, the Daughters of Charity were in the hospital in Frederick, Maryland, only a few days when they realized that they were in the midst of a prejudiced community that did not want their services. The sisters felt the townspeople had embittered the patients' minds against them so much that the soldiers often would not look at them or even speak to them. "We had no delicacies to give them," the sisters wrote, "the ladies had all. Therefore, we could do little for the poor soul, while we had not means of nourishing the exhausted body."[54]

Yet later in this same hospital, a sister was unexpectedly stopped one day by a convalescent soldier. She had often noticed that he viewed her with a surly countenance and only reluctantly took from her whatever she offered him. She wrote that he said:

Sister, you must have noticed how stiffly I have acted toward you ... but I could not help it as my feelings were so embittered against you, so much so, that your presence always made me worse. I have watched you closely at all times since you came to the barracks; but when you came in last night with the doctor to see the patient who lay dangerously ill, I noticed particularly that you did not come alone, but in company with a sister; and when you did all that was necessary for the patient, you returned. It was then my feelings became changed towards you, as I saw how clearly, how differently you acted from the female nurses.[55]

This soldier apparently felt the female nurses spent too much time alone with the men, especially at night. Thus, the other nurses were viewed with suspicion by the men. However, after reflecting on the actions and care of the sisters, this soldier changed his attitude.

Ultimately, among most soldiers, the sisters were highly respected largely because of their motivation, self-sacrifice, and skill. The sisters even recorded many instances of men who stopped swearing in their presence,[56] or that oaths or disrespectful words were not heard in the hospital in the years that they were there.[57] The Cincinnati Charity sisters, in fact, once overheard the remark, "Surely these ladies are working for God. Money is not the motive here!" The sisters felt that the great respect that some people held for them was remarkable, and even the "more ignorant never forgot themselves in the presence of the 'good ladies.' "[58]

One aspect of this admiration and respect was that the soldiers frequently gave credit to the sisters, rather than to the doctors, for curing them. The patients believed there was nobody like the sisters. They would often say, "Indeed it was not the doctors that raised me, it was the sisters."[59] A Daughter of Charity in a St. Louis hospital recalled that the soldiers would generally go to a sister rather than to a doctor, when given a choice. Thus, the sisters had to encourage them to have confidence in doctors. For example, every evening one sister visited a man whose hand had been amputated at the wrist. The man complained that the doctor had ordered hot poultices that morning, and he still hadn't gotten them. The sister, calling the nurse and wound dresser to find out what happened, discovered that no poultice was available. The sister immediately sent across the yard to the bakery and got some hops and had the poultice put on. The man was surprised and said, "The sisters found ways and means of relieving everyone and those who made profession of the business did not even know where to look for them."[60]

It was these direct, specific, and practical actions of the sisters, who were often carefully observed by the men lying on their beds, that resulted in a change from indifferent or negative attitudes to positive attitudes. In addition, the sisters' willingness to work with smallpox victims did not go unnoticed by the men. For example, Sister De Sales at the Confederate hospital in West Virginia wrote to Bishop Lynch to explain her action in quarantining a sister with the smallpox victims.[61] She wrote, "But things turned out such a way that I could not await your replies and consequently did what seemed to me right *under* the circumstances. Had not sister been *there*, two men would have died without baptism last week. The fact of a sister having gone there when those poor men were abandoned by the physicians has done more for religion at large and our community than all we have done since we left home."[62]

Because so many of the soldiers were young, the ministrations of the sisters, as well as those of other mature women nurses, tended to call forth in the soldiers memories of their own mothers. This also enhanced the positive feelings toward the sisters. Write to my mother," said a young soldier to a Daughter of Charity, "and tell her I was cared for in my suffering by a band of ladies who were as tender to me as mothers."[63] As a result of their experiences, the soldiers developed a loyalty to the sisters. If the men were wounded again and returned to the same hospital, they sometimes cried out, "I want to go to Sr. Frances's ward—I want to go to Sr. Helena's ward, I want to go to Sr. Agatha's ward."[64]

In addition, the condition of dying men and the horrors of the war put many of the soldiers in a receptive frame for religious instruction from the sisters. One Daughter of Charity recounted that often the men, when questioned concerning their future welfare, would reply, "I have not been of your religion, but wish to become what you are. The religion of the sisters must be the true one." "The religion of the sisters" became a common phrase among the men.[65]

In another incident, a Cincinnati Sister of Charity recalled a very young man in a bed at the extreme end of a ward who was suffering from a deep wound in the shoulder. The sister assisted the surgeon in dressing the wound, but the man closed his eyes, wouldn't speak, and avoided her every look. The sister realized "he had no love for the

Catholic Church or her children." Nevertheless, she observed that he noticed every word and every action of priests and sisters. Finally, after listening to the instructions and watching the baptisms, he was convinced by what he saw and asked for baptism.[66]

The soldiers' attitude and response toward the sisters was a reflection of the sisters' own care and concern for the soldiers. The men were often little older than the boys some of the sisters taught in their schools or cared for in their orphanages. Speaking for many sisters, one wrote, "It was heartrending to see those young fellows die hourly, often from fright, being too young to bear the hardships of a soldier's life or to withstand the scenes of battle; they seemed to me to be dazed and to die ere the scene passed their vision."[67]

Cincinnati Sister of Charity Agnes, returning to Cincinnati to assist in caring for the soldiers at St. John's Hospital after three months in Cumberland, was struck by the appalling sights of men without arms or legs. They were pale, haggard, and worn out with fasting and marching, and many died of broken hearts, she remembered. Long after the war, she wrote:

Faces and voices haunt me yet, calling for home and dear ones whom they were destined never again to behold on earth. The streets of Cincinnati . . . witnessed extreme suffering and misery. Frequently fine young men, seated on their own coffins, passed through them [streets] on their way to execution on some neighboring hillside. We cared for Unionists and Confederates alike. We knew no difference and made no difference.[68]

It was this attitude of impartiality toward Union and Confederate soldiers, whether a prisoner or a compatriot, that enabled the sisters to pass through the blockades and lines, getting supplies and sometimes attending to community matters. For example, discussing the need for an Ursuline Sister from Columbia, South Carolina, to go to Florida for health reasons, Bishop Verot wrote to Bishop Lynch that it would be safe. "The Yankees seem to be willing to do anything for the Sisters of Charity of Our Lady of Mercy," he said, "who have been so kind to their wounded soldiers in Charleston."[69]

A similar experience was that of a Daughter of Charity on duty in Mobile, Alabama, in 1864 who needed to go to New Orleans for clothing and also to take a sister for some community business. She obtained a pass from the Confederate soldiers without difficulty. Apparently, by this, the third year of the war, sisters were visibly established in many people's minds as nurses. The sister superior reported that the sisters were objects of excitement at every stopping place; the people even believed that there was going to be another battle because they thought the sisters were there to nurse. In one effort to test the sisters' neutrality, a woman on the train with them demanded to know what side they were on. "Now Sisters, I know you are for us, you know our cause is right, just say it is," she said. The sisters replied, "Madam, we are neutral and wheather [sic] the cause be just or not, it never gives us a thought, we devote our life to the suffering members of Jesus Christ and wheather [sic] they be Confederate or Federal, when placed in our charge, they are alike cared for by us." That response seemed to quiet the woman and she troubled the sisters no more.[70]

However, on the sisters' arrival at the Federal line, they found it more difficult to obtain a pass. The Union soldiers wanted the sisters to take the oath of loyalty to the Union. The sisters replied that they never took the oath because while they were nursing the sick and wounded Confederates, their sisters in the North were nursing the Federals. After some deliberation, the Federals allowed the sisters to pass with the greatest courtesy. When the sisters reached the Confederate line on their return to Mobile, the Federal officers sent for the Confederate officers and asked them to see the sisters safely home, which they did. This prompted a response from some refugee ladies traveling with them, who said, "How is it, sisters, that you are treated with so much courtesy by both parties while we are totally neglected."[71]

The sisters' reputation for impartiality to all soldiers was further confirmed by the Confederates when they had to evacuate Mobile in 1865 and were concerned about what to do with their sick and wounded who could not be removed from the city. After some deliberation, they decided to send them to the City Hospital, assured that "they would not be molested while in the charge of the Sisters of Charity." Though the hospital was already crowded, the men were sent, fully supplied with provisions. Somehow, the sisters made room for them.[72]

In the treatment of the soldiers, then, the sisters certainly seemed concerned about Union and Confederate soldiers alike. The most common attitude was that expressed by a Daughter of Charity who said she tried to impress on her sisters the necessity of "observing the greatest prudence in not manifesting partiality in any way whatever for either side but looking on them all as the wounded members of Jesus, which they did most faithfully I am happy to say." She added that it was "a beautiful and sad sight to look on those poor men, beautiful to see the union that existed among them in our Hospitals, sad to think that if they recovered they would be perhaps mortal enemies."[73] On the other hand, in 1862, Mother Angela Gillespie of the Holy Cross Sisters, wrote to Orestes Brownson, editor of *Brownson's Review*, remarking, "The bitter hatred expressed by Southerners without being able to express any other reasons except 'we hate the North' has entirely destroyed the highest sympathy I ever felt for the South and my heart now agrees with the article in the October issue on Slavery & War."[74] No other political reactions are recorded from her, however, and this may well have been an isolated remark. The only other known partisan comment was that of a Southern Mercy sister, originally from Charleston, who remarked in her diary that the sisters in Savannah were "heart and soul for the Confederacy."[75]

In general, however, the sisters maintained their reputation for impartial and excellent care of the soldiers, bringing them praise from officers and other high-ranking military officials. For example, the history of Charity Hospital, New Orleans, credits the presence of sisters with averting a disaster when the city was captured by Union General Benjamin Butler, called "the Beast" by the citizens after his takeover of the city on May 1, 1862. In spite of several acts of insubordination on the part of the medical officers and board of the hospital after Butler ordered them to take in wounded Federal soldiers, Butler did not seize the hospital or punish the doctor in charge. This had been the expected response considering Butler's other drastic actions in taking the city. Butler, in his memoirs, justified his martial-law actions in New Orleans by saying "the poor had to be fed, the streets had to be cleaned, the protection from yellow fever had to be made sure."[76] However, this same man gave $500 a month to the hospital for the seven months he remained in New Orleans.[77] The hospital historians believe that Butler's compassionate attitude probably came from the great respect he felt for the Daughters of Charity running the hospital, who would have shared the sufferings caused by any stringent means he might have evoked.[78]

Butler's attitude toward the sisters can also be seen in a letter to Sister Maria Clara, Superior of the Daughters of Charity in Donaldson, Louisiana, in September of 1862. In it, he apologized for the damage done by Rear-Admiral Farragut to their buildings in the general bombardment of the city, saying:

No one can appreciate more fully than myself the holy, self-sacrificing labors of the Sisters of Charity. To them our soldiers are daily indebted for the kindest offices. Sisters of all mankind, they know no nation, no kindred, neither war nor peace. Their all-pervading charity is like the boundless love of "Him who died for all," whose servants they are, and whose pure teachings their love illustrates.... Your Sisters in the city will also farther [sic] testify to you, that my officers and soldiers have never failed to do them all in their power to aid them in their usefulness, and to lighten the burden of their labors. [79]

He also promised to repair the damage as far as he could by doing as they asked—filling the order sent for provisions and medicine. [80] That his sentiments were probably more than mere appeasement may have derived from his early experience of seeing the burning of the Ursuline Convent in Massachusetts in 1834. This disaster later motivated him to introduce a bill into the state legislature, which ultimately failed, to make restitution for that act.[81]

In addition to Butler and other famous officers, such as General William Sherman,[82] recording their own views of the sisters, the sisters themselves also noted the reactions, both positive and negative, of some of the officers. For example, some Daughters of Charity, including a number who had been in the South for some time, were on a Union boat on its way to Richmond, where a flag of truce would take them to Maryland. When an officer visited the sisters, he exclaimed, "I need not question you, Sisters; all is right with you. You mind your own business and don't meddle with government affairs. Your society had done great service to the Country and the authorities in Washington hold your community in high esteem."[83] He further stamped the sisters' passes "Examined" without ever reviewing them and arranged for them to stay free on his boat, since he said he did not often have the honor of having Sisters of Charity as his guests.[84] The same officer also chartered a train for them from Annapolis to Baltimore, and the sisters said they "felt his kindness the more as he knew that we have been nursing the Southern soldiers.... To be sure," they added, "he may have seen us also at Portsmouth, serving the North; at least he knew that 'part' did not influence us in our labors for the men."[85]

This officers' attitude was echoed by government officials, who publicly expressed their gratitude for the sisters' services, and praise and admiration for their work. Among the most famous are those of Lucius E. Chittenden, an officer of the Treasury during Lincoln's administration.[86] This statement, incorrectly attributed to the President himself, included the following tribute: "Of all the forms of Charity and benevolence seen in the crowded wards of the hospitals, those of some Catholic sisters were among the most efficient. I never knew whence they came or what was the name of their order. [Because of the sisters] these scenes which were altogether the most painful I have ever witnessed, have ... a beautiful side."[87]

The efficiency and devotion noticed by Chittenden were also observed by other officials. The governor of Pennsylvania, Andrew G. Curtin, praised the efforts of the Sisters of St. Joseph at Camp Curtin. There, he said, "During a period of several weeks amidst the confusion of a constantly changing camp, and amidst an epidemic of measles with typhoid fever, the ... neatness, order, and sufficient ministrations immediately followed the sisters' arrival in camp."[88]

In spite of the general attitude of gratitude, praise, or at least respect afforded the sisters by the doctors, female nurses, soldiers, military personnel, and governmental officials, the sisters' work among prisoners or in the prisons sometimes drew suspicion and censure. The situation of the Daughters of Charity at the St. Louis prison in Alton, Illinois, is an interesting case in point. The sisters recalled that their first visit to the prison was by no means welcome. "Prejudice greeted us everywhere," they explained. "The patients would not even speak to us, though bereft of every consolation of soul and body." The sisters, however, were not discouraged, and they persevered. At their hospital they prepared broth and other delicacies that the sick were in need of and carried the food every day at noon to the prisons. Eventually, the sisters recorded, the "porrige pot" was hailed by the poor prisoners and caused many of them to bless God.[89]

Finally, arrangements with Colonel Ware were made by the sisters to visit daily in an ambulance provided for them.[90] Because of earlier experience, the sisters worked "with great prudence in the beginning in order to avoid misunderstanding." Eventually, the officers and the Sanitary Commissioners began to approve of their work, setting up a one-hundred-bed ward for the sick prisoners. In addition, the authorities proposed to give the sisters a place to stay where they could "remain day and night to attend more leisurely the wants of the sick."[91]

Unfortunately, though, according to the sisters' accounts, Colonel Ware was eventually removed and replaced with a prejudiced officer who did all he could to displace the sisters. Thus, they could no longer get what was necessary from the prison resources. The new guards at the gates sometimes even prevented them from going to the hospital. When some of the old guards noticed the difficulty, they became indignant and stepped forward, saying, "They are not ladies or women, but Sisters of Charity." Thus, the sisters were permitted to go on without further trouble.[92]

Official records provide a different perspective on this incident. In June 1864, about the time of the sisters' accounts of their dismissal, a Colonel W. Hoffman, Commissary General of Prisoners, wrote to Brigadier General Joseph T. Copeland, Commander of the Military Prison at Alton. Hoffman said, "As you will perceive by my letters to Colonel Sweet the employment of these sisters has not been authorized by me and as their services can be obtained only on unusual conditions viz, the renting and furnishing a house for them and the hire of a servant, their continued employment at the hospitals is not approved."[93] He then suggested that the general find men among the prisoners to serve as nurses, unless female nurses were absolutely necessary. If so, that fact would need to be reported back. In conclusion, he said, "I am under the impression that the Sisters [Daughters] of Charity take advantage of their position to carry information from and to prisoners which is contraband, and if this is so they cannot under any circumstances be employed at the hospital. Please furnish me a list of the articles purchased to furnish their house, with remarks to show where they now are."[94]

A week later, Copeland replied that he had notified the sisters that their continued employment was not approved, and their services would be dispensed with at the end of the present month. Copeland, however, concluded, "I feel that I ought in justice to these persons to express my conviction that the impression, under which you write, that they carry information to and from prisoners which is contraband, is not well founded."[95]

From the sisters' perspective, this event was not without its rewards. "Notified that our services were no longer required at prison," the sisters recorded that "the citizens were anxious for us to remain in Alton, and to convert our house into a hospital." Thus, they received full permission to open a civilian hospital for the citizens of Alton. The hospital, St. Joseph, continues today, though no longer under the direction of the Daughters of Charity.[96]

Another accusation that the Daughters of Charity were spies had been made earlier in December of 1861. Archbishop Francis Kenrick was apprised by Major General John A. Dix that "ladies in the costume of Sisters of Charity furnished by the Convent of Emmitsburg have passed the lines into Virginia, for the purpose of keeping up communication with the Confederate States." Concerned, Kenrick wrote to Father Francis Burlando, superior of the sisters. Kenrick acknowledged to Burlando that Dix "professes himself unwilling to believe that they [the sisters] have been guilty of so gross an act of infidelity to the Government which protects them in their persons and property."[97] Kenrick also indicated that he had explained to Dix that the sisters' "journeys were open and with formal passports from the Government at Washington and wholly unconnected with politics and not intended in any way to aid the rebellion."[98] However, Burlando requested the superior of the sisters, Mother Ann Simeon Norris, to draw up a short statement to be signed by himself and three of the administrative council to send to Dix.

The sisters' reply not only explained what might have caused the misunderstanding, but also reiterated the work that they had done for the Federal soldiers at the request of the Government. The letter stated that "at no time, under no circumstances directly or indirectly, have any of the sisters gone to Virginia or any other State for political purposes, or carried documents or messages, having political tendencies." Further, the letter clearly explained that the only object for which the sisters were sent to Virginia was to nurse the sick and wounded soldiers.

After explaining several specific instances in which sisters did cross the lines for health or community reasons, Mother Ann Simeon stated:

The fact that the sisters went to nurse the soldiers in the South, could not be interpreted as a disaffection for the Government since sisters from the same society were at the request of General Rathbone sent to Albany where they took care of sick soldiers and remained at the hospital until their services were no longer required.... In a word, the sisters have responded to every call without distinction of creed or politics, and are ready at any moment to give their services if asked by proper authority, nay they are willing to suspend their schools, and diminish their number in Hospitals and orphan asylums for the purpose of nursing the sick and wounded—of about eight hundred Sisters of Charity, there is not one but would readily obey the first summons for the same work of Charity.[99]

She concluded that the Superiors of the Daughters of Charity "are quite at a loss how to account for the odious charge." She suggested, however, that the accusation might have arisen from some ill-disposed source, or from some misguided female assuming a costume similar to that of the sisters, thereby obtaining a pass and abusing the privileges of the government. Mother Ann Simeon acknowledged this could have been possible since, a few months earlier, two individuals alleging to be from the South, and dressed like sisters, were seen in Baltimore feigning to be nieces of the Honorable Edward Everett, both of whom were members of the Community. Nevertheless, she emphatically concluded, "We take the liberty to remark that the duty of the Sisters of Charity is to strive to save their souls by the exercise of Charity towards their fellow creatures, the poor and suffering of every nation, independent of creed or politics."[100]

The belief that sisters might be spies or that others might dress as sisters in order to pass more easily through the lines plagued other communities beside the Daughters of Charity. For example, Bishop Augustine Verot, of Florida, whose territory was partially in Federal hands, had frequent difficulties passing between the lines of the two armies. In 1862, when he wanted to take five Sisters of Mercy from St. Augustine, Florida, to a school in Columbus, Georgia, he initially had difficulty obtaining a pass. Finally, receiving one, he was faced with a rumor that he was transporting slaves disguised as sisters. The fact that two of the sisters—one from Cuba and one from Virginia—were dark-skinned added to the rumor. After the sisters' fingernails were examined to see the natural skin color, however, they and Bishop Verot were allowed through the lines. In 1863, he and some sisters managed another trip without incident, but the following year, going to Columbus, he again had difficulty.[101]

Despite the prejudice, mistrust, and suspicion they met from some they worked with or served, the sisters, generally, were accepted and appreciated. While the change from a negative to a positive attitude toward the sisters and their religion is difficult to document, the sisters' own perceptions at the end of the war support the view that change did occur. As one sister working in a Washington, D.C., hospital noted: "Here we did not have the annoyances we had experienced in the beginning of the war since now our calling and costume were better known and understood."[102]

Regardless of the attitude toward them, the sisters themselves almost universally had a positive attitude toward their work. The Baltimore Mercy Sisters, after their offer to nurse at the Douglas Hospital in Washington, D.C., was gratefully accepted, summed up the attitudes of most people the sisters encountered. They noted the friendships they made with the doctors, the consideration they received from the chief of staff, the services from the orderlies who would do anything for them, and the appreciation of the patients. The soldiers, the sisters noted, seemed to regard them as holding the place of their mothers. When they came to know the sisters, they really loved them and could not understand why such noble services should receive no pay from the government. The sisters, of course, tried unsuccessfully to explain that the day would come when they would be "handsomely remunerated" in heaven. But, as the sisters said, their explanation was "all in mystery."[103]

Ultimately aware of the good they accomplished, the Daughters of Charity, recalling their Washington, D.C., hospital experience, expressed the feelings of most sisters. "Of the thousands who were under the sisters' care, we are able to assure you that nearly all were, not only well pleased, but also most grateful for the attentions given them by the sisters. They who at first spurned our kindest efforts, would tell us afterwards that our religion was so calumniated by those who were ignorant of it, that they had looked on us with horror, until they saw for themselves what Catholics were."[104] Nevertheless, the poignancy of the war experience was summarized well by a Vicksburg Sister of Mercy who wrote: "We had the consolation of the return of some to the faith, who had been negligent, and the baptism of others, sick and dying, but the demoralizing effect of the war was such that it was easier to die well, than to live well."[105]

Most of these reflections of the sisters on their experiences were written shortly after the war rather than during the actual events. As one sister explained, when asked later to write down information from her time of service, the sisters hadn't kept records, but rather did what needed to be done and let God keep the record.[106] Or, as another observed, "Sister was too busy in her young days rolling bandages and dressing wounds to be at all concerned about who came and went from Richmond."[107]

Nevertheless, because the sisters did see their primary role as one of spiritually ministering to the men, they were aware of and grateful for the positive effects their work had on changing attitudes about Catholicism. As one sister astutely observed:

Independent of what was done for individuals, thousands returned to their homes, impressed with kind feelings toward the sisters, consequently, towards our Holy Faith, also, which will benefit not only themselves but render in some degree our travel through the different states easier. The officers, doctors, and public authorities all concurring in their unlimited confidence in the sisters must, and did have, its silent effect on all.[108]

This increased tolerance for the sisters, their religion, and their activities, and the unlimited confidence in the sisters' dedicated work were the two predominant and lasting attitudes of those who became acquainted with the sisters because of the Civil War. The sisters' ability to establish cleanliness, quiet, and good order out of the dirt, noise, and confusion of war conditions, and their personal concern and hard work for the Union and Confederate wounded were all qualities that were noted by those who had contact with the sisters.

Understandably, those who requested the sisters' services expressed the most positive attitudes about the sisters' dedication and quiet, efficient service. Female nurses or other women who desired the prestige or attention the sisters generally received from doctors and soldiers expressed the greatest range of attitudes about the sisters. Soldiers, initially perplexed or confused by the sisters' external dress or what they had heard about Catholics, grew to love and appreciate them and their attentive care. Officers and other governmental officials, except those who suspected them of spying for one side or another, noted positively the sisters' willingness, competence, and commitment.

In spite of accusations about spying, the sisters, conscious of the fact that soldiers of either side were wounded and sick, were notably impartial in their care and treatment of them. The sisters' own attitude was that they were in the war to care for the wounded in body and soul, primarily as an extension of their religious commitment to serve those in need in the name of Christ.

Whether these qualities elicited praise, as was generally the case with the doctors, soldiers, and other military and governmental authorities, or were mistrusted or the source of conflict as was often the case with Dorothea Dix and her nurses, no one doubted that sisters of all communities possessed these qualities. This significant fact demonstrates clearly, then, that the effect of the sisters being called into service by many different people to perform a multitude of duties resulted in a consistent impression on other people and often caused a change in attitude about the sisters.

This change in attitude was noted on various levels. After the war, Catholic bishops, as well as doctors, Protestant soldiers, and noncivilians all attested to the impact of the sisters. In a pastoral letter of the American Catholic bishops, gathered for the Second Baltimore Council on October 21, 1866, the question of the condition and needs of the Catholic church were addressed. While not directly mentioning the Civil War the document's final section on religious communities concluded, "We discharge a grateful duty, in rendering a public testimony to the virtue and heroism of these Christian Virgins [Sisters], whose lives shed the good odor of Christ on every place, and whose devotedness and spirit of self-sacrifice have, more perhaps than any other cause, contributed to effect a favorable change in the minds of thousands estranged from our faith."[109] In addition, Dr. Samuel Gross, president of the American Medical Association, lamented at the 1869 annual meeting that the Catholic orders were still the only ones who seemed to see the importance of training for nurses.[110]

Changed attitudes were also apparent from the innumerable letters of support from Union officers who were prisoners in Charleston during the war and cared for by the Sisters of Charity of Our Lady of Mercy. These letters were included in the petition of the South Carolina legislature to Congress for funds for the sisters' orphanage. A representative response was that of a Michigan lawyer, formerly a Federal officer. In 1865, after acknowledging that his life and that of other Union officers had been saved by the Confederate sisters bringing food, clothing, medicine, and supplies to them, often at a great sacrifice to themselves, he said, "I am not of your Church and have always been taught to believe it to be nothing but evil; however, actions speak louder than words, and I am free to admit that if Christianity does exist on earth, it has some of its closest followers among the ladies of your Order." [111] Other letters particularly pointed out that though most men were Protestant, the sisters made "no distinction between us on account of religion or nationality."[112] This fact changed the men's attitude toward the sisters. Thus, they were willing to acknowledge this change and publicly support the sisters after the war.

More than anything else, then, the Civil War gave the sisters greater exposure to the lay public. The experience both revealed the religious values and beliefs that motivated their lives and also expanded the boundaries of their service in ways that could only happen in a national emergency. In the chaotic state of the country, the sisters willingly and easily moved from their often restrictive convent lives and Catholic institutions to constantly changing medical facilities caring mainly for Protestant soldiers. Yet, because the sisters saw this work primarily as an extension of their ministry to care for those in need, the adjustments to their lifestyle and work were smoothly made. Thus, the composite of attitudes toward them reveals a recognition that the sisters had both important skills and a pragmatic approach in applying them to immediate social needs. These skills, practically applied, stemmed clearly and directly from religious values and training that was uniquely acquired in a community of Roman Catholic women religious.

NOTES

1. John Brinton, *Personal Memoirs of John H. Brinton* (New York: The Neale Publishing Co., 1914), pp. 294, 199.

2. Brinton, pp. 44–45.

3. Brinton, p. 45.

4. Charleston Diocesan Archives (CDA), 27H6, Letter of Sr. De Sales to Bishop Lynch, July 11, 1862.

5. CDA, 28K4, Letter of Sr. De Sales to Bishop Lynch, Jan. 9, 1862. See also 27T4, Letter of Sr. De Sales to Bishop Lynch, Sept. 30, 1862.

6. CDA, 28S2, Letter of Sr. De Sales to Bishop Lynch, Mar. 12, 1863.

7. Archives of the Daughters of Charity, Emmitsburg, MD (ADC), *Annals of the Civil War*, vol. I, p. 13.

8. ADC, "Annals of the Civil War," Manuscript, p. 583.

9. ADC, *Annals of the Civil War*, vol. I, p. 30.

10. Jane Woolsey, *Hospital Days* (New York: D. Van Nostrand, 1868), p. 44. The nurse in question did not last with Woolsey, either.

11. Mary Livermore, *My Story of the War* (Hartford, CT: A.D. Worthington, 1887), p. 218.

12. CDA, 26W7, Letter of Rev. Lawrence O'Connell to Bishop Lynch, Jan. 11, 1862. He recommended that both parties be removed. See also 27P7, Letter of O'Connell to Sr. De Sales, Aug. 30, 1862.

13. Louisa May Alcott, *Hospital Sketches*. Ed. Bessie S. Jones (Cambridge: Harvard University Press, 1960), p. xxxi.

14. Congregational Archives of the Sisters of the Holy Cross, Saint Mary's, Notre Dame, IN (ACSC), Copy of General Order 351, Oct. 29, 1863.

15. ADC, *Annals of the Civil War*, vol. I, p. 23.

16. ADC, *Annals of the Civil War*, vol. I. p. 23.

17. Archives of the Sisters of Charity of Cincinnati (ASCC), Letter of Sr. Anthony O'Connell to Bishop John Purcell, Oct. 25, 1863.

18. ASCC, Letter of Sr. Anthony O'Connell to Bishop Purcell, Nov. 16, 1863.

19. ASCC, *The Catholic Telegraph*, Nov. 15, 1863, reprint.

20. Anna L. Boyden, *Echoes from Hospital and White House* (Boston: Lathrop, 1884), pp. 140–141.

21. Sophronia Bucklin, *In Hospital and Camp* (Philadelphia: John E. Potter, 1869), pp. 79–80.

22. Livermore, pp. 246–247.

23. Woolsey, pp. 42–43.

24. Lew Wallace Collection, Indiana Historical Society Library, Letter of Mrs. Lew Wallace to her mother, Dec. 18, 1861.

25. Kate Cumming, *Kate: The Journal of a Confederate Nurse* (Baton Rouge: Louisiana State University Press, 1959), p. 262.

26. Cumming, pp. 125–126.

27. William Q. Maxwell, *Lincoln's Fifth Wheel: The Political History of the United States Sanitary Commission* (New York: Longmans, Green, 1956), p. 68.

28. Jane Hoge, *The Boys in Blue* (New York: Treat, 1867), p. 280.

29. Livermore, pp. 224–225.

30. Livermore, pp. 204–205.

31. Livermore, pp. 218–219.

32. Hoge, p. 38.

33. Livermore, pp. 218–219.

34. Livermore, pp. 204–205.

35. ADC, *Annals of the Civil War*, vol. III, p. 125.

36. C. Vann Woodward, ed., *Mary Chestnut's Civil War* (New Haven: Yale University Press, 1981), p. 171.

37. Archives of the Sisters of Mercy, Vicksburg, MS (ARSMV), Sr. M. Ignatius Sumner, "Register of the Events from the Foundation of the Community of the Sisters of Mercy, Vicksburg, Miss.," p. 39.

38. ARSMV, p. 39.

39. ARSMV, p. 39.

40. Sr. Teresa Austin Carroll, ed., *Leaves from the Annals of the Sisters of Mercy* (New York: Catholic Publication Society, 1881–88), vol. III, p. 163.

41. ASCC, "Memoirs of Sr. Bernadine," n.p.

42. Carroll, ed., *Annals*, vol. III, p. 161.

43. ADC, *Annals of the Civil War*, vol. III, p. 111.

44. ASCC, "Memoirs of Sr. Cecilia," n.p.

45. ADC, *Annals of the Civil War*, Vol. I, p. 6.

46. ADC, *Annals of the Civil War*, Vol. I, p. 9.

47. ASCC, "Memoirs of Sr. Gabriella," n.p.

48. Livermore, pp. 218–219.

49. Gannon, p. 176.

50. ADC, *Annals of the Civil War*, vol. III, p. 116.

51. ADC, *Annals of the Civil War*, vol. I, p. 9.

52. ADC, *Annals of the Civil War*, vol. I, p. 16.

53. ADC, *Annals of the Civil War*, vol. I, p. 16.

54. ADC, *Annals of the Civil War*, vol. I, p. 28.

55. ADC, *Annals of the Civil War*, vol. I, p. 31.

56. ADC, *Annals of the Civil War*, vol. III, p. 111.

57. ADC, *Annals of the Civil War*, vol. III, p. 111.

58. ASCC, "Memoirs of Sr. Ambrosia," n.p.

59. ADC, *Annals of the Civil War*, vol. III, p. !25.

60. ADC, *Annals of the Civil War*, vol. III, p. 125.

61. Mother Teresa Barry had sent a letter disapproving the action of quarantining a sister, and Sr. De Sales had written to both Lynch and Mother Teresa. See CDA, 28M2.

62. CDA, 28M2, Letter of Sr. De Sales to Bishop Lynch, Jan. 27, 1863.

63. ADC, *Annals of the Civil War*, vol. I, p. 12.

64. CDA, 28K2, Letter of Sr. De Sales to Bishop Lynch, Jan. 6, 1863.

65. ADC, *Annals of the Civil War*, vol. I, p. 12.

66. ASCC, "Memoirs of Sr. Jane De Chantal," n.p.

67. ASCC, "Memoirs of Sr. Theodosia," n.p.

68. ASCC, "Memoirs of Sr. Agnes," n.p.

69. CDA, 29R2, Letter of Bishop Augustine Verot to Bishop Lynch, Oct. 5, 1863.

70. ADC, "Annals of the Civil War," Manuscript, pp. 478–81.

71. ADC, "Annals of the Civil War," Manuscript, pp. 478–81.

72. ADC, "Annals of the Civil War," Manuscript, pp. 478–81.

73. ADC, "Annals of the Civil War," Manuscript, pp. 478–81.

74. Archives of University of Notre Dame (ANDU), I–4-b, Letter of Mother Angela Gillespie to Orestes Brownson, Mar. 19, 1862.

75. Archives, Sisters of Charity of Our Lady of Mercy (ASCOLM), Annals of Sister Mary Charles Curtin, 1841–1892, n.p.

76. Benjamin F. Butler, *Autobiography and Personal Reminiscences of Major-General Benj. F. Butler: Butler's Book* (Boston: A. M. Mayer, 1892), p. 426.

77. Butler, p. 422.

78. Sheilla O'Connor, "The Charity Hospital of Louisiana," *The Louisiana Historical Quarterly*, 31 (Jan. 1948), p. 62.

79. Butler, p. 422.

80. Butler, p. 422.

81. Butler, p. 113.

82. Sherman's admiration of the Holy Cross Sisters, whom he knew through his wife's cousin, Mother Angela Gillespie, did not seem to extend to sisters in the South. In his famous "March to the Sea," the Ursuline convent in Columbia, South Carolina, was burned in spite of a promise by Sherman to the Superior, Sr. Baptista Lynch, Bishop Lynch's sister. See CDA, 32M4.

83. ADC, *Annals of the Civil War*, vol. I, pp. 17–18.

84. ADC, *Annals of the Civil War*, vol. I, pp. 17–19.

85. ADC, *Annals of the Civil War*, vol. I, pp. 17–19.

86. This quote was first misappropriated in Ellen Jolly, *Nuns of the Battlefield*, pp. 188–189, and subsequently quoted by almost every author writing about the sisters in the Civil War. However, the error was pointed out by Sr. Mary Ewens in her dissertation and Betty Perkins in her master's thesis. See bibliography.

87. Lucius E. Chittenden, *Recollections of President Lincoln and His Administration* (New York: Harper and Brothers, 1891), p. 259.

88. Logue, p. 125.

89. ADC, *Annals of the Civil War*, vol. I, p. 1.

90. ADC, *Annals of the Civil War*, vol. I, pp. 4–5.

91. ADC, *Annals of the Civil War*, vol. I, p. 5.

92. ADC, *Annals of the Civil War*, vol. I, p. 5.

93. US War Dept. *The Wars of the Rebellion: A Compilation of the Official Records of the Union and Confederate Armies* (Washington: US Government Printing Office, 1880–1901), Part II, vol. 7, p. 221 (Hereafter cited as *Official Records*).

94. *Official Records*, Part II, vol. 7, p. 221.

95. *Official Records*, Part II, vol. 7, p. 373.

96. ADC, *Annals of the Civil War*, vol. I, p. 6.

97. ADC, Letter of Bishop Francis Kenrick to Rev. Francis Burlando, Dec. 17, 1861.

98. ADC, Letter of Kenrick to Burlando, Dec. 17, 1861.

99. ADC, Letter of Mother Ann Simeon Norris, et al., to General Dix, Dec. 17, 1861.

100. ADC, Letter of Mother Ann Simeon Norris.

101. Willard E. Wight, "Bishop Verot and the Civil War,"*The Catholic Historical*

Review 47 (July 1961): 159–161. See also CDA, 27R5, Letter of Bishop Verot to Bishop Lynch, Sept. 2, 1862.

102. ADC, *Annals of the Civil War*, vol. I, p. 11.

103. Archives of the Sisters of Mercy of Baltimore (ARSMB), "Memoirs of a Sister," n.p.

104. ADC, *Annals of the Civil War*, vol. I, p. 27.

105. ARSMV, Sr. M. Ignatius Sumner, p. 17.

106. ADC, "Annals of the Civil War," Manuscript, various accounts. See especially p. 297.

107. ADC, "Annals of the Civil War," Manuscript, p. 119.

108. ADC, *Annals of the Civil War*, vol. I, pp. 7–13.

109. Peter Guilday, ed., *The National Pastorals of the American Hierarchy*, 1792–1919 (Westminster, MD: The Newman Press, 1954), p. 223.

110. Dr. Samuel Gross, quoted in Mary Adelaide Nutting and Lavinia Dock, *A History of Nursing*, vol. II (New York: Putnam, 1907–12), pp. 366–368.

111. "The Petition of the Members of the Legislature of South Carolina to the Congress of the United States in Favor of the sisters of Our Lady of Mercy, Charleston, S.C. for the Rebuilding of Their Orphan Asylum" (Charleston, SC: Edward Perry, 1870), pp. 16–17. Hereafter cited as "The Petition."

112. "The Petition," p. 20.

Conclusion

When the Civil War was over, the sisters returned home and took up again the tasks of teaching, care of the orphans, and nursing that they had engaged in before the conflict began. Those communities already in nursing continued to care for returning soldiers in their own hospitals, or sometimes remained for a time in government hospitals or homes for infirm soldiers. In addition, as a direct result of their war experience, the Sisters of the Holy Cross and the Sisters of Providence added nursing to their other educational and charitable works. Special recognition was also given to other sisters. For example, the Sisters of Charity of Cincinnati, who were nurses, were given a building which became Good Samaritan Hospital because of Sr. Anthony O'Connell's fame.[1]

The sisters in the South, however, found some of their convents and institutions damaged or destroyed. For instance, the Sisters of Mercy returned to Shelby Springs, Alabama, in May 1864 under a flag of truce to reclaim their convent in Vicksburg, Mississippi. The convent, though standing, was partially damaged by shells and had been occupied as headquarters by a Union general, whose servants had taken furniture and other articles.[2] In Charleston, South Carolina, a fire during one of the bombardments partially destroyed the orphanage of the Sisters of Charity of Our Lady of Mercy. However, supported by action of the South Carolina legislature and scores of grateful letters from Union prisoners the sisters had cared for, the community eventually received $13,000 from Congress for damages done to the orphanage.[3]

Though the sisters in the North did not have their buildings damaged, they sometimes suffered other hardships. The Sisters of St. Joseph, whose hospital in Wheeling, West Virginia, was turned into a government hospital during the war, recounted that they had to beg supplies from the market to make soup for the unemployed since food and money were so scarce.[4] These hardships, however, were typical of all the citizens of the war-torn states. Still, all communities of sisters, even those who did not directly serve in the war, received esteem and recognition from Protestants and Catholics alike for the quality of the work done.

Thus, Roman Catholic sisters emerged from the Civil War clearly identified in the minds of American Catholics and of the American population at large as women whose dedicated service deserved gratitude and praise and whose nursing skills offered a model for other women. Both the praise for their service and the recognition of their skills came as a result of the obvious contrast between the sisters and other female nurses, and from firsthand knowledge of the sisters gained by the experience of military and medical authorities and the soldiers. Both the striking contrast and the positive experiences resulted in improved attitudes about Roman Catholic sisters immediately after the war and increased recognition for their lives and work.

Three major but interwoven issues emerging from this study are the convergence of the sisters' values and skills with battlefield needs, the contrast between the sisters' abilities and those of other female nurses, and the resulting positive attitudes about the sisters. A careful examination of these themes clearly reveals the unique contribution of the Roman Catholic sister to the history of nineteenth-century women, of US nursing, and of American Catholicism. The sisters' place in these histories would not have been secured had not the sisters been concerned primarily about the religious purposes of their community lives. They were, as Protestant South Carolina Congressman C. C. Bowen said in a speech in the House of Representatives after the war, "faithful to their vows as the needle to the pole."[5]

When the war began, no one, least of all the sisters, realized that the Roman Catholic religious communities in the United States clearly had the values, experience, and skills needed to address the medical needs of the war. Unlike anyone else, however, the sisters had a sharply defined purpose and mission to care for other people, especially the sick and suffering—a mission that was religious in nature. Furthermore, the sisters, as they had demonstrated in other crises, notably the cholera epidemics, were willing to expand that religious mission to respond to new needs. In addition, the sisters had the experience of living and working in groups of women specifically organized to meet social needs. Many sisters also had the necessary nursing skills learned within their religious community through caring for the sick at home or in the hospitals they had established.

In sharp contrast to the antebellum situation of inmates or scrub-women giving minimal care to people in public almshouses or private city hospitals, the sisters regarded nursing as a religious calling, not a menial task. They saw the patient as a person in need of compassionate care, and they devoted their lives to giving that kind of care. The main purpose of the sisters' service, in peacetime as well as in war, was to serve people in need in the name of Jesus Christ and in imitation of His work through a life of dedicated service lived in community and expressed by public vows of poverty, celibacy, and obedience. Significantly for the wartime medical needs, the vows that the sisters took, which supported their religious mission and structured their lives, insured that they would be obedient to orders of legitimate authority, accustomed to living simply, and committed to celibacy. Thus, more than other female nurses, the sisters were used to following rules and regulations, would not demand special accommodations or other scarce resources, and would not be interested in the soldiers except as patients.

In contrast to the sisters, other women, whether motivated by patriotism or religious zeal, did not have the experience of directing their whole lives to the service of others. Neither were they accustomed to living and working in organized groups. Married women might be accustomed to obeying their husbands, making do with limited material resources, and being sexually faithful to their husbands, but they made up a distinct minority of those serving as nurses. Most of the female nurses in the war were single, and many may have been looking for a soldier-husband. More importantly, these lay women rarely had nursing skills, let alone experience, in establishing and staffing hospitals. Thus, though these women were eager to address the medical needs of the war, their presence in what was definitely a male environment was neither desired nor sought after by most medical and military authorities. Not only was nursing not a recognized job outside the home, but the idea of women attending to personal needs of strange men also was not considered acceptable for nineteenth-century women. Further, many doctors, though in need of assistance, found themselves unable or unwilling to cope with most of these women, whose enthusiasm far outweighed their organization, skills, or experience.

Thus, in retrospect, it is not surprising, but almost predictable, that against a background of weaknesses of the medical staff, (especially at the beginning of the war), the confusion of the nursing efforts, and the often negative attitudes of the doctors toward most women as nurses that the sisters would be sought after by military and medical authorities. Despite the Know-Nothing and nativist anti-Catholic sentiments of the decades before the Civil War, and despite popular literature depicting Catholic clergy, and especially sisters, as either engaged in various nefarious sexual activities or ignorant and bound by a corrupt clergy and foreign pope, the nursing experience, hospitals, dedication, and willingness of the sisters to serve was recognized. Certainly, the twenty-one communities of sisters responded differently to a variety of requests for service on battlefield, transport boat, and general hospital. While there are isolated instances of communities not responding to requests, the overwhelming evidence indicates that sisters everywhere in the Union and the Confederacy responded immediately.

In fact, nowhere is there a record of any community previously engaged in health care declining to serve in the war if asked. Rather, communities that had sisters in health care, especially the Daughters of Charity, responded generously. Even more significantly, perhaps, is the response of sisters who did not have a history of hospital work or nursing, notably the Sisters of the Holy Cross and the Sisters of Providence. Both responded to requests, nursed for a considerable part of the war, and then started hospitals and continued nursing after the war. Of even greater importance is the fact that the sisters' religious values and beliefs were generally not a deterrent to their being asked to nurse. Rather, those who asked for the sisters, whether government official, military officer, or doctor, were willing to accept the sisters on their own terms, something the authorities certainly were not willing to do for most other female nurses.

It has been suggested that unlike the sisters, the female nurses of the Civil War clashed with most doctors because the nurses' presence challenged male authority generally and the medical field specifically.[6] This theory perhaps implies that the sisters were preferred beause of their greater conformity to the image and ideals of domesticity. However, the situation may have been more complex. It appears that the sisters did challenge doctors and other authorities when they felt nursing care, nutrition, cleanliness, good order, and their religious practices demanded it. In addition, they were often able to get supplies that doctors or military authorities were not able to procure.

Although a certain tension and challenge did exist between other female nurses and the sisters, much of this was due to the fact that both before and after the war, appeals were made to American Protestant women to emulate Sisters of Charity. For example, Catharine Beecher in *The American Woman's Home* recounted a conversation she had with a woman who had seen much of military hospitals during the Civil War. Beecher asked, "Are the Sisters of Charity really better nurses than most other women?" "Yes, they are," the woman replied. "I think it is because with them it is a work of self-abnegation, and of duty to God, and they are so quiet and self-forgetful in its exercise that they do it better while many other women show such self-consciousness and are so fussy!" While aspects of Roman Catholicism or convent life may not have appealed to the American woman, the dedication, commitment, organization, training, and ability of sisters to meet various social needs did. Beecher challenged American women to emulate the Sisters of Charity: "Is there any reason why every Protestant woman should not be trained for this self-denying office as a duty owed to God?"[7]

There may have been no reason why Protestant women could not be trained, but certainly the four years of the war were too short a time to acknowledge a role of women in health care, let alone to turn nursing into a profession. Nevertheless, the Roman Catholic sisters, in that short period, did become known for the way their religious values, which were developed in community life, could contribute to an American need, and for the way their social-service experience and nursing skills could contribute to the medical field. These two contributions created a more positive view of the sister, her religion, and her Church and clearly demonstrated what a group of dedicated religious women could accomplish. All this might well have come about in time even if there had been no Civil War. However, the Civil War gave the Roman Catholic sister an unexpected opportunity to exercise these skills and values in a context larger than their own Catholic institutions. Because of the wider exposure of many Protestants and Catholics to the sisters' dedication and practical skills, the sisters were better known and more appreciated and respected at war's end than they had been four years before.

The sisters, of course, were not inherently professionals, reformers, or feminists, nor were they seen that way by themselves or others. Basically, the Roman Catholic sisters who nursed in the Civil War, while contributing a high level of care to the soldiers, saw their role (or the religious community saw its role) as continuing the mission of serving where needs and requests were greatest; thus, rather than believing that they were charting new paths and directions for moving nursing toward the status of a profession, they saw themselves as following in the long tradition of nursing care done from religious motivation. This is true partly because many of the sisters with special training themselves just passed this on as a matter of course to other members of their communities who served in the hospitals. This practice obviated the need for special training schools until such time as there were not enough sisters to handle the nursing. Also, in spite of some significant women religious who established health care and other institutions serving social needs of people, nursing for the sisters (as well as education and social service) was considered a "ministry," a service to and for others, rather than a profession.

These largely Irish and German immigrants and native-born women, living in a freely chosen, alternative lifestyle of a single-sex community rather than in marriage, and sometimes circumscribed by rules and regulations of a European, male-dominated hierarchical church, served as an example of what a skilled nurse could accomplish. This example helped pave the way for the beginning of professional training for female nurses within a decade after the Civil War. The familiarity with the sisters that the circumstances of the war provided also served to greatly enhance the positive image of the sisters and consequently of the Roman Catholic church during and after the war. It seemed to make little difference whether the sisters were from Union or Confederate states or nursed Northerners or Southerners. As Confederate nurse Kate Cumming observed, the six hundred Roman Catholic sisters who nursed in the Civil War on battlefields, in hospitals, and on transport ships seemed able to "do with honor"[8] what other women desired to do. This "honorable" work clearly has earned the Civil War nursing sisters a unique place in the history of nineteenth-century American women's history.

NOTES

1. Archives Sisters of Charity of Cincinnati (ASCC), file of Sr. Anthony O'Connell.

2. William H. Elder, *Civil War Diary* (Natchez-Jackson Diocese: Gerow, n. ed.), p. 112; p.57. See also Archives of Sisters of Mercy, Vicksburg (ARSMV), Sr. M. Ignatius Sumner, "Register of the Events from the Foundation of the Convent of the Sisters of Mercy, Vicksburg, Miss.," pp. 26–28.

3. "The Petition of the Members of the Legislature of South Carolina to the Congress of the United States in favor of the Sisters of Our Lady of Mercy, Charleston, SC for the Rebuilding of Their Orphan Asylum" (Charleston, SC: Edward Perry, 1870). Hereafter cited as "The Petition." See also *Congressional Globe*, Second Session of the Forty-first Congress, Mar. 21, 1870, pp. 171–173; Third Session of the Forty-first Congress, Mar. 3, 1871, pp. 2007–2010; First Session of the Forty-second Congress, April 18, 1871, pp. 767–812.

4. Sr. Rose Anita Kelly, *Song of the Hills: The Story of the Sisters of St. Joseph of Wheeling* (Wheeling, WV: Sisters of St. Joseph, 1962), p. 220.

5. Archives Sisters of Charity of Our Lady of Mercy, Charleston, SC (ASCOLM), "Rebuilding Orphan Asylum in Charleston, S.C.: Speech of Hon. C.C. Bowen," delivered in the House of Representatives, Mar. 21, 1870.

6. Ann Douglas Wood, "The War Within a War: Women Nurses in the Union Army," *Civil War History* 18 (Sept. 1972), 197–212.

7. Catharine Beecher, *The American Woman's Home* (New York: J. B. Ford, 1870), p. 346.

8. Kate Cumming, *Kate: The Journal of a Confederate Nurse*, ed. Richard B. Harwell (Baton Rouge: Louisiana State University Press, 1959), p. 178.

Selected Bibliography

ARCHIVAL SOURCES

AAC   Archives, Archdiocese of Cincinnati

ACSC   Archives, Sisters of the Holy Cross, Saint Mary's, Notre Dame, Indiana

ADC   Archives, Daughters of Charity, Emmitsburg, Maryland

ANDU   Archives, Notre Dame University, South Bend, Indiana

AOPK   Archives, Sisters of St. Dominic, St. Catharine, Kentucky

AOPT   Archives, Sisters of St. Dominic, Memphis, Tennessee

ARSMB   Archives, Sisters of Mercy, Province of Baltimore, Maryland

ARSMC   Archives, Sisters of Mercy, Chicago, Illinois

ARSMC   Archives, Sisters of Mercy, Cincinnati, Ohio

ARSMNYC Archives, Sisters of Mercy, New York City, New York

ARSMP   Archives, Sisters of Mercy, Pittsburgh, Pennsylvania

ARSMV   Archives, Sisters of Mercy, Vicksburg, Mississippi

ASCC   Archives, Sisters of Charity of Cincinnati, Cincinnati, Ohio

ASCN   Archives, Sisters of Charity, Nazareth, Kentucky

ASCNYC   Archives, Sisters of Charity, New York City, New York

ASCOLM   Archives, Sisters of Charity of Our Lady of Mercy, Charleston, South Carolina

ASOLMC   Archives, Sisters of Our Lady of Mt. Carmel, New Orleans, Louisiana

ASP   Archives, Sisters of Providence, St. Mary of the Woods, Indiana

ASPSF   Archives, Sisters of the Poor of St. Francis, Cincinnati, Ohio

ASSJP   Archives, Sisters of St. Joseph, Philadelphia, Pennsylvania

ASSJW   Archives, Sisters of St. Joseph, Wheeling, West Virginia

AUNG   Archives, Ursuline Nuns, Galveston, Texas

CDA   Charleston Diocesan Archives, Diocese of Charleston, S.C.
         Bishop Patrick Lynch papers

NA   National Archives, Washington, D.C. Dr. John Brinton papers

SECONDARY SOURCES

History of Religion in America

Ahlstrom, Sydney E. *A Religious History of the American People.* New Haven: Yale University Press, 1972.

Gaustad, Edwin Scott. *Historical Atlas of American Religion.* New York: Harper and Row, 1975.

————, ed. *A Documentary History of Religion in America.* 2 vols. Grand Rapids: William B. Eerdmans, 1982.

Handy, Robert. *A History of the Churches in the United States- and Canada.* New York: Oxford University Press, 1977.

Hudson, Winthrop. *Religion in America: An Historical Account of the Development of American Religious Life.* 3rd ed. New York: Charles Scribner's Sons, 1981.

Marty, Martin E. *Pilgrims in Their Own Land: 500 Years of Religion in America.* New York: Penguin, 1984.

Noll, Mark, et al. *Eerdman's Handbook to Christianity in America.* Grand Rapids: William B. Eerdmans, 1983.

History of Catholicism in America

Dolan, Jay. *The American Catholic Experience: A History from Colonial Times to the Present.* Garden City, NY: Doubleday, 1985.

————. *Catholic Revivalism: The American Experience, 1830–1900.* Notre Dame, IN: University of Notre Dame Press, 1978.

————. *The Immigrant Church: New York's Irish and German Catholics, 1815–1865.* Notre Dame, IN: University of Notre Dame Press, 1975.

Ellis, John Tracy. *American Catholicism.* Chicago: University of Chicago Press, 1956; rev. ed., 1969.

————. *Catholics in Colonial America.* Baltimore: Helicon Press, 1965.

————. *Documents of American Catholic History.* 2 vols. Milwaukee: Bruce Publishing, 1956; rev. ed. Chicago: University of Chicago Press, 1969.

Ellis, John Tracy and Robert Trisco, eds. *A Guide to American Catholic History.* 2nd ed. Santa Barbara: ABC-Clio, 1982.

Gannon, Michael. *The Cross in the Sand: The Early Church in Florida, 1513–1870.* Gainsville: University of Florida Press, 1967.

Guilday, Peter, ed. *The National Pastorals of the American Hierarchy (1792–1919).* Westminster, MD: The Newman Press, 1954.

Hennesey, James J. *American Catholics: A History of the Roman Catholic Community in the United States*. New York: Oxford University Press, 1981.

―――――, ed. *American Catholic Bibliography, 1970–1982*. Series 12, No. 1. Fall, 1982. Notre Dame: Cushwa Center Working Papers, 1982.

―――――, ed. *Supplement to American Catholic Bibliography, 1970–1982*. Series 14, No. 1. Fall, 1983. Notre Dame: Cushwa Center Working Papers, 1983.

Hutter, Donald, ed. *Mirror of 150-Year Progress (1810 to 1960) of the Catholic Church in the United States of America*. Cleveland, OH: Mirror Publishing, 1964.

The Metropolitan Catholic Almanac and Laity's Directory for the United States, Canada, and the British Provinces. Baltimore: John Murphy, 1861.

O'Grady, John. *Catholic Charities in the United States*. Washington, D.C.: National Conference of Catholic Bishops, 1930; rpt. New York: Arno Press, 1971.

Pillar, James J. *The Catholic Church in Mississippi, 1837–65*. New Orleans: The Hauser Press, 1964.

Sadlier's Catholic Almanac and Ordo for Year of Our Lord, 1864. New York: D. J. Sadlier Co., 1864.

Sadlier's Catholic Almanac and Ordo for Year of Our Lord, 1865. New York: D. J. Sadlier Co., 1865.

Shaw, Richard. *Dagger John: The Unquiet Life and Times of Archbishop John Hughes of New York*. New York: Paulist Press, 1977.

Shea, John Gilmary. *History of the Catholic Church in the United States*. 4 vols. New York: John G. Shea, 1886–92.

Wakelyn, Jon L. and Randall Miller, eds. *Catholics in the Old South: Essays on Church and Culture*. Macon: Mercer University Press, 1983.

Women and Religion in the United States—Nineteenth-Century America

Beaver, R. Pierce. *All Loves Excelling*. Grand Rapids, Mich: Eerdmans Publishing, 1968. (Revised edition *American Protestant Women in World Mission: History of the First Feminist Movement in North America*. 1980).

Cott, Nancy F. "Young Women in the Second Great Awakening in New England." *Feminist Studies* 3 (1975): 15–29.

Gifford, Carolyn DeSwarte. "Sisterhoods of Service and Reform: Organized Methodist Women in the Late Nineteenth Century. An Essay on the State of the Research." *Methodist History* 24 (Oct. 1985): 15–30.

James, Janet Wilson, ed. *Women in American Religion*. Philadelphia: University of Pennsylvania Press, 1980.

Porterfield, Amanda. *Feminine Spirituality in America*. Philadelphia: Temple University Press, 1980.

Ruether, Rosemary Radford and Keller, Rosemary Skinner, eds. *The Nineteenth Century: A Documentary History*. vol. 1 of *Women and Religion in America*. San Francisco: Harper and Row, 1981.

―――――. *The Colonial and Revolutionary Periods: A Documentary History*. vol. 2 of *Women and Religion in America*. San Francisco: Harper and Row, 1983.

Roman Catholic Religious Women in Nineteenth-Century America

Brewer, Eileen Mary. *Nuns and the Education of American Catholic Women, 1860–1920*. Chicago: Loyola University Press, 1987.

Byrne, Sr. Patricia. "Sisters of St. Joseph: The Americanization of a French Tradition." *U.S. Catholic Historian* 5 (Summer/Fall 1986): 241–272.

Code, Joseph B. "A Selected Bibliography of the Religious Orders and Congregations of Women Founded Within the Present Boundaries of the United States (1727–1850)." *The Catholic Historical Review* 23 (Oct. 1937): 331–351.

————, "Up-Date of 'A Selected Bibliography'." *The Catholic Historical Review* 26 (July 1940): 222–245.

Dehey, Elinor T. *Religious Orders of Women in the United States: Accounts of their Origin, Works, and Most Important Institutions*. Hammond, IN: W. B. Conkey, 1930.

"Destruction of Charlestown Convent from Contemporary Newspaper Accounts." *United States Catholic Historical Records and Studies* 13 (May 1919): 106–119.

Ewens, Mary, OP. "The Leadership of Nuns in Immigrant Catholicism." In Rosemary Ruether and Rosemary Skinner Keller, eds. *Women and Religion in America: The Nineteenth Century. Vol. 1* San Francisco: Harper and Row, 1981, pp. 101–149.

————. *The Role of the Nun in Nineteenth Century America: Variations on the International Theme*. New York: Arno, 1978.

Kenneally, James J. "The Burning of the Ursuline Convent: A Different View." *Records of the American Catholic Historical Society* 90 (Mar-Dec. 1979): No. 1–4, 15–22.

————. "Eve, Mary, and the Historians: American Catholicism and Women." In Janet W. Jones, ed. *Women in American Religion*. Philadelphia: University of Pennsylvania Press, 1980, pp. 191–206.

Mannard, Joseph G. "Maternity . . . of the Spirit: Nuns and Domesticity in Antebellum America." *U.S. Catholic Historian* 5 (Summer/Fall 1986): 305–324.

Monk, Maria. *Awful Disclosures of the Hotel Dieu Nunnery in Montreal*. New York: Howe and Bates, 1836.

Reed, Rebecca. *Six Months in a Convent*. Boston: Russell, Odeorne and Metcalf, 1835.

Ryan, Maria Alma, IHM. "Foundations of Catholic Sisterhoods in the U.S. to 1850." *American Catholic Historical Society Records*. Vols. 12–14, (1941–1943); vol. 12, 34–61; 87–109; 174–184; 219–243; vol. 13, 21–32; 96–100; 169–178; 250–257; vol. 14, 66–73; 134–146; 159–175.

Sullivan, Sister Mary Christiana. "Some Non-Permanent Foundations of Religious Orders and Congregations." *United States Catholic Historical Society Records and Studies* 31 (Jan. 1940): 7–118.

Thomas, Evangeline, CSJ. *Women Religious History Sources: A Guide to Repositories in the United States*. New York: R. R. Bowker, 1983.

Thompson, Margaret Susan. "Discovering Foremothers: Sisters, Society, and the American Catholic Experience." *U.S. Catholic Historian* 5 (Summer/Fall 1986): 273–290.

Women in Nineteenth-Century America

Beecher, Catharine. *The American Woman's Home: or The Principles of Domestic Science.* New York: J. B. Ford, 1870.

Clinton, Catherine. *The Other Civil War: American Women in the Nineteenth Century.* New York: Hill and Wang, 1984.

Cott, Nancy. *The Bonds of Womanhood: "Woman's Sphere" in New England, 1780– 1835.* New Haven: Yale University Press, 1977.

Douglas, Ann. *The Feminization of American Culture.* New York: Alfred A. Knopf, 1977.

Freedman, Estelle. "Separatism as Strategy: Female Institution Building and American Feminism, 1870–1930." *Feminist Studies* 5 (Fall 1979): 513–529.

Hales, Jean Gould. "Co-Laborers in the Cause: Women in the Antebellum Nativist Movement." *Civil War History* 25 (June 1979): 119–138.

Hogeland, Ronald W. "The Female Appendage: Feminine Life-Styles in America, 1820–1860." *Civil War History* 17 (June 1971): 101–114.

James, Edward T., Janet W. James, and Paul S. Boyer. *Notable American Women 1607–1950: A Bibliographical Dictionary.* 4 vols. Cambridge, Mass.: Harvard University Press, 1971.

Livermore, Mary A. *What Shall We Tell Our Daughters?: Superfluous Women and Other Lectures.* Boston: Lee and Shepard, 1883.

Melder, Keith E. "Ladies Bountiful: Organized Women's Benevolence in Early Nineteenth Century America." *New York History* 48 (July 1967): 231–254.

McDannell, Colleen. *The Christian Home In Victorian America, 1840–1900.* Bloomington: Indiana University Press, 1986.

Riegel, Robert E. *American Feminists.* Lawrence: University of Kansas Press, 1963.

Ryan, Mary. *The Empire of Domesticity: American Writing About Domesticity 1830 to 1860.* New York: Haworth Press and the Institute for Research of History, 1982.

Sklar, Kathryn. *Catharine Beecher: A Study in American Domesticity.* New Haven: Yale University Press, 1973.

Smith-Rosenberg, Carroll. *Disorderly Conduct: Visions of Gender in Victorian America.* New York: Alfred A. Knopf, 1985.

Treudley, Mary B. "The Benevolent Fair: A Study of Charitable Organizations Among Women in the First Third of the Nineteenth Century." *Social Service Review* 14 (Dec. 1940): 509–522.

Vicinus, Martha. *Independent Women: Work and Community for Single Women, 1850– 1920.* Chicago: University of Chicago Press, 1985.

Walsh, Mary Roth. *Doctors Wanted: No Women Need Apply.* New Haven: Yale University Press, 1977.

Welter, Barbara. *Dimity Convictions.* Athens: Ohio University Press, 1976.

―――――. "The Cult of True Womanhood, 1802–1860." *American Quarterly* 18 (Summer 1966): 151–174.

History of Nursing

Austin, Anne L. *History of Nursing Source Book.* New York: G. P. Putnam's Sons, 1957.

Bullough, Vern L. and Bonnie Bullough. *The Care of the Sick: The Emergence of Modern Nursing.* New York: Prodist, 1978.

Dolan, Josephine A. *Nursing in Society: A Historical Perspective.* 14th ed. Philadelphia: W. B. Saunders Co., 1978.

Dowling, Harry. *City Hospitals: The Undercare of the Under-privileged.* Cambridge: Harvard University Press, 1982.

Kalish, Philip and Beatrice J. Kalish. *The Advance of American Nursing.* Boston: Little, Brown, 1978.

Lagemann, Ellen Condliffe, ed. *Nursing History: New Perspectives, New Possibilities.* New York: Teachers College Press, 1983.

Nightingale, Florence. *Notes on Nursing; What It Is and What It Is Not.* 1860: rpt. New York: Churchill Livingston, 1969.

Nutting, Mary Adelaide and Lavinia Dock. *A History of Nursing: The Evolution of Nursing Systems from the Earliest Times to the Foundation of the First England and American Training Schools for Nurses.* 4 vols. New York: G. P. Putnam's Sons, 1907–12.

O'Connor, Robin. "American Hospitals: The First 200 Years." *Hospitals* 50 (Jan. 11, 1976): 62–71.

Reverby, Susan M. *Ordered to Care: The Dilemma of American Nursing, 1850–1945.* Cambridge, England: Cambridge University Press, 1987.

Rosenberg, Charles E. *The Care of Strangers: The Rise of America's Hospital System.* New York: Basic Books, 1987.

————. *The Cholera Years: The United States in 1832, 1849, and 1866.* Chicago: The University of Chicago Press, 1962.

————. "The Origins of the American Hospital System." *Bulletin of the New York Academy of Medicine* 55, No. 1 (Jan. 1979): 10–21.

Shryock, Richard H. *The History of Nursing: An Interpretation of the Social and Medical Factors Involved.* Philadelphia: W.B. Saunders, 1959.

Starr, Paul. *The Social Transformation of American Medicine.* New York: Basic Books, 1982.

Woodham-Smith, Cecil. *Florence Nightingale.* New York: McGraw-Hill, 1951.

Woolsey, Abby H. *A Century of Nursing with Hints Toward the Organization of a Training School.* 1916: rpt. New York: Putnam, 1950.

Roman Catholic Sisters and Nursing

Doyle, Ann. "Nursing by Religious Orders in the United States" *American Journal of Nursing* 29 (July-Sept. 1929): 775–786, 959–969, 1085–1095, 1197–1207, 1331–1343; 1466–1484.

Dwight, Thomas. "The Training Schools for Nurses of the Sisters of Charity." *Catholic World* 61 (May 1895): 187–92.

Jameson, Anna Brownell (Murphy). *"Sisters of Charity" and "The Communion of*

Labour": Two Lectures on the Social Employment of Women. London: Longman, Brown, Green, Longmans and Roberts, 1859.

"Sisters in the History of Nursing." *America* 92 (6 Nov. 1954): 144.

Stepsis, Sr. Ursula and Sr. Dolores Liptak, eds. *Pioneer Healers: The History of Women Religious in American Health Care*. New York: Crossroad Continuum, 1989.

"Who Shall Take Care of Our Sick?" *Catholic World* 7 (Oct. 1868): 42–55.

Civil War—General

Beitzell, Edwin W. *Point Lookout Prison Camp for Confederates*. Abell, Maryland: E. W. Beitzel, 1972.

Billings, John D. *Hardtack and Coffee or The Unwritten Story of Army Life*. Boston: G. M. Smith, 1887.

Butler, Benjamin. *Autobiography and Personal Reminiscences of Major General Benj. F. Butler*. Boston: A. M. Mayer, 1892.

Chittenden, Lucius E. *Recollections of President Lincoln and His Administration*. New York: Harper and Brothers, 1891.

Confederate States of America. *Official Reports of Battles*. New York, 1863; rpt. New York: Kraus Reprint Co., 1973.

Davis, William, ed. *The Image of War, 1861–1865*. 3 vols. Garden City, NY: Doubleday, 1981.

Glazier, Capt. Willard. *The Capture, the Prison Pen and the Escape, Giving a Complete History of Prison Life in the South*. New York: R. H. Ferguson, 1870.

Fredrickson, George. *The Inner Civil War: Northern Intellectuals and the Crisis of Union*. New York: Harper and Row, 1965.

Hesseltine, William B. *Civil War Prisons: A Study in War Psychology*. New York: Frederick Ungar, 1930; rpt. 1964.

Johnson, Robert and C. E. Buel, eds. *Battles and Leaders of the Civil War*. 4 vols. New York: Century Co., 1884, 1888.

Livermore, Thomas L., ed. *Numbers and Losses in the Civil War in America*. Boston: Houghton, Mifflin, 1901.

Moore, Frank, ed. *The Rebellion Record*. 7 vols. New York: G. P. Putnam's Sons, 1861–1866.

Thompson, Holland, ed. *Prisons and Hospitals*. Vol. 7 in Miller, Francis Trevelyan, ed. *The Photographic History of the Civil War in Ten Volumes*. New York: The Review of Reviews Co., 1911.

United States War Department. *The War of the Rebellion: A Compilation of the Official Records of the Union and Confederate Armies*. 70 vols. in 128 books. Washington, D.C.: U.S. Government Printing Office, 1880–1901.

Wiley, Bell I. *The Life of Billy Yank: The Common Soldier of the Union*. Garden City, NY: Doubleday, 1971.

————. *The Life of Johnny Reb: The Common Soldier of the Confederacy*. Garden City, NY: Doubleday, 1971.

Civil War—Medicine

Adams, George Worthington. *Doctors in Blue: The Medical History of the Union Army in the Civil War*. New York: Henry Schuman, 1952.

Barnes, Joseph K., et al. *The Medical and Surgical History of the War of the Rebellion, 1861–65*. 6 vols. Washington, D.C., Government Printing Office, 2nd issue, 1875–1888.

Blackwell, Elizabeth. *Pioneer Work in Opening the Medical Profession to Women*. London: Longmans, 1895.

Brinton, John Hill. *Personal Memories of John H. Brinton, Major and Surgeon USV, 1861–1865*. New York: The Neale Publishing Co., 1914.

Brooks, Stewart. *Civil War Medicine*. Springfield, Illinois: C.C. Thomas, 1966.

Cunningham, Horace H. *Doctors in Gray: The Confederate Medical Service*. Baton Rouge: Louisiana State University Press, 1958.

Letterman, Jonathan. *Medical Recollections of the Army of the Potomac*. New York: D. Appleton, 1866.

Loomis, E. Kent. "History of the U.S. Navy Hospital Ship *Red Rover*." Washington, D.C.: Navy Department Division of Naval History, 1961.

Mitchell, S. Weir "The Medical Department in the Civil War." *The Journal of the American Medical Association* 62, No. 19 (May 9, 1914): 1445–1450.

Shryock, Richard Harrison. "A Medical Perspective on the Civil War." In Richard Shryock, ed. *Medicine in America: Historical Essays*. Boston: The John Hopkins Press, 1966, pp. 91–108.

Stevenson, Isobel. "Medical Literature of the Civil War." *CIBA Symposia* 3, No. 2 (July 1941): 908–918.

US Surgeon General's Office. *Reports on the Extent and Nature of the Materials Available for the Preparation of a Medical and Surgical History of the Rebellion*. Circular No. 6, Nov 1, 1865. Philadelphia: J. B. Lippincott, 1865.

Whitman, Walt. *Memoranda During the Civil War [and] Death of Abraham Lincoln*. rpt. Bloomington: Indiana University Press, 1962.

————. *The Wound Dresser: A Series of Letters written from the Hospitals in Washington during the War of the Rebellion*, ed. R. M. Burke. Boston, 1898; rpt. Folcroft, Pa.: Folcroft Library Editions, 1975.

Civil War—US Sanitary Commission

Hoge, Mrs. A. H. *The Boys in Blue*. New York: Treat, 1867.

Maxwell, William Q. *Lincoln's Fifth Wheel: The Political History of the United States Sanitary Commission*. New York: Longmans, Green, 1956.

Olmsted, Frederick Law. *Hospital Transports: A Memoir of the Embarkation of the Sick and Wounded from the Peninsula of Virginia in the Summer of 1862*. Boston: Ticknor and Fields, 1863.

Stille, Charles. *History of the U.S. Sanitary Commission*. Philadelphia: J. B. Lippincott, 1866.

Thompson, William Y. "The U.S. Sanitary Commission." *Civil War History* 2 (June 1956): 41–63.

The United States Sanitary Commission: A Sketch of Its Purpose and Work. Boston: Little Brown, 1863.

Wormely, Katharine Prescott. *The Cruel Side of the War*. Boston: Roberts, 1898.

Civil War—Catholics

Blied, Benjamin. *Catholics and the Civil War*. Milwaukee: Bruce, 1945.

Conyngham, Major D. P. "The Soldiers of the Cross: Heroism of the Cross, or Nuns and Priests on the Battlefield." Typescript. n.d. University of Notre Dame Archives.

Elder, Bishop William Henry. *Civil War Diary, 1862–1865*. Natchez-Jackson, Mississippi: Most Rev. R. O. Geron. n.d.

Gannon, Michael V. *The Cross in the Sand: The Early Catholic Church in Florida, 1513–1870*. Gainsville: University of Florida Press, 1967.

Meehan, T. F. "Army Statistics of the Civil War." *U.S. Catholic Historical Records and Studies* 13 (Oct. 1919): 129–139.

Murphy, Robert J. "The Catholic Church in the U.S. During the Civil War Period 1852–1866." *Records of the American Catholic Historical Society of Philadelphia* 39 (Dec. 1928): 271–346.

Shannon, James P., ed. "Archbishop Ireland's Experiences As a Civil War Chaplain." *Catholic Historical Review*. 39 (Oct. 1953): 298–305.

Spalding, David. "Martin John Spalding's 'Dissertation on the American Civil War'." *Catholic Historical Review* 52 (Jan. 1966): 66–85.

Stock, Leo F. "Catholic Participation in the Diplomacy of the Southern Confederacy." *Catholic Historical Review* 16 (Jan. 1930): 1–18.

Wight, Willard. "Bishop Elder and the Civil War." *Catholic Historical Review* 44 (Oct. 1958): 290–306.

————. "Bishop Verot and the Civil War." *Catholic Historical Review* 47 (July 1961): 153–163.

————, ed. "Some Wartime Letters of Bishop Lynch." *Catholic Historical Review* 43 (April 1957), 20–37.

————, ed. "War Letters of the Bishop of Richmond." *The Virginia Magazine of History and Biography* 67 (July 1959): 259–270.

Civil War—Chaplains

Buckley, Cornelius. *A Frenchman, A Chaplain, A Rebel: The War Letters of Père Louis-Hippolyte Gaché, SJ*. Chicago: Loyola University Press, 1981.

Corby, William. *Memoirs of Chaplain Life*. Chicago: LaMonte, O'Donnell, 1893.

Durkin, Joseph T., SJ, ed. *Confederate Chaplain: A War Journal of Rev. James B. Sheeran*. Milwaukee: Bruce, 1960.

King, T. S. "Letters of Civil War Chaplains." *Woodstock Letters* 43 (1914): 24–34, 168–180.

"Letters of Kenrick to Hughes and to Lincoln." *Catholic Historical Review* 4 (Oct. 1918): 385–388.

Pitts, Charles F. *Chaplains in Gray: The Confederate Chaplains' Story*. Nashville: Broodman Press, 1957.

Quimby, Rollin W. "The Chaplain's Predicament." *Civil War History* 8 (March 1962): 25–37.

Trumbull, H. Clay. *War Memories of a Chaplain.* New York: Charles Scribner's Sons, 1898.

Wight, Willard E. "The Churches and the Confederate Cause." *Civil War History* 6 (Dec. 1960): 361–373.

————. "The Bishop of Natchez and the Confederate Chaplaincy." *Mid-America* 39, No. 2 (April 1957): 67–72.

Civil War—Women

Brockett, L. P. and Mary C. Vaughan. *Women's Work in the Civil War: A Record of Heroism, Patriotism, and Patience.* Philadelphia: Zeigler, McCurdy, 1867.

Collis, Septima. *A Woman's War Record, 1861–1865.* New York: G. P. Putnam's Sons, 1889.

Endres, Kathleen. "The Women's Press in the Civil War: A Portrait of Patriotism, Propaganda, and Prodding." *Civil War History* 30 (March 1984): 31–53.

Hancock, Cornelia. *The South after Gettysburg: Letters of Cornelia Hancock, 1863–1868.* Ed. Henrietta Stratton Jacquette. New York: Thomas Y. Crowell, 1937, reprint 1956.

Marszalek, John F., ed. *The Diary of Miss Emma Holmes, 1861–1866.* Baton Rouge: Louisiana State University Press, 1979.

Massey, Mary Elizabeth. *Bonnet Brigades: American Women and the Civil War.* New York: Alfred Knopf, 1966.

Moore, Frank. *Women of the War: Their Heroism and Self-Sacrifice.* Hartford, CT: S. S. Scranton, 1867.

Putnam, Sallie. *Richmond During the War.* New York: G. W. Carlston, 1867.

Quattlebaum, Isabel. "Twelve Women in the First Days of the Confederacy." *Civil War History* 7 (Dec. 1961): 370–385.

Simkins, Francis Butler and James Welch Patton. *The Women of the Confederacy.* Richmond: Garrett and Massie, 1936.

Swisshelm, Jane Grey. *Crusader and Feminist.* Ed. Arthur Larsen. Westport, CT: Hyperion Press, 1976.

Woodward, Comer Vann, ed. *Mary Chestnut's Civil War.* New Haven: Yale University Press, 1981.

Woodward, Comer Vann and Elizabeth Muhlenfeld, eds. *The Private Mary Chestnut: The Unpublished Civil War Diaries.* New York: Oxford University Press, 1984.

Civil War—Female Nurses

Alcott, Louisa May. *Hospital Sketches.* Ed. Bessie Z. Jones. Cambridge: Harvard University Press, 1960.

Austin, Anne L. "Nurses in American History: Wartime Volunteers, 1861–1865." *American Journal of Nursing* 75 (May 1975): 816–818.

————. *The Woolsey Sisters of New York: A Family's Involvement in the Civil War and a New Profession (1860–1900).* Philadelphia: American Philosophical Society, 1971.

Blake, John B. "Women and Medicine in Antebellum America." *Bulletin of the History of Medicine* 39 (March-April 1965): 99–123.

Boyden, Anna L. *Echoes from Hospital and White House, a Record of Mrs. Rebecca R. Pomroy's Experience in War Times.* Boston: Lathrop, 1884.

Bucklin, Sophronia. *In Hospital and Camp: A Woman's Record of Thrilling Incidents among the Wounded in the Late War.* Philadelphia: John E. Potter & Co., 1869.

Brumgardt, John R., ed. *Civil War Nurse: The Diary and Letters of Hannah Ropes.* Knoxville: University of Tennessee Press, 1980.

Cumming, Kate. *Kate: The Journal of A Confederate Nurse.* ed. Richard Barksdale Harwell. Baton Rouge: Louisiana State University Press, 1959.

Livermore, Mary Ashton. *My Story of the War: A Woman's Narrative of Four Years Personal Experience as Nurse in the Union Army.* Hartford, CT: A. D. Worthington, 1887.

Marshall, Helen E. *Dorothea Dix, Forgotten Samaritan.* New York: Russell and Russell, 1937.

Robinson, Victor. *White Caps.* Philadelphia: J. B. Lippincott, 1946.

Schwartz, Gerald, ed. *A Woman Doctor's Civil War: Esther Hill Hawks' Diary.* Columbia, SC: University of South Carolina Press, 1984.

Simkins, Francis B. and James W. Patton. "The Work of Southern Women among the Sick and Wounded of the Confederate Armies." *Journal of Southern History* 1 (Nov. 1935): 475–496.

Stimson, Julia C. and Ethel C. Thompson. "Women Nurses With the Union Forces During the Civil War." *Military Surgeon,* 62 (Jan. 1928): 1–17; (Feb. 1928): 208–230.

Wittenmyer, Anne. *Under the Guns: A Woman's Reminiscences of the Civil War.* Boston: E. B. Stillings & Co., 1895.

Wood, Ann Douglas. "The War Within a War: Women Nurses in the Union Army." *Civil War History* 18 (Sept. 1972): 197–212.

Woolsey, Jane Stuart. *Hospital Days.* New York: D. Van Nostrand, 1868.

Civil War—Sisters

Aubuchon, Marie T. "Sister Nurses in the Civil War." *Hospital Progress* 42 (May 1961): 182, 186, 188–89.

Barton, George. *Angels of the Battlefield.* Philadelphia: Catholic Art, 1898.

"A Brief Account of the Services During the Civil War of the Sisters of St. Joseph of Philadelphia." *American Catholic Historical Society Researches* 35 (Dec. 1924): 345–356.

Carroll, Sr. Teresa Austin, ed. *Leaves from the Annals of the Sisters of Mercy.* 4 vols. New York: Catholic Publication Society, 1881–88.

Code, Joseph B. *Bishop John Hughes and the Sisters of Charity.* (n.c.). Miscellaneous Historical reprint, 1949.

Constitutions of the Daughters of Charity of St. Vincent de Paul. Paris: Motherhouse, 1954.

Costello, Sr. Mary Loretto. *The Sisters of Mercy of Maryland, 1855–1930.* St. Louis: B. Herder, 1931.

Curley, Michael J. "The Nuns of the Battlefield." *Catholic Mind* 22 (Oct. 8, 1924): 179–180.

Donnelly, Eleanor C. *Life of Sister Mary Gonzaga Grace of the Daughters of Charity of St. Vincent de Paul 1812–1897*. Philadelphia: n.p., 1900.

Evans, Mary Ellen. *The Spirit Is Mercy: The Sisters of Mercy in the Archdiocese of Cincinnati, 1853–1958*. Westminster, MD: The Newman Press, 1959.

Franklin, Sr. Mary Lawrence. "Mercy from Eire to Erie: The Sisters of Mercy of the Erie Diocese." n.p., n.d.

A Guide for the Religious Called Sisters of Mercy, Part I and II. London: Robson and Son, 1866.

Harron, Sr. Mary Eulalia. "Work of the Sisters of Mercy in the Dioceses of the South." *Records of the American Catholic Historical Society of Philadelphia* 36 (June 1925): 155–161.

Hilleke, Sr. John Francis. "Holy Cross Sisters as U.S. Navy Nurses." typescript. Archives of the Holy Cross Sisters, South Bend, Indiana.

Jolly, Ellen Ryan. *Nuns of the Battlefield*. Providence, Rhode Island: Providence Visitor, 1927.

Johnston, Sr. M. Francis. *Builders By the Sea: History of the Ursuline Community of Galveston, Texas*. New York: Exposition Press, 1971.

Kelly, Sr. Rose Anita. *Song of the Hills: The Story of the Sisters of St. Joseph of Wheeling*. Wheeling, WV: Sisters of St. Joseph, 1962.

Kennedy, Hon. Ambrose. "Speech of Hon. Ambrose Kennedy of Rhode Island in the House of Representatives, Mon., Mar. 18, 1918." *Federal Register*. Mar. 18, 1918, 3–39. Washington, D.C.: U.S. Government Publications, 1918.

Lennen, Sr. Mary Isidore. *Milestones of Mercy: Story of the Sisters of Mercy in St. Louis, 1856–1956*. Milwaukee: Bruce, 1956.

Logan, Sr. Eugenia. *The History of the Sisters of Providence of St. Mary of the Woods, Indiana*. 2 vols. Terre Haute, Indiana: Moore-Langen Printing, 1978.

Logue, Sr. Maria Kostka. *Sisters of St. Joseph of Philadelphia: A Century of Growth and Development*. Westminster, MD: The Newman Press, 1950.

Ludey, J. M. "Arkansas Sisters of Mercy in the War." In *Confederate Women of Arkansas in the Civil War, 1861–65*. Little Rock, AR: J. Kellog, 1907, pp. 134–140.

Mackin, Aloysius, OP, ed. "Wartime Scenes from Convent Windows, St. Cecilia, 1860 through 1865." *Tennessee Historical Quarterly* 39 (Dec. 1980): 410–422.

Mallon, Edward A. "Sisters of Charity, St. Joseph's Hospital, 1859–1947." *American Catholic Historical Society Records* 68 (Sept. 1947): 209–213.

McAllister, Anna Shannon. *In Winter We Flourish: Life and Letters of Sarah Worthington King Peter, 1800–1877*. New York: Longmans, Green, 1939.

―――――. *Flame in the Wilderness*. Paterson, NJ: St. Anthony Guild Press, 1944.

McCann, Sr. Mary Agnes. *The History of Mother Seton's Daughters: The Sisters of Charity of Cincinnati, Ohio, 1809–1917*. 3 vols. New York: Longmans, Green, 1917.

McGann, Sr. Agnes Geraldine. *Sisters of Charity of Nazareth in the Apostolate, 1812–1976*. St. Meinrad, IN: Abbey Press, 1976.

McGuire, Mother M. Bernard. *The Story of the Sisters of Mercy in Mississippi, 1860–1930*. New York: P. J. Kennedy and Sons, 1931.

McHale, Sr. M. Jerome. *On The Wind: The Story of the Pittsburgh Sisters of Mercy, 1843–1968.* New York: The Seabury Press, 1980.

Melville, Annabelle. *Elizabeth Bayley Seton, 1774–1821.* New York: Scribner's Sons, 1951.

Metz, Sr. Judith. "150 Years of Caring: The Sisters of Charity of Cincinnati." *The Cincinnati Historical Society Bulletin* 37 (Fall 1979): 151–174.

Mug, Sr. Mary Theodosia. *Lest We Forget, The Sisters of Providence* of *St. Mary of the Woods in Civil War Service.* St. Mary of the Woods, IN: Providence Press, 1931.

O'Connor, Stella. "Charity Hospital at New Orleans: An Administrative and Financial History, 1736–1941." *Louisiana Historical Quarterly* 31 (Jan. 1948): 6–109.

The Petition of the Members of the Legislature of South Carolina to the Congress of the United States in favor of the Sisters of Our Lady of Mercy of Charleston, SC. Charleston, SC: Edward Perry, Printer, 1870.

Rafferty, Sr. Jeanette. *Mercy Hospital, 1847–1972: An Historical Review, Vol. I.* Privately printed typescript.

Roddis, Louis H. "The U.S. Hospital Ship *Red Rover*, 1862–65." *Military Surgeon* 77 (Aug. 1935): 91–98.

Semple, Henry C., ed. *The Ursulines in New Orleans, A Record of Two Centuries, 1729–1925.* New York: Kenedy, 1925.

"A Southern Teaching Order. The Sisters of Mercy of Charleston, SC, A.D. 1829–1904." *American Catholic Historical Records of Philadelphia* 15 (Sept. 1904): 249–265.

Spiritual Writings of Saint Louise de Marillac. Trans. Sr. Louis Sullivan. Albany, NY: De Paul Provincial House, 1984.

Walsh, Sr. Marie DeLourdes. *The Sisters of Charity of New York, 1809–1959.* Vol. I of 3 vols. New York: Fordham University Press, 1960.

Miscellaneous

Campbell, Sr. Anne Francis, OLM. Personal Interview. 12 Feb. 1986.

The Congressional Globe: The Debates and Proceedings of the Second Session of the Thirty-Eighth Congress. City of Washington: Congressional Globe Office, 1865.

The Congressional Globe: The Debates and Proceedings of the Second Session of the Forty-First Congress. City of Washington: Congressional Globe Office, 1870.

The Congressional Globe: The Debates and Proceedings of the Third Session of the Forty-First Congress. City of Washington: Congressional Globe Office, 1871.

The Congressional Globe: The Debates and Proceedings of the First Session of the Forty-Second Congress. City of Washington: Congressional Globe Office, 1871.

Tocqueville, Alexis de. *Democracy in America.* Eds. J. P. Mayer and Max Lerner. New York: Harper and Row, 1966.

US House of Representatives. *The Treatment of Prisoners of War by the Rebel Authorities during the War of the Rebellion,* Report No. 45, Serial No. 1391, Fortieth Congress, Third Session, 1869.

Unpublished Theses and Dissertations

Andrews, Rena M. "Archbishop Hughes and the Civil War." Ph.D. Diss. University of Chicago, 1935.

Campbell, Sr. M. Anne Francis, OLM. "Bishop England's Sisterhood, 1829–1929." Ph.D. Diss. St. Louis University, 1968.

Cavanaugh, William. "The Hospital Activities of the Sisters During the Civil War and Their Influence on the Catholic Hospital System Movement up to 1875." MA thesis. Catholic University of America, 1931.

Gallagher, Sr. Ann Seton. "A Study of the Nursing Activities of Sister Anthony O'Connell." MA thesis. Catholic University of America, 1957.

Gilgannon, Sr. Mary McAuley, RSM. "The Sisters of Mercy as Crimean War Nurses." Ph.D. Diss. University of Notre Dame, 1962.

Hickey, Sr. Zoe. "The Daughters of Charity of St. Vincent de Paul in the Civil War." MA thesis. Catholic University of America, 1943.

Misner, Sr. Barbara, SCSC. "A Comparative Social Study of the Members and Apostolates of the First Eight Permanent Communities of Women Religious within the Boundaries of the United States, 1790–1850." Ph.D. Diss. Catholic University of America, 1981.

Nolan, Charles E. "Carmelite Dreams, Creole Perspectives: The Sisters of Mt. Carmel of Louisiana, 1833–1903." Ph.D. Diss. The Pontifical Gregorian University, Rome, Italy, 1970.

Perkins, Betty. "The Work of the Catholic Sister in the Civil War." MA thesis. University of Dayton, 1969.

Smith, Nina Bennett. "The Women Who Went to War: The Union Army Nurse in the Civil War." Ph.D. diss. Northwestern University, 1981.

Tully, Sr. Angela. "Maryland in the Civil War." MA thesis. Catholic University of America, 1933.

Index

THE
ULTIMATE
GUIDE
FOR
GAY
DADS

Everything You Need to Know About LGBTQ
Parenting But Are (Mostly) Afraid to Ask

ERIC ROSSWOOD

For permission requests, please contact the publisher at:

Mango Publishing Group
2850 Douglas Road, 3rd Floor
Coral Gables, FL 33134 USA
info@mango.bz

For special orders, quantity sales, course adoptions and corporate sales, please email the publisher at sales@mango.bz. For trade and wholesale sales, please contact Ingram Publisher Services at: customer.service@ingramcontent.com or +1.800.509.4887.

Library of Congress Control Number: 2017951054

Eric Rosswood
The Ultimate Guide For Gay Dads: Everything You Need to Know About LGBTQ Parenting But Are (Mostly) Afraid to Ask

ISBN: (paperback) 978-1-63353-491-9, (ebook) 978-1-63353-488-9

BISAC - FAM006000 FAMILY & RELATIONSHIPS / Alternative Family
    - SOC064000 SOCIAL SCIENCE / LGBT Studies / General

Printed in the United States of America

To my husband, Mat.
07-07-07

PRAISE

"This is the parenting book gay dads have been waiting for! It takes the basic information you'll find in other parenting books and enhances it by including things specific to gay dads, like finding LGBT-friendly pediatricians, legal steps to protect your family, examples for how to answer questions like, "Where's the mother?" and tons of other valuable information gay dads will appreciate. If you're a gay dad, or you're going to be one soon, you'll definitely want to add this timely book to your library."
—**Stan J. Sloan, Chief Executive Officer,** *The Family Equality Council*

"A fantastic resource and an entertaining read of essential things that gay/bisexual men should know before becoming dads together." —**Chaz Harris, Co-Author of** *Promised Land*

"*The Ultimate Guide for Gay Dads* is an informative and practical book that covers a lot of the essential parenting tips! It includes advice from many parenting advocates, including professionals and gay dads who have helped pave the way for future gay dads. Rosswood has created a valuable resource and tool that should be read by all gay men considering parenthood. And for the existing gay dads out there, there are plenty of wonderful tidbits in the book for you too!" —**Dr. Ron Holt, best selling author of** *PRIDE: You Can't Heal if You're Hiding From Yourself*

"The journey to parenthood is not easy for anyone. For same-gender couples, this journey embodies many twists and turns that are not often documented or discussed in traditional parenting guides directed towards heterosexuals. Rosswood has created an invaluable resource for parents that not only covers traditional topics such as changing diapers and childproofing the home but also more nuanced topics, including traveling as a same-gender family, navigating birth certificate details, and deciding what your child will call you. Whether you already have kids, are deep in the process of starting a family, or only beginning your journey, you will find yourself referring to this book over and over again." —**J. B. Blankenship, author of** *The Christmas Truck*

"*The Ultimate Guide for Gay Dads* is a soup-to-nuts guide for gay fathers and covers all the small and large issues germane to two parents who are men. From choosing a baby name to selecting a physician, from changing diapers to bringing the right toys for airplane rides, from what to call each other to answering invasive questions, this book answers so many questions a gay dad might not even realize he has about raising kids, from babies to toddlers, from children to adolescents. Real-life examples are peppered throughout the book and offer more than one way of handling the many challenges that come up for parents, especially gay dads who face their own unique hurdles. This fun and accessible guide takes the anxiety out of becoming a gay dad. Told in the spirit of love and joy, this guide would make any gay man consider becoming a parent." —**Kathleen Archambeau, Author of** *Pride & Joy: LGBTQ Artists, Icons and Everyday Heroes and Climbing the Corporate Ladder in High Heels*

Thank you for reading **The Ultimate Guide for Gay Dads**. Gaining exposure as an independent author relies mostly on word-of-mouth, so if you see the value in this book and think others will benefit from reading it too, please consider leaving a short review online.
Thank you.

Contents

Foreword by
Writer, Director,
and Producer,
Greg Berlanti

Since I was a child I knew for certain three things about the adult life I imagined for myself. Most people would call these things dreams or aspirations and perhaps they were just that, hopes disguised as premonitions. But for what it's worth, I can't name any vision for my own future I've experienced before or since with the same degree of clarity and definitiveness. So here they are:

The first thing I was certain of as a kid growing up in New York was that I would spend my adulthood in California, and more specifically, Los Angeles. It wasn't because I wanted to work in the entertainment business, that dream was not yet hatched. When I was thirteen my family took a trip to Hawaii and we got stuck in Los Angeles for a layover for a few hours. I went exploring and came across a "Welcome To Los Angeles" sign above the down escalator into baggage claim. Though I'd never seen the sign before it looked familiar to me. And for a very brief moment, I wondered what it must be like to live in a city like Los Angeles with the beaches and Hollywood and the sunny days and warm nights. "I'll live here one day," I thought to myself. That was it. The dream remained but the memory of the sign drifted to the recesses of my brain until almost a decade later when I got an internship during college for a talent manager in Los Angeles. Upon my arrival at the airport, I saw the very same sign and that childhood memory flashed back along with the same feeling of familiarity. It is the same feeling I've had each of the hundreds of times I've seen the sign since...although now I just call that feeling "home."

The second thing of which I was one thousand percent sure was that my career would involve writing. I wrote a lot as a kid, acted in plays, built puppets and performed puppet shows, and like most Gen-X nerds made short films with my neighbor's first Betamax camera. Whether it was on a theatrical stage or behind a puppet theatre or with a camera on my shoulder, no profession or hobby has ever made me happier than dreaming up and crafting a story for an audience. However it is a craft that never came easy to me and still doesn't. And though I've gotten older, and those plays and puppet shows have become television shows and films that studios actually pay me to write, creating stories has never ever gotten easier. Like most if not all the writers I know, I find there is still nothing more daunting than sitting down to face a blank page. So why do so many of us torture ourselves by choosing a profession that makes us feel inferior for the majority of the time? I can't speak for the others, but for myself, in very fleeting moments where everything works and the story comes together and communicates emotionally exactly what I was feeling or trying to say, in those moments I feel certain, more certain than ever, that I'm doing what I'm supposed to do for a profession. I feel home.

The third and final thing I knew for sure about being a grown-up was that I would have a family. I didn't know if that meant I would have a partner for life. I was so young when I first imagined it, I didn't even know for sure I was gay. But there was never a moment during the time I wrestled with my own sexuality that I ever doubted my desire or capacity to be a parent. As young as I can remember, I read books to kids at the library, I started babysitting in eighth grade, and I was a camp counselor throughout most of high school. I had a very close-knit and wonderful family of my own. My parents, both by design and by example, taught my sister and me that family are the people that love you first and most. They are the ones you mark your life by, the people with whom you first bond and clash (and we clashed a lot) and who help you forge the person you are meant to become. That feeling of boundless love and support from those closest to you, through life's ups and downs, that feeling I was taught is also called home.

Now as fate would have it, all three of my "premonitions" came true. I now live in Los Angeles as a professional writer. As of February of last year I am a parent to our son, Caleb. None of these three things occurred in the time or the manner that I thought they would. For instance, I became a parent much later than I imagined—in my early forties—which was not conveniently the same time that my eyes went and I started developing new aches and pains that my doctor diagnosed as the incurable disease of "middle age." And for all my surety that I would one day be a parent, I've had nothing but questions ever since I became one. Simple questions like what's the best diaper to use on sensitive skin? Or what's the best formula to buy? Or do any sleep routines really work? And I've had more complex questions too, some of which pertain to being a gay parent, like what will our son call my partner, Robbie, and myself? Which of us will he call Dad? (He calls us both Dada by the way. Babies are much smarter than you are at figuring out what they want to do.) And I wonder almost every day if I'm a good enough parent. Robbie is great at changing diapers, dressing Caleb, putting him to sleep, comforting him, making him laugh, soothing him, etc. And I'm great at...delivering a running commentary while Robbie does those things. I wondered before Caleb came if I would feel inferior or be competitive. A weird thought, but something I've since learned is not uncommon amongst parents of the same sex. It's as simple as, "Will he have a favorite Dad?" As it turns out, Caleb doesn't seem to have a favorite Dad. He has no idea I'm not as good at changing him, in fact he seems to equally despise anyone trying to put a shirt on his head. But I do have a favorite parent, it's Caleb's other father. And when I watch the two of them together cuddling or playing, it's hard to describe how happy it makes me feel, so I'll just say again it is that same feeling of home.

I hope this book helps you with some of the many questions you'll have about your own family, I know it helped us. Wherever you're at on the journey to becoming a parent, best of luck to you. If you're still thinking and dreaming about it, don't give up hope. If you're about to become a parent, why are you reading this book—go get some sleep! And if you already are a Dad or a Mom, congratulations on fulfilling what was no doubt a life's dream of having a family and a home of your own. You are the luckiest person you've ever met. And so is your kid.

Greg Berlanti
Writer, Director, Producer

Introduction

Congratulations! You've decided to become a dad. You'll soon be entering a brand new world filled with fun and exciting adventures. This is a big moment for you and your family, one that will change your life forever.

Now, parenting is a big, life-altering challenge filled with many ups and downs. There's so much involved with caring for children that an enormous number of books have been written on the topic. A quick search for "parenting" on Amazon brings up more than two hundred and thirty thousand results! There are even entire degrees that revolve around child development. All this sounds like a lot to take in, but the good news is that much of parenting is instinct. Believe it or not, you'll probably know exactly what you need to do when you need to do it, and when you're not sure, there will be plenty of support out there to help you along the way: from your parents and doctors, to Google and, yes, even this book.

Now, I know what you may be thinking: "If so much of parenting is instinct, why do I need to read this book?" The answer is simple really. Parenting as a gay dad is different. "But isn't being a 'gay' parent just like being a 'straight' parent?" Well, yes and no. While it's true that gay parents do all the same things that straight parents do (change baby diapers, feed their children, do their laundry, take them to and from school, help them with their homework, read them stories, kiss their boo-boos, tuck them in at night, etc.), there are many situations that are unique to LGBT parents. For example, having to find LGBT-friendly doctors and schools, asking for paternity leave from work when you're not out to your employer, getting both parents' names on your child's birth certificate, and dealing with nosy, prying questions from just about everyone, everywhere.

One huge parenting difference for gay men is that having a kid is like coming out all over again on a daily basis, especially if you have an infant. Was coming out stressful for you? It's about to get more intense, and you will have a child watching your every move and listening to your every word. If you stutter or pause when responding to prying questions about your family, your children may pick up on you being uncomfortable, and they could start feeling like something is wrong about their family unit. So yes, while "straight parenting" and "gay parenting" are the same, being a gay dad is different and has its own set of unique challenges. That's why I decided to write *The Ultimate Guide for Gay Dads: Everything You Need to Know About Parenting But Are (Mostly) Afraid to Ask.*

This book is a direct follow-up to my previous book, *Journey to Same-Sex Parenthood: Firsthand Advice, Tips and Stories from Lesbian and Gay Couples*, which covered adoption, foster care, surrogacy, assisted reproduction, and co-parenting to help LGBT people make the best decision for expanding their own families. If you are looking to have children but haven't yet decided how you want to start your family, I recommend starting with that book first. *The Ultimate Guide for Gay Dads* picks up where that one left off and covers what happens when and after you welcome a child into your home.

While writing *The Ultimate Guide for Gay Dads*, I talked to doctors, educators, lawyers, and other dads to create a comprehensive book that covers the critical things you should know. I believe this is the perfect supplement to all those other parenting books out there, because it fills in the gaps with information specifically for us gay dads and leaves out all of the irrelevant info. You're not going to find information on how to best aim your nipple into your baby's mouth for breastfeeding. That wouldn't help you feed your baby, and you'd probably get hair in his or her mouth anyway. No—this book specifically covers the basics you need to know and includes a few things you might even be afraid to ask.

Whether you're a gay man welcoming a newborn, adopting an older child, or starting a relationship with someone who already has kids, this book is for you. Now take a deep breath and relax, because you've got this. You're going to be an awesome dad.

The Things About Parenthood No One Tells You About

We've all heard it before. The long list of things people tell you will change when you have kids. You won't be able to go out with your friends anymore. You won't ever sleep again. Your life will revolve around diapers, poop, pee, and puke. They either tell you how much your life is going to suck or how awesome it's going to be. Oh, you're going to have such a cute kid. You'll be able to get them cool clothes, wear matching outfits, throw the best birthday parties...blah, blah, blah. When the news gets out that you're going to have kids, it seems like everyone will want to tell you how they think your life is going to change. But the funny thing is that there are a lot of things that happen when you become a dad that no one tells you about. Here's a list of a few things you should probably know:

1. When you have a baby or toddler, you're going to get kicked in the balls...a lot. Seriously, like all the time. You turn into a play structure and will be climbed on, jumped on, body-slammed, head-butted, and more. Not only will your little dangly bits get kicked, but they'll also get punched, elbowed, kneed, and grabbed. Your kids won't know any better. It'll just be an accident when they're trying to play, but it will be an accident that happens over and over again. Other times, your kid may want to crawl into bed with you when they're sick or they've had a nightmare. Good luck keeping their knees, feet, and elbows still while they're sleeping. Maybe you should invest in an athletic cup.

2. The dad bod is real! Yes, guys with kids gain weight too! Researchers at Northwestern University's Feinberg School of Medicine tracked more than ten thousand men over a twenty-year period: they found that dads experienced an average 2.6 percent increase in their BMI ("Body Mass Index," a measurement of body fat based on a person's

weight in relation to their height), while similar men without kids actually slightly lost weight over the same period. For a six-foot-tall man, this worked out to be an average of 4.4 pounds of dad bod, while a similar man without kids lost an average of 1.4 pounds. This gain in weight may be the result of lifestyle changes, such as family becoming a priority over the gym or eating food off your child's plate when they don't finish. You and your partner may find that you like each other better with a little more junk in the trunk and a little more to hold on to, but if you don't want your weight to fluctuate, be conscious of this beforehand so you can make a better effort to stay healthy. Maybe take turns going to the gym while the other watches the children. If you're someone who likes to cook, maybe come up with a menu plan so that you have healthier options available to eat throughout the week. You can also search for "dad workout with baby" on YouTube to get a few exercise ideas. If nothing else, you'll see a bit of eye candy and can pretend you have the ability to lose weight just by watching.

3. Believe it or not, women are not the only ones who go through neurological and hormonal changes. Men actually go through these changes when they become parents too. Research shows that fathers who are more involved with their children experience a dramatic drop in testosterone and an increase in oxytocin, a hormone that acts as a neurotransmitter in the brain and influences social behavior and emotion. The more interaction fathers have with their children (responding to their baby's cries, playing with their kids, etc.) the stronger the effect. So if you find yourself questioning your sanity after listening to a sappy Top 40 pop ballad

and going through an uncontrollable crying spell because your child's whole life is flashing before your eyes and you think they are growing up too fast even though they're only six months old...don't worry. Your emotional breakdown probably won't last very long.

4. You might not feel an emotional bond right away. Some parents feel a massive rush of love when they hold their child for the first time; there's an immediate connection and the bond is instantaneous. Other parents feel absolutely nothing, and that's OK. For some people, the bond grows over time, as more interaction occurs. Don't freak out or feel guilty if you don't feel the immediate love.

5. There's a chance that you're going to get frustrated with the lack of changing tables available in men's restrooms because many places still limit them to women's restrooms only. When there are no changing stations available, dads are forced to change their baby's diapers on other surfaces (such as dirty bathroom floors or counters), and those unsanitary conditions can pose health risks. Plus, limiting these stations to women's restrooms isn't just a burden on male parents. It's also a casual reinforcement of sexism, hinting that it's a woman's responsibility to take care of children. In 2015, Ashton Kutcher famously launched a Change. org petition asking Costco and Target to stop gender stereotyping and to make changing stations available to fathers too. The petition gained over one hundred thousand signatures and resulted in both stores committing to making a change.

6. If you have an infant, you're going to be changing clothes multiple times a day. Not just your baby's

clothes, but yours as well. There's no escaping it. Even if you use a burping cloth during feeding, you're going to get spit-up and vomit everywhere! It'll get on your shirt, your pants, your shoes, in your hair, on your face and arms. Absolutely everywhere. Unless you want to bask in vomit all day, you're going to want to change. I suggest putting your designer clothes in storage for a year so they won't get ruined…that is, if you still fit into them. (See number two, above.)

7. Speaking of "number two"—if you have an infant, poop is going to take over your life in a way you never imagined. It's not just about how many smelly diapers you're going to be changing. You might even monitor how often your baby poops, the consistency, the smell, etc. You'll have poop horror stories like when your baby shits so hard it exits the top of their diaper and shoots all the way up to their shoulder blades. Or maybe your baby's feet touch his or her butt during a diaper change, and poo goes flying all across the room as they rapidly kick their feet. And yes, it's disgusting. No one likes dealing with it or cleaning it up, but you know what? You'll have great stories to tell, and trust me—you'll be dying to tell them.

8. Building blocks, both large and small, will become your mortal enemy. No matter how hard you and your kids try to clean up, by some mystical magical force, chances are that you will probably manage to find a stray one by accidentally stepping on it with your bare feet. And it will hurt like hell. When this moment occurs, your child will hear you and learn the art of stringing multiple cusswords together.

9. Your child learns to react to things by watching how you react to things. Parenting can be stressful, but if you show that you're stressed, chances are your child will mimic that stress. Take the example above, where the baby is kicking poop everywhere during a diaper change. You may be thinking, "Oh my god! It's getting everywhere, all over the walls and I can't stop it! Ahhhhhhh!" Your baby can pick up on the tone of your voice and your body language. If they pick up that you're stressed, they will probably start crying and screaming uncontrollably until you calm down. It's easier said than done, but try to remain calm when your baby is crying. You could try to ignore the chaos by focusing on singing a nursery rhyme or something. Or if poop is still flying around, maybe it's best to keep your mouth closed and hum the song instead so that you don't have to wash your mouth out later.

10. If you have an infant, keep in mind that about 80 percent of must-have baby products are worthless. You don't need a pee blocker, laundry detergent specially made for babies, or different wipes for butts, pacifiers, and boogers. Don't fall for clever marketing that will clutter your house and leave a hole in your wallet. Just stick with the basics. For a full list of recommended baby products and a list of gimmicks you can avoid, see page 70.

11. You will get looks from women every time you go out in public alone with an infant. Some will stand back and stare at you, watching your every move. Some will boldly approach you and ask where the baby's mother is. They may be suspicious, thinking you've kidnapped the child; or they may have admiration for you, thinking you're helping your "wife" by taking the baby out for a bit and doing

the grocery shopping. Some may even feel sorry
for you, thinking you need help—because a man
can't possibly know how to take care of a baby. I'm
not making these reasons up either: they are things
women have actually said to me in public when
I was out with my infant son. I'm not sure if it's a
maternal instinct or what, but I've never had a male
react the same way to me. Be prepared for these
awkward situations and see page 191 for ideas on
how to handle awkward situations and questions
from people.

REAL-LIFE STORY:
"When we were out with our kids or another set of
gay dads, various women felt absolutely no restriction
keeping them from invading our space or addressing
our children directly without even making eye contact
with us. One time, we were at a restaurant with another
gay dad family. A woman at the next table came over
and starting making baby noises to my friend's son.
She then picked him up without asking and tried to
walk him around the restaurant. If the gender roles
have been reversed, the cops would have been called."
–Rob Watson

12. Tons of people are going to want to give you advice
on how to take care of your children, even people
who aren't parents. Keep this in mind, though: every
child is different, so what works for one kid may
not necessarily work for another kid. Even with your
own children, what worked for your first child may
not work for your second or third. Most of parenting

is trial and error. Trust your instincts. You know your kids best, and you'll figure out what works best for them. Take suggestions if you want to, but don't feel like you have to listen to everything other people say. 90 percent of parenting advice is nonsense, except for what's in this book. This book is filled with fabulous information you can't live without, and even if you don't agree, you can still get some use out of it as a booster seat or doorstop or something. It also makes a great fashion accessory for your morning commute.

Coming Out as a Gay Parent

Do you remember coming out of the closet? Were you anxious and maybe a bit paranoid? Did it take you a while to get comfortable in your own skin? Well, get ready for all of those emotions to come flooding back. Having a kid is like coming out all over again, on a daily basis—especially if you have an infant. Strangers everywhere, from people in line at the grocery store to those working behind the counter at the dry cleaners, will want to tell you how cute your baby is...and then they'll want to know where his or her mother is. As your child gets older, you'll be coming out to their teachers, coaches, friends, the parents of their friends, and more.

In the beginning, if you have an infant or toddler, you may be able to control the conversation and choose how you'll respond to prying questions from strangers (See page 189). While you're waiting in the checkout line, do you want to go into the whole story about how your child was conceived and/or how your family was created, or do you just want to pay for your groceries and go home? Also, there may be times where you're not sure if the environment you're in is LGBT friendly. If that's the case, maybe you don't want to go into too many details.

When you have a toddler, or an older child who is able to speak, they may even be the ones outing you. They might be jumping up and down with joy to talk about their two dads, and the younger they are, the fewer filters they'll have. I'm not saying that you shouldn't be proud of being a gay dad. To the contrary, I think you should be out, proud, and loud, and we should foster an environment where our children are proud of their families too. All I'm saying is that having a kid is like adding a spotlight to your being gay, and before you just had to worry about yourself. Now you have to think about your little one too, and they'll be watching your every move. If you stutter or pause when responding to prying questions about your family, your children may pick up on you being uncomfortable, and they could start feeling that something is wrong with their family unit. So be ready for it, and practice what you're going to say and do before you get asked the questions. Talk to your family and friends about it too, so they know how to respond when your child is present.

GAY MEN TALKING ABOUT HOW VISIBLE THEY ARE AS DADS

"The three of us going out in public together is like putting a neon sign above our heads that says: GAY DADS. We get the stares; most are welcoming, but we have had a few judgmental glares. It's strange, going from being a couple that would not draw much attention (if any), to being a family that everyone notices. I knew prior to adopting that we would have to be out and proud because we would be more obvious, but I didn't expect it to be as much as it has been. We talked to our family about being proud of who we are because if we act ashamed of our family, our daughter will grow up feeling the same way. I've had a few arguments with my mom for telling her neighbors that I have a wife, and we can't have anyone showing our daughter that our family is less than any other."
—Chad Scanlon

"I'm divorced now, so people just see me and my son together, not two gay dads and a kid. Our son was three years old when we separated, and people don't really ask me prying questions anymore. We're lucky because we live in an accepting community, but I will say, though, airports are where it always got weird. There were lots of stares from people. I'm the type of person who just stares

right back. I literally don't stop until you look away."
—**Frank Lowe**

"At our daughters' former nursery school, we were the
only LGBT-headed family. During the second year with
the school, I arrived late to an All Parents Meeting. It was
standing room only, so I stood in the doorway near the
front of the room. Everyone in the meeting was facing in
my direction. A new parent had stood to ask the question,
'Have we done outreach to try and diversify attendance?
For example, have we reached out to LGBT-parented
families?' Every head immediately swung around and
looked right at me, standing there at the front of the room.
I just slowly raised my hand and, with a sheepish smile,
said, 'Um, that would be me?'"
—**Bill Delaney**

"The questions have decreased drastically since Harper
has been able to speak in complete sentences, and
because she is determined to talk to everyone. She does
not grasp the concept of 'stranger danger,' unless you
are dressed as the Easter Bunny. We are now 'outed'
everywhere we go. Whether we're at the hardware store,
our bank, or the TSA line—everyone knows that Harper
has two dads. Harper either tells everyone, 'This is my
dada and this is my daddy,' or she will quickly correct
someone, with sass, if they make a comment about her
daddy, and they are talking to Matthew."
—**Trey Darnell**

"Neither of us likes to harp on what we can't change. We
are visible. When we go out someplace, we are different
and people let us know that—whether they are asking kind
but inappropriate questions, or just staring and gawking at
us. At some point it will just be. Don't get me wrong, most

everyone is kind to us and genuinely curious."
—**Duke Nelson**

"As a gay man, I feel I had to learn not to care about what people thought about me. Holding hands in public, a slow dance with my college boyfriend, a kiss in public...I've found that attitude serves me as a dad too. Whether I was changing a diaper in public, walking around in a freshly soiled shirt, or dealing with a tantrum, I feel being gay prepared me to ignore the gazes of strangers."
—**Ian Hart**

Name-Calling

When straight people have a baby together, it's pretty much assumed that one of them is going to be called mom and the other will be called dad. Or mother and father. Or something else similar, based on societal norms. But what happens when a child has two dads? Can a kid refer to both of his or her parents as dad? The short answer is yes. People can choose whatever names they want for themselves. Chris and Josh may find that using the names "Daddy Chris" and "Daddy Josh" works for them and their family. Other parents may decide they want to assume a more unique name that differentiates them from each other, and that's fine too. It's all going to boil down to personal preference. What do you want to be called? If you haven't decided on a name for yourself yet, here is a list of various synonyms for a male parent.

- Dad
- Dada (Dadda)
- Daddy
- Father
- Poppy
- Pop
- Pops
- Pa
- Papa
- Papi
- Pappy

If you're still having trouble picking a name for yourself, or if you just want to be more creative, here is a list for how the word "dad" is translated in various different languages.

Language	Translation
Afrikaans	Vader; Pa
Albanian	Baba; Atë
Basque	Aita
Bosnian	Otac; Tata
Catalan	Pare
Croatian	Otac; Tata
Czech	Táto; Otec
Danish	Far
Dutch	Vader; Papa

Esperanto	Patro
Estonian	Isa
Filipino	Ama; Tatay; Itay;
Finnish	Isä
French	Papa
Frisian	Heit
Galician	Pai
German	Papa; Vater
Greek	Bampás
Hawaiian	Makuakāne
Hindi	Pita
Hungarian	Apa; Apu; Papa; Edesapa
Icelandic	Pabbi; Faðir
Indonesian	Ayah; Pak
Irish	Athair; Daidí
Italian	Babbo; Papà
Japanese	Otōsan; Papa
Korean	Appa
Latin	Pater
Latvian	Tēvs
Lithuanian	Tèvas
Luxembourgish	Papp
Malay	Bapa
Maltese	Missier
Norwegian	Pappa; Far
Polish	Tata; Ojciec
Portuguese	Papai; Pai
Romanian	Tata
Russian	Papa
Samoan	Tama
Scots Gaelic	Athair
Serbian	Tata
Shona	Baba
Slovak	Ocko; Otec

Spanish	Padre; Papá,
Swahili	Baba
Swedish	Pappa
Vietnamese	Cha
Welsh	Tad

The list above is not a full list, but it gives you a good idea of what's out there. If you are curious about more languages, or the pronunciations of any of the words above, Google Translate is a great resource.

DID YOU KNOW?

In a 2005 interview with Rolling Stone, while promoting Star Wars: Episode III - Revenge of the Sith, George Lucas explained that there is a special meaning behind Darth Vader's name. He was quoted as saying, "'Darth' is a variation of dark. And 'Vader' is a variation of father. So it's basically Dark Father. All the names have history, but sometimes I make mistakes—Luke was originally going to be called Luke Starkiller, but then I realized that wasn't appropriate for the character. It was appropriate for Anakin, but not his son. I said, 'Wait, we can't weigh this down too much—he's the one that redeems him.'"

> **REAL-LIFE STORY:**
> "We were going to do 'dad' and 'papa,' but that's not what
> our kids wanted to call us. We adopted our son when
> he was five years old, and he just started calling me
> 'daddy' and my husband 'dad'. When we later adopted
> his sister, she called us by the same names her brother
> used." –Jay Foxworthy

CHOOSING BABY NAMES

If you've thought about becoming a father, chances are
that you've probably had a few baby names floating
around inside you head. Maybe you've discussed names
with your partner and have jotted them down on a list
somewhere. Maybe the perfect name came to you in
the middle of the night. Should you go with something
unique and cool, or should you stick with something more
traditional? If you adopt an older child who already has a
name, you don't have to worry about any of this, but if you
are adopting a baby from birth, you're going to have to
pick a name for your baby, and it might not be as easy as
you think.

What If You Don't Get to Choose?

For example, if you are going through open adoption,
there's a chance the child's birthmother will want to
choose the name because it's something she can provide
for her baby. There's a lot to think about in this scenario.
If the birthmother wants to name the baby, will you keep
the name, or will you legally change it later, perhaps
when you finalize the adoption and get an updated birth

certificate? Before doing this, think about the impact this will have on your child growing up. Is there a possibility they will think you took a piece of their identity away from them?

Even if the birthmother wants to name the baby, that doesn't necessarily mean you can't be involved. Maybe naming can be a joint effort. Since people typically have three names (first, middle, and last), perhaps the birthmother would be open to choosing the middle name and letting you choose the first and last. There are many possibilities and things to consider.

What about the Last Name?

Speaking of last names, how will you choose one for your baby? If you and your partner have different last names, what will the last name of your baby be? Will he or she take one of your names, and if so, which one? Will the baby take both of your last names, and if so, will you hyphenate them? Which one will be first?

My husband and I never had to consider the last name scenarios because we combined our last names when we got married. My last name used to be Ross and his was Wood. We combined them to Rosswood and our son was given our last name when he was born. We feel that all of us having the same last name strengthens our family unit, but that's just us. You'll have to decide what works best for you and your family.

Teasing with Acronyms

Now, when choosing names for your child, it's important to take many things into consideration in order to limit the chances of them getting teased down the road. For example, what will the initials spell? Ashley Summer Smith would probably be referred to as an ASS, making high school a living hell. Daniel Ivan Kennedy would probably be called a dick; Trevor Ian Thompson would be called a TIT. But it's not just naughty words you have to consider. My name used to be Eric Alan Ross and my initials spelled EAR. Kids in school used to tease me by flapping their ears like Dumbo when talking about me. Also, names on school lists are often put in order by Last, First, Middle initial, so mine was listed as Ross, Eric A. Whenever I had a new teacher, or if there was a substitute, they would call out "Erica" during roll call. Since I was openly gay in school, everyone in class would laugh and use it as an opportunity to make fun of me for being gay. Kids are cruel.

Spelling

There are more than acronyms to take into consideration when it comes to teasing. I'm sure we've all seen the picture of the cake online that was supposed to say "HAPPY BIRTHDAY CLINT," but the letters were too close together so CLINT wound up looking like CUNT. If you haven't seen the picture, just Google "Clint birthday cake." I'm sure Clint was thrilled when he saw it. Best birthday ever.

Rhyming

Just when you think you've found the perfect name, you might want to run it through the rhyming test. If the name can be rhymed with something bad, making your child a target for teasing later in life, you might want to hold off and think about it a bit more. Here are a few examples of names that can turn into rhyming nightmares for your child.

- Cooper the pooper
- Jude the prude or Jude in the nude
- Tucker fucker
- Esther the molester
- Scabby Abby
- Colin colon
- Lucas mucus
- Lydia chlamydia

In the end, it's important to remember that kids will eventually get teased about something in their lives no matter what. Teasing is a fact of life and there's nothing we can do to prevent our kids from ever being teased, but we can raise them to be strong. In the end, if there's a name you're dead set on, it's up to you whether you want to use it.

Shh! It's a Secret.

One last thing when it comes to baby names. Keep in mind that if you mention any of the names you're considering to friends, family members, coworkers, etc., you are inviting people to give you advice, solicited or not. Unless you want it to become a debate, you may want to keep the list of names to yourself.

Taking Time Off Work

Am I Legally Allowed to Take Time off from Work When I Have Children?

According to the United States Department of Labor, at the time of this publication, the Family and Medical Leave Act (FMLA) entitles an eligible employee to take up to twelve workweeks of job-protected unpaid leave when they welcome a new child as part of their family. Some states have similar laws that may apply to more employers than FMLA does. This includes the birth of a baby via surrogacy, both domestic and foreign adoptions, and the placement of a child through foster care. Even though this family leave is unpaid, employers are required to continue employee healthcare coverage during this period.

Your employer may require that you use your saved vacation days and any other paid leave first, but that leave will not count towards your FMLA leave. So, if your employer requires you to take two weeks of paid vacation, you may still take an additional twelve weeks of unpaid FMLA leave (fourteen weeks total: two weeks of paid vacation, plus twelve weeks of unpaid FMLA leave).

Some states also offer some sort of paid family leave. At the time of this publication, only California, New Jersey, New York, Rhode Island, Washington, and the District of Columbia (starting in 2020) require paid family leave—but other states may quickly follow. Some companies have even added paid family leave as an employment benefit to become more competitive, even though the state they are in does not require it. Check with your employer to see what benefits you qualify for.

Can I Be Fired or Demoted for Taking Time off under FMLA?

Technically, your company cannot legally discriminate against you for taking qualified time off under FMLA. They are required to give you back your original job when you return or give you a new position with equivalent pay, benefits, and terms and conditions of employment. However things are not always cut-and-dried.

"More than half the states do not have explicit laws protecting employees from discrimination based on sexual orientation or gender identity," explains Cathy Sakimura, Deputy Director & Family Law Director for the National Center for Lesbian Rights, "although both federal and state anti-discrimination laws prohibiting discrimination based on sex should apply to protect LGBT workers."

So while a company can't technically fire you for taking time off under FMLA, some may try to get away with firing you if they find out you're in a same-sex relationship. If you are not out at work, and/or you fear you might be retaliated against for being LGBT, seek the advice of a lawyer before giving your employer information about your family expansion plans.

What If I Am Not Out at Work?

As mentioned above, over half of the states do not have laws that explicitly protect employees from discrimination based on sexual orientation and gender identity, so not everyone has the luxury of being out at work. If you want to take a leave of absence from your job, talk to a lawyer before telling your employer about your plans. Otherwise, you could always save up your vacation time and take a couple of weeks off instead of FMLA or state family leave, although that won't give you very much time to bond with your child.

Even if you don't plan on taking time off, consider what happens after you welcome a new child into your home. Do you need to add your child to the health insurance you have through work? If so, there's paperwork to fill out and someone in HR will have to process it.

Also, keep in mind that if you tell anyone at work that you are having children, or already have kids, they are probably going to ask you about your "wife" or the "baby mama." This could open up prying questions about your relationship status and your home life. Think long and hard about how you want to respond to these questions and what cans of worms you are comfortable opening.

While not impossible, it may be hard for you to keep it a secret that you have kids after you actually have them. You may need to rush home early to pick them up from school if they get sick, you may need to take time off to take them to doctor appointments, or something else may come up where your kids take precedence.

What Are Some of the Concerns Men Have for Taking Parental Leave?

In 2016, Deloitte and KRC Research conducted a parental leave study with an online poll of one thousand employed adults across America with access to employer benefits. They found that fewer than half of the respondents felt their company fostered an environment in which men were comfortable taking parental leave. While 64 percent of workers surveyed said that companies should offer men and women the same amount of parental leave, 54 percent felt their colleagues would judge a father who took the same amount of parental leave as a mother. The study also found that more than one-third of respondents felt that taking parental leave would jeopardize their position, more than half felt that it would be perceived as a lack of commitment to the job, and 41 percent felt that they would lose opportunities on projects.

In addition to the findings by Deloitte, the Toronto University's Rotman School of Management released a report in 2013 showing that involved fathers were looked down on by their colleagues and treated worse at work than men who stuck closer to "traditional gender norms." There is good news though: more and more men are choosing to take parental leave as more and more companies are offering it as a benefit. It also helps crush stereotypes when executives lead by example. Mark Zuckerberg, CEO of Facebook, made national headlines when he took a leave of two months following the birth of his daughter and Chad Dickerson, former CEO of Etsy, took nine weeks off when he adopted his son. When top executives take family leave, it demonstrates the company's values through actions and not just words.

How Can I Make Taking Time off Work Easier?

Many people fear that taking extended time off from work will be disruptive, so here are a few tips to make things as easy as possible:

1. **Tell Your Company Early** – Make sure you tell your company early so that you can work together to

come up with a transition plan, and so other team members can seamlessly fill in while you're gone.

2. **Be as Transparent as You Think You Can Be** – Births are not always on time, and you may be in a situation where you have to leave at a moment's notice. Or maybe you'll have to fly to another state to meet a birthmother a few months beforehand. Keep your employer aware of such possibilities if you can.

3. **Create a Plan** – Work with your supervisors and peers to come up with a handoff plan so that things will work seamlessly while you're on leave. Make sure everyone on your team knows who is covering what part of your job and whom they should contact if they need help.

4. **Talk to Other Fathers** – If there are other fathers at your company who have taken family leave, don't be afraid to reach out to them and talk to them about their experience. Ask them how it went and whether they have any advice on how to make the experience easier for you.

What Should I Do If I Feel Like I'm Being Discriminated Against?

If you believe that your rights under the FMLA have been violated, you can file a complaint with the Department of Labor by going to www.wagehour.dol.gov. Before doing anything though, you may want to consult with a lawyer. Lambda Legal, the National Center for Lesbian Rights (NCLR), American Civil Liberties Union (ACLU), and GLBT Legal Advocates & Defenders (GLAD) all help fight for LGBT equality in courts and have lists of attorneys who are LGBT friendly. They can provide legal information and contact information for attorneys in your area.

If I Become a Stay-At-Home-Dad, Will It Be Hard for Me to Re-enter the Work Force?

The number of stay-at-home dads has slowly been increasing over the last few decades. According to the Pew Research Center, there were roughly 280,000 men who stayed at home with their kids in the 1970s. That number increased to 550,000 in the first decade of this century. The study analyzed data collected in the Current Population Survey (CPS), conducted by the US Census Bureau and the Bureau of Labor Statistics. The data only included married couples with children where at least one spouse worked a minimum of 35 hours a week—and since the US federal government did not recognize marriage equality until 2015, the study did not take same-sex couples into consideration. The fact still remains the same though. As time goes by, more and more fathers are choosing to stay at home with their kids.

So what is it like for these fathers when they try to re-enter the work force? Unfortunately, many of these men find it difficult to find jobs. There's a stereotype out there that women who stay at home with the kids are caring, while men who choose to do the same thing are putting family over their careers and don't have the drive or dedication needed to fill leadership positions. Hopefully this stereotype will go away as more men choose to be stay-at-home dads—but until then, here are a few steps you can take to make it easier for you to re-enter the work force when you're ready:

1. Stay connected with your industry contacts. They can be references for you down the road.

2. Read articles, take night courses, volunteer, or do anything else that can help keep your skills up-to-date.

3. Keep networking and stay well-informed on the job market in your area.

4. Keep your LinkedIn profile up to date and let your connections know you are looking for work. Ask them whether they know of any job openings, and if they can help you get an interview.

Protecting Your Family

Why Should the Names of Both Parents Be Listed on a Child's Birth Certificate?

So what's the big deal with putting the names of both same-sex parents on a child's birth certificate anyway? Birth certificates are solely for identifying genealogical heritage, right? Wrong! Parents are often required to produce birth certificates to establish parental rights and/ or to prove they have the authority to take action on their child's behalf. If a same-sex parent is not listed on their child's birth certificate, it can sometimes prevent them from doing things like authorizing critical medical treatment or performing basic tasks such as enrolling their child in daycare, school, or extracurricular activities. Having both parents' names on a birth certificate can help provide LGBT couples and their children the privacy, dignity, security, support, and protections that are given to married opposite-sex couples and their children.

Can a State Refuse to Put Both of Our Names on Our Child's Birth Certificate?

They used to, but now every state must put both same-sex spouses on their child's birth certificate. Marisa and Terrah Pavan, a legally married lesbian couple living in Arkansas, gave birth to a baby girl in 2015 via an anonymous sperm donor; however, the Arkansas Department of Health refused to issue Marisa's name on the birth certificate and listed Terrah as the only parent. Leigh and Jana Jacobs, another legally married lesbian couple living in Arkansas, were also denied their request to add both of their names to their son's birth certificate when he was born.

At the time, a husband of a married woman was automatically listed as the father even if he was not the genetic parent—but that was not the case for same-sex spouses. So, with the help of the NCLR, the two couples sued for equal rights and won. In June 2017, the US Supreme Court ruled that states must treat married same-sex couples equally when issuing birth certificates and that this equal treatment was required by Obergefell v. Hodges, the 2015 marriage equality case.

"All states put the woman who gives birth on the child's birth certificate," says Sakimura, "unless the state allows surrogacy or there has been an adoption or other court order. This means that two gay dads—or a single gay dad—can be on the birth certificate if they used surrogacy in a state where that is allowed or they adopt."

Does My Name on My Child's Birth Certificate Give Me Full Legal Parental Rights?

Even if you are legally married, and both of your names are on your child's birth certificate, a birth certificate doesn't guarantee you will be protected if your parental rights are challenged in court. Because of this, it's important that all non-biologically related parents protect themselves by doing an adoption, or by getting a court order. If you have an adoption or court order recognizing that you are a parent, the law should treat you and your family like everyone else. If you are unmarried, you need an adoption or court order even more, because most unmarried parents who are not both biological parents cannot be on the birth certificate any other way. If you have any questions about your parental rights, you should consult a family lawyer.

What Else Can I Do to Legally Protect My Family?

Everyone, regardless of their sexual orientation or gender identity, should have a will in place to protect their families. A will should name all beneficiaries and be detailed in listing what you want to happen in the event that you are no longer able to care for your child due to death or injury.

Let's Go Shopping!

Yay! Isn't it great to have an excuse to go shopping? How much fun is it going to be to pick out adorable baby clothes, a decked-out stroller, and a cute, stylish diaper bag that's different from all the others and basically shouts out to everyone, "I'm the coolest, most fashionable daddy in the world"?

Stop right there! Hold on! While you may have mastered going to the mall and picking out fashionable clothes for yourself, navigating a baby store is a whole different monster, filled with gimmicky, money-sucking products around every corner. The packaging tells you that you need this item to keep your baby safe or to make a basic parenting routine easier. Do you really need a bathtub thermometer? How about baby kneepads to protect your child's knees while they're learning how to crawl? Protection is good, right? Check out the lists below to see what kind of products you really need and which ones you can live without.

Must-Have Products for New Babies

Car Seat – This goes without saying. They're required by law every time you drive somewhere with a child in the car, and hospitals won't even let you take your baby home without one. There are three stages of car seats for growing children: rear-facing (for infants), forward-facing, and booster seat. Convertible car seats are also available with the benefit of being specially designed to safely convert from a rear-facing to a forward-facing position.

When purchasing a car seat, make sure you get one that meets the Federal Motor Vehicle Safety Standards (FMVSS), and that you choose the correct seat for your child's age, height, and weight. The manuals for the seats will have the height and weight specifications; this information will most likely be found on the actual seat itself. Infants will need a rear-facing car seat—in fact, the American Academy of Pediatrics recommends that children ride in rear-facing seats for as long as possible.

Diapers – You're going to use a lot of these, so stock up...but not until you're 100 percent sure what size your baby will be wearing. The size of the diaper your baby wears will depend on his or her weight. While you may think a newborn baby will automatically need to wear a newborn-sized diaper, if he or she winds up being born at 10½ pounds, they're going to look like they're wearing a Speedo. It's best to buy a small pack of diapers for the first round, and then stock up once you know for sure what the correct size is.

TIP:
You'll have to buy diapers often, and the boxes can be big and bulky, taking up a lot of space in your car. The box might be difficult to carry back into the house when you're carrying a little one as well. If possible, consider ordering diapers and other big, bulky items online so they are delivered straight to your door.

Wipes – You will need plenty of these during diaper changes, but they're not just for butts! Wipes have many other uses too. You can use them to clean faces, hands, clothes, counters, and many other things. Wipes will become your new best friend. They come in a variety of scents, scent-free, and hypoallergenic versions. Keep stashes in various places around the house (bathrooms, baby's room, kitchen, etc.) and never leave home without them.

Baby Clothes – Obviously your baby is going to need something to wear, but what exactly do you need to buy, and how many of each item should you get? Be aware that babies grow fast, so there's a chance that your child could move up to the next size before they even get an opportunity to wear what you bought. Think about it. Baby sizes are 0–3 months, 3–6 months, 6–9 months, and 9–12 months. You're basically buying a whole new wardrobe every season! That can get expensive quick, so here are a few tricks to help you avoid needing to take out a second mortgage:

TIP:
You may have the urge to buy stylish designer outfits. Keep in mind that babies grow fast, and you'll wind up spending a lot of money for something your baby will only wear a couple of times–maybe even just once! Unless you want to get a designer outfit for a photo shoot, consider skipping it to save money.

---

1. Keep all your receipts and the tags on the clothes, until you're ready for your baby to wear the clothes you've bought. Even though you may have the urge to wash everything and put them in the dresser right away, try not to do this if you can. This way, you can return things if your baby grows out of them before he or she can wear them.

2. Buy a size up. Babies grow fast, so they'll be able to wear those larger-sized outfits in no time.

3. See what the clothes are made out of. The more cotton a piece of clothing has, the more it's going to shrink—so even if you buy the right size, it may not fit after you wash it.

4. Convenience and practicality should come before style, always! This may be one of the most difficult things, but try as hard as you can to resist the urge to buy clothing just because it's cute. Nothing is worse than waking up in the middle of the night to change a poopy diaper while in zombie mode, and then being stuck there with a screaming, squirming baby for what seems like forever because you can't unbutton their clothes. Why spend money on something that you'll never even want to put on your baby because it just frustrates you? At the end of the day, you're not going to care how cute that little sailor outfit is, even though it came with an adorable matching hat and tiny little socks. If it doesn't give you easy access for diaper changes, forget it!

5. Don't forget hand-me-downs. Many people store baby items after their children outgrow them and then give these things to other people in the community who have recently had children. If you know a friend or family member with children slightly older than yours, you might just score a few free toys and/or outfits. Also, consider saving items your child outgrows so you can pay it forward, or so you can have stuff available for your next child if you plan on having more.

Now, as for what clothes you should get, here are a few suggestions:

*   It typically takes about two weeks for a baby's umbilical cord to fall off. During those first couple of weeks, it will irritate your baby if anything (like

snaps, buttons, or zippers) rubs up against it.
Consider getting a few undershirts that open in the
front and have snaps on the side, to use until the
belly button heals.

- Onesies come in a variety of different styles. Some
  come with no legs and button up in the crotch. These
  are great for easy access when changing a diaper,
  and they don't ride up. Others come with legs, and
  some even come footed to keep your baby's feet
  warm without socks. Because onesies with zippers
  or snaps are easy to get on and off, it'll help keep
  your sanity if these dominate your baby's wardrobe
  for the first few months.

- Babies lose a lot of heat through their heads, so
  you'll want one or two beanie-style hats to keep your
  baby's head warm.

- Socks are a pain in the butt because they always
  wind up falling off. Just get a few to start with and
  see how it goes. Remember, footed onesies also
  keep feet warm.

- You'll probably need a sweater or hoodie to keep
  your baby warm while going outside. Look for
  something that's easy to get on and off and doesn't
  have drawstrings. If you go outside in the cold a lot,
  you may need a backup or two for times when the
  main sweater is in the wash.

TIP:
Two-piece outfits can be difficult for newborns. It can be hard to get a baby's head through the neck hole, and the shirts can rise up easily. Consider sticking to one-piece outfits in the beginning.

Bottles and Nipples – There are so many different types of bottles, the choices can be overwhelming. How do you know which ones you should get? To be honest, because every baby is different, you might have to deal with a bit of trial and error here. Some babies may take to a bottle instantly, with no problems whatsoever. Other babies might be fussy and refuse to feed from certain nipples or bottles. Here are a few basic tips for choosing the right feeding tools:

- **Nipple sizes** – Nipples have different-sized holes to control the amount of liquid that flows from them. They're marked with the suggested age range, but again, every child is different—so don't be concerned if your baby doesn't follow the exact recommendation. You'll want to start with a small nipple size in the beginning, for a slower flow. The nipple might be too big if you notice a lot of milk or formula spilling out the sides of your baby's mouth during feedings, or if he or she is choking and spitting up. If your baby looks like they are sucking fiercely and getting frustrated during the feeding, you may need to jump up to the next nipple size to allow for a faster flow.

- **Nipple Shapes and Textures** – There are generally two types of nipples: latex or silicone. Latex nipples are softer and more flexible, while silicone ones are more firm. The shape can vary too, from round bulbs to ones that are flat on one side. The flat ones are said to feel more like a woman's breast and are supposedly better orthodontically. Babies can be extremely picky about the shape and texture of bottle nipples, so it's a good idea to hold off on stocking up until you've found one that works well. Try one type out for a few days and if it doesn't work, switch it out.

- **Bottle Shapes** – Some bottles are straight; other bottles are angled, supposedly to make them ergonomic and easier to hold. And while no one really knows what causes colic (excessive and inconsolable crying for no apparent reason in a baby who is otherwise considered healthy), some bottles with angled tops and special venting features can reduce gas and spit-up by limiting the amount of air that flows through. Widths on bottles vary too. Wider openings are easier for pouring formula and are easier to clean.

- **Bottle Materials** – Bottles are most commonly made out of plastic or glass.

  - Plastic is inexpensive, light, and shatterproof. There used to be a concern about plastic bottles having a chemical in them called Bisphenol A (BPA), but the Food and Drug Administration (FDA) banned its use in baby bottles and cups back in 2012.

  - Glass bottles are heavier and more expensive than the plastic ones, but they last longer. You can even get special sleeves to go over them to protect the bottle from shattering, if that's a concern you have.

  - Silicone and stainless steel bottles are also available, but these are slightly more expensive and harder to find. Since plastic and glass are easier to find when you need last-minute replacements, it might make more sense to go with one of those. To make things easier for you, make sure the bottles and nipples you buy are dishwasher safe.

TIP:

You're going to need about 8-12 bottles. The smaller four-ounce bottles are perfect for the amount a newborn will drink in one sitting–but babies grow quickly, and it won't be long before they will need to eat more. Skipping the smaller bottles and going straight for the bigger ones could save you money.

Formula – There are various types of formulas aimed to reduce spit-up, fussiness, gas, and colic. There are also specialized formulas for premature or low-birth-weight babies, and even ones for babies allergic to soy or milk. See page 107 for a complete rundown on formulas, and to get a better understanding for which type you should get. Remember, babies can be picky, and you may have to experiment until you find a formula that works well for them, so don't stock up until you've pinned down one your baby likes. Also, don't change formula types frequently. If your baby is being fussy with what they eat, consult your pediatrician and ask for their recommendation.

Bottle Brush – You're going to be spending a lot of time cleaning bottles, and since they come in various shapes, cleaning them can be difficult without a bottle brush. Get one. You'll thank me for it later.

Burp Cloths – You're going to get puked on a lot and will probably go through about ten to twelve burp cloths a day. They're great because they're thick, absorbent, and small enough to fit a few of them in a diaper bag.

Receiving Blankets and Swaddling Blankets – Receiving blankets are like swaddling blankets, except they are a bit smaller. Most, but not all, newborns like to be swaddled (wrapped snugly in cloth), because it keeps them confined like they were in the womb. It's familiar and comforting for them. These blankets are good for more than swaddling though. They can be draped over strollers to keep the sun out of your baby's eyes, or even used to cover public changing tables. It's good to start with three to six of these. You can always buy more if you need them.

Place to Sleep – Your baby is going to need a place to sleep, and the American Academy of Pediatrics recommends they sleep in the same bedroom as their parents (but not on the same surface) for the first six to twelve months, in order to reduce the risk of Sudden Infant Death Syndrome (SIDS). Babies should sleep on their backs, on a firm surface such as a cradle, crib, or bassinet. Cradles and bassinets might make things easier for you in the beginning since they are more portable and easier to move from room to room. Also, consider a Pack 'n Play for the first few months prior to transitioning to a crib. Some even come with a convenient side-by-side bassinet and changing table, which can be a huge help for middle-of-the-night diaper changes.

Fitted Sheets – It's important that sheets fit tightly in whatever sleeping space you use, because loose bedding can increase the risk of SIDS. Since babies can spit-up a lot, consider getting four or five fitted sheets.

Blankets – It's possible that you can get away with just using swaddling blankets if you're in a warmer climate, but you may want to get a couple of blankets for the car seat or stroller just in case. Only use them if your baby is buckled in and can't move around. Blankets should always be snug and secure. Never use a loose blanket for your baby while he or she is sleeping, because it can increase the risk of SIDS.

Sleep Sacks – Since you shouldn't use blankets while your baby is sleeping, consider getting a few sleep sacks. They cover your baby's body and keep them warm while they're sleeping. Make sure you get the right size. It's important that you don't get ones that are too tight or too loose.

Bibs – These will work in conjunction with burp cloths to catch spit-up and drool. Consider getting four or five of these in the beginning since they'll get dirty quickly. Keep in mind that, just like clothes, you will need to get bigger sizes as your baby grows.

Diaper Bag – If you ever want to leave the house, you're going to want to get a diaper bag. This is going to hold everything you could possibly need while on the road: diapers, changes of clothes, bottles, toys, you name it. Basically, it's your magical British nanny bag. They come in different sizes and styles, and since times are changing, they're not all in bright pink or floral print anymore. Designers have started to cater to fathers and have created diaper bags that come in camouflage, branded with your favorite sports teams, and more. Some are made as backpacks and even murses/man bags. You can do a quick search for "diaper bags for dad" online and you'll see a ton of options. A word of advice though: this is another instance where substance beats style. Practicality is important. You want a bag that's easy to use so you can find things when you're in a hurry. Easy access to diapers, wipes, and bottles is more important than looking like a fashion model.

Stroller – This is another item you're going to need if you ever want to leave the house. Technically, you can hold your baby the whole time you're out, but if you ever want to get a break (and you will), a stroller is going to come in handy. Again, there are so many different types that choosing the best one can be overwhelming, and while jogging daddies can be sexy, are you really going to be using that jogging stroller, or are you going to give that up like a New Year's resolution in February? The thing with strollers is that none of them are perfect for every situation, so the key to getting a good stroller is finding one that fits your lifestyle. Here are a few questions you should ask yourself before splurging on one:

1. What is your budget? Strollers can range from about $25 to over $1,000! Keep in mind that more expensive does not always mean better. The most important thing is whether or not it fits your lifestyle.

2. Will you be traveling a lot? If you're going to be taking the stroller on trips, think about how easily it folds up and how much space it's going to take in the car. Will it fit with all your other luggage?

3. Will you have to carry it a lot? If you're going to be going up and down a lot of stairs, or constantly lifting it in and out of a car, you're probably not going to want the heaviest stroller.

4. Are you and your partner the same height? If not, you may want to get a stroller with adjustable handlebars.

5. Do you want a car seat that clips into your stroller? Some strollers come with a car seat that clips in and

out, making it easy to transfer from the stroller to the car or vice versa with ease. This will also make it less likely that you'll wake your sleeping baby while getting in and out of the car.

6. What kind of terrain will you be on? Your terrain will determine which type of wheel is best for you. Plastic wheels are fine for smooth surfaces like sidewalks and tile, but they may struggle elsewhere. Air-filled tires are great everywhere as long as you don't get a flat. They're like bicycle tires. Foam-filled tires are great in any situation. Also, consider the suspension: the more suspension, the better your stroller will handle various terrains and the less likely your baby will wake up while traveling on bumpy roads.

7. How easy will it be to keep clean? If you're going to be using the stroller a lot, you're going to want something that is easy to clean. Check to see if the seat is removable and washable. Can it be wiped down easily?

8. Do you need a lot of storage? Not all strollers are equal when it comes to storage space. Make sure there's enough for what you need.

9. What types of accessories does it have? Do you need cup holders? Snack trays? Rain covers? Don't fret if you found the perfect stroller without these. You can probably buy an accessory separately.

Baby Carrier – Strollers are not always the most practical mode of transportation for your baby. For example, if you're pushing a stroller around the grocery store, how are you going to be able to push a shopping cart around too? Baby carriers are amazing for situations like these! They cuddle your little one against your body, keeping your arms free to do various other things like grocery shopping or folding laundry. Just be sure to avoid chores that require movements that could put your child in harm's way.

There are many different types of baby carriers out there. For men, the most popular type of carrier is a buckle carrier, because they are comfortable, convenient, and easy to use. Most are versatile and can be worn in front or on your back like a backpack. When picking a carrier, make sure you get one that is adjustable and can grow with your child. Also, make sure your carrier is appropriate for your child's weight. Some carriers come with special infant inserts for smaller babies to make sure they are properly secured.

First-Aid Kit — You can buy pre-packaged first-aid kits that pretty much come with everything you need. At a minimum, make sure you have the following:

- A digital thermometer (and petroleum jelly if it's a rectal thermometer)
- Baby non-aspirin liquid pain reliever. Ask a pediatrician or pharmacist what they recommend.
- Saline drops to loosen mucus
- A bulb syringe to clear mucus from a stuffy nose
- Antibacterial ointment for minor cuts and scrapes
- Tweezers
- Adhesive bandages in various sizes

Because you can never be too prepared, here are a few other items you may want to include in your baby's first aid kit:

- Sunscreen
- Mild liquid soap
- Rubbing alcohol for cleaning thermometers

- Scissors
- Cotton balls
- A heating pad
- Instant cold pack
- Emergency foil blanket
- Eye wash
- Electrolyte solution for hydration after vomiting or diarrhea. Use only if your pediatrician advises you to do so.
- Microporous adhesive tape
- Gauze pads and gauze rolls
- Hydrocortisone cream
- Vinyl gloves
- First-aid manual

Always follow the directions on the packaging and use the recommended dosages for any medicines.

Toiletries – We all know the importance of staying well groomed, and your baby is no exception. The good thing is that you'll only need a few key items.

- **Baby Wash** – You'll need a gentle liquid or foam bath wash for your baby. Their skin is sensitive, so you'll want to avoid anything heavily fragranced. Some come in hypoallergenic and fragrance-free formulas. Some even come in a convenient two-in-one shampoo and body wash combo.

- **Shampoo** – Make sure the shampoo is tear-free in case it accidentally gets in your infant's eyes.

- **Baby Tub** – This isn't a necessity, but a good tub helps a lot! Babies can be slippery when wet, especially if you have used oil or cream on their skin. A baby tub helps to keep a baby in place while you bathe them. Some tubs are made to fit in the sink so you're not straining your back while bending over a full-sized tub. Other baby tubs are designed to fit inside a regular tub, and some are even designed to accommodate your baby while he or she grows. Look for tubs that provide support for your baby's head and have a nonskid bottom, both on the inside, for your baby, and on the outside, to prevent the tub from moving around.

- **Nail Clippers** – You'll find yourself trimming your little wolverine's nails often. They grow fast and they're sharp as razors too! Cutting your little one's nails for the first time can be intimidating because babies squirm a lot, but don't worry. You'll get used to it. You'll need a set of baby clippers, because adult clippers are too dangerous to use on infants. Some come with built-in magnifiers and/or lights to help make it easier to see what you're doing.

- **Moisturizers and Oils** – Baby skin can get dry easily, but a gentle lotion can help keep them moisturized. Coconut oil works great too. No need to soak them in it, but it's good to use every once in a while.

TIP:
Baby oil or coconut oil can help clean off sticky poop.

- **Diaper Rash Cream** – You'll need this to help ease your little one's pain when their bottom gets sore. A little goes a long way though, so use just a dab at a time.

- **Pacifiers** – These come in various different shapes and sizes, and you might have to try a few different ones until your baby finds a pacifier they like. Some pacifier nipples are bulb shaped; others are rounded with flat bottoms. The bases come in different shapes too. When you find one your baby likes, stock up on a few so you have spares. Also, it's handy to find ones that are dishwasher safe.

Things That Are Good to Have But Are Not Mandatory

Changing Pads – You can change your baby on the bed or couch, but small changing pads have the benefit of being soft, portable, and convenient. Technically, you can also just put a towel on the floor to keep the mess contained, but towels don't provide as much cushion.

Baby Swing – These are wonderful, because they free up your hands to do chores around the house like cleaning, dishes, laundry, cooking, etc. Not all babies will like the rocking motion of the swing, but many are comforted by it. If you get a swing, make sure your baby meets the weight requirements and can be strapped in securely.

Baby Monitor – If your house is on the smaller side, you may be able to hear your child cry no matter what room you're in, but if your house is bigger and has multiple floors, hearing your child in the middle of the night may prove to be a bit more difficult. Baby monitors alert you if your infant becomes active while you are in another room. Some are audio only, some have sound with a light indicator, and others come with cameras so you can hear and see your baby. There are even options to use your phone as a baby monitor, but keep practicality in mind and think about what happens if you have to take a call.

Things You Don't Need to Buy

Bottle Sterilizers – Previously, people needed to sterilize bottles before every use. Now, pediatricians say that if the water is safe enough to drink, then it's safe enough for cleaning. Some doctors recommend sterilizing bottles and nipples before the first use, but there is no evidence saying you have to. If you use well water, get it checked for impurities and make sure it is safe to drink. If there are any concerns with the quality of your water, then you may want to get a bottle sterilizer. Otherwise, you can just sterilize bottles when you need to by putting them in boiling water for five minutes.

Wipe Warmers – Some parents swear by these, but honestly, you don't need them. Keep in mind, if you start warming wipes, your baby will get used to it and expect all wipes to be warm from that point on. Do you really want to carry a travel warmer with you everywhere you go? It's just another thing to pack in the diaper bag and it takes a while to warm up too. Trust me. Skip the wipe warmer. If you think a wipe is too cold, you can always hold it between the palms of your hands for a few seconds to warm it up.

Bottle Warmers – While a warm bottle may be nice, a baby doesn't need heated formula. Room temperature is fine. Once you start warming the bottles, your baby will expect all bottles to be warm and may get fussy if given formula at a different temperature. Think about how this will impact feeding on the go. You may want to get a portable travel warmer if you go somewhere outside where the temperature will make the formula cold. Other than that, you can skip these and save the money.

Baby Towels – While baby towels can be cute, and the hooded ones can keep your baby's head warm, they're not a necessity. You can use a regular towel to dry your baby off after a bath. Just make sure the towel is soft. The same goes for washcloths.

Diaper Pails – These may sound great, and some parents swear by them, but you don't need one. Diaper pails are like mini trash cans for diapers with lids that hold in the dirty stench. The problem with these is that they take special liners that can get expensive quickly, and while it's true that the smell gets trapped in the can, just think about what the smell is like when it's time to empty the bag full of stinky diapers. Consider wrapping a soiled diaper in a doggy poop bag if you can't put it in an outside trashcan right away. Doggie poop bags are also great for changing dirty diapers on the go when you're away from the house and there isn't a trashcan nearby. Just bag the dirty diaper until you're at a place where you can properly dispose of it.

Pee Blockers – Seriously? While the concept may sound cute and useful, they're pointless. These whizz blockers are supposed to prevent baby boys from spraying you during diaper changes, but, in reality, they're hard to stay put on a squirming baby, and you'll most likely wind up getting peed on anyway. Putting a washcloth or second diaper over the crotch area can help if you're that worried about it. You don't need a special device.

Pacifier Wipes – You don't need special wipes to clean pacifiers that have fallen on the ground. Just run them under water to clean them or keep a few spares handy.

Baby Landry Soap – This is an example of clever marketing. You absolutely do not need special "baby laundry soap." Just use natural laundry soap, or something fragrance free or hypoallergenic. You can use this soap for all the clothes in the household.

Newborn Mittens – Again, these look cute and it may sound like you need them to keep your baby from scratching themselves. Unfortunately, they don't stay on well. If keeping your baby's nails trimmed isn't solving the issue, there are long-sleeved baby outfits available with tiny hand pockets at the end of the sleeves. Another option is to try putting baby socks over their hands, but again, those may not stay on.

Shoes – While they may look cute, babies don't need shoes until they start walking. Plus, they're restraining and may not even stay on. Save the money and wait to get shoes for when your baby is older.

Shopping Cart Covers – Shopping carts are so dirty and covered in germs! Who wouldn't want to protect their baby from them? Well guess what, the world is full of germs everywhere you go and unless you plan on raising your baby in a plastic bubble, he or she is going to come in contact with them. You don't need a special shopping cart cover to protect your baby while they sit in the grocery cart. Plus, who wants to drag one of those with them every time they go shopping anyway? If you are really that worried about it, use a wipe to wipe the cart down before seating your kid in one.

Baby Kneepads – Babies are so fragile. Wouldn't kneepads be great for protecting their little knees while they're learning how to crawl? Umm, no. They're babies, not professional skateboarders. Unless you're raising a mini Tony Hawk, you don't need baby kneepads.

Bathtub Thermometer — If you have no concept of what lukewarm means and you have an irrational fear that you're going to boil your baby alive, by all means get a bathtub thermometer. Otherwise, use your wrist or elbow to make sure the water is lukewarm.

Crib Bedding Sets — Bedding sets are cute, but you know what? They're also expensive. Plus, your baby's crib really shouldn't have most of the things that come in those sets anyway. The American Academy of Pediatrics says that blankets, comforters, pillows, crib bumpers, and soft toys increase the risk of SIDS, so you're better having your infant sleep prison-style, with a mattress and fitted sheet only.

Baby Powder — Baby powder used to be a staple in many houses across the country. It was used to prevent diaper rash, but has since become controversial in regards to safety. Diaper rash creams are safer for treating diaper rash, and you don't have to worry about your baby inhaling the powder from the air either.

When the Baby is Born – Creating a Birth Plan

If you are expanding your family via open adoption or surrogacy, chances are you're going to need a birth plan. A birth plan is a document that you'll collaboratively work on with the birthmother or surrogate to make sure everything goes smoothly during your time in the hospital.

This may be an extremely difficult time for birthmothers because the hospital makes the whole adoption more real. Even if you agreed to have a lot of contact going forward, she may feel like she is losing her baby. Because of this, compassion and understanding are crucial when you're making this plan. You may already have certain expectations in your head for how you want things to go, but when you're creating the birth plan with a birthmother, try to consider her point of view as well, so she doesn't feel obligated to do things she's uncomfortable with. Emotions will be all over the place, so it helps to have a well-thought-out plan to make things less stressful for everyone. Here are a few things to consider when creating your birth plan.

- Does the birthmother or surrogate have a preference for which hospital they would like to go to? If so, try to contact them ahead of time to let them know about your situation. It's important for the hospital to know that the birth is going to be an adoption or surrogacy so they will have an understanding of who will be present. Make sure you share your birth plan with the hospital as well, so things can run as smoothly as possible.

- Where will you be staying during the birth? Surrogates and birthmothers may not live near you. Check out the hotels ahead of time if you have the chance. For an open adoption, you may be staying in a hotel for a few weeks, so it's a good idea to make sure you have a variety of food options near by.

- What will you be taking to the hospital with you? At a minimum, you're going to need a car seat, because most hospitals will not discharge a baby without one. You might want to bring one or two outfits (for the baby, not you), a swaddling blanket, and a couple of diapers with you, too. Feel free to bring a couple of bottles of formula as well, if you think you'll need it.

- Does the birthmother or surrogate prefer a natural birth or a C-section? You're not the one physically giving birth, so you are probably not going to have much input on this, but it's important to understand how the birthmother or surrogate plans to have the baby. Keep in mind, even if she plans on giving birth a certain way, there may be circumstances where the plan has to change.

- Will there be a midwife or doula present?

- Does the birthmother or surrogate want medication during the birth?

- Who will be in the room during the birth? Maybe you want to be in the room to witness this once-in-a-lifetime moment. Maybe you're not sure if you can handle it and would rather stay in the waiting room. If you'd prefer to witness the birth, keep in mind that in regards to open adoption, this is a vulnerable moment for the birthmother. She may feel awkward, exposed, and uncomfortable with you present in the delivery room while she's dressed in a hospital gown with her legs up in the air. Make sure she doesn't feel pressured to do something she doesn't want to do. Also, if the birth is going to be a C-section, the hospital might have restrictions on how many people can be in the room.

- Who will cut the umbilical cord? Will there be cord blood banking and/or delayed cord clamping?

- Who will be the first to hold the baby?

- Will there be pictures or video allowed in the hospital? If so, when and where? Will the birthmother or surrogate be in any pictures with the baby?

- Who will primarily be with the baby during the hospital stay?

- Will the baby's first feeding be breast milk or formula? If it is decided that the baby will have breast milk, will the birthmother or surrogate breastfeed, or will she pump?

- If you are doing an open adoption, will the birthmother have alone time with the baby?

- Establish who will be making decisions regarding the baby's health while in the hospital.

- Who will give the baby their first bath? Your baby will get a bath while in the hospital. The nurses may be the ones to do this, or they may allow one of you to do it.

- If the baby is a boy, will he be circumcised?

- Who will be allowed to visit the baby in the hospital? Will it just be you and the birthmother/surrogate, or do you want friends and family members there too? Does the birthmother/surrogate want friends or family members present for support? Is there anyone that should not be allowed to visit?

- Who will choose the baby's name on the birth certificate?

- Whose names will appear as the parents on th
  birth certificate? Laws regarding this vary from
  to state.

- Make it very clear where you want the original
  birth certificate sent. In the case of adoption,
  the birthmother may not want to receive a birth
  certificate in the mail.

- Who will take home hospital mementos, like bo
  ID bracelets?

- What happens when it's time to leave the hospi
  For birthmothers, some may want to leave befo
  the baby is discharged, while others may want
  leave with the adoptive family. Who will carry
  baby out?

Keep in mind that the birth plan is designed to help thi
run more smoothly during the hectic time at the hospitc
is a living document, and things can change. It's possi
that an emergency C-section may be required, thus alt
who can be in the room. Or maybe you bond more w
the birthmother over time, and things change because
are more comfortable with each other. Be as detailed
honest as you can when creating this document, but be
open for changes down the road.

Circumcision

If your baby is born with a penis, one of the first major decisions you will have to make is whether or not you are going to circumcise your child. While it used to be automatically assumed that newborn males in the United States would be circumcised, the percentage of infants getting circumcised has significantly dropped over the last few years. Some insurance companies have even stopped covering the procedure because it is not a necessity. Ultimately, it's your choice whether or not you want to circumcise your baby, but if you're having trouble making the decision, here are some of the reasons people choose to go through the procedure or not:

Reasons Why People Choose to Circumcise	Reasons Why People Choose Not to Circumcise
Religion – Some parents choose to circumcise their babies because their faith tells them to.	**Lack of Medical Necessity** – The health benefits for circumcision are so minute, many wonder if they are enough to justify surgically removing part of an infant's body.
Tradition – Some parents choose to circumcise their babies because the fathers are circumcised.	**Tradition** – Some parents choose to not circumcise their babies because the fathers are not circumcised.
Cleanliness – Some people believe a circumcised penis is easier to clean, although that's not entirely accurate. For the first few years of life, the foreskin is stuck to the head of the penis by connective tissue that will dissolve naturally, so all you have to do is wipe the outside of the penis with a wipe during diaper changes, or a washcloth/ sponge when your baby is in the bath. Never attempt to retract a child's foreskin for cleaning. When the inside surface separates from the head of the penis and the foreskin's opening widens, it can be pulled back for easy cleaning.	**Consent** – Some people believe it is unfair to force a surgery on a child when it is not medically necessary. They say it is best to wait until the child is old enough to make the decision on their own, but it's important to note there is a higher risk of complications when performing circumcision on older children and adults.

Teasing – Some parents fear their sons will get teased in the locker room if their penis looks different from everyone else's. Keep in mind though: circumcision rates in the United States have dropped, so this may not be that big of an issue as time goes by.

Pain – Circumcision involves surgically removing skin from a sensitive part of the body, so there will definitely be pain. While there is pain relief that can be used, some people are uncomfortable putting that stress on a newborn baby.

Health – Uncircumcised males have a higher rate of urinary tract infections (UTIs) and penile cancer, but the percentages are so small: about 1 percent for UTIs and much smaller for penile cancer, which is already rare in the United States. Plus, we now have a vaccine that can prevent most, but not all, penile cancers.

Cost – Some insurance companies have stopped covering the cost of circumcision, and some parents choose to not incur additional costs.

Preventing HIV/AIDS – There have been studies that have shown circumcised males are less likely to contract HIV; however, the findings have been strongly contested. Most of the studies were conducted in Africa and only looked at adult subjects who had heterosexual sex. They didn't measure other risks and behaviors, such as condom usage, drug use, needle sharing, male-male sex, etc. Because there are so many different factors involved, it's important to note that correlation does not mean causation.

Feeding Your Baby –
No Boobie, No Problem

Newborn babies eat a lot, like every two to three hours, but with so many different options for what to feed them, how do you know what's best? Is formula OK, or should you opt for milk through a breast milk bank? And if you choose formula, what's the best kind? When should you switch to solids? Here you'll find the basics for feeding your baby so you can make an informed decision on how you want to proceed.

Donor Breast Milk vs. Formula

There are claims out there that breast milk is better for babies than formula because it's natural. Depending on whom you talk to, you may hear that breastfed babies are smarter and less likely to get diseases, but Dr. Raymond Cattaneo, a pediatrician in Kansas City, Missouri says we need to critically assess the claims.

For example, the Journal of the American Medical Association published a meta-analysis study in 2015 by Efrat L. Amitay, PhD, MPH and Lital Keinan-Boker, MD, PhD, MPH, which indicated that breastfeeding for six months or more "may" help lower the risk of childhood leukemia. The study showed the number of childhood leukemia cases decreased by 0.8 per 100,000, but guess what? There are so many other factors (the family's history of cancer, the breastfeeding woman's weight, whether or not she smoked, different environmental exposures, etc.) to take into consideration when comparing women who breastfeed to women who don't, that it's almost impossible to identify what is contributing to what. Also, much of the data was collected by having women complete a self-administered questionnaire, therefore introducing a potential recall bias. So, while the study showed that breastfeeding "may" reduce the risk of childhood leukemia, it didn't prove that it absolutely does, nor did it prove that breastfeeding is best.

So if you're looking for medical research to determine if you should feed your child breast milk or formula, there's honestly not enough information out there to determine whether one is conclusively better than the other. Formula has come a long way over the past few years, and as long as your baby is getting the proper nutrients, they should be fine. "When I see a child at five, six, ten, or fifteen years of age, I can't tell who was breastfed, who was formula fed, or who was fed both," says Dr. Cattaneo. "I don't tell people one is better than the other. My motto is 'Fed is best.'"

If you choose to move forward with formula, there are instances where some babies will have issues with certain types. They may get irritable, gassy, or fussy, or they may spit up a lot. This doesn't necessarily mean you should switch to breast milk. There are various types of formula, so you may have to experiment until you find a formula that works well for your baby. Keep in mind, there's a difference between the taste and consistency of formula and that of breast milk. If you switch between the two, your baby might become fussy, refuse to feed, arch their back, or more—so switching back and forth is not recommended. If your baby is being fussy with what they eat, consult your pediatrician and ask for their recommendation.

One final thing to seriously take into consideration is that donor milk from breast milk banks is expensive. You're looking at four to eight dollars per ounce, plus shipping! That price tag alone is enough to make the donor option out of reach for some families. Ultimately, choosing between breast milk and formula is a personal choice for parents, and there is no right or wrong answer. Just make sure your baby is getting the proper nutrients. Again, if there are any concerns with your baby's feeding, you should consult with their pediatrician.

Breast Milk Banks

If you decide to feed your infant donor milk, you can look online for a breast milk bank near you. A good resource is the Human Milk Banking Association of North America (HMBANA). They are a professional association that issues voluntary safety guidelines on screening breast milk donors, in addition to collecting, processing, handling, testing, and storing milk. More information about HMBANA can be found on their website at www.hmbana.org. Don't worry if you're not within driving distance of a breast milk bank, since most places will ship the milk directly to you.

There are possible health and safety risks for your baby if you feed them human milk from a source other than their birthmother. You could potentially expose your child to infectious diseases and/or chemical contaminants, like illegal or prescription drugs. Also, if breast milk is not handled and stored properly, it could become contaminated and unsafe for your child to drink. A few states have put in place required safety standards for breast milk banks, but the US Food and Drug Administration has not been involved in establishing those state standards. Dr. Cattaneo says that if you choose to go with donor milk, you should only use milk from a source that has screened its milk donors and has taken other precautions to ensure the milk is safe. Don't select random donors from online networks or get breast milk from a friend of a friend.

Formula

Choosing a formula for the first time can be overwhelming. There are lots of options, so to help you in your decision, here's a rundown of the different types available:

Powdered Formula – Powdered formula is the cheapest option, so if you're looking to keep costs down, this is the way to go. It does require a lot of measuring and mixing, though.

Concentrated Liquid Formula – This is a liquid that you dilute with water. It's a little more expensive than powder, and you'll still be measuring and mixing.

Ready-to-Use Liquid Formula – This is the most convenient option, because the water is already mixed in and the liquid can be poured right into the bottle. This can be handy when you're traveling and can't find a sterile water supply, but this type of formula is also the most expensive option.

After choosing what type works best for you, now it's time to choose what kind works for your baby. Most infants can do well on a regular, cow's-milk-based formula, so that is a good place to start unless your pediatrician says otherwise. It has a good balance of carbohydrates, fat, and protein. If your baby is spitting up a lot, try changing the way you feed. For example, keep them upright longer after a feeding, try switching bottle types, or burp them more. If they still seem to have trouble eating after about a week or two, consult your pediatrician and ask for recommendations. Here are a few other kinds of formulas:

TIP:
Even though some formula is cow's milk based, it is significantly altered so that babies can digest it. Infants cannot properly digest cow's milk for a while, and it is not recommended to give a baby cow's milk until after their first birthday.

Partially Hydrolyzed Formulas – With these, the protein is broken down to make them easier for babies to digest. This type of formula helps babies that have trouble absorbing nutrients.

Soy-Based Formula – This formula may be a good option for infants allergic to cow's milk; however, if they are allergic to the protein in cow's milk, they may also be allergic to the protein in soy-based formula. Consult a pediatrician before using this kind of formula. Also consult a pediatrician if you notice wheezing, hives, or rashes after feeding.

Premature Baby Formula – This formula typically contains more calories and protein, as well as a fat that's easily absorbed. If your baby is born premature or has a low birth weight, ask your pediatrician which formula is best to use.

Organic Formula – There is no research to date that proves organic formula is better than non-organic formula, so you will need to think about whether or not it makes sense to pay the higher price.

How Much Should I Feed My Baby?

For the first week, ease your baby into feeding by giving them one to two ounces every three to four hours, but never give them more than what they want. Take your baby's cue. After the first week, you can ease them up to about two to three ounces every three to four hours. As your baby gets bigger, they'll slowly increase the amount of formula or breast milk they eat. Every baby is different, but a good rule of thumb is to feed them approximately two and a half ounces of formula per pound of body weight each day. So if your baby is eight pounds, they'll eat about twenty ounces in a twenty-four-hour period. The frequency for how often they eat will slowly decrease as the quantity gets larger. Below is a good guide for the average baby, but check with your pediatrician to make sure you have a good feeding schedule for your child and that they are getting the right amount of nutrients.

Age	Bottles Per Day	Amount in Each Bottle	Total Amount Per Day
Newborn	6–8	2–3 oz.	12–24 oz.
1-2 Months	6–8	4 oz.	24–32 oz.
3-4 Months	6	4–6 oz.	24–36 oz.
5-6 Months	5	6–8 oz.	30–40 oz.
7-9 Months	3–4, in addition to solids	7–8 oz.	21–32 oz.
10-12 Months	2–3, in addition to solids	8 oz.	16–24 oz.

When Can My Baby Have Juice?

The American Academy of Pediatrics recommends that juice should not be introduced into a child's diet until after they are a year old, and even then, should be limited to four ounces a day. Dr. Cattaneo says parents should avoid juice altogether, if possible, because it provides no health benefits whatsoever, even if it says otherwise on the bottle. Most fruit juices have a high sugar content, lack dietary fiber, and may even contribute to excessive weight gain. Rather than drinking juice, children should be encouraged to eat whole fruits and vegetables. If you do wind up giving your child juice, make sure they drink it out of a sippy cup rather than a bottle to lessen the risk of tooth decay. Also, make sure it is 100 percent fruit juice with no added sugar. It's important to realize "no added sugar" can still have a hell of a lot of sugar.

> *TIP:*
> *You can lower the sugar content in juice by watering it down: half juice and half water. This will also give you peace of mind, knowing that your kid is less likely to run around like a raging lunatic from a sugar high, and that even if they do, it probably won't last as long as it would have if you hadn't watered it down.*

When Can My Baby Have Water?

Free water (that is, water not mixed in formula or already in breast milk) can cause electrolyte imbalances in babies, leading to seizures, coma, and even death. That is also why it is vitally important not to dilute formula which is designed to be mixed in a certain way. Using less formula and more water to save money can cause the same electrolyte imbalances.

It is ok to introduce free water in a sippy cup to infants six to nine months old. Limit it to about four ounces a day, and only allow them to have a few sips at a time to prevent them from getting too full or from getting a tummy ache. It is important they still get the necessary nutrients found in milk or formula. After they are a year old and well into eating solid foods, they can have more water. Check with your pediatrician if you have questions or concerns.

When Should We Introduce Solid Foods?

The American Academy of Pediatrics recommends that you introduce solids sometime between four and six months of age. Check with your pediatrician before introducing solid foods to make sure your baby is ready. Signs that your baby may be ready to try solid foods include:

- The ability to hold their head up on their own. They have good head control and can eat in a sitting position.

- Their extrusion reflex, where they push food on their tongue to the front of their mouth, has mostly disappeared.

- They become curious about other foods. Maybe they watch you eat or try to grab your food.

When we first introduce solid foods into an infant's diet, it's more about training them how to eat than about making sure they get more nutrients. It's also about teaching them different food textures, what to do with their tongues, and how to push food into the back of their mouths. The majority of nutrients should still come from breast milk or formula, and solid foods should compliment a bottled feeding in the beginning, not replace it. Also, when introducing new foods, only do one at a time. This makes it easier for your baby to digest and will also help you identify any foods your child may be allergic to.

Rice cereal made specifically for babies is a good place to start when introducing solids. For the first few times, try giving your baby a little formula, followed by half teaspoons of rice cereal (mixed with formula). After a couple of teaspoons, end the meal with a little bit of formula again.

Dr. Cattaneo says you don't have to limit yourself to rice cereal as a first food though. Pediatricians used to recommend it because they thought that cereal was the least likely to cause allergies. They later found out this is not necessarily true. He says a first food could pretty much be anything in pureed form, as long as it's not listed in the "What Foods Should Be Avoided" section below. Some people find that mild fruits and vegetables like pureed apples, bananas, carrots, and peas are good first foods, but you can even try some meats like pureed beef, chicken, turkey, and lamb.

Around eight to ten months, you can start giving combinations of foods, but you still only want to introduce one new food at a time. Your baby may be able to handle heartier foods, such as pureed broccoli, asparagus, and apricots. When your baby is able to sit up on their own, reach for food, and put it in their mouth, they may be ready to try other solid foods like wafer-type cookies and crackers. Around ten to twelve months, your baby may be ready for pasta and small chunks or pieces of food that can easily be mashed in their mouth.

What Foods Should Be Avoided?

There are many different types of foods that you should hold off on feeding your child, many which are listed below. When introducing your child to new foods, think about how they may eat it. Is the food easy enough to chew without teeth? Is it small enough to swallow without getting lodged in their throats? For the first few years, food should be cut into pieces no larger than half an inch. Below is a list of food items to avoid until your child is about three or four years old unless otherwise specified.

Cow's Milk – Cow's milk should not be introduced into your child's diet until they are one year old because before then, they won't be able to properly digest the protein in it. When you do introduce milk, avoid low fat because most children need the fat and calories for proper growth and development. Only feed your child low-fat milk if your pediatrician recommends it, which they may if your child is at risk for obesity.

Honey and Corn Syrup – Wait until your child is at least one year old before giving them honey or corn syrup, because it may contain spores of bacteria that can cause botulism.

Nuts and Seeds – These can be choking hazards, so hold off on feeding your little one nuts and seeds, such as peanuts, almonds, sunflower seeds, pumpkin seeds, etc. Also, make sure you carefully remove seeds and pits from fresh fruits.

Raw Vegetables – Cook vegetables to make them softer and easier to eat.

Whole Grapes – Grapes can be choking hazards when eaten whole. Cut them into halves or quarters.

Hard and Crunchy Foods – Avoid foods like popcorn, pretzels, mints, and hard candies, which can get lodged in your child's throat.

Peanut Butter – Nut butters of any kind can be difficult to swallow and can be a choking hazard. Avoid giving them to your child in large dollops or on a spoon. If you want your child to have peanut butter or another kind of nut butter, spread it thinly on something like bread or crackers.

Cheese – Avoid cheese that's stringy or melted, because it can be a choking hazard.

The above list is just a guide, and you should always check with your pediatrician before introducing new foods. Remember to wait several days after each new food item before introducing a new one, so you can identify whether your child has any allergic reactions to any of them. Also, because of allergies, check with your pediatrician to see when they recommend introducing foods like eggs, fish, shellfish, soy, and nuts. Alert your pediatrician if you notice any reactions such as diarrhea, rashes, or vomiting to certain foods.

Should We Feed Our Baby Organic Food?

Dr. Cattaneo says there is no definitive research proving that eating organic foods (and/or non-GMO foods) is necessary to prevent infections, helps growth and development, or has any other proposed benefits. And similar to what he said about breast milk vs. formula, when he sees a child at five, six, ten, or fifteen years of age, he can't tell who ate organic foods and who didn't.

From a health standpoint, there's no risk to going organic, but you're probably not going to prevent infections any more or less. The same goes for GMO foods. The science shows they are safe. If you are buying a non-GMO product, you are paying for the label, not a health benefit. If you can afford buying organic food though, and you want to do it, go for it. Organic farming is probably better for the environment, so that may be something you may want to take into consideration. In the end, it's ultimately a personal decision for you to make.

There's More Than One Way to Burp a Baby

When your baby is feeding from a bottle, you should burp them about every two ounces or whenever they start getting fussy. We often see people holding babies over their shoulder while patting them on the back, but the truth is, there are different positions for burping your baby, and sometimes you may have to try more than one. Here are a few different burping positions:

On Your Shoulder – Rest your baby's head on your shoulder and keep them in position with one hand under their bottom and the other on their back. Use the hand on their back to gently rub up and down, hopefully releasing any trapped air bubbles. If your baby doesn't burp after about a minute, try patting their back for a minute. Go back and forth between rubbing and patting until you are successful.

Sitting Up – Sit your baby on your lap. Use the thumb and pointer finger of one hand to hold the chin up and support their head. The base of your hand and wrist can be used to support your baby's chest and shoulders. Place your other hand on your baby's back and slowly lean them forward a bit so they are at a slight angle. Alternate between rubbing and patting your baby's back, while making sure their head does not flop around.

Lying Down – Place your baby across your lap facedown so their head is over one of your legs and their tummy is over the other. Hold them securely with one hand and use the other hand to rub or pat their back.

What If My Baby Is Constipated?

Every baby will poop on a different schedule, and that is usually OK. They may poop seven times in a day, or go several days without a bowel movement. They may even strain and turn purple while pooping, and that could be OK too. For a healthy child, constipation is defined by the consistency of the stool: hard, round pellets. Other signs may include straining for more than ten minutes, increased spit-up, or decreased feeding.

Constipation in infants is common, especially when they start eating new solid foods. Prune juice is a natural laxative that helps soften the stool and can make it easier for your child to go when they are having trouble. Pedialyte is another good option. Both of them may work quicker for some babies than for others, depending on the severity of your child's constipation—or they may not work at all. Consult your pediatrician if your child has gone several days without producing a bowel movement, or is crying in pain while going to the bathroom.

TIP:

For children six months to a year old, try diluting one to two tablespoons of prune juice in two to three ounces of water or formula at first. Keep in mind, a little bit of prune juice goes a long way! You can always add more, but you can't add less. Giving your child too much prune juice can give them diarrhea for days and result in a very sore bottom.

Diapers

This section tells you everything you need to know about diapers: how to pick the right type, how to pick the right size, and how to properly change them. Did you know there are differences between changing a boy's diaper and changing a girl's? That's all covered here in addition to tips on what you can do when you can't find a changing table.

The Big Debate: Cloth vs. Disposable

If you have an infant, you're going to be dealing with a lot of diapers, so it's important to use a type that best fits your lifestyle. Both cloth and disposable diapers have their own pros and cons.

Cloth diapers are better for the environment and are cheaper than disposables, as long as you're doing your own laundry and not using a service that rents out cloth diapers, washes them, and delivers clean ones back to your house. The downside is that they are messier and not very convenient. When you change cloth diapers away from home, you will have to carry them back to your house so you can wash them later. So if your baby poops while you're at the beach, park, or mall, you'll be carrying that smelly diaper around with you until you're ready to go home.

Disposable diapers are less messy, more convenient, and easier to use, but they're also more expensive and worse for the environment. The fastening tabs on disposable diapers can also rip easily if you pull too hard, which sucks if you're away from home and only have one diaper left.

Still not sure which ones to go with? Ask other parents what they use and what their experience with diapers has been like. You can also do a quick search online to see what other people say.

	Cloth	Disposable
Pros	• They are cheaper than disposable diapers, as long as you're not using a cleaning service. • They are more natural, without all the dyes and gels used in disposable diapers. • They are better for the environment.	• They are easier to change and more convenient than cloth diapers. • They are more absorbent than cloth diapers, so you will be doing fewer changes. • They are not as messy as cloth diapers. • You will have less laundry to do, because you just throw away the dirty diapers instead of washing them.
Cons	• They are messier and harder to change. • You will have a lot more laundry to do. • You will be doing more diaper changes because they are less absorbent. • When you change diapers away from home, you'll have to carry them back home with you, even the really smelly ones.	• They are more expensive than cloth diapers. • They are bad for the environment because very little breaks down. • Fastening tabs can rip easily if you pull too hard.

Benefits	Cloth	Disposable
Can be cheaper	✓	
Better for the environment	✓	
Less messy		✓
Less laundry		✓
Easier to change		✓
More absorbent (fewer diaper changes)		✓
Fewer dyes and gels	✓	
May make potty training easier	✓	
May help with having fewer diaper rashes.	✓	

How to Tell If a Diaper Is the Right Size

Unlike baby clothes, disposable diapers are sized by a child's weight, not their age. Don't automatically assume a newborn baby is going to need a newborn diaper. If your baby is on the bigger side, a newborn diaper will wind up looking like a speedo on them. Follow the recommended size chart on the package to ensure the diaper size is right for your child's weight range. Before stocking up on diapers (which you're definitely going to need to do), buy a small pack first and make sure they fit.

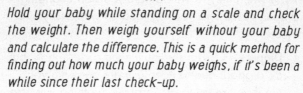

TIP:
Hold your baby while standing on a scale and check
the weight. Then weigh yourself without your baby
and calculate the difference. This is a quick method for
finding out how much your baby weighs, if it's been a
while since their last check-up.

Just like grown-ups, baby bodies are unique, and since
diaper brands are all different, you'll want to make sure
the brand you have fits your baby comfortably. Even
though diapers should fit snugly, there should also be some
give. You should easily be able to put one finger in the
waistband and two to three fingers between the diaper
and your baby's leg. If the diaper is leaving red marks, it's
probably either too tight or too small. And while leakage
does happen, if it occurs often, that's also a sign that you
probably need to change diaper sizes.

If you are going to use cloth diapers, they are available in
"one size fits all" options that fit most babies from birth to
potty training. Some also offer a variety of inserts so you
can customize the absorbency depending on the age and
size of your baby.

How to Change a Diaper

Needless to say, you'll be changing a lot of diapers. Your
baby will probably cry or get fussy when they're ready for
a new one, but there are other ways you can tell if they
need a change too. Sometimes you'll see their face turn
bright red as they grunt and strain while they poop. Don't
worry if you miss the cue though. You'll probably smell it
shortly after anyway. As for "number one" incidents, many

disposable diapers come with color-changing stripes that alert you when they're wet. Before you start changing the diaper, make sure you're prepared with everything you need:

- **Diapers** – Obviously you'll need a clean one, but it's a good idea to have a spare one with you too if you're using disposables. Nothing is worse than being on your last one and having the fasten tabs rip.

- **Wipes** – Just like you don't want your only diaper to rip, you don't want to start changing a poopy diaper, only to find out there's only one wipe in the packet.

- **Spare Clothes** – Diapers can leak, so make sure you have spare clothes with you. Store a few next to your changing table and take a few changes of clothes when going out for extended periods of time.

- **Diaper Rash Cream** – You won't need it for every diaper change, but it's a good idea to have it on hand in case you do wind up needing it.

- **Blanket** – If you're changing your baby in a public restroom, or any place other than your regular changing table, you should put a protective cloth down for your baby to lie on. You could use a receiving blanket, swaddling blanket, or any other type of cloth big enough to cover the area.

- **Distractions** – While not a necessity, you may choose to have something with you to keep your baby distracted or entertained during diaper changes. Maybe a rattle, toy, pacifier, or something else that will keep their interest.

Now that you have everything you need, you're ready to change a diaper. Follow these easy steps:

1. If needed, place the protective blanket down where you will be changing your baby.

2. Place your baby on the changing table or surface where you will be changing them. Strap them in to minimize their movement and keep them from rolling around. While strapping your baby in will help keep them confined, it's not a guarantee they won't roll off the changing table, so never step away.

3. Check to see if you're dealing with a wet diaper or a soiled one. If you're not sure, gently pull the elastic around the back of the legs to peek inside.

4. Undo the pull tabs. If the diaper is soiled, take the front of the diaper and slide it down towards the baby's bottom to wipe away the majority of the waste. Then fold the diaper closed and rest the baby's bottom on the outside of the front of the diaper.

5. If you're changing a baby boy, immediately place a clean diaper or dry washcloth over the penis to protect you from getting sprayed. Keep the little squirt gun covered while you clean everything with wipes.

6. Clean the front area first and make sure to get all the folds and crevices.

   - **For Boys** – Don't forget to clean underneath the penis, and the scrotum. If your baby is uncircumcised, do not pull back the foreskin to clean underneath. If your baby was circumcised, the penis will take about a week to heal and will look red and possibly even scabby during this time. You may even see a bit of oozing or a small amount of blood, which is also normal. If any of these symptoms persist beyond a week, consult with your baby's doctor. When the area is clean, apply petroleum jelly over the tip of the penis after every diaper change to keep it from rubbing against the diaper and getting irritated.

- **For Girls** – Always wipe from front to back (from vulva to rectum) to prevent the spread of bacteria that can cause urinary tract infections. Do not pull the labia back to clean inside. Also, it's important to note that staying in a wet diaper for too long could cause pediatric vulvovaginitis, a condition that causes irritation and/or discharge in the area of the vulva and/or vagina. Monitoring and making diaper changes when necessary can help lessen your baby's risk of getting vulvovaginitis. If you notice any of these symptoms, contact your child's pediatrician.

7. After you've cleaned the front, lift the legs to clean the bottom area, remove the dirty diaper, and place a clean one under the baby's bottom.

8. Before fastening the new diaper, make sure the baby is completely dry and diaper rash cream or ointments were applied if needed. If the umbilical cord stump is still there, fold the top of the diaper down so it doesn't irritate it and to allow the stump to get air so it can heal. Also, if you have a boy, point his penis down before placing the diaper over it to prevent him from peeing out the top of his diaper.

9. Fasten the diaper and dispose of the dirty one in a diaper pail or garbage can.

10. Change your baby's clothes if needed. Check the sheet on the bed to see whether it needs to be changed too.

11. Wash your hands thoroughly when done. If you are away from home and don't have access to a sink, use antibacterial wipes or hand sanitizer if possible.

> *TIP:*
> *Doggie poop bags are great for holding dirty diapers when you're away from home and can't find a trash can. They contain the mess and minimize the smell.*

Swim Diapers

If your child is not potty trained, they're going to need swim diapers when they go swimming. Unlike regular diapers (which are super absorbent and would swell up like a balloon in the pool), swim diapers allow liquid to leak right through. This prevents the diaper from swelling up and becoming uncomfortable. But what's the point of a diaper if it just leaks everywhere?

Swim diapers are specifically designed to be worn in water. Their main purpose is to decrease the spread of fecal bacteria (like E. coli) that would contaminate public swimming areas. Notice I said "decrease" and not "prevent." Swim diapers can hold in some solid waste, but they will not prevent diarrhea from leaking through. If your child has diarrhea, they should stay out of the pool so they don't risk contaminating it and making others sick. If there's a "poop incident," the pool will have to be shut down for a couple of hours until it can be properly drained and cleaned. Don't be that parent who ruins the day for everyone else.

The Poop No One Warns You About

Babies ingest a lot of things while in utero such as amniotic fluid, bile, mucus, skin cells, and more. Their first bowel movement contains all of this in a nasty, greenish black tar substance called meconium. It's disgusting and extremely sticky, making it difficult to remove from your baby's skin. If you're lucky, a nurse will deal with this alien substance for you so you'll never even have to see it, although since it does take about a day or two to completely pass all of the meconium, there's still a chance you might encounter it. A trick is to lightly coat your newborn's skin with petroleum jelly or coconut oil for the first couple of days to prevent the meconium from sticking to it. This will make the first few diaper changes a lot easier.

Changing Tables

As mentioned earlier in this book, society is still catching up on modern-day parenting. The country is stuck in a belief that women should be the ones taking care of babies, which is why many places only have changing tables in women's restrooms. Things are slowly progressing, but in the meantime, what's a dad to do? Well, you can change your child on the restroom floor or counter, but those places are unsanitary and can pose health risks. You can carry spare blankets with you everywhere you go to cover surfaces in emergencies. You could also change your child in the backseat or trunk of your car (SUVs are awesome for this). Or, if you're dexterous, you can sit on a toilet seat, change your child on your lap, and pray you don't get anything on you. We're dads, though. We can do it! Where there's a will, there's a way. Check out these stories of dads dealing with public changing tables:

"It has been a challenge to find changing tables in public places. There have been times when we used changing tables in single-stalled women's bathrooms and had employees guard the door."
—Mike Degala

"My biggest pet peeve is changing tables. I'm flabbergasted at how many places don't take into consideration that dads can change diapers too! Whenever I come across a place like that, I make sure to talk to the manager and take it to the company's social media page."
—Chad Scanlon

"Looking back when our son was little, we took him to New York and went to some pretty fancy restaurants. One time, he needed his diaper changed and there were no changing stations in the men's restroom, so we changed him on the chair next to us. Needless to say it was a stink bomb of a poop, and we cleared the tables around us fairly quickly! We thought it was funny, the other patrons not so much!"
—BJ Barone

"We have had challenges with finding changing tables in public restrooms. We used to speak to a manager and complain if we had nowhere to change diapers. A fun story: We were invited to the White House for a Father's Day celebration when our son was an infant. His diaper needed to be changed, so we took him to the men's room, which is located in the White House Library. Upon finding no appropriate place to change his diaper, we went into the library and placed him on the bench in the room to change his diaper. We covered the bench with a changing pad so we would not have any accidents but were quickly notified that the bench was a historical piece and that since the entire space was a museum, we should be more careful. We were given a 'pass' once we exclaimed we had no other place to go to change him and were very careful."

—Tommy Starling

What to Do With an Explosive Poo

If you have an infant in diapers, the chances are that you'll probably have to deal with an explosive poo at some point. And when I say "explosive poo," I don't just mean a big, nasty, smelly diaper. I'm talking about a poop that can't be contained and basically explodes out of the diaper. You'll know it when you see it. In the case of an explosive poo, it manages to squeeze out of both leg openings and out the top of the diaper. It will go up the back and maybe even all the way up to the shoulder blades. Inside the diaper, it will be everywhere: front and back. It's basically a 360 degrees poo! And if your child sticks their hands in their diaper, well, lucky you. It will get all over their hands and everything they touch too.

It's terrifying when this happens, because shit is literally everywhere! If this happens to you, try to remain calm and just take your baby straight to the bathtub. There's no point in even trying to use wipes. They can't save you. Turn on the water, make sure it's lukewarm, and just rinse your child off. Wipe them down with a washcloth and make sure they are completely clean before drying them off and putting them in a new diaper and outfit. When they are clean, go back and assess the scene of the crime to make sure nothing else was contaminated. If poop got on anything else, make sure to clean it thoroughly, especially if it's something that would go in the baby's mouth, like a pacifier or teething ring. In those cases, if the items can be cleaned and sanitized in the dishwasher, make sure you do that. If not, consider throwing them away. For other items, like floors and baby gates, bleach wipes can sure come in handy.

REAL-LIFE STORY:

"While on parental leave with my son, if I didn't know what to do with my time, I'd often drive to Babies "R" Us. We'd always need something... diapers, formula, and on one occasion we were all out of portable diaper wipes. When we got there, he was hungry and needed a bottle, and they're cool with people using their glider chairs for feedings. Halfway through his bottle, his diaper exploded. Poop everywhere. Up his back. Out the sides. All over my left forearm. I had a change in the diaper bag... but I didn't have any wipes. And I couldn't put him down. We slowly made our way to the cash register, holding him with my left arm, pushing the cart and paying with my right." –Ian Hart

Doctors

Can a Doctor Legally Refuse to Care for You or Your Child Because of Your Sexual Orientation?

In 2015, national headlines were made after a pediatrician refused to treat the infant daughter of a legally married same-sex couple. Krista and Jami Contreras had carefully chosen Dr. Vesna Roi at Eastlake Pediatrics in Roseville, Michigan: a doctor who came highly recommended by their midwife. Dr. Roi knew they were lesbians, and after the first prenatal visit, they were under the impression that everything was fine. But the morning they arrived for the appointment, another pediatrician in the practice greeted them instead, explaining that Dr. Roi had a change of heart. After "much prayer," she decided that she couldn't treat their baby because they were lesbians. Guess what. Using "religious freedom" as an excuse to refuse treatment for a baby with same-sex parents was not illegal.

Even though the American Medical Association (AMA) and the American Academy of Pediatrics have ethics rules that prohibit discrimination based on sexual orientation and gender identity, these "rules" are only advisory. Some states have laws that prohibit doctors from discriminating against people based on their sexual orientation, but there are no federal laws that explicitly prohibit discrimination against LGBT individuals. This means in that in some states, doctors can legally refuse to treat a gay person, or their children, if they cite "religious freedom."

Finding LGBT-Friendly Doctors

How can you find a supportive doctor who will treat you and your children fairly, with understanding, compassion, and empathy? Insurance companies can typically help you find a doctor based on gender, practice, and location, but I have yet to find one that uses "LGBT friendly" as a sorting option. It's not that easy to find one online with this choice either.

GLMA (previously known as the Gay & Lesbian Medical Association) has a database of online medical professionals and is a good place to start, but their database is still growing so you may not be able to find an LGBT-friendly pediatrician near you when you search. Dr. Cattaneo says there are many other things you can do to help find an LGBT-friendly doctor for your child, though. Here are a few things he suggests:

- Ask for referrals from your local LGBT center or your local LGBT chamber of commerce if you have one.

- If there's an LGBT parenting group near you, ask the parents in that group if they have any recommendations.

- If you're able to do so, ask your birthmother or surrogate's obstetrician.

- Ask the nurses helping you during the delivery.

You can also interview doctors too. Call their offices beforehand and ask how comfortable they are treating a child with two gay dads. Have they done any special research about children of LGBT families? Do they have experience with children of LGBT families? Do they have anyone that can be a reference and tell you about their experience with the practice? Finally, while it's great that we support people and businesses that are "family," don't be afraid of going to a non-gay pediatrician. The most important thing is that you go for someone you can mesh with and have a comfortable relationship with.

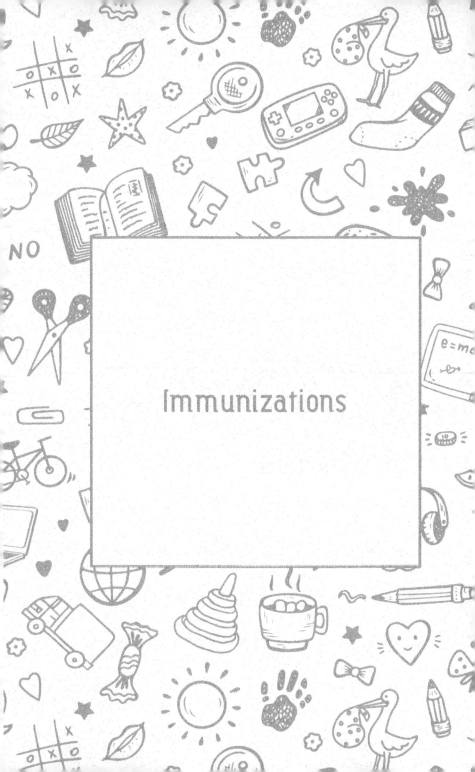

Immunizations

To Vaccinate or Not to Vaccinate, That Is the Question

There are certain situations where some people can't get vaccinated because they're undergoing medical treatment or have a certain medical condition, but other than that, keeping your child up-to-date on recommended vaccinations is one of the best strategies to help keep them safe and healthy. Immunizations are the reason we don't see widespread epidemics of viruses and diseases like measles, polio, and smallpox. Some vaccines may cause side effects, such as fever, excessive sleepiness, and even seizures, but Dr. Cattaneo says the symptoms of the virus or bacteria can be much worse, so staying current with vaccinations is extremely important. Talk about vaccines with your pediatrician beforehand and discuss the possible side effects. You can also visit the Center for Disease Control and Prevention's website at www.cdc.gov for more information.

Don't Be the Odd One Out

It's important to remember that vaccines don't just protect the person being vaccinated: they protect the people around them too. So, in order to keep your child safe and healthy, it's important for you to be current on your immunizations as well. In fact, everyone that comes in contact with your child (grandparents, aunts, uncles, friends, neighbors, etc.) should all be current with their vaccinations, especially within the first few months of your baby's life. This is called cocooning because when everyone is vaccinated, they form a "cocoon" of disease protection around the baby.

But If Everyone Else is Immunized, Doesn't That Mean My Child Can't Get the Disease?

When a high percentage of the population is vaccinated and protected, it's difficult for a disease to spread because there are so few vulnerable people left to infect. This is called "herd immunity," but a high vaccination rate doesn't mean unvaccinated people are immune to getting sick.

Just look at the Eagle Mountain International Church in Newark, Texas.

In 2013, the vaccine-skeptical megachurch was linked to at least twenty-one cases of the measles. The majority of the people infected had not been immunized, making them susceptible to getting the disease.

Can Vaccines Cause Autism?

In 1998, Andrew Wakefield and twelve of his colleagues published a case series in the Lancet, which suggested a possible link between autism and the MMR (measles, mumps, rubella) vaccine. The paper received wide publicity, even though there was only a small sample size of twelve patients and there was no control group. It was later found out that Wakefield not only falsified the data, but he was also being funded by lawyers who had been engaged by parents in lawsuits against vaccine-producing companies. This was a major conflict of interest. Wakefield was eventually stripped of his medical license and ten of the original twelve authors of the study retracted their support. Years later, the Lancet retracted the study too. Other researchers could not replicate the original study, and the American Academy of Pediatrics has released numerous subsequent studies showing no link between vaccines and autism. Still, for some reason, the myth hasn't gone away.

Are There Benefits to Delayed Vaccination?

To ensure their safety, all vaccines go through extensive clinical trials for safety and efficacy before being licensed, and they are monitored constantly afterwards. If your child is healthy and has no medical reason to not receive an immunization, there is no benefit to a delayed vaccine schedule, according to Dr. Cattaneo. In fact, delaying vaccines can put a child at risk for illness. However, there could be medical reasons why a delayed schedule might be necessary. For example, a child receiving chemotherapy may not be able to receive immunizations at the "appropriate" times/intervals.

Vaccines in a Nutshell

Vaccines save lives. It's as simple as that. Get your kids vaccinated according to your doctors recommended schedule, and make sure you're up-to-date on your immunizations as well.

Traveling with Children

Traveling is stressful, especially if it's your first time with a little one. Will you have trouble getting through airport security? Will your baby cry on the plane the whole time? Will your older child constantly kick the seat in front of them? How do you childproof a hotel? There's so much to think about, your head can spin—but with a little advanced planning, you can make things a whole lot easier for yourself, your child, and those around you. Here are a few tips for smooth traveling.

Infants and Toddlers

PACKING

If you're going to be traveling in a car or plane for a long time, strategically pack everything you need for the trip in a diaper bag and/or carry bag and keep it within arm's reach. If you're on a plane, your bag should go under the seat in front of you and not in the overhead bin. That way, you can access it during takeoff, landing, and any other time you're not permitted to get out of your seat.

The more organized your bag is, the easier it's going to be for you to access things quickly when you need them. Trust me, when you have a hungry, screaming baby on your lap in the plane, the last thing you're going to want to do is fumble around in a diaper bag trying to find a bottle, formula, and burp cloth. To make things easier on yourself, keep everything you need for diaper changes in one section, everything you need for feeding (bottles, formula, burp cloth) in another section, and distraction toys in another. Make sure the things you will need most are easy to grab, not at the bottom of the bag where you have to dig for them. If your child uses pacifiers, keep a few of them in a side pocket for easy access. Also, make sure you pack a change of clothes in your carry-on for yourself too in case you get puked, peed, or pooped on.

> *TIP:*
>
> *Consider using Ziploc bags to create multiple changing packs and fill each of them with a diaper and a change of clothes. When changing your baby, if the clothes are wet or soiled and need to be changed, you can seal the dirty outfit in the Ziploc before putting it back in your diaper bag.*

AIRPORT SECURITY

Going through airport security with an infant or toddler for the first time can be a challenge. In addition to holding your little one, you also have to get your bags in the bins, take out your laptops, and remove your shoes, belts, etc. There are a few things you can do though to make the process easier for you.

1. Make sure you have the right documents with you: either a copy of your child's birth certificate or an adoption document. The TSA agent may not always ask for this when you go through security, but if you look different from your child or have different last names, you may wind up having issues. It's best to always err on the side of caution.

2. If you have an infant, consider using a baby carrier to strap them to your chest when going through security. Not only will this free up your hands so you can manage your carry-ons, but many TSA agents (if you ask them nicely) will let you walk right through the metal detectors with these on too. This is

great, especially if your child is sleeping, because you won't have to wake them up when going through security. Strollers on the other hand, must be screened by X-ray. So, if you're in the security line and your child is asleep in the stroller, you risk waking them up when you have to take them out.

3. You can bring liquid and powdered formula through security, but you should let the agent know you have formula before it goes through the X-ray machine. If you don't want it to go through the X-ray, let them know so they can do alternative screening methods.

SURVIVING FLIGHTS

When people seated on the airplane see you walking down the aisle with a baby, they're probably secretly praying that you keep walking past them. Everyone assumes that babies are going to cry on airplanes. No one likes sitting next to a screaming baby, and let's face it, no parent wants their child to be the one screaming on the plane either. While there's nothing you can do to guarantee your child won't cry on the plane, there are definitely steps you can take to minimize the likelihood. Here are a few things you can try.

1. **Feed During Takeoff and Landing** – The pressure in the plane changes during takeoff and landing and the pressure will hurt your little one's ears. The pressure can make infants scream uncontrollably. Feeding from a bottle can release pressure and basically does the same thing for infants that chewing gum does for adults, so time your feeding to coincide with takeoff and landing. A pacifier may also work because of the sucking motion, but

feeding will calm a baby more and possibly even help them fall asleep.

2. **Coordinate Nap Time** – If you can coordinate it so that your child sleeps on the plane, you're in luck! If they're getting sleepy and you don't board for another twenty minutes or so, try to keep them awake until you can give them a bottle during takeoff. Hopefully they'll drift off to sleep then. Of course, there is no guarantee they will sleep on the plane, but whatever you can do to help make it happen will make things easier for you.

3. **Keep Plane Toys Separate** – Keep two sets of toys with you: a couple of toys to play with in the airport, and a couple that only come out during the plane ride. Babies lose interest in things quickly. Reserving a couple of toys for in-flight play only will hopefully keep them amused longer.

4. **Good Toys vs. Bad Toys** – You're going to be in a confined space, so choose toys wisely. Small cars, trucks, planes, or basically anything with wheels can easily fall on the ground and roll under the seat. They can even roll down the aisle and into other rows. Wheels are definitely a no-no. If your child is old enough to color, consider buying triangular shaped crayons. They're bulky, so they're easy for kids to hold and you don't have to worry about them rolling off the tray. Also, no-mess-markers are great because they only color the special paper they come with, so you don't have to worry about your child coloring the trays or seats.

5. **iPads, Tablets, and Phones** – Consider downloading a few age-appropriate games for the flight to keep your little one entertained. Keep in mind that some games require an Internet connection and your

plane may or may not have Internet capabilities. Consider downloading a few non-Internet games just to be safe.

6. **Be Creative** – Infants and toddlers can be amused by almost anything. When they've lost interest in their toys, see what other things you can do to keep them entertained. Maybe they can play with the plastic cups your drinks come in, or maybe they can play with your keys.

STAYING IN HOTELS

Hotels can be rough for little ones. Your child will be in an unfamiliar place so they may not feel as comfortable or secure as they do at home. Also, they will be in a confined space without a lot of room to run around, so they may get antsy. Stress can build up quickly, but there are a few things you can do to help make your stay more comfortable.

1. When making your hotel reservation, check to see what they can do to help accommodate small children. They may be able to provide things like a Pack 'n Play, crib, and high chair. They may even be able to childproof the room before your arrival.

2. Decide whether you would like to be near or far away from the elevators. Being closer to the elevator means you are in and out faster and won't have to haul your luggage very far. The downside is that everyone on that floor will need to use the elevator, so the closer you are, the nosier it might be. If noise is a concern, you can also ask if you can get a room far away from other guests.

3. While your home may be babyproofed to the nines, hotels are another matter entirely. Not only are

there safety hazards around every corner, there are also germs everywhere! How many people have touched that TV remote, and what were they doing beforehand? Chances are, it wasn't washing their hands. Here are a few suggestions for making sure your child stays as safe and germ-free as possible (you'll notice quickly that tape is your best friend). These are only suggestions, so do whatever you're comfortable with.

- When making your reservation, check to see whether the hotel has the ability to childproof the room.

- Put duct tape over any exposed electrical outlet. Make sure not to get the tape on the walls, because it can peel off the paint or wallpaper.

- Identify all the things you don't want your child to play with and move those items somewhere (like the top shelf of the closet) where they can't be reached. If they won't fit, call the front desk or housekeeping and ask if they will remove the items. Things to consider moving include alarm clocks, coffee makers, hair dryers, pens, books, magazines, baskets of snacks, phones, trashcans, etc.

- Tape cabinets and drawers closed so that your children cannot rummage through them or pinch their fingers in them. Remember, duct tape can remove paint and may even damage drawers, so use something like a painters tape for this.

- If there's a mini-fridge in the room that doesn't require a key to open, consider taping it shut too. Your little one doesn't need that bottle of rum, and you don't want to have to pay for it either.

- Jiggle the TV a bit to make sure it's secure. If it wobbles too much, push it back out of reach or put it on the floor so it doesn't accidentally fall on your child. Also, make sure the remote is out of reach. If you are OK with your child playing with the remote, consider wiping it down first. Those things are germ-infested.

- Make sure all windows and doors are locked. Make sure you also deadbolt the main door in case your child is able to open the door with the handle.

- If the curtains have pull cords, tape them up out of reach.

- If there are loose electrical cords, tape them back behind furniture.

- If there's an air-conditioning/heating unit on the floor with access to the controls, cover it with tape.

- Tape washcloths over sharp edges on furniture to prevent your little ones from hitting their heads on them.

- Move soaps, shampoo, lotions, and all other toiletries out of reach.

- Tape the toilet seat down to prevent your child from playing in the water and/or smashing their fingers under the seat.

These are just a few suggestions for making your room safer for children. Different hotel rooms may have different types of dangers, so it's important to do what you feel is necessary based on your environment. And of course, nothing is better than adult supervision, because no matter what lengths we take to secure the area, children are bound to find something we miss.

School-Aged Children

Traveling with school-aged children is completely different than traveling with infants and toddlers. They are more mobile and often able to entertain themselves. Still, they can get bored easily and may not have a lot of patience for long lines or waiting periods. Here are a few things you can do to make trips with school-aged children easier.

PACKING

Since younger children can go through a range of emotions, understanding these emotions and packing accordingly can go a long way. Think about things you can pack to help counter boredom, overexcitement, tiredness, and more.

- If your child is going to be sitting still for long periods of time (in the airport lounge, plane seat, car, etc.), consider letting your child pick entertainment kits, like coloring books and crayons or activity and puzzle books.

- Handheld game devices can keep your children entertained for hours.

- Download games and/or activities for your tablet or iPad if you have one. There are many educational apps disguised as games, so you don't have to feel guilty letting your child play on the device for long periods of time.

- Pack a set of headphones. This will allow your children to watch movies, listen to music, and play their noisy games without disturbing other passengers.

- Have plenty of snacks available to keep your kids from getting hungry and cranky.

- In case your child gets overexcited to the point where they're basically bouncing off the walls, pack something basic to help channel that energy. Maybe they could use a pen and paper to make a list of things they want to do on the trip, or maybe they could keep a journal to remember everything that happens along the way. Another option is to bring a map and have your child locate where you currently are and the places you will go. Talk about things like what you'll see on the trip and how far away the destination is.

AIRPORT SECURITY

Just like traveling with an infant or toddler, you'll want to make sure you have the right documents with you: either a copy of your child's birth certificate or an adoption document. The TSA agent may not always ask for this when you go through security, but if you look different from your child or have different last names, you may wind up having issues. It's best to always err on the side of caution.

If your child can walk on their own, getting though airport security should be easier. Depending on their age, they may be able to leave their shoes on and go through the metal detector as opposed to being screened through the Advanced Imaging Technology. One parent (sometimes both if the agent allows) can go through the metal detector immediately after their child.

If your child has a disability, medical condition, or medical device, mention this to the TSA agent so you can determine the best way to get them through security. Your child should not have to get out of a wheelchair or any other mobility device if they use one.

SURVIVING FLIGHTS

Long flights can be hard for children who don't like being confined in small spaces for extended periods of time. A little preparation can go a long way when it comes to helping your child get through this experience. Try some of these ideas.

- **Snacks** – Have plenty of snacks available. You never know when your child will get hungry, and it may be a while until a flight attendant will offer food.

- **Keep Plane Toys Separate** – Just like with infants and toddlers, school-aged children can get bored with toys and activities quickly. Consider keeping aside a couple of toys and/or activities for when you are actually in the plane. This could help make the flight more special for them and more bearable for you.

- **Good Toys vs. Bad Toys** – Again, just like with toddlers and infants, avoid things that can roll away (cars, crayons, etc.) if they fall off of the tray and onto the floor. Triangular crayons are great because they can't roll. Also avoid noisy toys unless your child can use headphones with them. Good toys at this age are handheld games, tablets, coloring and activity books, reading books, etc...

- **iPads, Tablets, and Phones** – Consider downloading a few age-appropriate games for the flight to keep your little one entertained. Keep in mind that some games require an Internet connection and your plane may or may not have Internet capabilities. Consider downloading a few non-Internet games just to be safe. Don't forget the headphones.

STAYING IN HOTELS

While you won't need to go through extensive childproofing like you do for infants and toddlers, there are still a few things you may want to consider. Parental controls are available on the TV to prevent your child from accidentally (or intentionally) stumbling across inappropriate channels. Also, keep in mind that some actions, such as removing items from the mini-fridge or making phone calls, may automatically put charges on rooms. Make sure your children know the rules for what they can and cannot touch and remove anything you have concerns with. Also, make sure all doors and windows are securely locked.

Childproofing
Round One – The
Early Years

Babies are constantly putting themselves in harm's way. Seriously, if there's anything dangerous around, your fearless, curious, death-defying stunt child will definitely find it. Luckily, most accidents are preventable, and there are lots of things you can do to keep your child safe. Below is a checklist for steps you can take to minimize the risk of an unexpected trip to the emergency room.

Basic Childproofing Checklist

Sleeping Area – Keep your baby's crib free of pillows, bumpers, stuffed animals, loose fitted sheets, and blankets. Your baby should be sleeping prison-style. All they get is a mattress and a fitted sheet. To keep them warm throughout the night, have them wear a sleep sack. Do not let your baby sleep overnight while swaddled. A swaddling blanket that comes unwrapped could cover your baby's face and increase the risk of suffocation. Also, make sure the mattress is on the lowest position to lessen the chance of them climbing out. Make sure your baby's crib is not next to a window, heating vent, or radiator. All loose items, such as toys, baby monitors, electrical cords, cords on the window blinds, etc. should be at least three feet away from the crib.

Doors – Secure all knobs on doors that go to off-limit areas such as the basement, garage, and outside. Consider getting doorstops or door holders if you are concerned about your child getting their fingers or hands caught in closing doors or door hinges. Also, regarding those little springy doorstoppers that prevent doors from slamming into walls: it's recommended that you glue the tips of them on or get the one-piece stoppers so that your child doesn't take off the tips and put them in their mouth.

Windows – Secure all windows by installing locking devices. Make sure you can still open them in case of an emergency, such as a fire.

Window Treatments – If you have window coverings with cords, make sure the cords are out of your child's reach at all times. Wrap them around hooks or get blind cord winders.

Electrical Cords and Outlets – Hide all electrical cords behind furniture if possible, to prevent your baby from chewing or playing with them. Tape or fasten them to a wall or floor if necessary. Make sure all electrical outlets are also covered, and don't keep lamps in places where your child can touch hot bulbs.

Stairs – Install baby gates on every stair access point, and anywhere else you want to keep off limits.

Balconies and Railings – Keep couches, chairs, and other furniture away from balconies and railings to prevent children from climbing over them. If you have posts or railings that are more than three inches apart, consider getting a mesh wall or another type of temporary barrier to prevent your little one from sliding through and/or getting stuck.

Furniture – Anchor TVs, dressers, bookcases, lamps, and any other type of furniture that could tip over.

Toy Boxes – Open shelves and bins are safer than chests; however, if you plan on using a chest around the house, make sure it has a lightweight lid that won't slam shut on your child's fingers. There should also be small air holes in case your little one climbs in.

Choking Hazards – Small items that can fit in your child's mouth should be kept out of reach. This includes loose change, marbles, stones, jewelry, hard candies, and other small objects.

Batteries – Batteries contain hazardous chemicals and can be extremely dangerous if swallowed. Fully-charged batteries should be securely stored. Dead batteries should be properly disposed of immediately after being removed.

Miscellaneous Items – Put breakables, valuables, and other off-limit items on high shelves out of reach, or store them in another location.

Plants – Keep plants out of reach, and make sure there are no poisonous ones inside or outside of your house. A quick search online can help you determine whether the plants you have are poisonous. If you're still not sure, replace them.

Fire Safety – Install smoke alarms and carbon monoxide detectors throughout your house and check them every month. Also, fireplaces, heaters, furnaces, and radiators should have protective barriers to keep children from burning themselves. Matches, lighters, and anything else that can start a fire should be secured.

Cleaning Supplies – House cleaners like bleach, glass cleaners, wood polishers, dishwashing tablets, and laundry detergents should be up high and out of reach. Pesticides and other chemicals should be stored out of reach too. You might even want to keep them in secured cabinets.

Plastic Bags – If you keep plastic bags in the house, make sure they are stored out of reach. Any other plastic bag that comes into the house (dry cleaning bags, produce

bags, plastic wrapping, etc.) should be disposed
of immediately.

Pets – Cats like to curl up to warm things, and they may try
to snuggle with your sleeping baby. This is dangerous for
many reasons. Cats could bite, scratch, or even smother
your baby. To train cats to stay away from the crib, cover
a large piece of cardboard in aluminum foil and place
it over the crib mattress (when your baby is not in it, of
course). Cats hate the crinkling sound and after placing
them on the cover, hopefully they will avoid the crib from
that point forward. If aluminum foil doesn't work, try
covering the cardboard with double-sided sticky tape.
Cats don't like sticky paws either. Other pet-related things
to consider include keeping dog and cat food bowls in
separate areas to prevent your child from getting in the
food or water, and making sure litter boxes are in separate
areas too. You definitely don't want your child playing in a
poop-filled sandbox.

Workout Equipment – Lots of people have workout
equipment in their homes, and while they may not look
dangerous, chances are that they most certainly are.
Treadmills, exercise bikes, elliptical machines, and other
equipment have various places that can pinch fingers,
bump heads, and more. Treadmills also have safety cords
that can shut a machine off in an emergency, but those
cords can pose a strangulation risk for your child. Children
should be kept away from exercise equipment at all times.
If you don't have a dedicated room where the equipment
can be locked away, use baby gates to section them off.
If your child has to be in the same room as you while
you work out, keep them in another area of the room
away from the equipment, but in a place where they are
still visible.

> **DID YOU KNOW?**
> In 2009, Mike Tyson's four-year-old daughter was injured in a treadmill accident at his home. A cable that was attached to the exercise machine had wrapped around her neck and strangled her. After freeing her from the cord, her mother called 911 and started CPR, but unfortunately it was too late. She eventually died in the hospital. Many people don't realize how dangerous exercise equipment can be for young children, but injuries from them are common and children should be kept away from exercise equipment at all times.

Pools – Fence off pools and hot tubs if you have them. Also, install a pool alarm, a device that alerts you when someone disturbs the surface of the pool, opens a gate to the pool, or removes a cover.

Firearms - Keep guns unloaded and locked away. Store bullets in a separate locked location.

The Kitchen

Sharp Objects – Knives, scissors, letter openers, sharp kitchen utensils, and other pointy objects should be secured in drawers that can't open.

Cling Wrap and Tin Foil – Plastic cling wrap and tin foil boxes have sharp cutting edges that can be dangerous. They should be kept out of reach of children.

Trashcans – It's a good idea to only use trashcans and recycling containers that have lids. Otherwise your curious child may decide to sample some new bacteria. They may also decide to make lovely new messes.

Sponges – These are bacteria cesspools and can make your child very sick. Plus, they are major choking hazards if a piece is bitten off. Keep sponges out of reach.

Stoves and Ovens – Install stove-knob covers on your burner controls. Also, appliance latches can be used to prevent your little one from opening conventional and microwave ovens.

Refrigerator – Keep your child out of the fridge by installing an appliance latch. Also, magnets are dangerous if swallowed. If you feel like you need to have them on the fridge, make sure they are larger in size (to lessen the chance of them being swallowed) and kept high enough that they are out of reach.

Appliances - Keep all items away from the edges of tables and countertops. This includes things like toasters, mixers, juicers, blenders, knife blocks, etc.

Dishwasher – Install an appliance latch so your child doesn't open the dishwasher and reach for something sharp or breakable. Also, remember to keep the detergent locked away.

The Bathroom

Doors – Make sure you install doorknob covers to prevent your child from closing the door and locking themselves in.

Toiletries – Colognes, perfumes, cosmetics, mouthwashes, toothpaste, skincare, hair products, and other toiletries can be toxic. They should be secured.

Medications – Prescriptions, medicines, vitamins, supplements, and anything else that can be potentially harmful if swallowed should be locked away. Yes, Viagra and PrEP too, so if you have anything bedside, make sure it's secured. While you're at it, if you have Viagra or PrEP, check the expiration dates because if you have an infant in the house, chances are you're not using them very often anymore.

Cabinets – Install cabinet locks to keep your child from getting into any contents you don't want them getting into.

Toilets – Install a lid lock to prevent your child from slamming the lid on their fingers or turning your toilet into a new splash pool. Also, children can drown in just a couple of inches of water, so unlocked toilets are drowning risks.

Hair Dryers – These can easily be knocked into the sink, bathtub, or toilet, and the cord could also get wrapped around your child's neck. Keep hair dryers out of reach.

Sharp Objects – Razors should not be kept on tubs or on sink counters. Make sure razors, tweezers, scissors, nail clippers, and any other sharp grooming objects are secured out of reach.

Bathtub – Install a faucet shield to protect your child from hitting their head on the faucet. Remember to never leave your child alone in the bath, not even for a second, and always drain the tub after use.

Water Temperature – Set the max water temperature in your home to 120 degrees to minimize the chance of accidental scalding. If you are unable to set the water temperature in your home, consider installing a scald guard which will slow the water flow if it reaches a temperature that is too high.

Bath Rugs – Use nonskid rugs to help prevent slips and falls. Also, consider getting a rubber bath mat for inside the tub.

Home Office

Computer Monitor – If you have a desktop monitor, make sure it's far away from the edge of your desk and consider bolting it down so your little one doesn't pull it on top of themself.

Choking Hazards – Make sure your desk remains tidy and there are no small items that your child can put in their mouth and choke on. This includes rubber bands, paper clips, pen caps, and things often found on desks and work spaces.

Electrical Cords and Outlets – If you have a lot of cords running into one outlet, consider threading them through a tube to prevent your baby from chewing or playing with them. Also use a surge protector cover.

Bookcases – Make sure all bookcases are anchored to the wall so your child doesn't pull them on top of themselves and get pinned down or hurt.

Childproofing Your Home Can Be Fabulous!

Baby-proofing products are not known for being particularly stylish, and let's face it—many of them can be downright hideous. They can be obtrusive or gaudy, and they can even clash with your home décor, but here's a little secret: it doesn't have to be that way! You don't have to stick foam corners on everything in your house in order to keep your child safe. With a little effort, it's possible to childproof your home in a way that doesn't cramp your style. Here are a few options that allow you to make your home safe while keeping it fashionable in the process.

Baby Gates – Most gates are made out of metal, mesh, or wood and stand out like a sore thumb. With a little effort though, you can find designer ones that are modern, elegant, and stylish. There are options for clamping around banisters and spindles instead of drilling into them, and you can even have fireplace gates stained to match your mantle or floor. There are retractable options too, so that the gate hides when it's not in use. Be creative! Try searching online for "stylish," "modern," "decorative," and "customized" baby gates to get a few ideas.

Electrical Outlet Covers – There are many options when it comes to childproofing electrical outlets. You can opt for the cheap option where you plug a small cover into the actual outlet, but these can be a pain to remove every time you need to plug something in. Also, if your child pulls a cord out from the wall, you now have an exposed outlet for them to stick their little fingers in. Look for options that cover the entire outlet and require you to slide or swivel the cover when plugging something in. When you remove a plug from these, they automatically slide shut. These types of electrical outlets offer more protection, they look better, and they're fairly inexpensive too.

Stove Knob Covers – You can find cheap options that are clear and don't make it difficult for adults to access. If you are going to be looking for new appliances in the near future, consider getting a cooktop with the knobs on top. They're modern and stylish, and the knobs are placed in a position that is more difficult for a child to reach.

Cabinets and Drawers – You're going to need to lock away those sharp knives and other dangerous things hidden in drawers and cabinets. Unfortunately, the majority of locks out there are bulky and just plain ugly! If you're looking for something that won't be an eyesore, consider magnetic locks or similar concealed locks that are easy to use and won't compromise the visual aesthetic of your home.

Coffee Tables – Hard and pointed edges on coffee tables can be major hazards for children because they're just the right height for toddlers to hit their heads when they fall. Consider getting a circular table without corners or a large ottoman that's soft and easy to clean. For ottomans, you can place a tray on top whenever you need a temporary sturdy surface for drinks or food. If you have tables with corners and you don't want to remove them, you can always get clear corner protectors.

Rugs and Carpet Tiles – If you have hardwood or tiled floors, you can create a stylish soft spot for your child with cute rugs or carpet tiles. They come in various styles, colors, and patterns, so you can find one that matches your décor.

Blind Cord Winders – If you have blinds on your windows, it's important that you secure the cords and keep them away from your little one. Blind cord winders allow you to wrap up loose cords and keep them securely out of reach. They're available in different colors to match your blinds and blend in.

Break-Resistant Glasses – Acrylic stemware and barware allows you to have nice glasses without the worry of having them shatter. They can look just like glass and are great for indoor and outdoor parties.

Picture Frames – Opt for picture frames with acrylic instead of glass. That way if your child gets ahold of the picture and drops it, you don't have to worry about pieces of shattered glass going everywhere.

Flameless Candles – If you love candles, don't worry. You don't have to live without them in order to keep your baby safe. Battery-operated, flameless candles are available in various different sizes, from pillars to votives and tea lights. Some create a nice glow, while others have flickering options to give the sense of a real flame. There are even scented options. Some are more realistic than others, so look around until you find something that you like.

Getting Professional Help

Childproofing a home can be overwhelming. If you don't have the time, or if you're afraid you might miss something, you might want to consider hiring a professional childproofing service. There are companies that will assess your home and address safety concerns accordingly. They can install gates and window guards, secure furniture and doors, and address any other risks. They can even safeguard your pool if you have one. It's not a cheap service, but if you're worried you might miss something, it could give you peace of mind. The International Association for Child Safety (IAFCS) can help you find childproofing services. Their website is www.iafcs.org. You could also do a general search online for childproofing services. Just make sure you check references and reviews.

Early Bonding with Your Children

Regardless if you are welcoming an infant or an older child into your family, early bonding with them is going to be extremely important. There are various types of bonding activities that you can do based on age level and background. Here are a few examples:

Bonding with Infants and Toddlers

SKIN-TO-SKIN CONTACT

Skin-to-skin contact, sometimes referred to as Kangaroo Care, is a wonderful way to bond with infants. It's simple and easy to do, especially during feeding and nap times. Just remove your shirt and your baby's clothes (except for their diaper), and hold your baby so that the two of you are skin-to-skin. For naps, hold your baby so you are chest-to-chest. Then place a blanket over your child without covering their face and…voilà! You instantly become a human incubator. There are numerous benefits to skin-to-skin contact including:

- **Enhanced Bonding** – Remember when we talked about oxytocin in the "Things About Parenthood No One Tells You About" section? It's that important attachment/bonding chemical that's released when you spend time with your child. Every time you experience skin-to-skin contact with your baby, your body releases oxytocin and enables that initial connection to occur naturally.

- **Regulating Your Baby's Body** – Your body can help regulate your baby's body temperature, and when you are chest-to-chest, your body can help regulate your baby's heart rate and breathing too.

- **Baby Cries Less** – The rhythm of your heart in conjunction with your warm body can help calm your baby, making them cry less.

- **Better Sleep for Your Baby and Less Stress for Everyone** – Since skin-to-skin contact can help keep your baby calm, it will likely be easier for them to fall asleep. Having a baby that sleeps more and cries less can also help keep you in a more calm and relaxed state. Well, as much as you can be with an infant in the house.

- **Better Growth and Development** – A calm baby that cries less and sleeps more can spend more time taking everything in, thus devoting more time to growth and development, both physically and mentally.

Even though feeding and nap times are perfect occasions for skin-to-skin contact, there are plenty of other opportunities for it as well. You can pretty much practice it anytime you're holding your baby, well anywhere it's appropriate for you to walk around shirtless.

EYE CONTACT

Another important factor of bonding is eye contact. Babies thrive off of it. Newborns are nearsighted for the first few months of their lives, so you'll have to be within eight to fifteen inches from their face while practicing eye contact. If you hold your infant in your arms during feeding times, your face will be the perfect distance, and when you lock eyes while practicing skin-to-skin contact during feeding times, you're basically emulating rock-star parenting skills!

OTHER PHYSICAL CONTACT

Babies love interaction, and there are many bonding techniques you can do with physical touch. Here are a few examples:

- **Kissing** – Kiss them on their foreheads, cheeks, hands, and feet.

- **Hand Grips** – Let your child grip one of your fingers. While they're holding on, try different types of interactions, such as slowly moving your hands in circles or tapping their hands with your thumb.

- **Apply Lotion** – A gentle massage can be calming for your baby. When using lotion, steer clear of ones that use perfume or dyes.

RESPONDING TO CRIES

Some people say that parents should allow their children to cry before responding to their needs, but it's important to keep in mind that infants are only able to express their needs through crying. When they cry, they are trying to tell you something (they're hungry, they're tired, they need a change, etc.). Quickly responding to an infant's cries can help build trust. In the beginning, try responding to their cries within thirty seconds and scale back in response time as they get older.

BABY CARRIERS

Carrying your baby or toddler against your chest via a carrier has many benefits. Not only does it free up your hands, but it strengthens the bond between you and your child since it allows you to stay close throughout the day. Your heartbeat and breathing patterns can also help keep your child in a calmer state, and you don't have to worry about maneuvering a stroller when you're out and about.

Bonding with Older Children

If you are expanding your family by welcoming an older child into your home, your bonding experience is going to be completely different than if you were welcoming a newborn. First of all, there are likely going to be trust issues that need to be overcome. Whatever living situation your child was in beforehand didn't work out, and they may be afraid that living with you isn't going to work out either. Your child may have had numerous placements before finding you, and they may be wondering how long it's going to be until they have to move on to another family. You're going to need to find a way to build trust and form a meaningful bond. This can take a long time, so patience and perseverance are key.

Also, keep in mind that children often wind up in foster care as a result of neglect, abuse, divorce, the death of a legal guardian, or various other unfortunate events that could disrupt a home. Every child's background and history is different, so what works for bonding with one child may not work for another. For example, a normal bedtime routine might include tucking a child into bed and giving them a hug and kiss goodnight, but that could be traumatizing for a child with a history of sexual abuse. Remember, social workers are there to help, so ask them for tips and ideas for what kind of bonding exercises might work for your family. You'll find a few examples below that may work for various ages. Periodically check in with your social worker to give updates and ask about different types of bonding exercises if the ones you are using don't seem to be working.

GETTING COMFORTABLE

Get on the Same Level – Some kids may not want to interact right away. If this is the case, you can still bond by being at the same level and sharing interests in close proximity to each other. For example, if your child is sitting and coloring at the table, you can sit next to them at the table and color too. If they are lying on the floor reading a book, you can lie on the floor and quietly read a book next to them. You don't have to interact or speak with each other, but you can get comfortable with being in the same space with each other while doing the same kind of activities.

ENCOURAGING EYE CONTACT

Use a Sticker – Without your child noticing, place a sticker on your face right between your eyes. Don't say anything about it and see how long it takes for them to notice.

Follow an Object – Play a game where your child has to keep their eyes on an object in your hand. Slowly move the object side to side, up and down, in a figure eight, and basically all over the place. Every few seconds, stop the object between your eyes so that your child looks at you for a couple of seconds before moving it again.

Peek-a-Boo – If your child has trouble making eye contact, you might be able to slowly work on it by playing a game of "Peek-a-Boo." It doesn't have to be covering your eyes with your hands like you would with a baby, but you could playfully peek around a corner and say, "I see you," before hiding again.

ENCOURAGING PHYSICAL CONTACT

Brush, Comb, or Braid Hair – It sounds simple, but brushing, combing, and braiding hair allows you to spend time with your child and have physical contact with them in a non-threatening way. Depending on the comfort and trust levels, you can do this in silence, hum or sing a song, or have conversations while brushing hair.

Painting Nails – Painting your child's fingernails and toenails can introduce physical contact and allow children to express themselves artistically at the same time. In addition to different paint colors, you can also use stickers and gems if you want to get fancy. And if your inner drag persona wants to express herself too, maybe your child can even paint your nails. Make sure you have nail polish remover on hand if you are concerned about looking too fabulous outside of the house.

Play Hand Games – Paper, Rock, Scissors, Patty Cake, and Thumb Wars are examples of games that involve non-threatening physical contact.

Three-Legged Race – It doesn't necessarily have to be a race. You could even try tying one of your legs to one of your child's legs and just walking around the house. This game involves physical contact and also encourages communication and teamwork.

ENHANCING COMMUNICATION AND INTERACTION

Read a Story – You can read a story to your child, or you can read together. This is a great bonding exercise because you can sit next to each other and increase vocabulary skills, literacy, critical thinking, and imagination.

Play Leader-Follower Games – There are many games that can be used to enhance communication and build trust at the same time. For example, "Red Light, Green Light" and "Simon Says" both involve people following someone's lead. "Mother May I" is also a great example too, although you may want to consider calling it "Father May I." It's completely up to you.

Play Ball – A simple back and forth game can be played with various types of coordination levels. You could roll a ball back and forth for younger kids. For older kids, you could kick a soccer ball back and forth or play a game of catch. A game of "Hot Potato" could also work for a child who has more energy.

Projects – Do a project together that involves working together physically to achieve a goal. Maybe complete a puzzle or build a model car.

Parenting Groups

Parenting groups can be extremely helpful for new parents. They're an opportunity for your kids to meet and play with other children; they give you an opportunity to get advice from others who are at the same stage of parenting as you; and they give you a chance to actually talk to other adults (something necessary for all new stay-at-home dads cooped up with someone who only knows how to say goo goo gaa gaa). But unfortunately, parenting groups can be a bit hit-or-miss for gay dads.

Many parenting groups are catered towards stay-at-home moms, because women have traditionally been the stay-at-home caregivers, and the groups give them an opportunity to hang out with other moms. This is blatantly obvious because many of the parenting groups reference mothers only, like "Mom's Day Out," or "Moms and Tots" or something along those lines. Sometimes, men are not welcomed into the group at all. Other times, they may make an exception for gay dads because they consider a gay man to be "one of the girls." Or maybe they've gotten past the whole gender-roles thing and accept parents regardless of gender.

There might also be an LGBT parenting group in your area, which is awesome if it's relatively close to you. Unfortunately, because there aren't as many LGBT parents as straight parents, there aren't as many local LGBT parenting groups either. You may find that you have to travel quite a distance to get to a play date or picnic, which isn't something that's sustainable in the long run when we all have busy lives. If you can though, try to get to an LGBT parenting group meeting a few times while your child is young so they can see other kids with same-gender parents. You can search for "LGBT Parenting Groups" plus your city and state to see if there's one near you. The Family Equality Council is also a great resource. Check them out at www.familyequality.org.

Finally, if you can't find an LGBT parenting group to attend in person, try looking for online parenting groups. They're great for getting advice from other gay dads, and you don't have to travel anywhere. Here are a few Facebook groups you may want to join.

Gay Fathers:
www.facebook.com/groups/15368945293/

Gay Dads
www.facebook.com/groups/7181147876/

LGBTQ + Parenting:
www.facebook.com/groups/1665204943700662/

Honestly parenting groups are a mixed bag. You may have bad experiences with them, you may have wonderful experiences with them, you may decide to skip them all together, or you may decide to create your own. To see what I mean, here are a few experiences other gay dads have had with parenting groups:

"We were not allowed to join our neighborhood mothers group. It would not have been much of an issue, except that one of my friends started the group (before we moved to the neighborhood). It got weirder because we've twice accidentally found ourselves at their Halloween party at the local playground, and our son is close friends with a number of the kids. He crashed the party. Somewhat awkward for the parents. Not for the kids. After several years we got an invite to their Easter Egg Hunt, but declined. The damage was done."
—Ian Hart

"There were many baby groups we attended that were specifically called 'Moms and Tots.' When suggested that they should change the name of the group they said, 'Well it's mostly mothers who attend the classes.'"
—**BJ Barone**

"We live in a very gay friendly area of the nation but there aren't that many gay parents (yet). I find playgroups and parenting groups to be one of the most discriminatory things I've faced. I'm a stay-at-home dad and have faced having to be approved by other moms on a regular basis, I've actually given up trying to expand my circle because it is exhausting having to be 'vetted' just to attend a play date. On a positive note, we have an 'all-gay' parents group that gets together monthly."
—**Chad Scanlon**

"An important factor for us has been our involvement with Modern Family Alliance, a local volunteer organization that hosts social gatherings and educational events for LGBT families. These gatherings gave our son the opportunity to meet and play with other kids who are part of non-traditional families."
—**Michael Hadley**

"Find other gay dads in your community. I never realized how many gay men have adopted in our area, until we started connecting on Facebook via foster/adoption pages in our area. They are great resource. Everyone parents differently, and you can all learn something from one another."
—**Adam White**

Questions You
Might Get Asked
and How to
Respond to Them

Knock, knock.
Who's there?
William.
William who?
William mind your own business?

Being attracted to someone of the same sex is not a new phenomenon. LGBT people have been around since the dawn of time, and we have been parents since the dawn of time as well. We may not have always been open about our sexuality while we were parents, but that doesn't mean we didn't exist. It used to be common for LGBT people to marry someone of the opposite sex and have children in an attempt to hide who they really were because they feared societal repercussions. LGBT people feared being disowned by their families, fired from their jobs, jailed, beaten, or even killed. While some of these fears still exist in our country, we've come a long way and have had numerous advances in LGBT equality over the last few decades. More and more people have come out of the closet and are proud of who they are. We can thank Stonewall, Pride marches, Harvey Milk, Obama, and numerous LGBT activists for that.

But just because we have more rights and are generally living more open lives, doesn't mean that everything is lah-di-dah. While same-sex parenting isn't a new phenomenon, "visible" same-sex parenting is. Television shows like Modern Family and The Fosters may have introduced people to the concept and reality of same-sex parents, but many people still haven't encountered LGBT families in person. We're like unicorns to some people: they've heard about gay parents but haven't really seen any. Because of this, you're probably going to be asked a lot of personal and invasive questions. Some people are genuinely curious and are trying to learn more about how adoption, surrogacy, and same-sex parenting works. Other people already have their heads full of negative assumptions.

It's OK to have mixed emotions when you get these kinds of questions, and your answers to them may change depending on your mood at the time or how much sleep you've had the night before. The challenge is finding a way to provide educational information while also protecting your child's privacy. Keep in mind that as your child gets older, they will be observing and listening to how you answer these prying questions, so you'll want to answer in a way that doesn't give them the assumption that something is wrong with their family unit. That being said, you don't owe anyone answers to questions about your personal life either. It's up to you whether or not you want to engage. Here are a few common questions you may get along with suggestions for ways you can respond.

Where Is His/Her Mother?

It's very common for strangers to ask this question, especially if a dad is out alone with an infant, and it could be asked for a variety of reasons. Maybe the person is just trying to make small talk with you. Maybe they think you have kidnapped the child, or maybe they feel bad for you, a male (who can't possibly know how to parent) being left to fend for himself while the mom (who obviously is the only one who can take care of a child) is somewhere else. Keep in mind that most of the time the person asking the question is not trying to be mean or negative. They might be assuming that there is a mother somewhere in the picture, or who knows, they may be curious about adoption, foster care, or surrogacy and are thinking you might be able to help them by answering a few questions.

Here are some possibilities for how you might answer this question. Remember, your child may be listening, so your answers might change as they get older. Also, it's best to keep your answers short with strangers unless you want to open things up for the person to ask additional questions about your personal situation. Try one of these answers.

- "My husband and I are the parents."
- "Why do you ask?"
- "There is no mom. He/she has two dads."

Which One of You Is the Dad?

If you and your partner are both out with your child, strangers may ask this question, assuming a mom is in the picture somewhere and dad is just hanging out with a friend. The quick and easy answer to this one is, "We both are."

REAL-LIFE STORY:
"Before our daughter could talk, we would often get, 'She is so precious, which one of you is her daddy?' We would then begin this eloquent and awkward dialogue of saying, 'We both are,' multiple times until we finally got the tilted head stare. We refer to this as the 'dog- whistle look.' You whistle, and a dog will tilt its head."
–Trey Darnell

Which One of You Is the "Real" Dad?

This is an attempt to find out whose sperm was used, with the assumption being that the one who is biologically related is the "real" parent. The person may even flat-out ask which one of you donated your sperm. If you're not comfortable talking about it, try one of these answers:

- "Does it matter?"

- "Why do you ask?"

- "We both are his/her 'real' parents."

> **REAL-LIFE STORY:**
> "The awkward question that we get most frequently is about the genetic relationship we have with our children. Again, we understand it is a natural curiosity, so we try not to be offended by the question. We have two sets of twins and both are mixed-race Asian and Caucasian, so it becomes a bit of a guessing game trying to figure out which half of the interracial gay couple is biologically related to each of these kids. Once, when our older children were still babies, we went out to lunch and the waitress asked us almost immediately after introducing herself, 'Who is the sperm donor?' We were so shocked with her forward approach that I frankly don't recall if we responded with an order for the avocado egg rolls appetizer or our standard response. We usually tell people that we keep that detail private because we want to be treated equally as parents to all our kids. The waitress' gay coworker overheard the exchange and was so mortified. He came to our rescue and took over our table for her." –David Hu

Which One of You Is the Mom?

This question assumes one parent is feminine and the other is masculine, or one of you does what they consider "feminine roles" and the other does what they consider "masculine roles." It's similar to when someone asks an engaged same-sex couple, "Which one of you is the bride?" You can joke around and say one of you is the mom if you'd like. Or you can say, "Neither. We're both dads."

What Is It like to Be a Gay Dad?

Well, the first thing we do in the morning is wake our kids up by playing loud dance music. Then we feed them protein shakes for breakfast, and spend time together gossiping while doing each other's hair. When it's time for school, we ride our magical unicorns there while waving rainbow flags, and when school is over, we hit the gym and work out for a bit before making our way to the club. No, gay dads are not different from straight parents. We feed our kids, clothe them, take them to school, read them bedtime stories, and everything else parents do. The simple answer to this is that we're just like other parents.

Who Does All the Mommy Stuff?

This question is horrible because it implies that it's a woman's job to do certain things like cooking, cleaning, feeding babies, and changing diapers. There are a few different ways you can answer this question:

- "We equally share parenting responsibilities."
- "What do you mean, mommy stuff?"
- "We don't believe jobs should be based on gender."

Why Did She Give Him/Her Up? I Could Never Give Up My Child.

Statements and questions like these stem from people having no real-life experience with how open adoption works. It used to be the case that the majority of adoptions in the United States were closed, and children grew up without knowing who their birthparents were. There was no contact between the birthparents and the adopted children, hence the thought process that mothers had "given" their children away and wanted nothing to do with them anymore. For many birthmothers, that couldn't be further from the truth. Many of them continued to think about their children, wondering if they were OK and whether they had made the right choice or not.

In today's day and age, the majority of infant adoptions in the United States are done through open adoption, allowing the birthparents and adopted children to have contact with each other after the adoption. Today, most birthmothers don't "give their children up" for adoption; they spend time trying to find the perfect family to place their children with when they know they are not in a position to parent themselves. Adoption doesn't mean the birthmother doesn't want the child, it means that she thought long and hard to make the best decision for her child. It takes a lot of thought, courage, and emotional strength to make a decision like that. Here are a few responses you might want to try out:

- "She didn't give him/her up. She made a difficult decision to do what was in the best interest of her child, and to give him/her a life that she could not provide."
- "She didn't give him/her up. She's still part of his/her life."
- "That's not my story to tell."

What If Your Child Turns Out to Be Gay?

As if something is wrong with someone being gay. If they are assuming a parent's sexual orientation determines a child's orientation, that's a false assumption. Here are a few suggestions for how you can respond:

- "I'd still love them, just like I would if they turn out to be straight."
- "Why? Do you think being gay is a bad thing?"
- "My parents were straight and that didn't make me straight."

What If Your Child Is Straight?

Maybe the person asking this question is assuming you won't be able to identify with your child if he or she turns out to be straight. A great way to respond to this question is to just repeat it back to them: "What if my child is straight?"

How Did You Get Him/Her/Them?

The person asking most likely wants to know how you formed your family. Did you pursue adoption, foster care, or surrogacy? Maybe they're being nosy or, again, maybe they are genuinely interested in learning how those avenues work. The way you should answer this depends on how open you want to be with the person. Do you want to explain the whole journey to parenthood with them, or do you want to change the topic? Again, remember: you don't owe an answer to anyone, so don't feel bad for not giving them the whole background.

> **REAL-LIFE STORY:**
> "People ask about how we created our family all the time. I try to remember that mostly people are curious, and the vast majority of the time this comes from a place of support. Still, it can feel quite invasive, especially in the wrong contexts. I try to answer completely because I think one of the important ways we gain equality is by educating people about our families. But I am also careful not to share too much—knowing that we are a family through adoption is usually enough." —Gabriel Blau

REAL-LIFE STORY:

"The question we get that sometimes irritates us is, 'How did you get them?'...like we went to a shopping market and picked them out from a display case. We recognize that these questions are often asked out of curiosity and not malice. We use this as an opportunity to educate people about how our family was formed and that we are not unique in our desire to be parents. If people are genuine about their questions, we will get as detailed as they want. We have even gone as far as to explain about our choices for egg donors and a surrogate if they really want to know. Sometimes they have just never had an opportunity to meet people with experiences like ours." –Tommy Starling

REAL-LIFE STORY:

"The most common question is, 'How did we get her?' While she was born here in the US, she looks Asian, and conversations start with something along those lines. Because of this, we get compared to the gay dads on Modern Family a lot. We were travelling to NYC, and the guy sitting in the seat next to me called his wife to tell her that he was sitting next to a real-life Cam and Mitchell. As I said it happens regularly–at first it was fun, but now it's just old." –Chad Scanlon

Where Did You Get Him/Her/Them?

This question is common when people adopt or foster children of a different race. Many times, there is an assumption that the parents adopted the child from a different country. The way you answer this, again, depends on how much you want to engage with the person. You could call them on it and ask, "Why do you want to know?" You could go ahead and tell them the details of your journey to parenthood, or you could even give a sarcastic answer. "At the bakery. I heard that's where they keep the buns in the oven." Keep in mind though, sarcastic answers may just lead to additional questions and your child might be listening to your answer too.

> ### REAL-LIFE STORY:
> "Because our children are adopted and are a different race, the most common question we get is, 'Where are they from?' While we do like to educate others and want to represent families that may look different well, we evade the question when it's asked in front of them. They are from here. Because they are black, there is this automatic assumption that we adopted from Africa. Sometimes I want to say, 'You do know that there are black people from the United States.' Of course we don't, but it would be nice if people used the filter, 'Would you want a stranger asking questions about your children in front of them?'" –Duke Nelson

How Much Did He/She/They Cost?

This could be another example of someone being genuinely curious about the practicalities of adoption, foster care, or surrogacy. They may be interested in starting their own family the same way, but not sure if they can afford the fees associated with it. Still, the question is as appropriate as asking another person how much their salary is. Your answer could be honest, blunt, sincere, or sarcastic. It's up to you.

- "He/she/they didn't cost anything."
- "Eighteen years of our lives."

REAL-LIFE STORY:
"The most awkward question (in the beginning at least) was, 'How much did she cost?' At first we just laughed uncomfortably and changed the subject, but two years in we tend to say, 'As much as a Prius.' That turns the table on who's uncomfortable. Who really asks how much a human being costs?" –Chad Scanlon

How Did You Get Stuck with the Kids? Is It Mom's Day Out? Are You Babysitting?

These questions assume dads are only taking care of the children because the mother is not available at the time. We have an opportunity here to change society's way of thinking. Taking care of children is not a "mom's" job; it's a "parent's" job. Try one of these responses:

- "I'm not 'stuck' with the kids. I cherish every minute I have with them."
- "Not every family has a mom."
- "Our child is lucky to have two dads."
- "Parenting is not a woman's job. It's a parent's job."
- "Fathers don't 'babysit.'"

> **REAL-LIFE STORY:**
> "I remember meeting a friend of mine for dinner and having my son in a stroller. As we were leaving, the hostess came up to me and patted me on the back saying, 'You are such a good babysitter!' That one comment has stuck with me for years. It felt like someone saying, 'You obviously couldn't be this child's parent.' We also had a lot of people come up so they could give us their unsolicited approval. 'You guys are so great,' or, 'It's so great that you're doing this!' I was never doing anything outside of what other parents would do, and I definitely wasn't doing anything great at the time. I would just be like picking my kids up from school or something like that." –Rob Watson

> **REAL-LIFE STORY:**
> "When we go grocery shopping or out to dinner, we often get the, 'Oh, you must be giving mom a day off' comment. We are quick to respond that there is no mom and that our kids are lucky and happy to have two dads. We never want our children to think there is anything wrong with their family or that they need to hide something." –Tommy Starling

How Old Was He/She When You Got Him/Her?

This question is quite common, and comes with an assumption that since you're a gay dad, you probably adopted or went through foster care. It's up to you if you want to go into details about your family expansion journey.

REAL-LIFE STORY:

"This type of question is usually presented to us as: 'How long have you had him?' or, 'How old was he when you adopted him?' Because our son was conceived via surrogacy and subsequently adopted, we typically say something like: 'We adopted him soon after he was born,' or 'He's been ours since he was born.' We provide basic information without going into detail." —**Michael Hadley**

REAL-LIFE STORY:

"Most people are capable of realizing that we are gay parents, but curiosity often leads them to question how our family came to be. People often assume our kids were adopted, and we have been asked, 'How old where they when you got them?' several times over the years. We understand that most people don't know about surrogacy, so we take no offense to these questions. We explain that our kids were born through surrogacy. This frequently starts a discussion about the complexities of gestational surrogacy. We would like to think we have opened some minds and educated some people in these conversations." —**David Hu**

REAL-LIFE STORY:

"We often get asked, 'How old was he when you got him?' Luckily we don't get offended very easily, and our lives are pretty much an open book, so we don't mind answering these questions. We explain our surrogacy journey and hopefully next time people will think twice about asking invasive questions." –BJ Barone

Aren't You Worried Your Child Will Be Bullied for Having Same-Sex Parents?

Look, everyone gets made fun of at some point. It's a fact of life. You are either too tall or too small, too skinny or overweight. Your hair is too frizzy, your teeth are too crooked, or your face is too pimply. Someone is always going to find something to tease you about.

The important thing is that we teach our children to be confident and proud of who they are. We can teach them to stand up for themselves, and we can foster an environment where our children are comfortable coming to us (or another trusted adult) whenever there's a problem. We can also lead by example.

What About Your Child's "Real" Parents?

The person asking most likely wants to know about the birthparents or the donors, but doesn't know how to phrase the question. First of all, you can answer the question if you are comfortable doing so, but it's none of their business and you don't have to answer if you don't want to. Second of all, you are the "real" parents!

Do You Think You Might Be Depriving Your Child of a Female Role Model?

Where do people come up with these ideas? It's not like we're raising our children on an island inhabited by men only. There are plenty of women in our lives that can be role models: grandmothers, sisters, aunts, nieces, teachers, friends, and neighbors. Take a pick.

How to Find LGBT-Friendly Schools

The school years can offer wonderful experiences for kids, but they can also be stressful too. It's important to find a school that will be welcoming to your child and your family, but how do you know if the school you're looking into is LGBT-friendly? Most schools will tell you that they're accepting and that they don't discriminate against anyone, but how do you make sure they are walking the walk and not just talking the talk?

It's important to keep in mind that all schools will tell you how great they are. Don't just talk to them on the phone and take their word for it. Visit the school yourself and check things out in person. Ask for referrals.

Below is a list of things to consider when researching new schools for your child. Don't feel obligated to get answers to everything on the list. Rather, use it as a guide and ask the questions that allow you to get a good feel for the school's acceptance of the LGBT community. Keep in mind that some of these points (like gender-neutral forms) are relevant to all schools, regardless of grade level. Other suggestions may be more relevant for secondary schools than for elementary schools or preschools.

> *REAL-LIFE STORY:*
>
> "When I was trying to enroll my kids in school, I noticed that several of the private schools had no issues with same-sex parents, but they did seem to have issues with kids that had learning challenges. They wanted to gloat about how smart their kids were and basically tried to screen out kids with challenges. My kids were from the foster care system and were exposed to drugs in utero, so they did have learning challenges. I remember one school wouldn't even talk to us. They wrote a letter to us saying we should do homeschooling. We tried looking into non-private schools too, but it was a challenge finding ones that weren't religious. The counselor at one of the Christian schools said our kids would be welcomed there, but he would tell them the same thing he tells kids with divorced parents: 'Your family is not God's plan for a family.' Yay, that seemed welcoming." –Rob Watson

What Is the Diversity Like in the School?

Understanding the school's diversity dynamics could give you a better idea for how sympathetic the staff is to the needs of students with various backgrounds. Are there other kids in the school with LGBT parents? Also look for other types of diversity that are not necessarily LGBT related: for example, race, religion, economic backgrounds, disabilities, etc.

Olivia Higgins, founder of Queerly Elementary, says that we can even go a step further. "Expand your evaluation of a school's diversity beyond just the demographics of the students and families. A faculty that reflects a broad spectrum of identities suggests the school may be a more welcoming place for everyone."

What Does the School's Website Look Like?

Sometimes you can get a good feel about a school from their website, so look over the information they provide online. What do their mission statement, vision, and school policies say? What type of school activities do they promote? Are staff pictures and bios posted? If so, remember to look for diversity within the staff.

What Do the Forms Look Like?

If you want your child to attend a specific school, you'll be required to complete their enrollment forms. Before filling anything out, look to see what type of language is used. Do they have words like "mother" and "father," or do they use more gender-neutral language like "parent" or "guardian"? The latter words are more inclusive and not just for kids with LGBT parents. They can refer to children who are raised by single parents or grandparents, too.

It's possible that a school can be accepting of diversity but may not have thought about changing their forms. If that's the case, you can help explain that by using more inclusive terminology, the school will be sending a more positive and welcoming message to students and their families.

Posters and Signage

When doing a physical tour of the school, be on the lookout for inclusive signage throughout the campus. Look for signs that show acceptance of all families or posters that say something like, "Everyone belongs here." Do the signs encourage people to be themselves and are they welcoming to everyone? Did you see a rainbow anywhere? You can also look out for GSA signs or "Safe Space" signs.

What Types of Books Are Used in the School?

Because books are used as teaching tools, you can get a good idea for the school's values by observing the types of books available in their library. Don't just ask if they have diverse books. Ask to see their library and then ask to see a few examples. Are their books diverse? Do they have any with LGBT families or diverse family structures? Do they have options where the main characters are different genders and races, or are they all the same? If religious books are present, do they favor one religion or are others represented as well?

Higgins says not to worry too much if you see a lack of these types of books in the beginning. "If your child's classroom or school library lacks books that reflect a wide range of perspectives, you can work with the librarian or classroom teacher to suggest new books to purchase. The Parent-Teacher Association (PTA) may be willing to help develop a book list and perhaps even raise funds for those new books."

For older grades, there's often a book list detailing what will be read during the year for each of the different grade levels. Don't be afraid to ask for a copy of the list so you can review it and see how diverse the reading is. You may even want to make suggestions for books that can be added. Regardless of grade level, being exposed to diversity in books can help students learn about acceptance while also giving them a greater chance to see themselves in the stories they read.

How Does the School Embrace or Honor Different Types of Families?

Families are discussed throughout our school journeys, from preschool to high school. Whether kids are drawing pictures of their families, mapping out their family trees, or taking courses on genetics, family structures are going to be brought up. Ask what types of projects the classes do on families and how they address various types of family structures. Are family pictures hung on the classroom wall, and if so, how will teachers address questions about your family from other kids or parents?

What Is the School's Anti-Discrimination Policy?

Reading a school's anti-discrimination policy is a good way to get an idea for how they feel about the LGBT community. Check to see if they prohibit discrimination on the basis of sexual orientation and gender identity. It's even better if they have language that prohibits discrimination based on the "actual or perceived" sexual orientation or gender identity of the student or because of anyone whom the student associates with. That means no one is allowed to discriminate against a student because he or she has LGBT friends or family members.

How Does the School Handle Bullying?

All schools pretty much have policies against bullying. Ask them how they define bullying, what they have in place to prevent it, and what actions they take when bullying occurs. Do they have classroom rules, and if so, what are they? Schools that take bullying seriously go out of their way to establish a safe school environment. To learn more about bullying at schools, go to www.stopbullying.gov.

REAL-LIFE STORY:

"It is important to us, living in Northeast Tennessee, that we are active in our daughter's life and her preschool. We are very open and forward with the school director and the preschool staff. Prior to enrolling our daughter in preschool, we visited the school, and we did not hide being a gay couple. Direct questions were asked regarding acceptance, behavior, and bullying. We do not just use the carpool line to drop off our daughter for school. One of us will always park and walk her in to her classroom. This allows us to become familiar with the staff and students.

"One day, my husband Matthew dropped off Harper for early care. Harper interacted with children of all ages during this hour before school actually started.

Harper's classmates know me as her Daddy, but were not familiar with Matthew. Harper began to cry when her classmates were telling her that Matthew was not her daddy. The teacher had everyone sit down and immediately began to teach the kids about how every family is different and Harper just happened to have two dads. Because we were present and active within the school, the teacher was able to take this opportunity and turn it into a learning experience for everyone. "While we see every family as different and find it fascinating, we do have to 'stay ahead of the game' and educate teachers and the school. At Harper's age, we are lucky that kids are still impressionable. We try to be positive male and fatherly role models and allow Harper's teachers and classmates to see that while we may be considered different, we are not that different. Harper's teachers are very good at recognizing who did Harper's hair that day. Is there a class for dads on how to do their daughters' hair?"
–Trey Darnell

What Does the School Do to Minimize Gender Segregation?

Sometimes schools can place limits and restrictions on people based on gender without even knowing it. For example, they may have boys line up in one line and girls line up in another. Other times it's more obvious, like requiring gender-specific dress codes. Is the school you're researching conscious of these practices, and if so, what do they do to minimize gender segregation? Here are some things you can ask about gender practices.

- **Activities** – Are students allowed to participate in sports teams and extracurricular activities in accordance with their gender identity?

- **Dress Codes** – Are gender-based uniforms required at the school, and if so, are students allowed to wear uniforms in accordance with their gender identity? Are students allowed to express themselves by wearing gender-neutral or gender non-conforming clothing?

- **Facilities** – Does the school allow students to use bathrooms and lockers rooms based on their gender identity, or do they require students to use facilities according to their sex assigned at birth?

These policies will not only give you insight into how the school treats transgender students, but it will show you how accepting they are to people's differences and if they foster a safe environment that helps students become confident and comfortable as individuals.

Does the School Honor LGBT Awareness and/or LGBT-Inclusive Events?

October is LGBT History Month, and it offers schools the opportunity to teach students about diversity and the important roles LGBT people have played in society. It can be celebrated in all grade levels, from talking about diverse family structures in earlier grades, to learning about significant role models like Alan Turing, Bayard Rustin, Renée Richards, Sally Ride, and Harvey Milk in higher grade levels. Research by GLSEN (originally called the Gay, Lesbian, & Straight Education Network) has found that LGBT-inclusive curricula contribute to safer school environments and increased peer acceptance. Here are a few other LGBT awareness events that can be honored or recognized in schools.

- **March 31** – International Transgender Day of Visibility
- **April** (day varies year-to-year) – Day of Silence
- **First Sunday of May** – International Family Equality Day
- **May 17** – International Day Against Homophobia and Transphobia (IDAHO or IDAHOT)
- **May 22** – Harvey Milk Day
- **June** – Pride Month
- **September 23** – International Celebrate Bisexuality Day or Bi Visibility Day
- **October** – LGBT History Month (USA)
- **October 11** – National Coming Out Day
- **Third Thursday in October** – Spirit Day
- **November 20** – Transgender Day of Remembrance
- **December 1** – World AIDS Day
- **December 10** – Human Rights Day

Does the School Have a Gay Straight Alliance (GSA) or LGBT Club?

GSAs are open to all students regardless of sexual orientation or gender identity, and their presence on campus may have a positive impact on a school's climate. They may also provide evidence of a school's commitment to LGBT students and their allies.

Does the School Provide Comprehensive Sex Education?

If sex education is taught at the school, check to see whether they provide information that is inclusive of LGBT youth, and make sure that the content covered is medically and scientifically accurate. If you want to take it a step further, you can even ask about the review process the curriculum goes through. Are there ongoing community groups that review the content? If so, who's involved? Parents? Teachers? Employees? Some schools may even have a parent night where they allow parents to ask questions about the curriculum. They can see what videos are being watched and what books are being read. If you want to verify the content, take the opportunity to do so.

What Are the Rules Pertaining to Student Relationships?

Are same-sex couples allowed to date and display affection at school on the same terms as opposite-sex student couples? If the school has dances, are students allowed to attend with someone of the same gender?

Do the Teachers and/or Faculty Go Through Any Type of Training on LGBT Issues?

There are all kinds of professional development courses to help teachers and faculty foster a welcoming school environment. Here are some of the things training can cover:

- Understanding different types of family structures
- Learning how to reduce gender stereotyping
- Using inclusive language
- Understanding the needs of LGBT students
- Learning how to answer questions relating to LGBT topics
- Recognizing and preventing bullying
- Providing safe spaces

If your school would like more information on training for teachers and faculty, the following websites are great resources:

Queerly Elementary
www.queerlyelementary.com

GLSEN
www.glsen.org

HRC's Welcoming Schools Program
www.welcomingschools.org

Southern Poverty Law Center's Teaching Tolerance Program
www.tolerance.org

There's a lot to consider when researching schools, and it's easy to get overwhelmed. Before you make the final decision, take a moment to breathe and reflect on the various things the school has to offer. "Same-sex families may be tempted to simply focus on picking a school based on how LGBTQ-friendly it seems to be," says Higgins. "However, don't lose sight of the many other equally important factors to help you decide on the best school for your child such as: location, before/after school care, cost, art and music programs, specific academic and social needs of your child, teacher-student ratio, curriculum, homework policy, adequate recess, physical education program, etc."

What to Do on Mother's Day

Some people have a mom and a dad. Some people have two moms or two dads. Some people only have one parent, while others may have multiple stepparents. Some children are raised by extended family members, like aunts, uncles, or grandparents, and some people don't have parents at all. All families are different. I know this, you know this, but other people don't necessarily know this.

Take Mother's Day and Father's Day for example. Lots of people, especially educators in schools, often assume that children have a mother and a father. They don't always take into consideration that some kids live in single-parent households, have LGBT parents, or maybe no parents at all. It may get awkward if your child has to make and bring home a Mother's Day gift. Will your child get confused? Will they get teased for not having a mom? Will they make the gift anyway and decide which dad to give it to?

One of the best things you can do is to take this opportunity to discuss family diversity with your child. Have a conversation about how all families are different and why their family is special. Remind them how much they are loved. In addition, explain your family situation to your child's school and ask them whether the classes celebrate Mother's Day. If they do, have a conversation about how you celebrate it in your home. It's important to keep in mind that not all families with gay dads celebrate Mother's Day in the same way, so even if the school has had children with gay dads in the past, this doesn't necessarily mean that they know how your family celebrates the holiday.

For example, look at all the different ways LGBT families are created. Some of our children were adopted and may or may not know their birthparents. Some of our children were born via surrogacy and may or may not know their egg donors or surrogates. Some of our children were in foster care and may or may not know their birth families. So on Mother's Day, do we celebrate birth families, surrogates, egg donors, or a combination thereof—or do we say our children don't have mothers? The answer honestly is, you do whatever you think is best for you, your family, and your child.

I talked to a bunch of other gay dads about Mother's Day. Here's what I asked them and what they told me.

How does Mother's Day work for your family? Do you celebrate the holiday? If so, how? If you don't celebrate it, what happens when your kids are in school and the class does a Mother's Day project?

"Mother's Day has evolved in our family. Our kids didn't know their birthmother when they were younger, so we wrote on balloons, said a prayer, and released them into the air to honor her. My son met his birthmother when he got older, but it wasn't a good experience, so we don't do that anymore. Now we spend the holiday with their grandmother."
—**Jay Foxworthy**

"Our family celebrates my husband on Mother's Day and me on Father's Day. As gay parents, we decided that we needed to take Mother's Day to celebrate one of us! Why not? The kids and I typically make something (hand/finger prints, art projects, cards, etc.) for my husband, and we cook or go out to dinner. Pretty typical of what straight couples with children would do for their mother on the day. We call it 'Daddies Day.'"
—**Adam White**

"We celebrate Mother's Day by honoring the women in our lives. At our son's daycare, they make Mother's Day cards and gifts, and we give them to our mothers (our son's grandmas). We buy gifts for our moms and take them out for Mother's Day brunch."
—**BJ Barone**

"Our daughter is still young enough not to realize Mother's Day is anything other than another day. As far as celebrating the day, we spend it with my husband's aunt, who is like a mother to us: she lives in the area and she is known as Nana. For our first Mother's Day we FaceTimed with our daughter's mother, but this past year she was on drugs and we skipped that for all of our benefits. Other family members acknowledge the day to celebrate both of us."
—**Chad Scanlon**

"My kids are not the only kids at their school without mothers. Some of their classmates take the opportunity to honor and celebrate their grandmothers, social workers, or other special women in their lives. For us, Mother's Day is Fommy (Father–Mommy) Day since my sons don't have a mom. As far as schools go, I think it's important that we, as gay dads, get involved and make an effort to get to know your child's teachers. That way, there are fewer chances of surprises."
—**David Aguirre**

"We have not found Mother's Day to be a major problem. Most teachers have asked us how we would like to handle Mother's Day projects, and we gladly let them know something can be made for their grandmothers, one of whom lives very nearby. This past Mother's Day, my husband's mother was able to be the guest of honor at the preschool Mother's Day show, where she was given

a decorated apron and treated to a song and dance performed by two of her grandchildren. She loved it! We are raising our children Jewish, so we have grown very accustomed to holidays being celebrated at school that are either not celebrated at all or occur without as much fanfare at our home. On the other hand, Father's Day and all the kids' birthdays fall after the end of the school year in Florida. So just like the Jewish holidays, we make sure to celebrate Father's Day and their birthdays at home or on vacation over the summer months, to make sure the kids don't feel like they are missing out."
—David Hu

"When my son was younger, the teachers would make it more inclusive and it would be celebrated as 'Parent's Day' rather than Mother's Day. If a project was made, he would make it for one of his grandmas instead."
—Del Hubers

"We adopted our son internationally, and he was in an orphanage from his first day. We don't know anything about his birthmother, but through comments, we acknowledge her and her gift/journey every year on Mother's Day. Our daughter was born via gestational surrogacy. We have an ongoing relationship with our daughter's surrogate and celebrate her directly on Mother's Day. Additionally, we celebrate the many mothers in our lives: aunts, grandmothers, godmothers, etc."
—Elliott Kronenfeld

"We celebrate by FaceTiming our mothers and avoiding brunch locations. Seriously, I hate long waits, even more so with kids. We literally got a family membership at the local zoo on Mother's Day in order to skip the line. I had not anticipated that the zoo was a Mother's Day destination. Our kids are in preschool and first grade. So far, the kids'

schools have been pretty respectful. We have received very nice non-gendered gifts from our kids that the other kids made for their moms."
—Ian Hart

"We celebrate Mother's Day by honoring aunts, grandmas, and other important women in our lives. We still have contact with our daughter's surrogate and we celebrate her for Mother's Day too since we couldn't have become parents without her. Our daughter is two now, and she has met our surrogate, but she doesn't currently do anything for her on Mother's Day. We think it's important to wait until she's older and can decide for herself if that's something she wants to do."
—Shawn Moore

"We celebrate Mother's Day over brunch with my husband's parents. Our son had a couple of Mother's Day projects when he was in preschool and kindergarten. He gave both of them to my mother-in-law."
—Michael Hadley

"We generally celebrate Mother's Day by celebrating with other members of our family who are Mothers. Typically, we would give Mother's Day cards to their Grandmother. In school the kids would make a project for Grandma and for Papa and Daddy."
—Mike Degala

"Mother's Day, for us, is a day to celebrate our children's grandmother. The school is very supportive and inclusive and allows my mom to attend their Mother's Day activities. Our children make cards for their grandmother and give her any crafts they may make at school."
—Tommy Starling

Mother's Day and Father's Day are based on good intentions to honor the roles that parents play in our lives, but in this day and age, do we really need to separate parents by gender? Especially when we look at same-sex parents. More often than not, we share parental responsibilities. If you're looking to be creative with how you celebrate your family, consider celebrating one of the following holidays:

- **Parent's Day** – 4th Sunday in July
- **Son and Daughter Day** – August 11
- **National Stepfamily Day** – September 16
- **Working Parents Day** – September 16
- **National Adoption Awareness Month** – November (whole month)
- **National Adoption Day** – Saturday before Thanksgiving
- **Universal Children's Day** – November 20
- **International Children's Day** – 2nd Sunday in December

Childproofing
Round Two – Older
Children

Childproofing isn't just something you do for infants and toddlers. It's something you're going to need to revisit every once in a while as your child gets older and becomes more independent, especially with technology. Here are a few suggestions to consider when childproofing your home for older children. Because each family is different, you will need to determine which rules, guidelines, and controls you are comfortable with implementing.

Television

There is a lot of content available on TV that may not be appropriate for your children to watch. Most television shows have TV Parental Guidelines to give parents more information about the age-appropriateness of each program; however, news and sports programs are exempt from these ratings. A device called the V-Chip has been built into most modern television sets and allows parents to block programs based on the TV Parental Guidelines.

Check with your cable company to see what controls they offer and how to implement them. You should be able to block individual programs based on ratings and channels. You can even block adult titles from showing up in the electronic program guide. Here are the different types of ratings used for television.

AUDIENCE LABELS:

TV-Y (All Children): Appropriate for all children, and the themes are specifically designed for a very young audience.

TV-Y7 (Directed to Older Children): Appropriate for children age seven and older.

TV-G (General Audience): Suitable for children and adults. The program may not be designed specifically for children; however, it contains little or no violence, no strong language, and no sexual dialogue or situations.

TV-PG (Parental Guidance Suggested): May contain material unsuitable for younger children, such as suggestive dialogue, coarse language, sexual situations, or moderate violence.

TV-14 (Parents Strongly Cautioned): The program may contain more intense suggestive dialogue, coarse language, sexual situations, or moderate violence.

TV-MA (Mature Audience Only): Unsuitable for children under seventeen and may contain offensive language, explicit sexual activity, and/or graphic violence.

TIP:
Some televisions have the ability to connect to the Internet and install apps. In addition to setting parental controls on your TV, you may need to set them up for your apps too. For example, you may want to consider enabling Netflix's parental controls to prevent your kids from watching inappropriate content through the app on your TV.

Computers, Laptops, and the Internet

Anything and everything is available on the Internet these days, so you'll want to make sure you proof the devices in your home accordingly if your child will have access to them. Each operating system and Internet browser will have different ways to set parental controls, and since technology changes frequently, I won't go into details on how to set them in order to prevent the information here from becoming outdated quickly. Rather, I will give you an idea for what you should be aware of. You can search online for how to set the controls on your specific device, and you can set the controls for what you feel is appropriate for your children.

The good thing is that you can set up different controls for different users. This means you can access the same device as your child, but you can give yourself freer rein than you allow your kids.

Time Limits – You can set time limits on your computer and/ or devices. You can allow a certain amount of time (for example, an hour or two a day) or you can prevent access during certain times. This is helpful for when you want a device to shut off when it's bedtime.

Email and Messaging – Some mail and instant messaging applications may allow you to set restrictions so that emails can only be sent to certain contacts.

Dictionary – You may want to check your computer to see if you can limit inappropriate content (such as profanity) from appearing in dictionaries and thesauruses.

Camera – You may or may not want to prevent access to the camera so that your children are not making themselves visible to strangers online.

Websites – You can set the controls to allow only specific sites geared towards children, or you can choose to block certain sites.

Web Browsers – There are various types of browsers that can be used to surf the Net: Internet Explorer, Safari, Firefox, Chrome, etc. Each of them runs independently of the others, so if you have more than one on your system, you will need to set up parental controls on each of them.

Internet History – If you share a computer, depending on what sites you visit, you may want to delete your own browser history.

YouTube – A Restricted Mode is available on YouTube to filter out mature content. This works on a browser level, so you will have to turn it on for each browser you use.

Online Games – Depending on your operating system, you may be able to restrict what games can be played or accessed.

REAL-LIFE STORY:

"I had to block a few video games because of inappropriate things, like excessive violence or cussing. If I saw them playing things they shouldn't be playing, I would talk to them about it and shut it down. It's sort of a losing battle in a way, but I think it's important to have these types of conversations with them. Many online games connect to the Internet and allow people to interact with other gamers. They talk about their characters and all kinds of things about their lives. When my son went online to play, he would be open about everything and would tell people he had gay dads. Eventually, he started getting harassed by other players online because of this, and they would call my son gay too: actually, not in a negative way. 'Dude, it's nothing to be ashamed of...' He got frustrated because it was not who he is. We had a conversation about blocking people who did not respect his identity." –Rob Watson

Gaming Consoles – There are lots of restrictions you can put in place such as restricting certain games based on ratings, restricting DVDs based on ratings, and preventing online usage and web browsing.

Social Media – Social media sites like Facebook, Twitter, and Instagram have become a major part of our lives, and eventually, your kids are going to want to be on those sites too. Consider taking a few precautions to keep your children safe from online predators:

- You can adjust the privacy settings on your child's social media accounts to make it harder for strangers to find them and prevent them from seeing posts.

- Some parents establish rules with their children allowing them to access their child's social media account upon request.

> ### TIP:
> Before your child uses the Internet, it's a good idea to talk to them and set a few expectations. Let them know what is acceptable for online usage and what sites to stay away from. Consider keeping the computer in a visible location, like a living room, so you can supervise online activity. Make sure your kids know they should never give out personal information online, such as names, addresses, email addresses, passwords, where they go to school, etc., and let them know that if someone bullies them online or makes them uncomfortable, they should talk to you, a teacher, or another grown-up they can trust.

Wireless Phones and Tablets

At some point in time, your kid is bound to get ahold of your cell phone. Maybe you decide to let them play a game, or they pick it up after you've set it down. Either way, you may want to consider having a password on your phone so they can't access it on their own. Other things you may want to consider:

- Make sure you don't have any compromising pictures on your phone that they could see by scrolling through your photos. (Don't worry, I won't judge.)

- Think about the types of apps you have on your phone and ask yourself if there's anything you wouldn't want them to see.

Many parents make the decision to give children their own phones or tablets when they get a bit older. Maybe you want to be able to call them when they are out with their friends, or maybe you want them to have the ability to call you in case of an emergency. Whatever the reason may be, if you give your child a device that can connect to the Internet, here are a few protections you may want to put in place:

Purchase Blocker – Unless you want your bill to skyrocket, it might be a good idea to put blockers in place to prohibit your kids from making purchases that are directly billed to you. This includes apps, games with in-app purchases, ringtones, and more.

Usage Restrictions – You can set limits on things like texts and data usage to keep your costs down. You can also apply other restrictions, such as who can be called and what content can be accessed online. Check with your wireless provider to see what kind of parental controls they have so you can make the best decision for your family.

Geotracking – This is the ability to identify a person's location by using the GPS data from their phone or other GPS-enabled device. You can do things like make sure your child arrives home safely from school, or set up alerts if they travel outside predetermined boundaries. If this is something you're interested in, your wireless provider can help you enable it.

Questions and Conversations Gay Dads May Have with Their Children

As a gay dad, there are lots of conversations you might have with your children that straight parents wouldn't typically have with their kids. For example, explaining how our families are different, conversations about LGBT bullying, explaining why people want laws passed that negatively impact our families, etc. Some of the topics are unique to our families, while others are common conversations that may be discussed differently in LGBT households. For example, some parents might have the "birds and the bees" talk solely to explain where babies come from. We, on the other hand, may take a slightly different approach. Here are a few examples of conversations and questions that have come up in other households with gay dads. Hopefully, they will provide a few ideas for how to have these types of conversations if or when they ever come up in your household.

How Your Family Was Created

"We had to explain the process of surrogacy to our children so they can respond to people with facts when asked if they were adopted or if their mother died."
—**Tommy Starling**

"We have open discussions about anything and everything with our daughter. It is very important to us that she understands she is adopted. She recognizes her biological parents from a photo. She knows them by name and talks about them often."
—**Trey Darnell**

"Our older daughter asked how she and her sister were conceived, which is a question that even the children of straight parents might ask. In our case, we began a co-parenting journey with two lesbians via the proverbial

turkey baster method. One of us dads provided the sperm and handed it off to one of the moms via a plastic syringe. After explaining this and also revealing which of us are their biological parents, our daughter had the follow up question of why was it those two who "made them" (her words), and not the other two parents? I doubt most straight parents have to field that one."
—**Bill Delaney**

Family Structures and Diversity

"We talk about what family means in a pretty expansive way. We talk about adoption, about biological family, and the different ways we inherit traditions, ethnicity, faith, etc. We talk about permanence and how it's OK to have complicated feelings about family, but that no matter what, this family is not going anywhere."
—**Gabriel Blau**

"We have had a lot of conversations about diversity in general, whether it's about them being Latino or having gay dads. We are both Christian, so we try to pass on those values of love, respect, and kindness to our children. We explain to our kids that they should respect people no matter what their beliefs are and they should be open to differing opinions and ideas. Sometimes people don't share our views and they may say or do hurtful things, but that's probably because they don't understand."
—**Jay Foxworthy**

"'Why do I have two daddies and where is my mommy?' We told our son, who is six, that there are families who have one dad and one mom, two mommies or two daddies, or one mom or dad."
—**Mike Degala**

"When our son was younger, we talked at great length about what makes up a family. He had another girl in his class that had two moms, one boy lived with his grandparents, and another spent part of the week with his mom and part of the week with his dad, as they were divorced. This gave us ample opportunity to explain to our son that families come in all different sizes and shapes and that it basically boils down to, 'Your family is whoever loves you and takes care of you!'"
—**Del Hubers**

"I think the special talks we have with our kids, especially in preparation for going to school, is the idea that their family is different, but that just being different is not a bad thing. We tell them that most kids have a mom and a dad. They don't have a mom, but they have two dads. We say it plainly without implying that anything is missing. It turns out that many of their classmates have parents that are divorced or otherwise split, so they are being raised by a single parent. There isn't necessarily anyone missing from those homes either."
—**David Hu**

"Our conversations really have been focused around inclusion. We talk about how we are different, but so is every other family. Our kids go to school with children in single-parent homes or a parent in jail. We make sure to explain that common social constructs like the nuclear family are not always common. We also talk about how being different is good. That we bring something special to the table that no one else can. And that everyone, no matter who they are or what they look like, contributes. Sometimes you may have to look for that contribution, but it is always there."
—**Duke Nelson**

"While we do not focus on our family being different than other families, we do talk about how families can be made in different ways. Being different is interesting and wonderful. We love how inquisitive a toddler can be and we try to capture those moments and turn them into an opportunity for learning. When we embrace being different and thrive in it, we become better dads and better people. If every family or person was the same, that would be pretty boring. We are not boring people unless we are binge watching a television show."
—Trey Darnell

Coming Out to Your Kids

"I grew up in the 70s and 80s when being gay was still kind of taboo. Even though I knew I was gay from an early age, I married a woman because I was afraid of being outed and didn't want to upset my parents. The marriage lasted many years and resulted in two children. I have now been married to my husband for ten years and he accepted me, the children, and my 'ex-wife' from the day I met him. When I finally came out to my son, he wanted to know why I had hidden my sexuality for so long and why I had married his mother. He went through a real rough patch of self-harming not long after I and my husband first met and got a flat together and my son needed medical help—it was a late response to my coming out and having a male partner. My husband has had chats with the kids regarding my love for them and my love for my husband. He has told them that I am still their father, despite the fact that I am gay and have a husband."
—Martyn Floyd

"My kids didn't know I was gay when they came to live with me after being in the foster care system. I eventually

came out to them a few months later. My oldest didn't believe me right away. 'No, you're not gay,' he said. 'Yes, I am,' I told him. Later that day, he came over to me and said, 'Dad, it's okay. I don't care if you're gay…but I just want you to know, I like girls.'"
—**David Aguirre**

Bullying and Violence

"The topic of the Pulse nightclub shooting came up at school in the aftermath of the tragedy. When my daughter came home from school that day, she told me that she found it really upsetting because I was gay and I could have been there. (She was only eleven years old at the time and didn't understand the distance between Florida and Canada, which is where we live.) She went on to ask why someone would do something so hateful. I told her that not everyone in the world is as accepting as we are, and in some places, people are taught to hate anything that is different from themselves. Sometimes people with hate in their heart do terrible things. I went on to say that we are very lucky to live where we do, and at a time when people are more accepting of other people who are not like them. Not long after, I got a T-shirt in memory of the victims of the Pulse shooting. My daughter liked the shirt and wants me to wear it the next time we go to Pride in Montreal."
—**Peter Leonard**

"I'm always thinking, how do I arm my kid with knowledge? We've talked about diversity like different races and religions. We've talked about not using the word 'gay' as 'lame,' and I've asked my son if he has ever heard the word 'fag' at school. We're pretty lucky though,

because we live in a bubble and his school is LGBT friendly."
—**Frank Lowe**

"We have had several conversations with our children that we know straight parents do not usually have with their children. We have prepared our children for the possibility of being bullied about who their parents are and how to respond. We tell them to be honest and unapologetic about having two gay dads. We tell them to be factual and stern in their response and consult with a teacher if the bullying continues."
—**Tommy Starling**

Discrimination, Anti-LGBT Laws, and Equality

"Our son is in middle school and we try to be proactive but not alarmist. In general terms, we share anything in the news that has (or could have) significant impact on gay families. We'd rather he heard it from us than at school. During the 2016 Presidential election, we had conversations with him about the backlash against the 2015 Freedom To Marry Act and that some people are uncomfortable with Marriage Equality and gay families. We tried to explain why they felt that way and shared that same-sex marriage is a new concept. We explained that attitudes are often slow to change and that some people have difficulty accepting those who are different in their eyes. We tried to prepare him for hearing negative comments about this at school, but he has not reported anything like that to us yet."
—**Michael Hadley**

"The hurtful conversations include explanations about laws that have discriminated against us. Our children do not understand why everyone is not treated equally."
—**Tommy Starling**

"We live in a conservative town. One day my kids came home from school with Trump stickers and they were excited about the election. I had to sit them down and explain that his beliefs on LGBT equality, women's rights, immigration, basically his whole platform didn't really agree with our lifestyle. The next day they went to school proudly telling everyone they were supporting Hillary Clinton."
—**David Aguirre**

"Social justice is discussed with our kids in broad terms. We try to demonstrate the importance of sharing and donations, of good manners, kindness, inclusiveness, and civility, and for expressing gratitude. Being in liberal San Francisco, we can't compete with some families in the expression of social outrage, but personally, I'm in no rush to delve into the subject of homophobia. It will come with time. Our kids will know that their dads grew up in a time that people were not very nice for no good reason, but that things are better and more people are more enlightened, and that if they need any proof of that they need only look at our family and friends. But that it's also our responsibility to help make it better for people who may live somewhere less accepting, or in a situation less fortunate than our own…and then we'll have a dance party in the kitchen."
—**Ian Hart**

Sexuality, Orientation, and the Birds and the Bees

"I think in most families, kids are presumed straight unless told otherwise. I never set an expectation on my kid's identities. That was the case when we eventually had the 'birds and the bees' talk. When I did research to see how other people had the talk with their children, I noticed that it often came up in families because someone got pregnant. The parents would start talking about the mother and father sex part and how a baby is made. I took a different approach and focused the conversation on what intimacy and bonding are. What is sexuality and what is sex? The whole conversation came up because one of my sons came to me and said his brother was misusing the 'F' word and saying it meant sex. I asked if he knew what sex was, and he said no—so we dove into the conversation and they got the whole scope of it. We talked about intimacy, what men's bodies do, and what female bodies do. I explained what happens when men do it, and what happens when women do it. We covered responsibility and sexually transmitted diseases, but the conversation started with intimacy."
—**Rob Watson**

"My parents never talked to me about sex, and I was sexually active very young. We've been very open with my kids about sex. They understand it can be a good thing or a dangerous thing. We stressed the importance of being protective of themselves and other people. For me, it's all about being open and honest with my kids, and creating an environment where they feel like they can come to us about anything. We have a rule in our house that if our kids do something wrong or bad but come to us and own up to it, there are no consequences. If we find out they

tried to cover something up or lie about it, there will be consequences. My son tried marijuana once and came to tell me about it. That was it. So far it's worked for us."
—**Jay Foxworthy**

> *TIP:*
> *If you're looking for a way to talk about reproduction with your kids, check out the book What Makes A Baby, by Cory Silverberg. It's targeted towards readers aged three to seven and covers conception, gestation, and birth in a way that is inclusive of all kinds of kids, adults, and families, regardless of how many people were involved, their orientation, gender identity, or family composition.*

Gay Dads Raising
Girls

As a gay man, there is a high probability that there may be a few feminine issues that you haven't had to encounter. So, if you happen to be raising a daughter, what do you do when she hits puberty? How do you know what kind of bra your daughter should wear? Should she be using tampons or pads? Here are a few basics you should know.

When Will My Daughter Start Puberty?

Children go through puberty at various different times. Most girls will start puberty sometime between eight and thirteen years old, but some can start earlier or later. The process normally lasts a few years and starts with the growth of breasts and pubic hair. A little later, hair will begin to grow under her arms and within 1–2½ years after breast development starts, most girls will get their first menstrual period. Every girl is different though, and not all of them follow this development pattern. If signs of puberty start before she is eight years old, or haven't started after thirteen years of age, your daughter should see their pediatrician to rule out potential medical concerns. You can also consult her doctor if you have any other concerns about the timing of her development.

To make puberty easier on your daughter, try to make sure she knows what's going to happen before it starts. If you're uncomfortable having the talk with her, there are plenty of age-appropriate books out there, and because young people tend to be savvy on the Internet, YouTube videos might even work better. There are tons of videos where people explain what it was like when they had their first period or when they went shopping for their first bra. Seeing someone else her age going through the experience and sharing their story may help your daughter relate.

REAL-LIFE STORY:

"As a gay dad, I had concerns about our daughter becoming a young lady, and we weren't sure if we would be able to help her through puberty. How would we talk to her about her period and would she be comfortable hearing these conversations from a man? We talked about the topic early on and even showed her videos online. When the time finally came, she had already been educated. She told us when she spotted so we could take her to the store, and she was very mature about it. There was no fear about coming to us about it, and, for me, that was one of my proudest parenting moments." –Jay Foxworthy

---

What Do I Do When My Daughter Is Ready for Her First Bra?

When it's time to go bra shopping for the first time, consider asking your daughter with whom she wants to go. It could be you or your partner, or maybe she would rather go with a female instead. If that's the case, you may want to ask (or maybe have her ask, if she's more comfortable doing so) someone she feels comfortable being around. This could be her grandmother, aunt, surrogate, birthmother, egg donor, or maybe even her best friend. If she wants you to go with her, here are a few tips to help you get through the experience:

- Discuss the shopping trip beforehand and set a few expectations to make sure you're on the same page. Does she want you with her, or would she rather have you wait nearby? How many will she be buying?

- Bralette, boning, compression bra, convertible, molded, racerback. Understanding bras is like learning a whole new language! Search online for "bra terminology" before you go to the store, so you understand the different types of bras and can get a better idea for what you're looking for.

- Determine how you will get the proper size. You can easily find sizing charts online if you want to measure at home, but doing it for the first time might be confusing. A salesperson at the store can measure and help your daughter get the proper fit. If you wind up asking a salesperson for assistance, do so quietly so that you don't embarrass your daughter.

- That brings us to the next point. You know your daughter best, and you may want to crack jokes with her, which is fine, but try not to do anything that will embarrass her during this vulnerable time. It's a big moment for your daughter, but it can also be awkward for her too. The last thing you want to do is make her feel uncomfortable or embarrassed about her body.

- Let her choose the style. This is a big moment for her, so let her pick a color and style that she likes. If you want to set a few guidelines, like nothing that looks like stripper underwear, that's up to you, but don't make her buy something she's uncomfortable with either.

Don't offer to help more than once. If she says she's fine on her own, give her space.

- Once she's selected a few bras, encourage her to try them on in the dressing room. Bras are intended to be worn for support and it's important she gets ones that fit her properly. Getting the wrong size can make her extremely uncomfortable.

- When you find bras that fit your daughter and are comfortable for her to wear, take note of the size, style, and brand name. That way you can order more online when necessary and save yourself a trip back to the underwear section. Her bra size is going to change as she gets older though, so make sure you always get the correct size before buying more.

TIP:

Don't put bras in the dryer, unless you have an air dry or delicate mode available. The heat from the dryer can melt the plastic underwire in bras and cause them to snap in odd places so the wiring pokes the skin. Air-drying is best, but if you need to put them in the dryer, make sure it's on the lowest heat setting, and take them out as soon as they are dry. Alternatively, you could also try to get bras with metal underwire instead of plastic.

How Do I Know Which Pads or Tampons to Get?

When your daughter gets to the point in her life where she's about to get her first period, she's going to need sanitary supplies, but how do you know what to get her?

Many girls start with pads (also called sanitary pads or sanitary napkins), which are rectangular pieces of absorbent material that go inside the underwear. Some have "wings" on the side that fold over the underwear to keep them in place. Other girls may want to use tampons, which are cylinders of absorbent material that are placed inside the vagina; these are especially suited for swimming, or for girls who are active in sports. Some tampons are inserted with a person's fingers, while others have applicators.

Both tampons and pads come in a variety of sizes, for heavier or lighter periods. Don't assume the most absorbent ones are better for every situation. It's possible that super-absorbent pads may wind up looking and even feeling like a diaper, and tampons that are too absorbent can cause discomfort or even gynecological problems. It's best to get the least-absorbent ones she needs. Some pads and tampons even come deodorized, but the scented ones can sometimes irritate the vagina, so you might want to skip those. Try getting a few different brands and types of pads/tampons so your daughter can determine what works best for her.

Also, make sure she knows how often to change them. The frequency will depend on how much blood she has, but it's a good idea to change pads at least every three or four hours even if she's not menstruating much. Tampons should be changed every four to six hours, or when they're saturated with blood. When one is left in too long, bacteria can grow inside it, enter the body from inside the vagina, and then enter the bloodstream. This can put girls at risk for toxic shock syndrome (TSS), a rare but very dangerous illness that can cause high fever, vomiting, diarrhea, muscle aches, dizziness, and/or rashes. Again, it's rare, but the illness can be severe and occasionally life-threatening, so make sure your daughter is aware of TSS and knows that she should remove the tampon and tell an adult immediately if she has any of these symptoms while using one.

Last, but not least, make sure your daughter knows that pads and tampons (even ones that say they're flushable) should not be flushed down the toilet. They should be wrapped in toilet paper and put in a trashcan. If you have dogs or cats at home, make sure the trashcan has a lid on it so that the animals don't get at them.

Tracking Menstrual Cycles

Pregnancy concerns are not the only reason for keeping track of menstrual cycles. Changes in menstrual cycles can also be a sign of a variety of different health issues, including thyroid problems, liver function problems, and diabetes. Irregular periods can also be a result of new exercise routines, gaining or losing a significant amount of weight, or extreme stress. While one late or irregular period isn't necessarily problematic, if it's prolonged or combined with other symptoms, your daughter should consult with a gynecologist or OB/GYN. Keep in mind, though, that it may take a year or more after the onset of menstruation for a young girl to develop regular monthly menstrual cycles that occur for the same number of days.

Every girl should maintain a menstrual calendar to keep track of her periods. It's as simple as marking the start and end date on a calendar. There are also apps for that so it's easy to track anywhere at any time.

How Can I Make Sure My Children Have Strong Female Role Models?

While our children have us as male role models, it's also important that they have strong female role models in their lives to understand that people can do anything, regardless of gender. Role models can be anyone from grandmothers, aunts, and cousins, to birthmothers, egg donors, and surrogates if you have good relationships with them. Teachers, coaches, and group leaders can also be possibilities.

In addition to real-life examples, we can go out of our way to make sure our children are exposed to strong female characters in literature, games, television, and movies. Do an inventory of books, movies, and games in your house every so often and see if there's a balance of gender in them. If not, consider getting a few new items to help offset it. If you need a few ideas for inspiration, A Mighty Girl is a great website that features a collection of books, toys, and movies for smart, confident, and courageous girls. The website can be found at www.amightygirl.com.

LGBT-Friendly
Books for Your
Kids

There are not many options when it comes to LGBT children's books, but as time goes by, more and more titles are becoming available. While this is not a complete list, here are a few books you might want to consider adding to your personal library. Also, I'm a big believer of: "If you can't find what you're looking for, write it yourself!" We need more books that represent our diverse families, and I'm sure you have a great story to tell.

The Family Book (By Todd Parr) – Written by New York Times bestselling author Todd Parr, this book uses colorful illustrations to show the various different ways that families are unique. Ages 2–5.

Families, Families, Families! (By Suzanne Lang) – This book features various types of family combinations, including same-sex parents and non-traditional family structures. It stresses the message that love makes a family. Ages 3–7.

The Christmas Truck (Authored by J. B. Blankenship; Illustrated by Cassandre Bolan) – This rhyming story tells of a child who works with Papa, Dad, and Grandmother to save Christmas for another kid they never met. Ages 4–8.

What Makes A Baby (Authored by Cory Silverberg; Illustrated by Fiona Smyth) – This picture book covers conception, gestation, and birth and does it in a way that is inclusive of all kinds of kids, adults, and families, regardless of how many people were involved, their orientation, gender identity, or family composition. Ages 3–7.

The Bravest Knight Who Ever Lived (Authored by Daniel Errico; Illustrated by Ida M. Schouw Andreasen) – A young pumpkin farmer goes on a quest to rescue a prince and princess from a fire-breathing dragon, and when the journey ends, he decides whose affectation he truly desires. Ages 4–8.

Rosaline (Authored by Daniel Errico; Illustrated by Michael Scanlon) – A modern take on fairytales that incorporates LGBT themes. A young girl named Rosaline must get past a tricky witch, a hungry wolf, and a bubbly fairy godmother before making it back home to her one true love. Ages 4–8.

Red: A Crayon's Story (By Michael Hall) – A story about a blue crayon wrapped in a red label, this book helps children understand the differences between how someone is on the inside vs. how they are labeled on the outside. Ages 4–8.

ABC: A Family Alphabet Book (Authored by Bobbie Combs; Illustrated by Desiree & Brian Rappa) – This book celebrates LGBT families while teaching the alphabet. Ages 3–5.

King & King (By Linda de Haan and Stern Nijland) – Turning the common fairy tale on its head, King & King tells the story of a prince who is being forced to marry, but he has no interest in marrying a princess. Ages 4–8.

Stella Brings the Family (Authored by Miriam B. Schiffer; Illustrated by Holly Clifton-Brown) – Stella has two dads and isn't sure what to do when her class has a Mother's Day celebration. She winds up bringing her whole family to the party. Ages 4–7.

10,000 Dresses (Authored by Marcus Ewert; Illustrated by Rex Ray) – Baily's parents tell him he shouldn't be thinking about dresses because he's a boy, but after meeting an older girl who is touched by his imagination and courage, the two of them begin making dresses together. Ages 5–9.

In Our Mother's House (By Patricia Polacco) – Marmee, Meema, and the kids are just like any other family on the block, but some of the other families don't accept them because they have two moms and no dad. Marmee and Meema teach their children what it means to be a family. Ages 6–8.

The Purim Superhero (Authored by Elisabeth Kushner; Illustrated by Mike Byrne) – A boy wants to wear an alien costume for Purim, but all of his friends are dressing up as superheroes. His two dads help him come up with a solution. Ages 4–8.

I Am Jazz (Authored by Jessica Herthel and Jazz Jennings; Illustrated by Shelagh McNicholas) – Based on the real-life experience of television personality and LGBTQ rights activist Jazz Jennings, this story details how Jazz and her family realized she was transgender at an early age. Ages 4–8.

Two Dads: A Book About Adoption (Authored by Carolyn Robertson; Illustrated by Sophie Humphreys) – A story about having two dads from the perspective of their son. Ages 4–8.

And Tango Makes Three (Authored by Justin Richardson and Peter Parnell; Illustrated by Henry Cole) – This book is based on a true story about two male penguins who created their own family with the help of a zookeeper. Together, the penguins take care of an egg and raise a baby penguin. Ages 4–8.

Daddy, Papa, and Me (Authored by Lesléa Newman; Illustrated by Carol Thompson) – This durable board book has rhyming text that shows toddlers what it's like to spend time with two fathers. Ages 0–3.

Mommy, Mama, and Me (Authored by Leslèa Newman; Illustrated by Carol Thompson) – This durable board book has rhyming text that shows toddlers what it's like to spend time with two mothers. Ages 0–3.

My Princess Boy (Authored by Cheryl Kilodavis; Illustrated by Suzanne DeSimone) – This book is inspired by the author's son who loves pink, sparkly things and sometimes even wears dresses and tiaras. Ages 4–8.

My Uncle's Wedding (Authored by Eric Ross; Illustrated by Tracy K. Greene) – Full disclosure: I actually wrote this book before I got married and changed my name. During the fight for marriage equality in the US, I got tired of people using children as pawns and saying marriage equality would hurt children, so I decided to do a picture book about a same-sex marriage from the perspective of a child. No struggles or hurdles—just an ordinary marriage like any other. Ages 3–7.

Promised Land (Authored by Adam Reynolds and Chaz Harris; Illustrated by Christine Luiten and Bo Moore) – A fairytale where a prince falls in love with a farm boy, but when the queen remarries, her new husband seeks control of the land the farm boy's family is responsible for protecting. Ages 4–8.

Zak's Safari: A Story About Donor-Conceived Kids of Two-Mom Families (Authored by Christy Tyner; Illustrated by Ciaee) – A boy explains how he was conceived using simple and accurate language. He covers sperm and egg cells, known-donors, donors from sperm banks, and genes. Ages 3–6.

The Princes and the Treasure (Authored by Jeffrey A. Miles; Illustrated by J. L. Phillips) – Two princes go on a quest to find "the greatest treasure in the land" so one of them can save and marry the princess; however, they soon realize "the greatest treasure in the land" is not what they expected. Ages 4–8.

Jacob's New Dress (Authored by Sarah Hoffman and Ian Hoffman; Illustrated by Chris Case) – Jacob wants to wear a dress, but some of the kids at school say he can't wear "girl" clothes. So what does he do? Ages 4–8.

Introducing Teddy: A Gentle Story About Gender and Friendship (Authored by Jess Walton; Illustrated by Dougal MacPherson) – A boy supports his teddy bear's transition from Thomas to Tilly. This is a story about being true to yourself and being a good friend. Ages 3–6.

Donovan's Big Day (Authored by Lesléa Newman; Illustrated by Mike Dutton) – Donovan is excited to be the ring bearer when his two moms get married. Ages 3–7.

Heather Has Two Mommies (Authored by Lesléa Newman; Illustrated by Laura Cornell) – Someone at school asks Heather about her daddy, but Heather doesn't have a dad; she has two moms. When the teacher has the children draw pictures of their families, the kids learn that all families are different. Ages 3–7.

A Peacock Among Pigeons (Authored by Tyler Curry; Illustrated by Clarione Gutierrez) – A colorful peacock finds himself growing up in a flock of grey pigeons, and winds up learning how to stand out when he can't fit in. Ages 4–8.

Worm Loves Worm (Authored by J. J. Austrain; Illustrated by Mike Curato) – When two worms fall in love and plan to get married, their friends want to know who will wear the tux and who will wear the dress. They soon find out, it doesn't matter. Ages 4–8.

This Day in June (Authored by Gayle E. Pitman; Illustrated by Kristyna Litten) – This rhyming book details what you will see at a Pride parade, from families, politicians, and equal rights organizations, to drag queens, shirtless dancers, and people dressed in leather. The main theme is one of inclusivity and the end of the book includes parental tips for discussing gender and sexuality. Ages 4–8.

The Boy Who Cried Fabulous (Authored by Lesléa Newman; Illustrated by Peter Ferguson) – A boy loves calling everything Fabulous, so what happens when his parents ban that word? Ages 3–7.

Emma and Meesha My Boy: A Two Mom Story (Authored by Kaitlyn Considine; Illustrated by Binny Hobbs) – A girl with two moms has to learn how to play nicely with her cat. Ages 3–6.

William's Doll (Authored by Charlotte Zolotow; Illustrated by William Pène du Bois) – William gets teased for wanting a doll, until someone understands that the doll will help him learn to be a loving parent someday. Ages 4–8.

Square Zair Pair (Authored by Jase Peeples; Illustrated by Christine Knopp) – Zairs are creatures that do everything in pairs, one round with one square. One day, two Zairs of the same shape pair for the first time and are rejected by their peers, until they realize different pairs of Zairs make their village stronger. Ages 4–8.

Adopting Our Two Dads: A Story About the Leffew Family (By Luca Panzini) – Based on a true story, this book shows how the Leffews formed their family through adoption. Ages 4–8.

Sex is a Funny Word: A Book About Bodies, Feelings, and You (Authored by Cory Silverberg; Illustrated by Fiona

Smyth) – This is a follow-up to the book What Makes a Baby. It covers bodies, gender, and sexuality in a gender-neutral way. It also includes children and families of all makeups, orientations, and gender identities. Ages 7–10.

Being Jazz: My Life as a (Transgender) Teen (By Jazz Jennings) – This memoir covers what it was like for Jazz Jennings to grow up as a transgender teen. Ages 12–18.

Gay & Lesbian History for Kids: The Century-Long Struggle for LGBT Rights, with 21 Activities (By Jerome Pohlen) – This book covers LGBT history for children. Ages 9 and up.

Resources

Family Organizations

Family Equality Council – National organization that has connected, supported, and represented LGBTQ parents and their children for over thirty years.
http://www.familyequality.org

Modern Family Alliance – Celebrates and supports LGBTQ parents, and prospective parents, in the Greater Kansas City area and beyond.
https://modernfamilyalliance.wordpress.com

Our Family Coalition – Provides support, education, and advocacy for LGBTQ families with children in the California Bay Area.
http://www.ourfamily.org

COLAGE – National organization that unites and supports people with LGBTQ parents.
https://www.colage.org

PFLAG – A national organization that provides information, support, tools, and resources for parents, families, and friends of LGBTQ people.
https://www.pflag.org

School Organizations

GLSEN – A national organization focused on creating safe and affirming school environments for all people, regardless of sexual orientation, gender identity, or gender expression.
https://www.glsen.org

HRC's Welcoming Schools Program – Works to create LGBTQ and gender-inclusive elementary schools by

providing lesson plans, books, and tips.
http://www.welcomingschools.org

Queerly Elementary – Provides workshops, professional development, consulting, classroom lessons, book lists, and other resources to help school communities embrace and celebrate LGBTQ diversity.
http://queerlyelementary.com

Southern Poverty Law Center's Teaching Tolerance Program – Works to reduce prejudice, improve intergroup relations, and support equitable school experiences for our nation's children.
http://www.tolerance.org

GSA Network – An organization that connect GSAs with each other to empower and educate their schools and communities.
https://gsanetwork.org

Campus Pride – An educational organization for LGBTQ and ally college students and campus groups.
https://www.campuspride.org

Advocacy Organizations

Human Rights Campaign (HRC) – America's largest LGBT civil rights organization.
http://www.hrc.org

GLAAD - A national organization that works for fair, accurate, and inclusive representation of the LGBTQ community in the media.
https://www.glaad.org

Equality Federation – An organization that works with state-based equality organizations to strengthen our

movement. Find a state-based equality organization near you.
http://www.equalityfederation.org

National Center for Transgender Equality – A national social justice organization devoted to ending discrimination and violence against transgender people.
http://www.transequality.org

National LGBTQ Task Force – Founded in 1973, this organization is the oldest LGBTQ advocacy group in the United States.
http://www.thetaskforce.org

True Colors Fund – An organization that works to end homelessness among LGBTQ youth.
https://truecolorsfund.org

Support Organizations

Center Link – Find an LGBTQ center near you.
https://www.lgbtcenters.org

The Trevor Project – A national organization that provides crisis intervention and suicide prevention services to LGBTQ youth.
http://www.thetrevorproject.org

The Born This Way Foundation – An organization with a focus on empowering youth.
https://bornthisway.foundation

It Gets Better – An organization focused on communicating the message "It gets better" to LGBTQ youth around the world.
http://www.itgetsbetter.org

Legal Organizations

Lambda Legal
https://www.lambdalegal.org

GLBTQ Legal Advocates & Defenders (GLAD)
https://www.glad.org

National Center for Lesbian Rights (NCLR)
http://www.nclrights.org

American Civil Liberties Union (ACLU)
https://www.aclu.org

Southern Poverty Law Center (SPLC)
https://www.splcenter.org

Transgender Law Center
https://transgenderlawcenter.org

Other Organizations

GLMA (previously known as the Gay & Lesbian Medical Association) – An organization dedicated to ensuring equality in healthcare for LGBT individuals and healthcare providers. They also have a directory of LGBT friendly healthcare professionals.
http://www.glma.org

International Association for Child Safety (IAFCS) – A network of child safety professionals and babyproofers.
www.iafcs.org

R Family Vacations – The first travel company to create vacations for LGBT families and their friends.
http://www.rfamilyvacations.com

Human Milk Banking Association of North America (HMBANA) – A professional association that issues voluntary safety guidelines on screening breast milk donors, in addition to collecting, processing, handling, testing, and storing milk.
www.hmbana.org.

Stopbullying.gov – A website that provides information about bullying from various different government agencies and offers ways to prevent and respond to it.
www.stopbullying.gov

National Gay & Lesbian Chamber of Commerce (NGLCC) – An organization that certifies LGBT-owned businesses and works to expand economic opportunities and advancements for LGBT people.
https://nglcc.org

You Can Play – An organization that works to ensure the safety and inclusion of all in sports—including LGBTQ athletes, coaches and fans.
http://www.youcanplayproject.org

Acknowledgments

I want to take this opportunity to give a shout-out to some of the people who helped get this book published.

First and foremost, thank you to my husband Mat, for all the love and support you gave me while I was working on this project. You helped me carve out time to write and you gave me a swift kick in the butt when I needed it.

Mom, thank you for babysitting while I went through my final edits. I couldn't have gotten through crunch time without you!

Kathleen Archambeau, thanks for reconnecting me with an old acquaintance, and jumpstarting this project

Brenda Knight, thank you for your faith, guidance, and mentorship throughout this journey. You've been a great cheerleader. By the way, I have an idea for another survey…

Christopher McKenney, Michelle Lewy, Morgane Leoni, Henryk Jaronowski, Hugo Villabona, Hannah Paulsen, and the rest of the folks at Mango Publishing. You all played a vital role in getting this book out there. Thank you for being such great partners. I'm so happy you were on my team!

Thanks to Olivia Higgins for helping with the LGBT-friendly schools section. You're a wealth of knowledge, and I appreciate you providing feedback on such short notice.

Thanks to Dr. Raymond Cattaneo for helping with the medical sections of this book. Your advice and feedback were invaluable.

Cathy Sakimura, thanks for coming through again with the legal expertise. You and the team at NCLR have always been there for me and I am forever grateful.

Thank you to everyone who shared their stories with me for this book. Adam White, Bill Delaney, BJ Barone, Chad Scanlon, David Aguirre, David Hu, Del Hubers, Duke Nelson, Trey Darnell, Elliott Kronenfeld, Frank Lowe, Gabriel Blau, Ian Hart, Jay Foxworthy, Martyn Floyd, Michael Degala, Michael Hadley, Peter Leonard, Rob Watson, Shawn Moore, and Tommy Starling. By participating in this project, you've helped tons of future gay dads.

Thank you Stan J. Sloan, Ed Harris, Kim Simes, and the rest of the team at the Family Equality Council for your help with this project and the continued support you've given me throughout my writing career. Christina Young, you're my superhero!

Robbie Hyne, thank you for being an awesome coordinator and for making things happen.

Greg Berlanti, I have admired your work for a long time and I am honored that you helped with this project. Thank you for carving out time during the busy pilot season to focus on this book and thank you for all you have done to increase the visibility of LGBTQ people on television.

And finally, I want to thank everyone who read Journey to Same-Sex Parenthood and encouraged me to write a follow-up. You're the reason this book exists.

HEADACHE

By: Tom Justic

To my wife.

All my life's accomplishments have
come from your inspiration.

"You live most of your life in your head.
Make sure it's a nice place to be."

-Unknown

now.

I am sorry, Rece. I'm sorry for destroying your family, and, again, my heart breaks for you and your children.

Take care. Find peace, if you may, in the knowledge that I will not allow myself to make these tragic decisions again, personally, or as a doctor.

All the best,

Frank

THE LETTER

December 11, 2017

Rece,

I don't even know where to begin other than to say I'm ॒
for everything. I let you down, and more importantly,
Kevin down, too.

You need to know that I have given up the practice of m
cine. I know this will not fix my mistakes, and I know this
most likely not give you peace, but you and your childre
serve to know that I will not have the ability to hurt an
else with my practice. No one has forced this move. In
I've been offered treatment and counseling to continue ᵗ
a doctor. I cannot, in good conscience, accept those offers

My heart breaks every time I think about you and K
which is often. Rece, I really thought I could help him
you, but my methods in medicine and personal choices
wrong. I think I know that now. I ignored the advice and ᶜ
seling from my peers, thinking that I was smarter than t
But I was sincere in my methods, Rece, believing them
the best way to practice, especially with Kevin. Every
sion I made was in his and your best interest, in my m
realize now, that those decisions were irresponsible and

I am not running away from this, nor am I running
from you. Please know that. If made to answer any allega
of negligence or willful mismanagement, I will answer
allegations. I will also answer any questions you may ʰ
know I owe you explanations, but I just cannot see you

WHAT STARTED AS A REGULAR DAY...?

July 27, 2015

Rece jumped from her sleep as the scream shattered throughout the bedroom like missiles screaming through the silent war zone night. The scream went on, and on, and on, and on. Rece jumped up, startled and groggy. Alarmed and afraid, she looked around and then down at Kevin. His mouth was open, and he was shaking. The sound coming from his mouth grew strikingly louder. She did what any mother with sleeping kids in the house would do; she covered his mouth with her hands. Both hands. Pressed against his screaming mouth.

"Kevin!" she whispered, the semi-muted screams pressing through her hands. "Kevin!"

The screams began to dim, barely able to release past her hands anymore. Kevin took a deep breath as Rece released the cover and awoke. He lay there in the bed. He stared at Rece. Rece stared back. They each then smiled and broke into laughter.

"You are insane, sir!" Rece blurted out as she twirled backwards onto the bed.

Kevin continued laughing.

"Again, huh?" Kevin asked, still giggling and smiling.

"Yes!" Rece responded. "And so, so loud this time!"

The two lay in the bed on their backs, waiting to hear the patter of feet of any one of their four children. They continued to chuckle a bit.

"Honestly, so honestly, I never even know I'm doing that," Kevin said.

"Oh my God," Rece responded, "I thought it was another panic attack."

"That hasn't happened in a while, and, no, this wasn't a panic attack," Kevin responded.

"Um, hm, let's see, about three months ago or so you had a huge panic attack," Rece said somewhat mockingly. "And you get them like every three months."

"You married who you married," Kevin said.

Rece reached over quickly and covered his mouth again with her hand.

Kevin pushed it off and laughed. "And what was with that?" Kevin said. "Suffocating your husband?"

Rece laughed back. "It's called not letting the kids hear their insane father scream for no reason in the middle of the night and wake them up!"

"Touché, baby, touché."

They lay in bed, both silent, not hearing anyone wake.

"Well, that was lucky," Rece said, "nobody woke up, which is very hard to believe."

"That loud?" Kevin asked.

"Yes, that loud," Rece answered. "What was it?"

"Like I said," Kevin responded quickly, "I don't ever really recall the screaming. But it's weird, I think today was a nightmare."

"Really?" Rece asked with extreme curiousness.

"Yeah, it's weird. I'm just remembering it now," Kevin said flatly.

"Tell me."

"Well, it was, I don't know, a thing or something, coming after me. And, and I was running. And I knew I couldn't let it catch me, so I ran, and ran, and I got to a door and I couldn't open it. But it was weird because it was just a door, you know, no building or walls, just a door in the middle of nowhere. So, it was dumb, because, like, I could have gone around it, but I kept trying to open the door instead, and it was coming at me, getting closer and closer, and that's when, I guess, I must have started screaming."

Rece looked at Kevin intently. "So bizarre," was all she said.

"I have to agree," Kevin responded. "Anyway, it's over."

"No E.R. visit needed?" Rece chuckled as she asked.

Kevin laughed loudly as he spoke, "I told you, this wasn't a panic attack, plus, I've never gone to the ER for those."

"Uh huh, I know, I know," Rece said, again mockingly. "Can we go to bed now?"

"No sympathy sex?" Kevin asked as he wrapped her up in his arms.

"I should get sympathy sex for having to live with you and your mental-ness!" Rece whispered loudly.

Kevin continued holding her. "Mental-ness?" he asked.

"Yes, dick, mental-ness. It's a word."

"Well, I'll give you sympathy sex for that, come on."

Rece laughed and pushed him away. "I love you, but not now. Now I'm too tired."

Kevin relented, kissed her cheek, and lay back on his pillow. "Good night, honey, I love you."

"Love you, too, sweetie."

--

The new morning sun shone through the big picture window into the master bedroom and onto the king-sized bed. The room lit up like a grand prairie sucking in the summer morning glow. On the bed, the light purple blanket was spread out unevenly. Rece was fully covered. Kevin had the middle of his legs covered; the rest of his body was left wanting. The white sheet was a bit crumpled underneath. The night stands next to the bed each held a glass of water. Hers was full, untouched through the night; his was drank, half of it left, with a spill next to the glass. On hers also sat two books. One book was old and weary looking, the other a shiny and pristine looking hard cover that had yet to be opened, except for her glancing occasionally. An old sports page, two lottery tickets, and some crinkled up candy wrappers were littered on his. On top of the candy wrappers sat a thick black hard cover novel with red initials on the bottom.

The sunlight caught his face and made him shake. Instinctively, he opened an eye. It was morning.

What day is it? Saturday, yes, it's Saturday. He paused in his thought and gained his bearings. *Oh my God. Last night.* He chuckled inside as he remembered his screaming last night. He looked at Rece. She was still asleep.

He gained some coherence. He couldn't, at that moment, remember if there was anything to do that day. But he was happy there was no work. He'd been bogged down there lately with deadlines and overtime, and he has missed his time at home with his wife and kids.

Baseball game.

His 14-year-old boy had a tournament game that day.

Something to do with the family.

As he contemplated that thought, he lay back and smiled. Next to him, Rece moved in her sleep and lifted her bare leg onto his. He smiled.

If you insist.

He smiled bigger and closed the one eye and started to turn towards his wife. It was then he heard a breathing noise near his face. Then he felt the breath. It smelled horrific, like rotten salami. He opened both eyes. It was Lou. Lou was their nine-year-old beagle. Lou was on the bed. He was two feet long and weighed fifty pounds. He was overweight by every stretch of the imagination. His white coat with brown spots glistened from a recent trip to the groomers. That morning, Lou was sleeping soundly on top of his wife Rece's pillow, right by her head. He shooed Lou off, but Lou wouldn't listen.

"Go on. Get off," he whispered very softly. He knew better than to speak loudly in this situation. It was imperative, to him, to keep quiet. Lou looked at him and licked at his face and buried his head into his curled-up body.

Kevin pushed at him. "Come on," he whispered again at Lou, a tad louder. Lou didn't budge. "Let's go, Lou, move," Kevin whispered even louder. After a long look at Kevin, Lou gave in and slowly walked his brown and white spotted self to the edge of the bed, then jumped off after much dramatic consideration and a drawn-out yawn. After his imperfect landing, Lou paused a long pause, yawned dramatically again, and ran very quickly into another room.

Kevin, almost exhausted from the Lou struggle, now rolled over and looked at his beautiful wife, sleeping and facing him. She was wearing one of his old tee shirts and a pair of his boxer shorts. He glanced down at her legs. The sight made him overly excited. He put his hand on her back and went in to kiss her.

"Uh-uh, honey," she said. She didn't even open her eyes.

"Oh, man!" he whispered undeterred, moving his hand down her back.

Rece shooed him off, like he had done to poor old Lou.

"We got four kids, Kevin," she said. "Plus, you kept me up all night."

"All night, my butt," Kevin responded quietly.

"Um, you did, loser. Plus, at any minute they'll be in here asking for breakfast. I love you, but not today, ok?" She kissed him on the cheek. "Now go get me some coffee." She smiled a wry smile.

He smiled back and sighed, "Yeah, ok. Um, you called me Kevin."

"Huh?" Rece asked with her eyes closed.

"Whenever you're mad at me you call me Kevin."

"My apologies, sweetie. Not mad at all."

Kevin laughed, "That's better."

"Good. I love you," she said quickly then flipped over.

"Maybe later, though, huh?" he said, glancing back at her, sitting up like a kid asking for candy later.

"Maybe later what?" Rece asked.

Kevin responded, "You know...."

"We'll see!" she smiled; her eyes still closed.

"Ok, then," Kevin said as he laid back and half smiled. "Love you so much!"

He rolled over and sat up at the edge of his bed. His head was down and his back ached. He knew the second he stood up his hip would hurt. His hip had been bothering him for a few months and he didn't know why. He stood, stretched up high with his arms and began to walk. A minor pain ran through his hip and his ankle was tender. He limped a bit then seemed to hit his stride.

Kevin walked out of his room and immediately stepped on a toy. He looked down and saw some sort of robot, pirate, army guy. The toy had a shield and armor and a pointy mask that went right into his foot.

"Ow!" he gasped. It really got him. "Jesus Christ."

He hopped a bit, then grabbed the wall, looked at his foot, saw no damage, and kept walking shaking his head back and forth.

He first passed the little boys' room. He looked in and saw the top bunk mysteriously empty. Below he saw two little heads immediately slam themselves back on the bed. They were pretending to sleep. Kevin walked slowly over the shiny, hardwood floor. He approached the oak bunk beds and pretended to look under the camouflage blankets. He heard giggling. He turned away from the bed.

"Well, too bad they're gone. I was gonna go get them doughnuts. Oh well!" Kevin then coughed uncontrollably.

"WE WANT DOUGHNUTS!!! WE WANT DOUGHNUTS!!" they yelled in unison over Kevin's cough. "DOUGHNUTS!! DOUGHNUTS!! DOUGHNUTS!!!"

Kevin smiled. "Ok, ok. Give me a bit and I'll go get some doughnuts, ok?"

"Yeah!!!" yelled James, the 9-year-old, his brownish gold hair glistening against his red-tanned face as he peeked out under his blanket.

"Best Dad ever!!" yelled Vincent, the seven-year-old, Kevin's twin in looks, right down to the dark skin and brown hair.

Kevin smiled and the boys then went back under their covers to their very important video games.

Kevin now continued down the yellow hallway lined with brown picture frames containing family photos and peeked into Kate's room. Her canopy bed was alone in the middle of the pink room. Pink linens hung down around her. Her very white headboard braced against the wall and her white quilt covered her in her sleep. His 13-year-old beautiful short blonde freckled faced daughter was still fast asleep. In her arms was Henry, her very worn, off brown stuffed dog, handed down from Rece. Kevin looked at Kate and smiled bigger.

Across her room he heard the patter of tiny, tiny legs. *The hermit crab!* Kevin walked over quickly, picked up the top of the cage, sprinkled some food inside and watched intently for more movement.

"Damn," he whispered. *I never see the damn thing.* They'd had the crab for three years, and Kevin still hadn't caught a glimpse of it.

He stared at the cage. He fixed his eyes on nothing as he was looking for any movement whatsoever from the crab. He waited. It never moved. He paused and looked back at Kate. He smiled.

As he left her room, he heard gunshots and mad screaming coming from down the hall. He approached Blaize's room. Blaize was his 14-year-old son. The gunshots grew louder and louder. He opened the door and the noise pierced through his head. Blaize was in his video game chair, the one they bought for him last Christmas. He sat in the center of the dark maroon room, littered with posters from famous movies. Next to the video game chair was a black mini refrigerator. Blaize had an open Coke can next to him, and his video game headphones were on. Clothes were strewn across the room. Candy wrappers littered the floor and there was a weird smell that Kevin had grown used to.

"Did you even sleep last night?" Kevin said loudly. He paused as Blaize did not respond. "Blaize!?"

"Oh, hey dad." Blaize smiled but didn't look up.

"I left you last night and you were playing this game, drinking Coke," Kevin said quizzically.

Blaize again didn't look up. He was killing zombies.

"Blaize!"

"All good dad. Just playing with Danny," Blaize said without looking up, his eyes so intense against the TV. Blaize started talking gibberish into his headphone. Kevin assumed it was Danny, Blaize's cousin.

"What...Blaize, what time does your coach want you there today?" Kevin said softer than before.

"Blaize?"

"What Dad?"

"Never mind." Kevin closed the door and shook his head. He headed down the long hallway to the staircase. He started down the wood stairs and looked out the perfect shiny glass window straight in front of him. The green grass of his lawn looked pristine, freshly cut the evening before and edged with perfect precision. His grass was very special to him. He worked hard to make it look good, and this morning he paused a bit to gaze at his fine work.

In the spring, he had raked the dead grass off, clearing up space for the healthy grass to flourish. He had rented an aerator to assure proper oxygen to the roots. Fertilizer with crabgrass preventer was the next step. Finally, he laid a nice layer of grub-be-gone so the bugs wouldn't hinder root growth. Every four weeks he re-fertilized.

The house was in the city proper, so he didn't have to deal

with water limits. The lawn was watered meticulously, probably more than necessary. He watered a lot but tried to let the grass dry out a bit. Kevin knew that letting the grass dry out allowed the roots to grow deeper. Kevin also made sure not to water too close to nightfall. Watering at night meant the grass would stay wet too long, which promoted disease.

That spring he had done everything perfectly. The lawn was perfect. It was a deep green, and upon close examination, there wasn't a grass blade out of place. And on this morning, Kevin took it all in, and was very happy.

Looking up from the grass, the trees looked still, and the sun was shining bright. An older couple walked down the street in shorts and what appeared to be matching shirts.

They look happy. He watched them walk until they disappeared past the corner house.

Down the street a bit, he saw kids riding their bikes. Two black dogs wrestled playfully on his next-door neighbor's lawn, a lawn that looked, to him, a little unkempt. As he approached the turn his eyes caught the glimpse of a few puffy clouds off in the distance. An old black car drove by noisily.

Kevin turned the corner of his staircase, ready to make the second leg of the journey downstairs. He turned and took a quick step. He was ready for some coffee! He saw Blaize's bat bag at the bottom of the stairs. The bat leaned against the front door. Next to the bat bag sat James and Vincent's basketball bags, both blue, and both very worn. The coffee was brewing as he reached the bottom stair. He had remembered to set the timer the night before. *This was perfect.*

As he hit the ground floor, he turned to maneuver around the light blue couch. As he turned, he put his right hand on the couch and lifted himself around the end. He hopped and landed on the hardwood floor beneath him. As he landed Kevin felt a shutter in his head. It felt like his brain was vibrating and a strange pain shot up the front of his face and landed at the bridge of his nose. The pain then radiated to the back of his head. He grabbed the couch to not fall, though he wasn't sure if he would. He put his fingertips on his forehead then he felt a minor rush in his head. He shook his head to clear the mess, but it made it worse. A small hammer came pushing down on the top of his head and jammed itself hard in the center. It was strange and annoying pain. It was pain he'd never felt before in his life. He stood at the edge of that couch and paused.

What the hell?

He sat down and tried to ponder this pain, but the hammer was a little too much. The pain split his head in half and the hammer now was forcing its way through his forehead. The pain centered at the bridge of his nose, up through the center of his skull. He lay down in the fetal position only because he wanted to sit down. His head was filling with pressure all at once. The pain radiated. His skull felt like it was splitting in half, and the pillow offered no help. Kevin lay down. He didn't want to move. *What the fuck?*

He grabbed a pillow and pressed it hard against his forehead. He wasn't sure how much time had passed since it hit him. He was on his back now. He pressed his forehead harder and harder. He released it and opened his eyes. He could see.

That I can see must be good.

He sat up. The pain was less, but an annoying pressure remained inside his head. It felt like the pressure was trying to push through his skull. Pain-wise, he felt somewhat better. But this pressure was like nothing he'd ever felt. It was relentless. It wasn't as noticeable as the initial knock-down, but it was relentless as hell.

"Fuck" he whispered. "What the..."

"Where's my coffee, dear?" Rece pleasantly called from upstairs. "I'm waiting". She let out a giggle.

He coughed hard. He didn't know why. It was just a reaction. He realized no time had passed.

"On my way," he said, softly under the cough.

He walked normally into the kitchen shaking his head calmly but vigorously. He heard the din of the refrigerator kicking in. He walked to it and pulled on both handles of the shiny silver double door. He saw last night's beef roast sitting right in front of him. He reached in and grabbed the cream. He turned towards the counter and saw the remnants of the ice cream they all had last night. Six bowls sat on the counter. He pushed them aside and put down the cream. The hammer was back. It was trying to work its' way through his forehead.

"Dammit!" he cried out, but softly enough so no one would really hear.

He shook his head and prayed that the coffee might make this go away. The hammer rattling was back. His brain was vibrating, and his skull was giving way to the force. The bridge of the nose felt the brunt. Pounding and filling with pressure, harder and harder. He worried a bit. He started to sweat.

Down the stairs ran Kate. He heard her whiz past the couch, and he knew she'd be there in seconds. He pressed his thumb and middle finger against his forehead, rubbing them back and forth on it. He prayed not to die in front of his only daughter. He didn't want her to know he was in pain.

"Hi Daddy!"

"Kate!!" he said, sounding fake in his excitement. "How are you? You were just asleep!"

"You ok?" she asked, looking down at her cell phone and not answering his question.

"Yeah, oh, yeah. Why?"

"I don't know, you look tired."

Kevin smiled at her. "Yeah, a little tired is all." He grabbed her head with both hands and placed a kiss on the top of her blonde head. "I love you." His kiss pressed against her head tight. His eyes remained closed, pressed tightly closed. His head hurt. His head hurt bad.

"You too, dad! You're such the best dad in the whole world!"" She ran and jumped on the couch and put the TV on.

He grabbed the counter with two hands. *This isn't right. This can't be good.*

--

"Well, I just couldn't wait anymore, hon." Rece appeared out of nowhere.

She entered the kitchen and Kevin had his head lowered and both hands were still on the counter.

"What's wrong? You ok?" she asked smiling. She had on very short shorts and one of his tee shirts. She looked amazing.

"Oh yeah, fine," Kevin said, smiling, not noticing her attire or her drop dead good looks. "I had one of those faint-y spells." Kevin paused and giggled nervously. "Phew. You ever get those?"

"Oh my God, all the time," Rece said, walking past him. He looked down and did notice her legs and feet. He then looked back down at the countertop.

Rece grabbed the coffee pot and poured into the two cups that Kevin had put out. Kevin pretended to look through the cupboard now. His head still pounded, and he felt like the room was tilted to the left. There was pressure between his eyes, and the left side of his head felt like it was inflating with a heavy liquid. His right temple now felt like a nail was being driven through it. As quickly as that pain came, it went, and then came back again. He grabbed the bridge of his nose with his thumb and index finger of his right hand. The pressure was intense.

"What's wrong, honey? You tellin' me everything?" Rece put her hand on his back and rubbed gently.

"Ah. Just got this crazy feeling headache, too, I think."

"Oh, ok. Do you want some aspirin? I know we have some. Get some and meet me upstairs. I have your coffee, ok?"

"Yeah." Kevin smiled. "Be right there."

Rece began to walk away and then stopped. "Hey," Rece said, "remember, tell me everything, ok? I don't want to go backwards, Kevin."

"I know, I know, I will," Kevin said. *Kevin, again.*

He didn't watch her walk away, her legs shining with the sunlight on them as it shone through the doors to the back deck. The glitter from the sun that was flickering off their pool and the water shined against the wall behind her.

Kevin stood there a bit then walked past Kate who had the black TV clicker in her hand and was watching something on the flat screen T.V. on the wall. The sound was very loud. Kate also had her cell phone working, quickly sending a text as she watched the TV. Kevin walked right in front of the TV as the sound seemed to get louder. He made his way to the bathroom and the medicine cabinet.

Inside he saw many medicines. There were bottles of children fever reducer, children pain reliever, children stomach medicine. He saw Ibuprofen for adults and adult acetaminophen. He had no idea what to take for this headache. He saw no aspirin.

I'm not a medicine guy. He had taken antibiotics before for the occasional strep throat, and one time for an infection on his hand. But he had never been the type to take over the counter medicine, mostly because he never really experienced any pain. He didn't really know what to take nor do at this moment.

He closed the cabinet and began to walk out of the bathroom.

This will pass soon.

The instant he said that, the pressure between his eyes heightened. The pressure pressed outward, from deep inside the skull towards the skin, like a geyser waiting to explode with no outlet. The pressure then extended outward from the bridge of the nose towards his temples. The throbbing was unbearable. It pressed on, over and over, from the nose to the temples. Meanwhile, his entire head felt like it could explode at any moment. *This cannot be right.* He decided to just go upstairs and be with his wife. Somehow, he reminded himself that he was walking fine, and had no other issues other than the pressure and the pain. *Weird.*

"What's so funny, Kate?" he asked as he approached the stairs.

"Huh?" Kate responded.

"I heard you laughing."

"Um, no you didn't, dad, because I wasn't laughing."

"Hm," Kevin said quietly. "Ok."

--

Lying in bed, he propped his head high on the pillow. The noise of the house was still high. Blaize was still killing zombies. The boys were knee deep in their own video games, and Kate was now blaring music from her iPad while watching loud TV. He buried the back of his head deep into his soft pillow. Rece had turned their TV on, as well. He stared closely. He didn't recognize the movie. He hit the 'info' button on the remote, after finding it deep beneath the covers. Nothing came up. He clicked the channel to a sports show.

His pain had subsided a bit. But he still felt clogged in the head. His forehead felt very full and there was still some pain between the eyes. Rece came out of the bathroom.

"Hey darling!" Rece's tee shirt was very loose fitting. Her brown hair hung down, and the short shorts were perfectly fit against her legs. She looked as if she had made herself up. But he knew she had not.

"Hey," Kevin said, wanting to be so turned on by his beautiful wife.

"The boys were in here," she said, plopping her body firm against his.

"Uh huh." He knew what she was going to tell him. He now remembered what he'd promised them.

"They're expecting, uh, doughnuts?" Rece put a kiss along his neck.

"Yeah, I mighta said something. Sorry." Kevin didn't respond to the kiss.

"I don't care, but they, uh, want 'em. Like, soon." She laid one more very nice kiss on his neck then flipped over on her back.

"I don't know, maybe they don't need doughnuts, ya know?" Kevin maneuvered his head deeper into the pillow. There was some relief there.

Rece responded, "No. I mean, I would prefer you don't get them doughnuts, but you promised them."

"What promise?" Kevin said grumpily. "I didn't promise. I just said we'd get doughnuts."

"To a 9 and 7-year-old, that's a promise, Kevin."

Kevin let out a deep sigh.

"What's with you?" Rece said. "You were all fun and festive this morning and now you're bein' all mopey."

"Eh, I know, it's just this…" Kevin didn't finish his sentence. He paused instead, not knowing what to say.

"Uh, yeah, this?" Rece wanted to know.

Kevin said to the ceiling. "I don't know, I just feel weird."

"You are weird, ya weirdo". Rece giggled and rubbed his head. Kevin didn't respond at all. Rece turned serious in her tone. "I don't want to go backwards, Kevin. I know you. When things go bad, or just get a little bit off, you do, too, you know what I mean? Is everything ok?"

"I know, Rece, I know, I won't, and, yes, everything is ok, it's just this…"

He sat up and a wave of pain and fullness engulfed his head. He immediately put his forehead down flat against both his palms.

"Honey, what is it?" Rece said, sounding somewhat concerned.

"This fucking headache. Fuck."

"I told you to take medicine. Did you?"

"No. What for?"

"Because medicine helps headaches, dumb-dumb."

"This isn't a headache, dear."

"Um, you just said you had a headache, and you're holding your head," Rece said putting a skeptical face on.

"Ha, ha, hon. I know, I'm not making sense, but…" Kevin didn't have the time to finish his sentence.

"We want doughnuts!!!!!" James and Vincent ran into the

room like middle linebackers attacking a gap. They jumped right on the bed.

Kevin grabbed them both and hugged them hard. The pressure was getting worse in the head. The boys squirmed about, giggling senselessly, having an absolute ball. Kevin began to tickle them a bit, and then lay back down. The hugging seemed to help.

"Kevin?" Rece raised her eyebrows.

The boys sat up. They stared at Kevin.

He stared deep into the two boys. "Yeah. Let's get those doughnuts."

"Yay!!!!!!!!"

Rece smiled and kissed Kevin on the cheek.

--

Driving down 103rd Street, Kevin stared blankly ahead, his head full of pressure. He drove past the 'Great Wall'.

"Look, Dad, the Great Wall of Chicago," James said as he pointed.

"What's that?" Vincent asked, looking out the window.

"You're so dumb," James said shaking his head.

"You're not dumb, Vince," Kevin said as he drove. "The "Great Wall' as your brother calls it, is just that. It's a wall. As you can see, it's about a block long. They were building a building a while back. Before they could really get it going, they ran out of money or something and because they had already put up that brick wall, and because it was nice, I guess, the city kept it and just uses it kinda as a park now."

"Yeah, dummy," James chuckled.

"James...." Kevin said, looking back at the boys.

Having not eaten, yet, he felt uneasy. His blood sugar was low, his hands shook, and sweat appeared on his brow. He gripped the wheel tightly, trying to focus on anything he could to keep his mind off his problems. The boys giggled in the back seat, sitting together looking at their minicomputer. Out of nowhere, Vincent yelled, "How far till the doughnuts?!"

"Ha-ha!" James yelped. "You said nuts!"

"I said dough-NUTS, James!" Vincent responded loudly.

They laughed loudly. Kevin stared ahead, hoping to not pass out as he drove. He glanced at his cell phone, sitting on the front passenger seat. He felt comforted that he brought it with them.

"Not so loud, ok boys?" Kevin asked quietly.

"Um, we aren't talking, dad," James said, looking at the computer.

The boys laughed. Kevin saw the doughnut shop ahead and put his turn signal on. The pressure in his head was constant now. A fresh pain appeared in his right temple. He rubbed it. He looked at the boys in the rearview mirror, and then turned into the lot. He parked near the door and sat, turning off the car. He sat feeling his pain. The pressure remained. He wiped his forehead clean of sweat. He heard a knock on the window. It was Vincent.

"Uh, dad!?"

Kevin shook his head to clear the webs. He tried to turn the car off again, but realized the keys were already in his hands. He took a deep breath, closed his eyes and exited the vehicle. The three of them went in for doughnuts.

DR. FRANK NOURZAD

The office of Dr. Frank Nourzad, M.D. is kiddie corner to Pete's Breakfast shop off Utah Drive. 'Pete's', as it is called, is known for its early hours and fantastic breakfasts. It is frequented in the early morning mostly by the elderly. The specialty is pancakes, but the corned beef hash with scrambled eggs is to die for, as well, they say.

Most of those elderly folks who are off to Dr. Nourzad's office across the street on any given morning usually stop in at Pete's for breakfast or to just talk to each other and share notes on their illnesses and discuss their treatment plans. If they have a blood test that morning with the Doctor, it's usually just coffee and a doughnut. If blood tests are in order, Pete keeps their secret.

Kevin and the boys drove by Pete's that morning on his way to get the boys their doughnuts. Kevin was oblivious to its existence.

That Saturday morning, 72-year-old Nate Young was seeing Dr. Nourzad for a checkup. He was in Pete's, killing time before his appointment. Pete stood at the counter. He was six feet, three inches tall. His five o'clock shadow was apparent at 7:30 a.m. that morning. He wore a tee shirt, his muscles flexing through it. Pete looked down as Nate spoke. The smell of fried eggs and bacon filled the room.

"Got a checkup with Nourzad today, Pete," said Mr. Young.

Pete responded without looking up, "Shame about what happened. He's a good young man, good young doctor too, huh, Nate?" Pete said dryly as he fixed a plate.

"Oh, he's the best, Pete. Yeah, that was sad. Real sad. So sudden. But, yeah, he's the best. Even for as young as he is. The best," Nate agreed. "Why, last week he cured my brother, I mean, you know, fixed him, I guess you'd say."

"Yeah?" said Pete inflecting the question part of his statement. He was still looking down at the plate he was preparing.

"Yeah", said Nate. "Ya know my brother had those stomach pains. They were really bad, and he had them for a while."

"I remember," Pete said, even quieter this time.

"Yeah, well, we thought it was cancer because he kept hurting, always in pain. He was constantly crouching over, couldn't sleep, couldn't eat much," Nate said.

"Yeah," Pete said.

"Well, Nourzad, you see he likes to be called that, he kept telling him about lifestyle changes, ya know, cleaner livin', I guess. Anyway, I'm boring you. Turns out he put Joe on some special diet, gave him some meds. More than anything, Pete, though, he talked to Joe a lot, ya know. Always talkin' to him. I mean Joe would go into appointments and I'd wait outside and it'd be 45 minutes to an hour sometimes, and I'd be asking him what the hell took so long, ya know?" Nate laughed as he finished his sentence.

"Yeah?" Pete asked, looking at the plate.

"Yeah," Nate said. "Well, Joe would always say the same thing: 'Dr. Nourzad likes to talk'. And, it wasn't just the doctor talking. Joe always said they'd just have these long conversations. I guess that's how Nourzad does it. I guess he learns a lot about us from talking, I don't know"

Mr. Young took a sip of coffee. Then he continued. "Yeah, so, it took a long time. Joe kept complaining that it wasn't really working. And sometimes I agreed because he was still hurting in there. But I also had heard that Nourzad wouldn't steer my brother wrong. Like, my buddy Nick had that neck thing last year and it took forever, but Nick said because of Nourzad, it went away. So, I kept telling Joe to be patient. Let Nourzad's plan work. And it did. So, the next week, I switched doctors to Nourzad," Mr. Young said, chuckling again. "Know what? The man loves to talk." Mr. Young laughed more. "At my first appointment, and I had nothing wrong, it was just a check-up, we talked for over 30 minutes. Some people just love to talk, I guess.

Pete chuckled. "That's great, Nate."

"Yeah. Anyway, with Joe, they ran some tests the other day. He's perfect."

"Tell Joe I said hi, will ya?" asked Pete.

"I will," said Nate.

Pete was walking away, then quickly looked back, "Say, you said just a checkup today? You're good?"

"I'm good. Just a checkup. I get 'em every six months. Feels good to get doc's seal of approval and all. I see him, we talk a lot, he sends me on my way, and I know I'm good." Mr. Young said.

"You got that right, Nate. You got that right," Pete said. He started to walk away and then turned back to Mr. Young. "By the way, does he just take elderly patients?"

"Who, Nourzad?" Mr. Young asked.

"Yeah," Pete said. "That's the rumor, that he only sees elderly patients."

"That's what I hear, too. He only sees us old folk," Mr. Young said as he chuckled again. "In fact, another guy told me last time I was in that Nourzad won't take anyone younger than 60. I don't know if it's true or not, but I think it is. In all my times there with my brother and then myself, I never saw anyone there to see him under 60, to be honest. Why do you ask?"

"My brother, he's 36, he was looking for a doctor. I've heard so many good things about Dr. Nourzad, but I've also heard from a few people that he only sees the elderly."

"Yeah," Mr. Young said after a sip of coffee. "I think that's the case."

Pete said thank you. Mr. Young finished his coffee and got up to leave.

--

"Hello, Mr. Young, how are you?" the female receptionist greeted Mr. Young with a smile.

"Hello, Jean," Mr. Young said. "How are you?"

"I'm just great."

"That is good to hear," he said "Oh, and I have told you to call me Nate, Jean."

"Well, Nate, the doc is running a few minutes late this morning, he's with a new patient, and it's taking a little longer."

"Oh, that's quite all right. That is expected here, Jean."

"Oh, certainly is, Nate," Jean said as she typed. "I mean, I've worked in offices like this for 25 years and I've never seen an office run behind schedule in a good way. Never one complaint about running late. It's wonderful."

"Well," Mr. Young said, "that has to do with the age of his patients, we are old, where do we have to go? Plus, the way he handles us, I mean, I've never heard or seen of a doctor care so much for each patient."

Jean smiled while continuing to type, then looked up, "Indeed, Mr., I mean, Nate."

Mr. Young smiled and nodded at Jean. "I'm going to take my seat."

"Call you soon, Nate."

Mr. Young turned to go sit down and then turned back to Jean. "Say, Jean, I wanted to ask, is Nourzad taking any new patients?"

"Oh, dear, Nate," Jean said at once, "I don't think so. He has so many already. I mean, in three years his patient total has tripled! If he does take any more, I'll quit!"

"Yeah, I figured," he said back to her, adding a chuckle. "And, certainly not a younger patient."

Jean laughed aloud. "Young? In Doctor Nourzad's office?" Jean laughed louder. "I don't think so, Nate. He just concentrates on the elderly."

"Like I said," Mr. Young said turning away from Jean, "that's what I thought."

Mr. Young sat in his chair and looked around at the crowded waiting room. "Yep, a bunch of old farts," he whispered under his breath.

"Mr. Young!" a voice cried out.

Startled a bit, Mr. Young did not respond.

"Nate..."

"Right here," he said, cutting off the voice.

"Dr. Nourzad will see you now." It was a younger nurse that he had never seen before.

"Thank you, dear."

Once inside the office, Dr. Nourzad sat down with Mr. Young.

"So, Nathaniel, how are you?" Nourzad asked.

"Great, doc," he responded. "Just here for a checkup."

"You can call me Nourzad, Nathaniel, remember?" the doctor said. "Been feeling ok?"

"Very good."

"That is wonderful," said the doctor to his patient. "And how is Myrtle?"

"As good as ever, doc," he responded with a grin a mile long.

"Ok, then, let us see…"

Mr. Young cleared his throat, and then interrupted the doctor. "Ya know, doc, every time I come in here, and the times I brought Joe, it's always about me."

Nourzad smiled.

"Well, I was hoping to hear about you," Mr. Young said directly.

"What do you want to know, Nathaniel?"

"Well, honestly, doc," Mr. Young said, "my biggest question, and it just happens to have come up lately, is why only the elderly?"

"You mean my patients? Why are they all old?"

"Yeah," Mr. Young said enthusiastically.

"Well, Nathaniel…"

"I'm not being nosey, am I doc, because if I am…"

"It's quite all right, Nathaniel."

Nourzad stood up and moved to the seat by the window. He sat and faced Mr. Young. "See, I went to medical school, Nathaniel, and I was working towards my specialty in psychiatry. And I probably would have gone that way had my parents not died when I was younger."

"Sorry to hear that, doc."

"It's ok. But, see, my parents died, both, at such a young age. In fact, we had kinda just moved here from India. And, being stubborn, neither of them spoke up about being ill. My dad died of a stomach aneurysm, which we found out as he lay dying, that he had felt that pain for months and did nothing about it. My mom died of heart failure a few months later. So, I was 9 by the time they both died. So, that was instrumental in me going to medical school, those two experiences. I loved psychiatry, but, thinking of my parents, it brought me to realize I wanted to help the aging, the elderly, help them identify and be able to express."

"Yeah, doc, again, so sorry, but that's great that you followed through with that."

"Well, I'm not special, certainly. I just hope to open up the lines of communication to those who need it and make them realize they can and should identify pain and report it." Nourzad paused, and there was a brief silence. "Anyway," Nourzad continued, "my uncle raised me after that. He was a dentist, with connections, as they say. I worked for him through college, he helped me get into Northwestern Medical School, and here I am, Nathaniel."

Mr. Young just smiled at the young doctor. No words were necessary.

"So," Nourzad broke the silence, "let us check that blood pressure while you give me that recipe you owe me."

It had been nine years since Frank Nourzad began his practice in the office connected to the back of James Hope Hospital near the south side of Chicago. His practice was geriatrics, only. His office was small, and he shared space with two older doctors. They accepted most patients with insurance and were part of an HMO service. As such, patients attached to the hospital could choose this group of three doctors as their 'primary physician'.

The doctors ran their practices together, sharing some patients. But most of the elderly had come to request Frank

Nourzad.

That Saturday morning in the office of Frank J. Nourzad, eighteen patients came in to see the good doctor.

"Eighteen smiling faces, doctor." It was Marge, one his nurses that day.

"A good half-day, huh, Marge?" Nourzad said to her as he signed off on his final file of the day.

"Very good, doctor," she replied to Nourzad, a sharp looking man standing six feet two, weighing 205 pounds. "Mr. Ravenswood really felt better about himself today. He came in a tad down, but those positive test results really brightened his spirits."

Nourzad smiled. "Ah, I don't think it was the results, Marge," the doctor said quietly. "He's come to an understanding with himself, Marge. He can deal with the reality of his disease, knowing what we are doing will keep him active for a couple of years. He wants to live. That is all, plain and simple."

The good doctor paused and took a breath. "He knows the results of the next test could change dramatically. He's seen that. He's no fool. But he's seen the way we work this. He believes in it, I think." Nourzad paused a moment, and then continued. "Positivity, Marge. It works. He knows he's not alone in this battle. We are always there for him. Always will be. It's freeing to him. But I'm boring you once again."

"Oh dear, doctor," Marge said, "you never bore me. I've been a nurse a long time, doctor. I've seen them come and go. I've seen the old ones, the young ones, the competent ones, and the idiots. I've seen them all, doctor, and I've never seen anyone do it like you, the way you talk to them, the way you care. I mean, I've never seen a doctor laugh and cry all in one visit like you did today with Mr. Ravenswood. He hugged you for over a minute, doctor. It's touching. It really is."

The doctor looked at her and smiled. He took a deep breath.

"Problem, doctor?" Marge asked while staring at him with a smile.

Nourzad paused a bit and then answered, "I feel bad for him, Marge. Those results were good, but the fact is the important levels weren't where they should have been."

The doctor looked down at his bag and paused again. "Anyway, those were kind words, Marge." He looked into the box that held today's patient files. He thumbed quickly until he found 'Ravenswood'. He grabbed the file and put it in his tan, faded briefcase. "Oh well, good day, nonetheless, Marge."

Marge knew she need not answer that question.

Frank Nourzad finished packing his bag, looked up, and walked out of the office. "See you Tuesday, Marge."

"Enjoy the rest of your day, Doctor," Marge said in response. Dr. Nourzad walked out into the overcast day. He did not respond.

VOWS, AGAIN

August 5, 2015

"Craziest thing," Kevin said. "Nope. It was just that one day and the headache went away. What was that, a week ago?"

"Yes," Rece said while smiling. "I kept meaning to ask you. I figured it went away. You know, I feel bad I didn't bring it up, but we've been so busy, and you really did seem ok."

"It did go away," Kevin said. "Otherwise, you would have known about it." Kevin laughed aloud.

"Oh," Rece said, "trust me, I know that!" Rece laughed, as well.

Kevin and Rece held hands as they walked to the church. The summer sunset peeked at them as it hovered over the trees to the west. The evening sky was perfect, and children played on the yards they passed.

"Are you nervous?" Rece asked out of the blue.

"Nervous?" Kevin said. "No! Why should we be nervous?"

"I don't know," Rece answered, and then laughed. She squeezed Kevin's hand tight. "I'm so happy we are doing this."

"Oh, me too," Kevin said. "This was such a good idea."

Rece laughed aloud. "Well, Mr. humble, I do appreciate and love it."

"It's going to be such a great thing."

"Thing?" Rece asked as she looked at him.

"Ceremony, baby. It's going to be so special."

She squeezed his hand tight again. "Thank you, sweetie."

Kevin smiled and they continued to walk. They crossed the busy street and entered the church. Father Donnelly was in the vestibule waiting for them as they walked in.

"Kevin and Rece," Father Donnelly exclaimed, "welcome. I'm so glad you are here."

"Thanks for seeing us," Kevin said.

"My pleasure," the priest said. Father Donnelly stood in black garb, a black shirt buttoned to the collar, and deep and rich dark black pants. Shiny black shoes covered his feet and his white clerical collar looked freshly shined. His grayish silver hair was cut short and perfectly, and he had not a facial hair in sight.

He led Kevin and Rece into the church and spoke as he walked. "The renewal of marriage vows is a wonderful moment in the eyes of God. Two people re-promising to God to live their lives together with His blessing."

"We are so happy to be here," Rece said as they followed behind him.

The three walked to the front of the church. Near the altar, Father Donnelly had set up three chairs. The smell of incense and candles filled the air. The lights were dim, except for the high beam shining on the crucifix over the altar.

"Let's all sit," the priest said. After a pause, he asked, "So, what brought about this desire to renew?"

Kevin looked at Rece and then back to Father Donnelly. "I, um, went through a few things. I'll just be honest with you, I wasn't the best dad or husband, and I, um, well, I want to start over with her. She put up with a lot and deserves a better ceremony this time. We were married in a courthouse originally, and I want to promise to God now that I will cherish and love Rece for the rest of my life." Kevin began to tear up as he looked at Rece. She reached over and squeezed Kevin's hand.

Father Donnelly smiled at them both. "It's so refreshing to hear the honesty and love from your voice." He then looked at Rece. "Rece, you are willing?"

"Yes, yes, I am," Rece said. "I know he went through a lot, too. I know what happened was based on things beyond his control, and this renewal is the perfect way to, as Kevin said, just start over." She reached for Kevin's hand and squeezed it hard once again.

"I would be honored to preside over this ceremony," Father Donnelly said. "I look forward to blessing this marriage under the cloth of the Lord, our God. Now, let's go over the details."

--

"That went well," Rece said, as her and Kevin walked hand in hand out the church door.

"I love you, Rece," Kevin said.

"Love you, too."

The two walked across the street. Instead of going straight, Kevin led Rece west, towards Meadow Lane.

"What's going on?" Rece asked.

"Well, to celebrate the occasion, I thought we'd go out to dinner."

"Kevin! Get out?" Rece said emphatically.

Kevin laughed and smiled. "I didn't think you'd be this excited."

"We never get to go out, with the kids and all, so, I mean, this is wonderful, Kev."

"The Italian Diner."

"Aww, Kevin, my favorite!"

"I know, baby, I know."

Rece and Kevin walked through the summer night into their bliss.

FAMILY ICE CREAM NIGHT

August 15, 2015

The family drove up to the baseball field for another base-ball game. Kate had her headphones on. She was singing music very loudly. Rece smiled in the front passenger seat of their 2011 black Honda Odyssey. Blaize was in the very back, uniform on, clanking his bats in a uniform rhythm. James and Vincent were playing their hand-held video games. They were in sync, playing each other in a baseball game.

"Ha-ha! You were out!" screamed Vincent.

"That was so lucky! You got lucky, Vince!" James yelled back.

The drive was 20 minutes. They were pulling in.

Kevin found a spot a little further from the prime spot. He nestled the van between two pickup trucks. He put the van in park. As he did, he let out a deep breath. He put his head back and rolled his head around, closing his eyes as he did.

"You ok?" Rece asked quickly but sweetly.

Kevin answered immediately. "Yeah, I mean, damn. Weird." Kevin shook his head aggressively.

"What is it?" Rece asked, extending her hand to Kevin's.

"My head," Kevin said. "That pain, from last week or so. It's back."

"Does it hurt?" Rece asked.

"Can I get out?" Blaize interrupted.

"Huh, yeah, yeah, get out guys," Kevin said quietly. "I'll, um, Mom and I will be right up with you. The games, uh, on field 7, so, we'll meet you there."

The kids scrambled out of the car like a hurricane, leaving a mess of juice boxes and candy wrappers behind them. They all began to run to the field.

"Are you ok?" Rece asked.

"I don't know."

"What is it?"

"It's like, um, crazy. Fuck, it just came out of nowhere."

"Is it the same pain?" Rece asked.

"Exact same. Right here," Kevin said, pointing to his forehead. "And it kinda pushes out, like my whole skull hurts."

Rece went through her purse. "Here, take two of these."

"What is it?"

"Motrin. It'll help, sweetie."

"Thanks, hon." Kevin took the pills and put them in his mouth. He reached in the back seat and grabbed an open juice box and swallowed them down. "Jesus, this hurt."

"Aw, honey, the Motrin will for sure work," Rece said assuring.

"Thanks," Kevin said. "Man, I hope. Fuck." *Jesus fuck.*

"That bad?" Rece asked.

"Huh?" he asked. "Yeah, it's a pain alright. Almost worse than last time."

"Well, let me know if it gets worse during the game. Hopefully the Motrin kicks it."

"Ok," Kevin said. He sat in his seat, not moving.

"Can you make it?" Rece asked.

"Yeah, yeah, I think so," Kevin said. "Ok, ok, let's go."

--

"You don't seem right. Still hurting?" Rece whispered in Kevin's ear about 20 minutes later, while staring ahead at the players running onto the field to start the game.

"My head is killing. It is so bad," Kevin said staring into the bleacher floor.

"Oh, sweetie, shit," Rece said. "Should we go home? I'll take you."

"That's sweet, hon," Kevin said, "but, no, I don't want to leave. But this is outrageous, Rece," Kevin whispered back.

"Well, if you think we need to go, let's go. I'll get Lisa to take Blaize home."

"She's here?" Kevin asked, looking around.

"She's at her nephew's game on field 3, I think. She told me last night that she'd be here today."

Kevin paused and then answered, "No, no, it's ok. I'll make it."

Rece hugged him with her right arm. "You'll be ok, sweetie. It'll go away. Like last week. Probably a one-day deal again."

Kevin smiled at her then hugged her. "Thanks honey. I think you're right."

--

"Dad!!!!"

Kevin jumped and turned. Someone had pushed him from behind.

"Kate. Geez," Kevin said

"Sorry, Dad. Had to do it," Kate said smiling and giggling.

Kevin put his right palm up to his head. "That's alright, Kate, but I thought you were with the boys. They went to the car."

"With Mom," Kate said, putting her headphones on.

"Mom..." Kevin was confused and cut himself off. He thought Rece was behind him.

Kate walked past Kevin and Kevin followed.

"Where's Blaize!?" Kevin yelled ahead to Kate.

She didn't hear him. He didn't care. He knew Blaize would meet him at the car but hoped people would think he was concerned about Blaize's whereabouts so they would not try to speak to him much more.

"Let's go, Dad! They're at the car!" Kate was walking fast now.

Kevin caught up to her. He put his hand on Kate's shoulder. The appearance would scare off any talkers. He was still confused how Rece and Blaize passed them to get to the lot first. *There's no way they passed me.* He and his only daughter walked forward. Kate's headphones were glaring. He could hear the music loud and clear. Up ahead he glanced in the area where his car should have been. He couldn't see it. His head was very full. There was a constant pain now between his eyes and he kept feeling like he would fall over. Between the pain there was fullness in the forehead, like cement being driven in. He was groggy. He grabbed Kate's shoulder tighter. She looked up at him and smiled. A soft calm came over his body as he smiled back at her. For a split moment, he forgot about his headache. He heard faint laughter, looked at Kate, and, once again, she was not laughing.

--

The ice cream cone towered forty feet into the sky. There were three flavors on the giant cone: chocolate, vanilla, and strawberry. In the night sky, the cone lit up. One could see it from a good distance as one approached. On this night, the kids had an idea the stop would be made. It always was after a hot night at the ball field. Being that it was on the way home helped their chances, too.

"Yeah!!" The two little guys cheered and smiled at each other as they saw the cone. "Ice cream!!"

"Nice, dad," Blaize said, his eyes on his iPhone.

"I want a sundae, dad," said Kate, her eyes peeled to Blaize's iPhone, as they sat next to each other in the way back seat.

"I don't think so tonight, guys," Kevin said quietly. His comment brought Rece to somewhat attention. *It's too late.*

Rece looked at Kevin and mouthed, 'Let's just get ice cream.'

Kevin winked at her and nodded an ok. He closed his eyes and took a deep breath. He kept driving. He reached to his forehead and rubbed it with the tips of his fingers.

"Wait, we're not getting ice cream?" Kate blurted out.

"Dad?" Blaize chimed in.

The little guys screamed in unison, "Come on, Dad! What gives? Why?!"

"It's late guys. No ice cream," Kevin said as he winked at Rece again.

"Sorry, guys, dad's right," Rece followed up.

"Aw, c'mon dad! Stop for ice cream!" Blaize yelled from the back.

"Ice cream, dad!" Vince and James yelled together, very loudly.

"Dad, c'mon," Kate said. "Mom? Tell him."

"He's the boss, sweetie," Rece winked at Kate and Kate smiled and giggled.

The light ahead stayed green. Just past the intersection was the ice cream Shoppe. Kevin drove through the intersection. The car was quiet. The turn had to come soon if they were going. He had to turn right into the first driveway, or they would miss it. Their eyes were peeled. No one said a word. The driveway approached.

"Thanks, Dad!"

It was Kate. Her head never peered up from her phone. They were getting ice cream. The little boys high-fived each other and giggled. Blaize was talking on his phone. Rece's eyes stayed ahead.

"Yeah!!!" the boys screamed.

"Ok," Kevin said as he put the car in park. "Let's go."

They all walked up to the door to the Shoppe. There was a giant menu outside. They all hung out a bit at the menu and shouted out what they wanted. Kevin led the way in after that.

Once inside, Kevin took a breath. There was a ringing in his ear and the right side of his head felt full. There was extreme pressure pain between his eyes, and, to him, his hearing was muffled. The pain between his eyes felt worse than ever. It was a constant pressure, like a blocked hose in which the water has no escape. The fullness in his right side tingled, as well. *Oh, Jesus.*

"You ok?" Rece said as she crept up behind Kevin and hugged him.

"Oh yea, all good," Kevin said. "Let's get some ice cream,"

Rece whispered. "You look miserable. Thanks for this. I

know you're in pain, but they love you for this. Thanks, sweetie. And I love you, too."

Kevin smiled the smile of a sad clown. Inside his head the pain radiated. The ice cream stop didn't make it go away.

"Ma! We're up!"

It was Blaize. It was their time to order.

--

"Thanks for the ice cream, guys," Kate said to both her Mom and her Dad.

Blaize mocked Kate. "It's a tradition, Kate! Gotta keep up the stupid traditions, right Kate? I mean, carving pumpkins on Halloween eve, Thanksgiving Day hikes, cocoa runs on Christmas Eve, and ice cream after baseball games, I mean, c'mon."

"We gotta keep the traditions, Blaize. Mom and Dad's traditions are what make our family fun, right Dad?" Kate asked.

"Whatever," Blaize said.

"Right, Kate," Kevin answered.

"Right Mom?" Kate asked again, this time to Mom.

"Absolutely, sweetie," Rece said, turning and smiling to Kate.

Kate looked at her Mom and smiled. She then went back to staring at her phone. The ride home was somewhat quiet as everyone ate at their ice cream. The little guys devoured their cones. Blaize scooped his sundae while watching his iPhone, which sat next to him on his seat. Kate was content in her phone, too. Rece and Kevin passed their waffle cone back and forth. Kevin handed it back to Rece and then gripped the wheel and stared ahead.

--

"The kids are all in bed," Kevin said, walking into the

bedroom while holding his forehead. The pain had subsided some, but there was still pressure in his forehead and fullness throughout. "I think they really liked that ice cream," Kevin continued, desperately hoping for a response. "Ya know?"

Rece was in bed, her glasses on, reading one of her books.

"Ya know?" Kevin said again.

"Oh," Rece said while laughing. "Sorry, was reading this and I dazed off. Huh?"

"Was a nice night, is all," Kevin said.

"Sure was, sweetie," Rece said. "Oh," Rece continued, "Thanks for handling the headache so well. Take two more Motrin and come into bed with me."

LET'S MEET RECE...

"Mom!"

"Yes, James, you don't have to scream," Rece said in a quieter tone than James, as she carried the cereal boxes to the table. Her hair glistened from her morning shower. She was dressed in black slacks and a white button-down shirt. Black sandals adorned her recently pedicured feet.

"I need that information for my report," James said.

"When is this due, honey?"

"Today," James responded.

"Of course it is, darling. Ok, let me get the milk and you can ask away."

Rece went for the milk and then sat down next to James. James poured his cereal and milk, and after one bite, began his questions.

"Name?" James asked like a reporter.

"Rece Ruscevich."

"It says here, maiden name?" James said.

"That's my last name before I married your dad. It's Sopo-wicz, S-O-P-O-W-I-C-Z."

"Weird name," Blaize whispered as he walked into the kitchen.

"Blaize," Rece retorted.

"Where were you born?" James continued.

"The moon," Blaize said softly.

"Blaize, please!" Rece said loudly to Blaize and then looked at James, "Pittsburgh, Pennsylvania."

"Pennsylvania?" James asked.

"Just put capital p, capital a," Rece said.

"Parents?" James asked.

"Jerry and Sylvia."

"Brothers and sisters?"

"None, James, you know that."

"Well, my teacher said I had to ask each question."

"Go on," Rece said patiently.

"Where do Grandma and grandpa live?"

"They're dead, numb-nuts." It was Blaize again.

"Blaize!" Rece said loudly. "Be respectful."

"What?!" Blaize said, raising his eyebrows as he said it.

"I meant to ask how they died," James said.

"Is that actually a question?" Rece asked back.

"Drinking and driving, Jimmy," Blaize said through the chewing of his cereal. "They were both drunk."

"Blaize, that's enough!" Rece sounded angry now. "Just stop."

"What, he's old enough to know, Mom," Blaize said and then ate at his waffle.

"What's drinking and driving?" James asked.

"Go to the next question, James," Rece ordered.

"What did grandpa do for a living?"

"He was a steel-worker."

"Grandma?"

"Waitress."

"Where did they raise you?"

"All over, James. We started in Pittsburgh, but then moved from city to city as grandpa kept trying to find work. We moved to Dallas, Oklahoma, Minneapolis, and then Chicago. I got here, in Chicago, I think when I was 10."

"When did they die?" James asked.

"Is that a question on the sheet?" Rece grabbed the sheet to verify.

"No," James replied as he put his spoon down and looked at his mom.

Rece glanced menacingly at Blaize, who looked but then quickly looked away from her.

Rece went on to explain more than she wanted to, as James listened intently. After about 5 minutes, Rece asked if that was enough information, and James said yes.

"Come here, sweetie," Rece said, reaching her arms out to James.

James got up and hugged his mom tight. "I love you," she said, "and your grandma and grandpa love you to."

"In heaven?" James asked.

"In heaven, yes, with Jesus."

James smiled and hugged his mom again. He then finished off his cereal and got ready for school.

--

"I'll just have a large café mocha with no cream and two Splendas."

After ordering, Rece stepped aside with Lisa, her best friend. They waited for their drinks and then walked to the table by the window. They both sat, Rece near the window, and Lisa across.

"So, how are you, how are the kids?" Lisa asked after a quick sip from her coffee.

"Oh my God, I wanted to kill Blaize this morning," Rece said, holding her coffee cup.

"Well, I've heard that before!" Lisa responded.

"He blurts out to James that my mom and dad died from drinking and driving or some shit like that, and I'm like, what?"

"Oh my God!" Lisa exclaimed. "Why?"

"Because I was answering some questions for James for school, and blah-blah-blah, they came up and Blaize is an ass."

They both laughed.

"What did you say?" Lisa asked.

"So, I had to explain the whole thing. The kid wouldn't let it go, and he's that age, I guess, he wants to know so I told him."

"Everything?"

"Yes," Rece answered, "everything. How they were alcoholics, what that meant, how they were driving one night when I was 12, and they never came home. Perfect morning with my kids."

"Oh my," Lisa said, looking compassionate as she did.

"Yeah, he was devastated, I guess. He had tears. But I told him they were in heaven and he was happy with that."

"Did you tell him about the crash, I mean, details?" Lisa asked.

"Oh. No, just that they crashed."

"Yeah, I can't imagine telling him they killed someone."

"Um, no," Rece said flatly.

"Oh, I'm sorry, sister; I know how difficult that is for you. Sorry you had to re-hash it again."

"That's ok. I mean, it's a part of who I am, so, I can't hide from it, and, as he was pressing me, I'm like, I'm not getting into this with him, but then decided he'd find out sometime, anyway, so I told him calmly and protected him from the bad stuff."

"You poor thing, Rece," Lisa said and then grabbed her hand and squeezed.

"So, then, Kevin comes downstairs, and James has a few questions for him, and of course Kevin gets the 'How did your mom and dad meet' questions."

Lisa laughed out loud.

Rece laughed, too, and then said, "He always gets the easy ones."

WHEN RECE AND KEVIN MET

"Excuse me; do you know where room 1035 is?"

The woman turned and saw Kevin standing there dressed in a blue suit, white shirt, ironed to perfection, with a light blue tie.

"Well, first of all", Rece responded with a smile, "You're on the wrong floor."

Kevin smiled. "Yeah, I'm not the brightest bulb in the batch."

They both laughed and smiled at that.

Kevin gazed upon the beautiful clerk. Her long brown hair flowed perfectly into her tan shirt. Her dark blue eyes captured him, and her perfect tanned skin engulfed him. Her body was perfect, and her smile was contagious. He felt weak and nervous.

"I have never really been to a courthouse before," Kevin said, still staring at her beauty.

"Well, well, then. You don't know what you've missed," Rece said as she stared back smiling. She shifted her weight to her left leg and put her hands behind her back, clutching her fingers together. "You see," she said while pointing, "that's a courtroom, and in it you'll find lawyers, and judges and sheriffs. And if you're lucky, you'll have an amazing clerk there to help you out."

"Ahhh. Let me guess", Kevin responded, their eyes locked, "you are that amazing clerk."

Rece laughed. "Oh boy, now that is one I've never heard before. I'm sure you're better than that."

Kevin thought, *Is this a thing here?* He then spoke, "Well, I think I, uh…" His face turned red.

"Aw," Rece said like she was talking to a baby. "Are you flustered, sir?"

"Well, now," Kevin responded, "now that's one I've never heard before."

"What, sir?" Rece asked quickly.

"Why yes," Kevin said. "You see my dad was a sir. Not me, though. Sir sounds so, I don't know, old."

"Ahhh, I see. You don't want to be the creepy old man flirting with a clerk?"

"Who said I'm flirting?" Kevin asked.

"Oh. Ok, then room 1035 is upstairs on the 10th floor."

He was thrown back by the comment. He didn't want this to end. "Well, maybe I…"

"Yes?" Rece interrupted.

"Maybe I am flirting."

"Oh, you don't want to do that," Rece said.

"I don't?"

"No. Because then you'll be late for court, counselor."

Kevin laughed. "Ohhhh! No, I'm not a lawyer."

Rece looked shocked. "Oh. Well then I don't want to talk to you."

Kevin stared. The moment seemed like an eternity. Rece

stared back.

"I'm kidding, sir."

Kevin laughed and smiled. "You are something."

"Yes, I am," Rece said and then turned away and walked.

Kevin followed quickly, catching up to her. He passed her and cut her off.

"Whoa, sir," Rece said. "Can I have a little space, please." Rece smiled as she said it.

"I think we weren't finished," Kevin said, looking into those eyes.

"Hm. The way I recall it, you asked where room 1035 was. And I told you. Seems finished to me. I don't recall any other questions." Rece looked at him then tried to move around him.

Kevin cut her off. "Will you go out with me?" The words just came out! He'd never been so upfront with a woman ever. His heart raced. His brow was wet. *What did I just do?*

Rece stared at him. Kevin stared back. In the hallway, the buzz of lawyers, witnesses, defendants, and police became loud. He desperately wanted her answer.

"I'd love to," Rece said. She then stepped around him and walked away. Kevin turned, watching her go. He didn't know what to do.

"How will I find you!?" Kevin yelled.

Rece turned, looked at him, and walked back towards him, but not all the way. "I'm the clerk for 1035, dummy." She then walked to him, grabbed his hand, smiled, let go of his hand, and turned and walked away. She took a few steps and turned back towards him. "I'll see you up there."

--

The cry of the baby started soft. It was staccato-like, almost a whimper. Then it stopped. A calm was over the home, not a noise o be heard except for the soothing buzz of the over-head fan.

Kevin lay still, comforted by his soft pillow. It was the same pillow he'd had since college. Oh, how Rece had wanted to toss that pillow for years, tired of the shreds of feathers that spilled from its 20-year-old cover. But she never did. It became more of a joke between the young married couple.

Next to Kevin lay Rece, her head resting against her flat long pillow. The single blanket covered them both, equally shared, keeping them cozy and warm. Their sleep was perfect that night.

The next cry started a little louder. The staccato quickened and grew a little stronger. Kevin heard it first. He opened one eye and listened intently. The whimpers came every few seconds. Then there was a pause. Kevin closed his eye and went back to enjoying his sleep.

Then it came again. Kevin opened his eye again, unsure of how long it was between cries. The pauses between cries shortened. It seemed inevitable at this point that the baby would not stop until fed.

Rece rolled over and tapped Kevin. "You hear that?" she whispered.

Kevin whispered back, "Yes. Shhhh."

"Maybe he'll go back to sleep," Rece said, holding Kevin tight now.

"This is no time for sex, honey," Kevin stated matter of factly.

"Oh my God, you wish," Rece giggled.

"Shh, shh, shhhh." Kevin covered her mouth with his hand.

"What is it?" Rece asked.

"Silence."

"I love silence," Rece whispered in his ear. "especially after having our fourth kid."

They laid still in the quiet of the night.

"Ahhhh," Kevin exhaled. "Goodnight sweetie."

"Good night, love." Rece kissed him on the cheek.

The scream came a second later. The baby was in full-fledged scream mode.

"Damn," they both said in unison.

"I think it's your turn," Kevin said.

Kevin grumbled and rolled back and forth in the bed. "Arg-gghh. Ok, my lovely. But just know this, when he's a star baseball player someday, I'll be sitting in the first row, you'll be in the upper-deck after I tell him about how I saved his life by feeding him every night."

"Aww, he'll love that, darling," Rece responded and then rolled over. "Good luck, dad. I love you."

"Mm-hmmm." Kevin sat up, rubbed his eyes, and got out of bed to feed young Blaize.

--

Blaize took his bottle like a champ. He finished it in what seemed like record time to Kevin. As Kevin sat in the recliner in the living room, he held him pressed against his shoulder, gently tapping his back to get him to burp. Kevin's eyes watched the sports highlights on TV. Blaize lay calm, his eyes closed as Kevin continued to tap. Kevin felt the gurgling inside Blaize and knew it was just a matter of time. Blaize let out a tremendous burp. Kevin brought him to his lap, looked at him, and whispered, "Good boy."

Kevin walked Blaize back upstairs, gently laid him down in his crib and covered him nicely with Blaize's new blanket. Kevin stood over him proudly, gazing upon his son. The sight brought him peace and calm. He took it all in, took a deep breath, thanked God in his head for his fortunes and walked back to his bedroom.

Rece was sound asleep. Kevin got into bed and pulled the covers over him. The bed was cool and easy to lie in. He rolled over and kissed Rece on the forehead. He whispered to her, "I love you."

--

"Kevin! Kevin! Be quiet!!" Rece shook Kevin as he screamed wildly. Rece was whispering her imploring's. "Kevin! Kevin!" Kevin continued to scream. Rece shook him harder. "Kevin!"

Kevin awoke, looking surprised and shocked. "What is it? I fed him," Kevin stated.

"You were screaming at the top of your lungs," Rece whispered.

Kevin thought a second then realized he, too, heard the screams. He just wasn't conscious of the fact that it was him. He continued to look at Rece confusingly. "Yeah. Yeah." Kevin paused. "I guess that was me."

Rece laughed quietly. "Oh my God, that was crazy."

"I know. Holy moly."

"Was it a dream?" Rece asked.

"No. I don't think so. I just was screaming," Kevin laughed as he said it.

Rece rolled back to her side of the bed, still amused. "But, I mean, why?"."

"Well, I'm a complicated person," Kevin said laughingly.

"Um, you think?" Rece said.

"Well, I haven't ever done that before though, huh?" Kevin responded.

"Crazy." Rece said. "Maybe it's a night terror. I've read about those."

"I don't know," Kevin said. "But, it don't happen often."

Rece laughed and chuckled. "Ha! Well, if it's not a night terror, then it's a racing heart, or night-sweats, or 'Rece, I can't breathe!'"

"Ha, ha, ha." Kevin said. "Very funny, ma'am. I thought I had issues in those moments."

"You do have issues, you weirdo," Rece leaned over and hugged him. "I love you. Even though you are insane."

Kevin held her close. "I love you, too."

Rece laid down and closed her eyes.

"Hey," Kevin said. "What do you say we drive off to Pittsburgh and see your old place soon."

"Kevin, I love you," Rece said as she sat up, "but that's not necessary."

"No, come on, let's. I think it will be good."

"I don't know, I mean, that property is sold now, and we don't even know who owns it. I'd doubt we'd get in."

"It's a farm in the suburbs of Pittsburgh," Kevin said. "Shouldn't be too hard to see from the fence, at least."

Rece chuckled. "Kev, you know that property is worth millions now?"

"Yeah," Kevin said softly. "I'm sorry. I shouldn't have brought it up."

Rece leaned over and kissed him. "You were just trying to be sweet."

"I just thought going back might be good, I don't know. Silly thought, I guess."

"Not silly at all," Rece said. "It's just that, my parents, after all I've been through with them, it would just be bad memories, sweetie."

"That property should have been yours. I was hoping to…"

"Buy it?" she said, interrupting his thought.

"I don't know."

Rece kissed him again. "You're so sweet. Maybe one day we'll look into it."

They cuddled up close and held each other. They fell asleep in each other's arms.

FAMILY ICE CREAM NIGHT

August 15, 2015

Rece was still reading her book and then kissed Kevin, told him she enjoyed the ice cream stop, asked him how his head was, and went to sleep after Kevin told her the head was 'fine'. Kevin tossed and turned for hours, though, trying to ignore the awful pain in his head. Rece lay sound asleep next to him, oblivious to Kevin's movement. Eventually, the pain subsided enough for him to fall asleep.

It was 2 a.m. In his dream, Kevin was cornered in the basement of the house in which he grew up. The cold cement floor, painted maroon, felt moist. The rain outside crashed onto the two-story brick house. The TV next to the desk was on, but no noise came from it. He heard steps on the hardwood floors above.

He couldn't sit still, he thought. He had to get up to his bedroom. It was the only chance. He moved towards the stairs. He saw a shadow on the giant fish tank near the stairwell. The fish seemed unconcerned of his perceived danger.

Kevin peeked upstairs and saw nothing. Along the wall was a shelf with his parents' old records. He spotted a Beach Boys album. He raced up the stairs.

He found himself in the kitchen. The light above the brick stove shone onto to the picture window leading out towards the deck. The double door refrigerator was open, with empty Tab cans strewn across the floor. The fire was out in the fireplace, and the circular staircase was ablaze.

He grabbed a leather jacket, threw it over his head and stormed upstairs through the flames. It was the only way. He had no choice. The attic door was open. The guest bedroom was empty. His bedroom was thirty feet away. He ran past the master bedroom. The laundry chute was open. He heard footsteps behind him. He pulled a painting off the wall and threw it behind him. There was the bedroom.

The door was closed. He turned the handle, but it was locked. He had to get in! He pounded his shoulder into that door repeatedly. The footsteps got closer. Again, he pounded and pounded. The footsteps stopped. He pounded one more time and felt a hand on his shoulder. Then he heard a wicked laughter. The laughter grew louder and louder. He turned and let out a scream.

As he slept, sweat poured off his head like he was in a shower.

Kevin awoke in a flash, dripping wet, and jumped flat off the bed. His mouth was dry, and his left arm was completely asleep. He opened his eyes.

The pain in his head cut through his skull like an axe. It was constant. He held his head and heard a faint shriek inside his head. He grabbed his head harder with both hands. It was the worst his head had felt since the headache started that morning. The shrieking inside grew louder.

"Oh my God," he said out loud.

He looked at Rece. She was asleep. The pain was pulsating now. The axe was wedged in his head and somebody was wrestling the axe to loosen it to get it out of the skull.

Kevin shook his head and took the deepest breath he'd ever taken. He reached skyward, trying to touch the ceiling.

The pain settled in, as if saying it wasn't going away. It was so constant. He wanted to bash his head against the wall to release the pain. He stared at the wall across from him and contemplated that. He shook his head and refocused. He knelt on the bed and put his head onto the quilt. He couldn't take it.

"Rece."

Kevin paused and rubbed both hands over his face while staring at Rece.

"Rece."

He stared at her more. He shook her shoulder.

"Hey, honey," Rece said in her sleep

"Rece."

He shook her again.

Rece finally woke up. In a daze, she looked at Kevin. "Hey, Kevin. You ok?"

"No. I don't think so," Kevin answered quickly.

"Ok, Ok, just relax." Rece sat up a bit and put her hand on Kevin's shoulder as he bent over, his head buried in his hands as he rubbed his head hard.

"How does it feel?" she asked, now putting both hands on Kevin.

"It just really hurts, Rece. So bad. So bad," he said. "I can't even, oh my God."

"You can't what, Kevin?" Rece asked, sounding a little more concerned. "You can't what?"

Kevin hesitated. "It's just so painful, and it's like, screaming inside."

"I know, Kevin. I know. It'll be ok," Rece assured him. "What do you mean screaming?"

"I don't know," Kevin said. "It's so fucking weird. It's like with the pain something is screaming, like a laughing scream. I don't know, that just kinda started. It's like, I don't know. I hear screaming or laughing when the pain gets bad. Like, vicious, wicked screaming." The pain accelerated. Kevin looked up at the ceiling. "No. No. No. This is bad. This isn't good, Rece," Kevin said. He then sat up abruptly, moving his head slowly side to side. His forehead was still sweating. His hands were shaking.

"You need to relax before anything right now, Kevin," Rece ordered softly. She now moved cross legged face to face with him. She grabbed both of his hands. "Look at me, Kevin. Look at me."

Kevin looked at her. Her long brown hair fell perfectly over the tee shirt she had borrowed from Kevin in which to sleep. It was big on her and hung low in the front. Her panties were pink. Kevin just looked at her.

"You need to relax. Just breathe. Let's calm down then we'll fix your head, ok?" Rece spoke so calmly. She pulled Kevin closer to her. "Look, look me in the eyes. You're freaking out over the head, but it's ok. You're not dying. If you want, we'll go have it checked out, but you're gonna be ok."

"How do you know?" Kevin said right into her eyes.

"Because it always turns out ok. You build these things up, sweetie. You get a pain, and right away you're dying. We've been here before, Kev. It's ok," Rece responded.

Kevin took a deep breath. He wanted to believe her. He felt this was different.

"The pain is just so bad, hon," Kevin said.

As he said this, the pounding in his forehead got worse. The axe was still wedged in his head. He heard a loud shriek and he closed his eyes so tight. The constant, pulsating pain radiated in his head and landed each time in his forehead. The pain did not relinquish. He grabbed his head with both hands. "It's not going away!" he said, sounding very scared.

"It will. It will." Rece grabbed his head and hugged him. "It will, Kevin. It will."

Kevin buried his head in her arms. He quickly felt a very small slice of peace, but at once the pain took over. It ate the peace and engulfed Kevin. His head felt hot. It felt full. It was pain at its worst. There was no peace.

He pulled away. "I can't stand it. I just can't!!" Kevin screamed.

Rece jumped out of bed. She ran to the bathroom and was back in an instant, pulling open a small white container. She reached over and grabbed her water. "Here, Kevin, take these!"

Kevin grabbed the three pills and jammed them in his mouth and then chugged the water, spilling a lot of it down his chin and onto his shirt. He breathed deep. Rece breathed with him.

"Ok. Ok, sweetie," Rece said calmly. "Hey," she continued, "do you want to go to the hospital?"

"I don't know," he responded, breathing heavily. "I don't know what they'll do."

"They'll make you feel better," she told him.

"What do you mean?" he asked quizzically.

"Kevin, they'll tell you you're not dying." Rece looked at him intently.

"How do you know that?" Kevin snapped a bit. "I mean, this isn't just nothing."

"No, I know. But it's a headache. And they can tell you that. Jenny suffers from headaches, Kev. She's in the ER all the time. It's migraines, and the pain, she says, is unbearable. You have a headache, it's bad, go to the ER and you'll feel better. C'mon. I'll take you." Rece turned to get off the bed. Kevin looked at her.

"Wait." Kevin held his head and looked down. "Stop. We can't leave the kids."

"Blaize can watch them," Rece answered as she stood next to the bed.

"I mean, I want to go, but no. There's no reason. They won't do anything." Kevin seemed confused.

"They can tell you you're ok," Rece said. "I know you. You need to hear that."

"I don't need that right now," Kevin said, now looking at her.

"Yes! Yes, you do. It will make you feel better, Kevin," Rece responded, leaning forward as she spoke. She kissed his lips. "I know you, sweetie. You need to."

"Get in bed. I'm not going." Kevin lay back on a pillow.

"Ok," Rece said and then crawled back on the bed and placed her perfect hand on his head. Kevin's eyes were closed, and he took a deep breath.

"I'm just scared, hon," Kevin said softly. "I hate this. I don't want them to tell me..." Kevin stopped in mid-sentence.

"Tell me what 'this' is," Rece said sweetly.

"Huh?" Kevin looked in her eyes.

Rece looked back at him. "This. Your headache. Tell me what it is."

Kevin took a deep breath. The pain in his head was centered down the middle running from the inside of his brain to the bridge of his nose. The pressure at the bridge pulsated.

The pain in the center of his brain was constant.

"It's just really bad pain," Kevin said. He took his right hand and placed it on top of his head. He ran his hand down the center of his head until his fingers reached his forehead. "It goes from here to here," he said.

"Ok, Kev." Rece leaned over and kissed his forehead.

"It's so bad, hon." Kevin buried his head in her chest.

Rece held him tight. She closed her eyes and rubbed his head gently, back and forth. She was tired, as was he. They lay down. After several minutes, Rece fell asleep, holding Kevin tight. Kevin closed his eyes and squeezed them tight. He didn't want to open his eyes. He stayed awake, listening to the scream in his head. Eventually, he passed out in pain, his wife still holding him tight.

--

"Want some coffee?"

Kevin's eyes were closed, but he was awake. He squinted up at Rece. She looked so hot in the mornings. He smiled.

"Yes. Yes. Coffee," he whispered at her.

Rece placed his cup on his nightstand. She bent over and kissed his head carefully so as to not spill her coffee on him. "I love you so much," she said.

"I know."

"Look," Rece said quickly, "I think we should go to the doctor."

Kevin looked at her funny. "Why?"

"Kevin," Rece started, "I really think you are ok, but I think we'd all be better off if you went and just got looked at."

"You think?"

"I do."

"I don't know," Kevin said.

"What worries you about going?" Rece asked.

"Nothing worries me, I guess."

"Kevin, c'mon. Who knows you best?" Rece asked.

"I just worry."

"About what it might be?"

"Yeah."

Rece reached in to hug him, and he accepted. "Aw, honey. It's going to be ok. I really think it'll give you peace of mind when they tell you nothing is wrong."

"I couldn't live with it, though, if there was."

"Well, could you think about it?"

"I will."

"Perfect," Rece said.

"How is it today, by the way?" Rece asked.

"No headache today, so far," Kevin responded.

"Perfect," Rece said again. "See, like last time. It was just one day."

She then turned to walk away. He watched her. He was excited. For a brief moment, he had no memory of the previous day. He wanted her.

"Where ya goin'?" Kevin said to her with a smile.

"Oh!" Rece giggled. "Five hours ago, you were dying and now you want some, huh? It's a miracle!" Rece was laughing out loud.

Kevin couldn't hold it in and cracked up.

"Give a dying man a wish, huh, my lady?" Kevin extended his arms to his gorgeous wife.

"Anything for my headache man." Rece crawled towards Kevin. "Kids should sleep in today..."

Their lips met. They kissed passionately. Their hands were all over each other. The excitement was overwhelming to Kevin. He pulled her shirt off and Rece pressed her body tightly against his. They kissed some more, and Kevin flipped her on her back. He pulled his shirt off and she ran her hands on his chest. They stared at each other until Kevin leaned in again to kiss her. Before he could get to her, the door creaked, and little feet were heard.

"James says we're hungry, dad!" It was Vincent, their 7-year-old; and, as usual, he was screaming his sentences.

Rece quickly pulled the covers over her and she scrambled for her shirt. Kevin collapsed backwards and lay on the bed, rolling over onto his stomach. He stared at Vince.

"James says you're hungry, huh?" Kevin said.

"Yep! He says we should eat." Vince held his blanket as he spoke.

Kevin smiled and turned towards the figure under the covers. He patted the figure.

"Y'all right down there?" Kevin was smiling.

"Take your son and go make pancakes, Kevin!" Rece struggled underneath the covers.

Kevin messed with the covers a bit more, laughed, and jumped off the bed. "C'mon, Vince. Pancakes."

Vince jumped up. "Yay!!"

--

"Dad!?"

"Yes, Vince, you don't have to yell."

"Who do you think? Spider-Man or Iron Man?" Vince looked up at his dad while walking down the stairs.

"Iron Man, for sure."

"Really?! Did you know Spider-Man came before Iron Man?" Vince told dad.

"I did not know that," Kevin answered. "Watch that toy."

Vince looked down and stepped over the toy car. The two continued down the stairs.

"Ok, big guy. Hop on the couch and I'll start the pancakes, cool?" Kevin asked.

"Mm-hm. Cool dad," Vince said as he jumped on the couch. "Don't forget the chocolate chips!"

"Ha-ha! I won't, buddy." Kevin smiled.

The food pantry adjoined the hallway leading to the kitchen. The door was originally pure white. The knob was silver. Surrounding the knob were smear marks from the four kids, a mixture of chocolate, cheese, crumbs, dirt and whatever. Try as they did, Rece and Kevin had a devil of a time keeping the pantry door clean.

Kevin opened the pantry that morning and pulled out the regular white flour, the whole wheat flour, the sugar, and the non-stick spray. He placed the ingredients on the counter. As he did, he thought about the headaches. *Where the hell did it go?* He told himself upstairs, when he awoke, to just go with the fact that he wasn't feeling any pressure or pain. He would continue to follow that advice. *I hope they're fucking gone.*

In the fridge, Kevin pulled out the butter, eggs, and the milk. He un-wrapped the salted butter and threw it in a dish. He set the microwave for 44 seconds and reached up into the cupboard for his mixing bowl. He placed it on the empty countertop and pulled open the utensil drawer. Out of there he pulled his measuring cups.

"Dad!" Vincent yelled.

"What's up, bud?" Kevin responded, laughing a little at the fact that Vince always yelled.

"Is it ready!?" asked Vince.

"Ha-ha! Not quite." Kevin smiled.

"What?" asked Vince.

"Not quite," Kevin said back.

"What does that mean?" Vince wanted to know.

"It means I'll call you when it's ready," Kevin said while smiling.

Kevin continued with the pancakes. He put the proper amount of white flour and whole wheat flour in the bowl. The stick of butter was softened, and he poured it over the flour. Next, he added the two eggs. He reached for the salt that he saw on the counter and added a bit. Then he scooped out a few tablespoons of sugar and added that in, as well. He walked back to the fridge and grabbed the milk. He poured two and a half cups in and it looked as though that wouldn't be enough, so he added a bit more. This was all standard procedure for his pancakes.

His spoon was on the island in the center of the kitchen. It was a wooden island with a black marble top, which also had a mini sink in it. On the island sat a marble jar and in it stood spatulas, knives, and big spoons, some of them wooden. This morning, Kevin grabbed his big silver spoon to stir his batter.

Once the batter sat a bit, during which time Kevin drank some more coffee and enjoyed the view out the sliding glass doors into his wood deck, he was ready to make his pancakes. The sun, which was bright earlier, seemed to be hiding a bit behind done clouds now.

The first cake cooked up perfectly. It was thick, brown with bubble holes throughout, and had crispy edges. The pan was at a perfect heat, and the batter was mixed well.

He made fifteen pancakes that morning, with only one dud, which he tossed in the garbage. The cakes were laid out on two plates for all to grab. The butter and syrup were out, and juice filled six glasses. Breakfast was ready

ON CALL

On-call doctors are available 24 hours a day, 7 days per week. They usually answer to an answering service which takes emergency patient calls and filters them through to the on-call doctor. The on-call doctor then determines if a phone call to the patient is warranted and, if so, calls the patient back and delivers an opinion on a course of action for any emergency.

For patients with HMO, the on-call doctor is an important rung on the health care ladder. In order to be approved for an emergency room visit, an HMO patient must receive approval from the on-call doctor of his primary care facility. If an on-call doctor approves, the patient may go to the ER, and his or her treatment is covered by insurance, less any co-pays. Of course, there are exceptions to this health care mandate. One exception is when a patient cannot take the time to contact the on-call doctor because the emergency is so great and there is no time to make a phone call. Such examples may be a car accident, a broken leg, or a heart attack.

On this day, Dr. Frank Nourzad was on call. The phone call came in at 9:07 a.m. The answering service had taken a cell phone call from a Marty Matthew. Apparently, he had passed out driving home from church. Marty was 74 years old and had been a patient at James Hope Hospital for years. His primary care physician happened to be Dr. Nourzad and the doctors at the office adjoining Hope Hospital.

The answering service mentioned the fainting and that the patient had felt chest pressure. In addition, the patient mentioned stomach cramps of a severe nature. Dr. Nourzad made quick work of the phone call.

"Tell Marty to head to Hope, if he's close, and if someone is there to drive him. If not, get to the closest hospital in a reasonable time. Please don't tell him to hurry. Again, if there's someone else with him, have them drive. In fact, can you check that? Then tell him I will meet him there, ok?" Nourzad waited for the answer.

"Sounds good, doctor. I will relay," the answering service responded.

Dr. Nourzad had just finished his three-mile run. He had had a bowl of oatmeal and some juice. He had to shower and get to Hope. He rushed for the shower when his cell phone rang again.

"Yes, doctor, Mr. Matthew is heading to Hope. He had a friend with him..." the service operator said.

Nourzad cut her off. "I'll be right there." Nourzad grabbed a bag, rushed to his door. He stopped at the door, grabbed a picture of his wife and kids, kissed it, stared at them a second, put the picture down, and ran out the door.

--

"Yes, doctor, we will," said the head nurse of the ER at Hope. "I see. Yes. And, can I say, we have plenty of doctors working today. We'll probably be ok."

The nurse paused. She looked straight into the waiting room, noticing the large crowd sitting and waiting. She saw several people hunched in chairs, blowing their noses and sneezing. In the corner sat a child with a bloody face, his mom holding him and caressing his back. Next to him was a man holding his arm which was wrapped in a homemade bandage. The nurse listened as Nourzad spoke.

"Ok, doctor. Yes." she said. "We will."

The nurse hung up. She walked to the front and called out a name.

"Marty Matthew?!" she called loudly. There was no answer. "Mr. Matthew?!" Still no answer as she gazed upon the patients. They all looked at her in disappointment from not hearing their name.

The nurse turned to Steve, the security guard working the lobby that day. Steve was a giant of a man with muscles oozing out of his tight blue security shirt. His blue pants were baggy with deep pockets on the thighs. He had a Billy-club hanging from his belt and a mini flashlight in his front shirt pocket. Steve had a straight face on that morning.

"Hey Steve?" the nurse said. Steve looked at her. "There's an old guy on his way in. About 75 years old, gray hair goes by the name Marty Matthew."

"Ok," responded Steve.

"When you see him, or, if you do, send him right to triage, ok?" the nurse requested as she made her way back into the ER. "His doctor thinks he might just sit here waiting."

"Ok, Sheryl. No problem," Steve responded.

"He's coming in on his own. No ambulance," she said over her shoulder walking away. Steve nodded.

--

Dr. Nourzad walked in through the back door of Hope Hospital. He swiped his I.D. Card and the door opened. Immediately, he saw a nurse wheeling a cart down the hall. The nurse was a redhead who was new to Hope Hospital. She was right out of nursing school and had landed this job as her first out of school. Nourzad had met her a week ago when he made his rounds. He had forgotten her name. The nurse looked up and saw Nourzad.

"Dr. Nourzad! Good to see you again!" she said with much enthusiasm and a genuine smile. "What are you doing here?"

Nourzad approached her quickly but slowed down a bit to answer her.

"Just seeing a quick patient," he said, smiling at her and then throwing her a wink.

"Lucky patient," she said back, smiling and winking back, but still moving her cart. "Have a good one."

"Yes," Nourzad responded while turning back to see her. As he did, he caught her looking back at him.

Nourzad composed himself and then moved quickly down the hall. He met resistance again at the E.R. door. He again swiped his badge and the door opened. It led into the back of the E.R. The white noise was apparent immediately, a soft hum throughout. As he turned, he saw Dr. Lufar wheeling a trauma patient into room seven. "Nourzad," said Lufar without even looking up.

"Need help?" Nourzad offered.

"All good, buddy," said Lufar, as three nurses rushed in behind him.

Across the hall he saw the nurse table. He rushed forward and asked about Mr. Matthew.

"Just came in, doc," said Sheryl. "He's in triage. Seems in deep distress, from what I hear."

"What room is open?" asked Nourzad.

"Um," Sheryl glanced at her intake sheet, "three and four, actually."

"I'll take four," Nourzad declared. "Can you see he gets there?"

"Sure thing, doc, but I think Walsh has him," Sheryl said.

"I thought he was in triage?" Nourzad asked.

"Well, he was, but there he goes with Walsh." Sheryl then pointed.

Nourzad groaned. "Thank you, Sheryl," he said walking away quickly.

--

Marty Matthew presented as a very pale, male white, complaining of severe stomach pains and shortness of breath. According to the triage notes, his pulse was 97 and his blood pressure was 137/92. His pulse-ox was 93%. He explained he was driving his car and passed out. He was assigned room three for Dr. Walsh, but a nurse came in and told Dr. Walsh the circumstances. Mr. Matthew was then placed in room four. Dr. Walsh was present with him. He was listening to his heart rate, when Nourzad entered.

"Marty, are you ok?" Nourzad entered room number four briskly. He did not acknowledge Dr. Walsh's presence.

"Hey, doc," Mr. Matthew said in a scruffy voice, looking up and making eye contact for the first time since he had entered the hospital. He was sitting on the examination table. He smiled.

"You got this one, Frank?" Dr. Walsh said as he carefully listened to the patient's heart. Walsh was a heavy-set doctor, looking every bit of fifty years old, or more.

"Yeah, I got him. He's a patient of mine," Nourzad explained.

"You were on-call, I take it?" Walsh asked.

Nourzad looked at Walsh. The question seemed irrelevant to Nourzad. He knew this might be an issue.

"Yeah, I was. Marty gets nervous without me, I think. It was no big deal. Had nothing else going on," Nourzad said softly.

"Except still being on call. Unusual for the on-call guy to

come in, Frank," Dr. Walsh responded quietly.

With that, Dr. Walsh patted Nourzad on the back and walked out. "Talk to me when you're done, ok, Frank?"

"Sure," Nourzad said now walking towards Mr. Matthew and grabbing the chart. He stared at the chart and looked at Marty.

"Looks ok on paper, Marty," Nourzad said. "Numbers are a tad high, but your pulse-ox is good. What happened?" As he asked, Nourzad looked into Marty's eyes with his ophthalmoscope.

"I don't know, doc. Just really passed out. I thought I was a goner. Didn't feel right at all. Real weak, heart raced, and boom, I passed out."

"You take your meds today?" Nourzad asked.

Marty answered directly. "Yes."

"Keeping up with them since our visit?" Nourzad inquired.

Marty responded in the affirmative again.

"Nurse, let's do a blood draw. Troponin."

"Ok," the nurse said going into a drawer.

"Marty," Nourzad spoke, "I'm going to check if you had any heart trouble. I don't think so, but just checking to be sure. Once that comes back, we'll go from there."

"Whad'ya think it is?" Mr. Matthew asked.

"I think you fainted. Low sugar, tired, too much coffee, nothing big," said Nourzad.

Mr. Matthew nodded. "I chugged coffee this morning. Not a good thing, huh?"

Nourzad smiled, sensing his diagnosis was accurate. "Not for you, Marty, especially if you didn't eat, and really especially if you took your meds without eating." He looked into Marty's eyes and asked, "Feeling better?"

"Yeah," Marty said quietly. "Ya know what, I really like that you were here, doc. Helps, ya know?"

"I know," Nourzad said patting Marty's shoulder. "Look, we'll get those results soon and I'll come back and talk to you. Sound good?"

"Yes. Sounds good. Thanks." Marty extended his hand to the good doctor.

--

"Come on in, Frank," Dr. Walsh said while seated at his desk in his makeshift E.R. office. It was a metal table and a folding chair. On the wall was a calendar. The desk had a phone and a legal pad. Two pens sat next to the pad. A copy of a medical journal sat on the edge of the table. Behind the table was a file cabinet. Nourzad noticed files sticking out of the drawers but wasn't sure whose files they were.

"It's not much, Frank," Dr. Walsh said to Nourzad as Nourzad perused the office. "But I like it. It calms me. My office upstairs doesn't relax me. This one does."

"I see," Nourzad said sounding very uninterested. "You wanted to see me?" He looked at Walsh quizzically.

"Look, Frank. Wait. Is the patient ok?" He looked at Nourzad.

"I think so," Nourzad answered.

"I thought so, too," Walsh responded, his eyebrows raised, looking at Nourzad.

There was an awkward pause, as Nourzad realized Dr. Walsh was going to lecture him. Nourzad sat and then shifted in his seat. He wanted to walk out but showed his respect by staying.

"I'm not your boss, Frank, ok, so, you really don't have to listen to me, I guess." Walsh paused. "But this is my E.R." Walsh paused again, staring at Nourzad, assuming Frank knew the point.

Nourzad said nothing.

Walsh continued. "In my E.R., there are protocols. One of which is when a patient comes in, he or she is assigned a doctor and that doctor has the patient up until admittance or discharge. Today, I was assigned..." Dr. Walsh paused and looked at a piece of paper in his hand, "...a Mr. Marty Matthew."

Nourzad said nothing.

"You disturbed my protocol, doctor," Walsh said straight to Nourzad.

Nourzad spoke. "I understand."

Walsh smiled. "Now, I get he's your patient. I get you want to help. But what you should have done, what other doctors do, is check in, see who is seeing the patient, and consult after initial screening."

Nourzad spoke again, after another awkward pause. "Ok."

"Ok?" Walsh repeated Nourzad's answer. "And that can be done over the phone."

Nourzad nodded.

"Now, I know this isn't the first time, either. You follow your patients here a lot. Why?" Walsh asked.

"I'm their doctor," Nourzad responded plainly.

"You're their primary physician, Frank," Walsh lectured. "When they come here, when you send them here, they become our patients. You have to let us do our job. You're affiliated here, right? But you're not an E.R. doctor. Consult afterwards if you have to be here. But don't do it again, what you did today."

Nourzad said nothing.

"Now, I see you ordered a blood test. Fine. But I'm going back in to see my patient and determine what should be done. Care to consult?" Walsh waited for an answer.

Nourzad was baffled. He sat staring at Walsh. *Who does this guy think he is?* Again, though, he chose to respect Walsh's authority. He took a deep breath and spoke. "He gets like this. Thinks he's dying. He likes to exaggerate his symptoms. I see it a lot. Wanted to reassure him. He's comfortable around me. I relax him. Was trying to head off useless tests, which would have sent him spiraling. He's fine."

Walsh looked at him for 10 seconds. "Yes, well, thank you for your input, doctor. I'm sure he'll be fine."

Nourzad turned to leave and paused. He was upset. Walsh showed him up for some reason. He felt he did absolutely nothing wrong. He knew his patient and how to handle him.

His instinct told him to leave, to walk away. It was Walsh's E.R. He could dictate. It wasn't easy for him, but he decided to let it go. Nourzad stood up. As he walked away, Walsh spoke.

"They all don't need a shrink, Frank. Remember that," Walsh said.

Nourzad turned. "What does that mean?" he said with a tinge of anger in his voice.

"It means you're a practicing MD. We treat ailments. We treat injuries. We treat trauma. They're not here because they need a psychiatrist!" Walsh's voice raised. "Now, I've watched you in here, I've heard from other doctors. Nurses, too. You spend hours and hours looking into their heads. That's not why we're here! If they need a shrink, we send them upstairs or refer 'em out. But that's rare! You're here too often, Frank. We know what we're doing. We don't need you here for every one of your patients because you think we can't handle their emotions."

"You are mixing your criticisms, sir," Nourzad said, staring at the imposing figure that was Dr. Walsh.

The two doctors stared at each other. Nourzad's lips pressed tightly together. His eyes squinted at the massively looking doctor across from him. Nourzad prepared to speak. He so desired to defend his ways. He was ready.

"Dr. Walsh! Trauma coming in! GSW to the head! 4 minutes out!" The nurse was frantic as she rushed in.

Walsh walked right past Nourzad. "Is he stable?"

"She! She! Not stable!" the nurse screamed.

The door closed behind the rushing Walsh and the nurse. Nourzad stood alone in the makeshift office. He took a very deep breath and walked out.

IT'S BACK

AUGUST 16, 2015

"That breakfast was amazing, Kev," Rece said as the two of them sat back in their chairs digesting. Sticky plates lined the table. Two bottles of syrup remained open. Spilled orange juice lay across the table in little puddles. All the plates were empty of any remaining pancakes.

Kevin smiled. "Oh my God, it was, right?"

"Very good," Rece said standing up to kiss him on the forehead.

"Ahhh." Kevin put his hands on his head. He looked outside and looked upon the overcast day. He turned back towards Rece. He took a deep breath.

"You seem good," Rece said.

"You jinx!" Kevin laughed. "No, just messin'. Yeah, I'm pretty good."

Rece laughed with him. She walked towards the table and grabbed a few plates. "I'm glad you feel better."

"Thanks. I was a little concerned there."

"Just a headache. Like last time, just a day," Rece said with a big smile. "Plus, I think the Motrin helped."

Kevin chuckled. "Is that what you gave me? I didn't even ask. Anyway, you were right. Again. But still, that was some serious pain. I really thought it was something. So weird."

"Well, it was, but headaches can be bad. Like I said, look at Jenny. Her headaches are so bad. She can't move sometimes."

"Yeah, I guess. Just never imagined they could be that bad."

Rece rubbed his shoulders from behind. "Just glad you're ok." She kissed the top of his head.

"Why don't you go up and shower," Rece said. "I'll take care of the dishes. Then I'll shower after you."

"Nice," Kevin responded. "Thank you."

"Love you, sweetie."

"You too."

--

The shower had a glass sliding door. Inside was a bench. The entire stall was brick lined, with a dark tan color. On the wall was the faucet. Next to the faucet were two switches. One switch activated the steam, one turned it off. Kevin dropped his towel and turned the faucet to start the shower. As he leaned back out of the stall, he switched the steam to 'on'. He looked into the mirror at his face. He hadn't shaved in a few days, and his beard was scruffy. He popped open the bottle of mouthwash and gargled a bit. It felt refreshing.

The steam began to escape the shower stall. It was ready. Kevin stepped in. He wet himself from the shower, putting his head under the stream and running his hands from front to back on his head. He let the water run down his body a bit, then turned and sat on the bench and let the steam run through his pores. He was as relaxed as he could be. He could have fallen asleep.

After a good five minutes, he stood up and did a complete shower, including a shave. He let the water run over his body a little longer, then turned off the steam. He turned the water off and opened the sliding door to reach for his towel. He stepped out and began drying off. After drying off, brushing his teeth and putting on deodorant, he walked out of the bathroom and into the bedroom.

He felt it then.

Oh, fuck.

The initial sensation in his head wasn't a pain as much as it was a feeling. It was a feeling of a slow rush into his head, like a thick sludge being poured into a bowl. It started as a gentle flow, but very quickly turned into a violent rush. His head went from perfect to tremendously full tremendously fast.

Fuck, fuck, fuck.

It knocked him onto his bed. He grabbed his head with both hands, his towel coming off in the process. He sat on the bed pushing his palms into his forehead as hard as he possibly could. He felt exhausted and anxious all at once. His blood flushed from his head into his chest. He was nauseous. He wanted to puke. His mind raced full speed. He wanted to scream.

He lay back onto the bed. The fullness now turned into pain. The pressure was pulsating outward, causing the center of his head to feel extreme pain. It was the feeling of the axe again.

"Fuck," he said out loud, but didn't scream it out. "What the fuck?!" he asked himself a little louder.

Kevin could not control all the physical and mental feelings he was having at that very moment. His body and mind were on overload. There was tingling in his fingertips and his brow wore sweat. Worst case scenarios sprung in his head. He tried to fight back at these feelings.

Fuck it. He stood up. He walked to his closet. *Fuck this.*

He grabbed his shorts and tee shirt, a pair of short socks and underwear. He threw them on his bed with disdain in his heart and looked for his shoes. He moved back to the bed to get dressed. He stopped at the edge of his bed and stood. He eyeballed his clothes for what felt like ten minutes. He stared at those clothes intently.

He finally dressed himself and then he just collapsed himself right back onto the bed. He laid his face flush with the quilt made on the bed and he placed both his hands on the back of his head. The feeling of pressure had now turned to pain and it was unrelenting. It pushed back at him in his attempt to ignore it. *It's fucking taunting me.* Kevin drove his hands into the back of his head to relieve the pain and pressure. It did not work.

He sat up. The pressure rested in his forehead, with most of it placing itself between his eyes at the base of his nose. He took his fingertips and rubbed the area hard. He took a deep breath. In his head, he heard a faint shrieking laugh. He opened his eyes and Kate was standing in front of him. As soon as he saw Kate, the laughter stopped.

"What's with you, dad?" Kate asked with a kid's quizzical look on her face.

Kevin faked a smile. "Oh, nothing, honey. Just tryin' to wake up a bit."

"Hm. Ok, dad. You look terrible. Maybe it was your pancakes." Kate smiled.

Kevin faked a laugh. "Maybe, funny girl, maybe."

"I'm going downstairs. Love you, daddy."

"Love you, too, sweetheart. Hey. Come here and hug your dad."

"Dad!"

"C'mon"

"Uhhhh, Ok."

Kevin hugged Kate tight. He held his head close to hers. It was a clean moment of peace for him.

--

"Kate says you're not yourself?" Rece said a few minutes later as she walked into the bathroom as Kevin finished fixing his hair.

Kevin rolled his eyes and breathed out. He then closed his eyes and turned his head slightly. He didn't answer. He continued combing his hair and looking into the mirror.

"What's wrong?" she asked him, placing her hand on his back. He felt a smooth rush go through his body.

"I don't know." He turned towards her, forcing her to release her hand from his body.

"Headache back?"

They stared at each other. He looked deep into her eyes.

"Fuck," he whispered. "How'd you know?"

"Your eyes. Looks like you're holding back pain."

"I'm so sorry, Rece, I didn't even want you to know, but it really hurts."

"Ok. It's not a problem. I'm your wife. Don't hide things. That's not healthy for us. I can always help, now go to the bed and sit down."

Kevin walked to the bed and sat down. He took a deep breath. Rece followed with a bottle in her hand.

"Take your shirt off and lay on your stomach," she ordered. "I'm going to fix you."

She walked to the bedroom door, closed it and locked

it.

The massage was deep and strong. Rece was a master. She took her time, finding the pressure points and manipulating the knots.

"You have some serious knots, honey," Rece noted to Kevin. "Wow. No wonder you have headaches."

Kevin responded immediately. "You think?"

"Yes! Do you know how bad this is for you? These knots affect your nerves and muscles. It's all related, hon, and it all leads to your head."

"Fuck. I hope you're right, Rece. This sucks."

"I am right." Rece burrowed her elbow into his back. She jumped off the bed and ran into the bathroom. She came out with a jar in her hand. After hopping back on the bed, he heard her twist open the jar. A few seconds later he felt her awesome caress, complemented by the soothing oil, which smelled of lavender.

"Oh God, that feels good," Kevin moaned.

"Yep. I know what I'm doing."

"Wow."

"Gonna cure this headache till it don't know who it messed with, right?!"

"Get it, hon." Kevin then moaned again.

He was really impressed with Rece's effort. She was more than into it, manipulating his back perfectly in every spot. He knew she more than wanted to fix this. He more than wanted her to. But as she worked, he felt no relief. At times the distraction of her touch, and the smell of lavender, distracted him from the pain, but in the end, the headache was still there. The axe in the skull was still present. The pressure seemed worse. He didn't have the heart to tell her. He wanted this to work so badly.

She pressed hard and deep into his back, kneading her palms into his muscles. She pressed as she rubbed upwards to his shoulders and neck. The pain released for moments as he breathed deeply and took in her touch. The pain came back as she released each time.

The smells and touch made him feel good, but in the end the pain was winning out, pushing back so relentlessly, and attacking the massage back. He put his face into the bed. Rece did a final once over on his back. She leaned in and kissed him on the neck and whispered in his ear.

"Bet that headache is gone now, huh?" She kissed him again.

"Thank you, honey. Thank you so much," he whispered back without answering her question.

Rece rolled off him and off the bed. "Love you, sweetie. I'll be right back."

"Love you, too," Kevin said.

Kevin lay on the bed and his head throttled with pain. His eyesight seemed blurry, but he wasn't sure if it was, or just a result of the pain. The massage was nice, and it relieved some anxiety, but the pain remained. He was at a loss. This wasn't going away.

Rece walked back, looked at him and paused. "It's still there isn't it?" she asked.

Kevin sighed and breathed in deeply. "Oh, Rece, yes."

"Oh, Kevin, I've tried everything I know to help you. I can't think of anything else. Look, last night and this morning you said you'd consider going to the doctor."

"Yeah."

"And?"

"To be honest, like I said," Kevin said, "I just don't know."

Rece looked at him lovingly. "It's your choice, honey. But I want you to and I really think it's the best idea. We need to know it's all ok."

"Are you worried, now?" Kevin asked.

"No, no, no, not at all. I just worry about you. I know when things weigh on you, they really affect you. I just want you to be ok, hon."

"I'll think about it," Kevin said.

Rece walked up to him and hugged him. "I love you.

WHITE ROOM

September 13, 2015

The church hall was very white. The floor tiles were white, yet somehow not dirty from years of footsteps. The walls were bright white with no pictures on the wall except a small portrait of Jesus on the wall in the back. The ceiling, too, was white. Kevin sat slumped over in his chair, dressed in a leather jacket and black knit cap. The meeting was set to begin after the 10 a.m. mass. It was 11:15, and Kevin sat alone. They had skipped mass that morning. Kevin's headache was too painful. He couldn't sit through it, he told Rece. She was busy. They would make it up for it next week, they promised each other.

Kevin sat with his thoughts. His forehead was pounding. His head was full. There had been no relief since the headaches began a few months ago. Rece had tried to convince him to go see a doctor, but Kevin refused. As he sat in the church basement, he thought on it again. *I just can't.*

Somehow, though, he felt at ease, a bit, being in the Church. He said a silent prayer for himself. He then felt bad about that. He wasn't one to ever pray for himself. His prayers always asked for others. He felt it was selfish to pray for himself when he has such a big family. He remembered, as he sat there, a priest once tell his grammar school class to never pray for yourself. But today, he felt out of hope for these headaches. He prayed for relief. He prayed that it wouldn't be fatal. His family needed him. He sat in silence afterwards. He dealt with the pain.

"Hi, Kevin."

Kevin looked up. It was Celia Jones. She handed him paperwork. Kevin glanced quickly at it. It was a budget.

"Thanks, Celia," Kevin finally responded.

"Looks like we'll need a few minutes. I know Davis is going to be late, and I think Joan may or may not be here. The rest should." Celia set up at the head table.

Two more men and three women walked in from the hallway. The men sat down opposite Kevin and the women walked up and spoke to Celia. Kevin remained seated with his head low, pretending to read the budget. From nowhere, three other men were sitting down, again, opposite Kevin, and four more ladies were lingering by Celia. He didn't know if he missed their entrance or had dozed off. It didn't matter to him. He saw the numbers and knew the meeting would start soon. He sat up straight and took a deep breath. The pain in his head grew intolerable.

He turned to his left and saw a woman walking towards him. She had gorgeous brown hair but wore a baseball hat over it. The tuck job was coming undone. Her skirt was black and hung just above her knees. On her legs, she wore black tights. He couldn't help but notice her legs and looked up and saw her powder blue sweater. She was making her way right to the open seat next to him.

"Hi," she whispered.

"Hello." She smelled amazing.

"Am I late?" she whispered again.

"Um, no. It hasn't started yet."

"Great, thanks," she said, a bit louder. She extended her hand to Kevin. "My name is Georgia."

Kevin paused. He shook her hand, looked her in the eyes and said, "Georgia, huh?"

"Yes."

"Nice name," Kevin said looking down, knowing that response was ridiculous.

She laughed, now turning forward.

Kevin thought it strange that this woman was there. He's never seen her before. He also thought it was strange that she chose to sit next to him. He was prepared to ask her why she was there.

"Ok, ok, let's start," Celia stated from her table, blocking Kevin's ability to ask Georgia questions. "I know we have to keep it quick today," Celia continued. "The Parish needs the hall by 11:45."

The meeting went on and by the time it was over, Georgia was gone. Although he had peeked at her a few times throughout, she had somehow disappeared before he could notice. When most of the others had already left, Kevin got up and walked out of the hall.

--

"How'd it go, honey?"

It was Rece, dressed to the nines, looking as pretty as ever. Kevin walked right past her to the couch. His head was pounding, and he felt as if he was going to faint. On the couch were James and Vincent. They were playing a video game. The noise was outrageous.

"Want us to turn it down, dad?" said James, his eyes never wavering from the T.V.

"Nah. Just give dad a hug, guys."

"Turn it down," Rece chimed in.

The two boys immediately dropped their controllers and jumped on Kevin and bombarded him with hugs. He squeezed them both tightly against his head and held them there. For a brief moment, he was at peace.

"No good, hon?" Rece walked up and sat down.

Kevin took a deep breath and told the boys he loved them. They went back to their game, turning down the volume.

"It didn't go well," Kevin said quietly, rubbing his face with his hands.

"No?" Rece moved towards him.

"No. They weren't going to change their minds and they wouldn't let me speak. Complete bullshit."

"Dad!! No swearing!" Vincent screamed.

Kevin continued, ignoring Vince, "They weren't going to listen."

"Sorry, guys," Kevin said to the boys then turned back to Rece, his eyes squinting as the pressure mounted in his head.

"There was a bit of a screaming match, and then it just ended."

Rece raised her eyebrows and smiled. "Did you start a fight in a church?"

"Church hall, technically." Kevin smiled a bit.

"Kevin." Rece smiled.

"I know, I know, they're just bad to do that and it pisses me off." Kevin stopped himself. "Ah, forget it."

"I'm proud of you, honey. It was a good battle. I love you.' Rece leaned over and kissed his head. "Oh! This was in the mailbox for you. I saw some woman drop it off a few minutes before you got home."

Kevin sat up. "Black skirt with black tights?"

"Yes. Pretty woman," Rece said, looking at Kevin.

Kevin sat up straight. "She was at the meeting. Do you know

her?"

"No."

"Oh my God," Kevin said with interest. "She like appeared out of nowhere, asked me if I was going to speak. Had no clue who she was. And to be honest, my head felt so bad at that point I really thought I was seeing things."

"Wait, your headaches are back?" Rece asked.

"Yeah, I mean, they really just haven't gone away, hon."

"Kevin..." Rece was disappointed.

Kevin interrupted, "No, but this woman. She wanted me to speak. It was so weird."

"Well," Rece handed him a note, "she thanks you."

Kevin read the note. It said, 'Thanks for trying, Kevin.'

RESEARCH

OCTOBER 5, 2015

"Fun Sunday, Kevin."

"It really was, Rece. I really enjoy the zoo."

"So fun, and the kids had a ball."

"They really did."

"And we made it to Mass, which was good," Rece said.

"Yeah, especially 'cuz we missed a couple weeks ago," Kevin replied.

"And the game was fun tonight, too, even though they lost," Rece said with a sad face.

"Yeah," Kevin responded, putting his head into his hands.

There was a pause.

"Oh, hon, still?"

"Yeah, Rece, it fucking won't go away, I mean, it's been what, months? And, as much as sometimes it dulls, it never goes away."

"I saw it in your eyes all day," Rece said, moving towards Kevin. She hugged him as he sat on the bed.

"It won't go away," Kevin said.

"It's only been about a couple months, though. It will."

"It's been longer," Kevin countered.

"What?" Rece sounded very surprised.

"I just never told you."

"Told me what?"

Kevin looked at her. "Look, I think I've been having little headaches, you know, on and off. No big deal kind of stuff. I didn't think much of it because they'd always go away."

"Wait," Rece stated. "You think you had them?"

"I think, yes. It's hard to say. But I've been thinking. I guess I didn't really think about them, I don't know. But I think I did." Kevin closed his eyes as he spoke.

"Well, were they bad?" Rece asked.

"Not like this. They were annoying, but they'd always go right away. So, I never told you."

"For how long?" Rece asked.

"I don't know. Six months?" Kevin answered. "On and off. But they were never like this. Ever!"

"I think that's actually good." Rece's eyes lit up.

Kevin looked at her funny.

Rece explained. "I know, I know, sounds weird; but if it was serious, well, I don't know. It just sounds like migraines probably."

Kevin just breathed out.

Rece continued. "You need to take medicine. The Motrin will work. "

"It hasn't, yet."

"You haven't tried it long enough," Rece said. "You're letting the headaches get ahead of you. You must keep ahead of them. Once that pain hits full stride, you're too late. Hit the pain early, then it won't peak. I asked Jenny that a while back. Let me get you some, then I'm going to tuck in Kate, you lie down and just rest."

Within minutes, Rece had fed him two ibuprofen tablets. She sat on the bed and looked at him. "Ready for the doctor?" she asked.

"I don't know," Kevin responded.

"Kevin."

"I know, I know. If they don't go away soon…"

"Kevin," Rece said, interrupting him.

"I know, I know."

"It's just time to do that, ok?" Rece said. "You've been avoiding it too long."

"I'll think about it."

"You don't have to worry, Kevin. Whatever it is, I'm here for you."

"Whatever it is?" Kevin asked. "You think…" Kevin cut himself off.

"I still think it's just a headache, but…" Rece cut herself off.

Kevin sighed and breathed. He looked at her. "Ok."

"Ok, sweetie, I'm gonna go tuck 'em all in."

He chugged some water and laid down with his laptop computer. He knew Rece would be a bit with her tuck -ins, so he thought he could relax and kill time on the laptop computer.

He went to check the scores. Then his head swooshed with pain. It went right to left and felt like pressure surrounding his head and pushing inward. He took his hands off the laptop and rubbed his head. He was distraught. He just wanted to know what the hell this was. He listened for laughter. There was none. *I don't need a doctor to know.*

He wanted an answer, so he went to Google.

'Headaches'

He punched it in and searched. In .21 seconds, 15,900,000 results popped up. He went to the first result that caught his eye:

'Headaches, symptoms, signs, causes.'

Headaches: one of the most common ailments in the world[i]. Understanding their causes is important, as most headaches aren't the result of a serious illness, some may result from a life-threatening condition requiring emergency care.[ii]

Kevin's heart raced. He glanced quickly down the web page. He saw words like brain tumor, aneurysm, clot, and stroke. He panicked immediately. He felt sweat building on his forehead. He took a deep breath. *I fucking waited too long. Fuck.* He clicked on the symptoms of a brain tumor:

'New onset or change in pattern of headaches'

It was the very first symptom of a brain tumor, according to this site. He told himself that his certainly were newly onset headaches.

"Fuck," he said under his breath. He kept reading.

The second symptom read:

'Headaches that become more frequent or severe'.

Oh my God.

'Unexplained nausea'

Kevin paused and thought. He remembered being nauseous yesterday during one of the worst parts of his day in relation to the headaches. He slammed his laptop closed. His head felt so full. The pressure pounded out at the sides, near the temples.

He re-opened the laptop. The search results reappeared.

'Vision problems'

His vision was fine. He never had a problem with his eyes.

'Difficulty in balance', 'trouble with speech', and 'confusion'[iii]

Kevin couldn't think of himself having any of these problems. But he remembered not noticing the coming and goings of people at the meeting yesterday. Plus, the first three symptoms had him very worried. He was starting to sweat even more. His heart raced on.

He clicked on the next web page. The first tab read, **'When to seek medical care for a headache'.** The first sentence read, **'When you're having the worst headache of your life'.**

To Kevin, this was absolutely the worst headache of his life. He remembered telling Rece earlier how he'd had headaches previously and that these were so much worse. And they were. The pain was debilitating to him. It had to be bad.

He read on regarding when to seek medical attention:

Different than usual headaches.[iv]

Kevin breathed deep and ran one hand over his face. The glare of the laptop shown on his face in the otherwise dark room. The T.V. on the wall had no sound. He couldn't hear any kids or Rece. His dog, Lou, slept elsewhere that night. He threw the laptop to the side and jumped out of bed. He bent over to touch his toes. He breathed deeply. His headache was still there. Kevin felt it was taunting him as he tried desperately to shake it off, but still didn't hear the laughter. The painkiller wasn't working. He felt dried out. His eyes watered, and pain shot down his neck. He sat down on his bed, grabbed the remote and lay down. He stared at the T.V.; his thoughts remained on the pressure and the pain.

He grabbed the laptop again and scrolled down the list of headache sites. He saw words such as: **migraine, cluster, serious, normal, common, and emergency**. He finally saw a friendly phrase. He clicked on the site.

'Most headaches are a common annoyance and not a serious health concern.'[v]

He slammed the computer closed. He breathed deeply, almost in relief. Rece walked in.

"Kate is good and tired, the boys are asleep, and Blaize is allegedly doing his reading," Rece said.

"Ha, ha," replied Kevin. His eyes stared at the T.V.

Rece adjusted in the bed. She flipped her pillows and pulled up the blanket. She snuggled close to Kevin and put her arm over his chest. She kissed him on the cheek. Kevin never moved. It was quiet.

"What if it's a brain tumor?" Kevin asked out of nowhere.

Rece didn't move. "What?"

"The headaches. What if it's a brain tumor?"

"Kevin. It's not, ok? If it was a brain tumor you wouldn't be walking around, going to basketball games, making pancakes, playing with the kids. Come on, sweetie. You're good. You got bad headaches."

"But what if?" Kevin asked. He put his palms over his face and rubbed.

"Sweetie come on. Get with me here. It's been two months or so. You still have pain, yes, but you have no other symptoms." Rece leaned up on her elbow and looked at Kevin.

"I get nauseous," Kevin whispered. "I've never had bad headaches before…"

"You just told me you'd had these before!"

"Yeah, but not this bad."

Rece looked into his eyes. "Oh my God, honey, it's really not a brain tumor, please. People with migraines have constant pain sometimes. It doesn't go away. Migraines cause you to puke. It's brutal. But it's not a tumor." Rece was starting to sound frustrated. "How is it now?"

"Bad. The same. It just isn't getting better."

Rece sat up now and put her hand on his forehead. "Where's the pain?"

"Right here." Kevin pointed at the very top of his forehead and moved his finger up and back about three inches from his forehead to the middle of his scalp. "It just pounds and pounds. It's blinding sometimes."

"The medicine isn't working?" Rece asked.

"No."

Rece crawled out of bed and went to the bathroom. Kevin stared at the ceiling; he was sure this pain would get worse.

Rece came out of the bathroom with two more pills in her hand.

"What's that?" Kevin asked.

"Tylenol. Acetaminophen. Take it."

"Really? I just took..."

Rece insisted. "Motrin is ibuprofen. This is different. You can mix. Won't hurt you so long as you wait a bit in between."

Kevin looked at her. He extended his hand and took the pills. Rece reached for her water and handed it to Kevin. He took the pills. As he swallowed, he paused. In the deepest recess of his mind, he heard faint laughter.

"Ok, now we're gonna lay down, relax, and get some sleep. You need to relax. Let this stuff work. You need sleep."

"Thanks, honey."

"You're welcome. I want you better."

"I want to be better."

"And we are going to the doctor." Rece said.

Brain tumor. No fucking thank you. "Let's see how this medicine works and then we'll see."

Rece looked at him for a long time. Kevin looked at her and then looked around the room. When he came back to her, she was still staring.

"Ok, sweetie," Rece said.

They hugged. Rece laid on Kevin as she snuggled into him. Together they laid there. Neither one fell asleep right away.

RAE

Doctor Nourzad's spacious living room had hard wood floors. The floors were spotless and had a perfect shine to them. The walls were light blue with fine white trim. Light yellow lamps lit the room. There was a giant perfect black flat screen T.V. on the wall, and a beautiful fish tank to its left. The living room opened into the kitchen which had an island in the middle, a double door all white refrigerator and a stainless-steel stove. The kitchen fan hung above the table, and a smaller flat screen T.V. carried the morning news of the day. Before the kitchen was a winding stairway to the second floor. Pictures of kids adorned the brown wall up. Each photo was in black and white. On the back end of the kitchen was a picture window, streak free, which looked out onto a lush green backyard. An all wood play set was set off in the back, and bikes and big wheels were lined up perfectly against the garage.

Nourzad stood at the window, dressed in khakis and a white collared shirt, perfectly pressed without a wrinkle, drinking coffee and looking out. He had already finished his run for the day and showered. He took a break before work. He envisioned his kids, running and playing. He pictured his wife pulling into the driveway, carrying her purse, waving to him and smiling. He missed his family. He looked down into the emptiness of his coffee cup. There was a knock on the door.

"Aunty Rae." Frank smiled as he pulled the door open completely. "How are you?"

Aunty Rae walked in, all six feet of her, and put her arms out and hugged Frank long and hard. "Oh, Franky."

"It's ok. I'm ok," Nourzad said reassuringly. "You don't have to say that every time we see each other."

Rae pulled back from the hug and they stared at each other, holding each other's arms. His aunt had deep black hair, and a picturesque face. Barely any makeup adorned her face, but she looked as if she had made it up. Her black leather jacket reached her waist, and she had on a white tank top underneath. Her blue jeans were tight to her legs and black boots were pulled over the bottom of her jeans.

"Thank you for stopping by," Frank told her so sincerely.

"It's not good for you to be here all alone all the time. You need people." Rae looked deep into his eyes.

"I have work. I have my colleagues. My neighbors stop by."

"Neighbors stop by? Uh-huh." Rae stopped as she walked towards the kitchen and turned. "You need family."

Rae and Frank sat and drank coffee and chatted. They shared some cake and smiled and laughed. They spoke about Uncle Charlie, and re-lived Frank's younger years. The conversation flowed, and it made Frank feel good. After thirty minutes, the conversation paused.

"What are you going to do today?" Rae asked suddenly.

Frank took his time. He whispered, "It's just a regular day, Rae. I'm going to work." He stared at his Aunt.

"It's not a regular day, Franky."

"It has to be. It has to be," Nourzad said, now looking back into his coffee cup.

"You need to discuss it," she said somewhat sternly.

"Why, Aunty Rae? Why?"

"Because it's the only way to move on."

Frank lowered his head. His right hand moved to his forehead. He rubbed it vigorously. He didn't look up. "I want to move on, Auntie, I do. This is my way."

"Your way isn't working. Discuss it with me, Franky, I'm here for you. Please."

"Auntie it's too hard. And how do you know that it's not working? It's working for me," Frank said still not looking at her.

"No, it's not, Frank. You are an amazingly strong man. You can do this, and you need to." Rae spoke sternly again.

"What do you want?" Frank asked quietly.

"I want to know what she'd be doing today."

Frank rubbed his eyes with his fingers and sighed deeply. "I don't know."

"Yes, you do." Rae reached over to Frank. "Tell me."

"This isn't therapeutic, Rae!" Frank yelled.

"Yes, it is!" Rae yelled back. "It's been months and you haven't said a word about them! They were your family, your life! You need to discuss them so you can move forward. You won't go to therapy; you won't see anybody at the hospital, and you don't discuss it with us."

"I'm dealing with it the way I know best," Frank said into his hands.

"Look at me Frank." Rae grabbed his hands tight. They looked at each other eye to eye. "Tell me."

"I know therapy, Rae. I went to medical school. I know all about the brain and how it works and how to deal with psychosis and emotional distress. I know it all, so when I tell you I'm dealing with it, I'm dealing with it. Now I mean no disrespect, but this is how I'm moving on."

Rae just stared at him for what felt like five minutes, still holding his hand.

Frank looked at her, took a deeper breath, looked down, sighed out loud and spoke. "She liked to walk in the morning. She did it for me. I didn't get much time with the kids and she thought it was important for me to bond with them during the mornings. So, she walked while I made breakfast and played with the kids."

Rae let go and sat back. "She was always so thoughtful, Frank."

"She was," Frank released a big breath. "And it was good. I was able to spend good, quality time with each kid. Johnny would talk my ear off while I cooked, telling me all about sixth grade issues." Nourzad continued and laughed. "Mickey would whip his baseball around and ask me to catch impossible catches. His arm was great for a nine-year-old. And Jory just watched TV and drew and asked me to critique everything she drew." Nourzad sighed again. "Just the cutest little girl ever. I really liked mornings. I loved them."

Rae smiled. "You and Jan found time at nights, no?"

"Oh yeah." Frank smiled. "Every Saturday night, actually, we went out, unless I was on-call or at the hospital. But if so, we made it a point to be together the very next day."

"You were a great husband and a great father, Frank," Rae stated as she stared deep into his eyes.

Frank shook his head no. "I don't know about that, Rae. But those four people were great people. They made me who I was."

Rae saw him quivering and shaking. A tear dripped down his face. She reached over to hold him but didn't get there in time. Nourzad stood and walked towards the picture window in the back.

"Ya know, Rae, I really should be going," he said without looking at her.

"You gotta deal with it eventually, Franky. You really do. And this was a good start," Rae said with much sympathy.

Nourzad stood quietly. Rae said nothing more. The moment seemed to last ages. Neither one of them moved.

PARANOIA

NOVEMBER 2015

'Cluster Headaches'

The search engine listed this first in Kevin's renewed search of **'headaches'**. It had been about a month since he first searched.

Cluster headaches appear quickly, with little or no warning and are characterized by excruciating pain. They occur in patterns, cycles or clusters. A cycle can last from weeks to months. Cluster headaches generally occur on one side of the head, with pain in and around an eye.[vi]

As Kevin read this on his laptop, at the desk in the upstairs office, the symptoms sounded, to him, very similar to his own. He took a deep breath and felt the pain of his headache that still had not gone away. He found some relief from the ibuprofen and acetaminophen, but only when taken together, at the highest doses. In those stretches, the pain didn't go away, but felt more like it was pushed back, held back by a tight net, pushing and pushing to try to get back at full force inside his head. He was on day thirty or so of the mixture of medicine. He wasn't sleeping well at all, he had taken four days off from work, and lay on the couch most of the time, fighting the pain that would not relent. He had not, yet, gone to the doctor.

Cluster headaches can wake you in the night (Id.)

Kevin had been awakened many a time during this stretch, but as he thought, maybe he was just never falling asleep.

Symptoms – Excruciating pain, one sided pain, restless-ness, stuffy nasal passages (Id.)

The pain had certainly been excruciating, right? At times, the pain was certainly on one side of his head, and the pain at the bridge of the noose was present. All these thoughts whipped through Kevin's head. He couldn't remember the last time he wasn't restless.

He hit the back button and searched more. Rece and the kids were out this morning. He had downplayed the headaches the last few days, not wanting to burden his family, but deep down it was eating away at him. He had such a sense of doom and despair, and the thought of death encircled him. He was so certain this condition would be fatal. He was certain he was dying.

'Tension Headaches'

He'd never heard of either of these types of headaches. In fact, up to this point, he thought headaches were head-aches. Tension headaches sounded interesting. He clicked on the site.

'Tension headaches are the most common headache among adults. They are commonly referred to as stress headaches.'

Stress. Maybe that's it.

'Symptoms of tension headaches: mild to moderate pain affecting the top, sides, or front of the head, headaches later in the day, difficulty sleeping, chronic fatigue, irritability, sensitivity to light(mild), general muscle aching.'

Kevin sat back and took a deep breath. He was encour-aged to see his symptoms on these websites. Surely, maybe, Rece was right. Maybe these were just headaches. He sat up and peered into the computer. He read more.

'Tension headaches affect 30-80% of Americans, while 3%

of Americans have chronic daily tension headaches.'[vii]

Huh. It was interesting to him to learn that one could suffer from non-terminal daily headaches. *Maybe I'm ok.* A sense of somewhat calm overcame Kevin as he sat at his desk. He took a drink from his water bottle and decided to check the basketball scores. He opened a new tab on his computer and searched for ESPN. Within seconds he was at the NBA page of ESPN's website. He eventually got to the scoreboard and checked on the previews of today's games. As he did, he felt pressure building in his head.

A rush of pressure and pain stormed up from the back of his scalp to his forehead. The pressure didn't relent but pulsated relentlessly. The pain seemed blocked by his skull, so it began to circle in his head, looking for a way out. He wanted to puke, though he really didn't have to. He rubbed his forehead, tried to block the pain by focusing on the basketball box scores, and took a big chug of his water. The pain tried to settle in. Kevin reached for the Tylenol and popped two in his mouth. He then popped in two Motrin. He closed his eyes and breathed.

'Headaches'

Kevin punched it into the search engine, again. More and more results popped up. He'd seen many of the results before and was losing track of which websites he'd already visited. Again, he saw many with the words **'brain tumor'**. He clicked on one.

Among the most common of all brain tumor symptoms, headaches have a range of types and causes. About half of all people with a brain tumor report experiencing headaches. [viii]

"Fuck!" Kevin yelled and slammed his hand on the brown oak desk. The yellow lamp with the grey lamp shade shook. He couldn't read on, yet he couldn't walk away from this information. He wanted answers desperately. He placed his right hand back on the keyboard when he heard the door open downstairs. He heard the loud din of the kids and Rece bustling in from their morning out. Kevin quickly closed the web page and turned the computer off. He stood up, took a deep breath, rubbed his eyes with his palms and walked out of the office. His face wore despair. His eyes ragged and tired. His body was sore. He walked towards the stairs and heard kids running up.

Fuck that, he thought to himself as he pondered his headache research. *I know it's a fucking brain tumor.*

"Dad! Dad! Look what we got!"

Kevin smiled his fake headache induced smile and hugged Vincent, as he was the first to get to him. He held him so tightly, as he listened to Vincent and James' story of their outing.

DATE NIGHT

December 2015

Rece walked downstairs dressed for the day. Kevin did what he'd been doing for weeks and weeks on end. He grabbed the Tylenol and Motrin and took two of each. He swallowed them down with water and waited for the pain in his head to deaden. It usually took about a half an hour for his head to turn into a dark chamber of chained horror. There wasn't necessarily physical relief, just a pause on the extreme ache. On the cocktail of mixed medicine, Kevin felt cold, hardened, and afraid. He was afraid because he knew the pain would return when the medicines wore off. But he was able to live and function. And he didn't have to go to the doctor.

The day was spent cleaning up around the house. The recent snow had melted, and garbage had shown up around the house. Candy wrappers, pop cans, popsicle sticks and paper cups appeared from the summer leftovers. The bushes and shrubs caught the litter with the help of the sometimes-heavy Chicago winds. On this day, Kevin walked slowly wearing his coat and hat with a small garbage can collecting the inevitable. His head was full. There was still no relief. And beyond that, he just felt plain drained.

"Pretty junky, huh?" Rece said as she snuck up behind him.

"Like always around this house," Kevin responded quietly.

"Headache?" Rece asked.

"How'd ya know?" Kevin asked, not looking at her.

"I know you. I told you before. It's always in your face. Ibuprofen working?"

"It does, but only when I take Tylenol with it. I need both for it to work. Been that way."

"Ok, well, that's good. At least it goes away. Just be careful." Rece looked at him intently as she said it.

"Be careful?" Kevin asked.

"Yes. Be careful. You tend to go overboard on things that make you feel, um, better, ya know?"

Kevin looked down at the weak grass and kicked at it. He knew.

"Well," Rece said again but more cheerfully, "At least they go away a bit."

Kevin didn't have the heart to tell her that they never really went away. He continued kicking at the ground below him.

"Ready for tonight?" Rece asked while smiling.

Kevin stopped kicking. "Oh my God. I cannot wait."

"It'll be fun. Like old times." Rece walked up to Kevin and kissed his cheek. "I'm off to the store. We need breakfast for tomorrow."

"Ok. Get O.J."

"I will. Love you."

"Love you, too."

Rece smiled. She gazed at Kevin with her head turned towards him as she walked away. *She's a vision.* He then tended to the bushes.

"Hey!"

Kevin looked up from the bush at Rece.

"Take some pain killers. I want you at full strength to-night." Rece then winked.

Kevin smiled.

--

"Ok, we're leaving!"

Kevin stood at the doorway. His new jeans cropped over his new brown leather shoes. He had on a blue long-sleeved shirt, and over that was the black leather jacket Rece had bought for him last Christmas. Lou laid beside him, his hind legs stretched out and his head on his curled-up legs.

"Dad!"

"Hey, James! Lookin' good."

"Thanks, Dad."

"Very cool pajamas."

James walked by and Kevin waited for Rece, standing still and looking forward. Rece then appeared on the stairs. Kevin looked at her and opened his mouth in amazement. "You are fricking stunning," he said.

Rece blushed, waved a hand at him, and shook her head with a smile. "Oh, stop."

"You look amazing."

"Thanks, sweetie," she said. "You, by the way, you? Wow."

Kevin rubbed his hand on his hair. "I gotta say, I still got it."

"Whatever, dad!" It was Kate. "Dork."

Kevin grabbed her, picked her up, and hugged her as she screamed and pushed away playfully.

"Dad!"

Kevin laughed and put her down. "It's cool that your dad is this good lookin', Katie, my dear."

Kate walked away, "Oh my word…"

"Ok, kids, where are Blaize and Vincent?" Rece was ready to go.

James responded from the other room. "They're playing video games upstairs."

Kevin and Rece looked at each other.

"What should we do?" asked Rece.

"Call them down?" Kevin responded.

"They know you're leaving!" James spoke from the T.V. room.

"Blaize!" Kevin called.

"What!?" they heard from the upstairs.

"We're leaving!" Kevin called out.

"Ok! Bye!"

"Bye dad! Bye mom!" Vincent screamed out.

Rece turned towards Kate. "Ok, we'll be at dinner, then a movie, then home."

"Uh huh," Kate said as she texted on her phone.

"We'll have our cell phones so, if you guys need anything, ok?"

"All good, guys." Kate looked up and smiled. Her blond hair hung just above her dark blue cheer tee shirt. Her legs were crossed, covering her pink shorts.

Kevin and Rece kissed her as she sat at the desk by the front door. They called out one last goodbye, locked the door, and went on the first date they had been on in a long time.

--

The sign still stood tall as they made their way down Cleveland Boulevard. Rece smiled.

"There it is." She grabbed his hand. "Kevin, this is so nice." Her voice was filled with pure, genuine, happiness.

"I know." Kevin's response sounded sullen, but he was overjoyed and couldn't express his feelings.

Rece did a quick turn to him. "You good? Headache?"

Kevin looked at her and smiled, "Actually, not too bad right now."

"I noticed!" Rece's smile grew. "You seemed really good while we were getting ready."

"I was. I took a butt load of Tylenol and Motrin." Kevin's voice rose, "I ain't letting these headaches ruin our night!"

They both laughed.

"No, but really, Rece, I feel pretty good. It's the best I've felt in a while, and I don't know, it's probably the medicine talking, maybe it is. But, I mean, after months and months or so of utter pain, it's just nice to have a way to kind of numb, ya know? What do you think?"

Rece looked at him and smiled. "I think it's great, sweetie. Headaches come and go. I think you had a really bad one and now it's getting better. I'm very happy. I know how much it hurt you and how it was affecting you. You tried to hide it, but I always knew." She leaned over and kissed him on the cheek. Kevin held back tears, and his love for her was never stronger.

"I'm just surprised you never went to the doctor," Rece said.

"I guess I wouldn't want to hear what they could say," Kevin responded. "Silly, I know."

"Ah, they'd just tell you you got a big 'ole headache," Rece said slowly for effect.

"Here we are," Kevin said excitedly, trying to push back his tears.

They pulled into 'Joe's Beef and Dogs'. It was a hot dog joint that served hot dogs, hamburgers, Italian beef sandwiches and the best French fries either one of them had ever tasted. It was lit up like a major city, with signs flashing and loud music playing in the parking lot.

As they pulled into a spot, Rece pointed and remarked, "That's where I'd wait for you!"

Kevin smiled. "I loved pulling in here and seeing you. Oh my God, Rece, we must have eaten here a million times!"

"A million and two!" Rece laughed. "I'm so glad we chose this as our first date. I love this place so much."

"So perfect for us, ya know?" Kevin said still smiling wide.

"Absolutely. Fifties music, nothing fancy."

"Right?" Kevin put the car in park. He leaned over and Rece moved into him. They kissed. Their lips met and to each it felt anew. They grabbed each other and wrapped in a passionate grip. The kiss went on for over thirty seconds. Kevin pulled away, looked at her and simply said, "Wow."

Rece giggled. "What?"

"You still melt me."

"We better curb this, huh?" Rece asked. "But cannot wait to get you home."

They kissed once more and went in to eat.

--

Rece gripped Kevin's hand tightly as he rested it on the console after starting the car.

"Enjoy the movie?" Kevin asked, eyes ahead.

"Enjoyed being with you, honey. Loved this idea. It brought me back to such good times, ya know? Not that these times are bad at all, because they're not, but just remembering when we first got together and how I fell in love with you, I just can't even express it, Kevin."

"Truly special, Rece. I'll never forget those dates we had. They meant everything to me." Kevin kept his eyes on the road ahead. Rece gripped his hand tight.

"I love you so much, Kevin. I'm truly so lucky to have found you. Thanks so much for this tonight." She turned to him and smiled.

Kevin finally looked at her, taking his eyes off the road. "Tonight isn't over, hottie."

Rece smiled as Kevin winked at her. She held his hand all the way home.

Once home, Rece kissed all the kids goodnight, as Kevin went in for his medicine cocktail. The pain curtailed again. He'd be numb again very soon, as the pain had tried, once again, to sneak in.

CONFIRMED

FEBRUARY 2016

"You know, Kevin, I was just thinking, I cannot believe it's been two months since our date," Rece said, lying next to Kevin in bed, naked and under the blankets.

"Time goes by fast," Kevin said.

"Yeah, it does, sweetie."

"I cannot believe you slept naked!" Kevin smiled as he scooted over next to her.

"Um, so did you!" Rece responded, her hand running on Kevin's leg.

"Well, I know, but wow, huh?"

"Kevin, it was amazing."

Rece leaned over and gave Kevin a kiss. Kevin put his hands all over her and dove in for a long hard kiss. They kissed passionately and rolled all over the bed, their bodies touching. Kevin pulled off her.

"We have to go, don't we?" he asked, his body pressed against hers.

"We so do, honey," Rece responded. She then grabbed his head and pulled Kevin in for another kiss. They made quick love then strolled into the shower and began their day.

--

"Mom!"

"She's in the shower," Kevin told Kate as he walked out of the bathroom and closed the door behind him.

"Why were you in there?" Kate asked, her eyes squinting.

"What?" Kevin said quickly as he walked by her to his closet.

Kate just continued her look then walked to the door. "Mom!"

"Yes?" Rece answered quietly.

"Is my dress in your closet?"

"Yes. I'll be out shortly, and we'll all get ready."

"Ok." Kate was content with Rece's answer.

"Dad." Kate turned to Kevin and spoke. "We need to leave by 10."

"Ok."

"Because we have to be there by 11."

"Gotcha," Kevin responded.

"Dad."

"Yes?"

"10."

"10, it is, sweetie."

"Ok."

"Ok," Kevin said smiling. "Tell the boys to go eat and then I'll start getting them ready."

Kate turned and walked out. She paused, looked at Kevin and said, "Why were you in there?" Kevin just looked at her. She squinted at him then left. As she did, Kevin heard her scream, "Boys!!" Kevin smiled and chuckled. He walked into the bathroom. The steam engulfed him as he strolled in. He couldn't see himself in the mirror, it was so foggy.

"Honey!" Kevin said, sounding shocked in his tone.

"What?" Rece said, giggling.

"What temperature is that shower?"

They both laughed.

Kevin peeked in, "I could never do that! It's way too hot!"

"Just hand me a towel, would ya?" Rece said as she cut the water off.

Kevin handed her the towel. As he did, Rece looked deeply into his eyes.

"What's up?" Kevin asked.

"I haven't seen it in a while."

"What?" Kevin asked.

"Your headache look."

Kevin smiled, "Ohhhhh."

"How long has it been?" Rece asked as she began to dry her perfect body.

"I mean, I'm not really sure."

"So nice. Glad those are gone."

"Me too, honey. Me too."

"Do you still take the medicine? The Tylenol and stuff?" Rece asked.

"Oh yeah, every day," Kevin answered. "I mean, they're gone, but I do get real minor pressure, so I keep takin both the Tylenol and Motrin, but I'm gonna stop soon, I think."

"So, they're kinda gone? The headaches?" Rece asked.

"Yeah." Kevin responded. "That really bad pain and pressure

is gone. Just real minor now. Totally tolerable. Thanks to the Motrin and Tylenol combo."

Rece finished drying her perfect body and walked by Kevin and ran her hand across his thigh. Kevin melted and took a very deep breath. Kevin grabbed her and pulled her close. They kissed long and hard, Kevin's hands all over her. They continued, locking the door.

--

"We still got it, baby," Rece said walking out afterwards.

"Boy do we ever," Kevin responded.

"Mom!"

The screech could be heard three blocks away. It was Vincent. He had on boxer shorts that were way too big on him. Chocolate covered his face, and his hair looked sticky.

"Yes, honey. You don't have to scream," Rece said back to him.

"I can't find my clothes."

"I'll get them. Just jump into the shower, please, and clean off."

Rece and Kevin glanced again at each other and smiled. They knew the day would now interrupt them, but they felt a passion for one another, and they secretly shared that passion with a quick look. They couldn't wait until the night brought them together again.

--

The Church glistened with tinsel, reminiscent of a Christmas Mass. Today, however, the tinsel was up for other unexplained reasons. It hung on the west and east walls, curling up and down. The smell of incense permeated the rear of the church, and bright lights hung high over the altar. Sixty-seven rows of pews were cut down the center by a walkway leading directly to the grey marble steps which led to the altar.

As Kevin held the door open for his family, he told Rece to try to get a row near the middle. Rece winked at him and led the troops forward. As he was about to let go of the door, Mike Miller came up from behind him.

"Kevin!"

Kevin turned and saw him, standing 6 feet 3, all 215 pounds of him. His black hair hung perfectly trim on his head, and his face had a perfect five o'clock shadow. He wore blue jeans and pressed white oxford shirt. Mike held out his hand.

"Mike!" Kevin yelled; way too loud for church.

They exchanged a very strong handshake.

"It's been forever," Kevin continued.

"It has, it has," Mike countered.

"How have you been?" Kevin asked, as they finally released the shake.

"Been great. Been very good."

"Oh my God," Kevin said. "What are you doing here?"

"My girl goes to St. Jude," Mike answered.

"Get out!" Kevin said loudly again.

"Yeah. We moved into the neighborhood about a year ago and put her here."

"Wow! I didn't even know you moved back here," Kevin responded.

"Yeah. Well, we were in the suburbs after college and then decided to move here."

"Wow. That's great."

"How about you?" Mike asked.

"Kate. My daughter Kate. She goes to Greenwood but does CCD here at Jude."

"So, they'll get confirmed together."

"Yes, yes they will."

They looked at each other for another moment and an awkward pause ensued. Kevin reached out his hand again and they shook.

"Great to see you, Mike."

"You too, Kevin. Let's try to get together. Do you have other kids?"

"Yeah, we have four. Three boys and Kate."

Mike looked amazed. "Wow. That's great. I have two boys, as well. 4th and 5th grade."

Kevin responded, "Freshman, Kate in 8th, 4th and 1st."

"Well, we should try to get together," Mike repeated.

"Definitely, definitely." Kevin smiled.

They entered the church together and walked to their families.

"Who was that?" Rece asked quietly as Kevin sat down next to her.

"Oh my God, that was Mike Miller. Remember him?"

"From college?" Rece asked, still being very quiet.

"Yes. Remember we went to his house…"

Rece interrupted him, "Oh my God, yes."

"They moved into the hood," Kevin whispered.

"No way," Rece whispered back.

"Way."

"Wow."

"I know, right?"

Rece continued, "Maybe they're cool now."

Kevin smiled and laughed, "He was always cool. She brought him down."

"Not so loud, goofy," Rece responded. Then she leaned into Kevin and whispered very softly, "He was never cool."

They both smiled.

The crowd filled in nicely, and not an open seat could be seen. The boys were all dressed in nice slacks, dress shirts and most wore ties. The girls all wore dresses in a variety of colors, though white stood out. The priests had begun to make their way from the back room to the vestibule. Some teachers milled about near the altar. Kevin sat and watched it all. He leaned into Rece.

"Why are we here?"

Rece laughed. "It's a pre-confirmation mass. They're just going over what they'll do when they actually have the confirmation."

"Oh," Kevin whispered. "And confirmation is when?"

Rece leaned closer to Kevin, "Now you decide to whisper? What?"

"Confirmation. When is it?" Kevin whispered louder.

"Next week."

"Gotcha!"

The mass and celebration went without a hitch. Afterwards, Kevin and Rece took the kids out to brunch then relaxed around the home the rest of the day. Blaize went out with his friends. Kate hung out with her girlfriends, and the two little boys played basketball in the backyard. Throughout the afternoon and evening, Kevin hung out with each group and shared stories and laughs. Rece made snacks and cleaned up after each mess.

After dinner, it was family movie night. Everybody had a vote. The votes were placed in a baseball hat, and Kevin picked the winner out each Sunday evening. This night, Vincent won. A kid movie about a toaster won out. None of the other kids were too pleased. Vincent was on cloud nine.

They sat on the couch, sharing popcorn, candy and pop. They laughed at the jokes, and thoroughly enjoyed the simple movie. Each one of them smiled throughout, and afterwards talked about how cute and hilarious the movie actually was.

"Great pick, Vince!" yelled Kate.

Vincent smiled.

Afterwards, Kevin and Rece tucked everyone in nice and snug. Kevin took the two little guys, while Rece tucked in the older ones. Kevin wrapped each boy in a blanket, kissed and hugged them, looked at them, turned the TV on, shut the light and blew them kisses. He met Rece in the hallway, who was smiling big.

"All good?" Kevin asked.

"Oh yes. All good," Rece responded, also smiling big.

They walked hand in hand to their bedroom. They cuddled and kissed good night under their giant blanket. Rece snuggled into Kevin's chest. A light rain began to fall outside. Kevin held her close. He hadn't taken his pain medicine during all the family action that afternoon and evening. They fell asleep within minutes.

WORST ONE EVER

Jesus fucking Christ.

Kevin opened his eyes in the darkness. The pain was horrendous. It found its way to the center of his forehead and built camp. It radiated upwards to the top center of his skull and began to throb. Kevin was in incredible pain. He sat up in bed, pushing Rece's arm off his chest. He put both hands on his head and massaged his fingers into his scalp as he grimaced in pain. The axe was back. It was dug deep into his head, slicing down from his mid scalp to his nose. The pain was deep and constant and appeared out of nowhere. He shook his head, hoping to shake the pain away. As he did, the pain only grew worse.
Kevin sat in agony for what seemed like an hour. He didn't want to wake Rece, but this pain was relentless. His head was full, the pressure was overwhelming, and the pain was all encompassing. He heard a dim shriek inside his head.

"Rece," he whispered, softly while gently shaking her arm, knowing she was sleeping heavily. "Honey, I need you, baby."

Rece didn't move.

Kevin lay back and buried his head into the soft pillow. He rolled it back and forth and then upwards again, trying to ease the pain. He grabbed the back of his neck with his right hand and massaged it rough.

"Rece," he said it louder. "Rece, wake up."

Rece jumped up out of her sleep and landed on her elbow, propping her head up with her hand and looked at Kevin confusingly.

"Hey," she said to Kevin. "What's up?"

"Headache." Kevin's eyes were closed.

"Oh, Kevin, really? Is it really bad?" Rece lay back down on her pillow.

"Worst one ever," Kevin said quietly, now looking into Rece's eyes.

"Ok, ok, let's think," Rece responded. "Did you take medicine tonight? Motrin?"

"No, I fucking forgot, and this fucking thing snuck the fuck in."

"Did you have a headache?" Rece asked.

"Just this minor pressure, you know, like I've been having, but nothing remotely bad." Kevin rubbed his face with both sweaty palms. "I've been taking it a lot just because it's been keeping the bad ones away. And tonight, I fucking forgot."

"Ok. You want more now?" Rece asked.

"Yes."

"Ok, honey."

Rece ran and grabbed the Tylenol. Kevin grabbed it and swallowed two.

"Where's the Motrin?" Kevin asked nervously, like an addict asking for Narco.

"Motrin?" Rece asked. "No, you can't mix them like that, you have to wait."

"No, no, no," Kevin said quickly. "You can take them together. Look, I've been doing that, and it has worked."

Rece shook her head. "Ok, we'll discuss that later. Drink some water and lay down..." Rece grabbed two Motrin and handed them to Kevin. He drank them down.

"Hon, this is bad. Really bad," Kevin said as he sat up off the side of the bed, his feet on the floor, his face in his hands with his elbows on his knees.

Rece crawled up to him and rubbed his back.

"I thought these were fucking gone, hon. I can't have these anymore!" Kevin said angrily.

"It's ok, sweetie," Rece calmly stated.

"It's not, Rece. This is bad."

Rece crawled around him and looked into his eyes. "Kevin, it's still headaches. You're ok. I promise."

"It's not. Headaches don't last like this. They don't get worse like this. This pain is horrendous, honey!"

"They do, Kevin," Rece said, still calm in her tone. "Headaches are brutal. Most people don't get them, but those that do, and bad ones, they're horrible and really hurt. But they don't kill you, Kevin."

"There are so many things this could be. You assume they're headaches, you do, but we don't know. It could be growing and I'm doing nothing about it," Kevin said very distraught.

"Kevin...."

There was silence.

"What?" Kevin said, looking at her.

"You know better," she said quietly.

"I used to. But I'm just not sure anymore." He responded. "This pain! Ahhhhhh!"

"Kevin!" Rece shouted.

"I can't stand it!!!" he screamed. "It's just pounding and pounding, Rece. Right here!" Kevin screamed, taking his hand and pointing from the middle of his scalp forward to his forehead. "It's like a fucking sledgehammer pounding over and over on a spike that's implanted between my skull. Fuck, honey. Fuck!"

Kevin stood up and walked around.

"What are you doing?" Rece asked, louder than her quiet tone from before.

Kevin continued to walk. "If I walk around, it helps."

"You see!" Rece yelled, sitting all the way up in their bed.

"What?" Kevin asked, mid pace.

"If you had a tumor in your head, you wouldn't think this clearly. You know to get up and walk. You're thinking. You wouldn't be able to walk around!"

Kevin stopped and looked at Rece. He stared at her and felt his forehead with his left hand, his right hand on his waist. "I don't know. It's too bad of a pain to be normal, Rece. I get what you're saying, but this is bad. I thought they were gone!"

"Honey, I love you, but this is going to get exhausting. You need to make a decision," Rece said, quietly again.

"Decision?" Kevin asked quizzically.

"You want to go to the hospital? I've been asking you to go to the doctor for months," Rece said.

"I probably should, Rece." Kevin stopped pacing. "It hurts so bad I don't know. This is the worst it's ever been. I can barely see, and all the websites say if it's the worst headache you've ever..."

"Kevin," Rece interrupted, "we are going, it's ok."

Rece stood up and walked to Kevin. They hugged tightly. Kevin grabbed her head and pressed their foreheads together. They stayed that way for over a minute, neither one eager to move. Kevin finally let go.

Rece raised her head back and looked at Kevin's eyes. They stared at each other long and deep. Not a word was said. They just appreciated each other in that moment. It was a moment they didn't want to end. They felt a genuine connection. It was 2:41 a.m. and Kevin and Rece felt so safe in each other's' grasp. They hugged again, for minutes, Rece rubbing his head. He pressed his forehead to her again and spoke.

"Let's go to bed."

"Are you sure?" She asked softly.

Kevin responded just as soft, "Let's go to bed, honey. The pain will be there in the morning. I got you tonight."

--

"It's time you went to a doctor," Rece said the next morning.

Kevin gazed at Rece, who was sitting up in bed, sipping coffee. The pounding headache had kept him up all night. His medicine of ibuprofen and acetaminophen was wearing off. The pain circled again, in search of a place to take hold. The pain in the bridge of his nose was excruciating.

"But I don't even have a doctor, do I?" Kevin responded.

"Yes, you do," Rece responded. "You have an HMO. We chose a site last year, remember?"

"No." Kevin placed his head in his hands.

They were sitting up in their bed. It was 9:18 a.m. Kevin had awoken with a pain very deep in his head. He had tossed and turned with it, eventually turning on the T.V. to try to forget about the pain. But the pain was too harsh. Every time he got comfortable, the pain worsened. It now shot up from his neck, over the top of his head and settled violently at the bridge of his nose. The pounding was horrendous. At times, it felt as if his head would collapse within itself. He had laid in pain all night, praying and hoping Rece would wake up. He couldn't stand it anymore.

As they sat in bed that morning, Kevin explained all the pain he was in. Rece consoled him and comforted him. They discussed going to the E.R., as they had several times since the headaches had started. Kevin decided against it, again. But this time, Rece was ready to get Kevin to a doctor.

She got up and left the room. Kevin was alone, wondering where she went, and for what purpose. It scared him that Rece was at this point. She had been steadfast in her opinion that he merely suffered from headaches. If she was concerned enough that she wanted Kevin to see a doctor, he thought, it must be bad.

Rece walked back in. She was wearing a pair of Kevin's boxers and his tee shirt. Somehow, after just getting out of bed, she looked absolutely beautiful. "Doctor's Perez, Smith and Nourzad," she said, reading from a piece of paper.

Kevin looked at her face, "Huh?"

"Those are your doctors."

Kevin's face showed confusion. "How do you know that?"

"Oh my God." Rece chuckled as she sat on the bed next to Kevin and showed him the brochure. "You picked them out last year. We went through that booklet you brought home from work. These guys were close, they were affiliated with Hope, Brian recommended them..."

Kevin nodded. "Yeah, I remember now, I guess."

"Later we make an appointment." Rece placed the brochure on her nightstand.

"It's bad, isn't it?" Kevin asked.

Rece placed her hands on his cheeks and moved his eyes to hers. "No. It's not bad, Kevin."

"You want me to see a doctor..."

Rece cut him off. "To see what's causing it, but more than that, Kevin, to help you. They have stronger medicine for headaches that might help you."

They stared at each other. Rece continued, "You can't go on like this. You don't sleep when you have these bad ones, you can't do your work, and you don't go into work and the kids..."

"What about the kids?" Kevin asked annoyingly.

"Don't get snappy at me, Kevin." Rece said back fast.

"I'm not."

"Look, the kids notice that you're not as playful and cheery is all when you get these bad ones. They notice things, Kevin. It's no big deal, but we all want you back to normal for good. It's hell when you have these bouts."

Kevin sat there in his thoughts. He was angry that she brought up the kids. He had tried so hard not to let these headaches affect his family life. He had pushed back all the excruciating pain. He sat through cheer practices and baseball games with a smile. He never wanted these headaches to win. Yet, his efforts weren't enough. It was noticeable. His headaches were affecting everything.

"I'm sorry." That's all Kevin could muster.

"Sorry for what?" Rece responded. "You've done nothing wrong. You have headaches. You just have to figure out now how we deal with them, so they don't affect us negatively."

"What if we can't?!" Kevin yelled, but not too loudly. "I mean, what if it doesn't go away, Rece? What if it's worse? What if it's killing me, Rece? What are we gonna do?" Kevin stared at Rece, who, in turn, stared back.

"Kevin, we'll call tomorrow and set up an appointment. That's the best thing right now, ok?" She stared at Kevin and grabbed hold of his hand. Kevin's eyes were shut tight. He shook his head side to side. The pain was exploding out of the bridge of his nose. Pressure was caving in all around his head. He looked miserable.

"I'm going to get you some more ibuprofen, ok?" Rece asked, without even waiting for a response.

In seconds, she was back. Kevin took three pills. He chugged the water and placed the cup on his nightstand. "Which doctor, hon?"

"What?" Rece asked.

"Which doctor do I see?" Kevin asked.

"Oh," Rece answered. "Well, we just call and set up an appointment. I think they tell you who to see."

"That's weird. Like roulette, huh. Spin the wheel..." Kevin said tailing off.

Rece chuckled. "Luck of the draw, Kevin. You'll get the new guy!"

Kevin smiled. The extreme headache kept him from laughing.

YOU WANT NOURZAD

MARCH 1, 2016

The van had just been detailed. It shone bright dark blue as they walked to it the next morning. Rece looked back at Blaize, who followed them out the door.

"We'll be back around 1," she told him.

"Ok," Blaize said, dressed in shorts and a white tee shirt.

"Make sure you let the dog out, ok?" Kevin spoke very quietly and monotone.

"Ok, Dad. Feel better."

"Oh, Blaize. Hey, this is nothing. Don't worry about it, ok?" Kevin sounded sincerer than when he gave his orders about the dog.

They both got into the van. Kevin drove. He always did. The drive was quiet, neither one having much to say. The streets were somewhat clear, just a few cars here and there, running their errands, or taking an early lunch.

As they approached the hospital, Rece pointed out Pete's Restaurant. "I've heard that's so good. We should go there one day."

Kevin looked out, "Never noticed that place."

"I think you go in there," Rece said, pointing to a parking lot.

Kevin turned into the spacious lot.

"How are you?" she asked.

"Ok," Kevin answered.

"Make sure you tell them everything, ok?"

"What do you mean?" He asked.

"Well, you know, sometimes you leave things out, like not telling me about your earlier headaches."

Kevin didn't respond right away. Rece looked at him. Kevin looked forward, looking for a spot in which to park.

Rece finally looked away from him. "Anyway, tell them everything so we don't have to come back, ok?"

"I didn't think they were a big deal, so I didn't tell you," Kevin said quietly.

"It's not that you didn't tell me when they were happening, it's that you left it out when we were going through this. Look, I just wish you would've told me, is all, no secrets, remember? All of it matters, but look, it's no big deal right now, let's just get fixed."

Kevin found a spot and parked the van. He did not respond to her. They sat in the car staring forward. The car was off. Neither one moved. Kevin felt a rush of heat pulsate through his body. Then he felt flush, like all the blood, water and emotion spilled out of his body at one moment. His head was full, and pressure pushed out from his forehead. His heart raced. Rece still looked forward, not speaking. He wished he knew why she was quiet. He didn't want to ask.

"I'm ready," Kevin said.

Rece opened her door. They walked into the offices of Dr.'s Perez, Smith and Nourzad.

The door creaked a bit as it opened. Rece walked in as Kevin stood behind her. She took an immediate left and angled towards one of the five available chairs. Kevin stepped into the office and looked around. Ahead of him was a second door closing, as a man's left calf and shoe escaped inside. Directly to the left of the door was a picture. He looked at it for a long moment. In the picture, a ship was disappearing into the horizon. The water was a deep blue around the boat but was turning grey towards the horizon. At the edge of the sunlight sat darker skies. The ship seemed calm, heading into the eerie unknown.

"Can I help you?" a voice asked.

Kevin turned away from the painting. "Um, yes. I have an appointment."

"Your name?"

"Uh, Kevin Ruscevich," Kevin responded as he walked towards the young receptionist. A glass window was open in front of her. On the counter in front was a computer, a sign in sheet and a cup full of different colored pens.

"Ok, Mr. Ruscevich," the receptionist stated, "I need you to take these forms and fill them out where I have marked red X's. As soon as you do that, bring it back to me, Ok? Oh! And I need your insurance card."

Kevin fumbled through his wallet and handed her his card when he found it right where Rece had left it. He took the clipboard from her hand and turned to find Rece sitting looking right at Kevin. He walked over and sat by her.

"All set?" Rece asked.

"I think so," Kevin responded. "I gotta fill these out."

"Ok, good. Need help?"

"No, I got it. Thanks."

Kevin filled out his forms. He didn't need help with any answers or information. He wrote clearly and legibly. Afterwards, he sat and looked around at all the older people sitting in the office. He noticed most of them had smiles.

"Bring it up," Rece told him

"Ok."

Kevin stood behind an older man at the counter. The old man was laughing. Kevin wasn't listening to the conversation. He was somewhat nervous, as his turn was coming soon. He hoped to himself to be laughing after his appointment. He heard the man in front of him say he couldn't imagine not having Dr. Nourzad. There was more conversation, but he couldn't make it out. The receptionist walked away for a second. Kevin had to ask.

"Dr. Nourzad is good?" Kevin asked the gentleman in front of him.

"Oh, son," the old man turned around to Kevin, "he's the best, the absolute best."

Kevin nodded his head. The old man continued, "Do you see him?"

Kevin answered, "No. This is my first time here. Don't know who I'm getting."

"Bah!" the man said loudly. He moved close to Kevin. "You get Nourzad. Don't let these fools tell you who to see. The other guys? Yeah, they're doctors, and they're good, but Nourzad is very special. He really knows his stuff. You gotta get him."

"But I thought, or was told, you get who you get," Kevin stated.

"No, no," the old man said. "It's HMO, I get it, but they're all tied to Hope, all three doctors. Technically, you're supposed to have one, but you get all three. It's like all three are your primary physician. Get Nourzad."

"Ok, ok, I appreciate that," Kevin said back.

"All set?" the receptionist asked.

"Oh, me? Yes, sorry." Kevin laughed a bit and thanked the old man again. He stepped past him as the old man grabbed an envelope from the receptionist and left.

"Ok, Mr. Ruscevich, I'll file these, and you can have a seat, Ok?"

"Um, who will I be seeing today?" Kevin asked.

"Dr. Perez," the receptionist said as she smiled.

"Um, ok, uh, anyway I can get Dr. Nourzad?" Kevin asked.

"Hm." The receptionist looked at her book while smiling, like she knew a secret. "Well, he's swamped today"

"Yeah, I'd really like to see him," Kevin told her, as he scratched his chin.

"Yeah, well, I don't think so, today, I'm sorry."

As the receptionist spoke, Dr. Nourzad appeared from behind her. Kevin saw him, not knowing who he was. *Young Doctor.*

"What's up, Nancy?" Nourzad asked. "I heard my name." He smiled.

"Oh, Dr. Nourzad. This gentleman is requesting to see you today," she said to Nourzad, looking up at him from her chair. She was smiling.

Nourzad smiled back then looked at Kevin. "With whom were you scheduled?"

The receptionist beat Kevin to the answer. "Dr. Perez."

"Well," Nourzad spoke quickly, "John actually wanted to step out to the Palos office this morning, so…"

Nourzad walked away. Kevin and the receptionist offered each other a quick, awkward smile and waited. Nourzad reappeared.

"All set. I'll take…" Nourzad looked at the paperwork, "… Mr. Ruscevich?"

"Yes," Kevin said.

"Ok. Set it up," Nourzad said. He then looked at Kevin, "See you in a bit"

Kevin nodded. Chelsea wrote in her pad and looked up at Kevin. She then looked over her shoulder then back at Kevin.

"Wow," she said. "I'd say you will be the youngest patient, by far, he has ever seen." Chelsea laughed.

"Really?" Kevin asked as he rubbed his forehead. The pressure was building in his head.

"Oh yeah, by far!"

Nourzad reappeared and smiled. "An old friend of mine told me I needed to start seeing younger patients. I think it'll be great."

They all smiled, and Kevin turned to go sit down next to Rece. The pain was sudden. It hit him in the center of his skull and moved to his forehead. It was pounding hard. He sat next to Rece.

"All good?" she asked.

"Yeah. I got this Dr. Nourzad. The guy ahead of me up there recommended him."

"That's good," Rece said softly.

Kevin paused a moment.

What's good? Was she upset?

He shifted in his chair. Rece was now skimming a magazine.

"Kevin." It was a voice from the recently opened door.

"There you go," Rece spoke.

"Yep." Kevin stood up. "Wish me luck." He looked at Rece.

She smiled and winked.

"Hey," Rece stopped him. "You want me to go in with you?"

"Nah, I'm good. Thanks, though."

"Love you," she said.

Kevin smiled back and walked in past the painting of the boat. He couldn't help but look at that doomed ship again.

--

"Kevin?"

A red headed smiling nurse met Kevin right as he passed the door. She extended her arm and Kevin shook her hand and responded in the affirmative.

"It's nice to meet you, Kevin. Ok, we're going to go back into room five," she said as they walked on down the hall.

Kevin saw two older men sitting in room two. Room three was empty and room four was full with two nurses, an old patient and what appeared to be an older male white doctor. Room five was empty and seemed very clean to Kevin as he followed the nurse inside.

"So sorry, Kevin. I didn't introduce myself, I'm Sheryl, and I'll be your nurse."

"No problem at all," Kevin responded.

The room was a light blue, with bright white trim. On the wall was an eye test placard. A small desk and table sat across the room from where Kevin sat. A green patient table sat in the opposite corner. Kevin's heart raced. He was nervous.

He had dreaded this day since his headaches began, knowing that if the headaches didn't clear up, he'd have to see a doctor. His concern was the diagnosis. He worried to death that the doctors would find a tumor. He couldn't shake that dread. As he sat there that day, he was certain the outlook would be grim.

"Ok, Kevin, we're just gonna check your blood pressure, ok?" the nurse said quietly.

"Yes," Kevin responded.

Sheryl wrapped his arm in the Velcro sleeve and began the test. The sleeve tightened slowly around his arm as Sheryl squeezed the air into the sleeve hose, cutting off the blood in his artery. Sheryl listened with the stethoscope and looked down, wearing a serious face. The pressure released. The tightness in his arm subsided, and eventually he felt the blood pumping through his arm again.

"Ok, 141/93," Sheryl reported. "Pulse is 98. Little nervous?"

"Yeah, I am."

"Ok, that's normal. Those numbers will come down when the nerves go down. I see that all the time."

"Ok, good," Kevin smiled.

"Alright." Sheryl wrote a few numbers down then placed the papers on the desk. "What seems to be the problem?"

Kevin didn't really appreciate the form of the question.

Problem?

He responded. "I've been having these really bad headaches," he said while touching his forehead. "Actually, they had gone away for a bit, but they came back really bad this week."

"How long have you had them?" she asked.

"I'd say several months, pretty much 24 hours a day. They were really bad. Then, like I said, they went away a bit, but came back bad this week."

"Ok. Were you taking anything?" she asked.

"Just Tylenol and Motrin."

"Ok. Sounds good," she said as she wrote more notes. "Dr. Nourzad will be in in a moment, ok?" Sheryl said as she stood up to leave. "It was really nice to meet you."

"Sounds good," Kevin said.

He sat alone. He looked out the window as he placed his thumb on his wrist to feel his pulse. It was still high. Outside he saw construction workers and trucks. The sun peeked through some grey clouds. The wind seemed strong based on the trees blowing right to left. He looked up and saw a bright white ceiling. He took a deep breath as he heard a knock on the door.

--

"I have four kids," Kevin told Dr. Nourzad, as they sat across from each other. Dr. Nourzad wore gray slacks with no wrinkles. His black shoes matched perfectly with his charcoal socks and black belt. He wore a lighter grey oxford shirt, with a shiny silver tie. His hair was perfect, combed to his right. It was a deep black. Kevin sat across as Nourzad sat cross-legged, straight up in his chair, never losing eye contact with Kevin.

"What are their ages?" Nourzad asked.

"14, 12, 8 and 6."

"A lot of work, huh?" Nourzad said while smiling.

"Oh yes. They give us a run, for sure."

Nourzad studied Kevin as he spoke. Kevin sat facing Nourzad, leaning forward a bit with his elbows on his knees and his hands clasped, wringing them back and forth.

"You mentioned 'us'," Nourzad spoke.

"Yes, I'm married," Kevin responded. "Been married almost 15 years."

"That's great. Where did you guys meet?" Nourzad asked.

Kevin looked at him quizzically. "Um..."

Nourzad smiled. "I know it may seem presumptuous, but it just interests me to know a few things before we proceed. If you feel more comfortable passing, I'll understand."

Kevin thought quickly of the great review of Nourzad he received in the waiting room. He assumed this guy knew what he was doing.

"We met at a courthouse." Kevin spoke somewhat quietly.

"That's interesting," Nourzad chirped. "Are you a lawyer?"

"No. I actually work at the Daily Sun newspaper. I'm a senior editor; she was a clerk in the courthouse I had to go to for work one day."

"That sounds nice," Nourzad said with a genuine smile. "Is it a good meeting story?"

Kevin laughed. "Actually, it was. I kinda didn't really know what I was doing there, and she helped me."

"That's how it happens!" Nourzad almost yelled. "I love it!"

"Yeah, she's actually in the waiting room right now." Kevin wasn't sure at all why he said that at that point.

"Well let's get her in here!" Nourzad insisted in his tone.

"I wasn't sure," Kevin whispered a bit.

"No. It's a good idea. I can get information from her, as well, that will hopefully help you." Nourzad stood up and opened the door. "Darlene? Or, um Chelsea? Can you call in Mrs..." Nourzad turned to Kevin, "I'm sorry."

"Ruscevich," Kevin spoke softly, wondering in his head why he mentioned Rece's presence.

"Ruscevich, Chels. Ask her to step in, please."

He closed the door.

"Ok, Kevin, your job. Tell me about your hours."

"Actually, the hours are good. I go in daily, but a lot of my work is done at home on-line," Kevin answered.

"Great," said the doctor, writing something on his pad. "The benefits of how many years?"

"18."

"Ok, great." Nourzad wrote more. "Now. Tell me about your sleep patterns."

Kevin adjusted in his seat as Rece interrupted and walked in slowly and quietly. Nourzad glanced at her immediately, directing his attention away from Kevin. Kevin looked at Rece, then back at Nourzad.

"I think I sleep pretty good. Six to eight hours a night," Kevin said as Nourzad looked at Rece.

Nourzad looked away from Rece and wrote, then stood up and approached Rece, who was dressed in a grey skirt, with a black tank top over a white tee. She wore sandals. As they shook hands, they looked like a perfect couple, Nourzad and Rece, both supremely good looking and dressed perfectly.

"My name is Frank Nourzad." He extended his hand and Rece obliged.

"Rece Ruscevich."

They shook and made good eye contact. Kevin looked on and shifted again in his seat. The handshake went on a bit and Kevin looked at them both. Nourzad released Rece's hand and asked her to sit in the seat next to Kevin. All three sat as Nourzad spoke again.

"Ok, so we have some good information here, to start," Nourzad said, looking at his pad. "Now, with headaches, I usually start straight off with that most times, they are pretty benign in terms long term health, ok? Meaning that headaches usually do not indicate any other health issues. Now, you mentioned work and the kids and the house earlier. Are you able to keep up with your daily life, and when I say that, I in no way diminish the pain you may be in on any given day, but I'm just curious if you can keep up with the daily grind."

"I mean..." Rece started, then stopped.

"Yes, Rece, you can answer," Nourzad said nodding at Kevin.

"I think he does great dealing with the headaches, and, yes, he has been keeping up with his responsibilities."

"Great," Nourzad said. "Kevin?"

Kevin looked at him and answered quickly, while turning to look at Rece as he spoke. "Yes. I'm good in that sense. I mean, I've taken a few days off here and there to deal with some serious pain, but I've kept up everywhere else."

"Any memory problems?" asked the doctor.

"No," Kevin answered.

"Any balance problems?" Nourzad stated rather than asked.

"Um." Kevin paused.

"I mean, ever fall over, feel faint, lose any ability to walk straight or stand straight up?" Nourzad asked.

"No," Kevin answered.

Nourzad continued. "Any difficulty raising your arms, moving your legs, anything like that?"

"No."

"Nausea?"

"No."

"Vomiting?"

"No."

Rece chimed in. "Well, he was nauseous a couple times."

Kevin responded right away, "Yeah, but it wasn't anything of note, I don't think."

"Well, with headaches," Nourzad opined, "it's all particularly of note. It's really important to know everything. Tell me about the nausea."

Kevin shifted again. "Sometimes, and not very often, I feel a little nausea when the headaches first start. But then it goes away."

"Great," Nourzad responded. "And never any vomiting?"

"None."

"Great." Nourzad wrote again. "Now, tell me about the headaches themselves."

Kevin sat still and thought. He wanted to get everything out and not leave out anything. Rece sat tight and looked at Kevin. Nourzad studied them both.

Kevin began. "It started about, I don't know, probably six to seven months ago. I was walking downstairs one morning, I remember, and I got this sudden pain and pressure right here." Kevin pointed to the top of his forehead and moved his finger down to the bridge of his nose. "It also filled up on this side of the head. It felt like immense pressure. It came on pretty suddenly and really knocked me back. Ever since then it's been pretty constant. The magnitude kind of comes and goes, but for the most part, the pain and pressure have been bad."

Rece looked at Kevin and chimed in. "Except he does have periods when they're not so bad."

Kevin looked at her. "Yeah, there are times when they dissipate a bit. Not a lot of pain at all. But, obviously, they come back."

"What was different about the times they dissipate, if anything?" Nourzad asked, looking at Kevin.

"Nothing that I can remember," Kevin responded.

"We had gone out on a date that one week, and I think after that is when the headaches kinda went away for a while." Rece spoke with a purpose, then looked from Nourzad to Kevin. "Right, dear?"

Kevin looked at her. "Yeah, I think so."

"When you have the worst pain, like you mentioned, what is it, from 1-10, 10 being the worst," Nourzad asked.

"10. Always. It really incapacitates me." Kevin answered without hesitation.

"Ok." Nourzad wrote some notes. "Has anything worked? Aspirin? Ibuprofen?"

"Yeah," Kevin responded. "I'm at my least pain when I double up on Ibuprofen and Tylenol."

"Yes, so long as you wait three hours between doses on each that should be fine," Nourzad stated. "And how do you feel today?"

Kevin and Rece looked at each other. Kevin then looked at Nourzad.

"It's been rough today. The pressure is right here." Kevin pointed to his forehead. "And it branches out here and here." Kevin ran his finger to the right and left from his forehead to the top of his skull.

"Ok," Nourzad said. "Is this pain at the worst point right now?"

"I don't know," Kevin said, running his palm onto his forehead and rubbing. "The absolute worst was twice, in the middle of the night, it felt like a lead pipe was jammed into my skull. Those were, by far, the worst two moments the last couple of months. Today isn't that. But today is bad."

Nourzad studied Kevin's face. He noticed Kevin's eyes stuck in an almost squint-like manner. Kevin rubbed his head a lot, and his voice was shifting to very monotone.

"Has the headache progressed since you came here today?" he asked.

"No," was all Kevin said.

"When you say your headaches incapacitate you, what do you mean, exactly?" asked Nourzad, the questions now coming towards Kevin a little faster.

"I just can't move. It hurts so much; I just lay there. Every movement of my body makes it worse," Kevin responded as he rubbed his head again. Rece sat, looking at Kevin.

Nourzad turned towards Rece. "Rece, do you see the effect of the headaches?"

Rece looked confused.

"I mean, is there anything out of the ordinary that strikes you about Kevin from Kevin's headaches? Do you see him struggle physically or mentally?" Nourzad clarified.

"Oh no, I mean, he's in pain, you can tell, but he doesn't stumble, or fall, or anything like that," Rece answered, picking up on the angle at which Nourzad was aiming. "But he is in pain, doctor. I see it in his eyes, like right now. When his headaches are really bad, it always shows in his eyes." Her voice trailed off.

Nourzad wrote. The three sat in silence for a bit. Kevin was feeling the headache get worse, the pressure building at the bridge of his nose. The pressure filtered to the side of his head. He rubbed his head with both hands. Nourzad took note.

"Does it hurt right now, Kevin, badly?" He asked.

"Yes."

Nourzad stood up and walked to the door. Rece's eyes followed him. Kevin's did not.

"Chelsea, inform June, Motrin 800, one pill, please," he said into the hallway.

"Kevin," Nourzad said as he walked back to his chair, "I'm getting you Motrin 800. When was the last time you had ibuprofen?"

Kevin responded. "This morning, about 8. Then Tylenol right before we left for here."

Rece looked at Kevin after he said that.

"Ok, good. You can..." June walked in after a quick knock of the door with a pill in a paper cup and a small cup of water. Nourzad thanked her, and June smiled and walked out.

Nourzad handed Kevin the pill. "Here you go, Kevin. This will cover you until tonight, but you can still keep up with the Tylenol. Just wait the three hours between the two, ok?"

Kevin took the pill and the water and swallowed the pill quickly. "Thanks," he said.

There was a brief pause, and Nourzad stood and spoke. "Is there anything else you'd like to tell me that might help me understand the headaches more?" He didn't direct the question to either one, but left it open as to whom could answer. Rece looked intently at Kevin. Kevin quickly glanced at her and then back to Nourzad.

Kevin said, "No."

"Ok, sit here and I'll be right back." Nourzad smiled and walked out with his note pad.

Rece and Kevin sat in silence. Rece stared at Kevin then spoke in a whisper. "Why didn't you tell him you mix the medicines?"

"What?" Kevin responded, sounding shocked.

"And your drinking," Rece whispered louder.

"I don't think that has anything to do with this, and I think it's none of his business." Kevin sounded frustrated.

"He told you, tell him everything." Rece sounded frustrated right back at him.

"I'm not telling him that."

"It was only like two years ago," Rece responded. "You never had headaches before, so maybe it has something to do with it."

"Don't you listen? I told you, I've had little headaches off and on..."

"But not like this." Rece cut him off. "Never like this when you were drinking. And you lied about the Tylenol and Motrin..."

Nourzad cut her off by walking back in after a very quick knock on the door. Rece and Kevin both looked up at the doctor, Kevin hoping for some favorable diagnosis, Rece wanting to tell Nourzad more.

Nourzad stood and looked at Kevin, then spoke.

"Ok, Kevin, first, it was a real pleasure to meet you. I think you are a very good man, and you have a wonderful wife here, and the two of you are raising a family and doing very well at it, so it sounds. Headaches are tricky, but for the most part, the headaches that you describe, the headaches that are affecting you, are always benign in nature. I don't see any signs that these headaches are a symptom of any other malady, ok?"

Kevin nodded.

Nourzad continued. "So, I don't think we need to run any other tests or anything like that. Now, we do have headaches here, and we want to fix this. It seems the over the counter meds are working for relief, yes?"

Kevin nodded in agreement.

"Ok, let's keep up with those, but I changed my mind and want to just go with the ibuprofen for now. I can prescribe the 800 milligram tablets, or you can take four of the over the counter 200 milligram tablets, that's up to you."

Rece spoke up, while looking at Kevin. "I think we should go with the prescription. It will be easier."

"Kevin?" Nourzad asked.

"Yeah," Kevin responded. "That's good."

"Ok, great. We'll do that." Nourzad scribbled on his pad then looked up. "Ok, so, let's keep up with the Ibuprofen, ok? Let's see how you're doing in, say one or two months, ok? I want you to come back and we'll evaluate you from there, but I think you're going to get better, Kevin. If you do, no need to come in, but that's up to you."

Kevin nodded, but thoughts ran through his head. *That's it? Where's the diagnosis? What if I'm dying and you didn't even look for anything?*

"Any questions?" Nourzad asked.

"What do you think it is?" Kevin asked, his eyes squinting.

"Long and short, Kevin. You have headaches. That's all," Nourzad said in a very soothing tone and voice. "You're going to be ok. Millions and millions of people suffer from these suckers. You'll get better. I've seen it."

Kevin nodded, and then said, "Should I have come in sooner?"

Nourzad laughed. "It's funny because most people with headaches are very frightened of them, yet most people put off going to the doctor for them. It's an interesting phenomenon, I guess, but you see it in the literature."

Nourzad extended Kevin his hand and a very big smile.

Kevin stood up, shook his hand and the two looked each other in the eye. Nourzad's eyes spoke promise, Kevin's spoke caution.

"You're gonna be ok." Nourzad squeezed Kevin's hand.

"Hey," Kevin said as Nourzad turned. "Why no Tylenol?"

"I just want to see how the Ibuprofen works on its own," Nourzad said, almost sternly. "No Tylenol. I know the nurse told you that you could keep up with the Tylenol, as did I, but let's not. There could be some issues with using both, so I want to see how the ibu works for now."

"Ok," Kevin responded, wanting to ask about those issues, but he didn't.

Nourzad then turned to Rece as she stood and shook her hand again, resting his hand on top of her palm, then clasping it tight with his other hand. "A real pleasure to meet you, Mrs. Ruscevich." They shook and looked at each other, Rece overlapping her left hand onto Nourzad's right hand as they shook. They looked long at each other, each with a genuine smile.

They released their grip and Nourzad turned to leave then stopped.

"Oh," he said with a gasp. "Pick up your prescription at the front counter as you leave."

"Thanks," Kevin and Rece responded in unison.

Kevin and Rece stood in the doctor's office in silence. Rece looked at her sandals. Kevin rubbed his head. They didn't say a word for what seemed like 5 minutes. Kevin finally spoke up.

"I think we should go."

Rece responded with a very quiet 'Yes'.

They walked out, Kevin picked up his prescription and the married couple walked to the car without saying a word.

--

Kevin drove as Rece sat in the passenger seat. She didn't stop talking. She mentioned Nourzad and the nurses and the questions asked and the plan for Kevin. She seemed very happy to Kevin. Kevin just looked ahead. Rece continued to go on about how pleased she was with the visit. She really wished he had mentioned the drinking and the mixture of medicine, but she understood Kevin's reasons. Kevin shifted a bit, looked at Rece and then back to the road ahead of him. He finally spoke.

"I thought he was a little inappropriate with you," he said.

"Really, Kevin? You're going to do that right after this doctor's appointment?" Rece shot back.

"What," Kevin said, "he was."

"How do you, I mean, Kevin, really?" Rece said, flabbergasted in her tone.

"He was flirting with you," Kevin said.

Rece let out a big laugh. "You're unreal, Kevin, you know that? No, I'm not doing this." She continued laughing.

"Doing what?"

"This. This jealousy thing again. You are crazy," Rece said, but with a smile. "You know how many times I've had to deal with this? Your jealousy? Come on, Kevin."

"I don't think…"

"Oh my God, Kevin, every time a guy talks to me you think he's flirting. Oh my God, Kevin, please."

"I don't…"

"Kevin, I'm asking you please, please do not do this right now."

Kevin didn't speak.

Rece started again. "You know, that was such a positive moment for you, Kevin. He basically told you that you are ok, something you've needed to hear for so long. You are under the care of a doctor now. All positive things, but what does Kevin do? You find another reason to be miserable. That's not healthy, Kevin."

"Alright, I get it," Kevin said, wishing he'd never mentioned anything.

"Kevin. Let's just go home."

"Ok."

WELL, LISA...

Rece picked up the coffee's and walked to the back of the coffee shop. As she did, two men who sat in chairs playing on their computers looked up and followed her with their eyes until she sat down next to her best friend Lisa. Rece pretended not to notice, but she did. She handed Lisa her coffee and the two sat in front of the big picture window. The overcast sky made the seats bearable, as no sun shone through the window.

"So how was the doctor?" Lisa asked.

Rece sipped her coffee and stared at Lisa. She swallowed before she answered.

"Oh my god, Lisa. Not sure."

Lisa sipped then responded, "Explain."

Rece obliged. "Well, look, I love Kevin, but he has headaches. He thinks he's dying. It's all in his head, really. I mean, I'm not denying his pain, but he's never been the type to be able to deal with pain or discomfort. He always jumps to the worst-case scenario and makes things worse for himself. Like when he got his panic attacks, which I think I've told you about, right?"

Lisa nodded yes.

"So, with those, he would get a little heart palpitation or a sharp pain, and in his head, he was dying of a heart attack and made the panic attacks a thousand times worse than they really were. And, Lisa, we'd be up for hours trying to calm him down." Rece paused. "I kinda feel bad talking about him like this because I love him so much, but I just need you to understand."

Lisa interrupted, "No, it's ok, I get it."

Rece took a deep breath and exhaled. "So, he creates these medical dramas, and I think that's what these headaches are. I mean, look, like I said, he has headaches, and I can tell they hurt. But I think he's telling himself it's a brain tumor or aneurysm or something horrible and it's making everything worse."

"That's rough, Rece."

"I know, but that's why I say I don't know how the doctor went. I think the doctor was important because Kevin needed to hear that he's really ok and not dying. If he gets that, then I really think Kevin will be way better off. He can deal with the headaches rationally, and not kill himself emotionally. Do you get it?"

"I do, I really do," Lisa said before sipping her coffee. "So, did it work? It was yesterday, right?"

"Yes, and, ugh, I don't know Lis, I really don't. I mean, on the way home from the doctor he said, well, I don't know. I mean, the doctor really just asked a bunch of questions and really didn't do much. I got what he was doing. He was seeing if there were any symptoms present that would indicate anything serious. He was really good. Good doctor, and pretty good lookin' too, if I may add."

"Wooooooo!" Lisa laughed and smiled.

Rece blushed, "Stop!"

"You said it!" Lisa retorted.

"I'm just commenting on the facts!"

They both laughed pretty hard.

"Ahhhhh...." Rece wound down here laughter. "Anyway, Kevin didn't say much on the way home. We were kind of fighting."

"Why?" asked Lisa, turning serious.

"Stupid Kevin stuff. I don't know, but all this has for some reason brought me back a bit." Rece spoke that a little softer

"To the drinking?" asked Lisa.

Rece looked astonished. "Oh my God, Lis. How do you know these things?"

"You're my best friend. I know you, bud." Lisa smiled. "Tell me."

Rece paused a bit. She looked at her coffee and sipped it a bit. She took another deeper drink, and then spoke. "When he drank, he hid everything. He hid the drinking, or tried to; he hid his work issues, his church issue, pretty much everything. Whenever I sniffed out an issue back then, which wasn't too hard, I'd ask him, 'Hey, everything ok?', 'Hey, is there something wrong?', "Hey, can I help you out?'. I mean, I knew things were going on, but he hid everything from me. I lost trust." Rece paused. Lisa stared at her like the best friend that she was, showing deference and concern and love. "And you know the huge problem we had with it. I mean, look, I dealt with the drinking, but it was the trust issues that hurt me most. I spent the last two years or so regaining that trust, and I have. I regained it with him. But this, I don't know."

"You see the same issues popping up, huh?" Lisa asked in the sweetest of ways.

"I do. I do. He's losing it at times, paranoia. I don't know. Minor things right now, but that's how Kevin starts," Rece answered. "And I don't want them to be popping up because I can't go through it again. If he keeps hiding shit from me, I cannot do it again. Like, he is now mixing the Tylenol and Motrin at the same time, and I knew this, but I thought he was taking one, waiting for three hours, and then taking the other. That's just not good for him, and he's got such an addictive personality. I don't know.""

Lisa grabbed her hand and looked her in the eye. "You went through a lot, Rece. You handled it so well. But you need to step back a bit. The drinking was the drinking. Ok, that was bad. And him hiding stuff from you back then, was just him always hiding the drinking, ya know? He wasn't hiding work issues. The work issues exposed the drinking, which he never wanted you to know about. So, remember, that was all the drinking. I see Kevin being scared here. I really do. I think he's in a lot of pain and just doesn't know what it is. Whatever you think he's hiding now, I think it's just him being scared."

Rece smiled. "You might be right. What would I do without you, Lis?"

The two friends squeezed each other's hands tightly.

"Look," Rece said. "He's just hiding little things now; like that he's had headaches before. He hides that he's in pain sometimes, stuff like that, and I know, seems minor, but I know him. When he hides, it hurts our marriage. I just don't want to go back there. But I really see what you are saying, that I shouldn't compare these issues. I get it. Thanks."

"Oh, my. No thank you's." Lisa smiled at Rece.

Rece looked at her deeply. "Thanks."

Lisa nodded at Rece, pressed her lips together and made the start of a smile. "You're welcome."

WHAT IF I'M DYING?

Kevin slouched on the couch. The T.V. was on, but he wasn't really watching. The boys were outside playing catch, and Kate was at her friend's house. Rece had gone out with her friend, Lisa. Kevin had just taken 800 milligrams of ibuprofen, as prescribed by Dr. Nourzad. The pain was unbearable this day, the pressure bursting at the bridge of his nose, and pressure radiating throughout his head. He was miserable. He prayed the pill would work. When Rece left, he told her he felt fine, not wanting her to be concerned or involved today.

As he lay there, he thought back to his visit with Dr. Nourzad. *Why didn't he investigate this? Why didn't he order tests? What if I'm fucking dying?*

Kevin sat up, rubbed his forehead, stood up, looked out the window at the boys and walked to his office. On his desk were piles of print that needed work. He'd put in for a week off on Tuesday and was due back at work in 5 days. The office had messengered the print to be worked on, but he hadn't touched it, yet. *I'll get to it.*

Kevin opened his laptop and went to Google. He typed in **'Brain Tumor Symptoms'**. The results flashed in seconds. He scrolled through the hits and clicked on BrainTumor.org.

'Headaches can be a sign of brain tumor'

It was the first line he saw as the web page opened. He scrolled through the sight to a page that listed the results of a survey completed by brain tumor patients:

The commonest first presenting symptoms were head-

ache (41%), vomiting (12%), unsteadiness (11%), visual difficulties (10%), educational or behavioral problems (10%), and seizures (9%).[ix]

The lists continued, but Kevin stopped looking. He lay back in his chair and rubbed his hand over his face and onto the top of his skull. The pressure was pounding throughout his head, and the head felt so full he wanted to pop it to release it all.

He went back to the Google results. He clicked on abta.org. Headache was a listed symptom of brain tumors, again. He clicked on **'headache'**.

Features:

Headache is one of the most common symptoms of patients with brain tumors.

Incidence:

About 50% of brain tumor patients experience headaches related to their tumor.[x]

Kevin breathed deep. 50% was too high, he felt. *Unreal. The doctor never really did anything to tell if I had a tumor!* He was angered, frustrated, and depressed. The pain in his head grew worse. He refreshed the page. He re-entered his search as **'Headaches'**.

Kevin clicked on a random page. He read.

Common primary headaches include migraines, cluster headaches, and tension headaches.

Secondary headaches

Secondary headaches are symptoms that happen when another condition stimulates the pain-sensitive nerves of the head. In other words, the headache symptoms can be attributed to another cause.

A wide range of different factors can cause secondary headaches.

These include:

alcohol-induced hangover

brain tumor

blood clots

bleeding in or around the brain

"brain freeze," or ice-cream headaches

carbon monoxide poisoning

concussion

dehydration

glaucoma

teeth-grinding at night

influenza

overuse of pain medication, known as rebound headaches

panic attacks

stroke

As headaches can be a symptom of a serious condition, it is important to seek medical advice if they become more severe, regular, or persistent.[xi]

Kevin read through the web page quickly. The information overwhelmed him. Nothing in it helped ease his mind. He desperately sought relief from the worry. He saw a link for migraines. He clicked on it.

A migraine can cause severe throbbing pain or a pulsing sensation, usually on one side of the head. It's often accompanied by nausea, vomiting, and extreme sensitivity to light and sound. Migraine attacks can last for hours to days, and the pain can be so severe that it interferes with your daily ac-

tivities.[xii]

Kevin sat back and breathed. He thought. His pain was usually in one area of his head, mostly in his forehead. He had some nausea at times, although not bad. His pain really did get so severe all he could do is lie down. *Christ. Do I have migraines?* He rubbed his hands on his face. The pain in his head began to radiate. He remembered reading about tension headaches and how they could last for 15 days straight. He had so many symptoms, but nothing narrowed down the diagnosis. He glanced at the screen and saw:

When to See a Doctor:

Migraines are often undiagnosed and untreated. If you regularly have signs and symptoms of migraine, keep a record of your attacks and how you treated them. Then make an appointment with your doctor to discuss your headaches.

Even if you have a history of headaches, see your doctor if the pattern changes or your headaches suddenly feel different.

See your doctor immediately or go to the emergency room if you have any of the following signs and symptoms, which could indicate a more serious medical problem:

An abrupt, severe headache like a thunderclap

Headache with fever, stiff neck, mental confusion, seizures, double vision, weakness, numbness or trouble speaking

Headache after a head injury, especially if the headache worsens

A chronic headache that is worse after coughing, exertion, straining or a sudden movement

New headache pain after age 50.[xiii]

Kevin took another deep breath. He heard the door open.

The pain was unreal. He heard Rece speaking to the kids and the boys laughing as they followed her inside. He held the mouse, turned his head towards the office door, and stared blankly, spacing out until his mind went numb. *It's not going away...*

MIXTURE

JUNE 2016

The grocery store parking lot was near full. Different colored cars lined the spaces. The sun shone overhead, though Kevin could hear thunder in the distance from the dark clouds in the far southeast. Kevin went around the near doors and pulled down lane number 7 and found a spot about 100 yards from the door. He put the car in park and sat back. His head pounded, with the pain radiating in the forehead. Sharp pains raced down his neck every 20 minutes or so, and pressure built in his skull. It was day 60, or so, since his visit to Dr. Nourzad, and the ibuprofen hadn't been working alone. Although there were moments where his head felt ok since the visit, the pain always came back stronger, it seemed. The only thing that worked for him was taking Motrin and Tylenol at the same time.

Kevin told Rece he'd run to the store for her.

"I need to just get out," he'd told her.

She gave him the grocery list, and off he went, his eyes squinting as he left. "You ok?" Rece asked him as he walked out the door.

"Not really," he responded to her. They said a quick good-bye, and Rece kissed his cheek. Kevin left.

Kevin's plan was to go get more Tylenol. He knew Rece would balk at that suggestion, as the doctor had said to just go the month or so on ibuprofen. It wasn't working, and the headaches were growing worse. The only time the headaches truly were put at bay was when he was taking the Tylenol and ibuprofen. Kevin was desperate. Rece didn't need to know. He didn't want to fight with her about it.

As he entered the store, he grabbed the cart and walked into the dark brown floored store. The fruit and vegetables met him first. He looked at his list and saw tomatoes, onion, grapes and apples on the list. He made his way around the section picking out the best-looking fruit he could. He was particularly pleased with the blue grapes. They looked perfect and were very fresh and ripe. As he turned his cart, he looked up.

"Hey! Hi Kevin!" she said very enthusiastically.

Kevin looked at her and froze a bit. He recognized her.

"Hey, from the church," he said.

She laughed. "Yes!" She laughed a bit more.

"How are you?" he asked.

"Very good! Just pickin' up a few things, you know?"

"Yeah. Same here. No big deal. Just a few things." Kevin smiled.

He looked her over again as she reached into her cart. She was very pretty, he thought. She looked up from her cart and showed him a package. It was lunch meat.

"Have you ever tried this?" she asked, still so enthusiastic.

Kevin looked closely. "No, I haven't. Did you get that at the deli counter?"

"No," she said quickly. "Over there by the cheese. Not a lot of people know about it. So good."

"Well, I think I'll try that. Looks good," Kevin said, still smiling.

She finally extended her hand. "My name is Georgia, by the way. We haven't really met."

Kevin shook her hand. "I don't think we've formally met at all."

"I'm new to the neighborhood," she spoke, and then paused. "Well, not really. I lived here my whole life but after I got married, we moved away, and we just moved back about 6 months ago, or so."

"Oh, nice," Kevin said genuinely.

She continued, "Yeah, my boys are at the school, and that's why I was at that church meeting. I had heard about it and thought someone should be there with you. I'd heard you were going. Anyway, I couldn't stay and that's why I was out of there before we could really meet. Sorry about that." Georgia looked at him.

Kevin responded, "Oh my god, no problem. Thanks for the support."

They both laughed a bit.

"Too bad it didn't work out, huh?" she said.

"Yeah, well, I didn't think they'd change their mind. Just didn't like the policy," Kevin said.

"So cool of you to be there, then," she exclaimed, cutting him off.

"Ah, no big deal," Kevin said, waving his hand at her.

There was a silence as they both looked at each other. Kevin thought quickly how nice the conversation felt. He noticed she smiled a lot as she spoke to him. He felt comfortable. For the briefest of moments, he didn't feel the unbearable pressure in his head.

"Well, Kevin. Nice to see you. Oh, by the way, what grades are your boys in?" she asked.

"Well, I have a son who will be a freshman, and then I have a daughter in 8th, and two more boys, one in 4th and one in 1st."

Kevin spoke almost like memorization.

She smiled even bigger, "Oh nice! I have an 8th grader and 4th grader, too!"

"Cool," Kevin responded. "We'll definitely see each other, then."

"Definitely!" she said, extending her hand again.

They shook.

"See ya soon," Kevin said.

"See ya!" Georgia said as she walked away, pushing her cart.

Kevin watched her a bit as she left him. He thought of Rece. He wondered if she would appreciate the conversation Georgia and he just had. He had a minor pause, as he wondered if he was too interested in Georgia. He shook his head. *Stop it.*

And just like that, the pressure and pain, which had never left, were felt again. Kevin grabbed his head with his right hand and squeezed his eyes tight. He pushed the cart with his left hand and headed right to the medicine aisle.

--

As Kevin pulled into the driveway, he noticed a scattering of bicycles and baseball gloves. Over on the yard he saw Kate and her friends doing flips on their pink gym mats. He parked and got out of the car. He gazed over the fence and saw Rece in her swimsuit, her body golden, looking perfect, lying out on the deck as the two boys swam and chased after a beach ball. In the distance, he heard the thunder again, but the dark clouds remained stationary to the south and east. No one by the pool flinched at the sound.

"Is that you, sweetie?" Rece yelled through the fence.

Kevin responded with a 'yeah'.

"Did you get everything?" Rece asked nicely.

"I think so."

"Great!" Rece responded. "Why don't you put it away and come on out here for a while?"

"Yeah?" Kevin asked.

Rece was walking over to the fence. "Yeah." she said quieter now. "I think the sun and relaxation will help your headaches. Plus, you can stare at me." Rece winked and smiled.

"Ok," Kevin said quietly. "I'll be right out." He winked back and cracked a forced smile.

Somehow, Kevin made it into the house without any of the other million kids around his house interrupting him. He made it to the kitchen and dropped the bags on the table. He still had a few more bags in the van, but knew he had the Tylenol. He found the bottle and opened it. He took two pills and put them in his mouth then walked to the refrigerator, opened a bottle of water, and swallowed the pills. He had taken ibuprofen an hour ago but ran out of Tylenol. He was hoping for relief soon.

After putting the groceries away, Kevin went up to his room to find a bathing suit. His head pounded away at him. He sat on the bed, lifting the suit up his legs. After adjusting the waist, he lay back on the bed. Georgia popped back into his head. He tried to shake her out. He didn't want her in there. He slowly made his way off the bed and walked to the window. He looked out onto the deck and gazed upon Rece. He grabbed two empty bottles of Tylenol that he had hid under his sock drawer. He replaced the old with the new. He then walked out of his room, down the stairs and out onto the deck. But first he strolled casually to the garbage can and buried his evidence.

"Hey! You made it!" It was Rece, gazing out from under her black shades. Her bikini was tight against her amazing body. Kevin gazed at her up and down and couldn't believe her beauty.

"Um, better wait on that. Too many kids around for that." Rece smiled cutely as she said this.

"Ha-ha, no problem, honey." Kevin sat back and took in the hot sun. It beat down on him and the rays felt good against his face and chest. He closed his eyes and Georgia popped into his thoughts again. *What the fuck?*

"Hey, Rece. What should we have for dinner?" It's just what came out of his mouth.

"Your spaghetti!"

"Ok, then."

"How's the head?" Rece asked and sat up.

Kevin closed his eyes and sat back. "Not too bad right now, actually. Sitting out here is already working."

Rece was happy. "I told you!"

"Yeah, you did."

"By the way," Rece started to say. "Declan and Mallory are sleeping over tonight. You ok with that?"

"Sure." Kevin kept his eyes closed.

"Be in a good mood, ok?" Rece asked, now lying back down.

Kevin opened his eyes and saw her lying back in her bikini. "When?"

Rece responded, "Tonight. Be in a good mood. The kids like it when you're cool to their friends."

"I always am," Kevin said, still looking at her body.

"I know. Just do it again tonight."

Whatever. He looked at Rece and wanted her right now. He was very turned on. "Hey, wanna sneak upstairs?" he whispered.

"Um, Kevin, no. Way too many kids about," Rece whispered

back casually, and then paused a bit. "But tomorrow night? You can have me."

At that very moment, there was a tremendous splash into the pool. The water jumped out of the pool and covered Kevin and Rece. Another splash followed, and then another. Blaize and his friends splashed away as Kevin and Rece shook off the water. Rece was laughing. Kevin sat quietly.

"Oh, honey, come on," Rece said to him. "It's kinda funny."

Kevin jumped up, grabbed Rece around the waist, lifted her up and walked towards the pool. Rece slithered in an attempt to escape. She screamed at Kevin.

"Do it, Dad!" Blaize yelled from the pool. His friends seconded it.

Rece flew into the pool. She splashed down and swam to the side. She popped up, her hair falling flat against her back as she wiped her face of the water. She looked at Kevin and stared a few moments at him, then said, "Now that was funny." Blaize and his friends hooted and hollered. Kevin smiled. His head felt full and stuffed, but the pounding was way down, and his neck didn't radiate in pain. In his mind, he thanked the Tylenol.

--

Kevin tucked in Vincent on the top bunk. Below him, James lay on his pillow, playing his hand-held video game. He kissed Vincent on the head and told him he loved him.

"Love you, too, Dad. You're the best ever," Vincent said.

"Thanks, Buddy." Kevin rubbed Vincent's head.

"Alright guys, time to hit it. I love you, have a great sleep, and if you need me, you know where I am."

Before he could finish his statement, the boys were clicking on their video games, peaceful as could be.

"Night, dad. Thanks," James said.

"Yeah, night dad," Vincent added.

As Kevin walked out of the room, they yelled in unison, "Love you!"

Kevin walked down the hall and peeked in cautiously to Blaize's room. To his absolute shock, he found Blaize and his friend, Declan, playing a video game quietly, with a bowl of popcorn and a few cans of pop by their sides.

"Hey, dad."

"Hey, Mr. Ruscevich"

Neither boy looked up.

"Ha-ha, hey guys. All good?" Kevin asked.

"Oh yeah! We're in a group game. So cool!" Blaize said.

"Yeah, Mr. Ruscevich. So cool," Declan added.

"Alright guys. Have fun," Kevin said as he walked away.

Turning towards his room he saw Rece sitting on Kate's bed, the two rehashing the day. On the floor was her friend, Mallory. It was the easiest, quietest sleepover ever, thought Kevin. He walked in.

"Hey, dad." Kate was the first to speak up. She smiled big at him.

"Well", Kevin started. "I just want to say this is the best sleepover of all time. So peaceful and quiet."

"They're just getting started, right girls?!" Rece yelled loudly.

The girls laughed hard. "Woo hoo!" Kate hooted, while pumping her fist.

"We're gonna party!" Mallory joined in laughing hysterically.

"Alright, alright, you animals. Have fun," Kevin said sarcastically. He walked out into the hallway.

"Be right in, hon!" Rece yelled to him.

"Sounds good," Kevin said, his voice trailing.

He walked into the bedroom. He plopped onto the bed and laid his head back on his pillows. He closed his eyes and was very relaxed. His head was full. He could feel the pressure, but it was currently at bay. That's how it felt at the full peak of his Motrin/Tylenol cocktail. His head would remain full. The pressure was still there, but the pain lowered, and he could relax a bit.

At this point, it was time to take another cocktail. The pills were next to his bed on his table. He took two of each, swallowed them down with water, and then lay back again. He put the TV on, and he had a moment of bliss.

He heard Rece say 'goodnight' to all the kids, then he heard her go downstairs. *Probably going to get water.* He had his, so that should be it for the night. He was ready to sleep. His head was in a good place to sleep. There wasn't a whole lot of pain, and he was tired. He wanted to take advantage of the situation.

Rece walked in with a medicine bottle in her right hand. She walked up to Kevin and stopped at the side of the bed. Kevin knew instantly what it was. Rece turned her hand outward and to the right exposing the Tylenol bottle.

"What's this?" she asked in an angry whisper.

Kevin's head and eyes were on the bottle. After her question, he raised his eyes towards her. "Look, you know what it is."

Rece stuck the bottle in his face. "You're not supposed to take these!"

"Whad'ya mean, 'not supposed to'? I mean, it was a suggestion by the doctor," Kevin responded, trying to whisper.

"No, it wasn't, Kevin. It wasn't a suggestion. It was your treatment plan." Rece was very aggravated. "You go to a doctor, after months and months of pain, you can't take it, you're going to die, and he gives you a plan and you're already blowing him off? Really?"

"Treatment plan? He told me to take pain medicine. That's not a treatment plan. Besides, it wasn't working. The pain was getting worse every day and it sucked!" Kevin's voice was rising.

Rece spoke back in a quiet yell, "Don't you dare raise your voice with kids sleeping over here."

"Oh my god, I was laying here quietly watching T.V.!" Kevin responded.

"Fine, you know what? It pisses me off you bought these. It pisses me off you're not following the plan and it pisses me off that, once again, you hide shit from me!" Rece stared at him.

"Hide shit?" Kevin questioned.

Rece laughed a sarcastic laugh. "Whatever, you dick. If you want to pretend to be clueless, go ahead."

"Now we're swearing?" Kevin wondered aloud.

"Whatever." Rece began to walk away.

"Look! Ok? Yes, I bought Tylenol." *How the fuck did she find that bottle?*

Kevin got up and followed her towards the bathroom. Rece stopped as Kevin continued. "I knew you'd disagree, Rece, so I bought them without telling you."

"Just like you always do, Kevin," Rece interrupted. "For how long, huh? You saw him two months ago. How long have you been sneaking?"

Kevin responded in a hushed and whispered yell, "Rece this fucking thing hurts every fucking day. Every day, all day, and sometimes I can't fucking take one more minute of it. It's not going away. And the one thing that works a little bit is when I mix the medicine. I need some fucking relief!" Kevin stopped and waited for her response.

"You don't get it." Rece walked into the bathroom. Kevin followed.

"Get what?" Kevin asked a little louder.

"You lie! Always!" They were toe to toe.

"How is that a lie?" Kevin asked, raising his hands.

Rece answered, "Because, it's sneaky, and sneakiness is a lie. You lie when shit gets bad. Always have, and, obviously, always will!"

"You don't care about this pain?" Kevin asked sympathetically.

"Ohhhhh! Now that's funny right there, Kevin. Fuck that." Rece reached around Kevin and closed the bathroom door. "You know I do! That's a bullshit question, and you know it. I've been helping you with these headaches from the start. I got you to go to the doctor, and I was making sure you did what he told you. You're the one who didn't listen to him. So, don't tell me I don't care. You're a sneak. You know it. Don't spin it on me now that this is at all about me not caring about you." Rece opened the door and walked back into the bedroom and left Kevin standing alone.

Kevin paused, looked at the ceiling, took a deep breath, and started to go back into the bedroom. He stopped short. A wave of pain raced through his head. A shudder violently erupted on the right side of his head and stuck there. Then he heard it. There was laughter in his head. *Is that laughter?* The laughter shrieked along with the steady jackhammer in his head, with waves and waves of pressure building and colliding on the right side. He felt sick to his stomach. He didn't want to move forward to let Rece see his pain. He walked back into the bathroom and sat a second on the toilet seat, his face buried in his hands.

"Are you coming in here?" Rece asked impatiently.

Kevin paused a bit, but answered, "One sec."

He pressed his eyes and forehead into his hands. He rubbed hard, hoping to dislodge the pain. He stood up and felt dizzy. He began to walk into the bedroom. It was dark. Rece had the T.V. on but didn't seem interested in anything that was on. He walked to his side of the bed and plopped down. The pain was violent. Rece didn't speak. Kevin lay there, more concerned about his head at that point. In moments, to him, Rece was asleep. Kevin was alone in his pain. He wanted dearly to wake her but didn't dare. He lay there until the new cocktail kicked in. Before too long he felt the isolated deadness of the medicine. In the faintest of faint sounds, he thought he heard muffled laughter. And then, it grew louder in his head. *Jesus fucking Christ.*

BURST

Dr. Nourzad lit the final candle on the table and sat himself down to eat. He had made a beef roast earlier in the afternoon, with hopes for a family meal that evening. The call from the hospital interrupted him. Marty Matthew had passed away.

'He was in route to the ER, doctor, and the aneurysm burst. The medics did the best they could..."

Nourzad cut in. "I know they did."

"So, Dr. Fry mentioned you were his primary, so I thought I'd let you know. He told me how close..."

"Thank you very much." Nourzad cut her off in the polite Dr. Nourzad way, being kind and quiet in his tone.

Nourzad blew out the candle, grabbed his keys and drove to Hope. He arrived as the funeral home was taking Marty away. He was able to convince the nurse to get him Marty's chart. He saw that Marty presented to Dr. Herr.

'pt presnts w/ aneu; arst imm up presnt0; crash cart; resus0 atts fail; tod 1801'

Nourzad gave the chart back to the nurse and walked out.

--

Once again at home, he set the table for his dinner. As he sat at the dinner table, he looked around at the 4 candles, each on an empty plate, corresponding to where his wife and children would sit each night at dinner. His hands were folded as his chin sat upon his knuckles. Thoughts of his parents, his family and Marty raced through his head. He took deep breaths as he went around the table and pictured first his wife, her deep black hair falling all around her as she smiled her pretty smile while listening to her children's stories. He then gazed upon each child as they ate and spoke and grew louder and louder, each vying for time to tell their stories.

Nourzad smiled as a tear ran down his right cheek. His stomach twisted in knots, and the pain of missing his family overwhelmed him. He sat back and pushed his plate away. The gravy from the potatoes spilled onto the table. Nourzad took a deep breath as a million memories and thoughts spilled through his brain: his wedding, his mother and father's funeral, the birth of his children, Christmases and Easters, birthday parties and intimacy with his wife. Nourzad stood in an instant and lunged over the table leading with his right arm. It landed on the table and he swung it violently to the left as he screamed and knocked the plates and candles off the table and onto the ground, the plates smashing as Nourzad lay on the table unable to move as the last breath of his scream escaped his mouth.

"Fuck! Fuck! Fuck!" Nourzad screamed. "I'm sorry! I'm sorry! I'm so sorry!"

Nourzad lay on the table, his eyes open, staring at nothing. He just breathed.

WANT THEM?

Kevin's eyes opened as the thought of Rece swooshed though his head. He wasn't sure how long he was asleep. The last time he looked, his phone indicated 4:12 a.m. His head felt very full, but the pain was minimal. *It's just fucking waiting*. He knew better than to move quickly, though. He knew with any movement he would awaken the pain. *I don't want to piss it off*. He just lay still. He turned his eyes to his left and noticed Rece wasn't there. It was Sunday morning, he knew. He remembered the sleepovers and how minimally intrusive they were. It was odd for Rece to be missing in the morning. She always asked Kevin to get her coffee. It was their thing.

Downstairs he heard the kids laughing and could faintly hear Rece talking to someone. He immediately wanted to be down there with everybody. He moved slowly as he sat up. The muted pain felt the movement and started to shudder. Pain raced into his forehead and sat against his skull. It was a pounding pain now, while the pressure had moved to the back. He reached to the end table for his ibuprofen. He twisted open the cap, grabbed a pill, threw it in his mouth and reached for a water. His bottle was empty.

"Fucking Christ," he said.

He walked very slowly to the bathroom, the pain and pressure mimicking his every move. He turned on the faucet and bent over to get water. He got enough to swallow the pill. He so desperately wanted to chase that with a Tylenol, but he knew better to wait a bit.

"God, fuck," he whispered to himself. He couldn't believe

this pain. He walked out of the bathroom and made his way to the hallway. He used the wall to keep him up as he walked to the stairs. He was going to fake it to make it this day. He didn't want anybody to see him in pain nor to notice how he felt. He took each step carefully, his hand still against the wall as he made his way downstairs. The voices grew louder, and he saw Rece by the back door as he turned down the final few steps.

"Dad!!" screamed Kate, as she sat on the couch with Mallory.

"Hey. Mr. R!" Mallory chimed in.

Rece turned. "Hey hon! How are you?" She was smiling.

Kevin smiled. It was fake, but it was a smile. "Hey, how's it going down here?"

Rece walked right towards Kevin. "What's wrong?"

"Oh, nothing. Just woke up. Little groggy, maybe, but all good."

Rece leaned in and raised up a bit to kiss Kevin's forehead. "Good. You have the headache face going. Glad you are ok."

"You made pancakes?" Kevin asked.

Rece turned back towards him as she walked into the kitchen. "Yes. I saved you a bunch. I'll get them for you. Hungry?"

"Actually, I am," Kevin responded. "Hey, where are the boys?"

Kate spoke up. "Outside. Baseball, basketball, I don't know. What did they say, Mall?"

"Basketball."

"Basketball, dad," Kate answered in her monotone voice.

Kevin smiled a bit, genuinely, as he glanced at Kate. He walked forward and sat at the table just as Rece placed his hot plate on the table.

"Orange juice?" she asked.

"Yes, please."

"Ice?"

"Nah, that's ok."

"It's really not a problem."

"No ice, thanks."

"Sure, you're ok?" Rece asked, staring at Kevin.

"Yeah," Kevin responded looking down.

Rece walked back into the kitchen and grabbed something off the counter. She paused a bit as she looked at it, then turned and walked to Kevin. She placed it right next to him on the table. Kevin looked. It was the Tylenol container. Kevin stared at it as the pancake on his fork sat in suspension. He looked up at Rece.

"Want them?" Rece asked, her eyes squinting a bit.

They stared at each other for what felt like hours, each one trying desperately to penetrate each other's' thoughts. Kevin was the first to look away, for the briefest of moments. He then looked right back at Rece, her eyes not blinking a bit. Kevin grabbed the container. "I'll hold onto it."

Rece blinked, pressed her lips together, and then breathed out. "Mm, hm."

"I'm not gonna take one, I'll just hold onto them," Kevin said, squeezing the bottle.

Rece looked back and smiled, "You can take them. It's your pain, Kevin. You know best. And you know what? I appreciate the honesty."

Kevin smiled. "I'm sorry. I love you."

Rece leaned in and kissed him. "I know."

Kevin began to eat his pancakes. Rece brought him his orange juice. She placed it right next to him, then bent over and kissed him on the head again. "I love you."

Kevin didn't hesitate, but said quietly, "I love you, too."

HOPE...

Hope Hospital presents as a bright smile on a dark day. Rows and rows of bright flowers adorn the driveways and walkways, and perfectly kept hedges stand at attention before the tall and shiny glass windows in the front. The bright red yellow brick walls flow upward as you look upon it. Bright lights shine downward at night, lighting up visitors and the fountain placed right by the front door.

Dr. Nourzad raced up the driveway in his black ford mustang, looking shiny and new. He screeched as he reached the front door. A valet walked towards him.

"Yes, can I...oh, Dr. Nourzad, everything good?"

"You can move this wherever you need to. I just need to get inside." Nourzad scrambled through the crowd to enter the hospital. He turned back to the valet and yelled, "Just leave the keys in the normal spot with a note!" Nourzad then entered the hospital.

He ran past the welcome desk that sat circular in the middle of the hallway of the entrance. A woman looked up and said hello to Nourzad as he ran past. Nourzad ran to the right hallway, moving quickly past patients, doctors and visitors. He reached the far back hallway and turned right. Fewer people blocked his way at that point. He noticed a few doctors looking at charts, not noticing him pass. He reached the back door which read, 'EMERGENCY ENTRANCE – PERSONNEL ONLY'. Nourzad burst through the big metal doors and looked up at the television screen above:

Ravenswood, Archibald – Room 4 – Walsh, Dougherty

Fuck.

Nourzad b-lined it over to room 4. He threw open the curtain and saw three doctors working over Archie Ravenswood. Dr. Walsh was one of the doctors. No one batted an eye when he barged in.

"What's the problem?" Nourzad asked loudly.

No one answered. The doctors worked furiously over the body. A nurse turned her head and recognized Frank.

"Doctor, I think we have this covered." She walked over to Nourzad and tried to passively lead him out of the room. Nourzad looked at her arm, and then refocused on the table.

"Guys, what is it?" he asked to the anonymous doctors.

"Cardiac arrest, Frank. Not looking good." It was a voice he recognized.

"What the fuck?!" Nourzad whispered to himself.

"Frank!" the doctor yelled while working on the patient. "We got this!"

"He's fighting leukemia...." Nourzad's voice trailed off into a conciliatory tone. "Why wasn't I called?"

Nourzad tried to peek through the doctors to see Archie one last time. The nurse put her hand on Nourzad's shoulder.

"Doctor"

Nourzad turned to her. "Huh? Yeah, ok. Um, alright." Nourzad wiped his face with his hand and turned and walked out.

Outside the curtain he heard a doctor say, 'That's it.'

Archie Ravenswood was dead.

Nourzad sunk his head low and breathed with purpose. His

head shook side to side as he looked up at the nurse. "How long was he here?" he asked.

The nurse looked at him gently and responded, "A couple hours."

"What do you mean a couple hours? For a heart attack? How'd he come in?" Nourzad now stood.

"He wasn't in arrest when he came in. He complained of some pain in his chest. They were testing and observing a while when he arrested." The nurse looked Nourzad in the eyes.

"Jesus Christ." Nourzad wiped his brow. "Did they even know?"

"Know what?" The nurse asked.

"That he had leukemia." Nourzad whispered hopelessly.

"Doctor, I don't know."

Nourzad placed his hand on her shoulder and thanked her. He put his hands on his hips, looked to the ceiling and walked out.

--

Outside the hospital, Dr. Nourzad sat alone. A soft drizzle had begun to fall. A tall man with a cigarette walked by and Nourzad waved his hand at him.

"Got an extra?" Nourzad asked.

The stranger obliged, and lit Nourzad's cigarette. Nourzad thanked him and sat back and took in a deep drag. The rush of nicotine into his body calmed his soul for the moment. He was completely relaxed in that single moment. He thought of his family. *I wish they were home right now.* He wished Jan was there. He wanted to tell her of his day, and how he lost two patients recently. He wanted to tell her that he missed his parents. He wanted to tell her he missed her! Nourzad dragged on the cigarette, and then looked at it to see how much was left. He felt a pat on the back.

"Those things'll kill ya, Frank."

Nourzad turned quickly. It was Dr. Phillip Jensen, an E.R. doctor at Hope. Nourzad had met him years ago and had worked with him on a few cases.

Nourzad smiled at him and laughed a bit under his breath. He extended his hand. They shook as Dr. Jensen sat down next to him.

"My second loss recently, back to back," Nourzad told him in a hushed tone.

"That's not easy, Frank."

"No, it's not." Nourzad dragged on the cigarette, drawing every last bit of smoke out of it.

Dr. Jensen crossed his legs and put his hand on his knee. He looked to the sky and spoke. "But you work with the old, buddy. Old people have a way of dyin' on ya." Dr. Jensen spoke deliberately.

"Shoulda went into pediatrics, huh?" Nourzad said laughing.

"Kinda the nature of the beast. You should be used to it by now, no?"

"Not really. And it's been a while. Hadn't lost a patient in a while. Now, two in short period of time."

"Well, that's the give and take, Frank," Dr. Jensen said.

Nourzad looked at him, "Give and take?"

"Give and take. The longer you keep them alive, the longer they live, the closer you get to them. Makes it harder when they pass."

The two sat in silence for a moment. The mist was turning more into a drizzle, but neither doctor seemed to mind. People filed in and out of Hope, walking right by, oblivious to the two doctors.

"E.R. is different," Nourzad said as a statement. He then crushed the butt of his cigarette against the bench. Dr. Jensen watched like a jealous ex-smoker.

Jensen then looked up at him, nodded and smiled, "Oh yeah. Very little attachment, Frank. They come in and out. I like it that way. Always have." He paused a bit.

"I don't know." Nourzad looked up at the sky and wrung his hands. He desperately wanted another cigarette. "I like the attachment. I like to know how it all turns out. I like being on that path with them as they make their way through it."

"Sure, you do, Frank. That's you," Dr. Jensen said immediately.

The drizzle steadied. Neither doctor moved much. Nourzad took a deep breath. "That's me?"

Dr. Jensen turned on the bench to look at Nourzad. "Look, Frank, it's just a different ballgame. In the E.R., the patient comes in, you evaluate them, and you save their life, in theory. It's a lifesaving, triage world in there. We sew 'em up and move them on. It's what I like. I like the challenge of the quick diagnosis in a critical stage. After that, what happens to them is what happens to them, but at that moment, assuming they move on from the E.R., I've done my job; I've had my effect on that person's life. The next one is always coming in soon after. I don't have time to follow them. Kind of understand?"

"Yeah, I do. I kinda wish I had that frenzy at times."

"I'm sure you do, Frank. It's just in a different setting."

Nourzad wrung his hands again, "I find myself so attached to each patient. I have this need to know what happens at each stage. I don't know."

"Like I said, that's you. That's in you, Frank. That's your need. Now, I know it probably weighs on you. And, I know I see you around here a lot. And I heard about you and Walsh."

Nourzad looked at him intently.

Dr. Jensen continued. "Yeah, look, he's a hot head. I see no problem with the primary physician showing up, I mean, that's the guy who knows, right? He's the guy, or girl, who has the best pulse of the patient, so, yes, I have no problem. On the flip side, I see Walsh's point to a tiny, tiny extent. Look, it's his E.R. Hell, I don't like some of his rules and I've been here longer than him. Still, he's the boss."

"He's not my boss."

"I know, I know, but he runs the E.R. and it's his show. He over-reacted to you, but what are ya gonna do."

"I should have kicked his ass."

"Frank, Frank, cigarettes and swear words? This ain't you."

Dr. Nourzad looked Dr. Jensen in the eyes. "Why'd you come out here, Phil?"

"I knew you'd be upset. I know you. Wanted to make sure you were ok."

"How'd you know I was sitting out here?"

"I asked Frida to come out here and look for you. She came back and told me."

"I appreciate it, Phil. I'll be ok. Thanks."

"Will be ok isn't ok, pal."

"I know, I know. I'm kinda working through some things here."

"You just lost your family, Frank. You got what appears to be a couple of rough work weeks going," he said, looking right at Frank. "Maybe a few days off. Go hang out with Rae and her family a bit."

"Nah, can't. I got patients all month," Frank responded. "No time to take off. Besides, it's the job that keeps me going."

Dr. Jensen looked at Nourzad very intently. "Look, Frank. I've been hearing that my whole life from doctors. But I gotta tell ya, sometimes, it's the job that brings you down. Just be careful. Just take care of you first." He stood up as the rain began to fall harder. "I have to go back in, Frank. You take care, and if you need anything let me know, ok?"

"You got it, Phil."

Dr. Jensen began his quick walk back into the hospital. As he approached the door, Nourzad stood up and yelled, "Phil!! Phil!!"

Dr. Jensen turned. Nourzad nodded at him. Dr. Jensen nodded back.

SOMETHING'S WRONG

"Are you ok?" Rece asked while carrying the full laundry basket into the bedroom. "Kevin?"

Kevin lay on the bed on his back. His knees were bent, and he had his hands covering his eyes. He was dressed the same as he was for breakfast.

"I thought you were gonna shower," Rece said to him as she laid the laundry basket on the bed next to Kevin. "Kevin!"

"Rece, fuck."

"Your head?"

"Yeah. It fucking hurts."

"What is it? You seemed good today," Rece said as she sat on the bed and touched Kevin's arm.

"The pressure is just so fucking bad. It's pretty blinding right now."

"Ok, tell me where it is."

"Right here." Kevin pointed to the bridge of his nose. "Then it moves upwards to here." Kevin rubbed the top of his head as he finished the explanation. "And the pressure is all over."

"Same as it kinda always has been?" Rece asked very business-like.

"I don't know, I mean, the forehead part, yes, I guess. But the pressure, I don't know, is usually just on one side. Now it's

190

everywhere."

"Ok. Did you take, well, what did you take today?"

"Just the ibuprofen," Kevin answered, still in the same position.

"What do you want to do?" Rece asked.

"This is, honestly, the worst it's ever felt, Rece."

"Is it?" she asked, rubbing his arm a bit.

"Yeah. This isn't right, man. Not to be dramatic, but something's got to be wrong."

"What do you want to do?" she asked again.

"I think I should go to the E.R., I mean, this, this is pretty fucking bad." He pressed his hands so deeply into his head.

"Ok." Rece took her hand off his arm.

"Really?" Kevin asked, his hands now off his face.

"If you want to go to the E.R., let's go," Rece said. "I think it's a good idea."

Kevin didn't respond. He lay motionless. He breathed heavy and Rece stood up and looked at him. Kevin finally sat up and looked at Rece, his eyes squinted, and pain showing all over his face.

"Kevin?" Rece asked.

"Ok. We need to go. This just isn't right," he said.

"Ok, let me tell Blaize." Rece walked out of the room.

He sat on the bed and heard her telling Blaize he had to watch the kids. Blaize sounded upset at first, but that changed to understanding as Rece explained more. He heard Rece walking back and debated confronting her on her apparent displeasure at the situation. He knew she'd be mad at any inquiry. The pressure in his head was relentless. There was faint laughter. He rubbed his hands all over his skull, messing his short hair. "Shut the fuck up," he said softly, but out loud.

"Huh?" Rece asked, suddenly standing at the doorway.

"No," Kevin said, embarrassed he was caught talking to his head, "no, I was just, look, it's nothing."

"Ok, well, are you ready?" she asked.

"Baby, you don't have to go," Kevin said while standing up.

"I already asked Blaize to watch the kids, plus, I'm just going."

"That's ok, I'll just go."

"Why?"

"Because it's stupid."

"No, Kevin, it isn't."

"You seem upset."

"Don't try to start a fight, silly. I mean, come on."

"No, I'm not, it's just…"

Rece breathed out hard and folded her hands, "Look, sweetie, it's all good. I mean, we were just at the doctor and he told you that you were ok. You didn't necessarily follow his plan, so the pain is still there. But I am not upset with you at all. Not one bit."

Kevin stared at her. "I appreciate that, Rece, I really do."

Kevin got up and walked towards the bathroom then bent over putting his hands on his knees.

"What is it?" Rece asked, walking towards him.

"It just hurts. It's killing me."

"Ok, ok, let's just go, Kevin."

"Rece, I haven't had a normal day in so long, I cannot even

remember." Kevin moved towards the bed and sat.

"Let me get my shoes and we'll go." Rece said, rubbing his shoulder quickly as she walked by. "It's going to be ok, Kev."

--

The walk from the parking lot to the E.R. felt long. Kevin and Rece walked side by side but said little. There was a breeze which made the air feel a bit cold. It was late September and the fall Chicago chills were approaching. Kevin zipped up his black jacket and turned his collar up. Rece buried her hands in her pockets. An ambulance whizzed by, and there were two police cars right outside the door of the E.R. Several people milled about, and Kevin and Rece entered.

"Crap," Kevin said right when they walked towards check in. "I didn't call in."

"Kevin," Rece responded disappointingly. "don't worry about all that stuff."

"Yeah, I'll call when we get home and say I was fainting from pain in my head and couldn't call. That's an exception."

"It'll be fine," Rece said.

"No. If you can't call because it's bad and have to get right to the E.R. they waive the phone call."

"Ok, hon," Rece said, looking at Kevin with a bit of sadness in her eyes.

"Yeah," Kevin said, seemingly to himself, "that'll work."

Rece patted his back.

--

"Next?" The older woman at the desk checked Kevin in.

The E.R. was quiet that early afternoon. There were very few people seated in the waiting area, and the hall to the E.R. rooms was empty, but for a few doctors and nurses standing around talking. Kevin had expected a very long wait, but was called in right after they were checked in. He entered the triage room greeted by a smiling male nurse. Rece followed behind.

"Hi, Kevin. My name is Mike. Have a seat." Mike sat down as well. He was dressed in a light blue shirt and darker blue pants. It was standard hospital employee garb.

Mike wrapped Kevin's arm in the blood pressure apparatus and asked Kevin what brought him in.

"I've been having really bad headaches for months and months now, and today it just exploded on me and just thought it was so bad I should come in."

"Ok," Mike said calmly as he began the blood pressure reading.

"The headaches have been for a couple months?" Mike asked.

"Yeah. More than that. Pretty much non-stop. I've had a few good days, I guess, maybe, but for the most part, I've had a constant one for too long."

"Any other symptoms that come with the headaches? Any today?" Mike asked, as he read the reading.

"I mean, I've had some queasiness, upset stomach, neck pains, but nothing real big."

"135/88. Not too bad, Kevin. It's a little high, but you're probably just nervous."

"Yeah," Kevin said quietly.

Nurse Mike then took Kevin's temperature and checked his pulse ox.

"Your temperature is fine, and your pulse ox is perfect."

"Ok," Kevin responded robotically.

"I'm going to take you into room 4. Follow me."

Kevin and Rece followed Mike through the two doors leading from triage to the main E.R. There were four rooms to the left as they entered. There was a din of constant noise, a sort of a buzz, with beeps and short sirens going off here and there. The walls were a light blue, with white trim. Two doctors stood and stared at a computer. To the left, other doctors were holding a woman down, trying to give her a shot. As they approached the far room, a cart with three doctors raced around past Kevin and Rece. It was an overweight, older gentleman who looked very much in distress.

"Right in here, guys." Mike led them into room 4. "The doctor will be right in."

Kevin and Rece sat in Emergency Room # 4 at Hope Hospital. They both studied the walls and floors. Kevin checked out the ceiling at one point. His head pulsated. The pain in his forehead was getting worse. He was glad they were here. As he sat there in the silence, he thought, *Finally, some answers.*

"Make sure you tell them everything," Rece asked while winking at him.

Kevin smiled. "I will," he responded quietly.

They sat some more, neither saying a word. It felt like a half an hour but was probably more like ten to fifteen minutes. Finally, a doctor and two nurses entered. They each introduced themselves. The doctor was a young female with long brown hair. She had freckles and looked to be 30 or 31 years old to Kevin. Her name was Dr. Herr.

"So, Kevin, you have headaches? Had them a while?" the young female E.R. doctor asked and stated to Kevin.

"Yes. Had them for quite a while now."

"And, you've been to the doctor before on these?"

"Yes," Kevin said. "I saw Dr. Nourzad a while back."

"Well, he is very good, so…"

"I've heard."

"Ok…" Dr. Herr looked into his eyes as she scooted close to him. She then asked Kevin to follow her finger as she moved it right to left and left to right. "Good," she said as Kevin followed all the directions.

"Raise your hands above your head," she ordered to Kevin as the two nurses watched. "Good. Hold them there." She looked at both arms.

"Ok, put your hands to the side," Dr. Herr asked. Kevin obliged. "Good, now take your right index finger and touch the tip of your nose." Kevin did. "Good. Now the other hand." Kevin did the same with the other hand. "Good. Now stand up and do the same thing."

The doctored stared intently at Kevin as he did it.

The doctor took a few notes. "Now, put both hands out like this." Dr. Herr straightened her arms out in front of her and made fists. Kevin followed suit. "Now, I'm going to hold them down and you push upwards." Dr. Herr pushed down and Kevin pushed upwards. It looked like an arm-wrestling match.

"Good. Now let's do it with the legs," Dr. Herr told him to sit and then grabbed his legs and pushed down. Kevin pushed them upwards.

"Ok, good. Stand up."

Kevin stood up off the table.

"See that thin line?" Dr. Herr asked and pointed.

"Yes."

"Walk it from here to there, turn around and walk it back."

Kevin walked the line steady and perfect.

"Good. You can sit down now."

Dr. Herr conferred with the nurses and the nurses then left. Dr. Herr grabbed a chair and sat down in front of Kevin.

"Ok, Kevin, the headaches are pretty bad?" she asked.

"Yes. They've gotten progressively worse, it seems," Kevin responded.

"Well, and I mean no disrespect here, but with headaches, we hear that a lot, that the headaches are getting worse. But sometimes it's just a factor of the time going by and the frustration level with the headaches. A lot of times, after a patient thinks about it, they kinda rescind and agree that the pain is probably the same and hasn't got worse."

She stared at Kevin.

Kevin spoke. "Yeah, I mean, I hear you. They were bad at first, too, then maybe got a little less severe, but now are bad again."

"Ok, so, the pain now and at the beginning were pretty similar, with a little break in the pain in the middle?"

"Yes, I guess, I don't even know anymore.""

"Ok, and you say about 8 months or so on these headaches?"

"Yes, I guess."

"Any throwing up? Fainting? Seizures?"

"No."

"Any blurred vision? Loss of sight? Hearing?"

"No."

"Does light affect your headaches? That is, does light ever trigger them?"

"No, I don't think so."

"But the headaches are a bit debilitating?"

"Yes."

"Where exactly does it hurt?"

Kevin told her the brunt was always in the forehead and the bridge of the nose. He told her of the constant pressure and the sledgehammer that occasionally hit. He told her the pressure was constant now, and the forehead pain was more prominent now.

"And, you've been taking ibuprofen? Acetaminophen?" she asked.

"Both."

Rece jumped in. "He was at Dr. Perez' office the other day and Dr. Nourzad told him to just take the ibuprofen."

Dr. Herr turned back to Kevin after briefly looking at Rece as she spoke. "Did you do that?"

"No. I mean, for a day or two, and then I just was in too much pain, so I took some Tylenol."

"Ok, well, he probably was worried about rebound headaches. Anyway, the cocktail of the two worked?"

"Yes."

"Did the ibuprofen work alone?"

"At first, then no."

"After you started taking the Tylenol?"

"I guess."

"Ok. Kevin, there are a lot of different headaches, with a lot of different symptoms."

"Ok." Kevin acted as if he'd heard this before.

"Migraines commonly occur with an aura, like vision loss, impairment, tingling in the arms, or even a speech problem. With the migraine comes excruciating pain, sometimes just on one side of the head, and it can pulsate, which could also mimic pressure, like you indicate. There are also what are called tension headaches, and tension headaches are common. Tension headaches can be like a vice around your head that just always feels like it's tightening. Tension headaches can go on and on, as well. Some people go fifteen to twenty days at a time, whereas migraines usually last under three days. Um, cluster headaches aren't as common but can bring very intense pain. Cluster headaches appear out of the blue, like that, and really affect an eye, one or the other, with the pain focusing around the eye or eyes. The thing about the cluster headache is the duration. I've read where cases can last months or even up to a year. Then they go away. Um, but, with the cluster headaches, we generally see red eye, stuffy nose, restlessness, um, droopy eyelid, stuff like that. Then you just have your general headache, Kevin, with no real label. I mean, here I did just describe three major types of headaches, each with symptoms of their own, but the symptoms do crossover. Also, you could have one symptom of, say, a migraine, but have no others. So, sometimes, we just label it as a headache."

Dr. Herr finally stopped.

"Ok," Kevin said, almost like a question.

"I don't see any major symptom here, Kevin. I think you have some serious headaches, but in terms of a diagnosis, we should probably defer to Dr. Nourzad. My job is to assess your immediate health, and I see no problem with that."

"Ok. So, just go home?" Kevin asked very disappointedly.

"Well yes, but, know, the over the counters work for you, in some ways, and Dr. Nourzad can offer other meds if the headaches continue."

"So, you see no real worry?" Rece asked.

"No," Dr. Herr said, not looking at Rece. "No, you're ok, Kevin, but you do have headaches which can be dealt with. So, I would check in with Dr. Nourzad in the near future and see where you go."

"Ok," Kevin answered.

"Ok, great, I'm going to give you 800 milligram ibuprofen pills, so you can take those, and I just have to fill out a few forms then you'll be set to go."

"Ok, thanks."

"Yep."

And with that, Dr. Herr was gone, and Kevin was left to go home and deal with the pain. Kevin and Rece sat in the quiet room.

"Whatever," Kevin said.

"I know, sweetie. I know you wanted more out of this, but this is two doctors now who say you're ok." There was a pause. "Doesn't that make you feel better?"

"I guess. I just want the pain to go away."

"I know, but the stress of worrying about your health should go down. You know you're not dying."

"Yeah." Kevin rubbed his face with his palms.

"Look," Rece said, "while you wait for the discharge papers, I'm going to step outside. I just need a breath of fresh air."

"No problem," Kevin said.

Rece kissed Kevin on the forehead and walked out.

--

She stepped out into the ER driveway and walked a bit to

the side of the hospital. The nice breeze caressed her face and the bright sun warmed her. She stood on the walkway admiring the people going in and out. She breathed in the fresh air and turned when she heard footsteps.

"Rece, right?"

Rece looked at the man and it took her a moment to remember. "Dr. Nourzad?"

Nourzad stepped closer and shook her hand. "Yes," he said, "It's so nice to see you."

Rece smiled big and returned the long handshake. "Good to see you, too."

"What brings you here?" Nourzad asked. "Is it Kevin?"

Rece looked around and then nodded. "Yes, he was in the ER, but he's ok."

"The headache?" Nourzad asked.

"Yes, it was really bothering him, but, um, they checked him out and said he was fine."

"Is he inside still?" Nourzad asked.

"Yes, he's just waiting on discharge papers, so I told him I'd wait out here for him. The stale hospital air was getting to me." Rece laughed.

"Ah, yes, well, eventually you get used to it," Nourzad said with a smile.

There was an awkward pause as the two looked at each other.

"Hey," Nourzad said, "well, maybe I should go see Kevin. I think I told him to come see me a month after we met. I didn't hear from him, so I thought he was ok."

Rece instinctively grabbed Nourzad's arm as he turned a bit. As she did, Nourzad looked at her face. Rece blushed. "No," she said. "Please don't. I think he's good. I think it's best for him that another doctor has told him he's ok. And, he didn't come see you, I guess, because that's just how he is."

Nourzad smiled at her. "You seem like a great wife."

Rece smiled. "I just need him to come to grips with his headaches."

"He will, Rece," Nourzad said. "I'm pretty sure he will."

After another short pause in the conversation, Nourzad said, "You remind me of my wife."

Rece's smile turned into a slight frown. "Oh."

"I'm sorry," Nourzad said somewhat embarrassed. "I'm not really sure why I said that, other than I really see her in you, especially your concern for your husband. It's nice to see."

Rece smiled at him.

"Well, I was going to go in here, but I'll sneak in the back, so Kevin won't see me." Nourzad then winked.

"I think that would be best for him," Rece said. "Oh, and, I know him. I think it'd be best if he didn't know we talked. He takes things…"

"I understand," Nourzad said. "As you wish."

"It was really nice to see you," Rece said, extending her hand to shake.

Nourzad shook her hand with two hands and held her hand tight. "It was a pleasure seeing you. If Kevin or you need anything, please let me know. I actually think we have an appointment set soon, so I'll see you both then." Nourzad released her hand.

"Thank you. Doctor."

Nourzad walked away to the back entrance of the hospital. Rece watched him walk away. As she did, she felt a tap on her shoulder. She jumped a bit. It was Kevin. She looked into his eyes and hugged him hard and long. She whispered into his ear, "I love you."

"What'd I do to deserve that?" Kevin asked.

"Just want you to know," Rece said, wiping down her clothes as if something had attached itself to her.

"Love you, too," Kevin said. "We can go now."

SOMEBODY HAS
TO LOOK...

Late that night, Rece lay asleep next to Kevin as he got out of bed to look for his laptop. He found it under the TV under a towel. He brought it back to bed with him and opened it up. He let it warm up and then opened a search engine. He punched in **'headaches'**.

He read up on migraines, tension headaches and clusters. The sites mimicked what Dr. Herr said about them. Migraines were excruciating and last up to 72 hours. Tension headaches could last from thirty minutes to a week, but some tension headaches can last up to 15 days. He read on and something caught his eye:

Tension headaches that last more than 15 days are called chronic tension headaches

He read on:

Most people have at one time or another experienced a tension-type headache. The pain is typically a dull tightening or pressure on both sides of the head, often described as having a tight rubber band around the head.[xiv]

Kevin took his thumb and index finger on his right hand and massaged his forehead. He then searched again. He punched in:

'Can a headache be the only sign of a brain tumor?'

The first site spelled out the following:

Around 50% of people with a brain tumor had headaches as

one of the complaints they went to the doctor with, and up to 60% will develop headaches at some time

Headaches are one of the most common symptoms of a brain tumor, but they are also common in healthy people, and can be due to many everyday causes

Headaches are rarely the only symptom of a brain tumor. [xv]

Kevin clicked on the next site on the list. It read as follows:

A common initial symptom of a brain tumor is headaches. Often, they don't respond to the usual headache remedies. Keep in mind that most headaches are unrelated to brain tumors.[xvi]

Jesus fucking Christ. He began to sweat.

The next site listed the common symptoms of a brain tumor. The first and most prominent symptom listed was:

'Headache'.[xvii]

Kevin threw his head back. He reached on the table and grabbed the ibuprofen. He was supposed to wait until 11:00 pm to take his next pill. It was now 11:23 pm. His head was full. The pain in the forehead pulsated. He took the 800-milli-gram pill, thought about getting some Tylenol, but looked at Rece and didn't. He went back to his search. He was frustrated at the brain tumor contradictions. He punched in the following:

'How to determine if you have a brain tumor'.

He saw the following terms on various sites:

Seizures, Clumsiness, Numbness, Change in Memory, Nausea, Change in Vision

Kevin grabbed his head with both hands. He rubbed his forehead with his fingers and stretched his legs towards then end of the bed. He heard Rece snore. He looked at her and breathed deeply. The computer screen was a blur. Kevin stared at it for what seemed like hours. Not one coherent thought entered his brain. He squinted at the screen one more time. The only script that entered his head was the bold-typed heading:

BRAIN TUMOR

He saw it again:

BRAIN TUMOR

And again:

BRAIN TUMOR

He walked over to his dresser. He reached under his tee shirts and picked up the bottle of Tylenol. He stared at it long, and then looked at Rece. He stared at her longer, still holding the bottle. He then opened the bottle, took two, re-hid the bottle, then returned to his computer. He looked on.

BRAIN TUMOR

He clicked on a few brain tumor sites:

Upon presentation, doctors will order either a CT scan or an MRI to scan the brain for any tumors. A CT scan may show tumors, but an MRI is the best method for this course of action

Kevin closed his computer and put his head on his pillow. The pain radiated in his head. He wondered why neither doctor had ordered a CT scan or an MRI. *It was the only way to know.* He knew he had read somewhere on these sites that a headache can be the primary symptom of a brain tumor. *What if I have a brain tumor? Why aren't they looking for it? What if it's growing!* For a half an hour, at least, he lay on the bed pondering his fate. He felt the pain hibernating under the cocktail's cover, awaiting its turn again at Kevin. In the recess of his mind he heard the laughter. Moments later, he was asleep.

WORK

"Honey? Honey? Are you going to work?"

Kevin opened an eye. His vision was blurry, and pain radiated through his head. He closed one eye and squinted at Rece with the other.

"Are you going to work, sweetie?"

Kevin stared at her with the squinting eye. "Um, yeah, I think."

"You think? You didn't put in for today," Rece said.

Kevin coughed. He heard thunder outside. "Yeah, I know. Ok."

"I'll get the coffee today. Lay here a bit."

Rece walked off towards the hallway. A sledgehammer pounded at his brain. He laid his head back on his pillow and closed his eyes hard, keeping them closed while feeling the tremendous pain. A sharp pain radiated from the back of his head down his neck. His right leg felt weak. He rolled toward his nightstand. He squinted to find the Ibuprofen 800. Somehow, he opened the container and took his pill, not even thinking about when it was he took his last one. Kevin listened as Rece spoke to someone downstairs. Kevin rolled slowly out of bed and walked to his dresser. He opened the main drawer. He shuffled through the contents. Growing frustrated, he started tossing things about. He listened for Rece. He opened drawer number two and squinted. He began tossing shorts and socks. He slammed the drawer, and stood, staring at the mirror and breathed heavily and deeply. *Where the fuck is it?* His head was full of pressure and pain. He heard the pain laughing at him. *Stop fucking laughing!* He thought of Nour-zad and the young ER doctor. *Fucking fools.* Turning towards the bathroom, he glanced and saw the acetaminophen on the bathroom sink. *How the fuck?* He went into grab it. He listened for Rece and glanced into the bedroom while leaning out of the bathroom. Kevin quickly opened the container then heard Rece approaching. He walked fast to his bed and laid down as he heard Rece coming up the stairs. He placed the container under his pillow.

"Here's your coffee, dear." Rece smiled her smile. Kevin thought how happy she seemed. He wanted desperately to be happy with her. His head pounded; the fullness overtook him. He squinted at her and thanked her.

"Headache?" Rece asked as she walked to her side of the bed.

"Little bit," Kevin said in a hushed tone.

"Work?" Rece stated.

"I know. I'm going."

"Good, I mean, Kevin, you know?"

"I know, it's been a while and I have to…"

"You gotta catch up, sweetie," she said nicely. "And, look, if you need anything today while you're there, you just text me, ok?"

"Ok, thanks."

"Now, take your ibuprofen with you, OK? Stay ahead of these fuckers!" Rece smiled.

"I will."

"You got this!"

Rece never left the bedroom as she dressed for the day. The pill bottle remained under his pillow. As the two walked out of the bedroom and started their days, Kevin glanced at the pillow.

--

Kevin pulled into the lot of his office. Cars of all shapes and colors lined the lot. The few open spaces were spread out. Kevin pulled in and placed the car in park. He breathed deeply and looked at his building. He felt his pulse and it seemed fast. He felt light-headed and worried he didn't eat enough breakfast. He clutched his ibuprofen bottle like a baby clutching its stuffed animal. Work was the last place he wanted to be.

As he walked the hall to the elevator, his head felt full. He didn't get a chance to double dose the acetaminophen. It always worked, but only in the sense that it put the beast to sleep. That was fine with him. As he walked, he noticed a pause in the pain. There was fullness, but not overwhelming pain. His head felt full as if filled completely with solid cement. The ibuprofen must be kicking in better than usual on its own. It dulled his senses, making him wander like a zombie, walking forward with no purpose. It was a respite. But he knew the demon was waiting to attack again. He felt deep in his pockets, wishing he had the other pill bottle.

--

That morning, St. Michael's Cemetery was pristine. It was a massive resting place, bordered by six total miles of busy streets and train tracks. The heavy looking silver gates were open from 7 a.m. to 7 p.m. each weeknight. The driveway in was wide, with a welcome hut in the middle. No one was ever present to welcome the visitors.

Nourzad arrived at 9:00 a.m. that morning, stopping there on his way to work. He pulled in and drove calmly through the winding cement roads, occasionally glancing at headstones and families. His drive through took him minutes, but time stood still to him that day. He finally pulled over and turned off his ignition. He sat, two hands on the wheel, staring straight ahead. He took a deep breath, opened his door and began to walk west. He stepped carefully, avoiding gravestones and flowers. A stray American Flag blew by his foot and he grabbed it, looked at the stones around him and found a military stone. He buried the flag's stick into the ground adjoining the veteran's grave. Nourzad thought of who the man might have been. *Did he leave a family behind? Was he missed? Was he brave at death, as in life?*

He continued on.

Several steps later, Nourzad turned left, then right by the dying oak tree. He stood and stared. Four headstones stared back at him. He didn't approach. He sat on an old tree stump, first shooing off some lost ants. His chin on his hands, his elbows on his knees, Nourzad gazed. He stared at the stones for over a half an hour, barely moving. He never approached. He thought deeply at first, then generally. He finally sat up, stretching his back and looking up to the sky. Stray clouds passed slowly. They were big, white, puffy clouds. A weak breeze blew in his face, and birds flew over the trees. In the distance, he heard the buzzing of the cars, and even further in the distance he heard a very faint train horn. He looked back upon the stones. He stood. "Maybe next time," he whispered. "I'm sorry." Nourzad walked back to his car. He sat for a second after starting it, looked around, drew a breath, and pulled away.

--

"Those copies complete, Kevin?"

He'd been at work for twenty minutes. He spent five conversing with his assistant, Leigh; five minutes clearing off his desk, and ten minutes sitting in his chair holding his head in his palm.

"I'm gonna need a day to finish, Martin. I know…"

"Kevin, I delivered them to you because..."

"I know why you did, ok, Martin. I need a day."

"I don't have a..."

"Yeah, you do. I know they're due the 11th, Ok? It's the 9th. I'll get 'em done."

"But I need to..."

"Martin, they'll be done! You don't need to proof them. Never have. My work is good. They'll be done."

"One day."

"I know."

With that, Leigh entered. She was 40-45 years old, she never said. She had rich dark hair, a semi-dark complexion and an infectious smile. She was skinny, but athletic looking. She was an avid runner and loved to read. She was Kevin's assistant for four years now.

"He looks pissed, Kevin." Leigh sat and smiled.

"He's a dick," Kevin said as he typed something on his computer.

"Whoa!" Leigh shrieked and laughed at the same time. "What's wrong with you? Vacation wasn't good?"

Kevin continued typing. "It wasn't a vacation. I just needed some time off."

Leigh shifted in her chair. "Everything Ok?"

Kevin stopped typing, turned towards Leigh, and said, "Everything is fine, Leigh."

"Doubt it, Kevin. I know you. But it's none of my business."

"See, now why do you always say that?" Kevin sat back; his voice loud.

"What?" Leigh looked puzzled.

"That! That, 'it's none of my business'," Kevin said in a mocking way.

"Look, dick, chill out," Leigh said.

"No, No. You always do that. You ask questions, get right up to the answer, then pull away and say that crap business crap."

"You said crap twice."

"Because it's crap. Why don't you ever want to know things? I mean, you ask, you ask, you search, then it's none of your business. I don't get it." Kevin stared at her.

"Look," Leigh said standing up. "You're in a bad mood. You got work. I'll let you do it."

Kevin stared at her as she left. As she did, she laughed and said, "Dick."

Kevin sat and closed his eyes. A small pain began on the right side of his head. He could feel fullness building up, and the bridge of his nose was cracking on the inside. His right arm felt weak, and he was sweating, he thought. He clutched at his pill bottle, still in his pocket. He turned to look out his window. The sun glared into his eyes, causing him to squint more. He saw cars passing on the street outside. People walked the walkway, and the landscapers were cleaning up the lawn. He stared at it all, cursing in his head at the beast as it awoke from its nap.

He heard the door close behind him.

"They're talking about you."

It was Leigh. She came in and sat.

"Who?" Kevin asked, rubbing his forehead with his thumb and index finger, his eyes closed.

"Martin, Rob and Q," Leigh said.

Kevin didn't respond. He sat with his eyes still closed.

Leigh spoke quietly. "Look, Kevin, I'm on your side. We are allies, right? But you gotta get it going here. If they want your work, you gotta do it. You've missed a lotta work lately. Things are piling up, plus, they're like kinda your bosses. You gotta listen."

"Fuck them. They are not my bosses. That's a bunch of bull-shit."

"I know, I know but they outnumber you!" Leigh giggled nervously as she said it. "They don't really like you; you know that. They can have you fired if they try."

"Like Alex? Yeah, fuck that. Alex didn't fight for himself. I will."

"Kevin." Leigh looked at him. "Come on. You got a family! You need this job."

"Why do you think they'll get rid of me, which they can't, by the way?"

"That's what Alex thought," Leigh responded quickly.

"Again, Alex was stupid."

"I think they can try to get rid of you because we've seen them do it. You had your issue a few years ago, too. They re-member."

"Issue?" Kevin asked in a harsh tone.

"C'mon, Kevin. I knew."

"You knew what?"

"You were drinking at work! C'mon, Kevin! It was obvious. Then you get a leave? Like I didn't know?"

"See? That's bullshit. Why didn't you ever ask me about it, or say something? If we're fucking allies, then why?"

"Because..."

"Right, right, right…" Kevin interrupted her. "…it was none of your fucking business, right?"

"It wasn't and you know it," Leigh shot back.

Kevin looked defeated. He sat back in his chair.

Leigh continued, "Look, you got it back together. Things were going well, and now you're taking so much time off and work isn't getting done."

"It's getting done!" Kevin yelled.

They sat in silence. Leigh looked at him. They stared eye to eye.

"Are you dr…?" Leigh stopped herself and didn't finish her question.

Kevin responded quickly. "You think that's your business?"

"No, I don't. I don't care if you drink, but I work with you and I fuckin' like what I do, and I need this fucking job. So, in that sense, yeah, it's a little bit of my fucking business."

"The work will get done. I'm here, Ok? I'm here."

"Are you, Kevin?" Leigh got up and walked to the door. She opened it and began to leave.

"Leigh," Kevin said softly.

Leigh stopped but didn't turn around.

"The answer is no, I'm not."

Leigh paused, looked at Kevin for a second, and then proceeded out of his office.

TO WHAT DO I OWE THIS VISIT?

"Nurse, can you get me the, um, Cates file? I think I left it on the desk in room 5."

"Sure, Doctor Walsh. Give me one second."

"Need it quickly."

"Ok."

Dr. Walsh sat in his make-shift office. He dabbled on his smart phone, in a way that looked like he didn't know what he was doing. He shuffled his feet as he sat, and constantly moved around in his chair. Growing frustrated with his phone, he placed it hard on his desk and sat back and stared at the door.

"Nurse! The Cates file, please!"

There was no response. "Jesus Christ," he said out loud. He picked up his phone again and dabbled, looking up every few seconds. He dropped the phone on his desk again and began to get up. "Nurse!"

As he yelled, Dr. Nourzad appeared at the door. He was dressed in khaki pants, a light blue collared shirt and a shiny brown belt. Brand new black and white gym shoes adorned his feet and his hair was perfect, combed over to the right with just enough spray to keep it together.

"Well Frank, to what do I owe this visit?" Dr. Walsh said while folding his arms together in front of his body.

"Archibald Ravenswood," Nourzad said sternly as he stood at the door.

"What do you mean 'Archibald Ravenswood'?" Dr. Walsh asked in a mocking way.

"He was one of your patients, recently, Doctor. You don't even know that." Nourzad looked intently at the bigger doctor.

Dr. Walsh sat on his desk and looked back at Nourzad as the anger shot to Nourzad from his eyes. Walsh breathed deeply, holding back the urge to lunge at the younger doctor. "Look, um, son," Walsh said, stressing the word son, "I don't need to tell you who may or may not have been a patient of mine, you understand me? And it's none of your fucking business who may or may not have been a patient of mine."

Nourzad spoke quick and fast with no pauses. "81 years old, a widower, four kids, one of whom was a minor league baseball player. He had 13 grandchildren. He loved baseball but preferred to watch basketball. His favorite city was Madison, Wisconsin. He loved pizza and Italian beef sandwiches and his favorite color was black. Black, doctor Walsh. Black."

Dr. Walsh stood up and expanded his chest. "I don't give a fuck if his favorite color was turquoise, you pompous piece of shit. Colors don't save lives, you maggot. Madison, Wisconsin doesn't save lives and I'm sure as all hell that I knowing that his son played minor league baseball would not have saved the life of that 81-year-old man who suffered from Leukemia, you fuck! He died as a result of a heart attack. Now get the fuck out of my office and if you ever approach me like this again, you'll see what happens."

Nourzad stared at the doctor. He bit his lower lip and thought about his family. He clutched at his pocket, feeling the fresh pack of cigarettes. He continued to stare.

"Dr. Nourzad?" The question followed a quick, brief knock

on the door. "Nurse Paul needs you. She said it was important."

The two doctors continued to stare at each other.

"Dr. Nourzad." The nurse grabbed his shoulder.

Like in a trance, Nourzad suddenly snapped to. "Yes. Yes. My apologies, nurse. Yes. Let's go."

Together, they walked out.

--

The hallway was empty outside of Walsh's office. The nurse clutched his arm and led him west down the hall. They turned right, and then left again, and into room 1234.

Nourzad spoke first. "Nurse Paul doesn't want to see me."

The nurse released his arm and grabbed his hands. "No."

They stared at each other, and Nourzad smiled. "Thank you."

"He's a dick, yes. But I've been his nurse for a real long time, doctor. And I've been a nurse here forever, and he's the best I've ever seen."

Nourzad nodded, tightening his lips together. "Thank you, Nurse. Thank you."

Nourzad walked out.

NO RELENT

Kevin shifted through his paperwork on his messy desk. He tossed an old candy wrapper into the small, black garbage can next to his desk. He leaned back on his cushioned black chair. As he did, the pain in his head worsened. It was full of pressure, and his forehead felt as if it was going to explode. He took a very deep breath. He stood up, walked slowly to his office door and closed it. He stood straight up, feet together and closed his eyes. He reached his arms straight out and brought his fingers to his nose. Both index fingers touched the exact tip of his nose. He opened his eyes and drew an imaginary straight line on the floor. He steadily walked it, straight as an arrow. He then stood straight again, arms out, eyes closed, and he touched his fingers to his eyes, then back out straight again, then touched his ears. He did this perfectly.

The pain did not relent. He sat in the chair again and closed his eyes. The only thought in his head was his pain. He reached in his pocket, opened the container that he pulled out, and took two more ibuprofen.

He sat with his thoughts. He knew Leigh had Tylenol. She always did for her muscle aches from running. He didn't flinch as he rose to go ask her for some.

Leigh sat at her desk, headphones in, as she typed away. "Yes, Kevin?"

"Hey, um, do you have any Tylenol?" Kevin asked.

Leigh opened her drawer and pulled out a small medicine container. "How many?"

Kevin responded, "Two will do?"

"How about 30, and just end it all," Leigh shot back, smiling.

"Don't tempt me." Kevin laughed as he said it.

"What's wrong?" Leigh asked.

"Nothing."

"Why the Tylenol, then?"

"Oh," Kevin said. "Just a little headache."

"Hm. Ok. Well, here's to ya." She handed Kevin the two little pills.

--

That night, Rece lay still on the bed as the dim light from the TV flickered throughout the room. Kevin lay still, awake and staring at the TV. He doubled up on the medicine again at 8:00 pm, the feeling of a solid fullness still permeating his body. The pain was in check, seething at the cage with which the medicine entrapped it. Kevin's eyes squinted, as if searching for an enemy with his periphery. He was exhausted yet couldn't sleep. His laptop was open, lying on the table next to his desk. His thoughts turned to his headache research that night. A dizzying array of terms and phrases raced through his head as he passed out on the bed:

Pain, nausea, pounding, brain tumor, cluster, migraine, vice, brain tumor, stress, E.R., doctor, immediate attention, benign, common, headaches, first symptom, brain tumor....

In his dream, he was watching a non-descript baseball game. The air was cold, he sat alone, watching the shadows run and catch on the field. Dark clouds over-shadowed the park. There was a hot dog, sitting on the bleacher next to him. He heard the murmur of the crowd but saw no faces. The sun peeked through in a moment, and then was gone. His breathing was labored and heard laughter. The laughter grew loud and sharp and he heard a voice say, 'Ok, that's enough of that, sir!", followed by more laughter that grew rapidly in intensity. He wanted to now open his eyes, but the laughter grew more intense. He shuddered.

"Oh my God!" he said as he woke. He could barely open his eyes, as they met the glare from the laptop staring back at his face. Laughter poured out loudly from the late-night talk show on the TV. He tried to sit up, but the pain was too much. It felt like an axe again wedged into the top of his head. *Holy fuck.* He had no idea what time it was. His head was full, swooshing around at record speed. He felt his fingers twitch. The pain was overwhelming. He reached for his pills but couldn't find them. He shuffled through his whole table, tossing things onto the floor.

"Where the fuck," he whispered. He looked on the floor and under the bed. He walked slowly to the bathroom, gazing at Rece as she lay quietly in her bliss. He couldn't find the pills anywhere. He sat on the counter in the bathroom, shivering. He put both hands on his forehead and rubbed it over and over and over again. He moved his head backwards, turning it from side to side. The battle was exhausting.

In that moment, he thought of his kids and what would happen when he was gone. He'd miss them so much. He thought of Rece, taking on the family load without him. His heart raced and sweat covered his hands. He wrung them together and breathed deeply.

"God," he said softly, "Please help me. Please make this go away. I implore you. Please."

He thought back to his school days, and the nuns saying to never pray for yourself, but to pray, instead, the Our Father. In his head, he said it:

Our Father, who art in heaven, hallowed be thy name. Thy kingdom come, thy will be done, on earth, as it is in heaven. Give us this day our daily bread, and forgive us our trespasses, as we forgive those who trespass against us. And lead us not into temptation, but deliver us, Lord, from evil, amen.

He stared at the ceiling, slowly rolled off the counter and walked back into the bedroom. He stared at Rece as he walked. He sat on the edge of the bed, on his side, and laid down, covering himself in the blanket. His body shivered, his hands shook, and the pounding in his head continued. In the vast space that was his mind, he heard the laughter again, roaring and squealing as he shut his eyes...

--

The alarm sounded like a canon in his head. He instinctively reached over and hit the snooze button. He immediately felt the tremendous pain in his forehead. There on the table sat both bottles of his pills. *What in the absolute fuck?* He looked at Rece, and she hadn't moved since last night. He based this conclusion on how she hadn't moved since he last gazed at her. He took two ibuprofen pills and two acetaminophen with water, as he sat on the edge of the bed. He immediately laid down hard again, squinting his eyes as he remembered his prayer last night. He breathed heavy and cursed the morning.

I'm calling the doctor today. Calling him right away.

Rece rolled over, opened her eyes, and smiled at Kevin. "Hey, sweetie. How are you?"

"I'm good," Kevin answered.

"Mmmm. That's good. Did you sleep well?" she asked.

"I did, thanks."

"That's awesome." Rece put her arm over his chest.

Kevin leaned over, held her tight and kissed her forehead. "I love you so much."

Rece responded immediately, "I love you, too."

--

Kevin raced through the hallway at work. His head was down, and he made no eye contact with anyone. He just wanted to be at his desk. He whisked through his office, oblivious as to whether anyone said hello. He didn't care. Once at his desk, he looked up his doctor's number. He couldn't remember his name but called the main office and explained his situation.

"It says here, Mr. Ruscevich, that you saw Dr. Nourzad last time," the receptionist said.

"Yes, yes, that's who it was," Kevin responded.

"Ok, well, he is in today, and we have an 11:30 cancellation if you want to come in then?" she asked.

"I will be there." Kevin didn't hesitate.

"Ok, I will mark you down," she responded kindly. "And, again, this for your headache?"

"Yes. It will not go away."

"Ok, hon, well, he will certainly take a look at you." She paused, and then continued, "It looks like it's been a while since you saw him."

"Yes," Kevin said having no clue. "And I'd had the headache way before that, too."

"Ok, well, we will see you at 11:30."

"Thank you," Kevin said.

Kevin hung up and sat back on his chair. He thought about how it should work out. He could get to the doctor and back to work, and then head home and no one would know he went. He didn't want to lie to Rece but justified in his head that not telling her about the appointment wasn't a lie. He just didn't want all the questions about the headaches from her. *Quite a fucking life, Kevin.*

--

As Kevin sat in the waiting room his head pounded with pain. The pain worsened as he walked into the office, fiercely pushing against the forehead and pulsing on all sides of his skull like an animal trapped in a cage futilely bashing itself against the bars in anger. His left leg shook as he sat, and he noticed his right fingers twitching. His heart raced again, as thoughts of doom and death filled his mind. An old man walked in with a newspaper tucked under his arm. He smiled at Kevin and sat down, crossing his legs and opening his news.

There was a din of conversation behind the receptionist, and the T.V. had a news show on. In that moment, Kevin saw the painting on the wall again. The ship looked more hopeless this time, as the impending storm closed in on it. Kevin stared at it. And stared at it. The painting engulfed his senses and he felt the mist of the ocean spraying against his face. He heard the thunderous waves crashing and crashing.

"Kevin?" an older red-haired nurse called out. Kevin shook his head back and forth quickly, awakening himself from the painting.

Kevin stood up slowly and squinted at the painting one more time. *It's too* late. He then made his way to the door, not noticing anything else around him.

"Hi Kevin!" The nurse held out her hand and Kevin shook it gently, saying a quiet hello back to the kind nurse.

"Let's go to room three right down the hall there," she said.

The two figures walked their way to room three, and the nurse closed the door behind them. She took his pulse, blood pressure and temperature. "Ok, Kevin. What seems to be the problem?" As she finished her sentence Dr. Nourzad walked in, dressed in black pants, a grey long-sleeved shirt, a shiny black belt and a black tie with grey stripes. His hair was combed over to the right perfectly.

"Hi Gail, I got this. Thank you very much for getting Kevin settled in," Nourzad said as he sat down. Gail smiled and walked out re-closing the door as she left.

Nourzad wasted no time. "Good to see you, Kevin," he said extending his hand. Kevin shook it back with a tight grip. The two held on strong for a moment and then relented.

"Thank you for having me in," Kevin said quietly.

Nourzad shifted in his seat to get comfortable and responded, "Never a problem, Kevin. I'm here when you need me, so I'm glad it worked out. Headaches, still?"

"Yes. Yes, and they just keep getting worse," Kevin said, gripping his hands in an interlocking way.

"I had heard," Nourzad said and then quickly added, "I mean, ok, I understand." Nourzad spoke and then stared at Kevin's face. "I see you're squinting."

Kevin processed Nourzad's last comments. He paused and then said, "Yeah, I guess."

"I know Rece said last time that the squinting was a sign of your pain, so she was certainly right about that," Nourzad said caringly. "She's not here today?"

"No, no, um, I'm here alone." Kevin shifted uncomfortably in his chair still processing Nourzad's comment about having heard.

"Ok, so, tell me about the headaches," Nourzad sat still and looked at Kevin.

What did he mean 'I heard'? Who woulda told him? Kevin waited to process his internal question, and then spoke. "They haven't gone away. In fact, they are worse, as I said." Kevin looked back at Nourzad. As he did, he felt the pain swirling around in his head, pounding aggressively at his forehead and skull. He closed his eyes for a brief second.

Nourzad leaned forward, "Does it hurt right now?"

I have no choice but to answer. "Yes, really bad."

"Tell me and show me where," Nourzad responded.

Kevin lifted his right hand to his forehead. "This is where the pain is constant. It is always here, like pounding outward. Then it moves around to all sides of my head, pounding and swirling and swirling around." Kevin paused, and then continued, "It just won't go away."

Nourzad stared at Kevin intently, studying his eyes and face. Kevin looked back, uncomfortable at the staring and silence. Nourzad continued to study the look on his face, then reached for a piece of paper and glanced at it. Softly, he spoke. "I see here you recently went to the E.R. I saw they looked at you for these headaches."

"Yes, it was, I don't know, recently, yes. Yeah, recently," Kevin responded.

"You're looking for peace," Nourzad stated knowingly, leaning in closer to Kevin.

Hmmm. "That's all I want," Kevin said.

Nourzad sat back. "Well, first off", Nourzad paused and glanced at a file, "I see they ran every relevant test for headaches when you went. The doctor noted all the tests." Nourzad turned the file to Kevin and showed him her notes. Kevin made nothing of the notes, other than that they did exist. "You, for lack of a better term, passed all those tests, Kevin. Meaning, there is no long-term health issue here, other than the headache itself. Does that make sense?"

"I guess. I mean, yeah, I get it," Kevin said back at Nourzad. *How the fuck had he heard?*

"It means that the headaches are not a sign of any life-threatening issues that would occur or last into the future.

Now, that said, you have the pain from these headaches, which cannot be understated in any way. So, we have to figure out how to deal with that pain and heal that pain."

Kevin just sat and listened.

"Let me ask you this, and, I'm asking this to kind of ease your mind. Do you know, Kevin, what the most complained about malady to doctors is, in the entire world?" Nourzad asked.

"Headaches, I assume," Kevin answered, showing the slightest of smiles.

"No," Nourzad said quickly. "Hunger. Hunger is number one. But headaches, headaches are number two. In the entire world."

Kevin stared at Nourzad.

"So, we see from that that headaches are just oh so common with a huge proportion of the world. People get headaches, and they get so bad, they go and report these headaches to their doctors. So much so, that it's the number two complained about malady. In the world."

"I see."

"And, let's think. When a person gets a pain, or a discomfort, they don't usually go right to their doctor, right? Most people hope it goes away, and most of the times it does. But if it doesn't, then they go to the doctor. There are exceptions, of course, but we are talking about for the most part. Ok. So, that tells us that the people with these headaches are suffering pain for extended periods. Like yourself."

Kevin stared again, not speaking during the pause.

"You're not alone, Kevin. They, being headaches, are a pain in the ass, and excuse my language, but they are. Headaches occur in the one area of the body where we, as people, cannot afford to have pain. A pain in the leg, well, that's down there. Stomach pain? It's here. Arm pain, it's over here. But headaches, headaches, they are right here." Nourzad brought his hands up to his head, covering his scalp and skull completely with them. "Understand?"

"I do," Kevin said.

"It causes one great grief and strife when there is pain up here in our heads." Nourzad sat back and looked at Kevin.

Kevin nodded, understanding the meaning, he hoped.

"So, Kevin, what I am hoping is that with some understanding, we, you and I, can lower the stress caused by this pain. We know it's wide-spread, headache diagnoses, so we know that people do get by with the pain, and with such a high frequency of complaint, we know people can and do function with headaches. And that you can, and will, do the same."

Kevin began a thought, but before he could express it, Nourzad beat him.

"Now, all that said, we also know that life is not an endurance sport. It's not a 'who is the toughest' event. We don't have to go through this hoping it goes away, which, it does, for the most part. We have medicine which can help."

"You said, for the most part the pain goes away," Kevin said.

Nourzad responded, "From my experience, and my studying the malady, headaches, even prolonged, do go away. Now, I've had patients who've had them for years, give or take. But then they went away, the headaches. I've had patients that have an extended headache, then it goes away, and then it comes back. And in my readings, I've seen a case where a gentleman had a headache for over 40 years, with no explanation of the reason, and no relief from pain despite medicine. I tell you that, Kevin, not to scare you, but to let you know, one, it's extremely rare, and two, to be completely honest with you."

"I appreciate that." *Fuck, he seems sincere.*

"Let me ask, and I should have asked before, but, have you ever had headaches in the past, and I mean your entire past, Kevin," Nourzad asked.

"I think I told you last time I had some headaches, although minor, in the past two years," Kevin answered.

"No, I know about those. I mean any others," Nourzad asked.

"No. I don't think so," Kevin answered again.

"Think," Nourzad asked.

Kevin sat, tilted his head to the right and responded. "As a kid, I guess, I used to get headaches, and they hurt, I remember, but that pain was always, always on the right back side of my head."

"See? You have a long history of headaches. And you are telling me about them here and now." Nourzad winked at Kevin. "See, where the pain was isn't that important. What is important is that you had them. You are a headache sufferer, who had a lapse in pain, but now it's back. This is good in the sense that we have some understanding now, Kevin, of your history."

With that came a knock on the door. It was Gail. "I'm so sorry to disturb you, Doctor, but your next patient is here. Just letting you know."

"Tell Darlene, I think it's Darlene, tell her I am with Mr. Ruscevich right now and that I will be right with her." Nourzad smiled.

As the nurse walked out, Kevin felt the pain in his head pounding and pounding and pounding, screeching its way around his head. He grabbed his forehead nonchalantly with his right palm.

"Pain?" Nourzad asked.

"Yeah, sorry," Kevin whispered.

"We will deal with that," Nourzad stated. "What I want to do is bring you back in one week, ok? I want you to stop using the ibuprofen. You've been using that? It's been working somewhat?"

"It seems less effective, doc, but to be honest. I mean, I guess it dulls the pain a bit. But not much." Kevin didn't mention the Tylenol.

Nourzad continued, "Ok, so this is going to be difficult, but, since they aren't giving much relief now, it's one week that you'll go without it, ok? I just want to make sure that the over the counter stuff isn't causing what they call 'rebound head-aches', which are caused, sometimes, by over-use of the over the counter variety of medicines used for headaches. It's not often we see that, but I just want to be sure. Sound good?"

Kevin just nodded.

"Ok, so none of those, back in one week, but, for sure, if you feel overwhelmed by this before that, just call in, ok?" Nour-zad said reassuringly.

Kevin sat, stared at the floor and took a deep breath. *How the fuck had he heard?*

"What is it, Kevin?" Nourzad asked.

"It's just that..." Kevin then chuckled. "It's not gonna go away. I know it. There's just something wrong."

Nourzad leaned forward. "What are you thinking, Kevin? Tell me."

Kevin stared at the floor as he spoke. "I think I'm dying. I think I have a brain tumor."

Nourzad leaned in even closer and put his hand on Kevin's shoulder and looked him in the eyes. "You're not dying, and you don't have a brain tumor. You don't. You have zero symptoms, Kevin, of any issue like that."

Kevin breathed deeply again, feeling the horrendous pain. "Ok, ok."

"We are going to get through this," Nourzad said. "We will talk in one week, right here."

"Ok," Kevin agreed. "Um, you mentioned other medicines?"

Nourzad paused as he stood up from his chair. "Yes. We will discuss all those options next week. If they are needed." Nourzad smiled. He began to open the door for Kevin. "Oh, and if you ever need to go to the E.R. again, call me first. I can meet you there." With that, he handed Kevin his business card, and the two walked out of the room together.

--

Kevin sat in his car after the appointment and sunk his head into his hands. He rubbed his forehead as he felt the pain taunting him, rolling around inside, pounding at his forehead. He contemplated all that was said by Dr. Nourzad, but in the end, he was alone with his pain, and no relief was in sight. He sat back in the driver's seat, pushing his head hard against the headrest, while tightly gripping the steering wheel. The pain pushed and pushed and pushed, his finger twitched, and his left ear began ringing. The one person who could stop this, in the one place that had any potential to help him, told him to go home. Kevin squeezed the wheel tighter and began banging his head over and over on the headrest at least 15 times. The pain did not relent, and Kevin let out a tremendous scream that echoed through the car.

"Fuck! Fuck! Fuck! Fuck! Fuckkkkkkkkkk!" Kevin released the steering wheel and pounded his palms on it as hard as he could several times as he yelled and yelled over and over.

"How the fuck did he know!!?? How did he hear??!!" Kevin then screamed just as loudly.

He then stopped suddenly, and it was dead quiet, other than the pant of his very heavy breathing. He closed his eyes, reached for the keys in his pocket, started the car, and began to drive back to work. His eyeballs ached, and the pain seared his skull. He pulled over immediately, took three ibuprofen and two acetaminophen pills, and then continued on to work. *Fuck.*

--

In his office, Dr. Nourzad sat at his desk, sipped his pop, and carefully scribbled notes regarding Kevin's visit:

'patient Kevin R presents alone today with same headaches, no relief exc occ'lly w/ otc meds

I see pain all over his face and in his mind – struggling to cope?

No signs/sympt's of any l/t issues – recently chkd in er – no signs of any l/t malady –

One-week re-visit – purpose? – need to c if there is dissipation w/o otc meds – if no relief then script meds option – more concerned with mental health than phys'l @ this pt'

He then put the file on his desk, put his feet up and his hands behind his head and closed his eyes. His children popped into his head and he saw them playing in the yard. He heard his wife's voice calling him. Nourzad's eye's closed. A tear ran jaggedly down his cheek.

"Doctor?"

He heard the nurse's voice and then her knock.

"I'm coming right now," Nourzad said as he looked up to the ceiling, took a breath, stood up, and continued his day.

WHAT CAN WE DO?

"How was work, honey?" Rece asked as Kevin walked through the door. She wore perfectly fit blue jeans and flip-flops. On top, she wore a light blue and white tie-dyed loose shirt which showed off her shoulders.

"It was good, hon," Kevin responded as he walked by her. He stopped, turned back, and kissed her cheek. "How was your day?"

"It was very good, thank you," Rece said, following Kevin. "How is your head, sweetie?"

Kevin stopped walking and Rece bumped right into his back. "Whoops!" Rece laughed as they collided.

Kevin turned to her, gave a small grin, and responded to the question, "It hurts, to be honest. Pretty bad, Rece."

Rece's smile turned to concern. "Aww, baby, I'm so sorry," Rece said as she reached for Kevin and hugged him with two arms. Kevin let his left arm drop down against his body, hugging her back with just that arm. Rece pulled back a bit, looked at him and said, "What can we do?"

Kevin looked at her. He thought of his visit to Dr. Nourzad and the pills he took against the doctor's advice. He gazed into his wife's eyes. "I don't know. I think I want to just rest on the couch tonight after we eat. I made an appointment for next week at the doctor."

"You just went to the ER," Rece said calmly.

"I know, but he said I should come back, so..."

Rece responded. "Oh good, sweetie. I think he mentioned we should go back for a checkup, right?"

"Yes, he did," Kevin replied. He then turned away from her and sat on the couch, crossing his legs, leaning his right arm on the armrest and laying his head in his palm.

Rece sat next to him, rubbing his thigh. "Why don't you go change, I'll feed you guys, and then you can rest here. Dinner is almost ready."

"Thank you, honey." Kevin held her hand as he spoke, "Where are the kids?"

Rece responded, "Actually, they are all in the back yard just hanging out."

"Ok, thank you, honey," Kevin said and then continued, "I'm sorry, Rece. I'm sorry I'm like this."

"Oh, sweetie," Rece spoke softly, "there's no need for that. We will get you better, soon. Now go change, you'll have a good meal, and then just relax."

Kevin walked towards the stairs, then turned and told Rece, "It smells really good."

Rece smiled and blew him a kiss.

Upstairs, Kevin collapsed back first on the bed and closed his eyes. The pain shot towards his forehead and out to the sides. It was pulsating and sharp. His head also felt completely full. *I've never felt that before, fullness and fucking pain. This is new.*

He rolled over onto his side and stared at the wall with no particular purpose in mind. He continued to stare into the wall. His mind was empty.

--

Kevin awoke to a shudder throughout his body. He lay in the exact pose in which he had fallen asleep, head back against the pillows, legs perfectly straight and his arms laying straight at his side. His head pounded and he felt dizzy. There was fullness in his head. This morning the pain was centered on the bridge of his nose. He stared at the wall in front of him, exhausted from the pain. He wanted it to be bedtime already. *Another fucking day. Did I eat last night? God damn, I don't even fucking remember.*

Vincent came strolling in in shorts and a tee shirt. He didn't say a word as he plunged head-first into the bed between Kevin and Rece. "Hey dad," he grumbled as his face hit the pillow.

Kevin didn't respond. He just rubbed Vincent's back as he continued to stare at the wall. He heard James and Kate talking downstairs, eating their breakfast.

I can't do this. He then pondered the long day ahead.

"Can you make me breakfast?" Vince mumbled through the pillow.

"One second, buddy," Kevin answered quietly.

The three lay in silence. Blaize then entered the room in a panic. His hair was everywhere, and he only had on boxer shorts.

"I need $50 today and you have to turn in all the permission slips!" Blaize yelled as he stood at the edge of the bed.

"Blaize, when did you know all this?" Kevin asked impatiently.

"I don't know, but it's all due today or I can't go."

"Go where?" Kevin asked.

"Oh my God," Blaize quipped, "To the boat trip."

Kevin sighed and reached past Vincent to nudge Rece.

"I heard him, sweetie," Rece said, half asleep. Kevin looked at her. *What the fuck?* "Blaize, the money is in the envelope on the table. The permission slips were dad's thing."

Kevin's head thundered and roared. Sweat dripped off his brow. He remembered the permission slip conversation with Rece a few days ago.

"Ok, um, I will get the slips. Vince, go down and get cereal, I have to take care of these slips," Kevin said calmly and decisively.

Vince squirmed off the bed, Blaize bolted to the hallway and ran down the stairs, sounding like a herd of zebras stomping through the brush.

"Sweetie, can you get me coffee?" Rece asked as she rolled over, covering herself up with the blanket.

Kevin sighed quietly. "Yes."

As he walked, the pain in his head swirled around in circles, while the sharp edge jammed his forehead. He stopped at the door, rubbed his head and breathed heavily. *What the fuck.* He then proceeded, step by slow step downstairs to begin his day.

--

Kevin heard Rece say the final goodbye to the kids as he lay on the bed with his hands over his eyes. The pain had not relented. He'd taken the mix of ibuprofen and acetaminophen 30 minutes ago when Rece was downstairs. He hid the pills in his drawer, under the mass of forgotten papers.

"You ok?" Rece asked as she walked in the room. He hadn't even heard her come in.

"Ah. You know. It still hurts."

"I know," Rece said as she sat next to Kevin and kissed his forehead. "I have to run around this morning. Are you working?"

Kevin paused, removed his palms from his eyes and blurredly looked at her. "Yeah, I am."

"You're gonna tough this out, Kevin, I know you will. It'll pass and one day we'll look back at this as a victory for you, you know? You are tough. You are so fucking tough. This is so painful for you, but I'm so proud of you for handling it well. I just want you to know that." Rece stood up as she finished.

"That means a lot, honey. I'm trying."

"I know. I know," Rece looked at him lying on the bed. "Call me if you need anything, ok, sweetie?"

"I will."

YOU SCREAMED
PRETTY LOUD

The first order of business at work that day was looking up headaches. He punched in **'Headache Diagnoses'**.

Neurological tests focus on ruling out diseases of the brain or nerves that may also cause headaches and migraines. The vast majority of headaches turn out to be benign in nature. Some of the tests look for a physical or structural abnormality in the brain that may cause your headache, such as:

Tumor

Brain abscess (an infection of the brain)

Hemorrhage (bleeding within the brain)

Bacterial or viral meningitis (an infection or inflammation of the membrane that covers the brain and spinal cord)

Pseudotumor cerebri (increased intracranial pressure)

Hydrocephalus (abnormal build-up of fluid in the brain)

Infection of the brain such as meningitis or Lyme disease

Encephalitis (inflammation and swelling of the brain)

Blood clots

Head trauma

Sinus blockage or disease

Blood vessel abnormalities

Injuries

Aneurysm (a "bubble" in the wall of a blood vessel that can leak or rupture)[xviii]

Kevin breathed heavily as he squinted at these results. He tried to comprehend the myriad of possibilities.

Fucking tumor, number one.

The pain throttled his skull at the bridge of his nose. The fullness continued to swirl in his head, as well.

Tests:

CT scan

MRI

Blood chemistry

Eye exam.[xix]

None of these fuckin things have been done.

Your headache pain may be serious if you have:

sudden, very intense headache pain (thunderclap head-ache)

severe or sharp headache pain for the first time

a stiff neck and fever

a fever higher than 102 to 104°F

nausea and vomiting

a nosebleed

fainting

dizziness or loss of balance

pressure in the back of your head

pain that wakes you from sleep

pain that gets worse when you change position

double or blurred vision or auras (light around objects)

face tingling and auras that last longer than an hour

confusion or difficulty understanding speech

droopiness on one side of your face

weakness on one side of your body

slurred or garbled speech

difficulty walking

hearing problems

muscle or joint pain

pain that begins after coughing, sneezing, or any type of exertion

constant pain in the same area of your head.[xx]

"This is fucking bullshit!" he yelled out loud as he slammed his hands on his desk.

He sat and breathed and closed his computer browser. He sat back and closed his eyes. His phone rang, but he ignored it.

There was a knock on the door.

"Come in."

It was Leigh. "You ok?"

"I'm fine. Why?

"Because, um, you just screamed pretty loud," Lee said as she tilted her head and raised her eyebrows.

"I'm fine."

"Ok." Leigh turned away.

"Uh, huh, ok," Kevin grumbled.

"W

Jesus, Kevin, what's your problem?" Leigh shot back.

"Ha. You don't give a fuck, so why even ask?" Kevin said staring at his blank computer.

"Fuck you, Kevin. If you have issues, fine, I get it, I do, but don't take your bullshit out on me, ok?" Leigh turned to walk away again.

"Fuck you, too, Leigh," Kevin said loud enough.

Leigh just walked away.

Kevin shouted, "You think everything is bullshit! You don't..." He stopped mid-sentence, looking at the door then turning back to his computer.

Leigh walked back into his office and slowly closed the door.

"Look," she said, still standing, "I don't know what is going on in your life, but you seem miserable, ok? And you really need to get your shit together, and I'm saying this as your friend."

"Pft. Friend. Don't make me laugh," Kevin responded.

Leigh just laughed mockingly.

Kevin continued, "You call me a friend, and sometimes I think you care, but deep down I know you don't. You are a cold person, Leigh, so please don't walk in here..." Kevin paused then raised his voice, "...and act like you give a fuck, then pretend to know I'm miserable but then walk away anyways, ok?!"

"You got problems, Kevin," Leigh said very quietly after staring him down, "I have no idea where any of this is coming from, but I hope you get some peace, I really do." She then walked out.

Fuck you. He sat in his own silence, staring at the work piled up on his desk. His head pounded. He looked at the bottom file drawer next to his desk. He stared at it. And stared at it. And stared at it.

Ah, fuck.

He opened the drawer fiercely. He bent over and looked inside from the back to the front. It was empty. He knew it would be. They weren't there anymore. They hadn't been for a couple of years. He was hoping one would still be there. He slammed it closed. His hands shook and he felt a pulling of his skin, like it was being pulled away from him. He could no longer sit still. He jumped out of his chair and clasped his hands.

Oh my God, oh my God, oh my God.

--

That Sunday, the alarm woke Frank from a deep dream. In it, Nourzad was back home in India with his mom and dad, eating dinner and smiling and laughing. His mom wore her favorite red dress, while his dad smoked on his pipe between bites to eat. His grandfather sat smiling. They laughed and talked and dreamt of what was to be. Frank then woke up.

As he opened his eyes, his body felt rested, but his mind was groggy. He rolled over and looked. He sighed and popped up out of bed. He walked to his window, smelled the coffee brewing, and looked out at his yard. He looked for a few minutes, glancing back and forth, up and back. He had no patients that Sunday, so there was no rush to run and shower, but he felt antsy. He wanted to work. He heard a knock on his door.

Rather early.

He quickly through on some slacks and a golf shirt. He looked at the mirror, fixed his hair a bit, then walked downstairs and opened the door without looking out first.

"Hi, Frank!"

It was his neighbor, Dan. Dan wore dark blue jeans and an over-sized grey sweatshirt. His hair was blowing every which way in the wind. He had a coffee mug in his hand and Nourzad saw the steam rising from it.

"How are you, Dan? It's nice to see you."

Dan extended his hand to Nourzad. "I'm good Frank. Thanks." Then he paused. Nourzad looked at him smiling. Dan then continued as he released the handshake, "I just want to make sure you're ok, Frank."

"Oh yes, I am," Frank responded quizzically. "Why do you ask?"

Dan shifted in his stance, "Well, the wife and I heard you screaming last night, and, you know, we didn't want to be nosey and all, but she did convince me to come over just to see."

"Oh my," Nourzad responded, "I'm so sorry if I disturbed you." Nourzad felt the wind and a chill. "Do you want to come in a second?" He motioned Dan to follow him. Dan closed the door behind him as he obliged.

They faced each other as Nourzad spoke, "I'm so sorry again. I have no excuse, really, and, quite honestly, I don't really remember screaming. Maybe it was in my sleep, I don't know. I also drank a bit of gin last night, so, who knows."

They both laughed heartily.

"Well, I've definitely been there, Frank," Dan said as they continued laughing.

"I'm sorry," Nourzad said.

"No, you don't have to be sorry, Frank, we get it," Dan said, "You've been through more than most, and if you want to scream it out, well, that's your right. We just want to make sure you're ok."

"I appreciate that, Daniel, and tell Lynn the same."

"I will, I will," Dan said turning towards the door, "We will see you soon."

"Looking forward to it, Dan."

And with that, Nourzad was alone in his home, again.

He sat on his couch with his legs crossed, his head half turned towards the sun peeking through the window next to him. He pondered the scream. He could not remember it. He peered over to his sitting chair and the small glass table next to it. His gin glass was sweaty and empty.

Doctor, heal thyself.

He walked towards his deck, opened the humidor next to the sliding doors, and grabbed a cigarette. He walked outside, breathed in the fresh cool air, lit his cigarette, leaned against his house and dragged. The rush of nicotine filled him fully. He relaxed and continued his smoke.

It has to be work, it's my best option.

But it was Sunday, and the office was closed. He finished his cigarette and grabbed another. As he exhaled his second in a row he thought of Kevin and his headache.

I wonder if he's better.

He tossed his finished cigarette into the small garbage can on his deck and walked back into his home. The hard wood floor shined below him, and the adjacent kitchen was immaculate. He roamed over to his den and started up his computer. He accessed his patient list and scrolled down to Kevin. There he saw a phone number for Kevin. He scribbled it down on a notepad, then picked it up and stared at the number.

I think I'll call him and see. Maybe Rece will answer. He quickly shook that thought out of his head.

SO, I'LL BE ALONE?

OCTOBER 2016

Kevin walked in from outside, leaving his kids at play. He saw Rece preparing lunch.

"What's for lunch?" Kevin asked plainly enough.

"Just some sandwiches. Lunchmeat." Rece smiled.

Kevin didn't respond and went to the couch.

"Pain, still?" Rece asked, walking towards him.

"Yeah, it just won't go away or stop." Kevin lay back on the hard pillow on the couch and closed his eyes.

"Well. What about that appointment with your doctor?" she asked.

"Yeah, I know."

"Well, whenever it is, tell me and I'll go with you," Rece said, "I know there are a bunch of medicines they can give you to help, other than the stuff you're taking, like prescription stuff. I was looking them up. We might have to go that route, sweetie."

"Ok. I think he mentioned that last time, no?" Kevin asked, then after hearing himself say it wanted to take it back.

Rece looked confused. "No, I don't think so. But we will ask this week."

Kevin sighed, realizing his dilemma. "Ok. You're going?"

"Yeah," Rece answered, "I really want to be with you

through all this, plus, and I forgot to tell you, I have to go away this weekend with Lisa. She has to drive to Michigan to pick up some stuff at her mom's and she asked me to go. I couldn't say no, even though I wanted to."

"Oh. So, I'll be alone?" Kevin asked. He wrung his hands together tightly, as they began to twitch when he asked if he'd be alone.

"Well, not alone. You'll have the kids."

"Yeah, of course." Kevin sat quietly.

"What is it?" Rece asked.

Kevin paused and breathed, then answered. "You know I don't. I don't, I don't really do well alone." He then chuckled nervously.

"Sweetie," Rece said looking at him, "come on. You'll be fine. It's just a night."

"I know," Kevin responded, Yeah, you're right. But with these headaches, and my emotional bullshit. You know?"

"I do, sweetie," Rece said walking to Kevin, "But you'll be ok. I'll have my phone and if you need me, you just call."

"Ok."

Kevin's cell phone rang, and he looked at the number. He didn't recognize it.

"Not gonna answer?" Rece asked after listening to five rings.

"Nah, I don't recognize the number."

"Gotcha," Rece said, "I do the same."

The phone rang again. Kevin Looked. It was the same number.

"Bill collector?" Rece asked laughingly.

"Probably."

When it rang a few minutes later, Rece suggested he answer. Kevin shook out the cobwebs from his head, rubbed his forehead, and answered.

Rece could hear him from the kitchen.

"Oh, well thank you. That's nice."

"Yes."

"Yes."

"Well, it's really not any better, no. Still a lot of pain. A lot."

"No, I haven't."

"Uh, huh."

"Yeah, I figured."

"Ok."

"Ok."

"I will."

"Thank you. I'll see you Tuesday."

"Ok, bye."

Rece walked towards him. "Who was that?"

Kevin looked at her. "Oh, that, um doctor. Ya know, the one we saw. Just calling to see how I was."

"Wow," Rece said. "How nice of him."

"Yeah, weird, but nice, I guess."

"It's not weird, Kevin," Rece quipped, "He cares. That's nice."

"It is. You're right," Kevin equivocated, "Fuck."

"What is it?" Rece asked quickly in response.

"My head," Kevin responded, then lay down on the couch, closing his eyes and rubbing his forehead, "Anytime I fucking move or do anything it just kills me."

"Do you want to eat?" Rece asked quietly. "Will that help?"

"No. I'll just sit here and watch TV while you guys eat if that's ok."

"That's fine. Not one bit of a problem." Rece gave him a quick kiss and went to the door and called in the kids for lunch. As she walked back past him, she asked, "What did he ask you? Sounded like you answered a lot of questions."

"Just a lot of how I'm doing."

Rece responded, "Hm. Ok."

"What?" Kevin asked regrettingly.

"If you don't want to tell me, no biggie."

"I'm telling you," Kevin said, "that he asked me how I was."

"Ok, cool," Rece responded, showing a fake grin, "Oh, hey, when's the last time you took medicine?"

"Oh, I don't know."

Rece walked to him. "Well," she said looking into his eyes, "that probably has a lot to do with the headaches being worse lately. That's why we should ask for the real stuff next time we see him."

Kevin stared at her as she walked back to the kitchen. He wanted to blurt out the truth, just to ease his mind. But he didn't mention a word. He knew when she was on to him. He knew she knew more than she was letting on.

--

As they lay in bed that night, the TV glittered in the dark room. Rece was still, her eyes fixed on the television, while Kevin shifted with each flare of pain. He wanted desperately for Rece to fall asleep so he could pop his Tylenol. The pain was excruciating, pounding each side of his skull. He heard a constant low grind throughout his head, and he couldn't sit still. As he lay, he noticed his left hand begin to twitch ever so gently. He grabbed it with his right hand and squeezed. He placed it back to his side and it trembled uncontrollably again. All five fingers quivered, and he could not stop it. He placed his hand over his head and then shook it. He looked at Rece and could see her eyes drooping. The fingers kept twitching, and the pain in his head thundered! His body felt weak, and his mind raced Kevin to the finish of this thought, which was his death. He then heard the laughter shriek in his head again.

Kevin got up and walked around the room, hoping Rece would wake. He opened and closed the window and turned on the light for a second. Rece didn't move. His head spun and the pain shot out from all sides. The bridge of his nose felt like it had a lead weight pushing down on it, and the fingers continued to twitch. In his computer research on brain tumors he thought he remembered seeing that twitching was a sign of a tumor. He walked to Rece's side of the bed and sat. The laughter shrieked louder and louder inside his head as the pain raced throughout it.

"Rece," he whispered, "Rece."

Rece opened an eye and gazed at her husband as he sulked over her in absolute pain.

"Honey, what is it?" Rece whispered.

"I'm going to the E.R."

EMERGENCY?

Kevin sat alone in one of the small rooms at the E.R. Rece kept texting him:

--r u there–

--yes...sitting in a room–

--Im so sorry I cant be there–

--its ok–

--Its just he's so sick. he's puking—

--I know. Hoping to get out of here soon—

--r u better?—

--No—

--Im so sry—

--its ok. Someone's coming in now—

Kevin put his phone in his pocket. An older female doctor appeared, looking at and reading a chart as she walked in. She wore a light blue coat, was about 5'7", medium build, with dark brown hair to her shoulders. Behind her was a young male doctor, so it looked like to Kevin. He wore a white jacket and had dark black hair that was short.

"Kevin," the doctor spoke, "I'm Dr. Russell, and this is Dr. Hughes, he's an intern here."

Kevin just quietly said hello and nodded.

"I see the headaches are back?" she stated. "You were in here recently, I see."

"Yeah, but they really haven't gone away," Kevin replied.

"Not at all?" the doctor asked.

"No."

The doctor took out her ophthalmoscope and looked into Kevin's eyes without even a mention of what she was doing. Kevin sat as she crept closer and stared deep into his eyes. She gazed deep and long, for what seemed like minutes. She then stepped back.

Without looking at Kevin, the doctor spoke. "What I was looking for, Kevin, were swollen disks in your eyes. Sometimes we'll find what we call papilledema, which is, again, swelling in the discs in your eyes. This would be one possible indication of pressure in your head."

The doctor paused and scribbled on her chart. She sat down. Kevin looked on and noticed Dr. Hughes looking at Dr. Russell intently.

"How did you get here, Kevin?" Dr. Russell asked.

"I drove."

"Were you able to walk from the lot on your own?"

"Yes."

"Are you dizzy?"

"No., but..."

"Can you stand up for me?"

Kevin stood.

"Walk to the hall and back for me, just a normal walk."

Kevin walked to the hall, turned, and walked back.

"Can you point to that table over there?"

Kevin pointed.

"Ok." The doctor wrote in her chart. "Ok, Kevin, so, I talked to Stanley, your triage nurse and he gave me the rundown of your headache situation. Then I looked you up and see that you've been here recently for the same thing. That's how I knew..."

Kevin interrupted her, "I know, I know, it seems weird. I keep coming here and to Dr. Nourzad, but these headaches will not go away."

"No, no, no, Kevin, no judgment at all. I understand, I really do. I used to suffer from headaches, too, so I completely under-stand where you're coming from." She paused and the room was silent. Kevin heard the buzz and grind in his head as the pain swirled and pushed. "You see Frank Nourzad?"

"I do."

"He's absolutely one of the best doctors I know. You're in good hands, there."

"Thanks, good to know," Kevin said quietly.

"So," the doctor continued, "Dr. Herr saw no signs of any long-term issues last time you were in, and I don't either, and I can assume Dr. Nourzad hasn't either?"

"No, he said I just have headaches, but..."

"Well, that's what I think, too, Kevin. I really do. But I get the concern you have. How long have you had these head-aches?"

"It's been so long. I don't even know anymore, but they are every day, and it's driving me crazy."

"What is the pain level now?"

"10." Kevin answered immediately. "It's always 10 now."

"Ok," the doctor responded, "What I want to do is order a

CT scan, ok? I really think it'll come back clear; I really do. But, with the pain not subsiding and it being to the point where you're coming in a lot, I think we should look, ok?"

"Ok."

"So, it's pretty light here tonight," the doctor spoke, "shouldn't take long. I'll go order it, they'll come get you and then bring you back afterwards, and we'll look at it. Sound good?"

"Yes, it does."

The doctors left and Kevin was alone with his pain and his thoughts.

God dammit they're gonna find a tumor.

He sat and closed his eyes and breathed. He noticed just then that his left fingers were no longer twitching. He closed his eyes and tilted his head forward, having his chin meet his chest.

Please God...

"Kevin?"

It was a big guy, maybe 30 years old wearing all blue scrubs pushing a wheelchair.

"Yes." Kevin mustered through his anxiety.

"Hi there, buddy, my name is Scott, and I'll be taking you for your CT scan."

Kevin looked at Scott, still sitting on the table, and then looked at the wheelchair. "Do I need a wheelchair?"

"Do you? No," Scott chuckled, "but do they make me? Yes."

Kevin turned his head to the side and rolled his eyes. "Why?"

"I'm not sure, buddy," Scott said as wheeled to Kevin, "I just do what I'm told. All CT patients have to be wheeled in."

Kevin sat on the table and stared at the wheelchair. *This is fucking ridiculous.*

"C'mon, buddy, it'll be fine. It's empty here tonight right now, so no one will see you."

Kevin slowly made his way off the table. He slid down on the chair and leaned back. Scott unlocked the brake, turned the wheelchair around and led Kevin out of the room. In the hall Kevin saw nurses at the main table writing and talking. In the room next to him lay an older lady crying and coughing. Two doctors stood outside the room and talked. He heard buzzing and beeps and a light above him flickered. His head roared as Scott wheeled him down the hall. The pain was a 10, and Kevin felt dizzy and scared. He felt he was being led to his destiny. *Fuck, just like that boat.*

Kevin broke the silence between the two with a question. "How long do these take?"

"Ah, a CT scan? Not long at all. You'll be in and out."

"And the results? They're immediate?" Kevin asked.

"No," Scott answered, "they're not immediate, but they don't take too long. It all depends."

"Ok."

"Don't worry, buddy," Scott continued, "the doc said to me, at least, that it looks like this one, for you, is just precautionary. They usually know when something is bad, and I really do not think she thought that, based on my experience."

Kevin didn't respond.

"You're gonna be ok," Scott reassured him.

Scott turned right at the end of the hall then quickly turned into a giant room with a couple nurses and techs in it. The first thing Kevin saw was the CT scanner. It was an ominous greyish white in color, with a long, thin bed jutting from a circular disk with a hole in the middle. Scott wheeled Kevin to the side of the machine and locked the chair in place.

"This is Kevin and he is here for a scan," Scott announced.

A red-haired younger nurse turned and smiled at Kevin then thanked Scott. Scott tapped Kevin on the shoulder and wished him good luck. Kevin just nodded in return.

As Scott walked out, he turned and said, "I'll be back for ya soon, Kevin."

The red-haired nurse introduced herself immediately after as Sawyer. She explained to Kevin the procedure as the techs readied the giant machine. Kevin felt his phone buzzing as Sawyer asked for his cell phone.

"I'll place it right here during the scan, ok?" she asked nicely.

Again, Kevin just looked and didn't respond.

Sawyer helped Kevin off the chair and onto the table. She turned and grabbed a vest-like garment from the adjacent table. She fitted it onto Kevin as she explained the vest to Kevin. "This will protect your chest area from radiation." She said, "We are just doing the head, so we don't need any radiation on the rest of your body."

With that short dialogue, she lay Kevin on the table and told him to sit still. He could not move during the test, she explained, which will only take about two minutes. Kevin lay on the table and took a deep breath. His head pounded and his heart raced. He made fists with both hands. Suddenly, the table moved Kevin towards the giant ring. His head and shoulders went into the ring and his legs remained outside as the bed stopped moving. All around him was the greyish ring. Light peered in from the room. He gazed around him at the machine.

"Ok, Kevin," the man next to the machine stated, "we are

going to start now, so don't move at all. Wait. Was there a contrast ordered?" the man asked Sawyer.

"No," she answered, "no contrast."

Kevin couldn't refuse himself as he asked, "What's contrast?"

The man leaned down to see Kevin in the ring and responded, "Contrast just helps us see the brain a little better, if needed."

Kevin lay and pondered that as he heard a whirl and a buzz begin within the ring.

"Ok, Kevin. Here we go. Lay perfectly still."

He wasn't even sure who said it. As it started, he felt the pain in his head subside, but he heard the shrieking laughter, although it was fading, as if it were running away. It was as if the pain and its fury had just suddenly scrammed. The buzz grew somewhat louder and he heard many beeps. He could see the man at the edge of his bed and saw Sawyer walk past the foot of the bed as the CT scanned him. He breathed heavy, pondered the contrast again, and lay still. The buzzing continued and Kevin could almost feel the vibration of the buzz. All movement stopped as Kevin peered out from under the ring. All he could see was the man standing next to him. Within a minute, the buzz slowed, and the beeping stopped. Kevin breathed out a sigh of relief, as he guessed the test was over. Soon enough, it was.

The bed moved outward from the ring and Kevin saw the man, Sawyer and Scott, with his wheelchair.

"Told you it was fast," Scott blurted out.

"Ok, Kevin, that's it," Sawyer said nicely as she helped him sit up. "You can go back with Scott and the doctor will be with you very shortly."

"Thank you," Kevin said quietly. He stepped down and Scott grabbed his arm to help.

"I'm fine," Kevin said as he looked at Scott.

"I know, I know, I just have to help. It's a guideline, buddy."

Scott wheeled Kevin back to the room in a hurry. As soon as they left the CT room, Kevin felt the pain again swooshing around his head and pounding at his forehead. *Fucking thing.* Scott moved Kevin back into his room. He helped Kevin back on the table and said his goodbyes. And like that, Scott was gone from Kevin's life.

Kevin sat and listened to the buzz in the hall. He heard small talk, beeping, and buzzing. He reached up with his right hand and massaged his forehead. The pain pounded with frenzy. Kevin rubbed and rubbed his forehead in an attempt to relieve the pain. He sat back on the bed, his hands and arms anchoring him as he leaned back and looked at the white ceiling. *Oh fuck, this is gonna turn out so bad.*

He waited impatiently, constantly moving and changing positions on the table. He rubbed his head, scratched his arms and ran his hands through his hair until it was a mess. Doctors, nurses and patients walked past his door, but they never entered. *It's gonna be a fucking tumor.* He stood up and breathed. He put his hands on his hips and leaned back, stretching out his stiff back. *Where the fuck is this doctor?*

Just then, he reached for his phone. *Fuck, I left it in that room.* He walked to the hall. As he peeked out, he saw Dr. Russell approaching and reading a piece of paper or something. He turned back into the room and sat down, closed his eyes, and breathed.

--

Nourzad sat in his dark study, wearing just shorts and a short-sleeved golf shirt. He held the chilled glass of gin in his right hand as he dangled a cigarette from his lips. His feet were up, and he stared at the television. His ash tray was filled with used cigarette butts, and there was spilled gin on his table and shirt. On the TV were old movies of his wife and kids. He stared, dragged his cigarette, and sipped his drink. He felt no physical pain at all. Above the TV, his clock read 12:27 a.m.

On the screen, his kids played in the yard as his wife spoke to him. It was a mid-July day, recently, and the sun was shining, and the grill was hot. The camera panned around the backyard from their deck as kids ran, threw balls and jumped around. His wife spoke of the food to be cooked and how beautiful the day was. On the screen, she approached him. She had long black hair, beautifully tanned skin and sunglasses. She wore a yellow sundress with straps. She came to him quickly and kissed him. "I love this man!" she yelled out.

Nourzad turned away from the TV and took a very long drink from his glass. The gin smoothly burned as it raced down his throat and perfectly coated his stomach. He lit another cigarette and continued watching the TV. His eyes grew heavy and his lungs began to burn. He drew in another drag of smoke as he stared at his wife on the TV sitting at the picnic table on their deck.

"Daddy! Daddy! Look!" he heard on the screen.

"I'm looking! That's great!"

The camera kept peering from the yard back to his wife, who now sat cross-legged, her perfect legs shining in the sun. She dipped her shades and winked at him. He turned away again from the TV and drank. He held the gin in his mouth then rushed the swallow. He followed up with another drag of the cigarette. He turned back to the TV and paused it on his wife. She was smiling, the sun beaming down perfectly on her. He just stared and stared. He dangled the cigarette from his fingers as the smoke trailed upwards. His drink was empty. The picture of his wife was still and perfect. He closed his eyes for the briefest of moments.

--

Dr. Russell walked in, still gazing at the paper she held. Kevin looked at her immediately for some sign of what the results stated.

"Ok, Kevin," she said as she pulled up a chair towards Kevin. "Hi."

"Um, hi." Kevin was confused.

She held up the paper. "These are the scans. I've looked them over."

"Ok."

"Now, I'm not a radiologist, ok? But I've been in this business a long time and I've read hundreds and hundreds of these. So, Kevin, we can see pretty much right away with the patient if there is something wrong, health wise, that is, in the head."

"Ok."

"I mean, if someone walks in with a brain tumor, we can tell usually, with how they walk, speak, move, etcetera. I didn't see that with you. And with these scans, you can usually tell right away if there is a malignancy or tumor or growth." She then looked at the scans one more time. "I don't see anything here, Kevin."

Kevin sighed.

"I know," she said, looking up at him, "you wanted some clarification, right?"

"I don't know what I wanted. Some answers, I guess."

"I know, but, sometimes, with headaches, a lot actually, you just don't get answers. And with these scans, there are no answers other than you are fine, health-wise."

"But I still have these headaches."

"You do. And we just don't know how long you'll have them. But it isn't anything to worry about regarding a disease that could harm you physically."

"Ok," Kevin said as he leaned back and looked at the ceiling. He looked back down at her and she stared at him.

"Now, I'll get these to the radiologist, who will look at them tomorrow. I'm sure he'll agree with my assessment. Then he will get them to Dr. Nourzad, and you can continue with him regarding treatment."

"Which is what? I mean..." His voice trailed off.

"There are a lot of good treatments for chronic headaches, which I think you have."

"Chronic?"

"Yes. That just means you have a headache more often than you do not. It's descriptive, not a diagnosis."

"Ok."

"And look, Dr. Nourzad is great. You're in good hands."

"Thanks."

"Ok," she said as she stood up, "I'm going to get you some 800 ibu to go home with for the pain. You can grab them in a sec. I just have to go do the paperwork. Meet me at my desk right out there in a couple of minutes"

"Sounds good," Kevin said. "Thank you."

"I hope they get better soon." And she walked out.

--

Kevin walked out of the hospital with a small bottle of ibuprofen and no answers. The half-moon peeked through the dark grey clouds as the pain thundered in his head. He was groggy and desperate. He wanted answers tonight, and he received none to his liking. The pain shuddered in his head. It was thunderous in its relentlessness. In the recess he heard a cackling, almost mocking laugh. *Fuck you!* He sat in the car for minutes, massaging his head on all sides. He swallowed a pill without water and began his drive home. Halfway there, he remembered he didn't have his phone.

--

Nourzad awoke to the smoke. It crept around his body quietly. He quickly jumped up, looked at the floor and saw a very small flame eating away at the throw rug by his feet. He stomped it out furiously with his shoes and waved the smoke to disburse it. He gazed at the source. His cigarette obviously dropped, he thought, as he fell asleep. Nourzad sat on the ground and tried remembering how he got here. He saw his glass and the mound of cigarettes in the tray. He breathed as he began to recall his night. His body turned so he could see the TV. It was still on pause. He slowly stood, staring at the screen. He reached for the remote control, shut the TV off, grabbed the glass, gulped down what was left and walked to his bedroom. He plopped down on the bed with his clothes on and passed out.

--

"Honey? Honey?" Rece shook Kevin ever so slightly. Kevin rolled over in the bed and looked groggily at Rece with one eye open.

"Oh, hey," Kevin said quietly and then shut his eye.

"How did everything go?" Rece asked, sitting up in bed now.

Kevin shifted and fully opened his eyes as best he could. "Oh, um, it was fine, it was ok, I guess. They did, um, a CT scan on my head."

"Oh my God! That's good, right?" Rece asked, putting her

hands on her face in surprise fashion.

"They didn't find anything wrong," Kevin said flatly.

Rece rushed into him and hugged him. "Oh my God, I'm so happy for you. I'm so happy you're ok."

"I know you are. Thanks. It's just that the headache is so bad still. I could barely drive home."

"I'm still so sorry I couldn't go with you, and I'm so sorry I didn't hear you come in. Vince was up most of the time you were gone puking and I just passed out. So sorry, sweetie."

"It's ok." Kevin rubbed his head and sighed.

"Did they give you more medicine?" Rece asked.

"Yeah, they did."

"Well, the CT scan should relieve you, no?"

Kevin held back an answer for a moment. Rece looked upon him. Kevin then spoke, "Yeah, I guess it should."

"But it didn't," Rece stated plainly.

Kevin looked at her, and spoke, "I mean, it did, but I looked up CT scans when I got home. They don't really use them to find brain tumors. MRI's are better at finding them. They can be missed with a CT scan. Plus, they didn't use contrast."

"Contrast?"

"Yeah, that's what I thought when I heard it last night. Contrast lets them see better in the brain, I guess."

Rece sat up straight and looked at Kevin. "Hm. I love you, sweetie, so much, you know that, but do you hear yourself?"

"What do you mean?" Kevin asked.

"I mean, look, every doctor you have seen has now told you that you just have headaches, that you don't have anything wrong with you. You don't have a brain tumor, yet you just won't listen to them."

"I know, you're right," Kevin said to her.

"There is no tumor. There's nothing there that's gonna kill you, and I know that's what you are still constantly worried about."

"I guess, yeah," Kevin said.

"Don't worry, honey, I'm telling you that you are ok. You always have looked for more than there is with your health. All your anxiety attacks, all your worries over minor pains, I mean, come on, Kevin. You always assume you are dying, and this time it's really bringing you down. You can't let it!" Rece raised her voice a bit as she said the last sentence.

Kevin sat up straight, his head pounding with pain. "I'm not letting it do anything. It's doing it on its own!" Kevin then lowered his voice a bit as he continued. "I'm just saying that something is really wrong with me and no one in that profession will do anything about it. Look, I can't even function anymore. It's there when I wake up, it's there all day, it's there at night, it wakes me up in the middle of the night," Kevin then raised his voice loudly, "and I just want it fucking gone!"

Rece stared at him and Kevin returned the stare. The moment was still and quiet as the couple both pondered how to continue and what to say. As per usual, it was Rece who spoke first. "Look, Kevin, you are going to get through this. I'm so confident that you are ok, health-wise. I'm confident that if you keep going to your doctor, you will fix this. You just have to stay strong."

Kevin stared blankly at her. Rece kissed him and got up out of bed.

"Where are you going?" Kevin asked.

"I have to shower."

"I'm a good husband," Kevin mumbled. "I'm a good dad."

Rece turned and leaned on the bed towards Kevin. "You are an exceptional husband and you are the best dad there absolutely is. What I love most about you is how good of a dad you are to our kids. I'm not saying you aren't. I'm saying, in all sincerity, Kevin, continue being that man."

RAE...

The knock on the door woke Nourzad. He shook out the cobwebs and looked at the clock. It was 6:30 am. He was groggy. *Another early knocking.* He went to put on clothes, and then realized he was fully dressed. *Oh my.* He did a quick look in the mirror and fixed his hair. Down the stairs he went and saw Rae standing on the front porch. *Oh, my word.* He sighed, paused at the door and then opened it.

"Hi Rae," Nourzad spoke first. "To what do I have the pleasure of this early visit?"

Rae walked in past him. "Well, you have work. I brought you donuts."

"Rae, you know I don't eat those."

Rae looked at him and said, "Well, you should. It'd be good for you to step out a bit from your norm."

"My norm," Nourzad said somewhat mockingly. He paused and looked at his aunt and then continued, "What is it, Rae?"

"I smell smoke. And you smell like liquor."

"Is that what you wanted? To tell me that?"

"No, I didn't smell it before I came in. Now I smell it, and I'm asking you why you smell like liquor and cigarette smoke."

Nourzad breathed in and walked past his aunt to the kitchen. Rae followed and sat at the table across from him.

"What's going on?" Rae asked worriedly.

"Nothing, Rae. Really."

"You never smoked before. Why now."

Nourzad responded quickly, "You never knew I smoked, that's all. I did. I just hid it from my family."

"You smoked behind her back?'

"You mean my wife? Yes, I did because I knew it would hurt her if she knew. It's no big deal, it was very little, but I did smoke, so you can't say I never smoked."

"Are you smoking more now?'

"More now?"

Rae looked at him angrily. "Why do you always make this so difficult?"

"Because I don't want to talk about it!" Nourzad yelled and stood up.

"But you have to. This is even more reason to!" Rae retorted.

"This what?"

"This smoking and drinking. You look hung over. Are you drinking everyday now?"

"Every day? Look, Rae, I'm not doing this with you. I have patients today and I have to get moving."

"Do you think your patients want a doctor looking at them who is hung over?"

Nourzad looked down and laughed. "Rae," he said, "this is really not a problem. I love you. I appreciate you. But I'm fine."

"You say that, but you aren't fine." Rae grabbed his arm as he tried to walk past her. "You need to speak with a professional."

Nourzad turned to her, "I am a professional. I know all about it, ok? I studied it. I'm the professional. I'm dealing with it, and Rae, my Rae, I am fine."

"Promise your aunt that you will talk to someone." Rae

stared at him. There was a long pause.

"Aunt Rae, I promise you, soon, I will talk to someone about it."

"About what, Franky?"

Nourzad smiled and raised his voice a bit. "About my wife and kids, ok, Rae, about them getting crushed and burned to death on a highway when I was at work, ok!? There! Are you happy?!""

Rae looked at her sweet nephew and stood up to hug him.

"No, no, no, Rae, no hugs. I really have to go, and I don't want to talk about this stuff with you anymore. I want you to visit, but it is becoming nauseating talking about this over and over and over. It's all you ever bring up."

"If you talk to someone else, a professional, I'll leave you alone about it."

"Ok," Nourzad said quickly.

Rae walked past him to the door. "I hope you eat a donut," she said. "If nothing else, bring them to work."

"Rae," Nourzad said as she opened the door. "I love you."

"I love you, too, Franky. Talk to someone." Rae then walked out. Nourzad stood and thought about the last few minutes and last night.

I'M A CALL AWAY

"Are you working today?"

Kevin looked at Rece and responded. "Yes."

"Ok, good. How do you feel?"

"The same."

"Can you work?"

"I'm going in. We'll see."

"Ok."

Rece approached Kevin and kissed him on the cheek. "Remember," Rece said, "I go away for the night on Friday."

"Ok." Kevin sat and stared.

"You'll be ok. I feel terrible, but I promised her long before all this was so serious."

Kevin looked at her. "I know. I just miss you and worry, that's all."

Rece sat next to him and held him. "You are going to be ok. I'll have my phone. We aren't going far. If you need me, I'm a call away from coming right home."

Kevin leaned over and kissed her. "Thank you."

--

Friday came quickly. Rece was up early, showering as Kevin lay in bed. His head pounded as he lay there still. The TV was off, and he heard the shower turn off. Rece walked out, just in a towel, beads of water glistening on her perfect skin. Kevin looked at her for a second, then asked, "What are the kids doing again?"

Rece smiled and sat next to him on the bed, her leg touching his. "Ok, things changed a bit. Blaize has a sleepover; he's leaving at 2 today. Your mom will pick the others up soon, actually."

"How long will she have them?"

"Till tomorrow night."

Rece got up, dropped her towel and reached into her drawer for underwear. Kevin looked, then asked, "So, I'm alone tonight?" He clasped his hands again, as they began to twitch at the thought.

Rece grabbed her panties and walked over to Kevin and sat on the bed, naked. "You'll be alone, but remember, I'm a phone call away, ok?" She leaned in and kissed his cheek. She waited there for a moment, then leaned back, looked at him, and then continued getting dressed. She then walked into the bathroom.

The pain in Kevin's head pulsated, and then swirled violently in his head. It was an eruption of new proportions. He buried his head in the pillows and squeezed his eyes shut. He leaned over, opened his eyes and gazed on the nightstand for pain relief. He didn't see any.

Rece came out of the bathroom dressed. "Want to come down and eat with me?"

"Sure."

They walked downstairs and Kevin sat at the table quietly as Rece made oatmeal and toast.

"I see you're in a lot of pain, sweetie."

"It's ok."

"Please don't worry too much. That always makes things

worse for you," Rece said.

Kevin sat and listened but didn't respond.

"Oh!" Rece blurted. "The hospital!"

"What?"

"Your phone. You should go get it today. It'll keep you busy."

Kevin shrugged. "I'll get it eventually. Not today, though."

"Kevin, you need it."

"We have the land-line."

"Ok, so you're not getting it today?"

"No, I don't think so."

"Get it tomorrow then, for sure."

"I will."

"Good," Rece said and walked the breakfast over to the table. "It's hard to believe you've made it this long without your phone." Rece then smiled.

Kevin giggled somewhat. "Right?"

Kevin and Rece ate as she spoke to Kevin. "Look, you're gonna be good this weekend. I'll be home tomorrow. Just use this time to relax, watch sports, get your phone and relax. I really think the downtime will help you."

"Thanks, honey," Kevin responded between bites. Then he put his spoon down. "It's just that…"

"What?" Rece asked.

Kevin paused then said, "It's just that I miss you and all, and I'm just so weak when you're not here."

"I know. But I'm here, ok? Just a phone call away for any-thing you need. Anything."

They looked at each other for a long moment. Their eyes were locked. Just then the kids stammered down the stairs.

Time's up.

--

Dr. Nourzad sat in his office with light background music on, studying from a book titled 'Headaches – Causes and Responses'. He took notes and flipped from chapter to chapter. On his desk was Kevin's file.

Nourzad wrote down on his notes:

Beta Blockers – propranolol?

Tricyclic? Anti-depress.

Valproate? Topiramate?

Botox?

Beta blocker best bet?

Nourzad sat back and thought. A call interrupted his process.

"Yes?" Nourzad answered.

"It's Rae, doctor. She said to not take 'no' for an answer."

Nourzad chuckled. "I guess I have to take it then?"

"Yes. I'll put her through."

"Yes, Rae. How are you?" Nourzad stated.

"Well, I don't matter, really," Rae responded, "I'm calling to check on you."

"I'm good, Rae, thank you."

"Have you, um, seen anybody?"

"Anybody?" Nourzad answered playing dumb.

"Doctor, you know what I mean."

"We just spoke about this, Rae. You are too pushy. But to ease your pain, I will tell you, I am set to talk to someone tomorrow morning."

"On a Saturday?"

"Yes, Rae. Doctors do work on Saturday."

"So, you're seeing a doctor then, good."

"I will be speaking with a doctor, so, yes, you can relax," Nourzad said courteously.

"Well, young fella, I'm so proud of you."

"Thank you, Rae. Anything else?"

"Are you going to Ralph's on Sunday?"

Nourzad paused. "No."

"Why not?"

"Rae, you know I don't go to Ralph's."

"Oh, Franky. They feel bad. You haven't seen them since it happened."

"I know. But there's really no reason. I just haven't seen them."

"Franky," Rae said, "It was an invite, like any other. Nobody could have known. They feel so badly."

"Rae, I have to go."

"Think about it, please."

"I'll talk to you soon, Rae."

"Good luck at the doctor's."

"Goodbye, Rae."

And Nourzad hung up. He immediately went back to studying headaches.

--

Rece walked back from the car dressed in blue jeans, a white long-sleeved shirt and gym shoes. Kevin stared at her from the window, sipping his coffee. He gazed upon her like it was the first time he saw her. *She's beautiful.*

The storm door closed and Rece stood, staring at Kevin. "That's it, I think," she said.

"Ok," Kevin responded.

"I already said goodbye to the kids, so come here," Rece said, extending her arms.

Kevin approached her; his eyes locked into hers. He reached her and they hugged, his arms wrapped tightly around her. Rece placed her head on his shoulders. No words were spoken during the hug.

"You're going to be ok," Rece spoke softly, as she pulled away from the hug. "This is going to be good for you."

Kevin held her hands. "Ok. I love you," he said.

"I love you, too, sweetie."

They looked into each other's eyes again. Kevin felt tears welling in his eyes, fear and loneliness gripping his insides.

"I'm really gonna miss you," he said

"I'm going to miss you more."

He walked her out to the car and opened the door for her. She sat down, put on her sunglasses, and looked at Kevin. "Remember, I'm just a call away. If you need anything..."

"I know. I love you." Kevin leaned into the car and kissed her cheek. "See you tomorrow."

"Call and text me," Rece said.

"I will."

He closed the door for her and Rece pulled away. He watched her turn left at the corner, and she disappeared into the neighborhood. Kevin took a deep breath and held it. His head was full of pressure, and pain circled his skull. As he walked to the door the pain increased, and the fullness inside expanded. He walked quickly to the couch and laid down. He had things to do to get the kids ready, per Rece, but the pain was too much at that point. He grabbed a pillow and squeezed it tight against his forehead and eyes. *I need something to stop this.*

He went up to his room and into his drawer. Buried beneath his shirts were two bottles. One had 800 milligrams of ibuprofen. It was the bottle he received from the ER. The other bottle was extra strength Tylenol. He looked at both, popped two Tylenol then dropped the Tylenol and buried it below some shirts. He took a white pill from the other bottle, placed it in his mouth, walked to the sink, ran the water and swallowed the pill. He rested his hands on the counter as he leaned into it. His eyes were closed. He heard feet walking into his room.

"You ok, dad?"

"Yes, Kate. I'm fine. Just give me a hug."

"Oh my God."

Kevin stepped towards her and hugged her. "Do you have everyone packed for the night?"

"Two nights, dad, duh."

"Mom said one," Kevin said confused.

"Mom was wrong."

"What the....ok."

"Grandma called last night. She wanted us 'till Sunday."

"Alright, alright, no problem. I'll have Blaize."

"Um, no, you won't. He's going for the week now."

"Did mom know that, too?"

"No. I just talked to Blaize and he's going to ask you. Just say yes. It's ok."

Kevin paused in the hectic conversation. "Great, ok, I will."

Kate reached out and hugged him. "Love you, dad."

"Kate, why'd you come in here?"

"Blaize wanted me to feel you out on him asking you."

"Ahhhh...." Kevin shook his head and smiled the smallest smile. "Tell him I said yes..."

Kate ran out.

"...but he's got to give me all the details!", Kevin yelled to her as she ran down the hall. *Ugh.*

"Dad!!!!!!"

Kevin heard the scream as he rubbed his forehead, hoping for a deadening of the pain.

"Vince!" he yelled. "If you want me, come here!"

He instantly heard Vince running full speed down the hall. Vince stopped and looked at Kevin. There was a long pause.

"Yes? Vince?"

"Oh. I don't have a bag to pack."

"A bag?"

"Yes. They all have bags, I don't."

"Mom said they would share a bag!" Kevin heard Kate scream down the hall.

Kevin clapped his hands, "There you go, little man. Share your brother's bag."

Vincent ran back down the hall. Kevin sat on his bed and buried his head into his hands. The ibuprofen hadn't kicked in yet. The pain was full. He heard the kids yelling, talking and packing. His parents would be there soon to take them. *What the fuck, I'm gonna be all alone.* "Fuck." His hands twitched.

--

For the second time in two hours, Kevin was on the street waving good-bye to loved ones. Blaize was inside packing, and soon he'd be gone, too. He squinted his eyes as he watched his mom's car drive away. His head felt still, but full. The ibuprofen and Tylenol trapped the pain for the moment, but the fullness was felt. His head weighed heavy, like it was full of cement, and his eyes hurt from the previous pain. He rubbed his forehead and went inside to sit down. He laid his head back for a moment, free of the extreme pain. But he knew it would be back, and soon. He closed his eyes, exhausted from the headaches, and he thought of Rece. *God, I wish she was here.* His eyes weighed heavier, as he laid back more, covering his eyes with a pillow.

What felt like a few moments later, he shuddered as he awoke. His head was full, and pain circled his skull again. The pain pushed sideways, attempting to escape through his skull. He looked around to see where he was. The house was quiet. *Blaize.*

He sat up. "Blaize," he said somewhat quietly. There was no answer. "Blaize!" Still no answer. He stood up and walked, his eyes squinting as he walked upstairs, overwhelmed by the pain. He looked in Blaize's room and saw that his bags were gone. "Fuck, what the fuck, Blaize?"

He reached into his pocket for his phone. "God-dammit! Fuck!" His phone was still at the hospital. He thought a million thoughts. He paced quickly down the stairs, looking for a note from Blaize on the table or fridge. There was nothing. He reached for the landline, then threw it down. *I don't know his fucking number!* He was sweating now, still reeling from the pain in his head. He ran upstairs and grabbed more pills. He swallowed them pills with water. He looked for the car keys and made his way to the car. *Fuck, they better still have my phone. Fucking Blaize.* Kevin raced down his street, barely stopping at the stop sign.

I LEFT IT HERE...

As he pulled into the hospital lot, Kevin felt nauseas and his head was pounding. The pain was exploding. He squinted as he drove into the lot. To his right, he caught the glimpse of a white car pulling out of the lot. A sudden burst of shrieking laughter ran through his head. He turned quickly. *Rece?*

He turned his head as far as he could to see if it was her. He lost sight of it but turned the car around and saw it driving away. It was too far to see the driver. All he could see was the similar make and color of Rece's car. *Was that her? Why would she be here?* "What the fuck is going on?" he whispered to himself. He reached around for his phone to call her. *Motherfucker.*

Kevin saw a parking spot in the middle of his pondering. He pulled in and parked. He looked down the road again, but the car was gone into the distance. For a split-second he thought he'd go follow it, but instead, he went inside to get the phone.

--

"Yes, I left it here a few days ago. In the ER." Kevin spoke quickly to the receptionist.

"Were you a patient?" she asked.

"Yes. I was. I called yesterday, and they said they had it."

"Who did?"

"I don't know, I called the number to the ER, a woman answered it, I explained my situation, and she looked for it then said, yes, we have it, we'll hold it for you."

"Ok. And your name is?"

"Kevin. Kevin Ruscevich."

"Ok, I will go check."

Kevin sighed loudly and turned towards the ER waiting room. He saw people coughing, some were bleeding, and most looked like they'd been waiting a long time. He didn't enter the waiting area. Instead, he leaned up against the wall adjoining the entrance. And he waited. He couldn't stand still, his legs shaking from the pain and the concern for Blaize. Pain shot up through his head. The Tylenol hadn't kicked in and the pain was enjoying its release, spreading all over his head. The fullness made him feel heavy as ever in his head. He wanted to lie down.

Leaning against the wall, he listened, looked and waited. Dozens of patients went by him as he slouched more and more against the wall. The woman who went to look for the phone had been gone over an hour now. He asked the next receptionist, but, to her credit, she didn't know where that woman was, or where the phone was. Kevin pleaded with her to check, and she did. And she did come back but could not find 'Sheila'.

"As soon as I find her, I will let her know," she said. "Oh, and I asked back there about the phone. Nobody knows. I'm sorry. Do you want to still wait, or come back?"

"I really, really need to contact my son," Kevin said. "I need that phone to do so. It's really quite important. I'm not sure how a receptionist just disappears. It seems really strange that she'd tell me she'd go look for it; she knows I'm here and waiting, yet, she doesn't come back. It's strange and it's really rude, as well."

"I understand your frustration Mr..."

"No, you really don't!" Kevin busted in.

"Let me go check again."

Kevin walked back to his wall and leaned. New patients

came in, looking for the receptionist. Kevin chuckled inside. *Unreal.* Through the new congestion, he saw the double-doors open just north of the waiting room. Three nurses walked in, and behind them was Dr. Nourzad. His head was down, reading some papers. Kevin didn't say anything; he just gazed out of his periphery to follow him. *Interesting.* Nourzad kept his head down as he approached Kevin, but Kevin almost surely saw Nourzad peek at him. *That motherfucker looked right at me.* Nourzad passed right by Kevin, with Kevin's eyes never losing sight. Kevin looked up at his back. Nourzad approached the west doors into the ER, and then stopped. He looked back and looked right at Kevin.

"Kevin?"

Fuck. Kevin stood up straight and responded. "Doctor." Kevin couldn't believe what just happened.

Nourzad approached and shook Kevin's hand. "Ah, I see you are squinting."

Kevin didn't respond.

Nourzad continued to hold Kevin's hand. He then turned his head and said, "Come with me. Let's talk."

He pulled Kevin by the hand for a split second, then released. Kevin followed without being able to say a word. They entered the ER and walked briskly, for some reason. Nourzad stopped at the first desk.

"Jo, do you mind if my patient and I use room two for a second? I saw it was open. We'll just be a minute or two."

"Sure, Dr. Nourzad, if we need it..."

"Of course, Jo."

The two men walked into ER room #2. Nourzad closed the door and stood, his arms crossed in front of his body. Kevin stood a few feet away.

"Please, Kevin, sit."

"My wife calls me Kevin when she's mad at me," Kevin blurted out. He wasn't sure why that came out.

Nourzad chuckled and released his arms. "I can assure you, Kevin, um, Mr. Ruscevich, I'm not mad at you. I just wanted to see how you were."

"Kind of happenstance that we bumped into each other, though," Kevin said.

"Yes, but I've been going over your file, and saw you, so, I just thought I could see how you were doing. If you are uncomfortable here…"

"No, no, it's fine. I'm just having a day, and the reason I'm here is because I left my cell phone here last time, and now they can't find it, and I'm in need of it badly."

"What's it look like?" Nourzad asked. Before Kevin could answer, he continued. "You know what, come with me."

The two walked through the ER to a small office in the west rear. Nourzad opened it. On the desk sat a box. Nourzad shuffled through it and pulled out two cell phones. Kevin immediately recognized his.

"That's it!"

"Lost and found box. Old school, I guess is what they'd say."

Kevin looked at him sideways then attempted to turn on his phone. "Crap. It's dead."

"Follow me."

They walked back the same way they came, Nourzad in front and Kevin following. Kevin looked into the passing ER rooms and noticed patients lying in pain, lying in wait and just lying. They scurried too fast for Kevin to get good looks at what was going on in each room. Finally, Nourzad stopped walking. Not paying attention, Kevin walked into him.

"Sorry."

"Jo, do you have a charger for an iPhone – Kevin, what is yours?"

"It's a 5."

"…an iPhone 5?"

Jo smiled and opened a drawer. "Hmmm, I think so, let me just see," she said like a grandma to a grandchild pretending to look for a toy that she knows is there. "Here ya go!"

Nourzad smiled and clapped. "Ah, Jo. Perfect. Kevin is going to use this to charge up his phone, as he has a very important call to make, and we will return it soon."

Kevin smiled at Jo and whispered a thank you.

"Now, Kevin, shall we?"

The two walked back to the room and Kevin immediately plugged in his phone. "I really need to get a hold of my son."

"I know," Nourzad said calmly as he sat on a table. "Why don't you sit, and as soon as it charges you can call."

Kevin seemed uneasy, as if he was in trouble. "Ok."

He looked at Nourzad and they stared at each other for what felt to Kevin like minutes. Nourzad finally spoke. "So, I see you and I just want to see how you are. You never came in."

Kevin looked at his phone. It wasn't charged, yet. He looked back at Nourzad. "Um, to be honest, doc, it hasn't got any better."

"I see…" Nourzad began. Just then the phone lit up.

Kevin ran to the phone, punched in his password and dialed Blaize. As it rang, he glanced at Nourzad, who looked at Kevin then glanced down at his shoes.

"Blaize!" Kevin yelled. "Where did you go?"

Kevin listened.

"But you didn't tell me."

Kevin rubbed his forehead and sat in a chair.

"Ok, I know, but I didn't think I was asleep, but ok."

Kevin rolled his head from left to right.

"Ok. But next time, no, I know. I know."

Kevin breathed in deeply.

"Ok, well, just know I love you."

He leaned forward, placing his elbows on his knees.

"Ok, bye. I love you." Kevin ended the call.

"Everything good?" Nourzad asked quickly.

"Yes."

"I'm glad."

"For me?" Kevin asked strangely.

"Yes, Kevin, for you," Nourzad responded. "Are you ok?"

"Yeah, yeah, it's just, I don't know, never mind. It just seems weird, us meeting here, I don't know." Kevin paused and then asked, "Why are you here?"

"I was just passing through that hall. You were picking up a phone you left here."

Kevin rubbed his forehead again, stronger this time. "I guess, yeah, you're right, but you don't work here."

There was a pause as the two looked at each other, a new dynamic had begun.

"Well," Nourzad said, ignoring Kevin's last statement, "the headaches?"

Kevin breathed. "Not better," Kevin said. "In fact, worse.

Much worse, and all this stress isn't helping."

"Stress, yes. Like?" Nourzad asked.

Kevin stood. "Well, ya know, doc, I don't know if that's something I want to tell you."

"It is, Kevin. Headaches are a quandary, and every little thing helps find the solution."

"I get that, but I'm stressed. The why shouldn't matter, should it?"

"Well, you're stressed," Nourzad spoke. "That should pass soon, and hopefully that will ease the headaches a bit as stress can definitely keep a headache going."

Kevin just looked at the doctor.

"So, you didn't take any over-the-counters, correct?" Nourzad asked.

"No," Kevin began.

"Since we saw each other last?"

"No."

"Then it makes sense you may not be getting any relief," Nourzad said.

"Yeah," Kevin said softly. "look, we can see each other soon. Can this wait?"

"Absolutely!" Nourzad said with zero hesitation. "I'm just following a colleague's advice, you see. Sometimes, Kevin, doctors need a lesson, too."

"Advice?" Kevin asked.

Nourzad breathed in. "I've had some, I don't know, personal issues of late," Nourzad said, in a story-telling way. "These issues may have been affecting my work mental state, so to speak. I know, I know, you don't need to hear the what's and so-forths; but, in a moment of, shall we say, stress, a colleague told me to focus on a patient, any patient, really, and work to get that one patient better. To do whatever I can to help that one patient. He advised me that this process would focus me. So, I'm trying it"

Nourzad paused. The two men looked at each other. Kevin squinted at the doctor, his pain worsening from not having any over-the-counter pain relief in a while.

"You, Kevin, are that patient," Nourzad said.

Oh, what the fuck?

"I'm going to help you deal with this pain."

Kevin pressed his lips together and nodded again. "Well, doctor, thank you. I, I guess I appreciate that."

Nourzad popped up off the desk like a child done with school. He extended his hand to Kevin. Kevin looked at the hand before extending. "I will see you soon."

Nourzad then walked out the door. Kevin took the phone and noticed the charger. He grabbed it and walked it back to Jo.

"Jo?"

Jo looked at Kevin and smiled. She had long brown hair, dark skin and beautiful eyes. She looked cute in her hospital blues. "Oh, my chord!"

"Yeah, the doctor forgot it, I guess."

"Oh, him? Yeah, he does that at times, but such a nice guy," Jo said bubbly.

Kevin just smiled. He looked at Jo and didn't know what to say. Jo helped him.

"Nice to meet you, Kevin!"

Kevin nodded. "Nice to meet you, too, Jo." Kevin turned

away and then quickly turned back to her. "Oh, and thank you."

"You're so welcome!"

Kevin looked at her a little more. Jo looked back and smiled an awkward smile.

"Look, Jo," Kevin said, "can I ask you a question?"

"Sure," Jo said, relieved Kevin's awkward stare was over.

"Dr. Nourzad," Kevin said, "do you know why he was here today?"

"He had rounds."

"Rounds, huh?" Kevin said.

"Yeah, in fact I was his nurse this morning during rounds."

Kevin nodded like a detective does when he learns a key fact in a case.

"So, he woulda been busy..." Kevin said under his breath and then began to walk away.

"But that was a couple hours ago," Jo said out of nowhere. "Sometimes Dr. Franky just hangs around." She then giggled.

Kevin turned and looked at her. He nodded the nod again.

STARING

In his walk to his car, Kevin circled around to the back lot. He eyed the cars, searching for Rece's. He saw no car looking similar to the one he'd seen that morning. He did a quick walk up and down the lot, then turned towards the front lot, where he'd parked earlier. *Weird.*

The pressure in his head made him dizzy. He walked slow and steady, making imaginary lines on the ground and attempting to walk them without veering off the line. He succeeded both times. Pain pushed out of his skull in all directions. *Fuckin' Christ.* He reached his car and sat in the driver's seat after turning on the car. He immediately turned off the radio. He sat and rubbed his head. He thought of Nourzad, and Rece. The whole meeting with Nourzad flashed through his head. *So fucking weird.* He grabbed his phone and called Rece.

"Hey hon!" Rece spoke loudly as she answered.

"Hey, for any reason, right?" Kevin said softly.

"Are you ok, sweetie?" Rece asked warmly.

"I'm ok, I was just at the hospital."

"Are you..." Rece began to ask, and then paused. "Oh, the phone?"

"Yeah, I got my phone," Kevin said with a giggle. "Obviously, right? Took a while, but I got it."

"Oh, that's good honey. I'm glad, but I thought...." Rece cut herself off, and then caught on. "Oh, yes, obviously you got it because you're calling me."

"Yeah," Kevin said. "So, anyways, I kinda thought I saw your car in the lot when I was pulling in here, so I was just seeing if you had come to see me."

Rece answered right away. "No, no sweetie. I didn't even know you were going there this morning, remember? I'm sorry. It wasn't me."

"Ok," Kevin said quietly.

"You ok, sweetie?" Rece asked again.

"Yeah, oh yeah, I'm just, uh, gonna go home now."

"Ok, sweetie, well, we are on the road, and we are about an hour out, so I'll text you or call you when I get there."

"Ok."

"Look, you sound miserable," Rece said sympathetically.

"No, no, no, don't worry about it, hon. Just have fun."

"Ok, baby." Rece sounded sad. "Look, you go home and relax, ok? I'll call you when I get there."

"It's ok, Rece. I'll be ok. I'm just gonna go home. You have fun."

"Relax, ok?" Rece reiterated.

"I will."

"I love you, Kevin."

"Love you too."

And with that, Kevin began his ride home. He drove in complete pain. His head was so full he wanted to pop it. The pain was excruciating. His stomach was nauseas. He drove by the local food mart and immediately pulled into the lot. He wanted a pop to soothe his stomach.

Inside the mart, he went down the aisles until he saw the pop. He grabbed a 6-pack of Coke and went around the back of the aisle. His head was pounding, he was dizzy. He thought of Nourzad. He thought of Rece's car. He thought of this unrelenting pain. As he opened his eyes from a strong squint, he saw the liquor aisle. He kept his periphery on the aisle as he walked by. He thought of his drawer at work. As he reached the end, near the checkout, he turned into the liquor section and went to the beer aisle. A slow laughter formed in his head. He looked around and saw no one laughing. He shook his head and went on. There he stood, pondering his pain, Nourzad, Rece and the fact that he was alone for the weekend. *I hate being alone.* "Fuck," he said softly. He looked at the cold beer. His hands twitched. *What could be the harm? It might help.*

He stood and stared at the beer for minutes. The twitching continued. He remembered how good it tasted and how good it made him feel. Rece was gone, the kids were gone. The pain was not. *I can try this.* "Yes, yes, I can," he whispered to himself. *I'm not drinking again, I'm just seeing if it'll help with the head-aches, that's all.* He first grabbed a 6-pack of beer. He walked two steps, turned around and replaced the 6-pack with a 12-pack. He stood holding the beer. *Just tonight, that's it.* He then quickly put the beer back on the shelf and stared at it. He breathed heavily. And stared at it. And stared at it. He rubbed his chin. His hands twitched. He then grabbed the 12-pack again and placed it in his cart.

He checked out, keeping an eye out for anyone who might see him buying beer. He asked the bagger to bag the beer. "Thank you," he said softly. He walked out of the store, again keeping an eye out for people he knew. He made it to the car, feeling like he had escaped being caught. He breathed deeply as he opened the bag to see his beer. *It'll be fine. Just one or two to see if it works.*

Once home, Kevin carried his bag inside and placed the beer on the kitchen table. He then sat down, his head in terrible pain. He put his elbow on the table and his chin in his palm. He stared at the beer. It had been a couple years since he had a sip of alcohol.

I never had a real problem. I can do this. It will help.

He continued staring at the beer, thinking about Rece, and what she'd think and say about this.

She's not here. She won't know. I have to see if this will work.

As he thought that, the pain in his head shuddered, like thunder railing through the sky. It was almost a whopping sound of thrills and excitement.

Drink it, it'll help.

The fullness expanded, causing him to wince. He continued staring at the beer.

His phone rang and he jumped up, grabbed the beer and threw it in the fridge. He held the refrigerator door closed as he stared at his phone, which he'd left on the table. He walked slowly to it, staring at it until he could see the caller ID. He didn't answer. The phone remained silent for a few moments, then rang again. Kevin stared at it and rubbed his head using both palms into his forehead. He breathed in deeply then reached for the phone.

"Hey, hon," Kevin answered as he rested the phone between his ear and shoulder.

Rece responded happily. "Hi! How are you?"

"I'm good, thanks."

"Feel any better?"

"No, not really."

"Aw, I'm so sorry," Rece said. "I wish I could be there to help."

"It's ok."

There was a long pause.

"You don't seem talkative," Rece said.

"I'm fine," Kevin responded. "I'm just tired."

"You ok?"

"Yeah."

"You sure?"

"Yes, I'm sure."

"Hm. Ok. Look, if there's anything you want to tell me…" Rece left her sentence incomplete.

How does she fucking always know?

"Honey?" Rece asked.

"No, sorry," Kevin said. "All good. I'm just sitting here. I, um, got home and now just gonna relax, like you said."

"Ok, sweetie. You do that," Rece said sweetly. "Listen, there are some bubble beads in the bathroom. Pour some into the tub and why don't you take a nice bath. It'll relax you and I think it'll help with the headache."

"Ok, I'll try that."

"Ok, good," Rece said back. "I'll call you tonight, ok?"

"Ok."

"You sure there's nothing else?" Rece asked quietly.

"No, I'm good. Thank you."

"Ok. I love you."

"Bye, hon."

"Bye."

Kevin hung up and realized he didn't say 'I love you' back. He texted Rece a heart emoji and placed the phone down. He sat back, placing his hand on his cheek. He stared at the fridge and stared at the fridge. He looked at it deeply and menacingly. He was almost studying it. He sighed. *Just a few.*

...THYSELF

Later that evening, Dr. Nourzad walked into the room and sat in the chair, waiting to begin his session as a patient, as he promised Rae. He had told her it was tomorrow, but he moved it up to the evening. He was uncomfortable. He didn't want to do this. But he knew Rae wouldn't stop bothering him unless he did. He decided on a doctor he could trust, someone who was familiar with his predicament, someone who would understand him, and someone with whom he'd talked to before. Still, as he waited to begin, he moved back and forth in his chair, adjusting his comfort level and showing his nerves.

He closed his eyes and wrung his hands together. He gathered his thoughts and imagined what he'd say. As he opened his eyes, the doctor was sitting across from him. Nourzad made eye contact.

"Good to see you again, doctor."

"You too," Nourzad responded.

"You look well."

Nourzad shifted in his chair. "Thank you."

"So, it's been a while."

"Yes," Nourzad said quietly as he looked around the room. "I didn't feel the need of late to do this. Oh, and thank you for seeing me earlier than tomorrow."

"Never a problem. So, what can we talk about?"

"I, um, I guess, um, my family," Nourzad said uncomfortably.

"Ah, yes. I don't think we've ever spoke of them."

"Well, there was never a need, until now, I guess."

"Until now?" Nourzad was asked.

Nourzad stared at the doctor across from him for a long time, minutes almost. He wrung his hands again and shifted forward. "My family is gone."

"Gone?"

"Dead."

"I see. I'm so sorry."

"It's ok," Nourzad said. "It's been a bit since they left."

"Losing a family member can have traumatizing effects. I can't imagine the burden of someone who lost their entire family. Can we discuss the circumstances of their deaths?"

"It was a car crash."

"I'm so sorry, Frank."

Nourzad sat quietly, waiting for the next question.

"Have you dealt with it?"

"Dealt with it?" Nourzad asked.

"Have you reconciled it with yourself? Is there pain, sorrow, blame?"

"Blame?" Nourzad asked impatiently. "Why do you ask that?"

"I'm just covering all possibilities, Frank."

Nourzad sat and thought. He wasn't sure what to say, but he was angry, now, for doing this. "I don't blame myself."

"That's good."

"Why is that good?" Nourzad asked.

"It's good because you aren't carrying that burden."

"Well, maybe I am," Nourzad said, looking down at the floor.

"Should you blame yourself?"

Nourzad breathed out. He shifted around in the chair and looked upward. He took a deep breath. "They wanted to go to the beach."

"Ok."

"They wanted to go to the beach with me."

"And?"

"And I said I had to work."

"Did you?"

Nourzad stared at the doctor. The doctor asked him again, "Did you have to go to work?"

"I went to work. I didn't have to, I guess." Nourzad closed his eyes and breathed.

"Please continue."

"Continue? I just told you."

"No, you explained a partial situation from your past. You didn't expound. I want you to expound."

"Expound. You want me to expound." Nourzad sounded sarcastic.

"Do you want help? Do you want to figure this out?"

"I'm fine!" Nourzad shouted and stood up. "This is stupid, Rae! I don't need this. I am fine!"

"Are you?"

Nourzad faintly heard the question. He turned his back and thought of walking out. He then turned back as his rage and anger built. He looked deeply across from him. He stared, seeing a blur across the room and wondering what may be asked next.

"Are you ok?"

Nourzad looked down and closed his eyes. He felt for the chair and sat back down.

"Take your time."

Nourzad sat and thought of his family. He saw each of their faces as he saw them the very last time. He wanted a drink. He wanted to forget.

"I want to forget them!" Nourzad shouted. The room was silent. Nourzad looked up and saw the doctor's pained face. Nourzad continued quieter as a tear fell down his cheek. "I want to forget them, ok? Every minute of every day, they are in my thoughts. I run from them, diving into work, drinking, and smoking, anything to forget them. If that makes me a bad person, then it makes me a bad person."

"Why would that make you bad?"

"Oh my God," Nourzad said exhaustingly. "This, look, this just doesn't help."

"No, no, Frank. You were expounding. You need to continue."

"I'm not supposed…" Nourzad began, and then stopped.

"Go on."

More tears lined Nourzad's cheeks. He rubbed them off with his hands. "I told my beautiful wife and my amazing kids that I couldn't go to the beach with them that day because I had to work. By having to work, I meant that I'd rather go into the office and see who I could help, who needed this treatment, who needed more time with me, who needed me! Me! Nourzad the Savior, they call me! I think I can save fucking everyone, they say, and no one will survive without me!"

"We've discussed this before. Is it true? Do you feel you must save everyone?"

"Oh, fuck that," Nourzad said. "I don't give a fuck about what they say. I do save people!"

"You do, I'm sure, but sometimes doctors…"

Nourzad interrupted. "Fuck. That."

"Then go back to discussing your family."

Nourzad yelled, "Go back to my family? Fine! They fucking needed me! My family needed me! I fucking killed them! They died in a blazing fire as I sat at work and now I have to live with it every fucking day, so I want to forget them, so I don't have to burden this fucking blame for killing my family!"

The doctor said nothing. Nourzad wept. The room was quiet, except for the sniffles and hiccups from the patient.

"The cliché response, Frank, is that we don't know why things happen. There are just some things we cannot control. My response, my trained, life-experience response is that every day people make choices, not because they are bad people, but because they prioritize and see a future wherein, they can make up time lost. But sometimes, for the reasons we can never understand, those futures are taken from us. It doesn't make them bad people that they made a choice. It just makes them human. We all take for granted a future that we envision, a future of family, happiness, and love. When it's taken from us, we look back and blame ourselves for being the one thing that we truly are, human. You made a choice that day. People go to the beach, or for drives, every day and they come home. Your family didn't because an accident occurred. It was nobody's fault. You made a human choice, with no evil intent. You thought you'd see them again. As for saving everyone, you know, Frank, you lost your parents at a very young age. It's wholly understandable that those experiences would force you to try to do anything and everything to heal everyone you come in contact within this profession. It's two separate issues, Frank."

Nourzad stared and cried, the tears flowing down, so much so he stopped wiping them. He heard every word spoken and had had enough. He wiped a cheek clean with his shirt and stood up and pointed at the mirror across from his chair which showed only his reflection.

"You know what?" He then paused. "Fuck you! You actually believe this crap you say? I don't need you. Fuck you!" Nourzad stared at the mirror across from him and only saw himself. There was no one else in the room. He looked, pointed, and told himself one more time, "Fuck you!" He picked up a glass and threw it at the mirror, shattering his image into pieces.

--

Kevin stood in front of the fridge, agonizing over the beer inside. He wanted it so badly. *Three fucking years.* He stood at the fridge, staring, thinking, wondering if the beer would help the headaches. *It'll at least calm me down.*

He opened the fridge, grabbed the 12-pack and put it on the counter. He walked over to the table and grabbed a chair and sat at the counter staring at the beer. Kevin wiped his brow. As he did, he felt the extreme pressure building in his head. He closed his eyes and thought, *What do I do?* The pain rattled in his head and he began to sweat. He stood up and wiped his wet palms on his pant legs. He turned and looked out the window. He looked at nothing, his mind solely on whether to drink that beer. He went back to the counter, grabbed the 12-pack and brought it to the couch. He pulled open the box and took one can out and placed it on the coffee table. He heard a distant shrieky laugh in his head.

Three years. The pain shuddered through his head and he

squinted at the beer. He heard a shrill scream in his head. He grabbed the beer and was about to open it when he thought of Rece. *I can't let her down. She told me…* "Fuck, fuck, fuck!"

He placed the beer back on the table and walked around the living room rubbing his fingertips against his thumbs. *Ok, ok, it's too early. I can have one or two tonight.* He grabbed the beer and stuck it back in the fridge.

The next few hours were a blur. He watched TV, ate, walked around the outside of his house and straightened out a few items in his garage. Now, as he sat on the couch, the pain in his head increased. His skull exploded outward and pressure engulfed the bridge of his nose. He felt a constant throbbing inside the head. *Fuck me.* He gazed at the fridge, then thought of Rece. Then he thought about seeing what he thought was Rece's car at the hospital. *What was she there for? Was she there? Fuck.* He rubbed his head and sat up. He thought of that car again and walked towards the fridge. He'd rationalized a reason to drink. Pity was a great motivator towards destructive behavior. *It'll clear my head.*

Kevin grabbed the beer and brought it to the table. Without hesitation he opened a can, put it to his lips and drank. The soothing carbonation poured down the back of his throat, as the full taste completely dominated his taste buds. The beer entered his body and soothed him as it planted in his stomach, coating it with pleasure. The next sip was bigger, as he took a full mouthful and savored the flavor and feeling. He sat down and finished the first beer and stared at the can as he swallowed the last sip of beer to come from the can.

"God, that tastes good," he said out loud.

He immediately opened the second can, drinking it with a purpose and feeling less and less pain in his head. *Amazing.* Before he knew it, four empty cans sat before him. He grabbed the fifth and closed his eyes, thinking of his head. For the first time in as long back as he could remember, there was no pain. He opened the fifth can and drank a very big gulp of beer. It eased its way down his throat as Kevin leaned back on the chair and breathed a sigh of relief. *Fuck, yes.*

For the next hour, Kevin found himself on the couch, watching TV and drinking his beer. He felt no pain now, as he lay with his feet up and head back. As he drank the next beer, his phone rang. He leisurely reached for the phone and saw it was Rece. He looked at the name for bit but didn't answer. *Fuck.* He put the phone down and sat back again. Within moments the phone rang again. Kevin drank from his beer and didn't reach for the phone. "Rece!!!! I love you!" *Fuck me, I'm terrible. Fuck, fuck, fuck, ok, I'll tell her I was asleep.* Kevin finished the beer and grabbed the next. As he did, tears ran down his cheek.

FILE REVIEW

The next morning, Dr. Nourzad sat in his office going over his patient list for the upcoming week. The list was up to almost 60 patients, which was over-whelming in a sense to him, but soothing in the time spent thinking of medicine. *I may have overbooked this week.* Then he chuckled. To his left sat Kevin's file, with notes and scribbles written all over the outside. Occasionally, Nourzad glanced at Kevin's file, while never looking at it directly. But his top thought was Kevin. As he sat, looking at file after file, his door swung open. It was Dr. Perez.

"Hello, Doctor Perez," Nourzad said with a smile. "To what do I owe the pleasure?"

"How are you, Frank?" Dr. Perez said as he sat down across from Nourzad.

"I'm doing very well today, John, thank you for asking."

"That's just great, Frank," Dr. Perez said. "You look well, too."

"Why thank you!" Nourzad responded. "So, what's up, as they say."

"File reviews."

"Ah, yes," Nourzad said, reaching into a drawer and pulling out a piece of paper. "I have that memo right here."

"I thought it would help us, as our clientele seems to have grown, as you know," Dr. Perez said. "I think we can all use a little advice or help with some patients. And, I think it keeps us on our toes. I actually got this idea from friends of mine in New York. They told me their practices do it, and that it has helped greatly."

"I don't see how it can hurt," Nourzad said, somewhat half smiling.

"So, I reviewed some of yours the past few weeks, Frank."

"Ok, and I'm fired?"

Both doctors let out a laugh.

"No, no, no, not yet," Dr. Perez said, still chuckling. "Anyway, have you reviewed your list? I think I have you five or six of mine and Scott's files."

Nourzad fumbled through a pile of papers behind him. "Yes, I think I've looked at a few, not all. My apologies."

"No apology necessary, Frank. I didn't put a timeframe on this."

"Yes, well, I've done a few if you want to do this now," Frank said, peering at the papers he grabbed.

"Yes, I'd like that," Dr. Perez said. "I think I'll go first."

"Great," Nourzad said, as he sat back.

Dr. Perez flipped through some papers and began the discourse. "So, with Ms. Nunez..."

"Yes, Anna," Nourzad said, assuring Dr. Perez he was on top of his client list. "Arthritis and osteoporosis."

Dr. Perez looked up at Nourzad and smiled. "Yes, well, I really like your analysis and treatment plan. The low dose of Boniva is great, but more than that, the diet and exercise plans are very well laid out, and, from your notes, it looks like she really is following this plan, well."

"Yes," Nourzad said and looked at his colleague.

"Good, well, I think she looks like she's doing so much better. I noted the pain thresholds that you document so well. She went from a, one second, ah, yes, from a 7 down to a 2! That's really good."

"Thank you," Nourzad said, sitting still and listening.

Dr. Perez continued. "You know, I have a hard time getting my older patients to listen. How do you do it so consistently?"

Nourzad shifted in his seat and responded. "Well, first, thank you for noticing. Secondly, I've made it a custom to just slowly build a relationship with my patients. I like to build the trust, get them to know me, and I them. Then we slowly build a plan together. I rarely push anything on my patients. I prefer to let them make the decisions, with myself just there to advise and discuss."

Perez smiled. "I think that's great, Frank."

"Thank you, John. It usually works."

"Very good," Dr. Perez said. "So, she's doing well?"

"Yes."

"Great."

Dr. Perez flipped through some more names, quietly saying the names and approving the care provided. Then he reached Kevin's name. "Oh, Kevin Ruscevich."

"Yes," Nourzad said.

"Headache sufferer," Dr. Perez said.

"Yes, chronic."

"Now, he's been here a few times, and I see some ER visits noted, um, a CT scan, over the counters..."

"Yes, that's all correct."

"Have we thought of referring him?"

"Referring?" Nourzad asked.

"To a neurologist," Dr. Perez said.

Nourzad shook his head and responded, "No, no, I haven't. I still think we can treat it together."

"Yeah," Dr. Perez continued as he shifted in his chair, "but, with the CT, and the meds and all the ER visits..."

"Two." Nourzad interrupted him.

"Excuse me?" Dr. Perez asked.

"He's had two ER visits."

"Yes, well, I just think with a case like his, we can refer him at this point, maybe." Dr. Perez sat and looked at Nourzad.

"I don't think we are there, yet," Nourzad said, holding his ground but showing the earned respect through his tone.

"The one thing we can do as doctors, Frank, is accept that maybe we can't always help someone, that maybe someone else, say, a specialist, has more of an expertise to handle a certain diagnosis."

Nourzad breathed in. "I understand that, but, not Kevin. Not right now."

"Frank," Dr. Perez said, removing his glasses and looking into Nourzad's eyes, "I hear about your clashes in the ER..."

"Look, John..." Nourzad tried to interrupt.

"No, Frank, let me just finish," Dr. Perez said very kindly. "Like I said, I heard about the clashes, and Walsh actually called me. But I told him that we needn't discuss Frank Nourzad because, although he may have some interesting methods, his patients never complain, and he works wonders with those who come in here. I refused to go there with him, Frank, because I know what a good doctor you are. There are times that I am amazed, actually. But all of us, good, great or bad, all of us, we all need to take advice sometimes, to look at a situation differently, and, quite frankly, to follow protocol."

Nourzad stared at Dr. Perez and didn't respond.

"I'm on your side, Frank. Completely," Perez said. "But we all need to look inside ourselves once in a while, and lose our egos, and follow the proper line."

"Dr. Perez," Nourzad spoke softly, "you gave me my job here, and I respect you more than any other doctor with whom I've ever worked. One of the reasons that I respect you so much, is that you let me work, and allow me to move forward in my practice untethered by protocols and lines, as you say. I work outside the norm, and my record is good. I do things differently, at a price of being looked at as a non-conformist. But, as you said, my patients do not complain. They love me, John, and I them. Now, I don't think for one second that this meeting was about Kevin Ruscevich, and whether he should see a neurologist…"

"I think he should," Dr. Perez tried interrupting.

"…I think this is about you telling me that I should check myself, and, how can I put it, um, conform more, which I do not mean in any derogatory fashion. Because it comes from you, I, of course, will do that. Trust me, John, no one looks inward more than I do. Probably too much so. I need a few more visits with Mr. Ruscevich. If nothing comes of it, I will refer him on. But I think I can help him, I really do."

Dr. Perez stood up and gathered his papers in his hand. He smiled at Nourzad. "I think this was beneficial, Frank."

"As do I," Nourzad said, as sincerely as he could.

Dr. Perez looked upon him and gathered his thoughts. He paused before adding, "Refer him, Frank. It's the right thing to do."

Nourzad didn't respond as Dr. Perez smiled, turned, and

walked out of his office. Nourzad placed his hands on his head and leaned back in his chair. He closed his eyes and thought. After a few moments, he reached for Kevin's file and grabbed a pen. Onto the file Nourzad wrote '**Neuro consult/refer?**'. Nourzad then shook his head and went back to reviewing his other files.

THUNDER

Kevin awoke with a thunderous headache. His mouth was as dry as the desert and sweat gathered on his forehead. He looked around to gather his bearings. On the table, he saw a blurry image of a can of beer. On the floor, he noticed several more. He tasted beer in his mouth and felt warn out and dry. *Oh my. What the fuck?* He rose to gather the beer cans. He walked to the cupboard for a plastic bag in which to put the cans. As he walked, his head cleared a bit, and he felt the sting of a hangover, a feeling he had not felt in a long time. *Jesus Christ.*

He grabbed some spray and cleaned up the spills on the floor and near the TV. He opened a few windows to air out the smell of stale beer. Then he sat. For the first time since he woke, he thought of the whole purpose of last night's experiment.

It fucking worked. It fucking worked. "The fucking pain went away," he whispered to himself as he grabbed his head. *Fucking back now, but Jesus it worked last night. Wow.*

He put all the cans in the bag and noticed there was one full can left. He placed that in the bag, as well.

Ok. No more. Never again. At least I know it worked. If drinking worked, it can't be a tumor.

Kevin walked the bag out to the alley and placed the bag of empty beer cans in his neighbor's garbage can. He closed it and looked around for witnesses. There were none. He walked back inside, his hangover still rolling. He cleaned down the kitchen table and sprayed air-freshener throughout the downstairs. He walked around and sniffed, assuring himself the house didn't smell of beer. When he was satisfied, he sat on the couch on which he had slept last night. His thoughts turned to Rece and how she could not find out about this. He walked around again, sniffing for the aroma of alcohol. He smelled none. Just then, his phone rang.

"Hey honey," Kevin said as he answered.

"Hey, baby, how are you?" Rece said enthusiastically.

"Good, really good, thanks."

"That's awesome, Kevin!"

"Thanks."

"No headache?" Rece asked.

"Well, not too bad right now, I'm still waiting to see if it will pop up bad."

"What about last night?"

Kevin paused. "Well, last night, no, um, the headache didn't really bother me, I guess."

Rece responded immediately, "Rest and relaxation, baby, that's what you needed."

"Yeah, I guess you're right."

"I'm always right," Rece stated and then laughed. "Anyway, hopefully it will last."

"Yeah."

"So, since you're a little better," Rece started, "Um, I was wondering if you'd mind if I stayed just one more night."

Kevin immediately thought of seeing Rece's car at the hospital last night. "Why?" he asked. His fingers then twitched.

"Well, we didn't get everything done last night, and Lis wants to go to some antique stores today; but, anyway, she was under the impression we were staying tonight, as well. I guess I didn't make that clear, it's my fault. But if you need me, please don't worry, I'll just come home."

I can drink again tonight. Fuck. His hands twitched some more.

"No, I don't mind," he said, "I'll be ok."

"Oh, and I talked to your mom, they're keeping the kids until tomorrow, as well, so one more night of peace and relaxation and feeling better, if you want it."

Kevin laughed. "How can I say no to that?"

"Right?" Rece said enthusiastically. "But, really, if you need me, let me know."

"No, no, it's ok. Just stay and help her," Kevin then paused and asked, "So, what time tomorrow?"

"Probably like three or four? Is that ok?"

"Yeah," Kevin answered. "Just, um, you know, text me or call when you're leaving."

"Absolutely, baby, I will. And I love you so much for this."

"I love you, too."

"And, look," Rece continued, "I'll text you later today, as well."

"Ok, sounds good."

"Love you, baby."

"Love you too, Rece."

Kevin hung up and immediately plopped himself on the couch. His head pounded, but he wasn't sure if it was his headaches or his hangover. The pressure built in his forehead, and pain stretched out from his brain towards his skull.

Ok, one more night. Get some beer, feel ok, then I'm done. He wrung his hands to stop the twitching. In the back of his head he heard a laugh. The pain began to build.

--

Nourzad turned the corner towards his street when he noticed it was blocked by cars. *Ah, the block party.* His face cringed a bit as he realized he'd have to park away from his home and then walk through the block fest to get there. He found a spot a half block from his street and locked the car as he walked. He heard children yelling and laughing and heard rock and roll music down the street towards his house. Many people filled the yards, and kids and adults crossed the open street to go from party to party.

Nourzad walked with a purpose, his head down, trying to make his way home unnoticed. A few people waved and some said hello. He was courteous, always waving and adding quiet hellos. He was two houses from his home when he felt a splash across his back. Immediately his entire back felt wet. He stopped in his tracks and felt the wetness with his hand.

"Oh my, Frank!" he heard from a short distance. "Billy! Apologize to Dr. Nourzad!" A little boy all soaking wet ran up to Frank and apologized. Frank smiled at him and told him it was no big deal.

"I'm so sorry, Frank," said the voice from behind him. It was Peter Simmons, his neighbor to his right. "I think he meant to hit his buddy and you crossed the path. So sorry."

"Like I told Billy, it's no problem at all." Nourzad smiled.

"Still, you're all wet," Peter mentioned.

"Not a problem," Nourzad repeated.

Peter then extended his hand. "How are you?"

"I'm good thanks," Nourzad said.

"Work today?" Peter asked.

"Yes, I had a full day."

"Well, at least you're done now," Peter said after he sipped on his beer. "You want a beer? I got whiskey and vodka too, by the garage."

Nourzad looked towards the garage and around Peter's house. "Um, you know, I think I'll go change and then maybe come out, if that's ok."

Peter laughed a bit. "Yeah, that might be a good idea – to change."

"Yes, let me just change, relax a bit, then I'll meet you back here later."

"Ok, Frank, I hope you do. Kelly made hamburgers and stuff, so you can eat, as well."

"Thank you." Nourzad shook Peter's hand again and walked into his house. As he entered, he checked the file in his hands to see if it was wet. There was a little dampness on the edge, but other than that, Kevin's file was ok. He placed it on his chair in the TV room then went upstairs to change. He could still hear the din of loud voices and rock music from outside.

Nourzad changed into new blue jeans, a white plain tee shirt and tan socks. He checked his hair in the mirror as he walked out of the room and went downstairs. He walked to the mini bar by the TV and poured himself a whiskey on ice. He turned, walked to the window, pulled the curtain slowly and peeked outside. The parties continued down the block. He sipped his drink, let go of the curtain and sat in his chair. He sipped his drink again and stared straight ahead at nothing. He closed his eyes and listened to the muted music from outside. The alcohol soothed him nicely as he relaxed with his drink in his hand and his feet up. The music's tempo kept him interested, and his first drink was complete. He poured another and walked to the deck to grab a cigarette. He lit it at the door and brought it in. He sat back in ease.

Occasionally, he'd glance backwards out the curtained windows, but felt so relaxed in his chair. He dragged more from a cigarette and drank his whiskey more vigorously. He closed his eyes and listened closely to the music. His hand clenched his drink as he thought of his family. He pulled the drink to his lips and drank the entire glass of whiskey. His throat burned but his stomach was soothed as the whiskey engulfed it. He staggered back to the mini-bar and poured himself another drink. He drank it with purpose as he walked to the door, put his sunglasses on and walked outside to the party.

--

Kevin sat looking at the fresh 12-pack of beer on his table. His head pounded at him all day. Between the short naps, the grocery shopping, and talking to his kids on the phone, he felt no relief at all. His forehead crushed down at him and pain shrieked out of his entire head. He knew the beer would soothe his pain, but he hesitated. He reached for his phone to check his messages, but there were none from Rece. They had spoken that morning, but not since. He gazed at the beer and then his phone again. He searched for Rece in his contacts and then called her. The line went right to her voicemail. He called again. And again. And again. He breathed out as he sat and rubbed his head. He tried calling her one last time, but, again, it went to voicemail. He sat and thought for one minute, about Rece, about the kids, about the pain in his head, about Rece's car at the hospital. He reached for the beer and opened it. He brought it to his lips as his phone rang. It was Rece. He drank the beer with a long slow pour into his throat. Immediately he felt relief, not from the pain in his head, but from the stress of that pain. His phone continued to ring until it didn't anymore. He stared at the phone as he reached for another beer.

Two hours later, the last beer was gone.

"Damn," he said to himself. *Weird. I feel drunk, but not as drunk as I'd imagined. Ah, but no pain.*

He physically felt his head with his hands. *No fucking pain.*

He went to the fridge to check for stray beers. There were none. He didn't hesitate as he grabbed his coat and walked out the door. *It's only five blocks away,* he thought as he reached for the back pocket of his pants to make sure he had a wallet.

The cool night breeze splashed at his face lightly. The trees waved to and fro ever so gently as the moon's light filtered through them. House after house seemed lit up, and occasionally people walked by, but it was dark enough to walk unnoticed. As he approached the main street bordering the neighborhood, he saw the bright lights of the gas station, which had the beer for which he was looking. He walked in, grabbed his beer and paid the elderly gentleman at the register. He wished Kevin a good night, and Kevin wished him the same.

As he walked back towards the street to go home, he heard his name called as a question. He turned.

"Kevin?"

Kevin stared at the woman from the church and the grocery store. He couldn't remember her name, but he remembered her. He waved at her, somewhat hoping she'd continue her business, but part of him hoping she'd come talk to him. One of his wishes came true.

She walked slowly towards him, her head turning back and forth almost in a nervous fashion. She reached Kevin and extended her hand. Kevin accepted. "It's been a while, how have you been?" she asked.

They held hands still as Kevin responded that he'd been well.

The woman looked down at the beer in his bag and said, "Got the essentials, do we?" Then she laughed.

Kevin laughed along. Then he stood there without speaking.

The woman broke the ice. "What are you up to?"

Kevin lifted his bag in the air a bit and responded, "Just gettin' a little beer and heading home."

"Ah, very nice," she responded back. "I was just grabbing some gas."

"Another essential," Kevin said plainly.

She laughed and said, "Yes."

They stood and looked at each other a little longer. The wind picked up a bit and a gentle mist began. She put her hand out to feel the light drizzle.

"Look", she said, "Um, if you want, I can drive you home, so you don't get wet."

"How'd you know I didn't drive?" Kevin asked.

"Um, I don't know, you were walking towards the sidewalk as I saw you?"

Kevin laughed. "Um, yeah, I think I can..."

She interrupted. "Look, wait one minute while I get cigarettes, then I'll drive you."

With that, she walked away into the store. Kevin stood in the mist, holding his beer. His buzz was dissipating, and his headache seemed to be breaking free. He walked to the side of the gas station and popped open a beer and drank most of it in one slug and threw the can in the alley. He then quickly walked back to where he'd been standing. The woman came walking out.

What the fuck is her name?

She approached Kevin with a smile. "Ready?" she asked.

Without answering, Kevin walked with her to the car. He opened the passenger door and looked around, nervous that someone would see him. He sat down, placed the beer on his lap, and breathed in.

"Gonna close the door?" she asked laughingly.

"Oh, yes." Kevin laughed back.

"So," she said, "turn left here and go east?"

"Yes," Kevin said quietly.

They drove towards Kevin's house without saying a word. The radio played music, but the volume was barely up, so Kevin couldn't recognize the song. Out of nervousness, he looked at her as she drove. She noticed it and looked at Kevin and smiled.

"So, just gonna drink your beer tonight?" she asked.

Kevin paused, then answered, "Yeah, I got the house to myself, so…"

Kevin didn't finish his own sentence and regretted spilling that information to her.

"That's nice," she said, "having the house alone."

"Yeah."

"The kids are with my ex tonight," she said.

Kevin just nodded.

"Where's your wife?" she asked.

Kevin looked at her quickly then gazed back at the street in front of him. "She's, uh, in Michigan."

"Nice."

"Yeah."

The car slowed to a stop. They were in front of Kevin's property, just behind the beginning of the actual house. She put the car in park.

"Well," Kevin began, "thank you for the drive."

"You're very welcome."

Kevin reached for the handle nervously, knowing it was time to get out. He turned again towards her. They stared as Kevin clutched the door handle. She looked at him. He stared. The woman moved very slowly towards Kevin, her eyes looking somewhat downward as she approached. Kevin felt a rush overcome his body as she neared his lips. Kevin never moved. Her lips reached his and touched. His stomach sank and the rush continued. He let go of the door handle and moved towards her, prepared to kiss her back.

Out of the corner of his eye he saw a light go off in his house. The rush of excitement turned upward, and the blood raced to his brain. He put his hands against her and pulled his head back. With a quick glance at the house he noticed his bedroom light on. He knew it wasn't on when he left. Kevin reached for the door again before the woman could ask what was wrong.

"I have to go," Kevin said very calmly and politely. "It isn't you. But I have to go."

He opened the car door. She said nothing as he stepped out of the car and onto the street. He closed the door and watched her pull away. His glance moved from her car to the house. He saw Rece walking into the kitchen. His heart pounded and sweat formed on his body. His thoughts raced. As he approached the house, he saw the woman's car reversing towards him.

What the fuck?

Her window was rolled down as she stopped next to Kevin.

"You forgot your beer," she said quietly.

She handed it to Kevin, winked, and drove away. Kevin

stood in front of his house, with beer in his hand. His wife was home. He stood and stared. His head pounded, and his neck was sore. He took a deep breath and approached his house.

--

Deep in the recesses of his mind, Kevin's thoughts raced in an instant. He remembered meeting Rece, their first date, and their first kiss. He remembered having their first child, Blaize. Kate, James, and Vincent flashed in his mind next. He remembered buying this house and their first night in it. Next, the schools entered his thoughts and the first days that accompanied them. He remembered baseball games and sleepovers, friends playing and parties out back. He saw Rece's smile in every flash.

His thoughts turned darker as he remembered his promise to her a few years back. How he never would again. How he needed help. How everything would be ok. How everything would be different. He'd never do it again.

His head was covered in rain and sweat as he threw the beer cans in the front bushes. He tried to smell his breath in his palmed hand, but couldn't, as the wind dispersed any chances. He couldn't stand out there all night. He loved Rece so much, and his memories reminded him so.

Be a fucking man. Kevin walked in.

LIGHTNING

He saw Rece standing in the kitchen. She was wearing her pajama shorts and shirt. Her hair glowed and her face shined. She looked up at Kevin, who stood like a prisoner awaiting direction. They stared at each other until Rece said, 'Hey.'

"How was your trip?" he asked.

"That's what you say right now?" Rece responded immediately.

"Wha-, what do you mean?"

"I was supposed to be home tomorrow. You were home trying to recover, and you ask me how was your trip?"

"Rece…"

"No. No, Kevin."

Rece walked towards him, threw two empty beer cans at the couch and walked past him. She began ascending the stairs. Kevin reached for her arm softly, and grabbed it gently, but Rece pulled away.

"You gonna hit me again?"

They stared at each other long and hard. Rece's eyes pierced at Kevin. Kevin stared blankly back.

"Rece, c'mon." Kevin's stomach dropped and he felt the blood rush throughout his body. He felt sweat building everywhere.

"C'mon? C'mon? You wanna c'mon?" Rece asked mockingly. She walked back past him to the kitchen. "Ok, Kevin," Rece waived him along, "Ok, Kevin, c'mon."

Kevin breathed in deeply and began to follow her. His head was exploding, and his hands tingled. Rece picked up her pace and turned into the kitchen. She pointed as she looked at Kevin.

"Since you're too chicken shit to just come out and tell me you're fucking drinking again, I'll point out to you that I found these, Kevin. And I smell beer on your breath. And you ignored my calls, and you mysteriously aren't home when I leave Michigan early to surprise you and take care of you, but no, you're not fucking home and I have to walk into this nightmare!"

She reached for a beer can and threw it at Kevin.

"How could you??!!" Rece screamed as a tear formed in her eye. "How...."

They both stood. Kevin gathered his thoughts. He looked at Rece and shook his head.

"Look," Kevin said after another deep breath, "I'm not drinking again."

"Fuck you, Kevin," Rece said quieter. "All you do is lie."

"I'm not," he said.

Rece began to walk away.

"You confront me on this and walk away? Rece, please?"

"Please what? You promised!"

"It's not the same thing, it's these headaches, Rece!"

"Ohhhh, the headaches, ok. You're drinking beer to fix the headaches, oh, yeah, that makes so much sense. Dr. Kevin, who knows everything and will not ever listen to his real doctor, prescribes himself beer to fix his headache. Bravo, doctor, bravo."

"Rece..."

Rece interrupted, "Yes, go on, I want to hear this."

Kevin took a deep breath. "I am in so much pain. I've had this headache for so long, and it's killing me, killing me. Nothing is working and it never ever goes away. The pain is indescribable. If I was writing a book, I couldn't even put into words how bad this pain is, but I've dealt with it."

Rece chuckled a bit and folded her arms.

Kevin continued. "I've dealt with it how I can, Rece. It hasn't been the best way, maybe, but I've tried. And it just built up. I was driving home and I stopped in the store and the pain was so great, so great. And I saw the beer and I just thought maybe, just maybe, I could have one night of no pain, no exhaustion, no fear of what the fuck is happening inside me. So, I bought it just to see if it would work. That's it."

Rece shook her head and squinted as she looked at Kevin. "Are you...are you crazy? You think that the best way to help yourself is to drink, when you know that you can't drink, that you cannot control your drinking, that drinking almost ruined your marriage and you promised your wife you'd never drink again, but that's what you think will help you?"

Kevin didn't respond.

"Ok, ok, so, how many nights, or wait, because I'm sure you drank during the day, too, once you had your first beer, but, how many?"

"How many what?"

"How, look, dick, don't make this hard on me, you know what the fuck I'm asking."

"I bought some the day you left, and look, it did help, honey!"

"And you drank today, obviously."

"It's helping."

"I'm so happy for you, Kevin."

"Rece, look, the pain…"

"Kevin, I know, I know. I know you've been in extreme pain. I do. And I've prayed for your recovery. I think about it day and night, and I have since it began. And I've done everything I can to make things easier for you, to guide you to recovery, to make you better. But you don't help yourself. You ignore what the doctors say, and…and, I don't know, Kevin. You know I've done all I could."

"I know…"

"Yet, yet, you decide to do this, knowing it would break my heart. And worse, you were never gonna tell me. You ignored my calls so that you could drink. Once again, you chose drinking over me. You could have taken my call, told me you were in crisis, but no, no, not Kevin. Kevin does what's best for Kevin only."

"Rece…" Kevin approached her.

"No, no…." Rece put up her hands to stop him. "You know, I can take a lot of things. I'm such a strong woman, and I took a lot from you when you were back-assed drunk for two years. I understand more than anyone that it's a disease, and maybe that's what it is again this time – but the lies, and you never, ever coming clean on anything, and the excuses, and the lies."

She paused a long time and then continued. "I saw you getting dropped off in front of our house, where you live with your wife and kids – I saw you get dropped off right now by a woman, who tried to kiss you, handed you beer, and who looked very happy for a woman dropping off a married man."

Kevin looked down and breathed out. *Oh fuck.*

"You shoulda led with that, Kevin."

--

Frank wrestled with the blankets as he woke, feeling a drag as he tried to cover up. He pulled harder, escaping the clench on the other side. He pulled them over and nestled in comfort.

"Hey, one way!" a voice semi-yelled with a tone of comic relief.

Frank's eyes opened in total curiosity. His mind analyzed the data, and then Frank closed his eyes hard and sighed too loudly. He felt a minor shove on the shoulder.

"I'm ok with just leaving. We made that clear last night."

Frank turned over and saw Janet lying blanket-less with just a pair of panties on and one of Frank's tee shirts.

"No, no, you don't have to go."

"I heard your, um, what would we call it, um, a sigh?"

"I, I just, ya know drank a lot...."

"Uh huh."

"No, that sounded bad," Frank said as he sat up in the bed. "I mean the alcohol just clouded my memory. I remember everything now, though."

Janet sat up, as well, and turned away from Frank. She stood up and face him.

"I'm not mad at all, ok." Janet smiled. "I need to go anyways. It was a lot of fun."

Frank just stared at her, not really wanting to say anything. Janet scrambled for her clothes that were scattered on the floor. She dressed then went into the bathroom. Frank closed his eyes and leaned his head back against the wall.

Janet looked at him when she came back into the room.

"Can I get you anything?" he asked.

Janet peeked her head out of the bathroom and smiled. "No."

Minutes passed until Janet walked out of the bathroom and into the bedroom.

"I'll walk you out," Frank said as he pulled on some shorts.

The two walked in silence to the front door. They faced each other as they reached the exit.

"Look, I really enjoyed learning about you last night. You are a great man, and you've been through so much. I just hope I helped you by listening."

"You did," Frank responded. "I needed an ear, a female ear, and you were there, and I really appreciate you listening."

"If you ever need that ear again," Janet said smiling, "Just let me know."

"I will," Frank said as he reached out to hug her. They embraced hard and long, Frank closing his eyes and breathing deep. As he let go, he looked into her eyes while holding her soft hands. "Thank you, Janet. Thank you."

Janet just smiled and reached for the door, opened it, and walked out. Frank watched her as she slowly ambled down the front sidewalk and turned. He watched her walk all the way to her house down the block. She entered her car, and then Frank took a deep breath and closed the door as neighbors milled about their front yards.

--

Kevin awoke with a headache. His forehead pounded, and a vice squeezed his skull. His eyes burned and his mouth was dry. The smell of alcohol was apparent. He shook off some cobwebs and realized he was on the couch. His head began to pound more immensely, and a sharp pain raced down the back of his neck. He rubbed his neck and shook his head softly. On the table, next to the couch, he noticed a beer can.

"Fuck," he said softly as he got up to throw it away. He walked into the kitchen and saw an empty countertop. He breathed out in relief. He squeezed the can softly and reached the garbage. He looked in and saw several empty beer cans. "Oh, Jesus," he said shaking his head. "Fuck." He then looked up to the ceiling, trying to peer through into his bedroom, where he assumed Rece lay. He opened the fridge and saw a couple beer cans left. He considered throwing them in the trash. He eyed them intently, and then closed the fridge. He turned and saw Rece standing there.

"Oh, hey baby," Kevin said softly.

"If you care, the kids will be home soon, so you may want to get dressed. Up to you. I'll be down here eating a bit if you want to use the bedroom while I'm down here."

Kevin curled his lips together then said, "What does that mean?"

"It means you can get ready while I'm down here."

"So that's it, we aren't going to discuss last night?"

Rece laughed mockingly. "Oh, now you want to discuss it. You don't want to have 12 beers first?"

"What?" Kevin asked, his eyes squinting.

"I waited upstairs for you to come up last night, Kevin. I waited. I never told you not to come up. Not once. But I hear you downstairs quietly cracking open beer after beer while I'm upstairs cry-..." Rece cut herself off. "You know what, that was the time to talk, Kevin. But you chose alcohol over me. Again. And you went back to sneaking. Again. I mean, you really think people can't hear you opening beer through your stupid fucking fake cough?" Rece laughed.

"I didn't think you wanted to talk last..."

"No! No! Don't you say that. Don't pretend to know what I want or needed last night!"

"I really didn't!"

"Fuck you, Kevin! Why don't you go talk to her!"

"Rece, nothing happened between me and her. Nothing."

"You were in her car. I was away. You ignored my calls. You were drinking without telling me. She leaned over to kiss you – yeah, I saw it, Kevin! There's nothing you can say. Whether or not anything happened doesn't matter, Kevin. You put yourself in a position for something to happen. Your mind and heart weren't with me. And I wonder if they ever have been, Kevin."

Tears ran down Rece's cheeks. Kevin stood silently.

"You broke my heart, Kevin. You broke my heart in different ways last night and being with her wasn't the part that hurts the most."

"Rece," Kevin said, his voice cracking, as he approached his wife.

"No, Kevin. No, stay away." Rece put up her hands. "I can't anymore. And I won't."

Rece turned and headed back to the stairs.

"I thought you were gonna…" Kevin said, and then stopped.

Rece continued walking.

"Rece!" Kevin said louder, but with no shred of anger or intimidation.

"Rece…." Kevin said softer.

Rece reached the stairs and looked at Kevin, who walked slowly behind her. He looked at her.

"Is that it?" he asked softly again.

"That's it, Kevin."

"You can't..." Kevin couldn't finish his sentence.

Rece grabbed the stair railing and stood waiting. "I can't what, Kevin?"

"I love you."

"I have no doubt that you do, Kevin."

"That's not enough?"

"Kevin, two years ago, or whatever it was, you said you loved me. You said things like 'never again', and 'I won't ever', and 'I love you, Rece', and 'I'll always come to you from now on'. Those are just words. Those were just words. But I took them to heart, and I believed you with all my heart because I was so in love with you. You were my whole heart, and what you did wasn't enough to break that bond of love. But in those two years, I could see it happening all over. I tried and I tried to steer you this way, to me, but it didn't work. All along you just couldn't wait, or couldn't help yourself, to go back to this. To this."

"To what?"

"To alcohol, and sneaking, and lying and just being who I guess you are, Kevin. And that may sound harsh, but who you are is who you are, and when someone shows you who they are you may ignore it once or twice because you love them so much, but after a while you just have to see who that person is, and really see that he is actually trying to show you who he is, and you have to see it, and listen, and accept. And as hard as it may be, to move on."

"Rece..."

"What, Kevin? What?"

"I didn't do anything, Rece."

"That's the saddest part. That you think that, Kevin. And

maybe people would look at this and say, oh, Rece, you're being irrational or a bitch, but they didn't live through my childhood. They didn't live through a few years ago. They didn't receive the promises and then live through the sneaking and lies and heartbreak. It can be the smallest thing that breaks your heart, and others may say that's so minor, but to the broken hearted, it's not. Look, I saw the beer, I couldn't believe it. I was hoping it was a friend of yours who brought it. I prayed that that was the explanation. And I loved you. Then I saw you in that van with that woman..."

"She tried to kiss me, and I refused."

"You're so magnanimous, Kevin. Good job. You led her on and then refused."

"I didn't lead anyone on."

Rece laughed a bit. "You got into a woman's car. A woman who you probably knew was interested in you, right? I'm right, probably. Then you turn her away when she just responds to your interest. Like I said, good job, Kevin. You didn't kiss her. Doesn't matter."

"Rece, Jesus," Kevin said, sounding exasperated. "Is this about her or the beer?"

"It's about you, Kevin. It's just about you."

"Rece...."

"Kevin, you can't even put into words what you want to say. You can't open your heart to me at a moment when it matters most. You're just stammering. You have nothing in there to give me. It was always about other things with you. I was just here."

"You know that's not true. We were in love...I mean, are, were, I mean, I love you, Rece."

"Kevin, look, forget that woman for a second, ok? Forget her for just a second. Two years ago, your drinking was so bad. And you were sneaking it, and you were good at it. Then you couldn't hide it anymore, and I accepted your problem and tried to help, and you pretended to get help and the drinking got worse and I threatened to leave because I cannot have you hurt this family with alcohol, and so you stopped, because you didn't want to lose this. It was never because you loved me. You didn't want to lose the wife and the house and the kids and the status. So, you pretended to quit again."

"What?!" Kevin said with conviction. "No way, I didn't pretend!"

"Yeah, ya did. Because you went right back to it when you wanted to."

"Wanted to?!" Kevin responded. "Do you have any idea how bad these headaches are?"

"Kevin, you tried this one last night."

Kevin placed both palms over his face and rubbed vigorously. "Jesus, Rece, I didn't try anything, I'm explaining it!"

"Do not yell at me."

"I'm not yelling, I'm explaining!"

"There's nothing to explain, Kevin. You are drinking again, after you promised, you swore, you promised that you would never drink again. Ok, sometimes promises aren't kept, and the person who promises breaks down and apologizes, but you never did that. You chose to sneak…"

"I didn't sneak, Rece! I'm trying desperately to fix these fucking headaches!"

"Fix? I mean, Kevin, c'mon. Fix?"

Kevin shook his head in frustration and laughed. "I don't even get what's going on."

"Kevin, it's pretty simple if you would just admit to what

you did, if you would just look inside and see. You're using the headaches to justify the behavior. You can't do that."

"I have had a headache, no, no, no, a brutal, uncontrollable headache for so fucking long, honey. It's fucking killing me. It's inside here and it won't fucking go away!"

"What's inside of you?"

"The headache! There's...Rece, there's something in there. It's causing these headaches and I've done all I can to get rid of it, but no one and nothing helps!"

"No one helps. You're unbelievable. But look, anyway, the doctor said, he told you, Kevin...look, I'm not doing this. You've been told that nothing is killing you, that you have headaches. That's it."

"They're wrong."

"All the doctors who have looked at you, examined you, they're all wrong?"

"Yes."

"So, you turned to drinking."

"I turned to a cure, a fix. Because I cannot live like this anymore. I can't stand the pain, Rece. It's killing me."

"It's pain, swee...it's pain, look, we've gone over this. Again, you're using the headaches as an excuse to drink. You don't get that, yet, because you're clouded by the alcohol, but that's what you're doing. And the worst part, Kevin, the absolute worst part, that you won't admit, is that you snuck it. You snuck it because you knew it was wrong and that you were lying to me. I'm done."

"Oh my God, honey, stop saying you're done!"

"I'm done, Kevin."

"I'll stop."

"Stop? No, no, I've heard it all before."

"I'll stop, honey! I promise!"

"Like you did last time, so many, many, times."

Kevin shook his head again. "So, I mean...I cannot believe this."

"What you're doing to yourself, Kevin, the drinking, the paranoia, the bullshit, Kevin, it led you to another woman."

Kevin laughed a bit. "No, it didn't! We bumped into each other and she gave me a ride home!"

"Bumped into each other as you were buying beer? To hide from me, right? And you were close enough with this woman to accept that ride and almost kiss her, you dick. You know how much that hurts me? You see what drinking does?"

"I didn't...I wasn't going to kiss her, and it had nothing to do with drinking."

"It had everything to do with drinking, but you refuse to see that. And, from what I saw, you were just about to kiss her."

Rece walked off the landing to the stairs and approached Kevin. "Wait, so, did you realize I was home? Is that why you didn't kiss her? Is that what happened? If I wasn't here, would you have? And where would that kiss have led? Or have you cheated on me with her already, Kevin?" They were face to face.

"Rece...." *How the fuck does she know everything*?

"No, no, Kevin, like I said, I don't even care about her. I mean, I care, but you lied, you snuck behind my back. Kevin, I can't anymore. I can't."

"What are you saying?"

"I'm saying what I told you a few years back, that if it happens again, I cannot stick around for the tragedy that follows."

"There wasn't any tragedy and there isn't now. I drank a little bit."

"How much, Kevin? How much did you drink this weekend while I was gone?"

"It doesn't matter because I only drank to fix this fucking headache."

"But you liked it, didn't you? You liked drinking, so you drank again the next day or night, whatever you did. And you're thinking about your next drink right now, and you drank last night! When I was upstairs. Oh my God. Forget it." Rece turned to walk towards the stairs and Kevin instinctively grabbed her arm. In one split moment Rece punched downward on Kevin's arm as hard as she could. As Kevin's grip came undone Rece then pushed him away with two hands. "Don't you fucking touch me. I told you that last time you dick. You want to hit me again?"

Kevin stared at her. The woman he loved.

Rece asked again. "Do you? Want to hit me again? And then ask forgiveness? Should we go through that all over again, Kevin?"

The two stared at each other for minutes. The pain in Kevin's head swirled through his brain like a roller coaster, up and down, around and around, with screeching cries and loud rumblings. A shriek of laughter followed the pain train in tune. Kevin closed his eyes with all his might and clenched his fists. Pain shot down his back and his fingers tingled. He took a deep breath, opened his eyes and looked right into Rece's. Kevin spoke in the driest, most unemotional way he could.

"Fuck you, Rece."

And he walked into the kitchen, grabbed his beer and walked out of the house.

WHO NEEDS WHO?

"I've definitely been drinking too much lately, and I'm, uh, yeah, I'm concerned about it."

"You paused in your admission. Why?"

"It's not easy to admit, I guess."

"No, it never is, and I probably shouldn't have called you on that. You've admitted an issue, and that's very good on your part. Do you think you need help?"

"Help in what way?"

"AA?"

"No, no, I'm able to stop when I want to. I think I just turn to it when things have gone bad."

"Bad?"

"Yeah, you know, like my life or situations in my life. When I can't handle things, sometimes I turn to drinking and I have now realized that maybe I shouldn't."

"Well, you certainly hedge your statements on it."

"I know. I know."

"Admitting to the problem is the right start. But setting that goal to fix it, that's a real difficult part. Are you ready, are you able to now go forward through the steps to deal with the issue? You know? That's where we have to get."

"I agree. But I consider myself able to handle situations with alcohol and without. I just think lately I've turned to it too much. I don't know. Maybe I'm seeing a possible problem that isn't there, yet. I'm just not sure. I know there's potential; I guess is what I'm saying."

"Your life isn't as affected by it as would be considered a problem?"

"Correct."

"And you bring it up to just throw it out there to recognize the issue, and be able to recognize it in the future, near or far, to be able to stop any possible course towards a spiral downwards."

"Yes."

"Look, I understand. I see. I'm just cautious. You've had tumult. Ok, and you see an issue. My concern is you're waiting to see if it inflates, instead of pulling that needle out now, thereby assuring, or making it much more difficult, to get too heavy."

"I feel comfortable where I am. I feel comfortable knowing, well, knowing that I have control."

"Well, control is important. As long as you can keep it or recognize quickly when you're losing it."

"I think I can."

"Very well. You certainly know where to find me when you need to talk about it – or, anything else."

"Thank you."

And with that, Frank nodded at the mirror, got up out of his seat, and walked away.

--

"Dr. Nourzad, Mr. Ruscevich is in room 4."

Dr. Nourzad looked up from the chart and acknowledged the information with a nod. He then continued reading the letter within:

In conclusion, we recommend that Mr. Ruscevich be referred out to a neurologist.

Dr. Nourzad then closed the file and walked towards room # 4.

"Sally," he stopped at the next desk, "when was Mr. Ruscevich's file updated in the system?"

"All files were updated Saturday."

"Including this letter?" He handed it to Sally. She glanced at it and affirmed its inclusion in Saturday's update.

"Thank you, Sally."

Nourzad entered room 4, greeted Kevin and sat down on a chair across from him. The two stared at each other for a moment. It was an awkward moment for Kevin.

"So, Kevin, how are the headaches? You missed our..."

"I know," Kevin interrupted. "They're still there. No, um, improvement. Still there."

"Ok."

"They just don't go away."

"I understand. Is it the same pain? Has it been better a little bit, or worse?"

"I'd say worse. I mean, they just won't go away. And the pain sometimes is just unbearable."

"Have you taken anything for them?"

Kevin paused before answering, thinking about the beer drinking, which had helped him. "Medicine? No."

"Anything else?" Nourzad asked.

"Like what?"

"Well, sometimes, Kevin, people change their eating habits, or anything like that. The literature shows that sometimes habit changing works for headaches. Have you tried that?"

"No."

"Ok."

"I mean, I think I eat pretty well."

"I'm sure you do."

"Ok, Kevin, so, I've thought a lot about this, and I've read up a lot on headaches, and re-studied the literature, the papers, the journals. Obviously, with you, we have headaches that won't go away. We have headaches that are somewhat affecting your everyday life, and when I say that, all I mean is that the headaches are noticeable enough to you that they affect your mental state. We've done all the tests, so we know that these are just headaches, not any life-threatening ailment."

Nourzad noticed Kevin look upward at the ceiling and shift in his seat.

"Everything ok with what I've said?"

Kevin thought a moment before responding. "I don't know. I just really still think that there is something wrong with me."

"You mentioned you thought it was a brain tumor last time."

"I still do," Kevin stated quickly in response.

"Ok, that's completely understandable. But we have tested you. The walking, the coordination tests, and the like. You had a CT scan which showed nothing, and there are no symptoms showing up which would correlate with a brain tumor. So, as much as I completely get your concern because the pain is so great, there is nothing to indicate brain tumor."

"I read where a CT scan can miss brain tumors," Kevin said intelligently.

Nourzad shook his head no as he answered. "They can, Kevin, but in this situation, I don't see that as the case."

There was a pause as the two looked at each other.

Nourzad broke the silence. "So, as I was saying, we have these headaches which are affecting you and they aren't going away. So, we have medicines that can help, Kevin."

"Ok."

"So, looking at the different options, we obviously have ibuprofen and acetaminophen, which you've tried, and they aren't presently working. We also have Triptans, which soothe blood vessels and can help with pain, as well. We have beta blockers. We have anti-depressants, which can help by affecting brain chemicals. We have anti-seizure medicines and we even have Botox, both of which I'm not going to recommend to you."

"What are you recommending?"

"I'm recommending lifestyle changes, Kevin. Something I touched on a bit earlier."

"Then why explain all those medicines?"

"Well, give me a second. Look, I really think your headaches can be managed with changes in eating, drinking, exercise, and the like. I want to try those avenues. In the meantime, I will prescribe to you the beta blockers, which are blood pressure pills. Your pressure has been a bit high during your visits, and so those can help you in two ways. I like the beta blockers because I can low-dose you, and work from there."

"Ok."

"Let's change your life, Kevin. A real healthy diet, a lot of water, decent exercise. I think this will lessen your headache tendency. We'll start on a low dose of blockers, and maybe even have some therapy."

"Therapy?"

"Studies have shown that stress and other mental health factors can cause headaches."

"I'm not insane," Kevin shot back.

"I'm not saying you are. But I'm a firm believer in mental health, meaning being healthy mentally. It's just an examination of your status. We talk out issues and see how we are doing."

"We?"

"You and me. I can certainly handle that aspect of your health, as well. I studied it greatly in med school and have been counseling others in my office. There have been fantastic results."

"With headaches?"

"No, not necessarily headaches, but overall health." Nourzad paused, leaned forward in his chair towards Kevin and clasped his hands. "Kevin, we change your life habits, we clean up, and we get better. Overall mind and body healing, Kevin."

Kevin looked at Nourzad, trying to process everything. The pain swirled upstairs and shot out at his skull at all points. As Nourzad had spoken, the pain howled louder and more extreme. Kevin rubbed his forehead. He wanted a beer.

"So, when would all this start?" Kevin asked.

"Right now, today. You change some eating and drinking habits, you come in once a month and we talk, and we see how it goes."

"The, um, blockers?"

"Beta blockers, yes. I'll prescribe those today. Again, for the pain. I mentioned last time, I think, that life isn't an endurance test. Certainly, if you continue to have pain, those will help."

"Ok. I guess that sounds ok."

"Great…"

"What do I eat?" Kevin asked.

"Great question. All we are doing is making change. If you ate a lot of red meat, we may switch to chicken or pork. If you ate a lot of salt, we cut back. If dairy was prevalent, we cut back. We just make changes to see if anything we are consuming now may be affecting the intensity of the headaches. Now, some people in the studies keep a journal, that way we can see when the effect of our plan will have begun."

"Ok."

"Ok, so, I will write up that prescription, we'll schedule a meeting for, say, about two weeks from now – and that will be a checkup and a therapy session, if you will."

"Great," Kevin said, thinking about getting home to have a drink.

"Keep a journal, if you can, and call me if you need anything or if you have pain still, Ok?" Nourzad handed Kevin his card. "My cell phone number is on there, as well."

"Thank you."

Nourzad extended his hand and shook Kevin's. "Thank you, Kevin."

--

Kevin raced into the house, his head pounding and swirling with pain. All during his ride home the pain screamed about in his head, pushing and pounding on all sides. He knew Rece was out until dinner time, and the kids were at school. He ran into the basement, reached under his bed and grabbed two cans of beer. He immediately drank one, and then opened another as he sat on the bed. He drank the second can just a bit slower but drank it until it was gone. He leaned back against the wall and closed his eyes and breathed. In his pocket was the prescription for beta blockers. He pulled it out and scanned it with his eyes. He reached under for another beer and drank as he pondered the prescription.

Beta blockers and food journals. He then finished the beer and opened another. He drank it fast, and as he finished off beer number four, he ripped up the prescription and threw it in the corner. He laid back a second. The pain had lightened in his head. The shriek of it all had dwindled to a mere whisper of pain, still there, but in check. He got off the bed, gathered the cans, and brought them outside to the neighbor's garbage can and deposited them. He walked back into the house, went back into the basement and lay on the bed. With his head soothed, he thought about Georgia and their near kiss. *Fucking stupid.* Down the stairs came Lou. He walked slowly and purposefully. Kevin spotted him. "there you are old boy, I haven't seen you in a while." Lou hopped up on the bed and snuggled next to Kevin. Kevin pet him as he sipped his beer.

--

"You smell like mouthwash," Rece stated as she sat by the boys and Kevin. Kevin had Vincent on his knees in the air as Kevin lay on his back while James and Blaize wrestled nicely next to them. Kevin just looked at Rece and returned his attention to Vincent. He laughed as Vincent wailed with delight. Blaize and James laughed too as they twirled about on the floor. Rece stared at Kevin. Kevin noticed the stare and spoke softly. "There's no problem." Rece got up and walked to the kitchen.

"Well, boys," Kevin said loudly as he dropped Vincent from his legs, "I gotta go talk to Mom. Be right back."

In the kitchen, Rece leaned against the counter as Kevin walked in.

"What?" Kevin asked.

"You need help, that's all I'm gonna say now." Rece stared at him.

"I don't need help. Everything is fine. Don't you see that? They are all happy."

Rece chuckled. "They're happy because they don't know what I know about you."

"What do you know about me, huh?" Kevin asked.

"That you're an alcoholic who won't admit it. That you're a husband who sneaks around with a..."

Kevin cut her off. "Rece, please."

"What? See? Lies and sneakiness, that's you. You think they'd be happy if they knew that?"

"Nothing happened with her, ok? And I'm not an alcoholic. I found a way to control my headaches, hon, and it's all ok. I love you."

Rece looked at him and attempted to walk around him back to the living room. Kevin grabbed her arm very softly. Rece stopped and looked eye to eye with Kevin.

"Please, sweetie, don't go there," Kevin said in a whisper.

Rece laughed mockingly.

"I never hit you," Kevin whispered.

"You don't even know you did it," she whispered back.

"Because I didn't. I love you, Rece. I know I would never do that to you."

"Do you remember telling me to fuck off the other day, huh?"

"Honey, that, that was just spilled emotions. I was at a loss and I just said that. I'm so sorry."

"Then get help."

"Daddy! Daddy!" Vince screamed as he ran into the kitchen. Kevin let go of Rece's arm and picked up Vince.

"You little stinker! You want another plane ride!?"

"Yeahhhhh!"

Kevin walked with Vince in his arms. He turned a bit to look at Rece as he walked into the living room with the boys and then said, "We love you, Mom."

"Yeah, Mom, dad loves you!" Vince laughed as he yelled it.

DRINK IT!

Kevin lay on the twin mattress placed in the corner of the basement. Lou was snuggled on his pillow. The twin was slightly bigger than the leather couch facing the television on the east wall. He had his blanket slightly on him, and the TV was on. He had his hands interlocked on the back of his head as he lay on the fluffy pillows. His headache had dwindled most of the day, and to Kevin's firm belief it was because of the alcohol. His last beer was over four hours ago, and the shrieking headache was coming back. It swirled around his head, pain shooting everywhere. His skull got heavy and squinting his eyes gave him little relief. He assumed Rece was in bed, and he knew the kids were, so he peeked under the bed to see his beer. It was there. He lay back again, taking a deep breath and contemplating this pain and his options. At that moment, his head split in half like a sword had sliced it down the middle. The pain wedged into the front of his skull and hung there, like he had a ten-ton weight hanging from a rope attached to his forehead. Sweat began to pour down his face, and his hands trembled.

Jesus fucking Christ.

He grabbed his laptop and searched headache pain. The results came up:

Headache and Brain Tumor Symptoms

He scanned the article quickly seeing **HEADACHE** and **BRAIN TUMOR** in the same sentence. The sweat poured out of his body even more and the pain in his head shrieked and moved more furiously.

Drink the fucking beer, Kevin. Drink!

The shriek in his head screamed louder as he thought that thought, and the pain engulfed his entire head.

He slammed the laptop shut and reached under the bed for a beer. The basement door opened as he did, and he heard footsteps coming down the stairs. It was Rece. He laid back again, putting his eyes on the TV like a teenager caught by his parents.

Rece walked to him, dressed in pajama pants and socks. On top, she wore a dark purple long-sleeved tee shirt. She stood by Kevin's make-shift bed and looked upon him. Kevin barely turned his head but saw her in his periphery.

"Are you not going to look at me?" Rece asked quietly.

"I am."

"Ok, look, I was going to try to talk to you, but I'll just go back up..."

"Rece, what?" Kevin snapped. "Don't go up, if you want to talk, then talk. I'm right here."

Rece chuckled mockingly and pulled a small child's chair to her and sat. She looked at Kevin and eventually Kevin looked into her eyes. The stare continued and Kevin shifted towards her and reached for her hand, which was on her thigh. Rece quickly pulled away.

"Kevin, really? No."

Kevin lay back and sighed.

"I don't know what you want, but I need to know," Rece asked calmly.

"I don't know what you mean by that," Kevin responded.

"Well, are you getting help? Do you want to stay here longer? But, um, you staying here, down here, and all, well, I mean, I can't have you here drinking all day, which, I think I've made pretty clear."

There was a piercing silence as Kevin grappled with the enormity of her statements.

Kevin looked at the ceiling and Rece concentrated on his face. "Kevin, I think we both know..."

"I don't know anything, Ok," Kevin snapped, but not angrily.

"Kevin, I told you last time that it would be the last time, your last chance. I'm not going back to that pain and suffering and watch you destroy yourself."

Kevin continued to stare at the ceiling. He didn't move on the bed at all. His head pounded inside. Shrieking screams of pain circled in his head, and they grew fiercer every second Rece spoke to him. He thought of the beer under his bed. He thought of the kids in bed.

"Anything, Kevin?" Rece asked.

Kevin breathed air through his nose and shook his head side to side.

"What, Kevin?" Rece asked rather kindly.

"Destroy myself. That's funny," Kevin said, still not looking at her.

"Kevin, you didn't see it then, and you don't see it now. It's a one-way path and it doesn't stop once you start drinking. It gets worse and worse, and I'm..."

"I didn't drink for two or three years, and it wasn't bad when I did drink."

"I'm not arguing this again, Kevin. I'm not. That's not why I came down here."

"So, you came down here to kick me out?"

Rece responded so quickly. "I'd never kick you out. Ever. But you can't stay if you're going to drink. Period."

Kevin now sat up in bed. The pain pierced his skull on all sides, and the shriek of it all grew more intense. *You need to drink that fucking beer.* Kevin shook his head aggressively and rubbed his forehead. As Kevin sat up, Rece instinctively moved back a bit in her chair.

"I'm not going anywhere, Ok? I love you, I love the kids, and I'm not leaving."

"Then don't drink. You can stay down here; we'll raise the kids..."

"Rece..." Kevin said quietly.

Rece stood up.

Kevin continued, "That's it? That quickly you are giving up on all of this."

"All of what, Kevin? All of what? You being drunk, sneaking off to drink, seeing another woman, all of that? You pretending again that you don't have a problem? You getting meaner and angrier?"

Kevin shook his head and smiled. "Fuck, you don't ever listen to me."

"Yeah I do."

"I never did anything with her."

"But you wanted to, and you were drinking, and you lie to me, so I honestly don't know if I believe you..." Rece cut herself off. "Look, I'm not doing this."

"So, that's it, huh?"

"That's it." Rece stood and stared at him. "Please, Kevin, please get help. We can do this. Together. Please see what I am saying.""

Kevin smiled, the shrieking wailed away in his head, and he reached under the bed and grabbed a beer. He looked into her eyes as he popped open the tab and started drinking the beer, pouring it down his throat, his eyes locked on hers in a taunting fashion, chugging the beer down until it was gone. In his head, the pain wailed and shrieked loudly as the beer entered Kevin's stomach. Rece, wanting to cry, held back and met his stare with confidence and strength. Kevin reached down for another beer, and Rece got up, walking away. Kevin popped it open and chugged again. As Rece reached the stairs he pulled the can from his lips and spoke loudly. "I'm not leaving, Rece."

YOU NEVER SEE IT COMING

Nourzad walked into the office dressed perfectly. His slacks were perfectly ironed with barely a crease. His brown leather shoes shined, and his pink shirt was neatly tucked under the sharp brown belted waist of his pants. He smiled as he sipped his coffee. The nurses and receptionists worked as he walked, none of them looking up at him. He desperately looked around for acknowledgment of his presence but grinned through the blissfulness of his arrival. He approached his office and saw two people sitting down near his desk. He recognized Dr. Perez as the gentleman closest to the door. He paused in mid-step, looked around again at the office, still no one looked at him. He stared at his office for a moment more, then walked inside.

"Ah, Dr. Nourzad." Dr. Perez stood and shook Nourzad's hand. "Frank, this is John Light, he's from the legal department…"

Nourzad interrupted Dr. Perez. "Yes, yes, I'm familiar."

"Well, Frank," Dr. Perez continued nervously, "this is really more of a reminder, formality, really."

There was a silent pause.

"What is?" Nourzad asked confusingly.

"Um, well…" Dr. Perez began but was interrupted by Mr. Light.

"Doctor, we've had some complaints, some paperwork, et-cetera on your, say, methods of late. We are just here to make sure you fall back on your protocols in all matters here and at the ER."

Nourzad looked at Perez. "What is this?"

"Like he said," Dr. Perez answered, "it's just a reminder."

"To follow protocols," Nourzad said quietly.

John Light repeated the response. "Protocols."

"Have I been reported? Have I been blamed for a death?" Nourzad asked.

John Light flipped through some paperwork, then looked up. "No."

Perez reiterated that. "No, Frank."

"When my mother called me by my first name as a kid, I knew I was in trouble. Am I in trouble here?"

"No," John Light answered. "Just follow the protocols, be a doctor as taught, and don't try to save the world, Dr. Frank Nourzad."

Nourzad stared at the lawyer. Perez stood up and placed his hand on Nourzad's shoulder. "Frank, doctor, sometimes we get to the point where we think we can do it all ourselves, without any help. It's ok. I've gone through that, as have others here. It's completely normal, doctor. This, this here today, is just a reminder that we have others to help us remember what we're doing here."

Nourzad stepped back from Perez, still eyeballing the lawyer. "I know, I know what I'm doing here. I'm helping patients. Did it ever occur to anyone here that the way it's been done, well, maybe that's the wrong way? Maybe, just maybe, my way is right?"

"God complex is a tricky thing," the lawyer said so matter

offactly.

"Fuck you!" Nourzad screamed.

Once again, Perez stepped between the two apparent combatants. "Frank, Frank, come on, now. You are taking this completely the wrong way. We are just reminding you to follow the norm, that's it. Do your thing, but follow what we do here, and it'll all be ok."

The lawyer stood up. "I think we are done here," he said to Perez. Then he turned to Nourzad. "Doctor, it was a pleasure. I've actually heard great things about your work. You don't know this, but my mother came to you not long ago. Catherine Winslow, a 76-year-old widow with lung cancer symptoms. I cannot tell you the hours I spent listening about the great Doctor Nourzad. Ends up, she didn't have cancer. She said you knew that immediately just from listening and talking to her. Now, I'm not sure if that meets up to the legal standard of care, but that's not the point. The point is, you helped her. You helped her in a way not many other doctors, if any, can. Because you humanized her, as she said – her words, not mine. See, doctor, nobody here is questioning your methods. We are just questioning if you will ever question your methods yourself. No disrespect intended."

With that, without an extension of a handshake, the lawyer walked out. Nourzad stared into nothing, his eyes glazed. He stood speechless, as Perez stood with his head down looking at the floor. Neither spoke until Nourzad fixed his daze and looked at Perez.

"You couldn't give me a heads up on this?" he said quietly.

"I didn't get a heads up on this, Frank." Perez whispered. "He was here when I got in. He gave me a 10 second run-down. I'm your supervisor, so-to-speak, so he wanted me in here with you when you arrived."

"You could have met me in the hall…"

"Frank, he was very insistent, ok? I had no choice but to sit in here and wait for you."

"That's bull crap, and you know it."

"Frank, look..." Perez began.

Nourzad interrupted him. "And what's this supervisor stuff, you're not my supervisor. What does that even mean?"

"Frank, I have the most seniority. The insurance insists on these protocols and all this other stuff, including us supervising each other. C'mon, you know this stuff."

Nourzad stared at Perez for a moment. "Where..." Nourzad began before pausing to sit. "Where did this come from?"

"I don't know, Frank."

"Yeah you do. Was it Walsh?"

Perez paused and then sat, too, across from Nourzad. "Yeah, I think. Look, he's just concerned. I'm concerned. We're all concerned, Frank. You lost your family. You took no time to grieve. You lost your parents young; you don't have much support. I mean, it doesn't, I mean, it's not a stretch to see you trying desperately to save all your patients; or not even always save but want to be the one who fixes them all. I'm not a psychiatrist, but it's easy to see."

Frank brushed off the lecture. "What did he say?"

"Who?" Perez asked.

"Walsh."

"Frank, who cares! I don't even know, ok? But the people in charge are concerned. Look, we have to look out for each other."

"That lawyer doesn't care. They just care about lawsuits."

"As they should, Frank. That's their job, and it's our job to provide care, and we have to make sure we are all providing the correct care."

"I give the correct care, always."

Dr. Perez stared at the younger doctor like a parent stares at a child in trouble who won't listen. Nourzad sat down, leaned back in his chair and stared at the ceiling.

"Frank..."

"No, it's fine. I'll abide. Whatever you want."

"It's not about me, Frank."

"Uh huh."

There was a long awkward silence. Perez finally stood and opened a folder. He took out some papers and handed them to Nourzad.

"What's this?"

"Your improvement plan."

Nourzad laughed out loud.

"Read through it, sign it, give it back to me and dammit, Frank, just go back to work and it's all going to be fine."

Nourzad didn't respond.

"Frank?"

"Ill, um, look through it."

Perez walked out, tapping Nourzad on the shoulder before exiting and closing the door.

Dr. Frank Nourzad sat in the chair, staring at the ceiling, then the wall, then his shoes. He thought of his wife and children. He had a vision of the crash. Then he winced. He breathed deeply, wondering what their last thoughts were. He thought of the daily pain of the empty house. He held the improvement plan papers in his hand and shook them as he glanced at them. He thought of his wife again. "I'm so sorry, my love," he said out loud. Then he stood up and threw the stapled papers hard against the wall, the sound of paper fluttering whistled through the stale office air. He reached across his desk with both arms, ready to violently throw everything thereon into the air. He breathed deeply several times, then walked over to the improvement papers, eye-balled them, ripped them in half and threw them into the trash.

I WILL NEVER UNDERSTAND HOW WE GOT TO THIS PLACE

NOVEMBER 2016

Kevin walked from the garage towards the house, a snow shovel in his hand. James met him chasing his basketball.

"I don't see snow, dad."

Kevin chuckled, and when he did, his head throbbed in pain. "Funny kid," Kevin said quietly as he patted James' head. "I'm preparing for winter."

"Great," James said then ran for his ball.

Kevin looked up and saw Rece walking towards him. She didn't smile as the wind blew her hair in every way. She brushed it out of her eyes as she made her way to Kevin. She stopped and handed him the papers. As she did, they rattled in the wind.

"What's this?" Kevin asked, grabbing the papers as they still flapped about. Rece didn't respond as Kevin glanced at them. He looked them over, quickly flipping through them. He then looked up at her. The pain in his head began to shriek inside his mind. He immediately thought of needing a drink. He chuckled a bit, but very discreetly, and then looked at Rece.

"Really?" he said.

"Yes, Kevin."

Kevin breathed in heavily and lifted his head, gazing up at the greyness of the sky, then spoke. "Till the day I die, I will never understand how we got to this point so fast."

"Kevin, I think if you really think, you'll know. I think you do know."

"It makes no sense to me. I'm not sure what..." He cut himself off.

"It's not always what you do," Rece began, "sometimes it's also what you don't do."

"Rece, Jesus, come on, the drinking helps, you gotta understand that, you gotta. Tt finally made them go away." Kevin had a begging tone to his voice.

Rece held strong, not allowing the wind to sway her. She shook her head as she spoke. "You need help, Kevin. It's been two months since I caught you drinking. Two months. You drink more now. I told you you could stay, we could live together, if you just stopped drinking – but..."

"So, this..." Kevin shook the papers. "This is what you want?"

"No, no, Kevin. No, no, no. It was never what I wanted. You know that."

"So, what, I have to get a lawyer?"

"That's up to you."

"I'm not working, hon. You know I can't afford one."

"You chose to go on leave rather than get fired, or, really, rather than cleaning up. You clean up, they'll take you back. You know that."

At that moment, Blaize and Vincent came running around

the corner and grabbed Rece, who laughed and grabbed them back.

"Save me, mom!" Vincent screamed in joy.

The three of them laughed and giggled and staggered about the sidewalk. The whole time Rece kept a concerned eye on Kevin. Kevin looked at the papers and then made his way into the house, shaking his head the whole time. Blaize and Vincent were oblivious to this, but Rece watched him enter the house as she faked another giggle and a laugh.

Once inside, Kevin went to the basement, sat on his bed, read through the divorce papers and cracked open a beer. Lou followed him downstairs once again and sat by his side. Kevin's head shrieked in pain, as the pressure pulsed and pushed its way around his skull. His forehead felt like it would collapse in on itself. He heard laughter in his head, drowned out only by the shriek. He chugged the beer fast, opened another one, and continued to read the papers.

--

Kevin woke up to Vincent standing next to him. His head was groggy, and his stomach was sour. His head pounded in a new and unusual way. He could barely open his eyes and wasn't sure if he really saw Vincent or not.

"Um, dad?" Vincent said.

Kevin sat up quickly, wiping his eyes and attempted to shake the cobwebs and pain out of his head. It didn't work.

"Hey, buddy," Kevin said in a very raspy voice, "What's up?"

"What's with all the beer cans?" Vincent asked.

Upon that question, Kevin noticed what looked like 15-20 cans laying around the bed. There were two on the bed, and a big spill by his feet. He now smelled the result of last night's excess.

"Oh, oh, this?" Kevin responded as he thought of an excuse. "This, well, my friends were here last night, and they left all their beer cans."

Kevin didn't look at Vincent when he said it. He got up and started collecting the cans. As he stood the pain in his head almost knocked him over, and his stomach swirled in disgust.

"I didn't see any friends here last night," Vincent said matter of factly with no judgment.

"Well," Kevin stammered, "They left, or, I mean, yeah, they got here and left while you slept."

Vincent shrugged his shoulders and began to walk away. "Ok, dad, love you."

Kevin watched Vincent walk away, holding five empty beer cans in his hand. He knew he couldn't let his youngest son just walk away from this but didn't know how to correct it.

"Vince."

"Yeah, dad?"

"You came down here for a reason?"

"Oh!" Vincent giggled. "Yeah, um, mom said she'll be right back and then you guys are going to go get coffee."

With that, Vincent once again began to walk to the stairs. Kevin stopped his momentum once again.

"Vince."

Vincent just turned without speaking.

"Vince," Kevin stated again, "I love you."

Kevin watched Vincent walk up the stairs, then continued cleaning up. He counted 14 empty beer cans. *Fuck, what am I doing to myself?* He then carried the cans to the garbage can in the laundry room. His head pounded and spun. It was difficult for him to walk. Once again, he wasn't sure if the pain was due to the headache, or from the drinking. But the pain grew worse as he walked. He had to sit down before he collapsed. As he sat on the bed, he looked under it with curiosity. All he saw was an empty box. There was no beer left. *Fuck.* "Fuck," he said softly.

He leaned back and then heard his phone buzzing. He scrambled slowly around the pillows, sheet and blanket to find it. It was a call from an unknown number, but, for some odd reason, he answered.

"Kevin!" The voice said in response to the quiet 'hello'.

"Yes?"

"It's Dr. Nourzad."

"Ohhh, hey doctor, how are you?"

"Well, my question to you is, how are you? I haven't heard from you in a month or so. I called two weeks ago but didn't hear back. I was hoping this meant you were ok, that the headaches had subsided."

Kevin paused in the conversation and in his head. He really wasn't sure how to respond. He bought him some time by saying, "Yeah, I'm sorry, I know we had some appointments, or whatever. And, I don't remember getting that call from you, but I apologize."

"No need for any apologies," Nourzad said. "Are you better?"

Kevin stammered at first, "Um, well, yeah, no, no, not really." He then began to speak clearer. "It's, it's not good, doc."

"I'm sorry to hear that," Nourzad said calmly. "Did you start the blockers?"

"No, no, I never, um, no, I kinda decided against those."

"Ok, that's perfectly ok. If you didn't feel comfortable with those, we can work another path."

Nourzad then paused and Kevin could hear the shuffling of papers on his end.

"Seems we were going to try a little therapy, as well. How are you on that?"

Kevin paused a second, then responded, "Yeah, I mean, I think I can do that. Might be good."

"Ok, good!" Nourzad sounded very excited. "Well, look, you can come in any day this week. My afternoons are free."

"Ok."

"And," Nourzad began then paused, "And, you now can meet me at my basement office at my home."

"Your home?" Kevin asked very quizzically.

"Yes, I'm working out of my home now."

"Um, ok."

"How's tomorrow afternoon, say two?" Nourzad asked.

"That'll work."

"Ok, great. I'll text you my address."

"Sounds good, and, um, thank you."

"See you tomorrow, Kevin."

"Bye."

Kevin put his phone down and heard Rece talking upstairs. *She's home. Great. Why the hell are we going for coffee?*

He got on his knees and crawled halfway under the bed, looking for just one beer. There were none. "Fuck."

"Dad!"

"Tell Mom I'll be right up."

He sat on his bed defeated. He wanted a drink. The pain was swelling. He wanted to puke. And he had to go face his future with Rece.

--

Rece drove silently, as the radio played softly. Kevin wore sunglasses and slouched in the front passenger seat looking out the window. The sun glared through the windows and the interior was hot. Kevin continued looking out the window and Rece didn't speak. Buildings passed through Kevin's vision, though he stared right through them, not noticing anything distinguishable. A few cars disturbed his bliss and forced him to focus more. As he did, he noticed the wall, standing strong and resolute. He shifted in his seat and stared at it intently, turning his body a bit to continue his intense glance. He thought for a moment, but was interrupted by Rece, who took Kevin's movement as a chance to speak to him.

"You ok?" Rece asked, turning down the radio, which was already barely loud at all.

"I'm fine," Kevin answered.

"Do you care where we go for coffee?"

Kevin looked at her through his sunglasses for at least 10 seconds without answering.

"Ok, then, we'll just go to Starbucks," Rece said.

Kevin then returned to looking out the window. More silent minutes passed before Rece again broke the silence.

"How's your head?"

Kevin responded quickly. "It sucks. It hurts constantly and it's getting worse by the day."

"I'm sorry," Rece said sincerely.

More silence ensued. Kevin didn't respond at all with sound or movement.

"How was the doctor? I know, or I think you went, right, recently?" Rece said, again, very sincerely.

"Look," Kevin began, "are we just getting these formal questions out of the way now?"

"God, Kevin, you are so angry."

"You...." Kevin started to say but stopped.

"What, Kevin?"

"Nothing."

"Kevin, I really want to know what the doctor said."

"You had time to ask and you didn't, so...."

"Ok, this is all poor Kevin again?"

Kevin didn't respond.

"Ok, well, I was sincere, Kevin. I wanted to know, and I still care."

"There's Starbucks," Kevin said, expressing relief in his voice that this series of questions was over. *I need a drink.*

Rece parked and the two walked in, ordered coffee and took a seat near the back by the refrigerated section. Rece sat against the wall on the cushioned booth and Kevin sat in the chair across the small table. His head pounded and his body craved a beer. He sucked down a big gulp of the coffee and felt the caffeine hit immediately. He chugged a little more, appreciating the feeling, though his body craved more. His sunglasses remained over his eyes.

Kevin broke the silence this time. "So why are we here?"

Rece smiled and looked into his hidden eyes. "Kevin, we need to work this out. You've decided to continue to drink. It's getting worse, and we need to have a plan. I don't want you living there anymore while you're drinking. It's getting worse and worse, Kevin, and I hope you realize that."

"It doesn't affect anyone. I'm in the basement, no one sees it. I think what we are doing is fine."

"Kevin, c'mon."

"No, Rece, I think it's fine and I'm not leaving."

"And you're not going to stop drinking?" Rece said almost helplessly, her face showing wear to these conversations.

"Rece," Kevin began and then chuckled, "I don't think you get it. I'm not sure anyone does, but I hope you do. This pain, this fucking pain does not go away. It stays and it stays, and it gets worse and it's absolutely trying to kill me. The only relief I get, ok, the only relief I get is from having a few beers. The pain goes away and I get moments of relief from an otherwise intolerable life. That's it. I hope you can understand that, being someone who has seen how bad these things are."

Rece drew in a deep breath. "Kevin, Kevin, I get it, I do, but you have to see what you're doing, and, look, I didn't want to go through all this again here. I thought we were pretty clear on how I felt about your drinking. It's zero tolerance, Kevin. You say it doesn't affect anyone, but it does. Number one, it affects you and number two, the kids. The kids, Kevin. You think they don't notice? Vince was so confused this morning seeing all those beer cans by your bed."

"He was fine, I explained it to him."

"Yeah, well, he didn't buy your explanation. He told Kate you were still drunk. They know, Kevin. And I cannot stress this, and I know you don't see it, but, Kevin, Kevin, it's getting worse. You're drinking more and more, and I see the change in your life. You're getting mean, and...." Rece cut herself off to stop from crying. She slowly took a quick sip of coffee.

Kevin looked at her and sighed without speaking. He thought of his kids. He thought of Rece and how long they'd been together. His head shuddered in pain as he thought. Rece wiped a tear from her cheek and Kevin handed her his napkin.

"I don't need that," Rece said softly.

"Don't cry, Rece," Kevin said.

"What are you going to do, Kevin. You need help," Rece responded.

"I'll quit."

"What?" Rece said quickly.

"I'll quit drinking, Rece. Look, I did it before, and I'll do it now. I'll quit."

"No, Kevin, no. I mean, yes, quit, that's what you have to do, but you have to do it for the right reasons and thinking you'll tell me you'll quit so things will go right back to normal....no, Kevin. You need help quitting. Real help."

Kevin stared at her and shook his head. The pain increased and he took a long sip of coffee.

"I, I, I don't even know," Kevin said, almost under his breath, but loud enough for Rece to hear.

"You do, know, Kevin," Rece said, another tear forming in her eye.

"I'll quit."

"That's great, and you should do that for yourself and your kids, Kevin, but don't do it for me."

"Do you know how cold that sounds?'

"Do you know how cold it feels inside your body when your spouse has the same problem your parents had, the problem that killed them? And then you realize your spouse actually has the same problem, and you see him going down that path, and he can't stop, and he sneaks drinks at work and secretaries have to call, and he hits you repeatedly one night?"

Kevin stared, taking the sentence in. His stomach dropped. "I, I didn't..."

Rece continued. "Do you know how cold it feels when you give that person another chance, and that love blooms again so well until one day you try to surprise that man you love only to find out he's drinking again, behind your back, again, and about to kiss another woman right outside your house? That's a feeling I don't wish upon you, sweetie. You promised me you'd never drink again. You promised you'd get help last time, and, hey, my bad for letting that slide, letting my love for you blind me to the fact that you were ok without getting real help. But you promised, Kevin. My parents, Kevin. Both of them. When I was a kid. I told you I won't have that with you. I can't. You promised."

Kevin was speechless and saddened by the counts levied against him. Each charge was accurate, yet defendable in his mind. But defending now seemed fruitless.

"Look," Rece said, "if you're looking for the reason. If you want that definitive reason so you can justify in your head why this is happening, I'll make it easy for you, because I know you pretty well, and I know you need that stamp upon every-thing in your life, that stamp that explains every facet of your life. Kevin, you beat the shit out of me a few years ago. You didn't even know it. You never apologized and most women, Kevin, most women would have left you then. I didn't. I for-gave you because I knew it was the alcohol, and I loved you so much. You were the true love of my life and I forgave you. I gave you that chance. But I'm not letting it happen again. You broke me when I got home and saw that beer and you with that woman. I'm broke, and I'm not letting you break me any-more. And I apologize, Kevin. I apologize for not forcing you to get clean. I let you hide in the shadows, thinking you were ok. I apologize for that, Kevin. And I'll always love you. So much. But, that's it, Kevin."

The pain swelled in his head. His body needed a drink. His brain comprehended what he just heard. He stared at his wife.

"Honey, I honestly don't remember…"

"I know you don't, Kevin. I believe you."

"Well," Kevin said softly, "let's just go. I'll figure out where to go. I'll make it easy for you, but I want to see the kids always. I'm not leaving them."

"I don't want you to leave them. You're a great father, Kevin. I'll always give you that. Fatherhood was never the problem."

"Mm-hmm," was all Kevin had to say.

"Kevin, you can beat these headaches," Rece said. "You can beat them the right way. You don't need alcohol. You don't."

"Let's go."

"Kevin…"

"Let's go, Rece. I have a lot to do."

--

Dr. Nourzad pulled into his driveway ignorant of the red car in front of his house. Had he seen it, he may have driven away, not wanting to deal with her. Instead, he gathered his file on Kevin and exited his vehicle. On the stairs was Rae, dressed in blue jeans and a red shirt. Her purse dangled from her shoulder as she smiled at Frank. He paused as he finally noticed it was her, then bowed his head and walked towards the stairs.

"Rae," he said. "You're here."

"Oh Franky, so good to see you."

"You, as well," he said, reaching out to hug her. They hugged a good hug and he patted her shoulder. "Let me guess…."

"Frank," Rae said in a drawn-out fashion, cutting him off. "Can't I just stop by and see you?"

"Yes, Rae, you can," Frank said laughingly. "But, you don't."

"Why are you working from home now?" she asked.

"There it is...."

"Frank," she said. "Imagine me hearing you're not working at the office anymore! What happened?"

"I'm sure you heard something, Rae," Frank said heading away from her and into the house. Rae followed.

"I honestly didn't. Marge just said she heard you had left."

"Ah, Marge. The knower of all."

"She loves you almost as much as I do."

"That's weird, Rae. She barely knows me."

"That's what people do, son. They love those that the ones they love, love."

"Rae. That's not even a sentence."

"Frank," Rae said more seriously now, "what happened?"

"Look, Rae," Frank said as he sat. "do you want a drink?"

"Frank..."

"I just left, Rae," Frank said while raising his arms in the air.

"Nobody just leaves. There's always a reason."

"Honestly, it was just time, Rae."

"Tell me, son." Rae sat next to him.

"Rae, look, I do things in a way that strikes other doctors as, um, different, or improper in their eyes, but they're stuck in their ways because that's just the way it's been done for ages. I have a different way of helping my patients, and I guess it rubbed a few people wrong, and I left. I left because I don't want to have to explain myself on every turn."

Rae looked at him and breathed. "Son, Franky, they just

wanted you to follow the procedures."

Frank stood and laughed out loud. "Rae, Rae, Rae, see? You did hear. Why don't you just tell me what you know before you do these things?"

"I heard they wanted you to sign some papers saying you'd follow their procedures, that's all I heard."

"Well, Rae, I'll tell you. I just didn't want to sign that. But, look, I was thinking about moving on, anyways." Frank moved towards the fridge.

"Frank," Rae said, standing up to follow him. "I think it's the wrong move. Marge heard from Dr. Perez that they'll welcome you right back."

Frank laughed again. "Rae, I love you. You are so sweet to look after me, but you don't have to. I'm ok, and I'm happy with my decision."

"You need structure in your life, Franky."

"I do?"

"Yes, you do. You need structure to help stay grounded about your loss."

"Who told you that, Margie?"

"Frank..."

"Rae, I've told you," Frank said, grabbing her shoulders lightly and looking her in the eyes, "if I need help, I have you and I'll come to you. I made that promise, and I promise you again now."

"Go back, son. Go back for your old aunt."

"I love you, Rae, but this will be good for me. It's less, um, stress."

"Franky, you need to go back. It's what you need."

"Look, sweetie, you tell Marge I'll be ok. I have all the support right here with you."

Rae stared at her boy and smiled a half smile. "Well, if you aren't going to listen to me, at least tell me how you're dealing with it."

"It?"

"Your family, you stubborn son of a gunner."

Frank sighed. "I'm doing fine. I think about them I do. I miss them. Every day and every minute. But this is what I'm left with. Finding meaning, as you want me to, isn't always possible. Nah, sometimes, in life, you are given situations that you just have to deal with, without ever finding a reason. And maybe there is one, but do I want to find that reason? Is it something I did? Was it my fault? No, no, sometimes you just leave it be and accept it. But I miss them, Rae. I cry sometimes, but, but, that doesn't bring them back."

"Oh Franky," Rae began to cry and hugged him hard.

Frank hugged her back. "I love you."

"I only bother you because I love you so much."

"I know, and, um, as much as I don't maybe tell you, I appreciate you. Always."

"I'm always here for you, Frank."

"Thank you. Now, Rae, how about a drink."

--

Kevin sat in the dark, looking around his new room with only the light from the TV guiding his view. His mom's guest room was small, and his bags took up most of the room. The pain of not seeing his kids ate at him as he sat there alone. *How the fuck did I get here?* He looked at his phone and saw text messages from Blaize, Kate and James. They all said they missed him already and that they loved him. Kate's text stood out the most to him:

'We understand – Mom said you did nothing wrong, that you guys just need a break. We love you and are happy you're at non's house and that you're ok'.

Kevin stared at that text and cried. He reached over for the beer his mom provided for him. She only had two and ran out for more. Kevin drank the beer furiously while still staring at Kate's text. He finished that beer and opened the second. As he drank it, he heard the front door open and close. It was his mom.

Kevin walked with his beer in his hand to meet her. His mom, Anne, stood five-foot two, and was skinny as a rail, yet she carried the case of beer in her right hand and two plastic grocery bags in her left.

"Mom, let me get that," Kevin said as he rushed to grab the beer.

"Thank you," she said back. "Let me settle in and then we can have a few beers and talk."

"Ok, mom."

Kevin put the beer in the fridge and then grabbed some pretzels from his dad's old pretzel jar. The imprint of 'Kevin's Pretzels' had faded with time. He took a deep breath, thinking about his dad. He then grabbed another beer out of the fridge and sat at the kitchen table. His mom walked in.

"Dad loved his pretzels," Kevin said as she cracked open a beer and sat with Kevin.

"He liked his jar better," she said. "He used to tell all his friends how you bought that for him."

"Yeah, but you bought it."

"He didn't know."

Kevin smiled and drank more beer.

"You're welcome to stay here as long as you need, Kevin."

"Thanks, mom."

"Do you think she'll change her mind?"

"Who, Rece?"

"Yes."

Kevin swigged his beer. "I don't think so."

"Do you want to tell me what happened, yet?"

"Mom, I really don't. Marriages just sometimes need a break."

"I know. So many of our friends divorced. A lot of them said they were better off afterward, so…"

"Yeah," Kevin said and then drank some more.

"It's none of my business anyway," his mom said

"No, mom, it's not that. I'd gladly tell you. I just don't feel like rehashing it."

They looked at each other.

"Mom, thank you. I know it was a shock, and I gave you no notice. I know this must be hard on you."

"Don't worry about me, Kevin. I just want you to be ok."

The time passed and they reminisced about dad, his childhood, and good times. Eventually, his mom tired and decided to go to bed.

"Are you going to be up more?" his mom asked.

"I'll head into the room."

"Your room," his mom said.

"Huh?" he said back at her.

"It's your room now."

Kevin just nodded. "Love you, mom."

She went off to bed and Kevin grabbed two more beers and went into his room. He opened one and sat on his bed. His phone was full of more messages from the kids saying they loved him. He drank more beer as he passed out staring at his phone.

--

The next morning the sun broke through the window and glared off the floor and into his eyes. He shook as he gathered himself and realized he was on the floor. A beer can was at his eye level. He shooed it away and sat up on the bed. He tried to shake off the cobwebs and in doing so he shook the monster in his head. The pain began in his forehead and then quickly and viciously swarmed around the rest of his head. He bowed it into his palms and groaned. *Jesus fuck.* He stood up and walked briskly around the room. The pain didn't relent. He breathed in and out quickly and stopped, placed his hands on his hips and twisted his body back and forth. *Fuck.* The pain continued to swirl and shriek, the pressure pounding and pushing. He walked deliberately to the kitchen and listened for his mom. He quietly opened the fridge and grabbed two beers. He walked into the bedroom and then into the adjoining bathroom. He turned on the shower to drown the noise and opened a beer. He drank it down, his stomach almost rejecting it. He pushed through that feeling to swallow even more. He leaned from the edge of the tub to the sink, letting the beer do the work as his elbow kept him from falling over in pain. The first beer was gone, and he opened the other, wishing he had brought three into his room. He chugged it down and breathed. He heard his mom shuffling in the kitchen and finished the beer and entered the shower.

The water streaked down his body and the steam entered his lungs. He continued to breath deliberately, letting in as much air as possible. The pain in his head dulled as the alcohol worked through his veins. He breathed in once more and felt a rush of relief. The pain was in check, but he could feel it lurking in his brain like a caged animal biding its time.

He dressed quickly, while hearing his mom in the kitchen. He grabbed his keys, his wallet and his phone. He had several new messages, but chose not to look at them, yet. He walked into the kitchen and his mom had breakfast on the table for him.

"Thank you, mom."

"Oh, honey, you're welcome. I hope you like pancakes."

"I love them."

Kevin ate quickly as his mom sat across from him and drank coffee.

"Slow down, Kevin and enjoy your meal," she said after taking another sip of coffee.

Kevin chuckled and wiped some syrup from his chin. "Sorry, mom. I have an appointment this morning."

"With the doctor?" she asked.

"Yes."

"About your headaches?"

"Yes."

"How do they feel?"

"I don't know, they still come and go."

"It's been a long time," she said. "Rece told me you've had them a long time."

Kevin looked up at hearing her name. He finished swallowing his food and responded, "Yeah, I have."

"They can't fix them?"

"No, not really," Kevin answered quietly.

"You know, your Uncle Jim had headaches."

"Yeah?" Kevin responded, interested in the information.

"Yes, he used to lie on the bed and just be miserable."

"When?" Kevin asked.

"Oh, during his marriage, before his divorce. Had 'em a few years, I think."

"What did he do? How'd he get rid of 'em?"

"I'm not really sure. I think they just kinda went away."

"Hm," Kevin said, then he finished his last bite of pancakes. "I wonder if they were this bad?" he asked.

"Not sure, honey. But if they're really bad, you have to demand answers."

"What do you mean?" Kevin asked.

"You have to push them for answers. Nobody knows your pain like you do. Nobody." She then sipped her coffee and continued. "If you don't fight for yourself, then nobody will. Remember that."

Kevin looked at her and she back. He nodded in understanding and then got up.

"Mom, I love you. Thanks again for everything."

He kissed her and went into his room. He waited for her to go to hers and he heard her shower running. He then scrambled to the kitchen quietly, grabbed two beers out of the fridge and a water bottle from her cupboard. He filled the large bottle with beer then stuffed the empty cans to the bottom of her garbage can. He sealed the bottle and carried it out with him to his car.

--

"You have a nice house," Kevin said, shaking the rain off his coat as he entered Nourzad's home.

"Thank you, Kevin," Frank responded. "Let me take your coat."

Nourzad led Kevin to the back room. They walked in, Kevin in front. Nourzad noticed the mirror in front of the chair and scurried to move it. Kevin noticed the mirror but asked for no explanation.

"Why don't you have a seat, Kevin," Nourzad said calmly.

Kevin obliged and shifted until he was comfortable. He looked around the room and noticed a lot of red. The walls were trimmed with an off grey. Pictures adorned the wall, but Kevin didn't recognize the historical figures painted thereon, except, he thought, the one on the east wall looked like Socrates.

"Would you like some coffee, or water?" Nourzad asked.

"I'll have a beer if you have one," Kevin said.

Nourzad chuckled, and Kevin smiled, sort of.

"No, I'm alright," Kevin said quietly.

"Are you a drinker?" Nourzad asked.

Kevin looked at the doctor and didn't respond.

Nourzad ignored Kevin's silence and opened his file on Kevin. He read it over quietly without looking up. Kevin shifted again in his chair and broke the silence.

"I, um, really didn't want to come; I just want to be honest. I know I cancelled a few times, but I just didn't see how..." Kevin stopped himself.

"Why's that, Kevin? Why didn't you want to come?" Nourzad asked, looking up from his papers.

"It's been tough lately, at home. I've been through, well, it's been tough. I didn't think this would help me out, especially with the headaches, but you mentioned we could, um, talk, like, um, therapy, and, I don't know, I just, I just thought maybe that would might, might help. I don't know."

"Well, certainly, Kevin," Nourzad began, "the headaches are my primary concern, and I wish we'd see some improvement. If not a cure for them, then I'd at least like to see some relief or an ability to deal with them in a better way. And when I say that, what I mean is that I don't believe or know how you deal with it, but when I see the amount of times you've come to seek help from me, or the hospital, it's certainly, again, concerning that you aren't getting the mental relief, so, with that said, I thought maybe we could talk them out, which I explained last time we saw each other. So, yes, yes, we can certainly talk and have therapy, as you call it. But we are here to fix the headaches."

"Ok," Kevin said, not knowing how to really respond to that.

"I think we can start with the problems at home, if you'd like," Nourzad said.

"Well..."

"Actually," Nourzad interrupted, "let's, let's start with the pain. Is it any better?"

"No."

"Ok, and, I gave you that prescription..."

"Yeah, I, I kinda looked it up and wasn't comfortable with it."

Nourzad looked puzzled and asked, "Why is that? What concerned you?"

"I didn't like the side effects, or the possible ones."

"Ok, that's completely understandable, and patients certainly look at those and sometimes choose against medications when weighing the benefits versus the possible side effects. What threw you off?"

"I don't know, really," Kevin said dishonestly. "I just looked them up and remember not liking what I saw."

"Ok, and where did you look them up?"

"Online."

"Do you do that often?"

"Huh?"

"Well, let's take the headaches, for example. Did you tend to research headaches?"

Kevin looked at the doctor and hesitated. *Jesus.*

"We are in therapy, Kevin. You can be completely honest here. In fact, that really helps."

"I did, well, and still do."

Nourzad stood and walked to his desk. He looked through some papers and pulled one out of the pile. "I was reading recently about patient self-diagnosis. It's a relatively new phenomenon, if that's the right word."

Kevin nodded affirmatively.

"Patients have so much access to what you called on-line diagnoses. People are looking up their symptoms and try to diagnose themselves. At times, this can conflict with any medical advice they may have received. Do you follow?"

"Yes."

"This article kind of talks of the dangers of self-diagnosis. I won't bore you with the details, but it says that we, as doctors, must recognize this phenomenon and try to work around it, in the sense that we must assure patients that the medical diagnosis is more informed."

"Ok."

"You may look up your headache symptoms and see a plethora of diagnoses, from migraines to cancer. But the problem is, and it's why you see so many possible diagnoses, is that there is no personal information being given. There's no discussion between you and the computer. The computer just takes the search, the symptoms, and pumps out information based on those words alone. I, in talking to you, to make this more understandable, get more information from you to help narrow down the diagnosis. Follow?"

"Yes."

"Agree?"

Kevin hesitated. "I, um, don't know. I mean, I get what you're saying, but you read and hear of doctors misdiagnosing patients all the time, which leads to death sometimes, from what I've read."

"Like any other profession, yes, sometimes mistakes are made. But the probabilities are better with a doctor than a computer."

"I get it," Kevin said, not sounding confident.

"You told me a few appointments ago, I think, that you thought you were dying," Nourzad said without continuing.

"Yes?" Kevin asked.

"Was that because of a self-diagnosis?"

"I guess."

"What was the diagnosis on line? A brain tumor?"

"Yes," Kevin said, now looking down at the floor.

"I can assure you, Kevin, based on all our interactions, medically and socially, you do not have a brain tumor."

"But see," Kevin said quickly, almost ready for that statement, "how can you be sure?"

Nourzad responded, "What would assure you, Kevin."

"An MRI."

"Of your head?"

"Yes."

"You don't have the symptoms that call for an MRI, Kevin. Believe me, and I think you know me and the way I do things, if I thought just a one little inkling that you needed an MRI, even if it was the smallest of inklings, I'd get you one."

Kevin answered back, "But it's really the only way to truly know."

"You had a CT scan which came up clean."

"I read where CT scans can miss tumors."

"In rare occasions."

"But they can miss."

"Yes, but yours didn't."

Kevin breathed in deeply and leaned back in his chair.

"Look, Kevin," Nourzad said, "I understand your frustration over that, but, really, you don't need an MRI. An MRI will show more than a CT scan, yes, but you show no symptoms of a brain tumor, other than a headache, which, taken alone, most definitely doesn't indicate a brain tumor."

Kevin remained silent.

"Kevin," Nourzad began to ask, "is death a concern with you? Is it a fear?"

"I don't know." Kevin refused to answer.

"I'll assume it is."

Kevin nodded slightly.

"This fear or, concern of death, can certainly add to your headache probability. You can develop stress on yourself because of your fears, which can constrict blood vessels, which can agitate the aches in your head."

"Ok."

"An MRI might alleviate that fear, yes, but, and what I'm about to say I say as your doctor trying to heal you, when that MRI comes out clean, you'll find another reason to fear. And I say this based on my interactions with you as my patient."

Kevin remained silent, his head beginning to pound and shriek. He wanted a beer. He began to think of reasons to leave.

"You look upset," Nourzad said.

"I'm not. I expected this coming in. I get what you're doing."

"Look," Nourzad said, "I've been talking too much. I want to hear from you."

Kevin shifted again and looked at Nourzad closely. He wondered if he could trust this man.

"Why, why are you doing this?" Kevin asked.

"What?" Nourzad asked back.

"Why do you care about me so much? I mean, you call me, you set up this therapy, you bring my file home. Why?"

"You're my patient. It's that simple, Kevin. I do this with all my patients."

Kevin nodded in the affirmative and didn't hesitate. "My wife kicked me out of the house."

Nourzad froze, not expecting that response, but his mind was ready, nonetheless.

"I'm sorry to hear that, Kevin. It certainly cannot help with your headaches."

"Yeah, a few weeks ago. It's because of the headaches."

"Explain," Nourzad said after a short pause.

"We were fine before these started," Kevin said pointing to his head.

"Stress from maladies can strain any relationship, Kevin."

"I see that now."

"Do you want to talk about it?"

Kevin didn't know if he should, but he did. "I used to drink. I guess Rece thought I drank too much. But, anyway, I stopped a few years ago when she asked me to. I just stopped cold turkey. I thought I handled it well, and I did it for her. I guess she knew that, or, I hope she did."

"Did you quit for her, or you?"

"What's the difference?"

"As wonderful it is to quit for your wife, to truly beat addiction, I think most would agree that you have to quit for yourself to succeed."

"It wasn't an addiction," Kevin said. "Well, anyway, I quit."

"Continue," Nourzad said, looking very interested.

"So, a few months back, I guess, I'm not really sure when, but I was distraught over these fucking headaches – excuse my swearing."

Nourzad nodded that it was ok.

"But," Kevin continued, "I stopped for some beer just to, I don't know, to see if it would help. I was desperate"

"Ok."

"And it did. It did work. When I drink, the headaches go away. I mean, they come back, I know it's not a cure, I'm not stupid, but for the time I'm drinking, I'm free, doctor, I'm free of this beast."

Nourzad sat and looked at Kevin, who looked back, desperate for a response.

"So many interesting comments there, Kevin," Nourzad finally said. "But continue."

"Well, she caught me, or, I mean, she found out."

"That you were drinking again?" Nourzad asked.

"Yes."

"I understand her strain, then."

Kevin looked at him quizzically. "Well, like I told her, the drinking helps."

"The relief seems so brief, Kevin, especially knowing the effects of that relief."

"Yeah, I guess, but as she doesn't understand either, it's relief. I've tried and tried to explain how bad these fucking headaches are, and nobody gets it!" Kevin yelled as his sentence trailed off. "It's fucking killing me! And the beer helps. Yeah, I get it, it pisses her off that I drink, but what about me and this pain?"

Nourzad sat and looked at Kevin, still not offering what Kevin wanted.

Kevin looked back at Nourzad. "Oh my God, well, look, I'll tell you. She says I hit her."

"When?" Nourzad asked, his expression remaining unchanged.

"Last time. Last time I drank. A few years back. That's why I'm out of the house."

"She doesn't want that to happen again," Nourzad stated, surprising Kevin. "She thinks if you drink, you may hit her again."

"I guess," Kevin said. "But I never hit her."

"Whether you did or not, she thinks, or says, you did. You cannot try to downplay that."

"Are you on her side now?" Kevin said unexpectedly and quickly.

"I'm on your side, Kevin. I'm trying to help you."

Kevin breathed in deeply again. "Well, ok, she thinks I did."

"Do you think she'd make that up?"

"No, Rece would never lie. She doesn't lie, ever."

"Ok."

"I just, I just, look, I'm a good guy, I'm a good husband, and I'm a great dad. I'm not the type of guy that would hit his wife."

"Nobody thinks that."

"She does!"

"Sometimes, Kevin, we unfortunately step outside our norm for the briefest of moments. It doesn't define us."

"It's defining me."

"What bothers you, Kevin? Why can't you accept that she says that you hit her?"

Kevin didn't answer. He sat there shaking his head back and forth.

"What is it, Kevin? Why can't you..."

"Because I don't remember doing it!!!" Kevin screamed in frustration as loud as he could.

Nourzad stood, walked to his water dispenser, poured a cup and calmly walked it to Kevin. "Take a drink."

Kevin cupped it with two hands and sipped the water and

then chugged it. Nourzad sat back in his chair.

"Do you wish to continue?" Nourzad asked calmly.

"Yes. I need to know." Tears began welling in Kevin's eyes.

"If you hit her?"

"Yes."

"Ok..."

"Because if I did, then, I don't know."

"You said before Rece would never lie."

"She wouldn't. She's perfect. She wouldn't lie, she wouldn't cheat, she wouldn't sneak around." Kevin then paused and looked at the doctor. After hearing nothing back, he continued. "But me, I guess I'm just, I guess I'm a fucking asshole."

"Don't beat yourself up. It's not helpful to you," Nourzad said. "But you firmly believe she wouldn't lie."

Kevin paused, looked at him closely and nodded. He then looked around the room in an attempt to not cry. Silence engulfed the room. Nourzad stared at his patient, waiting for the right moment. Kevin shook his head back and forth and breathed heavily.

"Do you know now, that you hit her?" Nourzad said cautiously.

"Yes," Kevin said as his tears ran down his face. His body began to shake.

Nourzad got up and placed his hand on Kevin's shoulder. "Do you feel better?"

"I don't. Not at all," Kevin responded. "Fuck. I mean, yes, thank you, I see what you did. I admitted it, I guess. But I still feel like shit about myself."

"Don't," Nourzad said. "You're a great person. I'm sure she's said that to you."

Kevin didn't answer.

"Did she ever tell you that?" Nourzad asked again.

"She said I was a great father."

"And she doesn't lie. She's a great woman," Nourzad said smiling.

Kevin looked at Nourzad and thought of everything he just said. "I should go," Kevin said as he stood.

"We are making good progress, Kevin. Don't go."

"No, I have to."

"Why do you feel you have to?"

"Because I just do!"

"Does your head hurt?" Nourzad asked, hoping to keep Kevin longer.

"It. Always. Hurts," Kevin said. "Oh my God, no one ever fucking gets that."

"Kevin," Nourzad said as he walked to the door to stop Kevin, "I do get it."

"No, no, no one does."

"Kevin…"

"I have to go, doc. I really do."

"Let's set up another day to come here and talk. Say, tomorrow?"

Kevin stared at the walls and the paintings on them. He looked again at whom he thought was Socrates. He then turned and looked at Nourzad. "You know, doc," Kevin began, his voice trickling with trepidation, "you know, you know that I sometimes think these headaches taunt me, that they are alive in there? Did you know that?"

"No," Nourzad said, hoping he swayed Kevin to stay. "Tell me."

"These headaches, they laugh at me. They taunt me. They let me know who for sure it is that is in control, and it's them. They are in control."

"Tell me more," Nourzad said, "come sit and tell me."

"But," Kevin said the word in a drawn-out fashion, "but you didn't know that. You didn't. You were more interested in me hitting my wife when, I think I heard when I got here, that you were more interested in the headache. Well, that didn't last, did it?"

Nourzad scrambled in reaction to Kevin's irrational thinking. "Kevin, I don't care about your relationship with Rece."

"Her first name, huh?" Kevin said and then mockingly laughed.

"Where are you going with this, Kevin?" Nourzad asked, feeling a loss of control.

Kevin trembled and cried as he spoke. "You didn't know the headaches laugh at me, that's where I'm going. But you sure seem to care about my wife's feelings."

Nourzad ignored the comment about his wife. "Kevin, the headaches aren't laughing at you. That's your mind reacting to the stress of the headaches."

Kevin began to walk out. "I think everybody is laughing at me."

"There is no laughter, Kevin. It's just a reaction!"

Kevin stopped to look at him. He stared at him without talking. Nourzad prayed that Kevin would come back and sit down. Kevin pressed his lips tight and continued to look at the doctor.

"Goodbye," Kevin said, appearing to want to say more. "I

appreciate all you did."

"Kevin," Nourzad said almost frantically, "tomorrow."

Kevin walked out of the house and Nourzad saw him run to his car. Nourzad stood in the doorway with the storm door half open as Kevin sped away. Nourzad closed the door and walked fast into his office. He scrambled through the papers on his desk and then scrolled through his phone. He saw her number on his phone, stared at it, moved his finger to the call icon, then paused, hit the home button, threw his phone on the desk, and stood, alone, in the red room.

--

Kevin reached below the seat and grabbed the water bottle that he had filled with beer. He took a long drink then drove as he scrolled through his phone looking for Rece's number. He found it and called. The phone rang a few times. Kevin's head pounded in pain. The pressure was unyielding, and the laughter was louder than ever.

"Shut the fuck up!" Kevin screamed. He followed with, "Answer the fucking phone!"

Rece did. "Hi, Kevin. How are you?"

"Did you fuck my doctor?" Kevin screamed into the phone.

"What?" Rece asked, astounded at the question.

"I saw you at the hospital the day you went to Michigan. Why were you there?"

The laughter shrieked louder inside his head, and he reached for the beer bottle.

"Kevin, I haven't been to the hospital since the time we went together, and how dare you accuse me of that!"

"Yeah, right, spare me, Rece. Why is my doctor so concerned with you, then?"

"Kevin, I'm not doing this."

Kevin squeezed the wheel so tightly and screamed, "Stop laughing you mother fuckers!"

"Kevin, I'm not laughing! Kevin!"

"I..." Kevin paused. "Not you, Rece. Look, I saw how you looked at each other that day you met him. I saw how long you held his hand. And I saw you at the hospital!"

"Kevin, where are you?"

"Are you fucking him?"

"Kevin, you're drunk, and you get mean and irrational when you're drunk."

"Yeah, well guess what, I'm not drunk. I just came from your doctor friend's house and I know he's fucking you!"

"I'm going, Kevin. Please go to your mom's and sleep this off."

"Why won't you say no?"

"What? Kevin, I'm not doing this."

"Why won't you say you're not fucking him?"

"Because you're an asshole, Kevin, for even thinking that."

Kevin grabbed the water bottle full of beer and took a long chug then responded, "Fuck you, you bitch."

Kevin threw the phone on the passenger seat and screamed. The phone immediately rang. He glanced at it as he drove. It was Rece. He reached over and hit the speaker button but didn't say hello. There was silence.

"What, Rece?!" Kevin finally yelled.

"I'm so worried about you, Kevin. Please go to your moms."

"No, Rece, you don't get to worry about me anymore. You kicked me out, that's over."

"Kevin, I didn't kick you...Kevin please go to your moms."

"Tell me you fucked him."

"What the, Kevin! Why would you want to hear that? Would that make you feel better? Another stamp to justify your behavior and why you're at where you're at?"

"You still haven't denied it."

"Fine, Kevin, I did not sleep with your doctor. I cannot believe I have to say that. Jesus, Kevin!"

"I saw your car, Rece. I saw it."

"Kevin, you didn't. Kevin, go to your mom's and sleep this off. You need help, Kevin. I'll come over in the morning and we will talk and figure out some help for you."

"Goodbye, Rece."

Kevin ended the call and drove on. He sipped the beer and then continued on to Steven's Bar, a few blocks from his old house and a few miles from his mom's place. He parked the car and went in, leaving his phone in the car.

He sat at the bar, ordered a beer, and then called the bartender over again.

"Hey, um, can I get a shot of whiskey, too? Any kind will do."

The bartender nodded. "Sure thing."

Soon Kevin had a cold draft beer and a tall shot of whiskey in front of him. He took a long drink of the ice-cold beer, then grabbed the shot glass. He sipped it at first, feeling the burn on his throat. He then chugged the rest and placed the glass back on the table. He noticed the bartender looking at him and pointed at the empty shot glass. The bartender understood his order.

An hour or so passed, and Kevin sat at the bar. He was loose, and there was no pain in his head. He took a drink of his beer and looked around the bar. In the far corner, he noticed her and quickly turned away. He chugged at his beer and then looked back at her. She noticed him now, too. Neither of them moved. She was sitting with a group of women, none of whom Kevin knew.

Kevin got up from his stool and let the bartender know he'd be right back. He nodded. He walked towards the back, barely glancing at her. He was headed towards the men's room. As he got close, she finally smiled and waved. Kevin didn't wave back, instead he made a quick left turn into the bathroom. As he stood there, he breathed heavily. *How the fuck can she be here? How is that possible?* He zipped up his pants and walked out. She was now standing, looking at him with a smile. He nodded at her and used his finger to request that she come by him. She walked to Kevin.

He nudged her shoulder and asked sternly if she could talk a second. She obliged. The two went deeper into the bar and sat in an empty booth. He looked at her as she continued to smile. He tapped his fingers nervously on the table.

"Why are you here?" Kevin asked.

She looked confused and raised her eyebrows. "Um, I'm out with friends."

"Oh my God," Kevin said exasperated. "Why here? Why now? While I'm here?"

"Kevin..."

Kevin interrupted her. "And how do you always know my name?"

"I'm good with names, Kevin. Unlike you." She then smiled and laughed. Kevin did neither.

"Kevin, I come here all the time since my divorce. In fact, I've never seen you here before. I had no idea you'd be here." She then paused as they looked at each other. "Would you like me to leave?"

Divorce. Unreal. The laughter faintly squealed in his head

Kevin turned his head away from her. "No. That's not what I'm..." He didn't finish his sentence.

"What's the problem, then?" she asked.

"I just find it weird, from my perspective. I don't know. And you're now divorced. Ah, you wouldn't get it."

Kevin heard more faint laughter in his head.

"Try me," she said.

Kevin downed his beer and waited for it to settle in before speaking. He motioned for the waitress to bring him another beer. He then began talking about the recent events at home with Rece. She listened closely and intently. They drank and ordered more drinks as Kevin poured out all the information as he poured in more and more alcohol. His head was spinning, and he could barely see.

"I'm sorry if I caused this," she said as Kevin finished up.

"No," Kevin said. "No, it's not your fault at all. That's not why it happened."

"Are you sure?" she asked. "You said she saw us almost kiss, and I don't want to be the reason..."

"It's not your fault," Kevin reiterated. "In fact..." Kevin breathed in as he spoke, and then breathed out. He didn't finish his sentence.

She smiled and grabbed his hand. Kevin didn't pull away. He looked at her eyes and then took another long drink of beer as the waitress placed it on the table.

"My car's out there, if you need a ride home," she said, still holding his hand.

"I shouldn't have told you any of that," Kevin said.

"Any of what?"

Kevin looked at her in the eyes. "C'mon, you know."

"What?"

"Rece," Kevin said. "I shouldn't be talking about her. It isn't right."

"Look, Kevin," she said as she began to gather her things, "I'm going to get going if…"

"Yeah," Kevin responded. He took a long hard drink. "Yeah."

They both got up and Kevin stumbled a bit. She grabbed him and straightened him out. "You ok?" she asked.

"No."

They walked out the back door and into her car.

--

The next morning, Kevin woke first, his eyes blurry and his head pounding. He had no idea where he was until he looked over and saw her laying there, her bare leg straddled over his. *Oh, Jesus fucking Christ no.* He plopped his head back on the pillow and looked around the room, not recognizing anything. His memory kicked in a bit, and he remembered driving here, to her place, with her. He remembered eating something with her, and he remembered them sitting on her couch. *What the fuck?* He squeezed his eyes closed and immediately thought of Rece. *Fuck, fuck, fuck.* The pain began to swirl in his head, he heard violent laughter, and his forehead felt like it had an anvil jammed into it. *Fuck.*

He tried to slip his leg out from under his to go to the bathroom, but she stirred and opened one eye. She smiled and placed her arm on his bare chest.

"Time to go?" she asked.

Kevin took the opening. "Yeah, I think I better."

"I understand completely."

"Georgia," Kevin said.

"Yes?" she asked.

"I just want you to know that I do know your name."

She smiled. "I know you do."

"Look..." Kevin began.

Georgia interrupted. "Kevin, it's all good. We will see each other around."

Kevin leaned over and kissed her on the forehead. "I'm not an asshole."

"If you were, Kevin, I wouldn't have had you over."

He looked at her and nodded. He asked her for a ride to his car, remembering he left it, along with his phone, at the bar. She looked at him and didn't answer, tilting her head a bit and raising her eyebrows.

"Yeah, I get it. Thanks anyway."

Kevin left. He walked to his car, which was a few blocks away. His head pounded, but he hadn't dared to ask Georgia for a beer. But he wished he had. He opened his car, looking around to make sure no one saw him, as if anyone cared. His phone was vibrating. He had 27 new text messages and 9 missed phone calls. The first 8 calls were from Rece, the last one was from his mom. *Jesus Fuck!* His phone rang again.

He answered Rece's call, but as he answered, he wished he hadn't.

"Yeah?" Kevin said.

"Yeah, Kevin? Yeah?"

"What, Rece?"

"Where are you? I was so fucking worried about you, oh my

God!""

"Why?"

"We said we'd meet at your mom's house this morning and you were so…"

"No, you said we would, but I never agreed."

There was a short pause before Rece asked, "Where are you? Where did you sleep?"

"Rece…" Kevin then paused. "It doesn't matter."

"Are you fucking kidding me?" Rece said instantly.

"What?"

"You know what, never mind, it's none of my business."

How the fuck does she know?

"Rece, I have no idea what you're…"

"Kevin, please. Ok, well, I had to deal with your mom this morning, and she was worried about you, too, so you may want to call her when you're done with whatever you were or may be doing."

"I didn't do anything, I just went out, and then…"

"Kevin, your lies get worse. Like I said, it's none of my business."

"Rece…"

"I have to go, Kevin. I just care about you and wanted to make sure you were ok. You still have kids that live in that neighborhood, you know. Remember that."

"What does that even mean?" Kevin asked loudly.

"Like I said," Rece responded, "I care about you, and I know that when you're well in your head, you care about your kids and what they may see or hear. Rumors move fast, Kevin."

Kevin hung up on her. His hands trembled as he sat in the car. His head pounded and he heard the shrieking again. He squeezed his steering wheel with all his might then banged his fists on the dashboard over and over again as he screamed out loud. The phone rang again. No name pooped up, but he recognized the number as a someone who'd called before. He didn't want to talk, but he answered anyway.

"Hello?"

"Kevin, this is Dr. Nourzad..."

Kevin hung up. *Fuck you, asshole.*

Nourzad called right back and Kevin ignored the call. He then put Nourzad in as a contact, so he'd recognize the call next time.

He then drove. He headed towards Rece and his house. He wanted to see the kids. He didn't care if Rece was there, as embarrassed as he was about her knowing. He just wanted to see the kids. His mind raced. He thought of the kids, Rece, Georgia, and what he had done. He thought about work and the possibility of losing his job if he didn't go back soon. He thought of his mom. *Crap.* He pulled over and texted her a quick message:

'Mom – all ok here. I slept at a friends house. My apologies for not letting you know Going to see kids. C u later. Love you'

He put the phone down and drove. He looked left and saw his church out of the corner of his eye. He slammed on the breaks. After stopping, he looked behind him and saw no cars approaching his. *Thank God.* He stared at the church. His head swelled with pain. He looked at the clock and saw it was 9:37. He knew confession ran from 9-11 each Saturday. He parked the car, placed his phone in his pocket, and went into the church.

He dipped his fingers into the welcoming holy water and made the sign of the cross. He walked in and saw one other person waiting by the confessional. He genuflected, made the sign of the cross again, and sat in the pew, looking at the crucifix hanging over the altar. He pushed back the pain in his head, assuring himself he'd get a beer right after this and then see the kids and then go to moms. He sat with his eyes fixed on Jesus. He prayed. *Please help, Lord.* Just then, the old woman by the confessional whispered to Kevin.

"I'm done, and I don't think anyone's in there, so go ahead." She smiled a warm smile.

"Thank you," Kevin whispered back and winked at her.

Kevin walked to the confessional and slowly opened the door. The dark space showed only a kneeler and a screen with a shadow on the other end. Kevin made the sign of the cross and knelt, making sure the door was closed first.

"Bless me father, for I have sinned. It's been way too long since my last confession," Kevin said with his eyes closed.

"Go on, son," the priest said from behind the screen.

"I have so many sins, Father, but I just wanted to confess to cheating, I mean, committing adultery on my wife. Yeah, I think I may have done that."

"I see," the priest said. "That, my son, has to stop, ok?"

"It has," Kevin responded.

"Good. The Lord considers marriage a sacred bond between two Catholics who pledged their devotion to each other before Him. It cannot be taken lightly, my son, what you have done."

Kevin bowed his head and listened.

"But the Lord above all else forgives. And if you truly are sorry, then I will ask the Lord for your forgiveness."

"I am, Father."

"Very well, my son. God, the Father of mercies, through the death and resurrection of His Son has reconciled the world to Himself and sent the Holy Spirit among us for the forgiveness of sins. Through the ministry of the Church may God give you pardon and peace, and I absolve you from your sin in the name of the Father, and of the Son and of the Holy Spirit. Your penance, my son, are your thoughts on what you did. Go and reconcile those thoughts with the Lord."

"Thank you, Father." Kevin then made the sign of the cross and walked out of the confessional. He turned to Jesus and made another sign of the cross.

Kevin ran out of the church and to his car. He sped rather quickly to the house to see his kids. His head pounded away, shrieking at an all-time high, the sounds piercing through his brain. *The fucking laughter.* He flew past the house and turned left, accelerating down the street, his eye ahead, looking for the bar and signs of life. He reached for his wallet in his pocket and opened it, seeing bills. He threw the wallet on the passenger seat and continued onwards. He saw a man walking into the bar and exhaled in relief. He parked and ran inside.

At the bar, he requested a beer and two shots and placed his money down. The bartender took his time and Kevin wrung his hands while he waited. The bar was dark enough, so he didn't feel exposed at such an early hour. Once his drinks were brought to him, he sipped the beer then downed the shot. The pain screamed in his head and he grabbed the other shot and drank it down. He felt the alcohol go to work instantly, caging the pain, dulling it for now. He drank the remaining beer quickly, counted the bills on the bar, and told the bartender he appreciated it.

"Keep it," Kevin said as he turned to walk out. He looked outside the door window to see if he spotted anyone he knew. He didn't. So, he walked out, got into his car, and drove to the house. He ate two or three mints before exiting the car and walking in.

"Dad!!!"

James and Vince jumped off the couch and ran to him, grabbing his legs and waist and hugging him. He hugged them back. From the kitchen, Rece appeared. She looked at Kevin and he at her.

"Hi," Kevin said.

"Hey," Rece responded, looking at him crossly.

"I, um, wanted to stop by and see the kids," Kevin said while still hugging the boys.

"Boys run out to the garage and get your brother and sister," Rece said, placing her glass on the table.

"Mom, do we have to?" James asked like a kid.

"Go get them. Both of you," Rece said like a mother.

"Both of us?" Vincent asked.

"Both of you," Kevin responded before Rece could answer.

The boys ran out.

"I wish you would have called at least," Rece said, walking towards Kevin.

"I didn't think of it."

"Why are you here?"

"To see the kids."

"I thought you'd come tomorrow."

"Tomorrow isn't guaranteed, Rece. I wanted to…"

"What does that mean?" Rece asked, cutting him off.

"It just means I wanted to see them."

"Why is tomorrow not guaranteed, Kevin?"

Kevin smiled a small smile. "Rece, it just isn't, and I wanted to see them."

"Are you ok? You're scaring me."

"Why are you scared, you don't have to be scared of me."

"Tomorrow isn't guaranteed. That scared…"

Before she could finish, the four kids ran in the house and surrounded Kevin. They all hugged him and talked loudly to him. Rece stood to the side and just looked at Kevin. Occasionally he looked up from the kids to look at her. They all sat on the couch and talked and laughed while Rece stood her ground, staring at her husband in almost disbelief.

"Ok, kids, daddy's gotta go, don't you, Kevin?"

Kevin looked at her, still smiling from the love the kids were giving him. But the smile turned flat. He looked at all four kids and then said, "Yeah, well, you know, I gotta go see Grandma, so, mom's right."

The kids all moaned. They all stood up and Kevin hugged each one separately and told them each how much he loved them. His hugs lasted long, and a tear ran down his cheek. He stood, "I love you guys so much, ok? Always remember that."

His head began to pound, as the pain had escaped the cage and swirled around in his head. The shriek was loud, and his fingers went numb. He looked at Rece and then his kids again. He fought back tears and told the kids to go on; he wanted to talk to their mother before he left.

Rece and Kevin stepped outside.

"Kevin," Rece began, "are you ok?"

"I'm fine," Kevin said, wiping any remnant of tears away. "I actually saw the doctor…" Kevin paused a bit, looking at her reaction to hearing that. Seeing none, he continued. "yeah, at his house…"

Rece cut him off. "House?"

"Yeah, I guess he left the office or something, I don't know. But he's, or was, he gave me a therapy session, like a shrink. It was supposed to help, and I don't know, maybe it did a little."

"Why are you crying?" Rece asked.

"I'm fine, hon."

"Why is tomorrow not guaranteed?" Rece asked, looking very concerned.

"It's just a figure of speech," Kevin responded.

"No, that's not."

"It is, Rece. To me it is."

"Kevin, please."

"Rece, what? I'm ok."

"Spend the night here. We'll make dinner for the kids."

"Rece, c'mon."

"I mean it."

"No, that's ok."

"What are you going to do now, then?"

"Going to my mom's."

"Let's renew those vows, Kevin."

Kevin stared at her and sulked his shoulders. He wiped a tear from his eye. "Oh, Jesus, honey, I'm so sorry."

"It's ok, Kev..."

"I was supposed to set that up. The headaches and all this. Rece, I'm so sorry."

"We can still do it!"

"You seemed pretty upset this morning, Rece."

Rece walked closer to Kevin and lowered her voice. "Kevin, I love you. Don't you see that? What you did yesterday in your personal time is what you did, I can't control that. Look, it's the drinking, I get it. It's always been the drinking. I know it's not you. I don't want you drinking because it affects you so much. Please spend the night and then we'll work on getting you help tomorrow. Even if it's just AA meetings."

"Rece, I don't need AA."

"Kevin…"

"I appreciate your care," Kevin said. "Look, ok, look, I'll go to my moms and I'll come back, sound good?"

Rece looked at his eyes closely. "Yeah?"

"Yeah, I mean, yeah, I'll be back."

"When?"

Kevin leaned towards her and kissed his cheek. She didn't back away. Kevin turned and said he loved her as he did. Rece watched him walk away. "You have four kids who love you, Kevin."

He turned towards her and just looked. He gazed at his house and then back to Rece. The shrieking in his head accelerated and screamed. Looking at her didn't stop the pain. Rece stared at him. The moment seemed frozen in time. Kevin began to walk away, when Rece spoke.

"Did you sleep with her?" She put her hands over her mouth and stared.

Kevin froze, that moment still holding him. He turned towards his wife and looked, not saying a word. Rece had her answer and her knees buckled a bit. Kevin moved slowly towards her and stopped a couple feet away.

"Rece, what you see here, this me, it's not me. Whatever I've become, whatever this has made me," Kevin said pointing to his head, "it's not me. But I know this, the man you loved, the man you know me as, he's gone, and I don't know how to find him. But me, right now, it's not who…" Kevin stopped in mid-sentence, and then continued. "To answer your question," Kevin said and then paused, looking at her eyes, "to answer your question, I don't even know if I did. I don't remember what we did. And that, that, that's probably worse." Tears built in Kevin's eyes and he took a deep breath and looked away from her. "I don't remember."

Rece just looked at him with a blank stare, almost as if she was looking right through him.

"You still want me to come back tonight?" Kevin asked as his voice cracked.

Rece just stared then answered, "Yes, of course I do." She began to cry uncontrollably.

Kevin paused and looked at her. "The Who," he said.

"The who?" Rece asked quizzically.

"The Who sang, I spit out like a sewer hole, yet still receive your kiss."

"Kevin…"

"Why, Rece? Why do you constantly keep accepting back me when I'm just a piece of shit."

Rece didn't hesitate. "Because I love you. I've always loved you. And I always will."

Kevin just stared at her. Both of them wiped tears from their eyes and cheeks. Kevin finally turned away from her and walked to his car. Rece watched her husband walk away slowly. Her eyes let go more tears and she wiped them away softly. Kevin drove away, looking at her in his mirrors.

"Come back, Kevin," Rece said under her breath,

--

When he arrived at his mom's house, Kevin's headache pounded and shrieked. His balance was weak as he exited the car, and he desperately craved a drink. The pain was so bad he could barely see where he was going. He entered her house and walked quickly to the fridge. He grabbed two beers and went into his room and drank. He scrolled his phone, seeing three missed calls from Nourzad. Nourzad had also left a voicemail. Kevin began to listen on his speaker.

"Kevin, this is doctor Nourzad. I was just calling to check on you. I didn't like how we left each other, and I really think we could both use another appointment. I can figure this out for you, and we can fix this all. Look, you aren't hearing the headaches laugh at you, Kevin. I yelled that as you left but wasn't sure if you heard. It's just your brain playing tricks on you. You aren't hearing things, Kevin. You have to know that. Trust me, I know medically and personally. So, when you get this, please call. I can meet you here anytime. I can also come see you if that's easier. You have my number. Take care."

Kevin immediately deleted the voicemail and walked to get two more beers. He lay on his bed and drank them both quickly as he just stared at the wall across from him.

--

"Frank, this is .... Perez. We need to talk immediately. Please call me back."

Nourzad hit the call back button as he drove. The phone was on speaker. He heard the ring and awaited Dr. Perez' voice.

"Frank," Perez said directly as he answered.

"Hello to you, as well, Doctor Perez."

"Frank, are you seeing patients at your house?" Perez asked. "More to the point, are you seeing patients that you procured from this office?"

"John," Nourzad began, "I don't really see how that's any of your concern. There are confidentialities involve...."

"Frank!" Perez interrupted. "Frank! I have given you every benefit of the doubt. I have had your back since you joined our office. Hell, the past two months I've gone to bat for you I can't tell you how many times. But you, you have gone too far now, Frank!"

"I appreciate your..."

Again, Perez cut him off. "You cannot see patients from this office at your house after you have left the practice, Frank!"

"Why not, John?"

"Frank, you are a great doctor, a great doctor. You have great instincts and your care is outstanding. But you don't ever consider the outliers when it comes to being a doctor! It's not all about you, Frank. You signed contracts, Frank. I have the contract right here. Non-compete. You cannot take patients with you when you leave the office. Those patients remain a part of this medical group. I mean, how do you not know that? Do you even realize he's not covered by insurance by seeing you outside this office?"

"Who, John?" Nourzad asked sarcastically. "Why don't you just say his name?"

"Mr. Ruscevich, ok? His wife called and mentioned him seeing you at your house! And you're now acting as his psychiatrist!!??" Perez screamed at Frank. "Frank! Have you lost your mind? I mean, did you ever even refer him to a neurologist, Frank? No, you didn't. Come on, Frank! You are not a psychiatrist! The man needs help and you've ran the gamut on him, Frank, and you have crossed the line in so many ways here! He needs a new voice!"

"Do you hear yourself, John?" Nourzad spoke clearly and calmly. "Do any of you hear yourselves? He needs a new voice? One that will tell him that he has a migraine, John? Is that it?

Get that diagnosis and move on him? 'Well, Mr. Ruscevich, you have migraines, thank you for your time and here is your bill'. No, no, John, he doesn't have migraines, and in fact, it'll take more time to figure out how to help this man. He has debilitating headaches, John, and he needs my help, not some neurologist who will run the same tests I've already run and shoo him away with a migraine diagnosis."

Perez didn't pause. "Frank, you're sounding very dangerous now. You are acting very dangerously now. You cannot see this man anymore; I need to hear you say that you understand this. I am calling him right after you and telling him he is not covered by seeing you anymore."

"John," Nourzad said, "you're a good man. You brought me into that office, and I appreciate you to the fullest. But you cannot tell me to not see this patient. I am not charging him, anyway, so, you don't have to worry about that. This man needs help, and I am not giving up..."

"Frank. leave the man alone."

"Call him, if you have to, John. I know you're just covering yourself. Again, I appreciate..."

Perez then hung up on Frank, just as he pulled up to Rece and Kevin's house.

--

Kevin shuddered as he woke. He had no concept of the time or place. He looked around to gather his bearings. He recognized the room after a few minutes. He was in his mom's living room. The morning news was on, and sunlight blared through the windows onto Kevin's face. The glare made the headache even worse. He had to hold his head with one hand as he used the other to help him stand up. *Fucking Christ.* "Fuck!!!!" Kevin screamed with all his might. He sat back down and waited for his mom to respond to the scream, whom he'd forgotten about and didn't want to have to explain the scream. He squinted around the room and hall but didn't see her. He didn't hear her, either. He got up to look for his phone. The pain was so bad he could barely walk. His head felt like it was full of set cement. He could barely hold it up. He picked up his mom's phone and called his cell. He heard it in his bedroom.

He had seven missed calls. Three from Rece, two from Nourzad and one unknown number. There were two voicemails, one from Rece and one from the unknown number. He immediately pressed the Rece voicemail icon. There were three seconds of silence and then a hang-up. *Crap. Why'd she not leave a message?*

He made his way to the fridge and grabbed a beer. His mom had re-stocked the fridge with beer at some point last night. He drank one down and started another, all the time standing next to the fridge. The pain wasn't subsiding. It was pushing and pushing, the cement inside expanding. The shriek was not present this morning, replaced by a jackhammer, inconveniently placed inside the forehead skull, bashing away relentlessly. Kevin opened one cupboard after another, over the stove, under the microwave until he found the hard liquor. He poured himself vodka, despite the fact that he hated it. He endured the burn as it travelled down his throat and into his empty stomach. He washed it down with a stale doughnut, leftover on the counter. He poured a little more vodka and drank it down. He sat at the kitchen table as the pain deadened a bit. He breathed and leaned back in the chair. *This fucking sunlight. Jesus.*

He walked into his bedroom again and lay down, hoping to pass out, but knowing he couldn't be asleep when his mom came home. His phone buzzed, and he answered without looking.

"Hello."

"You sound dead, Kevin."

"Who is this?" Kevin asked, not in the frame of mind to recognize any voice.

"It's Leigh, Kevin."

"Oh, Jesus, Leigh. Hi."

"Are you coming back soon. I've heard things and I think you need to get back to work as soon as you can."

Kevin didn't respond.

"Look, it's none of my business, ok? But talk is they're going to fire you if you don't come back."

"I'm on leave, Leigh, they can't..."

"Yeah, they can, Kevin," Leigh said, sounding like she knew exactly what she was talking about. "Come on. You know that. Let's not do this."

"Leigh, I can't really do this right now."

"Kevin, you need to come back if you want your job. That's all I'm telling you."

"Yeah, I don't think..."

"Kevin, if you want your job, come back and come back soon. Please, Kevin."

Kevin wiped the sweat from his forehead and sat up. His feet were on the floor and he had one elbow leaning on his left thigh and the other on the bed as he leaned forward. He held the phone to his ear, waiting to hear more from Leigh.

"Kevin, that's it."

"Ok, Leigh," Kevin said. "Thank you. And look, if I don't, or, if you don't hear from me..." Kevin paused. "...just, if you don't, well, just know that, well, just know, Leigh that, well, thank you for everything, Leigh."

He hung up and tossed the phone on the bed. He heard it vibrate and thought it was a call.

"What!?" he said to no one. It turned out to be a text. Frustrated, he looked at the text. It was from Kate.

'Hey dad, luv u. Ur doctor was here looking for u. Love u.'

Kevin stared at the text. And he stared. And he stared. *Unfucking believable.*

At that moment, the jackhammer cracked through the skull and shattered his head. Kevin keeled over in extreme pain onto the floor. Shrieking laughter filled his head. He shouted out and rolled along the floor. "Nooooo!" he screamed over and over. "Nooooo!" He crawled towards the adjoining bathroom but threw up a few feet short of the toilet. The puke covered the floor and his shirt. He lay in it after slipping on it while trying to use his hands to crawl away. He couldn't see, blinded by the pain deep in his forehead. Smelling the vodka in the puke, he licked some of it up, too weak to walk to the kitchen for more. He gathered a little momentum and crawled to the sink. He opened the drawer below it and grabbed a warm can of beer. He drank it fast and lay on the floor, the smell of puke enveloping the entire bathroom. He crawled to the tub and turned on the water. He took off his shorts and shirt. Puke had seeped through the shirt and onto the skin. Somehow, he found the ability to sit in the shower and wash himself. The pain didn't relent. The laughter continued. "Fuck you!!!!"

--

"Did you throw up, Kevin?" his mom asked as she placed some grocery bags on the kitchen table. Kevin looked up, now dressed in grey basketball shorts with a blue stripe down the side. He had sunglasses on.

"Oh," Kevin said, "yeah, mom, sorry. I cleaned it up."

"What was wrong?" his mom said as she approached and

hugged him.

"Something I ate, I guess," Kevin said, looking down at the glass kitchen table. "It just came out of nowhere."

"Was it your breakfast? Did you eat that doughnut that was out there?" she said, pointing to the counter.

Kevin shook his head yes. "Yeah, mom, I did."

He let her blame herself for leaving it around too long.

"I'm sorry, honey, it must have been that rotten old dough-nut."

"Mom," Kevin said, 'please don't worry about it. I'm ok."

"Ok," his mom said, accepting his diagnosis, "well, I hope you're well enough to go to the church with me. I really don't want to drive there."

"Oh, mom, what?" Kevin asked.

"Church. St. Jerome's," she said back. "It's a sit and chat day. I want to go, but don't want to drive."

"Sit and chat day?" Kevin said as a question.

"Yes, the day the congregation can just sit and talk about church and readings, and we have coffee, we sing."

"Yeah mom, I'm not up for that."

"You don't have to talk, you can just sit and listen, if you choose."

"Uh huh."

"It'll be good for you," his mom said as she began to put the groceries away.

"Mom."

"Kevin, please drive your mother to sit and chat day."

Kevin looked at her, contemplating the time and if he'd be

able to get a drink in before, realizing he may have to take her.

"What time?" he asked.

"12 until 1."

Kevin looked at the clock on the wall. It was 11:15.

"Well, I mean…"

"They have good doughnuts and then afterwards you and I can go to lunch."

"Mom, I'll drive you there and then come back and pick you up," Kevin said, offering his perfect solution.

"Oh, Kevin. Your dad used to sit in with me."

"Mom."

"I'm just saying."

"Look, I'll pick you up, too."

"Ok," she acquiesced. "I'll just go alone."

"Dad's been gone for six years, mom."

"I always have a friend go with me, but no one can today."

"You don't even go to St. Jerome's," Kevin said, the lawyer in him coming out.

"Yes, I do. I go to Pius and Jerome's."

Kevin rolled his eyes behind her back and then rubbed his eyes with the palms of his hands. "Alright, alright, I'll sit there with you but I'm not talking."

His mom smiled and continued putting the groceries away. "We'll leave soon."

Kevin waited for her to go into her room to get ready and then found a small water bottle. He gently poured some vodka in it and placed it in his jacket pocket. He looked in the mirror to see if the bulge was noticeable. After little shifting, he convinced himself that it wasn't. He took it out, drank a swig, and put it back in his pocket. He went off to the bathroom to gargle with mouthwash, went and sat on the chair by her front door and announced to her that he was ready.

--

"You could have dressed up," his mom said as they drove to the church.

"Mom."

"I'm just saying."

"You're always just saying, mom," Kevin said as he clutched the make-shift vodka bottle in his pocket. He then saw the church. "It's a lot closer than I thought."

"Of course," she responded. "You've lived here forever. You should know."

"I do, I mean I did," Kevin said. "Ok, well, I'm going to drop you off, then park, and I'll meet you inside."

"You can park right in front," she said, pointing to open spots.

Kevin stopped the car and told her he'd meet her inside after parking in the lot.

"Ok, ok, see you right inside. We'll be in the middle pews."

"See you in a sec," Kevin said.

Kevin pulled around the side of the church and found a spot among many. He took out the water bottle and drank a little vodka. The burn awoke his throat and he swigged a little more, trying to cage the pain. He shook his head after his last swig and placed the bottle in his pocket. *Just in case.*

The church was huge. The red brick glistening from the sun's rays that day. The stained-glass windows sucked in the sun, and the colors were beautiful. The long, heavy doors were open that day, propped open by strong thick chairs, welcoming the sitters, as Kevin called them.

Kevin quietly entered, hoping to not be noticed. He dipped his hand in the holy water and made the sign of the cross. He saw the group of chatters in the middle pews, as his mom had said. He walked quietly towards them and decided to sit towards the back. He sat still, still trying to just blend in. He heard the din of their voices and looked about the gigantic church.

Paintings adorned the walls, each painting depicting a Station of the Cross. The paintings led to an altar on each side. Above the main altar hung Jesus on the cross, and beside him on the altar sat statues of Joseph and Mary. Mary was on the left and Joseph on the right.

He looked over it all, taking in and appreciating its significance to the faith in which he was brought up. He remembered his old Catholic school, and thought of quick blurry memories of individual teachers and nuns who taught him the three 'r's' along with religion. Across the church he then noticed a man walking out of a confessional. The light above the door went out as the man exited, indicating an open confessional. Kevin chuckled to himself. *No.*

As he sat, the chatter continued. Kevin felt the pain building in his head, and he winced. He then thought of Rece and the doctor. He imagined them in an embrace and then physically shook that thought out of his head. *She said she didn't.* That embrace crept right back into his head. *Why the fuck was he at the house?* He quietly pulled his phone out of the pocket and looked at Kate's text again. He breathed out a frustrated sigh and then looked at Jesus above the altar as the pain grew worse.

God, what do I do? What is going on?

One of the chatters had stood up to speak. He could make

out the words. He sat up a little, leaned forward, and listened.

"God doesn't appear before us, because He wants us to have faith. Debbie, you lost your child a few weeks ago, and I can only imagine the internal struggles you had. I'm sure your faith was tested. Jeremy, your cancer came back, and you fight with all your might, but not once have you asked me or any of us, why. The Lord is always here. He's always here with us, and for us, without showing His or Herself. Why not? Why not come to us and let us know that all will be ok? Why not? God should do that, no?" The older gentleman paused.

"No," someone said loudly, answering his question. The man looked at the woman who said it. It was Kevin's mom.

"No, Anne," the man said softer. "No. No, he shouldn't. Because we don't need Him to show us. Through our faith, we know God is there and if we saw God, if we could only go to God for consolation, then this whole religion based on salvation through faith would just mean nothing." The man paused and looked at the other sitters. He then turned fully and saw Kevin, and he nodded at him. Kevin stared in disbelief. The man finished up. "Thank you all for listening to me this great day."

The others then applauded him. Kevin sat, wondering how the man knew to look at him.

The next speaker spoke quieter than the gentleman before and left Kevin to sit and ponder. *Faith, right.* The pain immediately began to rumble, push and spread. The pain pierced so hard through his head he could hear a screech, like metal scraping on the concrete after a car crash. The voices in the church became mute to Kevin as he blurredly looked around the church, trying to gain focus. His fingers trembled and his heart raced. He pulled out the bottle, bent over to his right a bit and took a big sip. He placed the bottle back into this coat.

The images of the church started to bombard him: Jesus,

Mary, Joseph, the altar, stain glass, the giant organ, and offertory candlelight glittering, two priests walking in black garments along the side of the church. The organ began to blare louder to him, and the images continued hitting him, faster and faster as the organ music wailed away. The sitters had stood and were singing loudly in unison with the organ.

"If-you-believe-in-me, Even-though-you-die, You-shall-live-forever – And-I-will-raise-you up! – And-I-will-raise-you-up! – And-I-will-raise-you-up-on-the-last-day..."

Kevin heard the singing blaring into his soul as he ran out of the church, covering his ears from the wailing organ. The shrieking was back in his head, screaming and parsing through his brain. The sunlight caught Kevin escaping the darkened church and blinded his vision. He pulled the bottle from his coat, chugged the remaining Vodka and threw the bottle into the street. He wobbled his way to the car and got in. He sat for one moment, looked at the church, fought back the extreme pain in his head and said out loud, "Please forgive me." He made the sign of the cross and then started the car and drove off alone.

--

Kevin drove through the streets of his neighborhood after stopping at the liquor store, looking around at all the houses and street corners. He remembered playing fast pitch against the brick wall of the old school on Springfield Avenue. He pulled over to see if the old square chalk outline was against the wall. As he looked, he sipped the beer, which he had poured into an old plastic cup he had found on the floor of the car. When he finished, he opened a new can, poured it in the cup, threw the empty can on the floor in the back area, and slowly drove on.

He drove by his grandma and grandpa's old house. The garage had been torn down, leaving just a backyard and a porch.

He remembered his grandpa sneaking beers in the garage after the doctors had told him he couldn't drink anymore. He chuckled. One time his mom and he delivered a 12-pack of beer to grandpa in that garage, out of the sight of grandma.

Around the next corner, he saw an open spot along the street, and he pulled over. As he did, his phone rang. It was Dr. Nourzad. Kevin pressed the 'IGNORE' icon. The phone rang again. Kevin ignored it again.

Kevin sat back in the driver's seat and sipped his beer. He thought of Rece. Every thought was of her: the way she looked so pretty the day he met her; the dinners she used to make him when they dated; her smile the day of their wedding. *Oh, Rece.* He chugged down the beer and relaxed his eyes. Rock music played low on the radio. He recognized the beginning of Led Zeppelin's "In the Light'. The foreboding beginning sounds oozed into his consciousness. He listened closely as he relaxed, letting every word make its way into his brain. The eight-minute song continued on as Kevin drifted more and more into bliss.

--

Nourzad stared at Kevin's chart. He read over every report, every note, every diagnosis given to Kevin since the beginning of his headache episode. When he was done, he read them again. He looked over the results of his CT scan, and the accompanying notes given by the radiologist.

IMPRESSION: No findings on the CT scan account for patient's complaint(s) – no further testing suggested – clusters?

Oh, man. Just a cluster? "But that long?" Nourzad said out loud.

He flipped open a journal and hurriedly flipped to the **'Headache'** section. He adjusted his reading glasses and underlined the following lines:

Cluster headaches:

One of the most painful types of headaches;

can last 6-12 weeks;

episodes can last from one week to a year;

cluster headaches can last for more than a year;

Treatment: 100% Oxygen, 12 liters per minute, 15 minutes provides relief; Intranasal anesthetic; calcium channel blockers; corticosteroids...

Oh, dear God. He rubbed his eyes then looked back upon the journal. He read the paragraph under the treatment section and thought, *oh fuck*, as he read the final sentence:

Once a cluster period begins, drinking alcohol may trigger more intense   headaches.[xxi]

Nourzad slammed the journal closed and picked up his phone. He called Kevin again and again, but there was no answer. He tried Rece's phone, but she didn't answer either. He collapsed onto his chair and pulled at his short hair, wanting to pull it out in frustration. *How did I miss that?* He tried Kevin's phone again, and then Rece's. He then tried Rece again after she didn't answer.

"Hello?" Rece answered

"Yes, yes, Rece, it's Dr. Nourzad..."

Rece cut him off. "Doctor, you can't keep calling here."

"Rece, yes, I know, it's very unorthodox, but it's imperative that I find Kevin."

"Doctor, he's very paranoid right now and if he finds out you're calling and stopping by, he's going to misinterpret that. You have to stop."

"Rece, it's the drinking. It's making it worse."

Rece ignored that and spoke back. "I spoke to your partner. He says you're not even supposed to be seeing…"

"Rece," Nourzad cut her off, using a calm voice to calm her, "where's Kevin?"

"I don't know," Rece responded, sounding distraught. "I've been calling him. What do you mean the drinking is making it worse?"

"He has cluster headaches," Nourzad said in a rush. "I think, I mean, I really, I, well, it looks like clusters. Long explanation aside, if it's cluster in nature then drinking will elongate and worsen his symptoms. I missed it. I'm sorry. There are options to him to make him feel better and I just need to find him."

"I'm trying to find him myself. His mom just called…look, doctor, I'll find him and let him know what you said, but I don't want you talking to him or letting him know that you've been calling…"

"Rece, please don't use us…"

"Us?" Rece interrupted Nourzad. "Us? There's no 'us', doctor."

"Look, Rece, please try to find him. Please."

Rece didn't respond.

"Rece?" Nourzad sounded louder. "Rece!!!!"

Nourzad hung up and called Kevin back. There was still no answer.

--

Hours later, Rece stood outside, calling Kevin's number over and over. The sun was setting, and a cool breeze ran through the front porch. She called again and then texted Kevin to please call her right away. She sat on the bench beside the front door and stared at her phone, praying Kevin would call her.

The last glimpse of sun desperately shone over and through the trees off to her right. Rece gazed upon the dimming as she clutched her phone, hoping to feel the vibration of a call. The sun was gone as she placed the phone on the bench and stood up. She looked right and left down the street and shook her head back and forth. She went to open the screen door when she heard her phone. She jumped like a scared kid in the dark night hearing a scary noise.

"Kevin!" she screamed loudly as she answered.

"Hi, Rece," Kevin said softly.

"Where are you sweetie?" Rece said calmly and softly.

"I kinda fell asleep in my car," Kevin said. "Rece, the pain is so bad."

"I know, Kevin," Rece said.

"Rece," Kevin said back, "it's not me. Remember that, ok?"

"Kevin, it's going to be ok. Just tell me where you are. You're scaring me, Kevin."

"I'm not trying to scare you. Don't be scared."

"You sound very drunk, Kevin, and that's ok. I understand why you drank. Just come here, or, no, tell me where you are, and I'll come get you."

"I'm getting rid of it tonight, Rece."

"Getting rid of what, Kevin?"

"The headaches."

"What do you mean, sweetie, the headaches? Kevin, come on now, just tell me where…"

"I'm getting rid of them. I woke up in my car here, and the pain was so fucking bad. I just can't anymore. I think I know how, and I'm ready. I'm just ready. I can't let them win anymore, Rece. These headaches, they, they, just ruined us and the kids and I…"

"They haven't won, Kevin."

"They're trying to destroy us, hon, and I can't let them."

"Kevin, you sound so drunk, please let me get you."

"I'll get rid of them and then it'll be over. It's best for you and…"

"Kevin."

"Rece, I love you. I always have and always will. You were my true love and sometimes you forget that, and whatever, but…"

Kevin stopped talking.

"Kevin," Rece said calmly.

Kevin didn't respond.

"Kevin!" Rece said louder.

"Yeah, I'm here, hon."

"Whatever you're doing, Kevin, please…"

"I know how to beat 'em, hon," Kevin said like a general going to battle. "They won't survive."

"Kevin, please," Rece said as desperate as ever. "Kevin!"

"I love you honey. I love you so much."

Rece listened and then heard the dead noise of a call ended. She screamed into the phone, "Kevin!!!!"

She called him back, but the phone went right to voicemail. She ran into the house and called for Blaize. She had to scream his name until he ran downstairs. She calmly explained that she was going to pick dad up. His questions regarding that went unanswered. She kissed Blaize's forehead as she held his head and then hugged him.

"I have to go get dad," she said while holding Blaize's head. "Watch your brothers and sister and have your cell phone by you."

"Is everything ok, mom?" Blaize asked her.

"Yes, sweetie, yes. I'm going to get him, and it will all be ok."

Rece left the house after telling Blaize to lock the door behind her. She dialed Lisa and asked her to come with to find Kevin. "I'm desperate, Lis. I'll explain when I pick you up."

Rece grabbed the steering wheel with both hands and sped down the street towards Lisa's house.

--

"Doctor Nourzad," Kevin said into the phone.

"Kevin!" Nourzad responded. "Thank you for calling. Look, I think..."

"Ya know," Kevin said, ignoring Nourzad's plea to speak, "I got a voicemail I just listened to that says you aren't supposed to be my doctor anymore. Said you shouldn't be giving me therapy and all because you're not trained in that. Imagine my surprise, doctor. So, I called the guy back and left him a voicemail and told him not to worry about it."

"Kevin, please..."

"Doc, ya know I'm kinda busy right now. I kinda passed out in my car and woke up with pain in my head that you'll never understand. I told you so many times how bad it is, and you did nothing for me, nothing. Go away, sir, they'll get better." Kevin laughed a bit. "Ah, but I get it, doctor. I do. But I'm in this horrendous pain, so excuse me but I don't really want to talk to you anyways, so I just called to say thank you for trying, I guess. I don't know. I'm fixing my head by myself tonight, so, so, you're off the hook."

"Kevin, how? Don't." Nourzad sounded frightened.

"No, no, no," Kevin said. "I gotta do it myself."

"Your words are slurring, Kevin. You're drunk. Look, cluster headaches get worse with alcohol, Kevin. That's why they're getting worse and not going away!" Nourzad said, still playing the doctor. "Clean living, Kevin, we talked about it."

"Fixing it myself, doc," Kevin said calmly and slow.

"Kevin, please," Nourzad said in a very exasperated tone. "Are you driving?"

Kevin sighed out loud and then answered, "Well, it isn't really your business, but yes. See, there's a wall in this neighborhood. Big wall really, and I'm gonna use it, see, to cure myself of this monster."

"Kevin, stop, Kevin look, I can help you, I can get you help. Please, Kevin, just stop. It's not a monster, it's just a bad headache!"

Nourzad cut himself off as he heard the loud sound of a raging whistling wind through the phone. He said nothing and his eyes bulged, and his jaw dropped as he heard Kevin screaming 'Ahhhhhhhhh!' The sound lasted an eternity in Nourzad's ear.

Kevin gripped the wheel tight, with two hands. His seatbelt was on. He floored the accelerator and no longer heard Nourzad's voice. The sound of the wind whipped through the open car windows. The headlights glared off every parked car he passed. The wall was within sight. He pulled his right hand off the steering wheel and clutched the seatbelt clip. The wall got closer and closer and the wind was howling through the car. His pain shrieked and wailed in his head.

"Keep laughing, you mother-fucker!" Kevin pressed on the gas.

His forehead pounded and pounded and pounded. Kevin approached the curb and started screaming as he unclipped his seat belt. The car hit the curb in front of the wall and bounced up, but quickly hit the grass. He pressed the accelerator to the floor and screamed louder. In an instant, he thought of Rece...

--

"Well you look wonderful tonight," he said as they sat down for dinner.

"Thank you," she said, smiling.

The restaurant was full that night and the smell of Italian seasonings spread through the room. It was dark, but candles lit each table just enough.

"I cannot tell you how thankful I am for you showing up," he said.

"Aww, thank you," she said. "I couldn't resist the invite."

"I've thought about you every moment the last two weeks and just feel so overwhelmed by this feeling about our meeting."

"Well, I kinda feel the same," she responded, still smiling.

"I don't ever want this feeling to end," he said, looking deeply into her eyes.

She looked back, reaching for his hand. "It won't, Kevin, it won't."

--

His head screamed a shrill shriek as the car sped closer and closer to the wall. Trying to match the screams in his head, Kevin wailed away. "Ahhhhh!!!"

The car was inches away when Kevin let go of the wheel and clicked off his seatbelt. The impact was loud and ferocious. The bumper hit and crumbled violently upon itself. The windshield glass shattered instantly sending shards of glass into Kevin's face. Inertia threw Kevin forward through the broken windshield, his chest and legs crushed from the steering wheel's drag as he flew forward.

The top of his head hit the wall with such force, his skull shattered. His brain was exposed and scraped down the wall as Kevin came to rest on the crushed hood of the car. Still conscious, Kevin noticed no feeling in his body and no pain in his head. Pedestrians screamed and yelled around him. Blood covered his body.

In the few moments left, Kevin heard silence. *No pain. No pain at all. No laughter.*

Sounds tried to batter him right and left. Voices were heard and sirens began to be noticeable.

"Are you ok? Oh my God! Call for help!"

Kevin lay there, unaware of his surroundings or any other people. He felt nothing, and it was welcome to him. He closed his eyes and thought of Rece. *I love you, baby. I love you so much...*

Then he was gone.

THE E.R.

Nourzad walked slowly, his shirt untucked and his face unshaven. His hair was a mess and his right shoe was untied. Nurses yelled and doctors rushed around him. They may have mentioned his name or said hello to him, but he didn't notice or care. He followed the noise and the rush into room 5. Doctors surrounded the patient, wailing and ordering, as nurses cleaned blood and administered more.

Nourzad stood at the door, leaning on his right shoulder against the trim. He didn't comprehend a word being said or screamed. He just stood and watched. Within moments, Dr. Walsh called it.

"That's it everyone," he said somberly. "We never had a chance with this one. Time of death, 10:52 pm."

Dr. Walsh removed his blood-stained gloves and stepped over bloody towels and tools. He patted a fellow doctor on the shoulder and walked towards the exit. He saw Nourzad staring blankly ahead.

"There was nothing we could do, Frank," Walsh said calmly. "I'm sorry. I know he was yours."

Nourzad looked at Walsh and nodded. Walsh continued out. As the nurses and doctors disbursed, Nourzad moved towards the bed and saw his patient laying there. Nourzad began to cry but wiped the tears away. He looked at his patient one last time, took in a deep breath, and walked out. He heard a nurse discussing the phone call to the deceased's wife. Nourzad's knees crumbled and he broke down in tears. Dr. Walsh saw Nourzad on the ground and lifted him up.

"It's ok, Frank," Walsh said, "It's ok."

"I killed him," Nourzad said, looking at Walsh with much despair.

"From what I've learned, he killed himself, Frank."

Nourzad leaned on the doctor in charge and cried. Walsh held him up, and eventually hugged him like a father hugs a defeated kid. Nourzad finally released his balance on Walsh and moved away.

"There will be questions, Frank." Walsh said. "But I got your back."

Nourzad stared at the imposing doctor. He bowed his head and breathed out deeply. He then looked at Walsh. "Why," he said quietly, "why would you of all people have my back?"

Walsh didn't hesitate. "Because I know, Frank. I hear. I investigate things. I know you're a good doctor. Sometimes we get screw up. It comes with the territory. People always second-guessing us, people always looking over our shoulders. We make decisions based on what we feel is right and proper." Walsh moved towards the younger Frank and placed his hand on his shoulder. "Plus, you didn't kill this guy, he killed himself. Sometimes, that's just what happens."

"But..." Nourzad tried to speak.

"No, no, Frank," Walsh said quieter now, "he killed himself, despite what you were trying to do. He killed himself."

Nourzad looked at him, still shuddering. He stared at Walsh. "No need to have my back, doctor, no need."

Nourzad put up a hand to indicate 'so long' as he walked away down the long E.R. hallway. The sights and sounds of the E.R. played on, without any sensory acknowledgment from Nourzad. He reached the exit and stopped. He took a deep breath, pushed open the door, and he was gone.

YES, MOMMY, I DO...

Rece read the letter from Nourzad and cried. She pulled her blanket tightly around her and sipped her tea. The picture of Kevin lay next to her and she cried more. She looked at the letter once more and then ripped it in half and laid her head on the couch.

"I'm so sorry, Kevin..." Tears ran from her eyes. She grabbed the picture and looked at her late husband. "I'm so, so sorry." Her emotions overwhelmed her and she cried and choked up relentlessly, barely able to catch her breath.

Just then, Kate approached out of nowhere.

Rece quickly composed herself, though the tears on her face were apparent. "Come here, sweetie," Rece said, extending her arms.

Kate saw the tears and instinctively cried in her mother's arms.

"There, there, sweetie, I know."

"Mommy?"

"Yes, Kate."

"I miss daddy so much."

"I know, sweetie, I know."

She held her daughter tight in her arms, feeling some comfort in the process. Kate just laid her head on her mom and breathed. Tears ran down her cheek.

"I miss him mommy," she said again. "I miss him so much

my head hurts."

Rece immediately sat up and looked at her daughter and studied her face. Kate was squinting. "You got a headache dear?"

"Yes, mommy, I do."

---

[i] https://www.insider.com/what-does-a-headache-mean-causes-2018-5; 08/05/2019.

[ii] https://www.mayoclinic.org/symptoms/headache/basics/causes/sym-20050800; 08/05/2019.

[iii] https://www.mayoclinic.org/diseases-conditions/brain-tumor/symptoms-causes/syc-20350084; 08/05/2019.

[iv] https://www.emedicinehealth.com/worst_headache_of_your_life/article_em.htm; 08/05/2019

[v] https://www.prevention.com/health/a20469104/when-to-see-a-doctor-for-your-headache/; 08/05/2019

[vi] https://www.mayoclinic.org/diseases-conditions/cluster-headache/symptoms-causes/syc-20352080; 08/05/2019

[vii] https://www.webmd.com/migraines-headaches/tension-headaches#1; 08/05/2019

[viii] https://www.abta.org/about-brain-tumors/brain-tumor-diagnosis/brain-tumor-signs-symptoms/; 08/05/2019

[ix] https://www.ncbi.nlm.nih.gov/pubmed/16547083; 08/05/2019

[x] https://www.abta.org/about-brain-tumors/brain-tumor-diagnosis/brain-tumor-signs-symptoms/; 08/05/2019

[xi] https://www.medicalnewstoday.com/articles/73936.php; 08/05/2019

[xii] https://www.mayoclinic.org/diseases-conditions/migraine-headache/symptoms-causes/syc-20360201;08/05/2019

[xiii] https://www.mayoclinic.org/diseases-conditions/migraine-headache/symptoms-causes/syc-20360201;08/05/2019

[xiv] https://www.verywellhealth.com/what-is-a-chronic-tension-headache-1719464;08/05/2019

[xv] https://www.thebraintumourcharity.org/brain-tumour-signs-symptoms/adult-brain-tumour-symptoms/headaches/;08/05/2019

[xvi] https://www.webmd.com/cancer/brain-cancer/brain-tumors-in-adults#2;08/05/2019

[xvii] https://braintumor.org/brain-tumor-information/signs-and-symptoms/;08/05/2019

[xviii] https://www.webmd.com/migraines-headaches/guide/making-diagnosis-doctors-exam#2; 08/05/2019https://www.emedicine-health.com/worst_headache_of_your_life/article_em.htm;08/05/2019

[xix] https://www.webmd.com/migraines-headaches/guide https://www.insider.com/what-does-a-headache-mean-causes-2018-5; 08/05/2019./making-diagnosis-doctors-exam#2;08/05/2019

[xx] https://www.healthline.com/health/headache/when-to-worry-about-a-headache#symptoms;08/05/2019

[xxi] https://www.mayoclinic.org/diseases-conditions/cluster-headache/symptoms-causes/syc-20352080;08/05/2019

Wait *for* *the* Rain

ALSO BY MARIA MURNANE

Perfect on Paper

It's a Waverly Life

Honey on Your Mind

Chocolate for Two

Cassidy Lane

Katwalk

maria murnane

Wait *for* *the* Rain

LAKE UNION
PUBLISHING

Published by Lake Union Publishing, Seattle

www.apub.com

Amazon, the Amazon logo, and Lake Union Publishing are trademarks of Amazon.com, Inc., or its affiliates.

ISBN-13: 9781477827413
ISBN-10: 1477827412

Cover design by Mumtaz Mustafa

Library of Congress Control Number: 2014951898

Printed in the United States of America

To Annie and Lynette

Chapter One

"You awake yet, hon?" Carol asked in her perpetually cheerful voice.

Daphne yawned into the phone. "Barely, but yes."

"Barely's good enough for me, and it's certainly good enough for the airline. Are you all packed?"

Daphne glanced at her bulging suitcase in the hall. "*Over*packed. It's the curse of motherhood."

"But Emma isn't going with you, right?"

"No, she's off to Utah with her dad. But I still packed way too much. I had to stop myself from tossing an iron in there. What is wrong with me?"

Carol chuckled. "Well, I guess it's better to be overprepared than the alternative, right? I'll be over in just a few minutes to grab you."

Daphne glanced out the window into the pitch-black Columbus winter and wondered how anyone could be so peppy at such an ungodly early hour. "Okay, thanks, Carol. See you soon." She hung up the phone and set it on the kitchen counter, then with another sleepy yawn opened the overhead cabinet. She reached for her favorite mug, the pink ceramic one Emma had made years earlier that said "I love you, MOMMY!" in wobbly blue lettering. It had been a Mother's Day gift back when Emma was in third grade. The pink was a bit faded now, and the handle had a small chip that seemed to be growing, but Daphne treasured it like gold. Despite her daughter's occasional groans of protest, especially those weekend mornings when she had a friend or two over—*Mom, that's so embarrassing!*—Daphne still used it nearly every day. If and when it became necessary, she would fix the crack with superglue. Retiring the mug to the back of the cabinet, much less to a dusty box in the garage with other mementos from Emma's early years, was simply not an option, at least for now. Daphne had never been one to hold on to possessions that had outlived their use, but when it came to her little girl's things, that was a different story. Going on sixteen now, Emma was growing up so fast, and Daphne was determined to cling to what little remained of her childhood for as long as she could. She couldn't yet bring herself to think about what her life was going to be about once Emma left for college. Just the idea of it was almost unbearable.

Her eyes still not entirely open, Daphne poured herself a cup of steaming black French roast, extra strong, and glanced at the time on the coffeemaker: 5:17 a.m.

She yawned again. It was much too early to be out of bed, much less on a day when she didn't have to rouse a slumbering teenager before school. She stirred cream and sugar into the mug and wondered how cold it was outside. It was certainly dark out there, and they'd been saying it would probably snow again today, or maybe there'd be freezing rain, which in her opinion was the worst weather of all. As she sipped her coffee, her mind traveled back to the period of her life when rising before the sun was the norm, not the exception, back when feeding Emma in the early morning hours was as much a part of her day as packing Brian a sandwich to take to the office.

Back when the house was rarely this quiet.

Or still.

Or . . . empty.

It was all of those things now, at least when Emma was at Brian's place. Or, as of last weekend, Brian and Alyssa's place.

Daphne stiffened at the thought. *I can't believe he's really getting remarried.*

She looked around the tidy kitchen and dining area, a bit too orderly for a house with a teenager living in it, even though Emma was only there half the time. She closed her eyes. *I can't believe this is my life now.*

She felt a pang deep inside as a vision flashed before her, one of Emma decorating her spacious new bedroom at the house in tony Westerville that belonged to the woman who would soon be her stepmother. It was a spectacular, magazine-worthy structure, one of several high-end properties Alyssa's family owned in the Columbus area. Daphne imagined her daughter giggling and gossiping with Alyssa as she unpacked, sharing her secrets and stories and crushes—things she never seemed to tell Daphne anymore. Daphne pictured the two of them chattering like classmates as they strolled arm in arm down the driveway of Emma's new home. Of Brian's new home. Of *their* new home.

Daphne closed her eyes and willed her mind to erase the painful visual. She took a deep breath. *Don't torture yourself like this. You know you're better off without him.*

She set down her coffee and glanced at Emma's monthly calendar on the refrigerator, secured front and center with an OSU magnet. As usual, her daughter's schedule was packed with volleyball practices and games, piano lessons, chorus rehearsals, study groups, and a smattering of birthday parties. Recent additions to the list were driver's training and an SAT prep course. Daphne had not only typed up and color coded the schedule but memorized it, and she took great pride in making sure Emma never missed an activity or appointment.

Daphne picked up the mug and made one last trip into her bedroom to confirm that she hadn't forgotten anything essential, although given that she'd triple-checked everything on her list after packing her enormous suitcase last night, she knew the chances were slim if not zero. Then she stopped by Emma's room to have a quick peek inside, something she often did when Emma was staying with Brian. She never *entered* the room, determined to give her daughter the privacy her own mother had never afforded her as a teenager, but she found it comforting to see Emma's things there, even if she was currently elsewhere. As usual the room was relatively clean, the bed made, the pink-and-white-checkered comforter smoothed evenly over the twin bed. The white walls were sprinkled with posters of pop stars and award ribbons from various events and competitions. A cork bulletin board above her white wood desk was covered with smiling photos of her and her girlfriends, the matching white chair tucked neatly underneath. A thick blue binder lay atop the desk next to a small stack of textbooks. Her daughter had inherited Daphne's knack for keeping things organized, something Daphne loved given how messy Brian was. It had been a daily battle just to get him to put his dirty clothes in the hamper, a battle Daphne had given up fighting years ago but had never been able to understand. How hard is it to toss clothes into a hamper or hang up a wet towel? Besides, they'd had bigger problems in their marriage than laundry.

On her way back into the kitchen she looked over at the empty oak table in the quiet dining room. Her imagination suddenly flashed to an image of breakfast time at Alyssa's place, where she pictured Emma, Brian, and Alyssa conversing energetically over pancakes about their upcoming adventure. It was Emma's spring break, and the three of them were headed to Park City to spend the week skiing, snowboarding, snowshoeing, sledding, and whatever else outdoorsy people do in the Utah mountains. Despite Emma's grumbling about a week away from her friends, not to mention her electronic devices, Daphne knew she was looking forward to the trip. No doubt she, Brian, and Alyssa would have a fabulous time together.

Just like a real family.

Daphne flinched at the thought.

In a few months it would be official. Alyssa would become the new Mrs. Brian White, assuming the title of Emma's stepmother.

Daphne felt another stab at the thought of Alyssa playing such a formal—and important—role in her daughter's life, one Daphne had wanted so desperately to keep all to herself. She glanced at the clock again, then peered through the white plantation shutters. A moment later she spotted Carol, the unofficial matron of their tidy block, emerging from the two-story Colonial-style house across the street. Bundled up in a massive red ski jacket and shiny black rain boots over what looked like a white flannel nightgown, she carefully navigated her way through the swirling snow flurries.

Daphne picked up the coffee and closed her eyes, again willing her anxiety to pass.

Be happy for Brian.

He's not a bad person.

Things will get better for you.

Things have to get better.

The divorce was now final, so it wasn't like she could expect him to stay single forever, even though part of her secretly wanted him to. He'd been dating Alyssa for more than a year, but for Emma's sake he had waited to move in with her until they were officially engaged, and Daphne had to give him credit for that. He was clearly trying hard to be an involved father now—much more than he had when Emma was younger. If he and Daphne didn't share a daughter, she'd be free to cut ties with him, but unfortunately that wasn't an option, emotionally or logistically. While no longer her husband, for better or for worse he was in her life for good.

This is how things are now.

She squeezed the pink mug tight, desperate to escape from the suffocating disappointment that her life wasn't what she thought it would be at this age.

She just wished she knew how to do that.

How to be alone after being part of a couple for so many years.

How to find herself again.

How to start over.

I could have had a career. Now I have just the shattered pieces of a family.

She blinked a few times to shake the visions from her head. It was time to focus on the reason why she was up so early this dark winter morning.

The birthday trip. I can't believe I'm really going.

Carol's knock on the door jarred her from her thoughts. She rinsed out the mug and carefully placed it in the drying rack, then hurried to open the front door.

Chapter Two

"A week in St. Mirika sounds just heavenly, especially given how darned cold it is here right now," Carol said as she carefully merged her SUV onto the freeway. It was snowing harder now.

Daphne was having difficulty wrapping her head around the fact that she was actually doing this. In just a few hours she'd be setting foot on one of the most coveted island destinations in the Caribbean. Home to soaring palm trees, a sparkling green ocean, and sandy white beaches, St. Mirika truly resembled paradise—or so it appeared in the photos she'd seen. For months her travel companions and longtime friends KC and Skylar had been sending around links to websites showcasing the dazzling beauty of the island.

She pressed a fist against her chin.

What will it be like to see them again?

They'd called themselves the Three Musketeers back in college, but it had been ages since the three of them had gotten together.

Daphne had changed a lot since those days.

I wonder what they're going to think of me now.

Carol didn't seem to notice Daphne's apprehension. "I've never been to the Caribbean, but I've heard it's just stunning. Norman's not much of a tropical vacation kind of guy. In fact, if it doesn't involve attending an OSU football game, he's not that interested in traveling." She shook her head with a sigh. "I adore the man to the moon and back, but I will never understand his obsession with that football team."

Daphne smiled to herself at the thought of Carol's equally good-natured husband, whose favorite activity in the world was lounging in his sacred leather recliner and watching his cherished Buckeyes take the field on his big-screen TV—if he wasn't attending the actual game, of course. And Norman was hardly alone in his passion. After all these years Daphne was still amazed at the affection the Columbus area had for the Buckeyes of *the* Ohio State University, as the school was officially called. Sometimes she felt like the only person in town who hadn't gone to school there. She saw Northwestern, her alma mater, as a university that had a football team. From what she could tell, OSU was *a football team that had a university*. On game days she still felt conspicuously out of place if she wasn't dressed in red, even if all she was doing was buying groceries.

"Where are you staying down there?" Carol asked.

Daphne glanced out the window toward the horizon, which was still dark. The first glow of the sun wouldn't appear for at least another hour. "I'm not exactly sure. Skylar's in charge, and she said my only job is to get myself on a plane and meet her and KC at the airport bar."

"Sounds like the perfect vacation for you at the perfect time." Carol knew about Brian's recent engagement. "You do so much organizing for Emma as it is. It will be good for you to sit in the backseat and take it easy for a few days."

Daphne nodded softly. "I can't remember the last time I wasn't in charge, not to mention the last time I went to a bar, so it should be an interesting few days, that's for sure." Despite Daphne's nervousness about the trip—her first as an unmarried woman in more than . . . fifteen years?—she was looking forward to seeing her old friends again. It had been so long since the three of them had gone on vacation together.

Too long.

Ten years in fact, when they'd spent a couple days in Chicago to "mourn" turning the Big Three O. They wore black all weekend and made silly jokes about being over the hill—while knowing very well their best years were ahead of them.

And now, here they were once again, reuniting to celebrate their fortieth birthdays.

Daphne tried to wrap her head around the vivid yet distant memory of the Chicago trip juxtaposed with the immediacy of the one she was about to embark on.

Am I really about to turn forty years old? How did that happen?

"Your friend Skylar sounds like she's on top of things," Carol said. "It's nice having people in your life like that: go-getters who can take charge once in a while, so it's not all on you."

Daphne nodded. "She's a redhead, and she basically meets every stereotype that goes with it. Strong willed, intelligent, no-nonsense, testy if provoked, and fiercely loyal. You don't want to mess with Skylar, but you *definitely* want to be friends with her." Daphne paused. *That's how Skylar used to be, at least. Will she have changed as much as I have?*

Carol smiled. "She sounds like quite the firecracker. Where does she live?"

Daphne frowned in thought. "She's in New York now, although I'm not sure how much time she actually spends there. She's in sales and has a lot of people working for her, so she's constantly on the road. It's been a while since I've seen her in person." *How have so many years slipped by? I used to see Skylar every day. Every single day.*

Carol patted the steering wheel. "Sounds like an exciting life she has. I've barely been out of Ohio, although when I was in my early twenties, I did spend a glorious week frolicking around Miami with a handsome—and much older—Italian man."

Daphne quickly turned her head. "You did what?"

Carol laughed. "It was *years* ago. Before I met Norman."

"How much older was he?"

Carol pursed her lips. "I never asked, but let's just say he was old enough to be my father. I knew it wouldn't last, but everyone needs a bit of adventure now and then, right?"

Daphne smiled wistfully and looked out the window again. "I guess so," she said, while thinking, *I used to be adventurous.*

Her mind began to wander again, traveling backward until it hovered over the last time she'd lived with Skylar. After graduation they'd both begun full-time jobs in Chicago, Skylar having landed a coveted spot in an executive training program at a software company, and Daphne working as an admin at a small travel magazine. Their entry-level positions were barely a notch above internships, but both young women excelled and were soon promoted—Skylar to sales associate, Daphne to fact checker. Thrilled with having taken their first official step on the corporate ladder, they'd celebrated by ditching their dingy futon and buying a real couch for the small yet cozy two-bedroom apartment they shared in Lincoln Park. In the following weeks they'd spent many nights sipping inexpensive wine on that purple velvet couch, laughing and dreaming about the spectacular careers they were about to embark upon.

Both of them were young, eager, and intelligent. Their energy and optimism was palpable. The road ahead was boundless, and they couldn't wait to make some footprints.

Then one snowy evening in January, Daphne and Skylar were tucked in a corner of their favorite wine bar a few blocks from their apartment, enjoying a quiet conversation. Daphne heard the chime of the bell and looked up to see Brian walk through the door with two coworkers, the three of them in town from Columbus for a conference. Brian and Daphne only briefly made eye contact, but a few minutes later he walked over to her, introduced himself, and said, "I'm going to kiss you tonight."

She and Skylar had laughed at his audacity, but there was something in his self-assuredness that appealed to Daphne, a little voice that whispered that if such a dashingly handsome man was so taken by her, it had to be for a very good reason. Brian just *knew* they were meant to be together, and that made her think he had to be right, because no man had ever looked at her that way before.

The introduction led to a drink, which indeed led to the predicted kiss, which led to a long-distance romance Daphne hadn't expected—but which she couldn't resist. She was completely swept off her feet by Brian's conviction that she was the One, and before she knew it, she'd quit her hard-earned magazine job and moved to Columbus to be with him.

Less than a year later they were married.

Once the wedding and surrounding hoopla was over, Brian's parents bestowed upon the happy couple a charming three-bedroom house in Grandview, which Daphne dutifully decorated with all the wedding presents and gift checks they'd received. It was fun playing house while she was still dizzy with the spell of newlywed bliss, still awed that a smart, handsome, successful man like Brian had chosen *her*, but once that domestic project was done, she had planned to find a new job in journalism and get the professional side of her life back on track. She'd worked hard at Northwestern and at her first venture into the working world, and she wasn't about to throw away a promising career just because she now wore a diamond on her left ring finger.

Nature, however, had other ideas.

Little Emma joined the family soon thereafter, and in what seemed like a blink, it was official: Daphne was now a housewife in suburban Ohio—with a newborn to look after. Almost overnight, her world became a blur of marriage, homeownership, and motherhood. She was woefully unprepared for all of it. However, despite her tender age, she did her best, and as the months went by, she became less overwhelmed and more comfortable in the role, although at times she still felt like a child herself.

Brian, who was five years older than Daphne, reveled in playing the part of provider to his young family, but early on it became clear that he had a very traditional vision of what that meant. While he was happy to *care for* Emma, he wasn't interested in *taking care of* her. He loved his daughter, but he loved her changed, fed, and ready for bed. Getting her that way was, in his opinion, Daphne's job. It wasn't what Daphne had envisioned, but he was paying the bills, so who was she to argue? If he wanted to relax with a drink at the end of a long day at the office, who was she to hand him a crying baby? She didn't mind, or she told herself she *shouldn't* mind. This was her life now, and it was okay, because that's what she'd signed up for, right?

She'd focus on the journalism thing once Emma was a little older. There was plenty of time. Eventually she'd go back to work, maybe get her master's, reboot her career, and everything would fall into place. Not quite in the order she'd pictured for herself, but it would fall into place nonetheless.

At least that's what she told herself.

Then came the miscarriages, four in total. The doctors had no explanation, but as it became more and more apparent that Daphne wasn't going to be able to carry another baby to term, she secretly feared she was being punished for not being a good parent, that her inability to bear another child was a direct result of a deep-seated remorse that she'd become a mother too soon. It was a shame laced with guilt that weighed heavily on her.

Not that she didn't love Emma. Of course she did. She adored her daughter and would do anything for her. After the miscarriages, however, she rededicated herself to motherhood, to doing everything in her power to ensure that her miracle baby had the storybook childhood she deserved.

Meanwhile, Skylar stayed at the software company, paid her dues, and slowly but surely proved her mettle. Now she was leading a global sales team and traveled the world, while Daphne had lived on the same block in Grandview for nearly seventeen years. And had never written a single article.

"Daphne, sweetheart, you there?" Carol waved a hand near Daphne's face.

Daphne blinked. "I'm sorry, I was daydreaming for a minute. What did you say?"

"I said you must be excited to see your friends."

"I am. I can't believe how long it's been." Daphne lightly touched her cheeks and wondered how much different she looked from when she was thirty. She'd seen the tiny crinkles that had begun to appear in the corner of her eyes when she smiled. Skylar and KC were sure to notice them too. She'd even bought some eye cream recently, although she hadn't forced herself to use it yet. It was still sitting unopened on her bathroom counter, almost smugly, as if daring Daphne to admit defeat.

"Why so long?" Carol asked.

Daphne shifted in her seat. "After the last trip there was talk here and there about planning another one, but nothing ever seemed to get off the ground. Then KC moved to California, and with her and Skylar on opposite coasts and me in the middle, geography got in the way. Plus Emma's activities take up most of my free time, which makes it hard for me to plan, so the years sort of flew by . . ."

She knew she was making excuses.

She'd been the one to resist getting together again.

Since she and Brian had split up, Daphne had been particularly remiss in communicating with her friends. Outside of Carol, she hadn't really spoken to anyone about the divorce, and what she'd shared had been limited at best. Talking about it only seemed to make her feel worse, so instead of working through her emotions, she'd stuffed them deep inside and focused on Emma, on her part-time job at the flower shop, on staying in shape, on cleaning the house.

On anything other than how much energy she'd poured into building a life that in the end didn't make her—or Brian—happy.

On anything other than the implosion of the illusion she'd been projecting to the world—and to herself—for years.

On anything other than coming to terms with reality.

Carol made a swirly motion with her right index finger. "I know what you mean about the years just zipping by. I'm still wondering where my fifties went. But given the way you talk about these gals, I hope it's not another ten years before you three get together again. Close friendships are like plants. They need tending to now and again, or they might dry up and blow away."

Daphne smiled at Carol, who at times felt like a mother figure to her—and nothing like her own mother. Daphne's mother, without ever engaging her daughter in meaningful conversation about *why* her marriage had broken up, had made it clear that she felt Daphne should have done more to save it, that she should have fought more for Brian. She'd also had the sinking feeling that her mother didn't think she was good enough for Brian. She'd never told anyone either of those things, and she wasn't sure which one hurt more.

When they reached the airport exit, Carol turned on her blinker and carefully navigated off the freeway, then slowed to a stop in front of departures. Before Daphne even unbuckled her seat belt, Carol jumped outside and popped the back hatch of the SUV, then pulled out Daphne's suitcase. "Sweet bejesus, you weren't kidding about overpacking," Carol said with an exaggerated groan. "This thing weighs a ton! Did you pack Emma in here?"

Daphne laughed. "Get back in the car. It's *freezing* out here. And you're wearing a nightgown!"

Carol waved a dismissive hand in front of her, batting away a few snowflakes in the process. "Nonsense. I may not be the most stylish cow in the barn, but I know a thing or two about good old-fashioned manners. Now give me a hug good-bye before I have icicles hanging off my nose. If I skedaddle, I can make it home in time to take a hot shower *and* walk the pooch before *Good Morning America* comes on. See how exciting my suburban life is?"

Daphne gave her neighbor a squeeze. "Your suburban life is wonderful. Thank you so much for the ride."

"When you get back, I'll take you to Jeni's for a double scoop of salty caramel, and you can fill me in on the details. It will be your belated birthday celebration."

Daphne winced. "Ugh, don't remind me about my birthday."

Carol wiggled her index finger. "Darlin', if I were turning forty again, I'd be jumping for joy. Now scat." She shooed Daphne away, then climbed back into the cabin of the SUV and tucked her nightgown inside before shutting the door.

Daphne waved good-bye as Carol drove away, then turned on her heel and headed into the airport, the heated air quickly enveloping her like a bear hug. She removed her wool coat and knitted hat, tucked the hat into her oversized tote bag, then rolled her suitcase toward the check-in counter. As she waited in line, she felt a stirring of gratitude for having a woman like Carol as a neighbor, especially since she and Brian had split up. Carol had been very good to her, always there to listen, never to prod or judge, unlike the chilly vibe

she'd felt from several of the mothers at Emma's school, a standoff-
ishness that subtly suggested that being a single parent was somehow an assault on the cherished institution of the suburban nuclear
family.

She thought about Carol's question, about why so much time
had passed since she and Skylar and KC had gotten together.
Daphne crinkled her nose. When was the last time she'd seen them?
Had it really been the Chicago weekend ten years ago? It couldn't
be, could it? Skylar had extended several invitations over the years,
but Daphne had always found a reason to refuse them.

Not that she didn't want to see her friends.

Of course she did, right?

She knew Skylar and KC were just as busy as she was, or at least
she figured they were. That's what she told herself. They were all
so busy, their lives so different. She still considered them to be her
best friends, but the truth was, she rarely talked to them anymore.
Outside of Emma's universe, for years now Daphne had barely
talked much to anyone. With all the carpooling back and forth for
all the activities, not to mention all the bake sales, fund-raisers, and
PTA meetings over the years, there never seemed to be enough time
to keep in touch with the outside world.

She sighed. *I'm still making excuses.*

It hadn't happened overnight, but Daphne had gradually
brought that isolation upon herself, reasoning that being a good
mother meant putting her own interests aside and focusing on what
Emma needed, even though that chapter of her life would eventually end.

She looked up at the departures display and had an unsettling
thought.

Where am I going?

Chapter Three

"Hey, hot stuff! Glad to see you made it in one piece." Skylar set her drink down and adjusted the designer sunglasses perched on top of her head, then stood up and held her arms open wide. "Now get over here and embrace me."

Her nerves fluttering even more than she expected them to, Daphne let go of her suitcase and hugged her friend, suddenly feeling like she might cry. She hadn't realized until right then how much she'd missed having Skylar in her daily life, how much she missed being able to share her deepest secrets—no matter how silly or foolish—with a friend who never made her feel silly or foolish.

Please still like me, she thought.

Not appearing to notice the conflicting emotions coursing through Daphne's psyche, Skylar returned her hug with affection and topped it off with a kiss on the cheek.

"It's really good to see you," Skylar said as they released each other. "I can't believe it's been ten years. We have so much to catch up on, I don't know how we're going to fit it all into just a few days."

"I know. It's hard to believe Chicago was that long ago already," Daphne said. She felt her heart beating faster than it should be and willed it to slow down. *Relax. You can do this. She's your friend.*

"Can you believe we're forty?" Skylar said, her green eyes expertly framed by black mascara. "I'd like to think we haven't aged a day since our last trip together, but we both know I'd be lying."

Daphne smiled, grateful to see that Skylar's straightforwardness hadn't diminished. For an instant she thought about mentioning the eye cream on her bathroom counter but decided not to. Skylar looked older than when Daphne had last seen her, but she wasn't any less pretty, at least in Daphne's opinion. She did, however, look more confident. It was clear she was a woman who knew what she wanted—and usually got it. *Why can't I be like that? I used to be like that.*

Daphne clenched her hands into fists. *Stop it. You're here to have fun, don't ruin this for yourself.*

She looked at Skylar's head. "I've never seen your hair so straight and shiny. It's like a shampoo commercial." Daphne knew the comment was a bit shallow for the circumstances, but she couldn't help herself. She didn't want Skylar to know she was mentally walking on eggshells, so she overcompensated.

Skylar smoothed a hand over her auburn locks. "That's because I ironed it this morning. Just watch, in this humidity it'll be a jungle in no time. I've decided that my new goal in life is to make enough money to have a stylist travel with me to blow out my hair every day."

Daphne laughed. "*That's* your life goal?"

Skylar shrugged. "Among others. I like to keep things interesting. How was your flight?"

"Uneventful, which is just the way you want a flight to be, I suppose. I slept most of the first leg. How about yours?"

Skylar rolled her eyes. "Ugh, a nightmare. I was in London last week and was supposed to fly here directly from there, but then at the last minute I had to go to Paris for a conference, then back to

New York for another two days of meetings. I'm exhausted. You have no idea how much I need this vacation."

Daphne remembered that Carol had made a similar comment on the ride to the airport, how in her eyes *Daphne's* life was hectic. What would she think of Skylar's schedule? Ferrying around a teenager and working a few hours a week at a flower store seemed utterly mundane in comparison to the professional canvas Skylar was painting.

Skylar resumed her seat on the barstool and patted the empty one next to her. "So enough chitchat. How are you doing? I haven't seen you in the flesh since you and Brian split up."

Daphne sat down too. "I'm doing great, just really busy. You know how it is, there never seems to be enough hours in the day to fit everything in." She spoke faster than she normally did, but in spite of that she was surprised at how nonchalant she sounded. When she and Skylar had been roommates, she'd never been able to hide her true feelings like this.

Skylar sipped her drink. "I'm glad to hear it. I'm still getting used to the fact that things didn't work out between you two. The way he approached you at that wine bar that first night . . . I guess . . . I really thought it was going to stick."

Daphne felt a stabbing sensation in her chest at the still-vivid memory of that first encounter with Brian, at what it represented, and suddenly she felt like she might cry. She wasn't prepared to deal with her emotions right now.

Please don't cry. Don't let her see what a mess you are.

She forced a smile that she hoped seemed genuine. "I'm doing fine, really."

"How long has it been since you called it quits?" Skylar asked.

"A little more than two years. The divorce took a while to get sorted out, but that's final now."

"So you just . . . grew apart?" The look in Skylar's eyes suggested she wanted to deepen the conversation. Both Skylar and KC had reached out by phone multiple times over the years, but Daphne almost always replied by e-mail, unwilling—or unable—to open up to her friends about her crumbling marriage, about the effect it was having on her. When she'd broken the news that she and Brian were parting ways, she'd made it clear that infidelity hadn't played a role, but she hadn't shared much more than that, not wanting to confess that they'd been unhappy for years.

Now Skylar was knocking on the door once again, but Daphne couldn't bring herself to open it. She was too afraid her stylish, successful friend would feel sorry for her, and she felt sorry enough for herself.

"Pretty much," she said with a shrug. That's all she'd really told anyone about the reason for the split. And it was true . . . in a sense. What Daphne hadn't been able to articulate—or admit—was that the main reason she and Brian had drifted apart was because neither of them was ever going to be the person the other needed for the marriage to work.

Brian was meant to be with a woman who was perfectly content being a wife and stay-at-home mom, one who dreamed about nothing beyond the white picket fence, one who didn't need anything else to be completely fulfilled. While Daphne loved being a mother and *did* want the white picket fence, she also wanted more than that. She needed a partner who wanted to share the caregiver role with her, one who supported her ambitious side, one who encouraged her to pursue the budding career she'd put on hold to have Emma.

It was a mismatch from the beginning, but at the time Daphne was too young, too naïve, too blind, to see it.

And now it was too late.

How had she wasted all those years, given up so much?

For what?

Her mind turned back to the cold, rainy Friday night when she and Brian had finally decided to pull the plug. Emma was sleeping over at a friend's house, so Daphne had made a reservation for two at their favorite restaurant, hoping an evening out together might rekindle the spark between them, might help them rediscover the connection that had been gone for so long that she could no longer remember what it felt like. Not that she and Brian ever fought that much. They bickered on occasion as every couple does, but for the most part they got along fairly well. The fundamental difference between them was deeper than either of them wanted to admit, so almost without realizing what they were doing, they centered their relationship around the one thing they both cherished: their child. They continued to communicate about the day-to-day logistics of running the household, an approach that let them keep their family intact without acknowledging that something between *them* was dying.

Until that rainy night.

Midway through dinner, after yet another conversation focused nearly entirely on Emma, Brian had looked up from his pasta, a weariness in his eyes, and said, "What are we doing, Daph?"

She had no response, because she didn't know either. She'd just stared blankly back at him, wondering how they'd gotten to this place, wondering what had happened to them, wondering how she could be *married* to this man . . . yet feel so completely alone.

That night he'd packed a suitcase.

"Daphne?"

The sound of Skylar's voice yanked Daphne back to the present. She blinked and looked at her friend.

"I just want you to know that I'm really sorry it didn't work out," Skylar said.

Daphne kept the smile on her face. "Thanks, but that's all in the past now. I'm doing great, *really* great actually. Life goes on, right?" *Where is my life going? Please don't cry.*

"How's Emma?"

"She's doing wonderfully. She's almost as tall as I am now, can you believe it?" Daphne felt a surge of emotion at the thought of her daughter, a mixture of love and heartache as she realized Emma, Brian, and Alyssa would be well on their way to Utah now. She briefly looked over Skylar's shoulder, unable to maintain extended eye contact, but her smile remained frozen. "She's got a lot on her plate, juggling school and friends and all her extracurricular activities; you know how teenagers are. She's spending this week at a resort in Park City with Brian." *And his fiancée. Why can't you say it? Brian is getting remarried. Just say it! Just tell her!*

"How old is she now?" Skylar asked.

"Who?"

Skylar looked confused. "Emma."

Daphne swallowed. "Yes, of course, I'm sorry. She's fifteen."

Skylar slightly narrowed her eyes. "Daphne, are you okay?"

Daphne nodded. "Yep, I'm good, just a little tired from getting up at the crack of dawn." Knowing she wouldn't be able to fight off the tears much longer if she didn't change the topic of conversation, she cleared her throat and pointed to a suitcase propped against the bar. The bright green bag had a sticker across it that said, "Running Is Cheaper Than Therapy." "I'm guessing that's KC's?"

Skylar laughed. "You think it's *mine?* My therapist would love that."

"Where is she?"

"I'm right here, sweet cheeks." Daphne felt a tap on her shoulder. She swung around to see her much shorter friend, smiling and freckled and looking as tan as if she'd already been on the island for a week. She was wearing a light blue baseball hat that read "USA

Volleyball," her sandy-blonde hair pulled back into a ponytail. Like Skylar, she looked older than the last time Daphne had seen her, with noticeable crinkles around her eyes when she smiled.

Before Daphne could speak, KC practically hurled herself forward and wrapped her tiny arms around Daphne's torso. "I'm just thrilled that we're all together again. Thrilled! Poor Max has had to listen to me babble on and on about this trip for months. I think he's as happy as I am that it's finally here just so he can get some peace and quiet with the babies. He practically pushed me out of the car at the airport this morning."

"The babies?" Daphne asked.

"Martha and Oreo, our kitties." KC gestured to her purse. "Want to see a video? Cutest things you've ever seen."

Skylar sipped her drink. "We'll take your word for it."

Daphne smiled at KC. "I've missed your random chatter. It makes me think of all those late nights we had in the dorms, talking about everything under the sun."

"And sometimes until the sun came up." KC pointed to the ceiling. "Think how many pizzas we must have eaten."

The memory of those long-ago marathon conversations, which bounced effortlessly from topic to topic, from romance and religion to politics and pop culture, stirred up more internal angst for Daphne. *Why don't I engage with people like that anymore? What happened to me?*

"Where have you been?" Skylar asked KC. "Were you doing laps waiting for Daphne's flight to get in? Or maybe some sit-ups?"

KC smiled and put her hands on her hips. "You mock me now, but we'll see who's laughing when I make you two do my beach workout with me."

Daphne adjusted her tote bag over her shoulder. "Beach workout? I don't think I like the sound of that." She looked at Skylar. "Do you like the sound of that?"

Skylar set down her glass and put her hands behind her ears. "I'm sorry, what was that? My only form of exercise these days is exercising selective hearing." She stood up and clapped her hands together, then gestured to the bartender for the bill. "Okay, ladies, let's get this party started. I'm *so* excited to be the hell out of Manhattan. It's absolutely arctic there right now."

Daphne held up the black coat she'd been carrying in the crook of her arm. "Same goes for Columbus. What am I going to do with this thing all week?"

KC grinned. "It was eighty-two when Max chucked me out of the car on his way to go surfing."

"Are you teaching fitness classes at the beach now?" Daphne asked.

KC nodded. "I'm still mostly at the gym, but now I also run an outdoor boot camp on Tuesday and Thursday mornings. The sand is great because it's low impact but high resistance."

"I'm highly resistant to this conversation," Skylar said. "If you seriously plan to do some crazy-ass workout while we're here, I may have to lay my towel out on the other side of the island from you. I haven't been to the gym in ages." She pointed to her rear end. "If you want proof, feel free to have a squeeze."

KC's eyes lit up, and she looked from Skylar to Daphne. "I was kidding before, but maybe I *could* lead you both in a beach class while we're here! That would be so fun."

"My selective hearing is acting up again," Skylar said as she reached for her phone. "Sorry, just have to quickly check my e-mail."

"I'm in okay shape, but I definitely couldn't keep up with you," Daphne said.

KC patted her on the shoulder. "Sure you could! Many of my students are divorced women in their thirties and forties, so you're right in my demographic."

Daphne felt another twinge deep inside. *I'm a demographic now. I'm a cliché.*

"That's not a criticism, not at all," KC quickly added when she saw the look on Daphne's face. Skylar, who was now typing furiously into her phone, didn't seem to notice. KC kept her hand on Daphne's shoulder and gave it a squeeze. "My divorced clients are usually in fantastic shape, or well on their way there. Most of them are back in the dating scene—or easing their way there—so they want to look and feel their best. I think that's a positive thing. Not that you need help in any of those departments." She removed her hand and placed it on her own cheek. "Am I talking too much? I feel like I'm talking too much. I hope I'm not putting my foot in my mouth here."

"Don't worry, I get what you're saying," Daphne said. *I hardly look or feel my best lately. For a long time, actually.*

"Are you seeing anyone? They must be lining up for you," KC said.

Daphne cleared her throat and tried to sound casual as she answered, "Not right now." The truth was, she hadn't gone on a single date since she and Brian had split up.

She knew she needed to put herself out there. *Doing so* was a different story. Columbus was hardly a hotbed of single men her age, and it wasn't as if people were clamoring to set her up with eligible candidates. She was too shy to attend singles' mixers alone, and she didn't have any single female friends to drag along—or to drag *her* along. She knew of a handful of divorced fathers through Emma's school circuit, but that road seemed laced with too many gossipy thorns. More than once (usually after a couple glasses of wine) she'd started filling out an online profile, carefully uploading the most flattering photos on her laptop, but when it came to describing herself to the world, she was embarrassed at how little she had to say. Hobbies? Career highlights? Notable accomplishments or adventures? She couldn't think of a single thing to write that didn't revolve around Emma, so inevitably she ended up pressing "Delete."

She wanted to believe in herself, to trust that her limited résumé "outside the home," as it were, was no reflection on her value as a person.

But the truth was, she didn't.

Deep down, she felt it wasn't enough. She *wanted* to expand her life, to climb her way out of the structured world she'd built for herself, but she was paralyzed by fear of what that represented: that she'd somehow failed.

Her marriage had been far from perfect, but that didn't mean she hadn't put a lot of work into it, and its dissolution had been crushing. She didn't know if she could take another blow like that. The idea of starting all over was daunting. *I'm almost forty years old. How do I begin dating again?*

Skylar, who was still focused on her phone, typed furiously for a moment longer, then tossed the device into her purse. "Okay, ladies, let's make some noise. We're here, we're forty, and it's time to stir up a little trouble in St. Mirika." She polished off her drink and signed the bill. "I know that didn't rhyme, but I don't really care. Now let's get out of here."

As they followed Skylar toward the taxi stand, once again Daphne felt her heart begin to beat a little faster, knowing that stirring up a little trouble was exactly what she needed, yet still a bit anxious at what that might entail. "I'm not sure I'm ready for this," she whispered to KC.

"Ditto," KC whispered back.

"I heard you both," Skylar called over her shoulder. "Selective hearing goes both ways."

Chapter Four

"Wow, Skylar, this place is *gorgeous*." Daphne let go of her suitcase and took in the spectacular scene around her.

"Well done." KC craned her head back to marvel at the high ceilings.

The three of them were standing in the foyer of the sprawling beachfront property, which led into a spacious living room lined with floor-to-ceiling glass windows that opened to a large wooden deck overlooking the beach. The tile floors were a soft tan color, the walls a crisp white. The structure of the house was slightly curved like a half moon, with rounded hallways on either side. A number of seashell-themed prints dotted the walls, the watercolor hues a mixture of blue, green, and yellow that blended seamlessly with the bright sky and sparkling ocean outside.

Skylar studied a note on her phone, then pointed left and right without looking up from the screen. "Parker's secretary says there are three bedrooms down each hall. All of them face the ocean and have their own bathroom and entrance to the deck."

"Who is Parker?" Daphne turned and looked at her. She knew Skylar had arranged a beach house, but she'd assumed it was a rental. This place looked too nice to be a rental. Then again, Skylar didn't fly coach.

Skylar tossed her phone into her purse. "Our CEO. This is one of his vacation homes. He told me we're welcome to it as long as we don't trash the place."

KC laughed. "*Trash the place?* You sound like we're still in college."

Skylar held up a finger. "I'm aware of my tendency to regress verbally, but I promise it's only in social situations. I sound like the consummate professional whenever necessary. Now, who wants a margarita before dinner? Parker's secretary said she'd make sure the bar was stocked for us."

KC adjusted her baseball hat. "I'm digging Parker's secretary."

"She dresses like she's stuck in the eighties, but she's efficient; I'll give her that." Skylar headed toward the large island in the center of the enormous—and pristine—kitchen. "So who wants that margarita?" Just then her phone beeped. She pulled it out of her purse and glanced at the display, then made an annoyed face. "Oh sugar, I have to take this. Just a sec." She answered briskly. "Hi, Geoffrey, did you track down those figures on the Halston account? Yes . . . I heard about that . . . okay . . . yes . . . Hold on a minute, I just landed, let me open my laptop." She covered the phone with her hand and whispered, "I'm sorry, ladies, can you get the drinks on your own? I need to deal with something first."

KC pointed toward the beach. "No worries, I think I'm going to go for a quick run anyway. I also need to call Max to let him know I made it here in one piece."

"I should check in on Emma too," Daphne said, although Brian was pretty sure they wouldn't have much reception in the mountains. "Where should we put our things?" She peered in both directions.

Skylar pointed down the hall to the left, then to the one on the right and continued to whisper, "Choose any bedroom you like, except for the one on the end that way. That one's mine, *suckahs*. Parker said it has a steam shower."

Daphne looked at KC. "I could get used to this lifestyle."

KC put her hands on her hips and nodded. "I know I live on the beach, so shouldn't complain, but this place puts my little cottage to shame."

The two of them wheeled their suitcases into bedrooms down the hallway to the right. Daphne carefully unpacked her things into a large white dresser and matching armoire, then turned on her phone and watched the screen flicker to life.

No messages.

She dialed Emma's number, but it went straight to voice mail. With a start she wondered if she'd be able to connect with her daughter at all this week; she felt unsure how well she'd handle such a lapse of communication. Not that Emma communicated all that much lately, even those precious days when they were under the same roof. Once a cuddly chatter bug who couldn't get enough of Mommy, Emma was now a typical overscheduled teenager who spent most of her limited free time in her room, studying, playing with her phone, or hanging out with friends—oftentimes simultaneously. Girl talk with *Mom* wasn't high on her priority list, which left *Mom* alone most of the time. In her head she knew Emma was only doing exactly what teenagers do, that in fact her behavior was perfectly normal and indicative of a healthy, supportive upbringing, but that didn't make it any easier to experience.

Maybe the adjustment to the changing relationship with her daughter wouldn't be so difficult for Daphne if she weren't a single parent now.

If she had a husband to hold her hand as together they watched their baby girl prepare to leave the nest.

If together they took another figurative step toward the rocking chair on the front porch, one imperfectly perfect day at a time.

If she didn't feel so alone.

She pressed a palm against her forehead. *Stop it! Stop being so negative! Stop dwelling on the past!*

She felt a few tears welling up in her eyes, then glanced at the closed door of her bedroom, not wanting Skylar or KC to see how fragile she was, desperate to keep up the illusion of the person they thought she still was, of the person she wished she still were. If her old friends saw her the way she used to be, maybe Daphne could see herself that way too, if only for a few days.

Try to have fun, she told herself. *These women care about you.*

She stepped into the immaculate bathroom to inspect her face in the mirror for evidence of tears. She heard a noise and glanced out the window. KC was standing on the main deck, dressed in gray running shorts and a pink sports top with the same baseball cap she'd worn on the plane. She carefully pulled one foot up behind her to stretch her quadriceps, then the other. She followed that with a stretch for her calves and hamstrings, then adjusted her hat, walked down the steps onto the beach, and took off running, a tiny cloud of sand swirling around her sneakers.

Daphne felt a sense of admiration at the familiar sight of her old friend's ponytail flapping out of the back of her trademark baseball cap. KC was now a grown woman and the proud stepmother of two young men about to embark on their own journey through adulthood (not to mention the mother of two cats, apparently), but she clearly still embraced life like the bubbly teenager she was when Daphne had first met her, back when Daphne had the good fortune of being paired up as her roommate in the freshman dorm.

Daphne looked at herself in the mirror. In college she had been bubbly too. And relatively sporty—not in KC's league by any stretch of the imagination, but she'd played on various intramural teams, taken dance electives here and there, and generally enjoyed staying in decent shape. Eager to experience everything the venerable institution had to offer, she'd also popped in and out of multiple clubs on campus, dabbling in art, drama, photography, and even debate before setting her focus on writing for the school newspaper. She'd excelled in her classes, joined a sorority (Skylar was in her pledge class), made lots of friends, and over four years of coed life in Evanston, gradually checked off the standard rites of passage of the typical college experience. She was walking the colorful, exciting, interesting path she'd always imagined for herself. Following in the footsteps of many a Northwestern University graduate, she would have a successful career in journalism, where she'd crisscross the globe as a freelance travel writer to discover exotic, far-flung destinations, or maybe patrol the sidelines at major sporting events for *Sports Illustrated*, or perhaps even win a Pulitzer as a rookie beat reporter at the *New York Times* for uncovering local election fraud. At some point down the road, marriage would be the next box to check off on the list, followed eventually by homeownership and children, everything tracking according to plan.

Then Brian came along, and the distant future of that picture suddenly became the present, propelling her ahead of schedule on the itinerary. Now, as she studied her aging reflection and thought about what had happened since that fateful night she'd met him, she felt . . . defeated. What did she have to show for all those years of hard work, of everything she'd invested in their family, of the budding career she'd sacrificed?

She had a wonderful daughter; there was no denying that. Emma was bright and friendly and growing into a delightful young woman. Daphne adored her, and she was proud of the way she was raising her.

But she also had a broken marriage.

And a broken spirit, if no longer a broken heart. She'd given up on salvaging the connection that had once existed between her and Brian, but that didn't make it any easier to face a future that looked nothing like the one she'd envisioned for herself.

She used to be full of joy and optimism like KC, at least most of the time. That was one of the reasons the two of them had always gotten along so well. Where had that side of her gone? When had she stopped seeing promise in the inkblot and started seeing . . . spilled ink?

She lightly slapped her cheeks. *Stop feeling sorry for yourself. Look where you are right now. You're going to be fine!*

If only she believed that.

She looked outside again and watched KC disappear down the shore, then decided to change and go for a walk on the beach herself. It would be fun to explore her new surroundings, and she could use some fresh air. Plus, she had no idea how long Skylar would be on that call.

Back in her bedroom Daphne changed into a pair of white shorts and a fitted purple Northwestern tank top, slathered sunscreen over her fair skin, then reached for her straw hat and headed back toward the kitchen. Skylar was in full work mode at a desk in the living room, staring intently at her laptop, and talking with Geoffrey. She wore a wireless headset and pecked feverishly on the keyboard.

"Uh huh . . . uh huh . . . and did the German office confirm when they'd get us that report? Uh huh . . . got it . . . and what about France? We need them both by Wednesday or Parker's going to have my head. Okay . . . yep . . . got it. And yours too. I really need yours." She glanced up at Daphne and mouthed the words "I'm sorry."

Daphne smiled as she put on her hat, then pointed to the beach and mouthed "Going for a walk." She wondered how many people were on the other end of that phone call, and if any of them knew where Skylar was at the moment. Her friend played down her professional success, but Daphne knew how hard she'd worked to achieve it. Skylar had been like that in college too. A social butterfly who was frequently the first girl in line at the keg on the weekends, she was just as frequently the last girl to leave the library during the week. Not too many people back then seemed to know that Skylar had a stealthy studious side, which was just the way she liked it. But Daphne had been her roommate in their sorority house and had seen the more ambitious aspect of Skylar's personality firsthand. While KC spent much of her nonclassroom time on the soccer field, Daphne and Skylar spent a good chunk of theirs studying, and that shared work ethic—or was it fear of falling behind in a sea of over-achievers?—had firmly cemented their friendship.

As she watched Skylar in action on the conference call, Daphne's mind drifted from their college days to her suburban life in Grandview, where she often felt a similar, if less overt, sense of competition within the stay-at-home-mom community. The pressure to excel, even in something as innocuous as a bake sale, was often palpable. She knew it was absurd, but that didn't make it any less real. She'd seen the raised eyebrows for the store-bought goodies on those fold-out card tables. How much could be said without a single word being uttered.

Skylar half nodded to acknowledge Daphne's gesture, then flickered her eyes across her laptop and resumed typing. "Got it. And what did Melissa have to say about the delay in the China roll-out? That market's not going to wait. If we don't move soon, next quarter's going to be a steep climb. Okay, let's see what data Thomas has. Can you get him on the call?" Her fingers flew effortlessly across the keys, as if they belonged to a piano and not a computer.

Daphne tiptoed toward the glass door and quietly exited the house. Once outside, she crossed the deck and climbed down the short flight of stairs to the beach, where she saw the footsteps KC had left in the soft white sand. She decided to go in the same direction, figuring they'd run into each other on KC's way back. She kicked off her flip-flops and held them in one hand, then trotted toward the water to let the tiny waves wash over her bare feet as she strolled along the shore. The sea was a bit warm yet refreshing, the color a spectacular shade of green. She'd never been in an ocean this warm—or seen one this beautiful. It was a far cry from Lake Erie, that was for sure.

She walked for about a hundred yards, passing two additional houses as she went. Both were larger than the one she and her friends were staying in but similar in design, each with floor-to-ceiling windows opening to a sprawling deck facing the ocean. She saw no sign of life inside either place and wondered if they were vacant.

Are all the homes here used only a couple weeks a year?

She couldn't imagine that kind of wealth. She and Brian had always lived comfortably by most standards, especially in the Midwest. His parents' generosity in buying them a house, and his partnership at the firm had made Brian's expectation that she be a stay-at-home mom hard to overcome, although a few months ago she'd taken the part-time job at the flower shop just to keep herself busy on the days when Emma was at Brian's house. Before Daphne and Brian had split up, every summer their family of three had taken an annual trip, usually to Hilton Head or Naples. They'd always stayed in relatively fancy hotels, but owning deluxe beachfront property on a tropical island was in a completely different league.

She looked down and kicked up a wedge of powdery sand.

I wonder if Alyssa's family owns a beach house somewhere? It was certainly within the realm of possibility. Alyssa's family was one of the most prominent in Columbus.

Daphne pressed her palms against her eyes and willed herself to think about something else. She wasn't jealous of Alyssa because she was with Brian, but she *was* jealous of the life they were now leading. That was all Daphne had ever wanted for herself and for Brian—to be happy together.

She turned her gaze back to the ocean, mesmerized by the green hue of the water as she walked. Out in the distance she spotted a catamaran cruising by. She stopped to pick up a shell, then waded out a few feet into the gentle waves, the water not yet reaching her knees. She studied the shell in her hand for a few moments, then lifted it to her ear and wondered where it had come from. She stroked it with her fingers, then reached her arm back and flung it awkwardly into the air. She watched it wobble in a high arc, then plop harmlessly into the water maybe twenty feet in front of her.

"Nice throw," she heard a voice shout behind her. "Go, Cats!"

She turned around and saw a man standing on the deck of yet another spectacular oceanfront property, his hands spread along the railing. He held up a beer bottle in a toasting gesture and appeared to be smiling at her, although it was hard to tell given the distance.

"You've got quite an arm there. Did you play softball at Northwestern?" he yelled.

She put her hands on her hips and squinted. She couldn't see him very well, but she could tell he was tall. He was wearing a straw fedora and green swim trunks, no shirt. She guessed he was probably in his early thirties. He also appeared to be in very good shape, at least physically.

Before she knew what she was doing, she cocked her head to one side and yelled back at him. "Are you making fun of me?"

He chuckled. "Guilty as charged. Are you a Northwestern grad?"

She nodded, then felt her cheeks flush as something dawned on her. *Oh my gosh, I think he's flirting with me. And I'm flirting right back.*

The unfamiliarity of engaging in playful conversation with an attractive stranger, not to mention one who wasn't wearing a shirt at the moment, was unnerving.

And, Daphne realized, kind of fun. *Keep talking to him! You can do it!*

She started walking toward the house. "Did you go to Northwestern too?" She immediately regretted asking him, afraid that he would answer yes and follow up by asking her when she graduated. Her momentary surge of courage began to wilt, replaced by a fear of appearing foolish—and forty. *Please don't ask me when I graduated.*

She slowed her pace. Maybe if she didn't get too much closer, he wouldn't notice the fine lines around her eyes. Just in case, she decided to keep her sunglasses on. *I should have opened that jar of wrinkle cream.*

"What did you study there?" he asked.

She swallowed. "Journalism." *Please don't ask me what I did with the degree.*

He took a sip of his beer. "I wanted to go to Northwestern, but unfortunately the powers that be in the admissions department didn't share that sentiment, so I ended up at Michigan. Not as expensive, just as cold. Much better football team, however."

Daphne smiled. "Touché. I live in Columbus now and have learned a thing or two about college football." Now that she was closer to him, she could see he was undeniably handsome, with tanned skin, broad shoulders, thick and wavy brown hair that looked like it could use a trim, and light green eyes. He was good-looking, but his smile seemed genuine, which eased her nerves a bit and helped quash her inner monologue, at least temporarily.

He gave her a knowing look. "Oh yes, Buckeye Nation is a force to be reckoned with, especially in the Midwest. Anyhow, while I'm a Wolverine and not a Wildcat, I *do* like purple." He pointed to her tank top with his left hand, and when he did so, she caught herself glancing at his ring finger. It was empty.

She felt her face flush and hoped he hadn't noticed where her eyes had just been. She stiffened. *Why did I just do that?*

She couldn't remember ever checking the ring finger of a man who was clearly so much younger than she. *Thirty-two, maybe?*

He bent down and reached into a large cooler on the deck, then fished out a bottle and held it up. "Can I offer you a frosty cold beer? I can't drink these all by myself."

She shook her head. "I'm fine, thanks."

"Are you sure? It could be my way of making up for heckling you about that tragic throw, although truth be told, that tragic throw needed to be heckled."

She smirked. "Thanks, but my tragic arm and I are good. I'm guessing you're not alone?" She gestured to the cooler. "That's a lot of beer for one person."

He pointed a thumb behind him. "Bachelor party."

"Is that so?" She hadn't attended a bachelorette party in . . . how long had it been? KC hadn't had a bachelorette party. Before that . . . her mind drew a blank. She reached into the far corners of her memory and tried to clear away the cobwebs.

He removed the bottle cap. "This is my *seventh* in the past year."

Daphne felt her eyes open wide. "Seventh? You must be quite popular."

"I wouldn't say that. Then again . . . maybe I would." He gave her a wry smile.

She put her hands on her hips, then realized it was the second time she'd done so. She quickly removed them. "Are you holding down the fort all by yourself?"

He took another sip of his beer. "It's a hard job, but someone has to do it. I only get rattled when a pretty woman walks by."

She immediately looked at the ground, secretly thrilled by his comment but at a complete loss as to how to respond. So she said nothing. Instead, she just stared at the sand, stunned that such a handsome man had recognized her not as a mom or a new divorcée, but as a woman.

She'd forgotten what that felt like. *He's really flirting with me!*

She still didn't speak, however, and the seconds began to tick away.

Just before the pause in conversation became awkward, he cleared his throat. "*Anyhow*, to be honest, I'm not sure why all my friends decided to get married at the same time, but I'm going broke with all the festivities. Last month it was Florida, now here, and next month a bunch of us are going down to Patagonia to go ice climbing."

Finally she looked up and regained eye contact, albeit through her sunglasses. "Are you here with a big group?"

"Thirteen, plus the groom."

"Wow. That's quite a turnout for such a far-off destination. I don't think I've ever had thirteen friends who would travel so far, no matter what the occasion. The groom must be a great guy."

He held up one finger, then two, then a third. "Beach, beer, golf. Yes, he's a great guy, but men, especially this crew of clowns, will travel far and wide for those three little words."

She smiled. "I suspect you're omitting a select word or two for my benefit. That sounds pretty PG for a bachelor party."

He laughed and tipped his beer at her. "Nothing wrong with being a gentleman."

She pushed her sunglasses on top of her head and peered over his shoulder at the house. "Are all of you staying here?"

He pointed toward the deck floor, then down the beach. "There are nine of us here, and five more in a smaller place a couple houses that way. I kind of feel like I'm in a fraternity again, although this place is a hell of a lot nicer than the rat hole I used to live in." He gestured over his shoulder toward the glass doors. "I've been waiting for my turn in the shower for a while now. I've long given up any expectation of hot water. I'm just hoping to get in the shower before I turn thirty."

She stiffened as the comment yanked her back to reality. *He's not even thirty?*

Suddenly feeling foolish for flirting, however awkwardly, with him—not to mention for thinking he'd been flirting with *her*—she quickly put her sunglasses back on. He was clearly just being friendly, and she was too out of practice to know the difference. Her internal monologue returned with a vengeance. *What were you thinking? Why would a man like that flirt with you? He's in his twenties and gorgeous, and you have a teenage daughter and newly signed divorce papers in your desk drawer at home.*

"I'm Clay, by the way. Clay Hanson," he said.

She glanced down the beach, mentally plotting how to exit the conversation without appearing rude. "It's nice to meet you, Clay."

"Do *you* have a name?" He looked amused. Could he tell how flustered she was?

She clenched her hands into fists and forced herself to look at him. *Stop being so awkward!* "Oh gosh, I'm sorry. I'm Daphne."

He raised an eyebrow. "Daphne? That's not a name you hear every day. I like it."

She smiled slightly but didn't reply. Instead, she looked down at the ground and wondered why it was so hard for her to accept a compliment.

"What's your last name?" he asked.

She looked back up at him and responded, "White." She didn't feel the need to mention that White was her married name and that she wasn't married anymore but that she'd kept it because she wanted to have the same last name as her daughter. What was the point?

He nodded slowly. "*Daphne White.* I like that, sounds like the name of a movie star."

She scratched her cheek. "You think? I've always felt it has the ring of a Disney character."

He chuckled. "It's a pleasure to meet you, Daphne White. When did you get to St. Mirika?"

"About an hour ago." She moved her fingers to the tip of her nose and wondered if she was already getting sunburned in spite of her hat. She'd never been one to tan, somehow always going straight from pale to pink. "What about you? How long have you been on the island?"

"This is our third day. I think I'm still a bit hungover from the first afternoon. I'm afraid to know what I'm going to feel like by the end of the week." He pressed a palm against his forehead.

"I've heard how those bachelor parties can go." *My ex-husband's was more than fifteen years ago, but I'm not going to mention that.* She gestured toward the ocean. "I can't believe how beautiful it is here. The water is so clear and *green.* It's mesmerizing."

He turned and pointed behind the house. "If you think this is pretty, you should go explore the cliffs on the other side of the island. The rock formations are off the hook."

She caught her breath at the thought. Daphne was terrified of heights.

Clay kept talking. "They also have a cool bridge up there you can walk over. It's a bit steep getting there, but definitely worth it for the view. I've also heard the monkey forest here is pretty cool, but I don't know if we're going to make it there."

"Thanks, maybe we'll check them both out. My friend Skylar's sort of in charge of our schedule this week, so I'm not really sure what we have planned."

"What brings you here? Bachelorette trip?"

She flinched. "Not quite, more like a reunion."

"Oh yeah? What kind of reunion?"

She hesitated. *Should I tell him the truth? That I'm here to celebrate my fortieth birthday? Do I have to tell him?*

"Daphne White, earth to Daphne White," he said.

She blinked and touched her nose again, even though it wasn't itching. *Stop overthinking this!* "Oh, I'm sorry. What did you say?"

"I asked what kind of reunion are you having?"

"Oh, um . . ." She turned her head to the left and was relieved to see KC a hundred yards or so down the beach, doing jumping jacks. Daphne waved, but KC didn't appear to see her, and Daphne couldn't help but smile at the sight. *Who does jumping jacks at all, much less on the beach?* She loved how KC simply didn't care what anyone thought of her.

"Just with some girlfriends from college. I haven't seen them in a while." She pointed in KC's direction. "I just spotted one of them, actually. I should probably go catch up with her."

Clay finished his beer and stood up straight. "I should probably get a move on too, or I'll never get that shower. I may have to break down a door soon. This really is like living in the Sigma Chi house all over again, minus the beer-soaked floors."

Daphne laughed and waved as she turned to go. "It was nice meeting you, Clay. Good luck salvaging that hot water."

He tipped his head slightly before stepping toward the glass door. "Have fun with your girlfriends. Don't get into *too* much trouble, but speaking of my shower situation, be sure to dip your toe in the figurative hot water, at least a little bit. How often are you on a tropical vacation?"

She smiled. "I'll try my best."

As she walked away, she felt the smile remain on her face. She knew he was just shooting the breeze, but she was proud of herself for having flirted at all, even if it was just for fun. It was a tiny step, but for her it was an important one in the right direction: forward. *That wasn't so bad, was it?*

On her way toward KC, Daphne was visited by memories of her own housing experience in college. Her first year in the dorms, she and KC had shared a room with two other girls, the four of them essentially existing in Habitrail-like conditions, yet not once had any of them batted an eyelash. Everyone did it, no one thought twice about it, and that was that. It was college! Looking back *now*, however, she had no idea how she'd managed in such a cramped space. She and Brian had shared a bathroom, but she had her own sink. She'd also had her own closet.

She looked at KC, who was no longer doing jumping jacks. Now she was chatting energetically with an older couple, all three of them gesturing up at the sky. Daphne's eyes followed. A cluster of dark clouds had appeared over the mountains from the east, heading their way.

As Daphne walked up to the threesome, KC held out an arm game-show style. "Here's one of my pals right now. Daphne, we were just talking about you. I was telling these nice folks about how you and Skylar and I have reunited to *ring in our forties*." She made a swirly motion with her finger in the air, then wiggled her hips.

Daphne smiled. "It's nice to meet you."

"I'm Harry Lewis, and this is my wife, Eleanor. Welcome to the best years of your life . . . so far," the man said with a knowing wink. His hair was silver white, as was his wife's. "We're from Connecticut and are here celebrating forty years as well, but of *marriage*, if you can believe it."

KC put a hand on Daphne's shoulder. "Isn't that awesome? It's so inspiring."

"Forty years is impressive, that's for sure," Daphne said. "What's your secret?"

"Are you married, dear?" Eleanor asked.

Daphne shook her head. "I'm divorced." She didn't elaborate, suddenly dreading that the conversation might pull her backward again, the tiny swell of optimism she'd felt after her conversation with Clay evaporating before her eyes.

"What's the secret to a long and happy union?" KC asked. "I'm happily married, but it's only been five years. I'd love any tips on how to make it to the Big Four O."

Eleanor interlaced her arm around Harry's. "For *me* . . . it's a romp in the sack with the pool boy every Tuesday afternoon while Harry plays golf. Keeps me feeling playful."

Daphne and KC both stared at her, wide-eyed.

"I'm kidding, kidding!" Eleanor let out a hearty laugh that belied her petite frame, then looked up at her much taller husband. "Look at their faces, Harry. I told you, *it's funny.*"

"She's used that line before," Harry said with a mock eye roll. "Gets people every time."

KC put a hand on her heart. "You got me, that's for sure. Nice one."

Daphne was struck by their energy, their vitality, and the obvious joy they gave to each other just by being together. She could never imagine her mother interacting with her father like that. Her parents' relationship, as Daphne had always perceived it as a child, was much more distant. They got along fine and rarely argued, but she'd never seen them laugh or express sincere *affection* toward each other. A peck on the cheek was the extent of what she'd witnessed, and Daphne could probably count those instances on two hands. Much like the way her own marriage had been toward the end, to

Daphne her parents' union at times appeared to be more of a business arrangement than a relationship founded on romantic love. But they were still married, and Daphne wasn't, so who was she to judge what worked for them?

Standing at that moment before Harry and Eleanor, whose marriage was so unlike her parents', so unlike her *own*, Daphne felt an unexpected—and welcome—flicker of inspiration. *Maybe happily ever after does exist? With the right person?*

"So what *is* the magic recipe for making it work?" KC asked. "Or is there one? I grew up thinking I'd never get married, and because of that I'm secretly afraid that I'm going to mess it all up." KC's parents had divorced when she was five.

Daphne quickly turned her head. She'd assumed KC's skepticism about the viability of "until death do us part" had disappeared after she'd met Max.

Maybe I'm not the only one wondering if I'm . . . the only one?

"I believe laughter is the secret to the success of our relationship," Eleanor said as she looked at Harry. "For forty years this man has been making me laugh, and when you're laughing, you're being *yourself*. If you're not being yourself, you're not in a good marriage. Plus, a man might be quite dashing in his younger years and get away with a less than pleasant personality, but what woman wants to spend her golden years with a saggy, old coot who doesn't have a sense of humor? Not me, that's for sure!" She let out a little cackle and patted Harry's arm.

Harry shrugged. "I just stick around because Eleanor's easy on the eyes."

Eleanor touched his nose with her fingertip. "You're not so bad yourself. Then again, my eyes aren't what they used to be."

"I *love* you two." KC interlaced her hands in front of her. "Will you adopt me?"

Daphne sighed. "Will you adopt me too?"

Harry chuckled. "Our four children might object to that. They're grown and have kids of their own now, but they still want their share of the Christmas loot."

Just then a deep rumbling sound interrupted the conversation.

"Was that thunder?" Daphne asked. Where had that sound come from?

"Check it out." KC pointed to the sky, which was now quickly filling with dark clouds that just moments before had seemed so far away. "We're about to get drenched!"

Daphne watched in wonder as the clouds moved with a ferocity she'd never seen. Before anyone could speak, the sky erupted above them. As the heavy drops came pouring down, Daphne turned to run for shelter, but KC grabbed her arm. "Where are you going?" she asked her.

Daphne looked from KC to Harry and Eleanor, neither of whom had moved an inch.

Eleanor tilted her head back and opened her arms. "Isn't this just fabulous? I told you!"

"You weren't kidding: it's *amazing*!" KC raised her voice so that they could hear her over the din of the rain. "This happens every day here?"

Harry nodded. "Just about. It's one of the reasons we love St. Mirika so much."

Eleanor twirled around in a circle, her arms out like a cross. "It's my favorite time of day here. So magical and pure."

"How long does it usually last?" KC asked through the din.

"Just a few minutes, sometimes a bit longer," Eleanor said. "Sometimes I wish it would go on forever. There's something about a burst of rain that makes everything fresh and new, don't you think? It's as if Mother Nature is giving us another chance."

Daphne wiped a few drops from her forehead. "I guess I never thought about it that way." She looked up at the ominous sky, intrigued by the unfamiliar sensation of warm rain running over her skin. It felt refreshing . . . soothing . . . *healing.*

She made eye contact with Eleanor as the significance of what was happening to her began to take shape, an invisible beauty that made sense only to her. Or maybe to all of them. "I think you're right," she said with a tiny smile.

"That's the magic of this seaside oasis, my dear." Eleanor gave her a knowing smile in return. "It makes you see things in ways that never occur to you in the real world."

.   .   .

"*There* you two are. The margaritas are ready, they are de-li-cious, and they aren't going to drink themselves." Wearing an oversized yet stylish straw hat and a white linen tank dress, Skylar was standing on the deck as Daphne and KC approached the house. The rain had stopped and the skies had quickly cleared, allowing the hot sun to resume its beating down on them—nearly drying their clothes and hair on the walk home. Save for a few drops lingering on the railing of the deck, there was scant evidence that just a few minutes earlier their stretch of beach had been smack in the path of a tropical thunderstorm. It was like magic.

Skylar held up her glass, then pointed to the kitchen. "There's a pitcher in the fridge. I tried to wait for you, but I couldn't hold out any longer. After that call from hell, I needed to self-medicate."

"No need to apologize," KC said as she trotted up the stairs. "I'd love a margarita, but I need to hydrate before I partake in any self-medication. Otherwise, I might not make it to dinner."

Skylar scoffed. "Please. As if *self-medicating* is even in your vocabulary. When's the last time you had more than one drink?"

KC pointed to Daphne. "If you have a vocabulary question, she's the queen."

"I wasn't asking a *vocabulary question*. I was asking a question about *your vocabulary*," Skylar said.

"Who's on first?" KC asked with a grin.

Daphne held up her palms. "I'm not getting involved in this conversation."

Skylar gestured inside. "Fine, fine, I concede defeat. Filtered water's in the fridge. How was your run?"

"Beautiful," KC said. "Although I got a little overheated toward the end. I did a bunch of jumping jacks when I was done, and at one point I was tempted to run right into the ocean to cool off."

Skylar looked at Daphne. "Did she just say *jumping jacks*?"

Daphne smiled. "Right on the beach. It was quite a sight to behold."

KC tapped her chest. "Hey now, there's nothing wrong with the good old-fashioned jumping jack. It gets the heart rate up, that's for sure." She patted Skylar on the shoulder on her way into the house.

"I prefer sex for that," Skylar called after her.

KC disappeared behind the glass door, and Daphne looked up at the sky. "Did you see that crazy rain?" she asked Skylar.

Skylar nodded. "I heard it from my desk, then came out here after my call and caught the tail end of the downpour. Amazing how quickly it came and went, isn't it?"

"It was incredible," Daphne said softly. Eleanor's words were still bouncing around in her brain. *"There's something about a burst of rain that makes everything fresh and new. It's as if Mother Nature is giving us another chance."*

I want that chance, she thought.

Skylar took a seat in a reclining patio chair and reached for her margarita. "We're bound to get soaked a few times this week, although that's not too unusual for this part of the world."

"Yet another reason to love it. I'm so glad you brought us here," Daphne said. For a moment she considered sharing what Eleanor had said, but something held her back, as if she needed to keep it to herself for now. Instead, she stretched out in a lounge chair and inhaled deeply. The fresh, salty air stung her nostrils a little bit, but she didn't mind.

She didn't mind at all.

KC reappeared holding a large glass of water, then pointed down the beach. "I saw a neat little spot we should check out at some point. It was a thatched hut with a big banana on the roof and a good-sized line in front of it, so they must be selling something yummy in there."

Skylar sat up and removed her designer sunglasses, then squinted down the beach. "Ah, the hut with the banana. Parker mentioned that place. I think he said it's called Banana Banana. Or maybe it was Bananarama? It was definitely Banana something or other. Regardless, he said they make really good smoothies. We should definitely go there."

Daphne looked at her. "If it's really called *Bananarama*, I want to go there just because of that name."

"Me too." KC took a seat on a bench. "I loved that band. And I *love* tasty smoothies. You think they have kale?"

"Kale in a smoothie? That's disgusting," Skylar said.

"Says you." KC rubbed a hand over her abdomen. "Leafy greens are good for the digestion."

Skylar put her sunglasses back on. "Leaves belong on trees, so if you think I'm getting them in a freaking *smoothie*, you need to up your medication."

"I'm not on any medication," KC said.

"Well, maybe you should be," Skylar said. "The pharmaceutical industry is what keeps our economy running, you know. It's practically your civic duty to take *something*."

Daphne laughed. "You're both nuts."

KC grinned. "Nuts are good in smoothies too."

"Will you shut up already?" Skylar said. "I'm losing my appetite."

"Fine, fine. Maybe we could go tomorrow after our beach workout?" KC said.

Skylar sipped her margarita. "Do as you will, but I'd literally rather be sitting on a conference call than sweating my ass off while on vacation. Ergo, while I'm game for a leaf-free smoothie, I won't be joining you in any self-inflicted torture."

"I love sweating while on vacation," KC said. "It's the best."

"Sometimes I wonder how we're even friends," Skylar said.

KC pumped her fist. "Too late! I'm grandfathered in. You're never getting rid of me."

"Lucky me," Skylar said with a mock sigh.

"Speaking of conference calls, did yours turn out okay?" Daphne asked Skylar.

Skylar shrugged. "Okay enough. Unfortunately, I have a feeling I'm going to be on the phone a lot this week. It's just impossible to disconnect entirely."

"It's a cruel . . . cruel summer . . ." KC sang as she skipped into the house to refill her water glass.

"Will you grab me some water too?" Daphne called after her.

"I'm on it," KC yelled over her shoulder.

Skylar took another sip of her margarita and looked at Daphne. "So how was your walk?"

Daphne felt a rush of energy at the question, an unexpected reaction that secretly thrilled her. "Beautiful! I still can't get over how white the sand is, and the water is so *green*. Everything is so calm and serene here."

"That's island living for you. It's like going back in time, before iPhones and Facebook took over the world."

Daphne looked out at the beach. "I take a lot of walks at home, and I can't remember the last time I didn't pass at least a handful of people on their phones. Counting KC I saw exactly four people during my walk here, and definitely no phones."

Skylar leaned back in the patio chair. "That's what I love about tropical vacations: the relaxed, low-key energy that seems to permeate the air. When I'm not on a soul-killing conference call, that is."

"You work so hard, it's really impressive," Daphne said. "You've *always* worked so hard. I think that's one of the reasons I did too, when we lived together. I had to keep up with you."

Skylar shook her head. "I highly doubt that. You were pretty driven, even more so after we graduated. I had no doubt you were going places."

An awkward silence followed.

"If you *wanted* to, I mean. I hope you know what I mean," Skylar added. "You know how smart and capable I think you are, right?"

Daphne smiled and hoped it looked convincing. "I do, and thank you. You deserve to take a break for a few days. That's all I'm saying."

Skylar glanced at her watch. "Easier said than done. I still have to check on one more thing before dinner."

Daphne gestured toward the shoreline. "KC and I met a sweet older couple when we were walking on the beach. I think they said they're from Connecticut."

KC emerged, carefully carrying three glasses of water. "Did I hear my name?"

Daphne reached for a glass. "I was just about to tell Skylar about Harry and Eleanor." She turned toward Skylar. "They're here to celebrate their *fortieth* anniversary."

KC handed Skylar a glass, then took a seat on the bench. "Pretty cool, huh? They seem really happy together."

Skylar nodded. "Forty years is quite a milestone in and of itself, but forty years and *happy* is almost unheard of. Good for them."

KC took a sip of water. "They told us laughter is the key to a successful union, because when you're laughing, you're being yourself, and if you're not being yourself, what's the point? I liked that."

"I liked that too," Daphne said softly. She tried to pinpoint when she'd stopped being herself with Brian. *Too long ago.*

"Funny how hard it is to be yourself sometimes, isn't it?" Skylar said. "Doesn't make a lot of sense when you think about it."

Daphne felt her neck get hot and hoped the conversation wasn't leading in a direction she didn't want to go. She cleared her throat. "Anyhow, it was wonderful to see them happy together after so many years."

"My parents were never happy," KC said. "If my mom hadn't gotten pregnant, I doubt they would have married."

Skylar looked at Daphne. "Your parents are still together, right?"

Daphne nodded, grateful for the shift in course, however slight. "They're hanging in there, for better or for worse, although the way my mom loves to complain about everything, I suspect that for my dad it's mostly worse. What about yours?"

Skylar held up her glass as if in a toast. "They hit fifty years last summer."

Daphne tried to wrap her head around the idea of being married for that long. "Wow. I think my parents are at forty-two."

"Max and I are heading on six," KC said. Then, as if reading Daphne's mind, she leaned over and squeezed Daphne's knee. "For what it's worth, my parents didn't even make it to five." Daphne gave her a grateful smile in return, but she didn't say anything.

Skylar sipped her drink. "Half a century. Insane, right? I don't know how they do it. They seem pretty content too. I mean they bicker here and there, but for the most part they genuinely enjoy each other's company. If I were married to the same man for that long, I think I'd kill the poor guy. I can't even imagine being married for *one* year, much less fifty." Marriage and children had never been in Skylar's plans.

"Did they have a big party to celebrate?" KC asked.

Skylar nodded. "We all went to Hawaii."

Daphne turned her head. "You mean *all of you*, including your million nieces and nephews?" Skylar had three sisters and two brothers who were all married with multiple kids.

Skylar took another sip of her margarita, then set it on the bench next to her chair. "The whole burrito. It was a zoo. Total chaos. I swear to God we took up half the hotel. It was fun, but also exhausting. I spent nearly every night at the bar trying to de-stress."

"More self-medicating?"

"*Exactly*. Perfect use case." She glanced at the dwindling liquid in her margarita glass. "Speaking of which, I might be in need of a refill soon."

Daphne closed her eyes and leaned back in her chair. "I can't imagine having a family that big. When I was a kid, by default our family vacations were always so tame." Daphne was an only child.

An only child with an only child.

She'd never been on a vacation with her own parents as an adult, although she and Brian had once gone on a cruise with his parents when she was pregnant with Emma. The elder Mr. and Mrs. White weren't unkind people, but they were so formal and reserved that for the entire week Daphne felt like she was still auditioning for the role of daughter-in-law—even though she was already married to their son.

Throughout the duration of their union that feeling had never gone away. *Will they like Alyssa better?*

She tried to push the negative thoughts aside as she heard KC asking Skylar a question. "Did everyone get along okay on the trip?"

"Pretty well, or well enough. There were at least two tantrums a day, but usually only one was by an adult."

Daphne blinked. "What?"

Skylar pushed her arm. "I'm joking."

"Oh, got it." Daphne was still only half paying attention, still thinking about how Brian's parents had never quite warmed to her. In the early part of her marriage, she'd tried so hard to get them to like her, and while they'd defrosted slightly over the years, she'd grown to accept that they were never going to embrace her with open arms, figuratively or literally. They just weren't that type of people. But it still stung that they had never seemed all that interested in the person she was, treating her instead as their son's wife, now ex-wife, or as their granddaughter's mother. Never as Daphne. *And I let it happen.*

Skylar gave her a strange look. "Daphne, are you okay?"

Daphne forced a smile, but she knew it was a bit stiff. "Yes, sorry, I'm just a little scattered right now." *I'm a mess. Can't you two see that?*

"You clearly need to get used to hanging out with me again. You're way out of practice," Skylar said.

"Agreed. We need to break you in," KC said.

Daphne stared out at the water, unable to look her friends in the eye. "I'll take that." It pained her that she couldn't open up to the people she'd once shared everything with. She wanted to, but she just couldn't do it. She felt pitiful for her inability to break free from her stagnation, to make changes she knew she needed to move herself forward.

After a few moments of silence, Skylar sat up in her chair and stretched her arms over her head. "So *anyhow*, the big Aloha Family Adventure went well, and no one ended up in the hospital, although one of my sisters nearly lost it when my nephew sailed out of one of the swinging hammocks at the hotel and landed right on some tiny old Japanese lady."

KC covered her mouth with her hand. "Oh my gosh! Was he hurt? Was *she* hurt?"

Skylar shook her head. "Luckily no, but when he landed on the lady, it startled her so much that she farted, like *really loud*. She didn't speak a lick of English, but apparently flatulence is a universal language."

Daphne laughed, and KC let out a little shriek. "That's hilarious!"

"My nephew thought so too. We all did, but my sister was mortified. She's a bit uptight if you ask me, although I'm not one to judge anyone's parenting style. I don't even have a cat."

"Parenting is tricky, that's for sure," Daphne said. "It's not like anyone gives you an instruction manual, you know? So you end up feeling your way through, learning as you go."

"Same goes for being a stepmother," KC said. "I pretty much walked in blind and still have no idea if I'm doing it right. But neither one of them is in jail, so that's a good sign."

Daphne smiled at KC, wishing she could be as forthright with her lack of confidence. *I'm still hoping I'll figure it out too.* Why couldn't she just admit that?

Skylar stood up and stretched her arms over her head again. "I honestly don't know how people do it. I have no problem running a global sales operation, but for the life of me I couldn't handle raising kids." She pointed at Daphne. "I'm so impressed that you have a *teenager* and still look so good. I think being a mom would age me rapidly."

"I bet you'd make a great mom," Daphne said. She meant it. Skylar was perhaps the most competent person she knew.

Skylar turned toward the house. "I guess I could do it if I had to, but to be honest I don't think I was born with that gene. I'm more than happy being the cool aunt who lives in New York City."

KC pumped a fist in the air. "That's the spirit! Who wouldn't want a cool auntie who lives in New York City?"

Skylar tipped her glass at her. "Exactly. Now come on, ladies, let's get you each a margarita."

. . .

Twenty minutes later, Daphne leaned over the granite island in the kitchen and looked at KC, who was stretching on the floor next to the barstools. A sea of gleaming copper pots and pans hung overhead on an oval rack. Daphne wondered if they'd ever been touched. "You're really still playing soccer?" she asked. KC had just shared her plans to participate in an adult tournament the following weekend.

KC moved her legs into a straddle position, then leaned to the right to grab her toes. "Why wouldn't I still play? I love it."

"I think it's fantastic that you're still playing," Skylar said. "I bet you run those young whippersnappers into the ground."

KC looked up at her with a grin. "I don't know about running anyone into the ground, but I do a pretty good job of holding my own out there."

"Are you the oldest one?" Daphne asked KC.

KC shook her head. "Not by a long shot. Tons of older people play soccer. In fact, the tournament next weekend is over-forty."

"A whole tournament for people over forty?" Daphne raised her eyebrows. "I've been to a few volleyball tournaments with Emma, and they're pretty intense even for the kids. Seems like a soccer tournament would be really hard on your body."

KC sat up and stretched her hands over her head. "It's a lot of running, but it's not that bad if you have subs. I've been playing in tournaments for years, but this is the first time I'm old enough to play in the over-forty division, so I can't wait."

Skylar gave her a strange look as she reached for the pitcher of margaritas. "Do you realize how weird that sounds?"

KC laughed. "They have over-thirty, over-forty, over-fifty, even over-sixty. That way you can always play against people your own age, so it's competitive. I'm really looking forward to it. After all these years of chasing around youngsters in the over-thirty division, in the over-forty I'll get to be the fastest one again."

"Only you could make turning forty sound like something to aspire to," Skylar said. "You should work in advertising. You could probably package up sand and sell it at the beach on spring break."

"Wouldn't it be nice to be on spring break again?" Daphne said with a wistful smile. "To be that young again?"

KC switched her stretch to the other leg. "Guys, we *are* young."

"We're not *that* young," Skylar said.

KC nodded. "Well sure, we're not twenty anymore, but who cares? We're not *old*, just older than we used to be."

Skylar pointed at her. "Seriously, you should join an advertising agency. You could make millions."

"I feel old," Daphne said softly, surprised at her candor. She thought of her conversation with Clay, how she'd been too embarrassed to tell him the reason behind her reunion with her friends.

KC looked up at her. "Well, you shouldn't. Didn't you hear what Harry and Eleanor said to us? To them, *we're* the youngsters. Just because I can't run as fast as I did when I was in college doesn't mean I'm *old*. It doesn't mean I can't still play soccer and have fun."

"Harry and Eleanor seem to have made quite an impression on you," Skylar said.

KC nodded. "They seem like good people."

Daphne nodded too. "Supersweet. A little, um, *feistier* than I expected for people their age, but they have a warm aura about them."

"Oh, now I want to meet them," Skylar said. "I like me some feisty."

KC pulled one foot behind her and moved into the hurdler's stretch. "Trust me, you guys, as a woman who is married to an older man, I know from personal experience that age is just a number. It means nothing unless you *let* it mean something. It's all in how you think."

"You should say that in a Yoda voice," Daphne said. She remembered how Clay said he wasn't even thirty yet. What would he think of this conversation? Was KC just kidding herself into believing forty wasn't over the hill? Then again, KC had never looked healthier, or *happier*, than she did right now. Maybe she was onto something. Daphne leaned over again and gently nudged KC with her foot. "Speaking of age, are your stepsons in their twenties now?"

KC lifted her head and smiled. "One is! Isn't that nuts? Josh is nineteen and a sophomore at UCLA, and Jared is twenty-two and living with his girlfriend in a cute little bungalow in Santa Monica. Can you believe I have a stepson old enough to be living with his girlfriend in a cute little bungalow in Santa Monica?"

Skylar held up a hand. "Please change the subject immediately. This conversation is too horrifying to continue without more alcohol in my system."

KC grinned, then stretched both legs in front of her and leaned forward to grab her toes. "Okay, fine, we'll go back to soccer. It's a fantastic workout, but it's also supersocial, especially the coed leagues. Going out for beers after the game is practically mandatory. Max and I love it."

"I love going out for beers," Skylar said. "Maybe I should find a league that just does that. No actual exercise, just socializing and drinking."

Finally done with her stretching, KC jumped up and put a hand on Skylar's shoulder. "I think they call that *going to a bar.*"

"Semantics," Skylar said. "But a league like that would be a better investment than my gym membership, which I barely use."

"You and Max met through a soccer league, right?" Daphne asked KC.

KC nodded. "Another perk of the coed system. I found myself a husband, and I wasn't even looking for one."

"I wish I were athletic," Skylar said.

Daphne looked at Skylar. "You mean so you could meet your husband that way too? I thought you didn't want to get married."

"I don't. But what's not to like about coed recreation? Sweaty, athletic men in shorts? Count me in."

"I can't imagine playing soccer with men," Daphne said. "Do people get hurt a lot?"

KC opened the refrigerator and pulled out a pitcher of water. "The men in our league are pretty chill. Once in a while some Rambo type will go in crazy hard for a tackle, but those types don't usually stick around too long because they get the evil eye from everyone. Most of the people I play with go out of their way *not* to hurt anyone. Everyone knows we all have to go to work the next day."

"Well, it sure keeps you looking great, that's for sure." Skylar looked at her own upper arm, then gave it a squeeze. "I keep telling myself I need to work out more, but the truth is I hate exercising too much to do anything about it. After a long day at the office, if I'm actually home and not on an airplane or at a work dinner or a client event or on a date, I'm like, why go to the gym when I can stay right here on my supercomfy couch and drink wine?"

KC laughed. "You *sure* you don't want to try my beach class tomorrow morning? I've already got Daphne signed up."

Daphne coughed. "You have? I uh . . . I thought that was just a suggestion."

KC removed her baseball hat and pointed it in the direction of her bedroom. "It was a suggestion that we will be converting into a reality. Okay, ladies, I'm off to take a shower. What's next on the itinerary?"

Skylar held up her nearly empty margarita glass. "I need to shower too, but first I'm going to finish this delicious beverage. Then, unfortunately, I have to make another work call, but I promise it won't take long. I was thinking we could have dinner at a place not too far from here called Captain's Grill. It's right on the beach, and apparently the food there is amazing."

"Sounds perfect," KC said. "How dressy is it?"

Skylar gave her a look of mock surprise. "You brought a dress?"

KC grinned. "I brought *one* dress. So let me know which night I should wear it."

"I can't imagine you in a dress," Daphne said. "Did you even wear one to your wedding?" Max and KC had gotten married at City Hall in a family-only ceremony.

"I wore a white tank dress from J.Crew," she said. "Does that count?"

Skylar rolled her eyes. "For *you*, that counts. And to answer your question, Pippi Longstocking, tonight is casual. We'll do the dressy dinner thing for Daphne's birthday. But I have a proposition for you. If Daphne and I do your beach workout, you have to go shopping with us for girly stuff, deal?" She turned and looked at Daphne. "That's a fair deal, right?"

Daphne nodded. "Sounds equitable to me."

KC hesitated for a moment, then shook Skylar's hand. "Okay, I can live with that. Deal."

Skylar smiled. "Nice. I heard there are some cute stores in the main downtown area. Maybe we'll head over there tomorrow and gussy you up."

KC trotted toward her bedroom. "Do what you must. I'm not wearing makeup, though!" she called over her shoulder.

"Once a tomboy, always a tomboy," Skylar said as KC shut her door. "God help her."

Daphne lifted her margarita for a toast. "And here's hoping she never changes."

Skylar clinked her glass against Daphne's. "I'll drink to that."

Chapter Five

Captain's Grill wasn't technically *on* the beach, but without bur-
rowing the table legs and chairs into the sand, the outdoor seating
area of the charmingly rustic restaurant was about as close to the
shore as it could be. The tables were spread over a raised wooden
deck, each one flanked by a large white umbrella ready to be opened
for protection from the sun, or perhaps the sudden onslaught of a
rainstorm, which, as Daphne now knew, was not an uncommon
occurrence on St. Mirika. A string of white lanterns dotted a high
fence lining the three edges of the deck not facing the water, which
secluded the deck and created a protective illusion that it was the
lone dining spot on the beach.

"Wow, that's tasty," KC said as she sipped her mango sangria.

"Isn't it?" Skylar said. "St. Mirika is famous for it. I don't know
why it hasn't taken off in the States. Maybe I should quit selling
software and start selling mango sangrias instead."

"Maybe I'd come work for you," KC said. "You said I'm good
at selling things, right?"

Skylar nodded. "With your charisma and my connections, we'd
make a fortune."

Daphne gazed out at the ocean, utterly mesmerized by the view. The sun was just beginning to set, casting a soft orange glow across the sky and spreading over the water, which gently rolled up against the shore.

"You okay there, sweets?" Skylar asked her. "You look a little dazed."

Daphne nodded slowly and kept staring at the horizon. "I feel like we're on a movie set. I've never seen anything like this."

"It really is paradise," KC said. "I love living in Hermosa Beach, but this takes the word *beautiful* to another level." She cocked her head at Daphne. "What's a word for more beautiful than beautiful?"

Before Daphne could respond, Skylar held up her glass. "Sangria."

Daphne laughed. "Well done."

Skylar took a sip of her drink. "Thank you. I'm no Daphne White, but I do have a pretty extensive vocabulary when it comes to cocktails. And this sangria is spectacular."

Daphne glanced out at the ocean. "I think St. Mirika is the most, um, *sangria*, place I've ever been."

"Me too," KC said. "Max and I went to Maui for our honeymoon, but this blows that out of the water."

Daphne put a hand on KC's arm. "Speaking of the water, have you ever seen water so *green*? It's like toothpaste, don't you think?"

Skylar made a sour face. "What kind of toothpaste do people use in Ohio? That sounds disgusting."

"This place really is out of a movie set," Daphne said. "Not that I have anything to compare it to, but high rolling with Skylar kind of *feels* like hanging out with a celebrity, so it's almost like we're in a movie right now."

KC turned her head as if on a swivel. "So is this the scene where the handsome stranger sends over a bottle of champagne? Skylar, does that sort of thing happen to you?"

Skylar smirked and picked up the menu. "Shush, both of you. My job is light years from Hollywood, and you both know it. Now, let's order." She reached into her purse and removed a pair of designer reading glasses from a sleek black case.

KC laughed and pulled out her own glasses case, although decidedly less fancy. She waggled it in the air. "You too?"

Skylar nodded and frowned. "Horrifying, isn't it? I was in denial for months, but I finally caved over Christmas after my nieces and nephews made fun of me for holding the presents away from my eyes so I could read who they were from."

KC laughed. "I was in denial until Max threw his pair across the breakfast table and told me to put them on. He said for weeks he'd been watching me do the same thing with the newspaper and he couldn't take it anymore."

Skylar looked at Daphne. "What about you? Have your eyes betrayed you yet?"

Daphne shook her head. "Not yet. But then again, as we know, I'm still in my thirties."

"Touché," Skylar said with a dry smile. "What about your hair? Have you yanked out any wiry grays yet?"

Daphne immediately touched the sides of her head. *Do I need to be pulling hairs out?* She'd noticed a stray gray here and there but hadn't done anything about it. Were they obvious? She was too afraid to ask. "Not yet," she said.

Skylar tapped her left temple. "I call the worst offenders *angry hairs*, you know, the ones that grow in every direction besides *down*? I hate those little buggers. I started yanking after my little niece asked me if I had tinsel in my hair. That was quite a rude awakening, to say the least."

KC laughed. "That's hilarious. In my book, gray hair is a badge of honor, like you've earned it!" She tapped her heart.

"I have zero interest in reading that book," Skylar said. "My hairdresser says I'm not ready to color it yet, but when the day comes, I'm heading straight to the salon to take the plunge."

"I'm going natural all the way," KC said. "Like a cotton ball."

"I bet even with a head of white fluff, you won't seem old," Daphne said. "You're too much like a little kid."

"I wear compression socks when I run sometimes," KC said. "Does that count for something?"

Skylar laughed. "I don't even know how to respond to that."

As they perused the menu, Daphne stole a glance at Skylar, who, even with reading glasses perched on the bridge of her nose, looked put together *and* on top of things, as if she knew something no one else in the room did. She looked confident. Successful. Classy. An impeccable package she'd created all on her own.

When was the last time Daphne had felt any of those things about herself? Where had her self-confidence gone? Where had *she* gone?

"Daphne, hon, you there?" Skylar said.

Daphne looked up from her menu to see KC, Skylar, and the waiter all staring at her. She felt her cheeks flush.

"Are you okay, Daphne?" KC looked concerned. "You disappeared for a moment there."

Daphne nodded. "Yep, totally fine, just taking everything in."

"Are you ready to order?" Skylar gestured to the waiter.

Daphne looked up at him. "Oh yes, of course. Sorry. I'll . . . I'll have the mixed green salad and the glazed salmon, thank you." She closed her menu and handed it to him.

Once he was gone, Skylar tapped her fork against her glass a couple times, then lifted it up. "I'd like to make a toast to *us*: the Three Musketeers together again, at last."

"Aw, I love you guys," KC said.

"You love everything," Skylar said. "But seriously, can you believe we met when we were eighteen years old, and now we're forty? That means we've been friends for more than half our lives."

"Wow," Daphne said under her breath. "That's cool but kind of scary too."

"Totally," KC whispered back.

Skylar kept talking. "Yes, my dears, we've been friends for more than twenty years now. It seems like just yesterday the three of us were wearing scrunchies and drinking wine coolers from a straw in the dorms. Thank God the digital age wasn't around when we were in college. If any of those photos got out, my meticulously constructed image as a serious businesswoman would be in serious jeopardy."

Daphne sipped her drink. "That's for sure. Remember that time you made out with Jason Green in the study lounge with the glass windows and didn't know there were like ten of us watching?"

KC raised her hand as if in a classroom. "I remember! That was awesome. People were taking bets on when you two would come up for air."

Skylar closed her eyes and took a deep breath. "Apparently I had blocked that incident from my memory, but thank you both for reminding me. Now I get to relive it in all its classy glory."

Daphne smiled. "You're very welcome. And for the record, you were very classy. It was quite PG-13, from what I remember."

KC held up a finger. "Also for the record, I never wore a scrunchie because they fall out too easily when I run. *My* go-to look was the reverse french braid, if you remember. I rocked that thing."

Daphne held up a finger too. "*Also* for the record, while I admit to the scrunchie thing, I'm not forty yet. I still have two more days in my thirties, so don't drag me down with you just yet."

Skylar sighed dramatically. "Jeez, Louise, I'm trying to give a *toast* here. Will you two please shut down the peanut gallery and let me finish?"

"Of course, I'm sorry. We didn't mean to cause a kerfuffle." Daphne reached for her sangria.

KC giggled. "You and your SAT vocabulary. Who uses the word *kerfuffle?*"

Skylar snapped her fingers twice. "Focus, ladies, focus. It's clear you're not used to drinking sangria."

Daphne and KC both sat at attention and looked at her as she stood ceremoniously.

"Okay then," Skylar said with a nod, then cleared her throat. "*Anyhow*, I'd officially like to thank both of you for joining me in what I'm sure will be a trip I will remember forever. Despite our earlier conversation about age, turning forty is a big deal, and I can't think of two women I'd rather celebrate the occasion with than you, two of the smartest, kindest, most interesting people I've had the pleasure of meeting in my life. And believe me, I've met a *lot* of people. I know I don't see either of you very often, but I *think* of you often, and I want you to know that I love you both very much. So here's to the Three Musketeers, together forever." She sat down and clinked her glass against KC's, then Daphne's.

KC reached over and put a hand on Skylar's shoulder. "That was a beautiful toast. You're going to make me cry."

"No I won't." Skylar immediately shook her head. "You never cry. You're always too freaking *happy* to cry. Of all those people I just said I've met in my life, *none* of them has ever been as happy as you."

"I could cry tears of joy?" KC said, a hopeful expression on her face.

Skylar rolled her eyes. "I'll believe that when I see it."

KC grinned at her. "Okay, you're probably right."

Skylar set down her glass and reached for her purse. "To commemorate the occasion that has brought us here, I thought you both might like to see something. Do you ladies remember this?" She removed a small pink notebook.

Daphne caught her breath at the sight of the leather binding. "Is that . . . Daisy the diary?"

Skylar held the book against her chest. "The one and only."

"I can't believe you still have her," Daphne said. "Do you still make entries?"

Skylar laughed. "Oh God no. I haven't touched the thing since college. I can't believe I found her, to be honest. But I'm so glad I did. I thought you two might want to read what you wrote in good ol' Daisy at the end of our senior year. Do you remember when we each predicted what our lives would be like twenty years after graduation?"

"No way! I forgot all about that!" KC said.

Skylar smiled. "I know it hasn't been quite twenty years, but close enough. Should we see what we each wrote? I haven't read it yet because I thought it would be fun to wait until tonight. I have absolutely no memory of what I predicted."

KC wiggled her fingers at the diary. "I wanna see! Gimme."

"Only if you read what you wrote out loud," Skylar said. "I'll go first." She opened the diary to a bookmarked page in the back and began to speak. *"In twenty years I will be CEO of a large company, probably in New York or London."* She shrugged, then handed the book to KC. "Getting there, I guess."

"You're *more* than getting there," KC said. "You're a rock star." She began to skim the page. "Okay, what did I write . . . Here it is! *In twenty years I will be leading a Peace Corps unit in South America or Africa.*" She laughed and handed the diary to Daphne. "Hey, that's not bad! I'm hardly leading a unit, but I did join the Peace Corps for a couple years."

"Well done," Skylar said. "Your turn, Daphne."

Daphne scanned to her section of the page, then quietly began to read. *"In twenty years I will be an award-winning journalist."*

A brief yet undeniably awkward silence followed, none of them sure what to say. Skylar looked like she was about to speak, but then the waiter returned with their entrées, followed by a busboy who refilled their water glasses. Once they were gone, Skylar quietly tucked the diary back into her purse and pressed her palms together. "Alright then, my official work at this dinner is done. Enough of the speeches and emotional mumbo jumbo, blah blah blah. Let's get to the good stuff."

"Good stuff?" KC raised her eyebrows. "You mean as in dessert?"

Skylar sighed. "I mean as in *girl talk*, Einstein. We're forty. We're not dead."

Daphne lifted a forkful of salmon and willed herself to smile at Skylar. "I think I'd pay to watch you in a meeting with your staff. I bet it's pretty entertaining." *I was going to be an award-winning journalist.*

"Oh yes, I run a tight ship," Skylar said, then tilted her glass toward KC. "So tell us, what's it like being married to a man in his fifties? I've never dated anyone that old, I mean that much *older*. You know what I mean."

KC cut into her mahimahi. "It's pretty great. He's emotionally mature, a fantastic life partner, my best friend and confidant: everything I could ask for, to be honest."

Skylar narrowed her eyes. "Really?"

KC swatted Skylar's arm. "Yes, *really*. Why are you so surprised?"

"I guess I'm just cynical that you can find all that in one person."

"Then I guess I'm just lucky," KC said with a grin.

"*He's* lucky," Daphne said to her.

KC put a hand over her heart. "Aw, thanks, Daphne."

Daphne took a big sip of her sangria. *I used to think I'd found all that in Brian. I couldn't see that it was an illusion of my own making. I was too young.*

Skylar looked at KC. "How old exactly is Max?"

"He'll be fifty-three in August," KC said.

Skylar leaned back in her chair. "No wonder you're not fazed by the idea of turning forty. You're always going to feel young in Max's circle. Maybe I should start dating older men too, then I won't have to worry about my wrinkles when I smile."

Daphne pictured the wrinkle cream in her bathroom.

"I'm thinking about trying Botox," Skylar added. "It might be time."

Daphne turned her head. "You are?" She'd never heard anyone outright mention Botox before, although she suspected a good chunk of the women in Columbus had done it. Daphne was one of the youngest mothers at Emma's school, but many of the others appeared to defy their age in ways that seemed less than natural. Then again, she'd bought wrinkle cream, so who was she to judge? They were all fighting the same war, just with different weapons.

Skylar nodded. "I figure if it makes me feel better about my appearance, what's the harm? When I feel good about my appearance, I feel good about myself."

KC smiled at her. "I've always loved that about you. You do what makes *you* happy, period. Screw what anyone else thinks."

Skylar tipped her head. "Why, thank you."

"You have that quality too," Daphne said to KC. "I've always admired that."

"We *all* have it. That's why we gravitate toward each other," Skylar said. "The cream rises to the top for a reason."

Daphne wished she were half as secure as her friends. For better or for worse, they knew who they were inside, and they were at peace with it. She struggled to stay focused on the conversation, trying to dissolve the images floating around in her head. Of her empty house in Ohio. Of the family photos now boxed up in the garage. *Stop it! You weren't happy in that life! It's time to move on!* This time she dug a fingernail into her palm to snap herself out of the trance. KC and Skylar had moved on to another topic of conversation.

"So how was your fortieth anyway?" Skylar crossed her knife and fork on her plate to indicate that she was done with her entrée.

"It was fun," KC said. "Nothing crazy."

"What did you do to celebrate?" Daphne asked, grateful that they hadn't noticed her drifting off . . . again. Or if they had, that they hadn't pointed it out.

KC's eyes got a little brighter. "*Well*, in the morning Max and I went for a long run on the beach."

Skylar pretended to shoot herself in the head. "Of course you did. I'd rather wax my lady bits than go for a long run on any morning, much less my *birthday*. But go on."

KC looked from Skylar to Daphne. "After our run Max showered and went to the office, and then a couple of my girlfriends took me to a yummy lunch at my favorite Mexican restaurant. Then that night Max put together a little dinner party at the house. Nothing crazy, just three couples, including us."

"He cooked for you?" Daphne asked. Brian had never cooked for her. Actually, that wasn't true. Before they were married, he'd made her a handful of candlelit dinners, but that stopped after Emma was born. So much had stopped after Emma was born, and then the miscarriages happened. *I was going to write for the* New York Times.

KC nodded. "Max loves to cook. I think that night he made shrimp scampi. That man has many talents, I tell you. Then after dinner we all walked downtown to play Bingo."

Skylar coughed. "Please tell me I heard that wrong."

KC grinned. "I can't say that you did."

Daphne cocked her head to one side. "You really played *Bingo*?"

"You bet we did," KC said. "And we rocked it."

Skylar groaned and set her drink on the table. "You realize that you turned *forty*, not *eighty* right? Good lord."

"Trust me, it's not as bad as it sounds," KC said. "This time of year they have Bingo every Friday at this bar called Watermans, which is on the main drag off Hermosa Beach that runs right up to the shoreline. It's all for charity, and it's packed with people of all ages. Trust me, we weren't the youngest people there, and we weren't the oldest either; kind of a rowdy crowd, but all in good fun. It's a blast, and they have some cool prizes too. Max won a pair of really nice snowboarding goggles."

Daphne flinched at the word *snowboarding*, her mind suddenly yanked to Park City. Her imagination began to torment her again, pinching her insides with a vision of a smiling Emma, Brian, and Alyssa perched on top of a snowcapped mountain, posing for a new family photo.

Grieving for the future she thought would be hers, for the family unit she'd spent years trying to keep intact, Daphne took a sip of water and balled her free hand into a fist under the table. *Please stop torturing yourself. You don't deserve this. Let it go.*

"So what's going on with your love life? Who's your latest boyfriend?" KC was asking Skylar.

Skylar took a sip of sangria. "Currently it's an Italian named Antonio, although his turn in the rotation is just about up."

The comment jolted Daphne back into the present, and she looked at Skylar. "You're still doing the rotation system?" she asked.

"I am. It's not necessarily what I envisioned for myself at this age, but it works for me, and if I've learned anything in my life, it's that you have to go with what works for you."

"Amen to that. How many are in the rotation right now?" KC asked.

Skylar closed her eyes and counted on her fingers. "These days it's Antonio, Michael, and Trevor. Oh! And Kristoff. Yikes, almost forgot Kristoff. He's new."

KC laughed. "I've never been able to keep track of all your men. You're amazing."

"It really is impressive," Daphne said. "When we were roommates, our answering machine was always on overdrive. Remember that time when you were dating two guys named Ben at the same time? I have no idea how you pulled that one off."

Skylar shrugged. "I like men, what can I say? Plus, my system keeps life interesting."

"So how does the rotation work exactly?" KC asked.

"There's no formal structure to it. They just kind of come and go in waves, and some of them circle back around after a while. Some never cycle back in, however. It really depends on a lot of factors. Some move away or get married. Or it just fizzles. I hang out with each guy for a month or two, and then before we get a chance to start bickering or anything, I move on to the next one. I have enough drama to deal with at work; I don't need it in my personal life too. With the rotation, I'm able to keep things light and playful, which is all I really want from a relationship. I have my sisters and girlfriends for the deeper stuff."

"You don't ever wish you could settle down with just one man?" Daphne asked. It was all *she'd* ever wanted.

Skylar frowned. "I don't know. Maybe if I met one who made me want to, but that hasn't happened yet. When I was younger, yes, I figured I'd get married someday down the road, but then I got so focused on my career and my priorities kind of changed. I'm not sure if that's because I haven't met the right person or because I'm just wired differently from other women. You know I have issues with commitment. I can't even decide which city I want to live in. Okay, I'm officially rambling. Damn, this sangria is good."

KC laughed and kissed her glass. "I'm kind of in love with it."

"How do you meet most of the men you go out with?" Daphne asked Skylar.

"It depends. Some through work, others through friends. Once in a while I do the online thing. There's no real formula," she said.

"Seems like a lot of couples meet online these days," KC said. "It's amazing how much the world has changed. Remember the days when a guy would actually call you on the phone to ask you on a date?"

Skylar gestured for the waiter to bring another pitcher of sangria. "Trust me, that doesn't happen anymore. It's all done over e-mail and text now. And while online dating is an easy way to meet a lot of men, it's not an easy way to meet the *right* men."

"Why is that?" KC asked. "Can't you just weed out the bad ones before ever meeting them? I would think that would make it a lot easier."

Skylar held up a finger. "*Theoretically*, yes. But in my experience, what you see in the profile and what you get in real life are usually quite different, and not in a good way." She looked at Daphne. "You know what I mean, right?"

Daphne bit her lip and shook her head. "I haven't tried the online thing."

Skylar looked surprised. "Really? Is it that easy to meet men in Columbus?"

Daphne didn't know what to say, so she took a big sip of her sangria and didn't say anything.

KC jumped in with another question for Skylar. "So how are the guys different from their profiles? You mean their photos are really old?"

Skylar nodded. "That happens sometimes, a lot, actually, especially with men in their forties. Another thing I've learned is that if a guy's photos are all faraway, it's probably because he doesn't look good up close, and by that I mean he's ugly. Same goes for if he's wearing sunglasses. Sunglasses usually equals ugly."

KC laughed. "You don't mince words, do you?"

Skylar shrugged. "I'm just being honest." Then she tapped her head. "I've also learned that if a guy is wearing a visor or a hat in his pictures, it's because he doesn't have much hair, if he has any at all. And most men claim they are at least an inch, if not *two*, taller than they really are, which for the life of me I don't understand, just like the hair or sunglasses thing. Do they really think I'm not going to notice they're short or balding or ugly the very moment we meet, like *immediately*?"

"Maybe they plan to be sitting down the whole date?" Daphne said with a hopeful look. "And wearing a hat and sunglasses?"

Skylar pointed at Daphne. "That happened to me once, not joking. The guy was sitting on the barstool when I arrived, and when he stood up like a half hour later, I thought he was still sitting down. That's how short he was. Lesson learned. Now if they don't list their height on their profile, I ask."

KC tapped her own head. "I'm shrimpy, so I've never really cared about the height thing."

Skylar gestured to herself. "Try being five nine. Trust me, you would care."

KC frowned. "You're right. Online dating sounds less awesome than I thought."

Skylar shook her head. "It's not *all* bad. I know a lot of people who have met some great people through it. You just have to know what to watch out for so you don't waste your time. And it's not just men who embellish their profiles. Women do too."

"How so?" Daphne asked.

Skylar framed her face with her hands. "For example, my male friends tell me they won't go out with a woman if her profile only includes photos that are up close."

Daphne touched her own cheek. "Why not?"

"Because that usually means she's overweight."

"Oh." Daphne sucked in her breath. "I never thought of that, but I guess it makes sense."

KC made a sad face. "That sounds mean."

Skylar shrugged. "It's reality. And those are just the superficial things. I think the biggest problem with dating sites, at least at our age, is that they're so female heavy that the most appealing men get bombarded with messages, and they just can't keep up. I know some quality guys from work who have profiles up, and they're so overwhelmed that they barely have enough time to weed through everything coming in, much less proactively search for women to contact."

"Women are really that aggressive?" KC asked.

"Yep. Apparently some women offer sex for money too."

"What?" Daphne's jaw dropped open.

Skylar rubbed her fingertips together. "I went on a date with a guy who told me a woman once cut to the chase after a few messages. She made it pretty clear that if he was willing to pay, she was willing to give."

Daphne's mouth was still open. "Wow."

"I don't think I could contact a man on a dating site. I'd be too chicken," KC said.

Daphne nodded. "So would I." *I'm too chicken even to post a profile.*

"It's not really my style, but women today are assertive, so if I see a guy I want to meet, I'll reach out," Skylar said. "But I don't expect to hear back because I'm not sure if they'll ever even read the note. My friend Jay says he gets *hundreds* of messages a month, and he's not even that attractive, although if you ever meet him, please keep that information to yourself. I've also learned that the men in their late thirties or forties are usually looking for younger women, so even if they *are* proactive in their searches, I don't even show up in the results—unless I were to lie about my age, which apparently a lot of women do for that exact reason. So the men who contact me are usually way older or way younger. It's rare that I hear from someone who is remotely attractive *and* relatively age appropriate."

Daphne frowned and took another sip of sangria. "This conversation is getting depressing."

"Totally," KC said. "It's depressing *me*, and I'm not even single."

Skylar shrugged. "It is what it is. Another fundamental flaw in the system is that the profiles have to be written, and not everyone is a good writer." She gestured to Daphne. "I know I don't have Daphne's gift for words, but at least I can put together a freaking sentence. If a guy doesn't know the difference between *you're* and *your*, it makes him look dumb, no matter how many advanced degrees he may have. Am I right?"

KC winced. "I have terrible grammar. You'd hate me online."

Skylar winked at KC. "*You*, I could never hate. But that's the problem with online dating. It forces you to notice things you wouldn't if you met someone organically, but when all you have to go on is the profile, it's tough. That virtual first impression sticks."

KC frowned. "This is not what I thought online dating was like *at all*. They make it look so fun in the commercials."

Skylar laughed. "Everything looks fun in commercials, Little Miss Sunshine. Buying Cialis looks like a trip to Disneyland in the commercials." She pretended to use a megaphone. "*Hey, everybody! I have erectile dysfunction! Isn't that fantastic?*"

Daphne laughed, grateful to be doing so in the midst of such a disheartening conversation. "What kind of men do you, um, *search* for?" she asked Skylar. The process sounded so clinical to her. "For example, what do you consider age appropriate?"

"I'll go older or younger by a decade or so, but I won't do married," Skylar said.

KC's eyes got big. "*Married?* Married people do online dating?"

Skylar nodded. "I hate to break it to you, Little Bo Peep, but married men do a lot of things."

KC covered her ears with her hands. "I don't know if I want to hear this."

Skylar reached over and removed one of KC's hands. "Please. I'm sure Max is as loyal as a German shepherd. I've just met a lot of married men over the years who don't seem to be all that concerned with the fact that, you know, their *wife* is at home waiting for them." She turned to Daphne. "I'm sure you've been hit on by married guys, right?"

Daphne shook her head. "Not that I'm aware of."

Skylar gave her a look. "I find that hard to believe."

Daphne stared at her lap. She'd been in such a fog for so long that she'd almost stopped paying attention to men entirely.

"How do you know they're married?" KC asked.

Skylar took a sip of her drink. "You mean online or in person?"

"Both."

"*Online,* sometimes they say it outright. But when I've met them in other situations, like at a trade show, for example, it depends. Sometimes they're wearing a wedding ring, but not always."

Daphne looked back up. "If they don't have a ring on, how do you know?" For the first time, she wondered if Brian had ever cheated on her. She certainly hadn't strayed, even when things between them were beyond repair.

Skylar set her glass on the table. "Sometimes the tan line gives it away."

KC laughed. "That's so sad, it's funny. Men think they can get away with that?"

Skylar reached for the sangria pitcher and refilled all their glasses. "Yes, some men are that stupid. A few weeks ago, after work, I met a man at a bar who told me he was in Manhattan for a few days for business. Very handsome, charming, the whole deal. And no ring, no *tan line* either. He bought me a couple drinks, then asked if he could take me to dinner the following night before heading home over the weekend."

Daphne and KC both leaned in closer.

"And?" KC said.

"And I said sure. Why wouldn't I?"

KC grinned. "Your life seems so fun. Most weeknights I go to bed at nine thirty."

Skylar continued. "So he pulled out his phone to get my number, and I noticed that his wallpaper backdrop was a picture of a little boy. I asked if it was his son, and he said yes. He didn't immediately follow that up by explaining that he was divorced, so I asked if he was married."

"And?" Daphne asked.

"And he hesitated for a moment before responding that yes, he was married, but that I should give him credit for being honest."

KC laughed. "Wow, that guy had some balls."

Skylar sipped her drink. "Oh, it gets better."

"What happened?" Daphne asked.

"He told me I should sleep with him because married men never have sex, meaning he'd put a lot of effort into it."

"That's not true!" KC shouted, then immediately covered her mouth with her hand. "Oops, sorry I got a little fired up there."

Daphne looked down. In the last years of their marriage, she and Brian rarely had sex. Early on they were intimate nearly every day, but after Emma was born that tapered off. Not overnight, but gradually, so gradually that it wasn't noticeable—until one day when it was.

"What did you say to the guy?" KC asked Skylar.

Skylar held up her index finger. "Before I could respond to his comment, he told me that I should *also* have sex with him because—and I swear I'm not making this up—because he has a big dick. Those were his exact words. 'I have a big dick.'"

"No way!" KC yelled, then covered her mouth with her hand again. "I'm sorry, I'm not used to drinking sangria. Or to hearing awesome stories like this."

Skylar laughed. "It's okay. You're funny when you drink."

"He really said that with a straight face?" Daphne asked.

Skylar crossed her heart. "You know I would never lie to you two."

"What did you say back to him?" Daphne asked. "I'd be speechless."

"I think I would have up and left." KC pounded her fist on the table.

Skylar gave them a sly smile. "I did leave, but first I came up with something pretty good. I stood up and casually reached for my purse, and then I smiled and told him *he* was a big dick. Then I calmly strolled out of the bar."

KC pumped her fist. "That's my girl!"

Daphne clapped her hands. "Well done. I'd probably still be sitting there with my mouth open."

Skylar bowed her head. "Thank you, thank you."

"I'm so fired up right now," KC said. "Can't no man be messing with my Skylar!"

"I love it when you drink," Skylar said to her. "Anyhow, the online thing isn't all bad. It just depends on what you're looking for, and when getting married and having kids isn't priority number one, you can have a little more fun with it. I have some girlfriends in New York who are hell-bent on finding a husband, so they treat online dating like a full-time job. They're basically managing a spreadsheet, trying to keep track of everyone."

"Sounds exhausting," Daphne said.

"I agree, but sometimes it's a necessary evil if you don't want to sleep alone, or if you want to procreate. So enough about *my* love life. What about you? What's the story in Columbus? If you're not online, how do you meet most of the men you go out with?" Skylar asked.

Daphne felt her neck get warm. She took a sip of water, then pretended to be looking at something on the beach.

Skylar and KC both turned their heads to follow her gaze.

"What are you staring at?" KC asked.

Daphne awkwardly pointed toward the ocean, which was barely visible in the moonlight. "Oh, I, um, I thought I saw a dolphin jumping."

"For real?" Skylar squinted. "Your eyes really *are* good."

"That's an understatement," KC said. "I can't see anything out there."

Daphne swallowed and looked at Skylar. "So getting back to the men in your rotation. What do they do for a living?"

Skylar set her glass down. "Kristoff's a banker, Michael's in pharmaceutical sales, Trevor's an attorney . . . and Antonio's a bartender. I've learned that bartenders are usually a lot of fun to date because they have hilarious stories. Drunk people do funny things."

"What are all their ages?" KC asked.

Skylar closed her eyes again to think. "Give me a minute . . . okay . . . Antonio's twenty-seven, Michael's thirty-three, Trevor's thirty-nine, and Kristoff is forty-two." She opened her eyes. "I think that's right."

KC whistled. "*Twenty-seven?* Wowsa. That's twenty-five years younger than my husband. A quarter century!"

Skylar shrugged. "What can I say? I don't discriminate. Plus, you're the one who said age is just a number, right?"

"I did say that," KC said. "I guess I never really thought about it backward like that."

The waiter returned to clear their plates, and after he was gone, KC picked up her drink and looked at Skylar. "The rotation thing sounds fun, but complicated. And maybe a little draining," she said.

"All of those adjectives are accurate, but enough about *me*." Skylar looked at KC. "I want to talk about you and Max again. How's the sex? Do men get better at it in their fifties? Or does it, you know, start to wilt a little bit?"

Daphne felt her cheeks flush. "Don't you think that's a little personal?"

"No," Skylar said without looking at her. "We're in the inner circle here, no subject is off-limits. So how is it? Is he paying close attention to the aforementioned Cialis commercials?"

KC laughed. "*No.* I have zero complaints in that department. Max is in great shape all the way around."

"He must be to keep up with you," Daphne said. "Although I don't know if anyone could keep up with you."

"How's his business going?" Skylar asked.

"Fantastic! Commercial real estate is booming in LA right now, so they're growing like gangbusters on the construction side. Jared's been there since graduation, which Max is thrilled about. He doesn't want to push, but it's sort of his dream to groom his firstborn to take over the business when he retires."

"What does Josh think about that? Is there any competition there?" Daphne asked. As an only child she'd always been curious about the sibling dynamic. Why were some adult siblings such close friends, while others rarely spoke to each other?

KC reached for her napkin. "Trust me, there's no rivalry there, at least where the family business is concerned. Josh would *never* want to work for his dad, much less have an office job of any kind."

"Not his vibe?" Skylar asked.

KC shook her head. "Far from it. He's only a sophomore, so we'll see how it pans out, but as of now he's planning to do Teach for America for a couple years. And after that, who knows? But I doubt commercial real estate is in his future. He's too much of a free spirit for an office job. I love that about him. Personally, I think he'd make a great elementary schoolteacher because he has such a gentle way about him."

"I could say the same about you," Daphne said to her.

KC smiled at Daphne and used her fingers to make a heart.

"I would be a horrible teacher," Skylar said. "I don't have the patience for it."

"Your dream of making enough money to hire a traveling hairstylist would be out the window on a teacher's salary, that's for sure," Daphne said.

Skylar held her glass in the air. "An excellent point. Yet *another* reason why I could never be a teacher."

"So to finish up on your original question: Max is great, Josh and Jared are thriving, there are no complaints, all is good on the home front." KC clinked her glass against Skylar's.

"You really love those boys, don't you," Daphne said to KC. It wasn't a question. The glow she saw in KC's eyes when she talked about her stepsons was how Daphne felt when she thought about Emma. A love so unconditional and pure, it was overwhelming at times. Emma was nearly old enough to drive now, but sometimes when Daphne looked at her, she still saw the miracle baby she'd carried home so gingerly from the hospital, and in those moments it took every ounce of Daphne's willpower not to smother her daughter with kisses, be it in the middle of a piano recital or volleyball match—or God forbid in front of other kids at school. She'd learned her lesson about that.

KC's face lit up. "You have no idea. Biggest surprise of my life."

"I'm glad you found Max," Skylar said. "I remember you used to say you would never get married and have a family, but I always felt that you would make a great mom. You're such a positive role model."

"I certainly didn't expect to become a stepmom of two teenage boys at age thirty-five, but it turned out to be one of the best things I ever did. Life can really sneak up on you, you know?"

Daphne felt a pang in her gut. *It sure can.*

"So speaking of kids, tell us about how Emma's doing," KC said to Daphne. "Is she in high school now?"

Daphne nodded. "She's a sophomore, which I still can't believe. She's getting her driver's license soon."

"Wow, I remember during our last birthday trip, you were telling us how you'd cried when you'd dropped her off at kindergarten," KC said. "Soon you'll be dropping her off at college."

"Oh gosh, don't remind me."

"Is she dating?" Skylar asked.

Daphne shook her head. "Not yet. Not ever, I hope." *Not that I know of. I bet Alyssa knows. Stop thinking about Alyssa!*

"Do you have a recent picture?" KC asked.

Daphne reached for her purse. "I have millions." She pulled out her phone and scrolled through the photos, then handed the phone to KC. "Here's one from her volleyball tournament last month."

KC smiled at the phone, then handed it to Skylar. "Look at that adorable face. Where did all those freckles come from? She looks more like my daughter than yours."

Daphne touched her own cheeks, then looked at her arms. "Brian and I have no idea. I have like ten freckles on my entire body, and he has even less."

Skylar studied the photo, then handed the phone back to Daphne. "She's still in that awkward gangly stage, but it's pretty clear she's going to be a swan once she emerges on the other side. Prepare yourself."

Daphne held the phone against her heart. "The thought of her going on a date makes me feel a little sick."

"So speaking of dating, what about *you*?" Skylar asked Daphne. "Are you dating anyone worth mentioning?"

Daphne felt her cheeks flush, and then she reached for her water glass. "No, not really." *Not at all.*

"Are you dating anyone *not* worth mentioning?" Skylar asked. "Those guys make better stories anyway."

KC grinned. "I agree. Any exciting flings? My divorcées are always regaling the class with tales of their romantic adventures, most of which don't really qualify as *dating* but sound pretty entertaining."

Daphne shook her head slightly, her nose still in her water glass.

Skylar raised an eyebrow. "A smart, attractive, single woman like you, and no stories to share? That doesn't add up."

Daphne suddenly felt a familiar sensation in the back of her head, and she knew that within seconds, her eyes were going to well up with tears. She noticed the waiter approaching them with dessert menus and was grateful for the forced break in conversation.

Skylar put her reading glasses back on and studied the list. "Do either of you want anything? I'm too stuffed for anything big, but I could be convinced to share something."

Daphne stood up. "I'm pretty full as well. I think I'll pass. Will you excuse me for a minute? I'm just going to run to the ladies' room." She tucked her chair close to the table and struggled to keep the tears at bay before her friends could see them. *Don't cry. Don't cry.*

KC held up her purse. "I have dark chocolate squares if you want one."

Skylar's eyes lit up. "Ooh, perfect. You still carry dark chocolate with you everywhere you go?"

"Always."

Skylar waved her fingers at the purse. "Gimme."

Daphne forced a smile. "Save me a square, okay? I'll be right back." *Please start talking about something else while I'm gone.*

She hurried inside toward the restroom, her eyes fixated on the wood floor. She didn't feel any tears yet, but she could feel her cheeks getting hot. The restaurant was filled with strangers she would most likely never see again in her lifetime, but she still hoped none of them would notice how upset she was. How embarrassed she was for losing her composure, *again*. How frustrated she was for still feeling like this: socially paralyzed, afraid to start dating, afraid of everything it represented. *Let the past go!*

Once safely ensconced in the empty restroom, whose bright white walls were adorned with nautical-themed paintings, she dotted a few tears away with a Kleenex. A small smudge of mascara under her left eye was the only evidence that she'd been on the verge of crying. She wiped it away and took a deep breath, then took a step back and looked at herself in the mirror, grateful to finally be alone. *What happened to you?*

The face looking back at her was the same that Skylar and KC remembered, but the person behind it wasn't. Where was the wide-eyed optimist who loved to laugh, who loved to try new things, who never backed down from a challenge, and who was excited about her future? *Where did you go?*

She splashed cold water on her face, then patted her cheeks with a paper towel—hard. *Get it together. You're stronger than this!* She dug around in her purse for some lipstick and blush, then did her best to conceal the fact that she'd been inches away from dissolving into tears. *You're going to be fine.*

Less than satisfied with the results but knowing she couldn't spend the evening hiding inside the restroom, she forced a less than convincing smile into the mirror, patted her cheeks one more time, and then made her way back outside.

．　　．　　．

"I still vote for the Monkees," Skylar said as Daphne returned to the table. "Davy Jones was dreamy."

KC shook her head. "No way. *Definitely* NSYNC. Justin Timberlake all the way, baby."

"JT is hot, I agree. But *DJ* was timeless. You'll see."

"What are you two talking about?" Daphne took a seat, relieved that the conversation had turned away from her dating life.

"We're debating who was the best boy band ever," Skylar said. "Super Jockette here is overlooking the obvious choice."

"What about the Beatles?" Daphne said.

"I don't think the Beatles count as a boy band," KC said. "They're so famous that they're like a regular band."

"Agreed," Skylar said.

"Emma likes One Direction," Daphne said.

Skylar shook her head. "History will prove me right. You just watch, my friends." She tapped her palms against the table. "So speaking of bands, who's up for a nightcap? I heard there's a great spot just down the beach that has live music."

KC began to speak, but Skylar put a hand in the air. "Wait. That wasn't a question, so allow me to rephrase. *Time for* a nightcap. There's a great spot just down the beach that has live music."

Daphne made a sheepish face. "Can we take a rain check? I woke up at five this morning."

KC followed suit. "I was up at three thirty. And you guys know I need my sleep."

Skylar gestured for the bill. "You can sleep when you're dead. Chop chop."

"What time is it?" KC asked.

Daphne looked at her watch. "Nine thirty."

KC yawned. "I may have to take back what I said about not being old. I'm kind of exhausted."

"Me too," Daphne said. "I can barely keep my eyes open. I'm sorry, Skylar."

Skylar signed the credit card receipt and stood up. "You're *really* too tired to go?"

KC and Daphne nodded in unison.

"Even for one drink?" Skylar looked incredulous.

They nodded again.

Daphne looked at her hands. "I'm sorry. Can we go there tomorrow night?"

"The bed in my room looked so comfortable," KC said in a tiny voice. "And that sangria made me so sleepy."

Skylar sighed. "You two are somewhat pathetic. If you were this lame in college, I don't know if we would have been friends."

"We know," KC and Daphne said in unison, although now they were kind of laughing.

Skylar held up a finger. "Okay, fine, I'll give you *one night* to get acclimatized, but only one. Our time together on this fabulous island is limited, so I want to make sure we get the most out of it."

"I promise I'll be more fun tomorrow," KC said.

"I don't know how fun I'll be, but at least I'll be awake," Daphne said.

KC poked her in the rib. "Stop it, you're always fun."

"Thanks, KC." Daphne gave her a weak smile. *I wish I felt that way.*

"Let's walk home," Skylar said. "I need to work off that amazing meal I just inhaled. Unless you wimps are too *tired* to walk?"

"I'm up for that," KC said.

The three of them descended the back steps of the restaurant, then removed their shoes and began strolling along the sand. They had taken a cab to the restaurant, which had wound through the quaint streets leading into the center of town, but in a straight line their house was barely a mile down the beach. It was dark out now, but the gentle air was still warm, the sand soft and squishy between their toes. The beach was dotted with couples and small groups meandering about. An older man sat alone on a large towel, staring out at the water. Daphne wondered what he was thinking. *Is he happy? Or is he hurting inside? Does he feel all alone?*

"I love the sound of the ocean," KC said. "There's something about it that's so soothing."

"I feel that way about a nice glass of wine . . . or three," Skylar said.

KC and Skylar kept walking, but Daphne didn't move or respond to Skylar's joke. Instead, she stood still and kept her eyes on the dark water.

"You okay, Daphne?" KC returned and put a hand on her arm.

"You left us again," Skylar said.

"I'm fine, just . . . tired." Daphne kept gazing out toward the sea.

"You sure?" Skylar didn't sound convinced.

Daphne nodded and forced yet another smile. The act was beginning to wear on her.

Skylar put an arm around Daphne and pulled her along the beach. "Hey, I just realized that you skipped to the restroom right when we were about to delve into your love life."

KC clapped her hands and did a little skip. "Ooh yes, let's hear about that."

Daphne wiggled out of Skylar's embrace and kept looking out at the water, afraid to make eye contact, afraid she would start crying if she did. "There's not much to tell."

Skylar waved a dismissive hand. "Nonsense. There's always something to tell. The magic is in *how* you tell it. So you're not dating anyone seriously, no big deal. Tell us about the last guy you smooched."

Daphne felt the tears coming back. *Please don't make me do this.* She began walking a little faster.

"Hello?" Skylar said.

Daphne didn't reply.

"I can't imagine dating again," Daphne heard KC say behind her. "I wasn't very good at it when I was single. I'd definitely be worse at it now."

Then Skylar spoke. "What are you talking about? I hope you'd be bad at dating, given that you're *married*."

Daphne glanced behind her and saw KC give Skylar's midsection a squeeze. "You know what I mean," KC said to Skylar.

Skylar and KC quickened their pace and caught up to Daphne.

"So spill and tell us something juicy," Skylar said. "And for the love of God, will you stop walking so fast? I'm going to get a cramp here."

Daphne slowed down—but just barely. She studied the sand in front of her, her toes sinking into it with each step.

"What is going on with you, Daphne?" Skylar said. "You're acting really weird."

Daphne suddenly stopped in her tracks. She took a deep breath, then finally let her eyes flicker toward Skylar. "I'm not ready to date yet, okay?"

Skylar glanced at KC, then back to Daphne. "Wait a minute. Are you saying you haven't dated since you and Brian split up?"

Daphne nodded.

"At all? In two-and-a-half years?" Skylar said.

Daphne began walking again. Fast. Then the tears arrived. This time for real. *Is it too late for me? Am I capable of having a healthy relationship? Do I even know what that means?*

She wiped the tears away with the back of her hand and kept moving, as if by staying in motion she could somehow escape the embarrassment of what she'd just shared. Skylar and KC were her best friends, but she didn't want them to see her this way. She didn't want them to know how much she was hurting inside, how empty she'd become. She kept walking as fast as she could, the tears now streaming down her face.

"Daphne, hon, please stop," Skylar called from behind.

KC trotted to catch up to her, a concerned look on her face.

Daphne tried to will the tears away, but it didn't work this time. She began crying harder, then coughing in a futile effort to make herself stop. Finally, she gave up walking and stood there, her shoulders slumping.

KC put a hand on her arm and squeezed. "Are you okay?"

Skylar joined them and caught her breath when she saw Daphne's face. "Oh, hon, what's wrong?"

Daphne didn't respond. Instead, the three of them stood there on the beach, Daphne now sobbing uncontrollably.

KC began to pet Daphne's hair. "Whatever it is, it's going to be fine."

After a few moments in which no one spoke, Daphne finally choked out the words. "Brian's . . . getting remarried."

Skylar sighed. "Damn it."

"Oh sweetie, I'm so sorry," KC said. She kept petting Daphne's hair.

Daphne coughed again and wiped the tears away from her eyes. "I haven't been on a single date since we split up, and now he's marrying *Alyssa*. Beautiful, perfect, thirty-three-year-old *Alyssa*."

"She sounds like a bitch," Skylar said.

Daphne let out a weak laugh, then dropped her flip-flops and crumpled downward to sit on the beach. She pulled her knees up to her chest, the tears still streaming down her cheeks, although with less intensity now.

Skylar and KC sat down next to her.

"I'm sorry," KC said. "I know that must sting."

"I'm forty years old and have to start all over. I'm a failure," Daphne whispered into her knees.

But Skylar and KC heard her.

KC began to rub Daphne's back. "Oh sweetie, that's not true, that's not true at all."

"Don't think like that, Daphne," Skylar said. "You're a *mother*, for crying out loud. How can you feel like a failure when you've raised a sweet girl like Emma, when you've done so much for her?"

Daphne rested her forehead on her knees. "Emma doesn't need me anymore."

KC began petting her hair again. "That's not true. Girls *always* need their mothers. I still talk to mine all the time."

Daphne kept her forehead pressed against her knees. "I know it's just a phase she's going through, but it hurts that she doesn't talk to me like she used to. Some days she barely talks to me at all."

"She's fifteen," Skylar said. "Who talks to their mom at fifteen? I think I went my entire junior year in high school without talking to mine. I was too busy obsessing over which pair of acid-wash jeans to wear with my Reebok high-tops."

Daphne coughed out a laugh. "I remember those high-tops."

"Me too. You rocked those kicks," KC said.

"My sisters have gone through this exact same thing," Skylar said to Daphne. "You can't take it personally."

"Rationally I know that, but I just miss her," Daphne said.

"I think it's good for teenagers to pull away from their parents a little bit. It means they're experimenting with the idea of becoming adults one day by testing the boundaries a little bit, which is an important step for them," KC said.

Skylar pushed KC's shoulder. "Look who's playing the role of the wise old lady."

KC laughed. "Josh and Jared each went through a bit of a phase, not exactly rebellious, but definitely a period where Max and I were hardly topping the list of people they wanted to spend time with. Yes, it takes some getting used to, but you'll adjust. In the meantime, try not to let it eat at you."

"But you and Max had each other to turn to during that phase," Daphne said, finally lifting her head. Then she looked at Skylar, her eyes watery. "And your sisters have their husbands. I have . . . just myself." She began to cry again, her shoulders slumping.

"Hey now, you have us," Skylar said. "We're not going anywhere."

Daphne wiped more tears from her cheeks. "I just feel so guilty . . . and sad . . . that I couldn't give her the family that I wanted for her." *That I wanted for myself.*

"Don't do that to yourself," Skylar said. "Lots of kids have divorced parents."

"I can't help it. I'm trying to keep it together in front of her, but I'm terrified she's going to see that I don't know what I'm doing with my life anymore, and that it's going to mess her up somehow."

"My sisters all tell me that kids come with their bags packed anyway," Skylar said. "You can do your best, but at the end of the day they are who they are."

"I agree," KC said. "Divorce doesn't mess children up. Living with unhappily married parents does."

"Besides, married or divorced, no family is perfect," Skylar said.

More tears streamed down Daphne's cheeks. "I'm so embarrassed," she sniffled.

KC gave her a strange look. "Embarrassed? Why in the world would you be embarrassed?"

"Because it's been more than two years, and I can't get over it."

"Over Brian? Or over the end of the marriage?" Skylar asked.

Daphne sighed and stared out at the ocean. "I'm not sure anymore."

"There's a big difference there," Skylar said.

"Do you still love him?" KC asked.

Daphne took a deep breath. "I think . . . I think part of me will always love him; I mean he's the father of my child . . . but no, I'm not *in love* with him anymore." The truth was, she hadn't been in love with him for a long time, and he certainly hadn't been in love with her. Was that what hurt so much? That they'd both wasted so many years on a marriage that wasn't working? Going through the motions just to keep up outward appearances?

"Then that's a *good* thing," KC said. "It's okay to mourn the demise of the relationship. You were together for a long time."

"I think it's more than that," Daphne whispered.

Skylar and KC exchanged a glance, then remained silent, giving Daphne time to elaborate.

Finally, Daphne spoke the truth. The complete truth. She told them the entire story, unvarnished.

When she was done, she stared at the sand. "I think . . . I think I feel like a failure for entering into a marriage that was probably doomed from the start," she said quietly.

"Don't say that," Skylar said. "You and he were madly in love. How were you supposed to know it wouldn't work out?"

Daphne pushed a strand of hair out of her eyes. "I just wish . . . I just wish I could go back and tell myself to wait until I knew him better, to focus on *myself* before molding my entire life around someone else's. All those places I was going to go, all those stories

I was going to write . . . I never did any of it." *I was going to win a Pulitzer.*

"I'm sorry for bringing the diary," Skylar said. "That was a boneheaded move. I didn't think it through."

"It's okay," Daphne said. "I know you didn't mean anything by it."

Skylar and KC kept watching her, KC still lightly stroking her hair. A few moments passed before Daphne spoke again. "I was too young to get married," she whispered. "I gave up too much."

"I know you were young, but that doesn't mean it was the wrong thing to do," KC said. "You can't beat yourself up about it."

Daphne sighed. "I was so naïve."

"Naïve how?" Skylar asked.

"It never occurred to me that the intense feelings Brian and I had for each other would go away . . . that one day they would just be . . . gone."

"No one can ever know that," KC said.

"But *I* would have known that if I'd known him better," Daphne said. "I rushed into it, and then once we were married and I had Emma, I lost who *I* was." Tears started sliding down her cheeks again. "I was so stupid to let it happen."

Skylar narrowed her eyes. "What do you mean? Let what happen?"

Daphne didn't reply.

Skylar's eyes became dark. "He didn't . . . *hurt* you, did he? I swear to God, if he ever touched you—"

Daphne quickly shook her head. "No, never. It was just that when we met, I was on my way to *becoming* someone, you know? I had a real future, and then—poof—it was gone." *I was gone.*

"That's not true, Daphne. You have a wonderful daughter you adore. That's *huge*," KC said. "You have to be proud of that."

Daphne wiped a tear from her cheek. "I know, and I am, but we all know I used to want to be something *in addition to* a mom. Brian was never going to be on board with that, but I was too blind to see it."

Skylar nodded slowly. "Ah, now I get it."

"He's old-fashioned?" KC said.

Daphne laughed weakly, her eyes still wet. "He never even changed a diaper. Can you believe I married a man like that?"

"I think a lot of women marry men like that," Skylar said. "They don't discuss the division of labor before kids enter the picture, but when they realize they aren't on the same page as their husbands, it's too late and they're stuck doing all the work."

Daphne nodded slowly. "That's exactly what happened to me." *I can't believe I let it happen to me. I thought I was smarter than that.*

"Did you ever, you know, ask him to help?" KC asked.

Daphne squeaked out a laugh. "If it were only that easy."

"I'm sorry, that was a dumb question," KC said.

Daphne smiled and put a hand on KC's arm. "That's okay. It's just, or I should say it *was* just, hard. I was so young, and I didn't know what I was doing, and I think I just gave up battling him because it didn't seem worth wrecking my marriage for. I decided it was better to . . . keep the peace." *I always kept the peace.*

"Do you think it would have wrecked your marriage if you had spoken up?" Skylar asked.

Daphne frowned. "I don't know, but at the time I thought it would. So I gave up on the career thing and put all my energy into being a good mother, but when I look back now, I realize that while I love my daughter, that decision probably contributed to the deterioration of my marriage because I stopped being *myself*, stopped being the Daphne Brian fell in love with, and the Daphne who fell in love with Brian." *I miss that person.*

"You're still Daphne to me," KC said. "It's been wonderful hanging out with you again."

Daphne closed her eyes. "You're just being nice. You know I'm not the same. I'm a fragment of who I used to be."

"None of us are the same as we were in college," Skylar said. "We're adults now, Daphne. We've all changed."

"But at the core, where it really matters, you two seem the same to me," Daphne said. "I don't think you could say that about me."

KC shook her head. "You're being too hard on yourself."

"I think what you're feeling is totally normal," Skylar said. "Not that I have any experience with divorce, but I have several friends who do, and you'd be surprised at how often the word *failure* creeps into the conversation. Failure for having chosen the wrong person. Failure for not trying hard enough to make it work. Failure for not living up to society's expectations."

Daphne sighed. "I don't know anyone in Columbus who's divorced. I feel like a pariah at Emma's school sometimes. Some of the other mothers, the way they look at me . . ." Her voice trailed off. "It's like they think there's something wrong with me."

"They're probably just resentful because they're not happy in their own marriages," Skylar said.

Daphne frowned at the thought. "You think so?"

Skylar shrugged. "You never know, but I wouldn't be surprised. No one knows what's going on behind closed doors in a relationship, so who is anyone to judge when two people decide to pull the rip cord?"

"Amen," KC said. "I don't like people who judge. Except real judges, of course. They're cool."

"What about your friends out there?" Skylar asked. "They support you, right?"

Daphne felt her cheeks flush, then picked up a handful of sand. "I don't really have any close friends, just people I know from

Emma's school and around the neighborhood. There's Carol, a nice older lady who lives across the street, but she's the only one." She'd never officially admitted that before, but there was no use hiding it now. There was no use hiding any of it now.

Skylar and KC exchanged a look but didn't say anything. They understood.

Daphne watched the sand slide through her fingers. "Everyone thinks he left me, and I guess technically he did, but I knew a long time ago that it wasn't working anymore, maybe even before he did."

"How long?" Skylar asked.

"Years," Daphne whispered.

"Oh hon," Skylar said.

"I'm so sorry you had to go through that," KC said.

Daphne sighed. "I knew it wasn't working, but I was *committed*, you know? And we had Emma, and all her activities, and there was so much to do to keep the household running that I wouldn't let myself face it . . . I couldn't bring myself to face it. It was almost like I was subconsciously waiting for Brian to be the one to wave the white flag and say he wanted out, and one day he finally did."

KC and Skylar remained silent.

Daphne took a deep breath. "I know it's for the best that we're not together anymore, I really do. But I'm still . . . and I know this probably sounds crazy given everything I just told you . . . but I'm still hurt that . . . that I was so easily replaceable," she whispered the last words.

"Oh sweets," Skylar said. "Don't feel that way."

"I can't help it. It's bad enough that everyone thinks he left me. Now he's found someone else first, and I feel like a cliché because I gave up my career to be a stay-at-home mom. I was an honor student at Northwestern, and now I'm working part-time in a flower store."

"I love flowers," KC said.

Daphne gave her a weary yet grateful smile. "I love *you*," she said.

Skylar held up a finger. "First of all, it doesn't matter *who* pulled the trigger. If it wasn't working, it wasn't working, and prolonging the inevitable would have only hurt you both more."

"Exactly. Who cares who blinked first?" KC said. "Who would even know something like that?"

Skylar held up another finger. "And *second* of all, who cares if he found someone else first? That has nothing to do with you. It's not like he left you *for* this Alyssa woman." She hesitated. "He didn't leave you *for* her, right?"

Daphne shook her head. "No, he didn't meet her until after we split up. I'm sure of that, but it's still hard to watch. I just wish I'd found the strength to leave, to rebuild my life instead of behaving like a passive bystander in it. If I'd done that, I don't think I would care so much about where Brian's going because I'd be focused on where *I'm* going. Instead, I feel stuck."

"I'm sorry if the moms are being catty about it," KC said. "I've seen that side of parenting, and I'm not a fan."

Daphne groaned. "Tell me about it. The gossip in our town is terrible. It's like high school, only meaner, because people aren't talking about your prom date, they're talking about your *marriage*."

KC nodded. "I witnessed my share of the chatter when I entered the picture at Josh and Jared's school. Divorces, affairs—everyone knows everyone else's business. Suburban gossip can be fierce."

Skylar made a face. "Remind me never to move to the 'burbs. Don't any of these women have jobs?"

"I'm sure some of them do, but they're not the ones I interact with," Daphne said.

Skylar pointed at her. "Now you know who your new friends need to be. Women who have too much going on to be digging through other people's laundry baskets."

Daphne laughed weakly. "Trust me, I've been thinking that for a long time."

"Why didn't you tell us any of this before?" KC asked. "If I were this upset, I probably would have brought it up while we were still at the airport."

Daphne smiled and wiped a tiny tear from her cheek. "That's because you're you. The truth is, I didn't bring it up because I didn't want you two to see me this way."

"What way?" Skylar asked.

Daphne laughed and gestured to herself. "*This* way. Hysterical, insecure, racked with self-doubt, an emotional train wreck."

"But we're your *friends*, Daphne," KC said. "You shouldn't have to pretend around us. We take you as is, remember? The Three Musketeers, together forever?"

Skylar nodded. "She's right, you know. We love you no matter what."

"I guess I just didn't want you two to see how differently my life has turned out than what . . . than what I expected it would be," Daphne said.

Skylar shook her head. "We care about *you*, not your résumé." She looked at KC. "Is your life résumé the way you expected it to be at this age?"

KC shook her head. "Not even close. As we just saw in Daisy the diary, my plan was to be a lifer in the Peace Corps, remember? Look at me now. I drive a *Mercedes*, for crying out loud. And while I do love being married to Max, dealing with his drug-addicted brother is another story. I can't say *hosting an intervention* was on my bucket list, but—boom—there it is."

Skylar tapped KC's arm. "Forget what I said earlier about refraining from gossip. That sounds juicy, so I'll be following up on it later."

KC smiled and looked at Daphne. "See? No one's life goes exactly the way they think it will when they're in college. We all have hiccups and detours along the way. That's what makes it interesting."

Skylar nodded. "Definitely. Anyone who tells you otherwise is probably hiding a dead body in the basement."

Daphne laughed, softly but sincerely. "You guys are so great. I'm sorry for turning our first night here into a sob show."

Skylar held up a hand. "Stop that. From now on, no apologizing for your feelings, okay? If you want to cry, then cry. If you want to laugh, then laugh. If you want to complain about your ex-husband, then complain about your ex-husband. This trip is about celebrating the fact that we've been alive for four decades, and I don't want any of us to feel like we have to put on an act and make our lives look like something they're not."

"Well put," KC said with a smile. "I can totally picture that on a greeting card."

Daphne smiled. "I wish I shared your sunny take on the whole *turning forty* thing. Right now I just feel like a middle-aged woman with a broken past and nothing to look forward to."

Skylar stood up and clapped some sand off her hands and backside. "Okay, I realize that ten seconds ago I said I wanted us to speak freely on this trip, but that might be the biggest load of crap I've ever heard." She held up a finger again. "*First* of all, you're not middle-aged. As you yourself pointed out over dinner, you're still in your thirties; is that not correct?"

Daphne nodded.

"Good. Now, thirties is hardly middle-aged, and anyone who would suggest otherwise is an idiot." She held up a second finger.

"And *second* of all, as we also discovered during dinner, your eyes are still functioning like they did when you were a teenager, is that not also correct?"

Daphne nodded again.

"Good. More evidence that you're not ready for a senior living community anytime soon. And for the record, only those whose eyes aren't working *at all* couldn't see how gorgeous you are for a woman of any age; is that not correct as well?" She looked at KC.

KC agreed. "I was shocked to hear you haven't been dating. I figured you'd have men chasing you down the street, or the cul-de-sac, or wherever it is that you live."

Skylar clasped her hands together. "Good, we're all on the same page. Daphne, you are intelligent, genuine, and more beautiful than you've ever been, so for the love of God, let's get you back on track to living the life you deserve, which is one filled with love, friendship, happiness, and—for this week at least—lots of mango sangrias, margaritas, and rum punches. Are you with me?" She held her hand down to Daphne.

Emotionally exhausted but no longer despondent, Daphne looked at her friends and felt an enormous wave of relief begin to wash over her. She'd been so scared of revealing her true feelings, yet now that she had, she wondered what she'd been so afraid of. They loved her then, and they loved her now. *I'm still the same person to them,* she realized. *Maybe I'm not as lost as I think I am.*

Feeling drained yet hopeful, she held out her hand to Skylar. "All right, I'm with you. That sounded like another greeting card, by the way."

"Maybe I should look into that as yet another side business," Skylar said. "Apparently I'm full of creativity this week."

KC jumped up. "You're full of something, that's for sure."

"Watch it, pip-squeak," Skylar said. "I could squash you like an ant just by sitting on you."

Skylar and KC each took one of Daphne's hands, then pulled her up to a standing position. As KC wiped the sand off her backside, Skylar stood in front of Daphne and put her hands on Daphne's shoulders. "Are you feeling better now? Even a little?"

Daphne nodded, then smiled as she wiggled her feet back into her flip-flops. "I am." *I really am.*

"Good." Skylar slipped an arm around her and gently nudged her back toward the beach house. "Now let's get some sleep. Tomorrow night I'm not taking any excuses about how tired you two are."

"Uh oh," KC whispered from behind them.

"I heard that," Skylar said without turning around.

"What happened to your selective hearing?" KC asked with a groan.

"What did you say?" Skylar put her hands behind her ears, then looked over at Daphne and winked.

Chapter Six

When Daphne woke up the next morning, she yawned and stretched her arms overhead. Slowly the deliciousness of her new surroundings washed over her. *I'm in an extravagant house on spectacular St. Mirika. With Skylar and KC.*

That was quickly followed by another realization. *I broke down last night. They know now. But it's all right.* The budding sense of hopefulness she'd felt on the beach last night was still there. *I'm going to be okay.*

Then a third realization hit her, this one not as easy to swallow. *Tomorrow I turn forty. Forty! Wow.*

She stretched her arms again, then froze. Perched high on the far side of the ceiling, over near the glass doors leading to the deck, was a small gecko.

"Hey little guy, what's your name?" Daphne said softly. She held a hand to her ear, pretending to listen, then made up a name for her new friend.

"Fred, did you say? It's nice to meet you, Fred. I'm Daphne, and I'm going to be forty years old tomorrow. What do you think of that?"

She chuckled to herself. *What is wrong with me?*

Whatever the impetus, it felt good to laugh. She pulled the duvet to one side and gently swung her legs to the tile floor. She wiggled her feet into a pair of disposable slippers she'd found the night before in the closet—they looked just like the ones she'd seen in hotel rooms and were wrapped in a tidy band made of thick white card stock—then shuffled into the bathroom to get ready to face the day.

As she brushed her teeth and looked at her reflection, she realized how much better she felt than she had just twenty-four hours ago. Something was missing now: a weight she'd been carrying around for so long that she'd forgotten what it felt like not to have it dragging her down. She hadn't planned to confess her struggle to come to terms with her failed marriage, but breaking down and opening up to her friends had lifted an enormous burden off her psyche. It was liberating.

She set the toothbrush down on the sink and spoke silently to the woman in the mirror. *This is your last day in your thirties. You're on a beautiful tropical island with your two best friends. You'd better make the most of it!*

There was no use fighting it. Like it or not, at this time tomorrow, she'd be forty. She was still dreading it, but not nearly as much as she'd been just yesterday. She was smart enough to recognize that for the mental victory it was. *At least I don't need reading glasses yet.*

After finishing up in the bathroom, she returned to the bedroom to check her phone. Her face lit up at the notice of a text message from Emma, the first she'd received since before she left for the airport. With the message was a photo of Emma and Brian on a chairlift, waving at the camera through snowflakes, silly grins on their pink faces.

Hi Mom, having a great time! Hope you are too. Happy early birthday if this reaches you!

She smiled at the message and briefly held the phone close to her heart. It had been a long time since Emma had sent her a friendly text like that. She typed a quick reply, then set the phone down on the desk, trying not to think about who had taken the photo.

She looked up at the ceiling. "Hey, Fred, my daughter's on vacation with my ex-husband and his new fiancée. Isn't that *great?*"

She chuckled again to herself. *I think I'm losing it. But at least I'm laughing and not crying, right?*

She finished dressing, then glanced up at the gecko one last time and waved good-bye before shutting her bedroom door and making her way down the hall.

.   .   .

"Good morning, sunshine, did you sleep okay?" KC said in a hushed voice from the kitchen, then put a finger to her lips and jutted her chin toward the living room. Daphne turned her head and saw Skylar hunched over her laptop, headset on, her dexterous fingers once again flying over the keyboard.

"Yes . . . got it . . . yes . . . got that too. Wait a minute, Jason, could you please repeat that last number? Hmm . . . okay, yes this time around, but that can't happen again. No really, it can't, trust me."

Daphne glanced at KC, who responded with an "I have no idea" gesture.

Skylar kept talking. "You've *got* to get me a meeting with Alfonso next week, okay? Yes, yes. Got it. And what about Germany? We have an analyst call in two weeks. Without that report, they're going to be at our throats. Julie, did you hear that?"

"She never stops, does she?" Daphne whispered.

"I guess not," KC whispered back. "Want some coffee?" She held up her mug. "They've got one of those superdeluxe machines that brew one delicious cup at a time. I was about to go enjoy this on the deck and admire the view. Come join me!"

Daphne smiled. "Sounds heavenly. You go ahead, I'll make myself a cup and meet you out there."

KC pointed to the half-and-half and sugar she'd left out on the counter, then carefully made her way past Skylar. She quietly opened the French doors leading outside as Daphne tiptoed into the kitchen. She pulled a white ceramic mug from one of the cabinets and set it under the nozzle of the coffeemaker, then pressed the button. As she watched it brew, she listened to bits and pieces of Skylar's side of the conversation and wondered what the discussion was about. It had been ages since Daphne had been in an office environment, so much of the jargon sounded like a foreign language to her.

"Have they finished the RFP yet? If not, they're going to drag down the entire CRM implementation . . . The data for that IBU is in the cloud. Yes, check the content management system for Asia Pac . . . How's the pipeline visibility for Germany?"

Daphne stirred sugar into the mug, then picked it up and watched her friend. Skylar's brow was furrowed in concentration, her mouth tense. In Daphne's mind, Skylar's corporate life had always seemed so glamorous, especially when compared to her own suburban existence, but right now it didn't look all that appealing.

She took a sip of her coffee. *Is that what my life would be like if I'd gone down that route? Would I be working right now too? On my vacation?*

She tiptoed toward the glass doors leading to the deck, which KC had left slightly ajar. Skylar looked up and gave her a weary smile as she passed. Daphne thought she looked tired. And a little stressed.

Daphne smiled back, then gently shut the doors behind her.

• • •

"Maybe it's because I've had a good night's sleep, but I think it's even prettier here today than it was yesterday," Daphne said as she settled into a deck chair next to KC.

KC propped her legs up on a bench. "Probably because you had a good cry too. Remember what Eleanor said yesterday about how rain makes you see things in a new way? Tears are a form of rain, in my opinion."

Daphne flinched. "Can we maybe not talk about my meltdown? Or at least not yet? It's eight o'clock in the morning."

KC grinned. "Meltdown, that's cute. Spoken like a true mom."

Daphne smiled weakly, then gazed out at the clear water. "*Anyhow*, I think the water has a little blue in it today. Yesterday it was more green. The sand looks just as white, though. Stunning, isn't it?"

KC reached over and clinked her mug against Daphne's. "Here's to another day in paradise, and yes, I realize I kind of just plagiarized a Phil Collins song. Who knows what other adventures await?"

"In all seriousness, thanks for being there last night," Daphne said as she sipped her coffee. "I know that wasn't one of my finer moments."

"Nonsense. It was one of your *finest* moments."

Daphne gave her an incredulous look. "How so, exactly?"

KC set her mug down and sat up straight. "Do you know how many people go through their entire lives pretending everything is okay when it's not, burying their feelings, never being able to confide in anyone? It's toxic to keep all that bottled up inside, but people do it because they're terrified to admit that their life isn't perfect."

Daphne frowned. "I never thought about it that way. I guess I knew *I* was doing it, but it never occurred to me that other people were doing it too."

"I'm proud of you for having the guts to pull the curtain back a little bit." KC pointed to the cloudless sky. "And it's only rained once. Remember what Eleanor said? Think how enlightened we're going to be by the end of the week. Geniuses, probably."

Daphne laughed. "I guess we'll see."

"So are you still up for a workout on the beach? We should go before it gets too hot."

Daphne grimaced. "I want to, but I'm kind of scared."

KC waved a dismissive hand. "Don't be scared. It will be fun, I promise. I'm not out to kill anyone. And afterward we can walk to that hut with the banana on top and get a smoothie."

Daphne glanced down the beach and had an unsettling thought. If they did their session on the stretch between here and the smoothie shop, there was a decent chance Clay from yesterday and his bachelor-party friends would see them at some point. She wasn't thrilled at the idea of *anyone* seeing her suffer through a sweaty exercise session, much less a group of men in their twenties.

She blinked. *Why am I thinking about this? What is the big deal? Although, it was kind of fun talking to him.*

She swallowed and casually pointed in the other direction. "I'll do it, but I'm thinking it would be cool to check out a new part of the beach. Maybe we could do the boot camp down that way?"

"Sure, I'm easy." KC took another sip of her coffee, then kissed the mug. "Have you noticed that even the *coffee* tastes better here than at home?"

Daphne smiled. "I think that's because the machine that brewed it probably cost more than my car did."

"Perhaps, but part of me thinks tiny fairies sprinkled St. Mirika with magic dust that makes everything here beautiful and yummy." She used her fingertips to make pretend droplets fall from the sky.

"Good morning, ladies, sorry for having to begin our first full day here with another work call, but it is what it is." Skylar's voice suddenly boomed from inside the house, then returned to a normal decibel as she stepped out on the deck. "Wow, it's already getting warm out here."

"Everything okay at the office?" KC asked. "That call sounded a little tense."

Skylar shrugged. "A minor crisis, but nothing I haven't been through before."

"You were right about your work demeanor," Daphne said. "You sound so professional on the phone. It's impressive."

Skylar did a little curtsy. "Well, thank you, my love. I do my best."

"We were just talking about doing a beach workout, then heading over to check out that smoothie place," KC said. "You in?"

Skylar shook her head. "I was *planning* to, but . . ."

KC raised her eyebrows.

Skylar laughed. "Okay, I'm totally lying, I wasn't planning to, and yes, I know I shook your hand, but in court I would swear that was under duress. Plus, I've been doing supported squats all morning."

"Supported squats?" Daphne said with a cough. "As in . . . sitting down?"

Skylar winked at her. "Indeed. I might be able to join you for the smoothie part, though."

"If you're breaking our deal, does that mean I'm off the hook for shopping?" KC said.

Skylar gestured toward the glass door. "Anyone want some more coffee while I'm in the kitchen?"

Daphne and KC both raised their hands. "I assume you didn't hear my question about the shopping?" KC asked.

"You assume correctly," Skylar said. "Two coffees, coming right up."

. . .

KC adjusted her baseball cap, this one purple with "NU Soccer" embroidered in white across the bill. She clapped her hands together and began to twist her torso back and forth as Daphne was laying out a large beach towel on the warm sand—and wishing she could lie there with it.

KC pointed about thirty yards down the beach. "Let's start with some light stretching, and then we'll do some easy shuttles from here to that rock. Sound good?"

Daphne stood up straight, gave her beach towel a yearning glance, then lifted her arms out to either side. "We've already established that I don't have much of a choice in this particular matter, so I think that's a superfluous question."

KC squinted at her. "What's *superfluous*?"

"Unnecessary. What's a shuttle?"

"Just a light jog. We'll do ten up and back, no break in between."

"Does up and back count as two?"

KC laughed. "No. Now let's get these vibrant bodies of ours moving. Did you put sunscreen on? Your skin looks a little pink."

Daphne adjusted her ponytail. "Trust me, I practically took a bath in the stuff. And for the record, I prefer *rosy glow* over *pink*."

KC grinned. "Okay, just checking. The sun is a wonderful life force, but it can be dangerous. I'm liking that your argumentative side is making a comeback, by the way."

Daphne smiled as they began to jog. *I'm liking it too.*

. . .

Forty-five minutes later, Daphne feared her legs were going to give out. She felt the sweat dripping down her face as she jogged in place, tapping her palms to her knees as KC counted out loud. She couldn't remember the last time she'd been this exhausted. In addition to the shuttles and running in place, they'd done multiple sprints, squats, sit-ups, planks, and lunges.

She looked over at KC, her breath heavy. "Are we almost done? I think I might actually collapse in a heap, right here on the sand." *At least I wouldn't be sobbing this time.*

KC grinned at her. "Almost done, pal. Just twenty more. Come on, you can do it. Watch me. Knees high, knees high."

Daphne lifted her tank top and used it to wipe the sweat off her face. "I feel like we're in one of those commercials they show for exercise videos at three in the morning. Not that I watch TV at three in the morning, of course."

KC laughed, but didn't stop. "That's it, just like this. Keep it going, keep it going."

Daphne did her best to imitate her diminutive friend, who never seemed to run out of energy. "How can you be so cheerful right now? I'm dying!" she squeaked out.

KC didn't slow down. "You'll get the hang of it. That's it, knees high, knees high. Count down with me now, we're almost done."

Together they counted backward from ten, then KC clapped her hands together. "That's it, Daphne; you did it! Nice job!"

Daphne immediately put her hands on her hips and began to walk in small circles, trying to catch her breath. "Oh my God, I'm so glad that's over."

KC trotted over and put a hand on Daphne's shoulder. "Seriously, Daphne, you did amazing. You're in much better shape than I expected, given the way you were talking."

Daphne gave her a look. "You think I'm in *shape*? I think I just almost died."

KC laughed. "Says you. It will be easier tomorrow, I promise."

"Tomorrow? Are you crazy? There's no way I'm doing that again tomorrow. I'm already afraid I'm not going to be able to walk tomorrow."

KC shook her head. "I wasn't planning for us to do *this* tomorrow. The key to staying fit is to mix things up so you don't get bored. So we can do another workout like this again later in the week. Tomorrow . . . I was thinking we could go for a nice run along the beach, or maybe a hike."

Daphne began walking back toward the house. "Are you trying to kill me? Is that your plan? I always had a suspicion that you never really liked me."

KC quickly caught up to her and pinched the flesh above her hip. "You finally figured that out, did you? But really, you did great just now, and I love how it's brought out the fiery side of you."

"Just think what a bitch I'd be if we lived in the same town."

KC laughed and adjusted her baseball cap. "I'd have you playing soccer before you knew what hit you. Now let's go see if Skylar's done with her call. I'm dying for a smoothie!" She picked up her beach towel and shook it out, then rolled it into a log and trotted ahead toward the house.

· · ·

A half hour later, Daphne, Skylar, and KC were sitting on a bench at the smoothie place—officially named Bananarama, to Daphne's delight—each with a fresh, cold drink in hand.

"Delicious," KC said as she took another sip. "I have zero idea what's in this, and you know what? I don't care."

"What's yours called?" Daphne asked. "Skylar and I both got a Mango Madness."

"That's island speak for *no leaves*," Skylar added.

KC licked the side of her cup. "Mine is Taste Explosion. That's a pretty accurate description of what's going on in my mouth right now."

Skylar studied her mostly orange-colored smoothie. "Can you imagine if these had alcohol in them? Maybe that's another business we should explore along with the mango sangrias." Then she looked at Daphne. "So you survived the workout?"

Daphne groaned. "*Survived* being the operative word. It wasn't pretty."

"Please, you did great." KC lightly punched Daphne's arm.

"Ouch." Daphne covered the spot with her hand. "I'm fragile, remember?"

KC laughed, then looked at Skylar. "Maybe you can go for a run with us tomorrow?"

Skylar shrugged. "We'll see. I may have another conference call."

"For real?" Daphne asked. "Or are you just avoiding the torture chamber?"

"I take offense at that," KC said.

Skylar sipped her smoothie. "Depends on what I hear from a few people on my team later today. But I'd rather not think about work right now. I suggest we go back to the house and relax on the beach for a while, then shower and head to the center of town for some lunch and shopping."

"Shopping?" KC did not look thrilled. "What about our deal that was declared null and void?"

"C'mon, tomboy, throw me a bone, okay? I promise it won't be that bad. Plus, we're going dancing tonight, remember? Maybe you can find something fun to wear. And I *definitely* want to see you in something girlie for Daphne's birthday dinner. I'm thinking pink. And flowers. Maybe even a bow. Although I'm kidding about the bow."

KC ran her fingers over the bill of her baseball cap. "Can I wear this with a dress?"

"Only if you want to be eating alone. Daphne, what say you? You up for a trip into town?"

Daphne nodded. "Sounds good to me, although just to warn you, I may need to sit down on a bench at some point, or maybe lie down when we get back. My body is already rebelling from what I just put it through." She put a hand on her lower back and grimaced.

Skylar smiled and stood up. "Lying down is what the *beach* is for, my dear. Now let's get a move on. The golden tan I don't have is waiting for me to claim it."

Together they headed back toward the house, flip-flops in hand, their feet ankle deep in the clear water. The sun was hot but not unbearably so, a cool breeze dancing across the shore. There were a fair number of people sunbathing on the soft sand and frolicking in the gentle waves near the smoothie hut and neighboring area, but the farther they got from the hotels marking the center of town, the less crowded the beach became. For a stretch it was just the three of them, and they strolled in a brief yet comfortable silence. As she admired the quiet beauty surrounding them, Daphne thought about what had happened as they'd covered the same route after dinner, how she'd finally opened up—and the sky didn't come crashing down.

She glanced up at the handful of clouds swirling above them. Were they due for another rainstorm soon? *I hope so.*

"Any word from Emma?" KC asked Daphne.

"I got a text. Sounds like she's having fun, although it makes me nervous that she's in a different state without me."

"Try not to worry so much. She's with her *father*, not a gang of convicted felons. It's not like she's going to get into any trouble," KC said.

"I know, but still, it's hard. As I'm sure you've noticed, when it comes to Emma, I'm kind of a worrier."

"I can't believe you have a teenage daughter," Skylar said. "Did you freak when she got her period?"

Daphne coughed out a laugh. "You have no idea. I'm still a little traumatized."

KC gestured toward the ocean. "Remember how traumatic going swimming used to be before we started using tampons?"

"I've never used anything but tampons," Skylar said.

KC looked at her. "Even in the beginning? In the beginning I was way too scared to try them."

Skylar shook her head. "I have older sisters, remember? From day one they refused to let me use a pad, said it was like straddling a surfboard."

Daphne laughed. "That's a pretty accurate description. A little too graphic for my taste, but accurate."

"My sisters don't sugarcoat things," Skylar said. "Hard as it may be to imagine, I'm the soft one in my family."

"Hey, check it out." KC pointed down the beach to what appeared to be a game of touch football.

The trio came to a stop about thirty feet away from the action, which looked a little rowdy and not all that organized, yet quite fun. A pair of wireless speakers set on a beach towel played reggae music, providing a tropical, low-key backdrop that belied the very American competition playing out on the sand.

"Babe alert," Skylar said under her breath.

"Which one?" KC asked.

"Take your pick," Skylar said with a little whistle.

Daphne scanned the group. Of at least a dozen men running here and there, none caught her eye until she spotted a familiar face.

It belonged to Clay Hanson.

She immediately smoothed a hand over her ponytail and found herself wishing she didn't feel quite so . . . frumpy. Skylar was wearing a pretty green sundress and looked as put-together as ever, but she and KC were still in their sweaty workout gear. She knew it was silly to care about her appearance, but she did.

Sure, Clay was a few years younger than she was, but there was just something about him that made her want to look . . . *attractive.* Or at least more attractive than she felt right then.

She glanced at the tote bag she was carrying. It contained sunscreen, two bottles of water, her wallet, a visor, a pair of sunglasses, and a beach towel. As always, she'd brought an assortment of practical items with her, *mom* items that were of absolutely zero use to her right now. No lip gloss or blusher, not even a hairbrush.

"Now *that* guy's hot," Skylar said in a hushed voice.

Daphne looked up from her bag and wondered which one Skylar was talking about. Her eyes surveyed the section of beach the group had carved out as their playing field. A dozen or so shirtless men running across it, barefoot on the sand, most of them appearing to be in pretty good—if not extremely good—shape. Only a couple of them had any trace of a beer belly, and just one of them appeared to be losing his hair. She wondered which ones were married, or if any of them had children. By the time Daphne was in her late twenties, she had a daughter in school, but she knew that wasn't typical.

The guys were playing seven on seven, all of them horsing around and clearly having a ball, acting like overgrown versions of the kids they weren't anymore. They were using a bright green Nerf ball, the likes of which Daphne hadn't seen in years, and which brought back a few childhood memories of her own. During her elementary school years, flag football with a Nerf ball had been a popular lunchtime activity, right up there with Red Rover, dodgeball, jump rope, and marbles. She'd never been very good at flag football or dodgeball, but she'd *dominated* at marbles.

"If they were playing volleyball, I'd swear we'd died and gone to heaven," Skylar said.

"Good call," KC said.

Daphne snapped back to the present. "Are you referring to that scene in *Top Gun*?"

Skylar smiled and pushed her sunglasses on top of her head. "You bet I am."

"Best scene ever," KC said.

"There's a surfeit of toned skin out here, I'll give you that," Daphne said.

KC looked at her sideways. "Does that have anything to do with surfing?"

Daphne laughed. "Just means there are a lot of fit bodies in front of us."

"Should we go around them?" KC pointed to the water, then looped her finger up toward the houses. "I'd hate to interrupt their game."

Skylar put a hand out to stop KC. "What's the rush? I say we stay and enjoy the view for a while."

KC laughed. "Okay then, stay and enjoy the view it is."

"I'm not opposed to that," Daphne said with a slight smile. *What's the harm in looking?*

"Nor *should* you be opposed to it," Skylar said. "Let's get a little closer."

The three of them inched their way toward the group, not wanting to draw attention to themselves. Once they were in earshot of what the players were saying, it became apparent that the chatter had much more to do with heckling than discussing the score or rules of the game.

"Come on now, Bates! My grandmother could have caught that!"

"I'm sorry, Wilson, did you say something? I can't hear such a high-pitched voice."

"Eric, dude, could you be any slower? You're like a dial-up Internet connection for chrissake."

KC grinned and put her hands on her hips. "These guys are awesome. They remind me of my brothers. Josh and Jared would fit right in too."

"Awesome and *cute*. I like the quarterback. I wonder what his story is." Skylar gestured to a tall, dark-haired guy in hunter-green board shorts. From that distance Daphne couldn't tell if he was wearing a wedding ring. Then again, given what she'd recently learned from Skylar about married men, that probably didn't mean much.

"They could pass for a boy band shooting a video, although it would be a pretty large band," KC said. Then she looked around the surrounding beach area. "I wonder why they're all here? I don't see any significant others cheering them on."

"Bachelor party," Daphne said.

Skylar and KC both looked at her.

"Is that a guess?" Skylar asked. "Or do you know something we don't?"

Daphne pointed at Clay, then up toward the deck. "I met the tall guy in the blue shorts yesterday when I was taking a walk on the beach. A bunch of them are staying in that house."

Skylar checked it out. "Nice place. I wonder which one is getting married?"

"I have no idea. Clay's the only one I met. He was on the deck by himself."

Skylar turned to watch the game again. "I hope it's not the quarterback."

"We could always just ask them," KC said.

Daphne felt her cheeks turn red. "Oh, I don't think we should."

"Why not?"

"Because they're so much, you know, *younger* than we are," Daphne said.

"So? Who cares?" KC looked puzzled.

Skylar put a hand on KC's shoulder. "I think what she's trying to say is that if we approach a big group of younger guys and ask them which one of them is getting married, it will make us look like cougars."

"Like what?" KC looked even more confused now.

"Cougars." Skylar made a clawing motion with her fingernails. "You know, older women who prey on younger men."

KC opened her eyes wide. "That's really a word?"

"Where have you been?" Skylar asked. "That's been a word for years."

KC frowned. "Well, it doesn't sound very nice."

Daphne nodded. "I agree. I don't like that term. I think it's disrespectful to women."

"I'm not particularly fond of it either, but I didn't make it up," Skylar said with a shrug.

"You date younger men," KC said to Skylar. "So you're a cougar?"

Skylar shook her head. "I date them, but only if they approach *me*. Big difference, at least in my opinion."

"Is there a term for men who date younger women?" KC asked.

Skylar laughed and put her hand on top of KC's head. "Yes, my tiny friend. It's usually called *rich*."

KC pushed Skylar's hand away, but she was laughing. "*Hey now*, I think my husband would take offense to that."

Skylar laughed too. "Then don't tell him."

Now Daphne was also laughing. She glanced up at the sky. *It feels so good to laugh like this.*

Just then a stray football came flying their way. KC bent down to pick it up, then effortlessly tossed it back to the group in a perfect spiral.

"Wow," yelled the blond guy who caught it. "Nice arm." He looked genuinely impressed.

KC smiled and adjusted her baseball cap. "Thanks! I played a little as a kid!" she yelled back.

Skylar chuckled. "Of course you did."

The majority of the players were now looking at Daphne and her friends from afar, Clay included. He clapped some sand off his hands and waved. "Hey, Daphne White, good to see you again!" he yelled.

She waved back and forced herself to yell loud enough for him to hear her, although she could feel her cheeks burning at the attention. "Hi, Clay Hanson!"

"You and he are on first- *and* last-name basis?" Skylar said. "Well done, *Daphne White.*"

"Please behave," Daphne whispered back to her.

Skylar slipped her sunglasses back over her eyes. "Clay *Handsome*, is it?"

"Clay *Hanson*," Daphne said, still in a whisper. "And please keep your voice down."

Skylar smiled without looking at her. "You call him whatever you like, and I'll do the same. All I'm saying is that he's quite the eye candy, and it's been a long time since you've visited the candy store."

KC rubbed her hands together and grinned. "Can I just say I'm *loving* hanging out with you two again?"

·　·　·

"Halftime!" someone called out, and the game quickly broke up as nearly everyone headed up to the deck, where a large red cooler filled with ice-cold bottles of water—and beers—awaited.

Two players stayed behind. One was the blond who had caught KC's throw. The other was Clay. They chatted with each other for a moment, then turned and began walking toward Daphne, Skylar, and KC. When Daphne realized what they were doing, she swallowed and hoped her friends wouldn't say anything to embarrass her. *He's coming over here!*

As if reading her mind, Skylar patted Daphne's arm. "Don't worry," she said under her breath.

"Thank you," Daphne said, her voice hushed.

"Great game," Skylar said in a normal decibel as Clay and the blond approached.

"Thanks," Clay said with an easy smile. Then he looked at Daphne but pointed the Nerf ball at KC as he spoke again. "I gotta say, your friend here could show you a thing or two about throwing."

"*Both* my friends here could show me a thing or two about a *lot* of things," Daphne said with a smile of her own, one that didn't feel as forced as she feared it would be. "This is KC, and this is Skylar."

"Clay Hanson." He shook both their hands, then gestured to his pal. "This is Doug Bates."

"Ah, *Bates*, the one who runs slower than a grandmother," KC said with a slow nod.

Doug pretended to stab himself in the heart. "Coming from someone with an arm like yours, that hurts."

Skylar narrowed her eyes at Clay, but not in an unfriendly way. "Do you always speak to people using first and last names?"

Clay laughed and scratched the top of his head. "Sorry, force of habit. I meet a lot of people through work."

"What do you do?" Skylar asked.

"I'm in finance. Nothing too exciting. Doug here's the one with the cool job." He patted his friend on the shoulder.

"Oh yeah? What would that be?" Skylar looked at Doug.

"I'm the host of a sports talk radio show."

KC's face lit up. "Did you just say sports talk radio? I *love* sports talk radio!"

"Doesn't he have the perfect face for radio?" Clay said.

"Shut it, pretty boy," Doug said, punching Clay's arm.

"That's my husband's dream job," KC said.

Clay punched Doug's arm back. "It's pretty much *every* guy's dream job. Lucky bastard."

"What can I say? Someone has to do it. So what brings you three to St. Mirika?" Doug asked them.

"Just a girls' reunion," Skylar said. "What about you?"

Daphne glanced at Skylar, amazed at how she was able to pose the question without giving any indication that she already knew the answer.

"Bachelor party." Doug turned toward the deck and pointed at a sandy-blond-haired man standing next to the quarterback Skylar had been eyeing. "That's the betrothed over there."

"Which one?" Skylar asked casually.

She's so smooth, Daphne thought. No wonder she was so good at her job.

"See Scott, the tall, dark-haired guy who was playing quarterback? It's the one standing next to him. His name's Perry," Doug said.

"*Perry?* That's fancy," Skylar said. With the guys' backs briefly turned to them, she discreetly gave Daphne's arm a little squeeze, then leaned toward her and whispered. "I'm calling him *Hot Scott.*"

Daphne smiled. For now at least, the quarterback was still in the game. *This is fun.*

Clay turned around. "It's a family name. We rib him about it all the time." Then he gestured toward their makeshift football field. So you three want to join us for the second half? We could use some fresh legs out there."

"Fresh legs?" Skylar gave him a skeptical look. "I don't mean to sound rude, but from what I saw, it didn't look like anyone was running all that hard."

"They were running harder than you were," Daphne said to her.

"I'll take that," Skylar said with a shrug.

Doug laughed. "Wanting fresh legs is code for *some of the guys want to stop playing and start drinking.*"

"I think 'some' is probably an understatement," Clay said.

"They want to start drinking already? But it's not even lunchtime." KC looked a little horrified.

Skylar patted her shoulder. "We're on island time, Missy Franklin. Relax. No one here's training for the Olympics."

"So what do you say?" Clay asked KC. "We all saw that arm, so you can't pretend you don't know how to play."

KC grinned and raised her hand. "Okay, I'm in! Can I play quarterback?"

Doug snatched the Nerf ball from Clay, kneeled down, and handed it to her. "You took the words right out of my mouth—well, not exactly—but you know what I mean. It would be an honor." Then he looked up at Skylar and Daphne. "What about you two? Up for a scrimmage?"

Daphne swallowed. She was decently coordinated but hadn't played touch football since . . . how long had it been . . . *elementary school*? "Um . . ."

"Come on, Daphne," Clay said. "It will be fun. You can be on my team."

"Go ahead." Skylar gave her a nudge. "I'll watch. That will keep the numbers even."

KC pinched Skylar's waist. "Way to weasel out of it."

Skylar laughed. "I'm just being helpful. No one likes to play with odd numbers, and besides, I'm not dressed for it. Now go, scat." She gave Daphne another push.

"Okay, why not?" Daphne smiled weakly. *I hope I don't regret this.* She was proud of herself for trying something new—while simultaneously terrified that she'd make a fool of herself.

"Come on up to the deck, we'll introduce you to the crew." Clay waved the three of them toward the house. A few of the guys were already drinking beers, but most were drinking bottled water. Clay raised his voice. "Everyone, this is KC, Daphne, and Skylar."

An assortment of greetings filled the air as the guys waved back.

"Where'd you learn to throw like that?" Perry called to KC.

"I have brothers." She held up three fingers.

Skylar put her arm around KC. "Don't underestimate this one. She's tiny, but she's also not human. It's only a matter of time before some government scientist shows up and hauls her away for research."

KC leaned her head against Skylar's shoulder. "Aw, thanks."

Doug pointed to KC and Daphne, then to Skylar. "These two are going to join the game in the second half, and this one wants a beer." He looked at Skylar. "That was an assumption about your wanting a beer, but a correct one I hope?"

"Very correct," she said with a strong nod. "You're good. If you ever want to get out of the radio business and explore the world of sales, give me a call. I'm always looking for talented people."

Doug laughed. "I'll keep that in mind."

"Good. Now beer me, please," she said.

Scott quickly leaned over the railing and handed Skylar a frosty bottle. "I gotcha. Skylar, was it?"

"Yes, and you are . . . ?" She looked up and took the bottle with a casual smile and a subtle bat of the eyelashes, again providing no hint that she was already well aware of his name. Daphne watched her friend in action and felt like she was taking a clinic in how to remain calm, cool, and collected in any social situation. *I need to learn from her.*

She glanced at her tote bag and again wished it didn't look so . . . practical, if not downright maternal. At least it didn't have a sippy cup and little plastic bags filled with Cheerios inside.

Doug clapped his hands together a few times and shouted. "Okay people, let's get moving. Lactic acid's a bitch; can't let it build up."

KC smiled up at him, her eyes bright. "You know what lactic acid is?"

He tapped his temple. "I'm a radio personality. My entire profession is based on knowing just enough to make people think I know a hell of a lot more than I actually do."

She put her hand up for a high five. "My husband would love you."

After a few minutes most of the players had come down from the deck to reassemble the teams and prepare to start the second half. Daphne, who was now standing next to Clay, bit her lip. "I hope I'm not too much of a weak link." She pointed to KC, who was already on the beach, jogging in place and stretching. "If you haven't already noticed, Mia Hamm over there's the athlete of our trio."

"Hey, don't be stealing my nicknames," Skylar said to her.

Daphne turned her head. "Have you already called her Mia Hamm this trip? I've lost track."

Skylar took a sip of her beer. "Well, if I hadn't yet, I would have at some point this week. That one's definitely in my rotation."

Daphne laughed. "You and your rotations."

Skylar winked at her. "Don't be knocking my systems."

Clay gestured toward the rest of the group. "I don't think you have much to worry about. Half the guys are still recovering from last night, and the other half are in terrible shape. We're getting old."

Daphne smiled to herself. *That's what* you *think.*

Ignoring the last part of his comment, Skylar calmly took a sip of her beer. "What did your gang do last night that requires recovery?" She directed the question to Clay but turned her gaze to an approaching Scott, who was among the last to arrive from the deck.

"We went to the Castaway," Clay said.

Skylar raised her eyebrows. "How was it? We were supposed to go, but these two pansies said they needed their beauty sleep." She gestured to Daphne and then to KC, who was now jogging in place about twenty feet away.

"It was fun, definitely the most happening spot in this part of the island," Scott said. "I'm sure we'll end up there again tonight if you want to come check it out."

"Then maybe we'll see you there. Even if I have to drag these two by their ponytails, we're going out tonight. They already promised me. *Right*, Daphne?"

Daphne protectively reached for the back of her neck, imagining what that would feel like. "Right."

"Can I grab you another brew or some water before we kick off again?" Scott asked Skylar as he pointed toward the deck.

Skylar smiled at him. "A water would be lovely, thanks. I'll join you."

As Scott and Skylar made their way up toward the house, Clay watched after them for a moment, then looked at Daphne. "She's a spirited one, isn't she?"

Daphne nodded. "You have no idea. You do *not* want to get on her bad side."

"Well, for the record, I think it worked," he said.

She turned and looked up at him. "You think what worked?"

"The beauty sleep you got last night. Now come on, let's go play some football." He jogged onto the beach.

Before she could react, KC yelled and waved for her to join them. "Come on, Daphne!" Doug was standing next to her now.

Daphne kept her head down as she walked quickly toward the sandy field, hoping no one could see how much Clay's comment had just made her blush.

Or how good it had made her feel.

•   •   •

Daphne and KC played the entire second half of the game, which lasted a hair over thirty minutes before everyone decided to throw in the towel and head back to the deck—and the cooler of beers sitting on it. Daphne successfully met her modest goals of (a) not getting hurt and (b) not embarrassing herself. She also had much more fun than she expected to. Once the game got going, she didn't feel self-conscious about the age gap between her and KC and the guys, and she was surprised by how friendly the players on both teams were to her. She caught three passes and only dropped one, so for her, it was a resounding victory, even though her team lost.

While Daphne was thrilled just to have made it through the game unscathed, KC, on the other hand, stole the show from the opening drive. Her athletic prowess impressed not just Doug, but anyone who knew anything about football. Not only did she throw multiple touchdowns from the quarterback position, but on the last play of the game she discreetly changed roles with Doug to move to wide receiver. Under normal circumstances she wouldn't have been able to outrun anyone on the other team—except for Daphne, of course, whose job to that point had been to watch for a quarterback sneak. The surprising switch caught the other team on their heels, and Daphne on the wrong part of the field, or, more accurately, the wrong part of the sandpit. Terminology notwithstanding, the momentary confusion allowed KC to run down the beach unimpeded—and catch the winning pass unguarded. Once she was safely inside the end zone, she chucked the green Nerf ball high in the air, then plowed straight into the water, diving headfirst under a wave in celebration. Her team quickly followed, all of them splashing and hooting and hollering. The team began to pump their fists and chant: "KC! KC! KC!"

Clay and Daphne stood on the beach with their fellow teammates, watching the celebration erupt.

"She's like a goddamn hummingbird," one of the guys said.

"Amazing," another guy said.

Clay nodded. "I get tired just watching her. Where does she get all that energy?"

Daphne made the universal "I'm clueless" shrug. "She's been bouncing off the walls since the day I met her. Sometimes I think she has caffeine in her veins instead of blood."

Clay laughed. "You and she have been buddies a long time?"

She nodded. "We lived in the same dorm freshman year. Skylar too."

"Ah . . . so you're all Northwestern brainiacs," he said with a slow nod. "That explains a lot."

She cocked her head to one side. "Explains a lot about what?"

He smiled. "I'm just messing with you."

She swallowed and felt her neck get a little hot. "What about this group? How did you all meet? Or is it kind of a hodgepodge whose only connection is the groom?"

Clay put his arm around the guy standing next to him, the one who'd compared KC to a hummingbird. "The bulk of us went to business school together, and a few of the guys, like this chump here, are Perry's buddies from undergrad at Rutgers," he said.

"Do you have a fancy name too?" Daphne asked the friend.

"Hardly. I'm Steve. Doesn't get much more common than Steve."

She smiled. "I don't know about that. What about John?"

He laughed. "My last name's Johnson."

She laughed too. "Okay, you win. I can't help you." *I'm joking around with attractive younger men!*

"She sure showed them how it's done, didn't she?" a female voice called.

Daphne turned her head and saw Skylar approaching them, gesturing toward the water. "Check out our girl," Skylar said.

Daphne's eyes followed Skylar's arm. KC was now perched on top of Doug's shoulders, horsing around and hollering like one of the guys.

"I want to be like her when I grow up," Skylar said.

Clay laughed. "Me too."

"Me three," Daphne said.

As they stood there watching the revelry continue, Daphne realized that it had been a long time since she'd been surrounded by so much lightheartedness. It felt great.

Chapter Seven

After hot showers and lunch at a tiny beachside café, the three friends went window shopping along the main drag marking the center of town—a charming, picturesque area lined with winding cobblestone streets that didn't appear to follow any sort of grid or structured pattern whatsoever. Most of the buildings were quaint one-story structures, with the occasional two-story unit housing an array of assorted businesses. Daphne noticed two law firms, two dentist offices, one accounting firm, and one sign for a shared chiropractic/acupuncture outfit. The rest of the storefronts dotting the sidewalks were a mixture of restaurants, boutiques, combination coffee/dessert shops, and nail salons, their white stucco facades freshly scrubbed and practically sparkling; each roof was topped by the rounded clay caps emblematic of the Mediterranean style, and many boasted matching ceramic pots full of brightly colored flowers on the windowsills.

As they wandered the free-flowing streets and explored the tiny alleys of the hamlet, Daphne felt like she was in another era, light years away from Grandview Heights. Had she really been out of Ohio for only two days?

Most of the storefronts they encountered presented modest, tasteful window dressings. A handful, however, featured bolder offerings inside. One shoe store displayed a particularly outrageous rack of boots.

"Check those out." Daphne pointed to a thigh-high pair made with red, white, and blue snakeskin. The spiked heels looked to be at least four inches long.

Skylar held up a defensive hand. "Beyond tacky. They're clearly going for the shock value."

KC looked down at her midsection. "Those things would go up to my vagina."

Skylar laughed as they moved away from the store. "That brings new meaning to the term *shock value*." She pointed to a sundress on a mannequin in the next window, then spoke to KC. "I can't picture you in those boots, but I bet that little number would look great on you. Let's go try it on."

"Do I have to?" KC asked. "Can't we go in there instead?" She pointed to a store across the street called Ryan's Sports Shack.

"You can't possibly need more workout gear," Skylar said. "C'mon, show some estrogen for once and try on a pretty dress for me?"

KC sighed. "Okay, fine. Will you at least work out with me if I try it on? A dress *up* for a work*out*?"

"Perhaps . . . definitely maybe . . . we'll see." Skylar opened the door to the boutique. "But first, let's see that baby on you."

The three of them ducked inside the pleasant yet slightly cramped shop, and Skylar and Daphne perused the jewelry display while KC took the dress to the tiny fitting room in the back.

"You doing okay today?" Skylar asked, her voice a bit hushed. "You seem to be, but I don't want to push."

Daphne picked up a dangly gold earring and held it to one ear in front of a mirror. "I'm doing much better than yesterday, but given where I was yesterday, that's not saying a lot."

"It'll take time. I'm just glad you finally opened up to us. I knew there was something off with you, right from when we met at the airport, but I wanted to wait until you were ready to talk about it."

Daphne looked at her. "You did?" She thought she'd done a pretty good job of concealing how she was really feeling. Maybe not a spectacular job, but a decent job.

Skylar nodded. "It was pretty clear something was eating at you."

"How so?"

Skylar sorted through a rack of colorful beaded necklaces. "The best way I can think to explain it is that you didn't seem like yourself. You seemed, I don't know . . . *vanilla.*"

Daphne didn't respond, but her eyes said, *Could you elaborate?*

"You know, a little bland, a little going through the motions, which is unlike you," Skylar said.

Daphne frowned. Vanilla *was* the perfect word for how she'd been feeling. For way too long. *And I'm supposed to be the one who's good with words.*

Skylar held up a necklace for inspection. "One of the things I've always loved about you is how *engaged* you are, Daphne. I don't mean bouncing off the walls like KC, but that you have a spark about you, you know?"

Daphne nodded slowly. Skylar was right. *What happened to that part of me?*

Skylar returned the necklace and put a hand on Daphne's arm. "I know the old Daphne is in there somewhere—I've seen little glimpses of her today. We just need to figure out how to get her back full-time."

Daphne felt a few tears welling up in her eyes, but for the first time in a long time, they weren't entirely tears of sadness. They were also tears of optimism.

"Please don't give up on me, Skylar," she whispered.

Skylar shook her head. "Never. I'm a bulldog, remember? I don't give up on anything I care about, and I care a *lot* about you."

"Thank you," Daphne said as she wiped a tear from her eye.

"Okay, pals, what do you think?"

They both turned their heads at the sound of KC's voice at the back of the store. She took off her baseball cap and flung it at her friends, then held out her arms and did a little twirl.

Daphne caught the baseball hat and carefully tucked it into her tote bag for safekeeping. She also removed a tissue and discreetly dabbed at the remaining tears.

"Well? Am I a Greek goddess?" KC shimmied her hips side to side, runway-style. The white dress she had on had spaghetti straps with thick horizontal pink stripes.

Skylar chuckled and covered her mouth with her hand. "I know I picked it out, so hate to say this, but you kind of look like a candy striper."

KC looked crushed. "Darn. For real? I was kind of digging it. The stretchy material is supercomfy."

Skylar turned to Daphne. "Back me up here?"

Daphne shook her head. "I'm sorry, but I'm with Skylar on this one. I feel like I'm in a hospital right now."

KC held up her palms in surrender, then turned on her heel and mock-stormed into the dressing room with a laugh. "Okay, fine. But don't say I didn't try!"

"Now we know who to go to if we need some first aid, though," Skylar called after her.

"Wow, she really did look like a teenybopper in that thing," Daphne said. "From the neck down she could have passed for one of Emma's friends."

Skylar began sifting through the dress rack. "We'll find her something. I'm determined to put a little salsa in that señora if it kills me. So speaking of Emma, earlier you said she was in Utah. Is it her spring break?"

Daphne hesitated before replying. "Yes, she's in Park City with Brian . . . and Alyssa." *All three of them. Together. Get used to it.*

Skylar saw the strain on Daphne's face. "I gather this is the first time she's gone on a real vacation with Alyssa?"

Daphne nodded. "The first of many, I suppose. Alyssa's got all kinds of money."

"That might not be a bad thing. Sometimes traveling opens the mind a lot more than a textbook can," Skylar said.

"I know. I just need to get used to the idea that there's another mother figure in her life now. I hate that."

"I'm sorry, hon. You know it'll get easier, right?"

Daphne sighed. "I know. I just want it to get easier faster."

Skylar smiled. "There's that wit. But you'll adapt. That's the roughest part of anything difficult, getting used to it."

KC appeared next to them. "Okay, my personal shoppers, have you found me anything else, or am I off the hook?"

Skylar held up another white sundress, this one strapless and embroidered with tiny blue-and-green flowers. "Try this one. It's supercute."

"You want *me* to try on a *strapless* dress?" KC asked.

"Did I stutter?" Skylar said.

Daphne reached for the dress. "Wait a minute. I think this is the same pattern as my duvet cover at the beach house."

"It is?" Skylar held the hanger up and studied it. "My duvet cover's white with blue swirls."

Daphne nodded. "It's *exactly* the same as mine. This dress could have been made from the same fabric."

KC grabbed for the dress. "That's awesome! I could lie on your bed wearing this and I would be completely camouflaged. Strapless or not, that alone is worth seeing if it fits."

She skipped into the dressing room, and Skylar and Daphne watched her.

"She really is like a kid," Skylar said.

·   ·   ·

After an afternoon of shopping and wandering around town, they returned to the beach house, a bit tired, sunned out, and ready for some downtime before dinner. KC ducked into her room for a nap, saying she was too wiped out even to make herself disappear on Daphne's bed wearing her new dress.

Skylar had to dial into yet another conference call and quickly settled at the desk in the living room. "I feel like this is my office," she groaned as she reached for her headset.

"At least you have a nice view, right?" Daphne said.

"That's the spirit." Skylar chuckled and put on the headset. "Now shush, I need to switch gears into professional mode."

Despite all the activity of the day, Daphne wasn't feeling sleepy, so she decided to go for another walk on the beach, this time in the opposite direction. She and KC had explored a sliver of that stretch during their workout, but she was interested to see what else lay beyond the patch they'd covered.

Before leaving the house, she popped into her bedroom to check her phone—which she'd left plugged in on the dresser while they were out shopping—to see if Emma had returned her text from earlier in the day. The screen was blank.

Daphne frowned. While a part of her hoped her daughter's lack of communication was because she was having too much fun on her vacation to even think about her phone, a bigger part of her hoped it was due to poor cell reception. She felt a bit self-centered admitting that to herself, but it was true. She missed her daughter, and she wanted her daughter to miss her back. At least a little bit.

She set the phone down on the dresser, then reached for her straw hat and tote bag and quietly made her way into the kitchen so as not to disturb Skylar's call. She heard snippets as she retrieved a bottle of water from the refrigerator and tiptoed through the living room toward the French doors, the sound of Skylar's fingers flying over the keyboard providing a musical backdrop to the conversation.

"Walk on the beach," Daphne mouthed the words and pointed to the ocean.

"Sounds *bueno*," Skylar whispered with a quick smile, then immediately returned her focus to the conference call. Daphne was amazed at her ability to slip in and out of worlds so seamlessly.

Daphne gently closed the glass doors behind her, then walked across the deck and glanced up at the cloudless blue sky. She'd applied and reapplied sunscreen a couple times already, but she could still feel her fair skin burning in the hot sun. She hunted inside her tote bag for a bottle of sunblock and her sunglasses, sprayed herself down one more time, then put on the straw hat and glasses and made her way down the steps. Once off the deck, she removed her flip-flops to enjoy the feel of the beach between her toes, but it was too hot for her skin, so she quickly trotted down to the shore. The clear green water felt soothing on her bare feet, the wet sand soft.

She took a quick look back at the deck, then set off on her walk.

●　　●　　●

After wandering quietly for a few minutes, Daphne noticed that the houses lining the beach were becoming more secluded, the gaps between them noticeably larger. Soon what she was passing no longer qualified as *houses* so much as mansions. Or full-blown estates.

Each one seemed to be more stunning than the next. The architecture differed from structure to structure, but nearly all of the residences were white. To Daphne the collective effect was reminiscent of the pristine, shingled, white-and-gray houses of Nantucket.

It was simply . . . beautiful.

Daphne stopped and put her hands on her waist, gazing up at one of the mansions. These were clearly the vacation homes of the über rich, toys of those so wealthy there was no need to even consider renting them out. It was hard to fathom that kind of wealth. She was still getting used to the gorgeous place Skylar's boss was kindly letting them borrow. The house she was staring at right then was from another world entirely. She wondered what that type of life would be like. Were the people who owned it happy? The popular refrain said that money can't buy happiness, but Brian had always told Daphne that he wondered if whoever had coined that saying didn't have a lot of money.

"How could you not be happy if you were rich?" he would say. She'd never really challenged him about it, but looking back now, she saw the comment for what it was—a reflection of his immaturity, of his relatively shallow values.

Come to think of it, she'd never challenged him on most of what he said. *I used to think he was wise just because he was five years older, but he wasn't even thirty when we met.* Oh, how her perspective on age had changed.

She turned around to look out at the ocean. A memory of Skylar's comment from earlier flickered to life: she'd described Daphne as *vanilla*.

It had stung to hear Skylar choose that word to describe her, but Skylar was right. It had been gradual, but over many years of pouring her energy into her daughter's activities, of struggling to calm the waters with Brian, of smoothing the way for everyone *else* to be happy, Daphne had lost track of what made *her* happy. And it wasn't money.

When she and Brian had met, she'd loved dancing and traveling and taking chances. She loved staying up late and drinking wine and laughing over lively conversation. She loved exploring and wandering and wondering. All the seeds for a picture-perfect future were there, but then everything started to change. Daphne began to wonder what their marriage would have been like, what her *life* would have been like, if he'd just . . .

She balled her hands into fists. *Stop thinking about it. It's over.*

She glanced up again at the extravagant house, then picked up a rock and hurled it into the ocean, farther than she had yesterday. As it sailed through the air, she was surprised to hear herself repeat the thought out loud—as a shout. "It's *over!*"

She watched the rock hit the water, making a small splash that quickly disappeared. Almost immediately the sea regained its smooth veneer, leaving no trace of the rock or its impact. Daphne stood there for a few moments, then checked her watch and decided it was time to head back to the beach house. She took a deep breath and felt a jolt of buoyancy as she exhaled. *It's time for more in my life. No more vanilla.*

Skylar would be proud.

•   •   •

"Hey, woman, how was the walk?" Skylar greeted Daphne with a broad smile. She was still sitting at the desk in the living room, her headset now dangling around her neck.

Daphne pointed outside toward the new swath of beach she'd just explored. "Gorgeous. I think we're at the tail end of a ritzy neighborhood. Some of the houses that way are unbelievable."

Skylar closed her laptop, then removed her headset. "So I've been told. That's a glimpse into how the other half lives."

Daphne laughed and looked around the expansive living room. "Like we have it so bad. This place is amazing."

"Hey, I'm not knocking it or complaining in any way. I'm just speaking the truth, which is that I'm well aware that our current digs are hardly extravagant. Some of the estates along that part of the island have their own helipads."

"Well, for *me*, this place is certainly extravagant. But I agree that it's just because I haven't been exposed to the lavish things you have. You're pretty much the only high roller I know." She knew Brian's parents were well-off, but she couldn't imagine their flying all over the world like Skylar did. They were too reserved to actually *enjoy* their money.

Skylar shrugged. "Extravagance is relative. Trust me, my life in New York is far from the upper echelons. You ready for a drink?"

Daphne glanced at the kitchen. "I don't know if I can do alcohol yet. I think I need some coffee, to be honest. I should have followed KC's lead and taken a nap."

Skylar waved a finger at her. "Don't even think about pulling the rip cord early again tonight. You promised, remember? And if there's one thing I admire more than your vocabulary, it's that you never break a promise. It's hard to get you to *make* one, but once you do, I know it's golden."

"I know, I know: enough with the guilt. I'm well aware that I told you I would rally tonight, thus the suggestion of a caffeine infusion. Is KC still passed out?"

"I think she's in the shower."

"When do we need to leave for dinner?"

Skylar glanced at her watch. "In about an hour. Just enough time for you to shower and change and have a cocktail with us on the deck. After your caffeine infusion, of course."

Daphne nodded. "Got it."

"Did I hear someone say something about a cocktail on the deck? I feel like a new person after that power nap."

Skylar and Daphne both looked toward the hall. KC was standing there, her wet hair pulled back into a ponytail. She wore a pair of cutoffs and a bright teal T-shirt that read "St. Mirika!" in white lettering.

Skylar held up her forearm as if to shield her eyes. "What in the name of Holy Jesus are you wearing?"

KC glanced down at the shirt. "Isn't this great? I bought it when you two were in that jewelry store."

"Why is it *shouting* at us?" Daphne asked.

KC laughed. "I have *no idea*, but I love it."

"What happened to that adorable white dress with the flowers?" Skylar said.

"I thought that was for Daphne's birthday dinner."

"Then what about the dress you brought with you?" Skylar asked.

KC shrugged. "I can't find it in my suitcase. I must have forgotten to pack it." She glanced down at her shirt. "No worries, though. I'll just go with this."

Skylar covered her eyes with her palm. "God help us."

KC grinned and raised a hand in the air. "So what about that cocktail? I'm in!"

Chapter Eight

"What's the plan for tomorrow?" KC sipped her rum punch, then set it down as the waiter handed her a dessert menu. "And you'd better not say shopping. I already paid those dues."

Skylar gave Daphne a look. "What is wrong with her? Who doesn't like shopping? It's like not liking chocolate. Or sleeping. Or breathing. It's just not natural."

Daphne smiled and took a sip of her drink. "Don't ask me. I gave up trying to understand what makes her tick about a week after we met. It was easier just to watch her run around like a wind-up toy."

KC rubbed her hands together. "*So*, what's on the docket? Doug told me about some gorgeous cliffs on the other side of the island. Should we go check them out? Or maybe go zip-lining? Do they have that here? Or parasailing? I've always wanted to try something high-flying like that." She turned toward Daphne, her eyes bright. "Any of those would be a killer way to celebrate your birthday, don't you think?"

"I guess so," Daphne practically mumbled, not wanting to let on how much the idea of anything *high-flying* frightened her.

"I'm exhausted just listening to that list," Skylar said. "Did you know that some people go on vacation to relax?"

Daphne was grateful for Skylar's objection. When she was younger, she hadn't been so scared of heights, had she? She didn't think so.

"Well, we have to do something adventurous to ring in Daphne's fortieth," KC said, then leaned over and patted Daphne's arm. "Maybe we'll kick it off with a nice run on the beach."

"Can we call an audible on that?" Daphne asked. "After today I'm afraid to find out how much my body's going to hurt when I wake up. I'm already feeling it."

"A little soreness is good," KC said. "It's like a receipt for your hard work."

"We'll see," Daphne said. *Is this what it feels like to get old?* She glanced at the dessert menu, wondering how much time she had left before she'd be reaching inside her purse for her own pair of reading glasses.

Skylar tapped her fingernail against her drink. "If *I* have anything to say about it, your muscles won't be the only thing hurting in the morning." She gestured to the waiter for another pitcher.

"Oh no," Daphne said. "More rum punch?"

"Oh yes," Skylar nodded. "More rum punch."

"Oh mama," KC groaned.

"Oh shush," Skylar said.

KC looked at Skylar. "Anyhow, back to tomorrow. What are we doing? You still haven't told us the plan, but I know you have one. You *always* have one."

Skylar paused to let the waiter set a fresh pitcher on the table. When he was gone, she refilled their glasses, then picked up her drink and smiled. "You are correct. I've made arrangements for us to spend the afternoon at the nicest spa on the island."

Daphne's ears perked up. "A spa?" She hadn't been to a spa in ages. *I could use some pampering.*

"There's a pretty famous one on the island called Serendipity, and from what I've seen, it's gorgeous. I booked us each a facial and a massage, my treat."

"You don't have to do that," Daphne said.

"Please. I *want* to. I've been itching for a fancy spa trip myself lately, so it's not like my motives are purely altruistic."

Daphne smiled. "Okay then, you can treat."

"Where is it?" KC asked. "Will it take all day?"

"It's at the Four Seasons on the north shore, but God forbid you spend an *entire day* relaxing, so I thought we could stop at the monkey forest on the way. How does that sound?" Skylar said.

KC pumped her fist in the air. "Now we're talking!"

Skylar pressed a palm against her forehead. "Only you would be more excited at the idea of seeing a monkey than of getting deluxe spa treatments."

KC grinned. "Come on, even *you* have to admit that going to a monkey forest sounds awesome."

Skylar shrugged. "Okay, I'll take that. Who doesn't like a good monkey?"

"How does it work?" Daphne asked. "Is it like a zoo?"

Skylar shook her head. "Not at all. The monkeys run around completely free, no cages or anything. You can even feed them bananas if you want. They sell them right there. I've been to the one in Bali, and it's pretty cool. But you have to be careful with your sunglasses, because the monkeys will jump on your shoulder and take them right off your face."

"For real?" Daphne asked.

"Oh yes. They're not afraid of humans at all. In Bali I saw this guy holding a yellow-and-orange-striped Popsicle, and a monkey ran up and stole it right out of his hand, then bolted up a tree. The monkey must have thought it was a banana."

KC clapped her hands together. "I can't believe we're going to see real monkeys! I might not be able to sleep tonight."

Skylar shook her head slowly. "Once again, I don't know how to respond to that."

KC pointed at Skylar. "Hey, city girl, if you're allowed to dream about having someone travel with you just to make your hair pretty, I can get excited about seeing some monkeys."

"She has a good point," Daphne said to Skylar.

Skylar laughed and touched the sides of her head. "I have a lot of hair. It's hard to deal with."

KC did a little dance in her seat. "Monkeys! Woo, I'm so excited!"

Skylar looked at her askance yet again, then picked up her dessert menu. "Okay Curious Georgia, let's order something sweet, then get out of here. We need to change venues so you can re-create that move you just did on an actual dance floor. The night is young, *we* are young, and the Castaway is awaiting."

.   .   .

The Castaway was hopping. As the trio approached the entrance, they were greeted with the unmistakable music of a Jamaican steel drum, whose sound Daphne had always thought had the mystic ability to elevate the mood of everyone within earshot. The inside area of the bar was long and a bit cramped, especially near the front door, but the entire backside of the structure was open, leading onto an expansive deck area off the beach. A dance floor front and center was surrounded by cushioned chairs and love seats, the talented three-man band tucked away in a corner. A string of white paper lanterns lined the inside walls and also framed the outdoor area, wrapping the entire place in a warm, festive glow.

"I already love it here!" KC snapped her fingers and began to bob her head from side to side.

Daphne inconspicuously glanced around to inspect the demographics. The place wasn't packed, but both the inside and outside areas were quickly filling up with revelers. Inside, most people were tucked up close to the bar, chattering loudly over cocktails and rows of shot glasses. On the deck area, some couples and small groups of friends were already having fun on the dance floor, while others huddled together and watched from their seats. Still others stood by themselves or nestled in small groups, and nearly everyone swayed gently to the music. The Castaway was inviting and friendly, and as Daphne scanned the crowd, she saw faces smooth, wrinkled, and somewhere in between. She was also hard-pressed to find one that didn't have at least a hint of a smile on it.

Including hers.

Skylar ran her hand over KC's ponytail. "I completely agree. The vibe is groovy, and I don't throw that word around lightly. Now, who wants a drink? I've heard this joint has the best rum punch on the island."

KC raised her hand. "I'm in. I'm not gonna lie. I'm loving the rum punch."

Daphne shook her head. "I'm good for now."

"You sure?" Skylar gave her a look that asked, *Are you doing okay?*

Daphne smiled. "I'll have one in a little bit, I promise. For now I'll take a water."

"Okay, be right back. Why don't you grab us a place to sit if you can find one."

Skylar squeezed her way toward the bar, and as soon as she was gone, KC pinched Daphne's waist. "All good with you? You look a little uncomfortable."

Daphne smiled. "It's been a while since I've been in a scene like this, but I'm fine, really. I'm just a little tired. I should have been smart and taken a nap like you." She thought it ironic—and somewhat humorous—that her friends were now worried about her state of mind when she was finally feeling a little better about it. *I should have opened up to them a long time ago.*

"Power naps are the fountain of youth," KC said. "Twenty minutes and I feel like a new person. Sometimes, when I *really* need one, I don't even make it to the bedroom. I just lie facedown on the living room carpet."

Daphne laughed. "What?"

KC pointed to the floor. "Yep. Facedown on the carpet. Max thinks I look like a corpse, but I swear it works like a charm. You should try it sometime."

Daphne laughed again. "I'll keep that in mind." She looked out at the deck. "I can't remember the last time I went dancing. Maybe our girls' weekend in Chicago? I used to love to dance." *I used to be pretty good at it too.*

"I hear ya. Seems like I only dance at weddings these days, but I'm feeling the urge to shake my booty tonight."

Daphne put her arm around her. "Are you going to do one of your trademark moves?"

KC snapped her fingers in the air twice. "It is not beyond the scope of possibility, my friend. I guess we shall see."

"We shall see what?" Skylar returned, carefully holding three glasses of rum punch. She handed one to both KC and Daphne, then took a big sip of her own to keep it from spilling.

"What's this?" Daphne asked.

Skylar batted her eyelashes. "I'm sorry, did you not want one? I don't have the best hearing."

Daphne laughed and shook her head. "You're evil."

Skylar shrugged and lifted her drink in the air. "I'll take that. To the Three Musketeers, back together at last."

"To my last night in my thirties." Daphne raised her glass too. "Tomorrow it's all over."

Skylar rolled her eyes. "Oh please. We've been over this like a thousand times. It is *not* over. In fact, it is *far* from over. Mark my words, ladies. Forty is the new black."

KC coughed back a laugh. "Huh?"

"You heard me, Peppermint Patty."

"I thought the expression was *life begins at forty*," Daphne said.

"I like to be original," Skylar said as she pointed to KC's glass. "Now, consume."

KC lifted the glass and studied it. "What exactly is in rum punch that makes me love it so much?"

"Rum," Skylar said. "That's all you need to know. Now, what were you saying? Something about we shall see?"

"Remember those random dance moves I used to do at parties when I was a bit, um, inebriated?" KC asked.

Skylar cocked her head to one side. "Is that a fancy way of saying when you were *schnockered*?" She elbowed Daphne. "What's the SAT word for a more agreeable phrase?"

"Euphemism," Daphne answered immediately.

Skylar snapped her fingers. "Yes, *euphemism*. Is that a euphemism for when you were three sheets to the wind, which by the way is a euphemism for *drunk*?"

KC grinned. "Whatever the word, you know I've never been much of a drinker." She took another sip of her rum punch. "This is the most alcohol I've had in a long time. And I'm not gonna lie. It tastes pretty darn good."

"That's like the third time you've said a variation of that exact same thing," Skylar said.

Daphne smiled. "I love how entertaining KC gets when she's tipsy."

Skylar sipped her own rum punch. "I love it too. Remember the time she did a full-on *backbend* at the SAE formal?"

"I'd pay to see that again," Daphne said.

KC laughed. "I'd probably get myself thrown out of here if I pulled that move. I'd probably throw my back out too, come to think of it."

Skylar gestured toward the young couple making out in a corner. "I beg to differ. While watching you get punted from a bar at age forty would most definitely be the highlight of the trip, I suspect the threshold for what's considered appropriate behavior isn't very high here."

"Why exactly did we choose Chicago to celebrate turning thirty?" KC furrowed her brow. "I remember wanting to go to Vegas."

Daphne felt her face flush. "Um, that was me. Emma was so young, and Vegas was so far away . . ."

Skylar put a hand on Daphne's shoulder. "Methinks it was Brian who put the kibosh on the idea, but that's water under the bridge now, correct?"

Daphne gave her a grateful look. "Correct."

Skylar winked and pointed toward the back. "Let's check out the deck."

They wandered outside and surveyed the landscape in search of open real estate. For a few minutes it was standing room only, so they were forced to sway with the crowd, but soon Skylar noticed a couple getting up to leave a cushioned bench. Like a seasoned pro, she pounced the moment they were gone, somehow managing to look dignified as she did so. She took a seat and gracefully crossed her legs, then smiled and patted the open spots on either side of her.

"The view's much better from here," she said.

Daphne plopped down next to her, but KC remained standing.

"Do we have to sit?" KC said. She began hopping side to side like a boxer. "I'm kind of itching to dance. I love this music."

"Then go for it." Skylar gestured to the dance floor. "No one's stopping you."

KC stopped hopping and let her arms fall to her sides. "You won't dance with me?"

"I will, but not yet. I want to soak in the scene first." Skylar's head turned as if on a swivel. "This place is a gold mine for people watching. I love the way everyone lets loose on vacation."

"If you've got moves on the dance floor like you do on the grid-iron, I'll dance with you," a man's voice said.

The three of them looked to KC's left. Doug from the football game approached, a big smile on his face.

"Hey, teammate!" KC gave him a high five. "Fancy meeting you here."

"What can I say? Word got out that you would be here, so how could I *not* come?"

KC glanced behind him. "Where are your buddies?"

Doug pointed over his shoulder with his thumb. "At the bar. Where else would they be?"

"All of them?" Skylar craned her neck through the crowd. The *Is Hot Scott here?* went unspoken, but Daphne didn't need to hear it to know that's what she was asking, just as Skylar didn't have to hear the *Is Clay here?* Daphne was thinking.

Daphne smiled to herself. *I love that we don't have to say it out loud.*

The playfulness and subtext of their communication was like going back in time for her, each new interaction quietly nudging her dormant persona back to life.

"About half of them are here," Doug said. "The rest of the crew are still at the bar where we had dinner. They may come by later." He turned to KC. "So what about that dance, champ?"

She grinned. "You don't have to ask me twice."

The two of them disappeared into the crowd, but Doug was so tall that Daphne and Skylar could see the top of his head bobbing up and down in the middle of the dance floor.

"I wish I had half her energy," Daphne said. "I'm proud of myself for even being here right now, and she's out there cutting a rug."

"You *should* be proud of yourself for being here," Skylar said. "We're all wired differently, so for certain things you can and should only compare yourself to yourself. I work with some people who never sleep more than four hours a night, and they're completely fine. I know I can't function like that, so I don't try. I need at least six hours to get by."

Daphne pressed a palm against her chest. "I could never live with just six hours. I don't do well without sleep. I was a zombie when Emma was a baby." Her mind began to drift as she remembered that phase of her life. Brian needed to work in the mornings, so it went without saying that Daphne was the one to take care of the moonlight feedings and rocking sessions—even on the weekends. It was during those quiet hours that the first seeds of doubt began to take hold, when she began to wonder if her marriage wasn't what she'd thought it was going to be.

Now she knew better. Now she knew he should have stepped up. She also knew she should have spoken up.

"Daphne." Skylar snapped her fingers. "Earth to Daphne."

Daphne blinked. "I'm sorry, got lost in my thoughts there. Did you say something?"

"I asked if Emma is having fun on the ski trip? Have you heard from her?"

"Not since this morning. I don't think she has very good reception there."

"I'm sure she's having a great time." Skylar put her arm around Daphne's shoulder and squeezed. "I'm *also* sure she's missing you a little bit, even if she's too cool for school to tell you so."

Daphne smiled, grateful that she didn't need to explain. "Thanks. I think I'm going to the restroom. Watch my seat?"

"I'll try, but if Hot Scott makes his way over here, I won't try that hard."

Daphne laughed. "Fair enough." She stood up and smoothed her sundress, then reached for her purse.

Skylar lowered her voice. "Here comes your birthday present."

"What?"

"Babe alert, two o'clock."

Daphne glanced to the right and saw Clay and Scott emerging onto the deck. Scott was unquestionably good-looking, but it was the sight of Clay that got her attention. Tan and with a slight stubble now, there was something about him that made her just a little bit . . . uncomfortable. Or was *nervous* a better word choice? Anxious?

As Daphne stood there mentally evaluating appropriate adjectives, Skylar gave her a nudge from behind. "Don't be shy, go say hello."

"You think I should?"

"Of course. And send his buddy my way while you're at it."

"I'll try," Daphne said.

"Don't try, *do*. There is no *try*."

Daphne gave her a look. "Didn't Yoda say that? I'm pretty sure Yoda said that."

Skylar sighed. "You are such a nerd. Will you get going already?"

"Okay, fine." Daphne took a deep breath and smoothed her dress again, then headed in the direction of the restroom. *Smile. Be friendly. Loosen up. You can do it. He thinks you're pretty, remember?*

She weaved her way through the crowd, her eyes scanning the dance floor as she walked. She spotted Doug and KC among the sea of people but now didn't see Clay and Scott anywhere. She turned back to look at Skylar, who was gently nodding her head to the music, clearly content to be sitting by herself. At least for now.

"Careful there, neighbor."

Daphne turned around and nearly bumped into Clay. He had one hand high in the air, and she had a feeling he'd put it there to keep her from knocking the drink out of it.

"Oh gosh, I'm so sorry. I didn't see you."

He laughed. "Talk about stating the obvious. Have you been here long?"

Daphne shook her head. "We just came from dinner. KC's dancing with Doug, and Skylar's sitting over there. Doug said some of your crew was here, but I wasn't sure if that included you." She gave him a half smile. *Another feeble attempt at flirting, but at least I'm trying!*

He smiled. "I told you this place was fun. Isn't it great? I love the energy here. Everyone's so chill."

"Skylar calls it the vacation vibe, although it could just be the alcohol. Speaking of which, KC's pretty funny right now. She doesn't usually drink very much."

Clay held up his beer in a toast. "You're a *great* dancer, said the tequila."

Daphne laughed. "That's good. Did you make that up yourself?"

He shook his head. "I stole it from a buddy. You know what they call a margarita?"

She cocked her head to one side. "I do not. What *do* they call a margarita?"

"A snow cone of bad decisions."

She laughed again, but before she could say anything more, an attractive young blonde appeared out of nowhere and grabbed Clay's arm. She didn't look a day over twenty-five.

"*There* you are, big guy. I was wondering where you'd wandered off to. Come dance with me." She began pulling him toward the dance floor.

Daphne blushed. *I can't compete with that.*

She held her arm out to let them pass. "Don't let me hold you up, I was just on my way to the ladies' room. If you see KC out there, tell her we have a rum punch waiting for her when she gets thirsty."

"Will do. Good to see you, Daphne." Clay gave a quick wave as the blonde dragged him into the crowd.

Daphne watched them for just a moment, then turned and headed straight for the restroom, which had two stalls. Surprisingly, one of them was open. *Thank God,* she thought as she pushed open the door. Waiting in the restroom line at a crowded bar was one thing from her younger days that she did not miss.

After exiting the stall she washed and dried her hands, then hunted around in her purse for her lip gloss. She glanced in the mirror and smiled politely at the two women huddled together at the adjacent sink. She didn't mean to eavesdrop, but it was impossible not to given their proximity. From the conversation Daphne inferred they were about a year removed from college.

"Going back to work's gonna blow. This week has been off the *hook*," the first woman said.

Her friend stuck out her tongue. "Don't get me started on how much I'm dreading walking into that office. I hate my boss. She's such a bitch."

"I saw your post about her on Facebook. Sounds like a nightmare to work for."

"You have no idea. As soon as I can line up something else, I'm out of there."

As Daphne opened her lip gloss, she realized that she felt a bit sorry for the women, despite their youth. Actually, *because* of their youth. Granted her own career hadn't progressed past the bottom of the totem pole, but she couldn't imagine not knowing better than to criticize *anyone*, much less an employer, in a forum as public as social media. She made a mental note to set Emma down and explain the permanence of a digital footprint.

She stole another glance at the women as she applied a dab of color to her lips. Both of their complexions were unlined. Flawless, actually. Not a wrinkle between them. Daphne couldn't help but wish her own skin still looked that good. Not that hers looked *bad* by any stretch of the imagination. It just looked . . . older.

Their conversation continued. "Did she really sleep with him again?" the first woman asked. "I thought she said she was done with being treated like that."

The second woman shrugged. "He's an ass, but she's in love with him. She keeps hoping he'll change."

The first woman sighed. "Why is it so hard to find a good guy? I just want to get married already and be done with it. I'm so sick of the dating game."

"Me too. If it were up to me, I'd have a ring on my finger by now."

Daphne put her lip gloss away and slung her purse over her shoulder. As she turned to leave, she took a last glance at her reflection in the mirror and remembered when she used to talk like that, when she used to dream about the day a dashing Mr. Right would come along, sweep her off her feet, and carry her into the future she'd been dreaming of since she was a little girl.

Be careful what you wish for, she wanted to tell them.

. . .

"How'd it go with Clay Handsome?" Skylar asked as she handed Daphne her drink.

Daphne plopped down on the seat next to Skylar. "It went. He's not alone, so I aborted."

"Let me guess. A pretty young thing?"

Daphne nodded and took a big sip of rum punch.

Skylar crinkled her nose. "Sugar. What about Hot Scott?"

Daphne glanced around the deck. "I didn't see him, but I imagine he's not alone either. Pretty young things are a dime a dozen here. Although I see a handful of gray heads too, which I've got to admit makes me feel less like a senior citizen. When I get home, maybe I need to start going to Bingo parlors like KC."

Skylar rolled her eyes and stood up. "I'm pretending I didn't hear that. As for the boys, oh well: easy come, easy go. I'm activating Plan B."

Daphne gave her a curious look. "And that would be . . . ?"

Skylar pointed to the bar. "Alcohol. Need I say more?"

Daphne laughed. "You needn't."

"I hold down the fort, will you? Barreling my way to the front of the line might take a while."

"I'll do my best." Daphne took another sip of her drink and again surveyed the deck area, which was now packed with partygoers—and pulsating. "But don't blame me if I fail miserably. This place is getting kind of rowdy, and I don't want to end up with a black eye trying to save your seat."

"You're almost forty years old. I'm sure you can manage to save my seat."

Daphne smoothed a hand over her hair. "*Thank you* for reminding me of that. That's *just* what I needed to hear at this exact moment in time."

"Anytime, babe." Skylar blew her a kiss, then turned and slipped through the crowd. Daphne turned her attention back to the spot where she'd last seen Clay. While she'd been in the ladies' room, the band had been replaced by a DJ, and the dance floor, which had gradually expanded to cover most of the deck, was now so full she couldn't locate him. And despite Doug's height, she'd long ago lost track of him and KC. She scanned the entire area again, then gave up and took another sip of her drink.

When the song ended, the DJ, who had been playing hip-hop, changed gears and began to play a slower piece of reggae music. In response, the population on the dance floor collectively slowed down its pace, but there was little attrition. Daphne peered through the crowd, wondering what had happened to KC, but she still couldn't see her.

She took another sip of her rum punch, then closed her eyes and softly rocked her head back and forth to the music. *KC will be fine. I will be fine too.*

Daphne loved reggae music. There was something so soothing about it, so happily mellow, that it always made her smile and feel like everything was going to be fine. Perhaps it was because she usually only heard it playing at barbecues, which by their nature are, typically at least, inherently void of major stressors. Whatever the association, reggae made her feel relaxed and happy, which was exactly what she needed right now.

The rum punch was also helping her unwind and enjoy herself. Outside of the occasional glass or two of wine (perhaps three on those nights when she'd dabbled with the online dating sites), she wasn't much of a drinker anymore, and while she had drunk less than her friends tonight, she was beginning to feel the effects of the alcohol. However momentarily, the edges were softened, the nerves calmed, the awkwardness of her encounter with Clay soothed.

She smiled, her eyes still closed. *Things are good. I'm on gorgeous St. Mirika with my dear friends and having a really nice time. Who cares if I have crow's feet.*

"Excuse me, is someone sitting here?"

Daphne opened her eyes and saw a slender brunette standing in front of her. She looked to be in her early twenties. She also looked like she was about to cry.

Without thinking, Daphne pushed her purse to one side and patted the empty seat next to her. "Not anymore. Please, sit down. Are you okay?"

The girl pressed her palms against her eyes and sighed. "I'm so embarrassed."

Just moments ago Daphne had felt intimidated by the age gap between herself and a good chunk of the female patrons at the Castaway, but all that melted away at the sight of this teary-eyed young woman. Her maternal instinct kicked in with a force that surprised her.

"What's wrong?" She put her hand on the woman's svelte arm.

The young woman slowly removed her palms from her face, but her birdlike shoulders remained slumped. "I feel so stupid," she said softly, not making eye contact.

"Why? What happened?" Daphne asked.

The woman didn't reply right away, but it was clear she was collecting her thoughts, so Daphne waited patiently for her to respond.

After a moment the woman took a deep breath, then wiped a tear from her cheek and began to speak, still without making eye contact. "I met this really cute guy here last night, and he seemed kind of interested, so I was hoping to run into him again tonight. That's basically the reason I came here, to be honest. But . . . but . . . he's with someone else. I just saw them together."

Daphne made a sympathetic face. "I'm so sorry. Men can be so fickle." Her brain suddenly recalled a similar situation from her freshman year in college. It had been two decades, but she still remembered it vividly because of the anguish she'd felt. She'd had her eye on a cute sophomore in her American history class, and she went out of her way to sit next to him whenever she could do so without being too obvious. After a handful of brief yet flirtatious conversations—mostly initiated by her—he'd asked her over to watch a movie at the off-campus apartment he shared with two buddies. When she arrived, he opened up his refrigerator and offered her a beer, which turned into several, and they ended up making out on the couch until his roommates came home. It was all quite innocent, but it was dreamlike to Daphne. She barely knew him, but their evening together cast a spell over her that left her giddy and literally unable to eat, something that had never happened to her before. That same night she'd begun making plans in her head for all the fun things they would do together—picnics, dinners, date nights, more movies on the couch—all under the intoxicating haze of romance.

The very next afternoon, as Daphne was still floating in the warm memories of his kisses, she spotted him walking arm and arm with another girl—and not in a platonic way. She was crushed.

More than twenty years later, she still remembered what that felt like, how hurt and humiliated she'd been. She also remembered the jarring realization of how quickly she'd begun planning a future with someone who had already left her in his past.

How eager she'd been to find her Prince Charming at such a tender age.

"I'm sorry," she said again to the devastated young woman sitting next to her in Skylar's seat.

The brunette gave her a weary smile. "Thanks for being so nice. I'm Janine, by the way."

"I'm Daphne. And there's no need to thank me. We've all been there. It stings now, but eventually it goes away, I promise." Daphne couldn't even recall that young man's name now. Was it Jim? John? Maybe James? She remembered that it had been something nondescript, and while she'd found him dreamy at the time, over the years both his name and face had been absorbed into the massive blur that was now *the past*.

"Are you here with your family?" Janine asked. "I'm on spring break from Florida State."

Daphne smiled and shook her head. "Not this trip. I'm with two girlfriends. My daughter's with her dad this week. I'm . . . divorced." *There. I said it. And the world didn't end.*

Janine's eyes got a little bigger. "You're here with two *friends*?"

"Yep, from college actually. We met in the dorms."

"That's so cool. I hope when I'm, um, older, that I still do fun things like that."

Daphne laughed. "I'm not *that* old."

Janine blushed and pushed a loose strand behind her ear. "Oh, I didn't mean to . . . um . . . you know . . ."

Daphne smiled. "It's fine, really, I'm just giving you a hard time." She knew Janine wasn't trying to insult her, and while Daphne *was* feeling quite maternal at the moment, it was clear that Janine viewed her as a mother figure and not a contemporary of any sort. Then again, back when Daphne was in college, she would have thought the exact same thing at the sight of an older single woman at a bar. She probably would have been horrified, to be honest. When she was in college, she thought twenty-five was old. Truly old, as in time-to-hang-it-up old.

She snickered to herself at the memory. How could she have ever thought twenty-five was old?

She took a sip of her drink and looked at Janine. The young woman was nice-looking, there was no denying that, but her little black dress was a little too tight, her makeup a bit too heavy. She'd come to St. Mirika to enjoy her spring break with her friends, but here she was, fretting over a boy she'd just met and would probably never see again. She was trying too hard and wasting her time, but she didn't know it . . . yet. *She'll learn.*

Daphne remembered how she used to do the same thing when she was younger. She kept barking up the wrong romantic tree and could never understand why it didn't turn out the way she wanted it to. Over time, with the benefit of hindsight, she'd realized that's what a lot of young women do. Not all of them, of course, but a *lot* of them. In college Daphne often put so much mental energy into trying to figure out what guys wanted that it never occurred to her to focus on what *she* wanted from a relationship, to consider if the men she was chasing would make *her* happy. Now she understood that it was free spirits like KC and Skylar who were the happiest of all. KC and Skylar never cared a lick about what other people—male or female—thought of them, and finding "the One" at such a young age, if ever, was never on their radar. In college KC was a tomboy who loved to play soccer and wear baseball hats, and she was still that person today, currently on the dance floor and having a blast with a guy a decade her junior who was clearly thrilled to be her dance partner. Eighteen-year-old Skylar was an ambitious honors student who loved to banter with many boys and kiss even more of them, but first and foremost she focused on herself. Now she was running a global sales operation, dating multiple men, and still setting her own rules.

"Where are your friends?" Janine asked Daphne. "I lost mine."

Daphne gestured inside, then toward the dance floor. "One's at the bar; the other's somewhere out there."

Janine looked surprised. "The dance floor?"

Daphne nodded. "She may have a few years on you, but KC will outlast you *and* all your friends. Trust me."

"That's cool. She sounds fun."

"Yes, KC is definitely cool *and* fun." Daphne felt a stirring of pride at her friend's perpetual youthfulness, just as she had during the football game earlier. And, by association, she began to feel a little bit of pride in herself. After all, while not on the dance floor, she *was* in a bar right now. And she *had* played football earlier in the day. She was also enjoying herself along the way. There was definitely something to be said for that.

"How long are you here?" Janine asked.

"Just a few days." Daphne smiled at her, and while she envied her radiant skin and cascading hair—as she had the young women in the restroom—she didn't envy the insecurity that emanated from her. With even more clarity, Daphne realized just how much she'd grown up since her college days.

She also realized something else. *I don't want to be that age anymore.*

Instead of mourning the air-brushed memories of her lost youth, she was now seeing that while she'd certainly had fun in that period of her life, it hadn't been without its bumpy patches, and she was glad it was over. For better or for worse, Daphne now knew who she was at her core, even if she'd allowed herself to stray from it during the time she'd been married to Brian. But her personal detour was a different story, one that she knew she needed to address. Janine, however, was still navigating those internal waters, still trying to figure out who she was.

Daphne had already done that. Now it was time to get her back.

She took a sip of her drink and smiled at Janine. "Actually . . . we're all here to celebrate our fortieth birthdays." She felt a sense of relief as she said the words. She'd stepped across the line, spoken her impending age out loud for the first time.

Janine looked shocked. "Forty? For real? I never would have guessed."

Daphne smiled. "Thanks. Mine is tomorrow, actually. Kind of hard to believe, but I'm slowly getting used to it."

"Happy birthday," Janine said. "Really, you look amazing. My mom's forty-three, but she looks way older than you."

Daphne laughed again. No wonder her maternal instinct had kicked in around Janine. She wondered what Skylar would think of her new friend: Where *was* Skylar exactly? She should have been back by now. Daphne craned her neck toward the entrance to the bar but couldn't see her. *Where is she?*

"Oh God, there he is," Janine whispered.

Daphne turned back to look at the young woman, who was now shielding one side of her face with her hand.

"The guy you were with last night?" Daphne asked her.

Janine nodded, not looking up. "I wasn't *with* him, but I kind of wanted to be, if that makes sense. I thought we were having fun, you know, flirting and dancing, and we even kissed a little bit, but then we kind of lost each other in the crowd."

"Which one is he?" Daphne knew men didn't often "lose" women they were interested in.

Janine kept her eyes averted, her hand still shielding her face. "Tall, green T-shirt, tan cargo shorts. Please don't be too obvious."

Daphne casually scanned the dance floor until her eyes rested on the man in question. She covered her mouth with her hand to stifle a gasp . . . and a laugh. It was Scott. Hot Scott. *Okay, this is bizarre.* There was no question about it: she was caught in a generational time warp. Daphne bit her lip. *Oh jeez.*

Out of respect for Janine's feelings, she tried not to show her amusement at the situation, but she found it pretty . . . amusing. *Don't laugh. It will crush her if you laugh.*

"Hey, hot stuff, I'm sorry that took so long." Skylar reappeared from the crowd, holding a small cardboard box filled with fresh drinks.

Daphne squinted at the drinks. "Did you get a job here?"

Skylar smirked. "The line was crazy long, so I decided to stock up. There's no way I'm waiting in that thing again." She smiled down at Janine. "Looks like you made a new friend in my absence. Hi there, I'm Skylar."

"This is Janine," Daphne said. "She's here on spring break with her girlfriends."

"Nice. I like to think I'm on a spring break with my girlfriends too. You want a rum punch, sweetie?" Skylar held up the cardboard tray.

"Did I take your seat? I'm so sorry." Looking a bit embarrassed, Janine stood and reached for her purse. "I should try to find my friends anyway."

"Don't go on my account," Skylar said. "We can all fit. Come on, stay put and have a drink with us. You look like you could use one."

Janine sat back down and gave Skylar a weak smile. "Is it that obvious?"

"Kind of, but then again I work in sales and have a freakish ability to read people." Skylar sat down and handed Janine a glass. "What's up?"

"Boy trouble," Daphne said.

"*All* boys are trouble." Skylar surveyed the deck. "Is the culprit here?"

Daphne looked at Janine. "Can I tell her?"

Janine nodded softly as she took a sip of her drink.

Daphne shifted her eyes to the dance floor. "Tall with dark hair, green T-shirt, tan cargo shorts. He was kissing Janine here *last* night, but tonight he's here with another girl."

Skylar's eyes followed Daphne's, then flickered with recognition when they landed on Scott, who appeared to be dirty dancing with a young blonde about Janine's age. She quickly looked at Daphne and gave her a *Got it* nod. The amused look on her face showed she shared Daphne's outlook on the peculiarity of the situation. Janine was in knots over the tenuous love triangle, but for Skylar the triangle—make that *square*—was hardly a source of drama. Quite the contrary, and Daphne knew they would laugh about it as soon as Janine was out of earshot.

Daphne stole a quick glance at Janine. She looked sad, disillusioned, and, well, a bit clueless. Just as Daphne had been at her age. *Score another point in favor of being older.*

Skylar sipped her drink. "I'm sorry he kissed and bailed, but better that than to *sleep with you and bail,* right?" She gave Janine a sympathetic smile, and Daphne again admired her friend's compassion. Just a few minutes ago Skylar had been planning to put a few moves of her own on the man in question, and here she was comforting a woman roughly half her age about him.

Janine half smiled, then set down her unfinished drink and stood up. "I guess so. I think I'm going to go back to the hotel."

"You sure?" Daphne asked. "What about your friends?"

She pursed her lips. "They won't miss me, trust me." Her eyes darted to the dance floor.

Daphne and Skylar exchanged a glance, and then they understood.

Skylar narrowed her eyes at the crowd. "Is the blonde he's dancing with one of your friends?"

Janine nodded slightly.

"Ouch," Daphne said. That had to hurt.

"Does she *know* you like him?" Skylar asked.

Janine nodded again. "I think so. I mean, she was here last night."

"So she saw you two kissing?"

Janine swallowed, and her cheeks flushed red. "I wouldn't say we were *kissing*, exactly. I, um, I kind of tried to kiss him, but he didn't really, um, reciprocate very much. I was . . . I was pretty drunk." She looked mortified, and Daphne's heart broke a little for her. "I didn't tell my friends about it."

"Kiss or no kiss, if she knows you like him, then she's not your friend," Skylar said.

Janine wiped a tear from her eye. "I think she's just drunk right now and doesn't know what she's doing. She's usually really sweet, I swear."

Skylar scratched her cheek. "Then you're a nicer person than I am. Then again, a lot of people are nicer than I am."

Daphne put her arm around Skylar. "I think you're very nice."

Janine laughed weakly. "You two have been really kind, thank you." She turned and gave them a slight wave, then left.

After she was out of earshot, Daphne shook her head. "Poor thing."

Skylar sipped her drink. "Girls can be so horrible to each other at that age, especially when alcohol and douchey men are involved. I remember once freshman year at Northwestern I was at this party, and a girl I'd become friendly with in one of my classes made out with a guy she *knew* I had a crush on, like almost right in front of me. And she didn't even *like* him. I think she just did it to get back at her boyfriend. I never spoke to her again, although I don't think she even knew how much I hated her because we didn't run into each other that much after the semester ended, but in my mind she was blacklisted forever. I got even, though."

"You did? How?"

Skylar smiled and pointed to herself. "Years ago she applied for a position at my company, and *I* got to interview her. Trust me, she didn't get the job."

"Remind me not to get on your bad side," Daphne said. "You play hardball."

Skylar sipped her rum punch. "I don't care how drunk you are, or how much the world has changed since we were in college, or any of that crap. It's pretty black and white. You don't engage with a guy if you know your friend likes him, period." She held up her palm. "To people like that I say *unsubscribe*."

Daphne laughed. "You unsubscribe from people?"

"All the time. Life's too short to deal with unstable personalities." She scanned the area for KC. "Where's Serena Williams?"

"Still on the dance floor, I suppose. I haven't seen her since you went inside."

"There she is." Skylar pointed through the crowd.

"Where?" Daphne's eyes followed in search of KC yet saw nothing but a mass of pulsating bodies. The DJ was back to playing hip-hop, and the crowd was now practically jumping up and down in unison.

"At the bar on the other side of the dance floor."

Daphne raised her eyebrows. "There's *another* bar here?"

Skylar stood up. "Apparently so. I wish I'd known that before I wasted half the evening waiting in line for these drinks. Let's go find the little one."

Daphne glanced at their bench. "Do you think we should give up our seats? They're kind of comfortable."

"All good things must come to an end. Besides, I promised KC we'd dance with her."

Daphne put a hand on her own chest. "You promised KC that *we'd* dance with her? I don't remember being part of that discussion."

Skylar grabbed Daphne's arm and pulled her up. "You are now. Let's go."

They carefully skirted around the swarm on the dance floor and spotted KC sitting on a stool at a small outdoor bar at the very edge of the deck. To her right was Doug. They were both holding a drink and laughing.

"There she is," Skylar said.

Daphne squinted. "Are my eyes playing tricks on me, or is that an empty shot glass in front of her?"

Skylar smiled. "Your eyes are still working just fine. I'm so happy to see that right now."

When she noticed her friends approaching, KC grinned and held her arms open wide. "*There* you are. I was wondering what had happened to you."

Daphne laughed. "What happened to *us*? This is the first time we've moved since we got here."

Doug put his hand on the top of KC's head. "The captain here's a little tipsy."

"The captain?" Daphne raised her eyebrows.

"As in captain of the football team," he said.

Skylar held up her drink. "Nice. I may add that to my arsenal of nicknames."

KC stood on her tiptoes and hugged Skylar and Daphne. "I'm having so much fun on this vacation! Skylar, thanks so much for organizing it rock-star-style! And Daphne, thanks so much for finally getting that pretty face of yours out of boring *Ohio* to come hang out with us!"

Skylar looked at Daphne and mouthed the word "hammered."

KC hugged them even tighter. "Have I told you two how much I mean to you?"

Daphne laughed. "What?"

Doug chuckled and pointed to the empty shot glass. "That was our third."

"Three shots?" Skylar's eyes grew wide. "The woman's smaller than my twelve-year-old niece."

Doug held up his hands in a "don't shoot" gesture. "She insisted. She said we were celebrating our victory in the football game."

"We were *celebrating*!" KC pumped her fist. "We are *champions*!"

Skylar looked at Daphne and mouthed the words "She's going to die tomorrow."

Daphne laughed. It had been nearly twenty years since she'd seen KC like this, and she was thoroughly enjoying it.

"Guess what!" KC said in a voice way louder than necessary. "Doug said he's *never* seen a girl throw a football as well as I did today. And I'm *forty*!"

Skylar gave Doug a little nudge with her elbow. "Don't you love how she just owns that?"

He smiled and nodded. "She's the best. I've never met anyone like her."

"We should figure out how to bottle her positive attitude and sell it," Daphne said.

Skylar whistled. "Can you imagine? We'd make a fortune. Yet another business to start when we get home."

"We'd make a fortune on what?!" KC yelled. "On being *champions*?!"

Skylar put an arm around her. "We're right here, peanut. No need to shatter any eardrums."

"Hey, people, we wondered where you'd gone off to."

They turned and saw Clay approaching the bar, followed by Scott. Daphne waited to see if the blonde from earlier was trailing behind Clay, but she didn't spot her. *It's probably only a matter of time before she resurfaces.* Scott appeared to be solo as well. For now, at least.

Not wanting to experience that awkwardness again, Daphne touched Skylar's arm and gestured toward the other side of the deck. "Maybe we should take KC back to where we were sitting," she said in a hushed voice.

Skylar gave her a strange look and kept her voice at a normal decibel. "Why would we do that?"

"We wouldn't want to, you know, *intrude*," Daphne practically whispered.

"Since when are attractive women an intrusion?" Suddenly Scott was behind them, one hand on Daphne's shoulder, the other on Skylar's.

Daphne gave him a sheepish look. "How did you hear that?"

"It's a gift. I can't see twenty feet in front of my face, but I can hear a pin drop in the other room."

"Skylar has superhuman hearing too!" KC yelled.

Scott smiled at Skylar. "Yet another thing we have in common."

"What was the first thing?" Skylar asked him.

"I'll tell you later. First things first." He turned and gestured to the bartender. "Anyone need a drink?"

"I'll take a brew," Clay said.

"Those are the magic words," Doug said with a nod. "Grab me one as well."

Skylar nodded too. "You don't have to ask me twice. A rum punch would hit the spot."

"I'm in," KC raised her hand.

Skylar pulled KC's hand down. "I think the muppet here's had enough."

Scott looked at Daphne. "What about you, Daphne? What's your poison?"

Daphne smiled and pointed to the rum punch she'd been nursing. "I'm good, thanks."

As Scott leaned toward the bartender to order, Daphne turned her head and scanned the crowd. *If she comes back, she comes back.*

Doug put his arm around KC but spoke to Skylar. "Think this one is going to make it out of bed tomorrow? She might have a monster hangover."

"I'll make it!" KC shouted. "Just watch me!"

Skylar shrugged. "We'll see. Our only formal plan for the day is to go to a spa, so all she really has to do is go from lying down in one place to lying down in another. How hard can that be?"

"What about the monkey forest?" KC frowned. "I want to feed them bananas!"

Skylar smiled. "That's right, we're going to the monkey forest too. Can't forget the monkeys."

KC pumped a fist in the air. "We're going to the monkey forest tomorrow! And it's Daphne's fortieth birthday! Can you *believe* that? Doesn't she look *amazing*? She's so *pretty*! Isn't she *pretty*?!" She reached up and began to pet Daphne's hair.

Daphne felt her face turn beet red. Doug clearly knew their age, but until now Scott and Clay hadn't, at least not officially. *I guess that cat's out of the bag.*

Clay looked at Daphne. "Forty? Really? I never would have guessed."

Daphne did her best to mimic Skylar's trademark *What can you do?* shrug, although part of her wanted to run onto the beach right then, dig a big hole in the sand, then jump into it and hide. But Clay didn't have to know that, right? She added a smile to her shrug. "As Skylar says, forty is the new black." *Maybe I am learning from Skylar.*

Clay laughed. "Well, whatever color forty is, it suits you."

"Thank you." *I'm beginning to think so too.*

The DJ began playing "Dancing Queen" by ABBA, and KC suddenly jumped up from her barstool, wobbled slightly, then steadied herself. "Okay, people, this is a tune that simply *must* be danced to! Who wants to join me? Skylar, you promised."

"Okay, let's go," Skylar said, setting her drink on the bar. "Who can say no to ABBA?"

Scott put a hand on Skylar's lower back. "Show me the way," he said.

"Let's rock this thing." Doug pointed toward the dance floor.

As they all made their way toward the pulsating crowd, Clay caught Daphne's eye, then jutted his chin toward KC, who was waving her arms in the air. "I think the tequila's been whispering in someone's ear," he said.

.   .   .

After what seemed to Daphne like hours but in reality was just a handful of songs, KC finally ran out of steam. When the band stopped to take a short break, she put one hand on her hip and raised her other in the air. "Okay, I think I just hit the wall."

"Thank God." Skylar immediately bolted off the dance floor in the direction of the exit. "I hit that thing like three days ago. Let's get out of here."

Daphne quickly followed her. "I thought you'd never say the word."

"I'm pretty beat too," Clay said.

"Anyone want a roadie?" Doug asked, pointing to the bar.

Clay shook his head. "I'm good, thanks."

Skylar pointed to the beach. "I'm walking home if anyone wants to join me."

"You guys are really leaving?" Scott ostensibly asked the group, but he was clearly looking at Skylar.

"Why don't you go find your friend?" Skylar said over her shoulder. "She seemed fun."

"What friend?"

"The sorority girl who was hanging off your arm earlier. I bet she'd love to dance with you."

Scott laughed. "She's a kid."

Skylar shrugged, still not looking back. "I could say the same about you."

"Ouch."

She turned around and put her hands on her hips, then smiled at him. "You want to walk us home?"

"You have anything to drink there?"

"Perhaps."

He smiled back. "Then yes."

"Okay, then walk us home." She intertwined an arm with KC's on one side and Doug's on the other, then gestured with her head for him to follow. "Let's hit it, people."

Daphne watched Scott trot to catch up with the group, figuratively as well as literally chasing her friend. *Bravo, Skylar.*

"You ready to go?" Clay asked Daphne.

"More than ready." She placed her hands on either side of her head. "My ears are ringing."

In a staggered formation, the six of them made their way down the beach. A number of people were milling around, many of them fellow refugees from the Castaway. As they approached the shore, Daphne turned back for another look at the bar, which had thinned out a bit but was still quite crowded.

"I wonder what time it will finally quiet down?" she said to Clay.

"Not for hours. We were there pretty late last night."

"This is plenty late for me. I'm glad our house is close enough to the action to be fun, but not too close to keep me awake all night."

"Are you a light sleeper?"

"Light enough." She didn't feel the need to tell him that she had earplugs in her travel bag. And an eye mask. *He knows how old I am. That's enough information for one night.*

Daphne and Clay eventually caught up with the others. Skylar glanced back at the fading lights of the Castaway, then looked at Doug. "What happened to the rest of your crew?"

"God knows," Doug said. "Attrition is pretty normal for a group our size."

Scott, who was now walking on the other side of Skylar, put a hand on her shoulder. "I can't say I have a problem with it."

Ignoring his overture, Skylar yawned and stretched her arms over her head. "I haven't danced that much in ages. I may fall asleep before I make it home."

"Aw, don't say that," Scott said. "You promised me a nightcap."

Daphne glanced at Skylar to see her reaction to his comment, but Skylar didn't seem to have one. At least a visible one. *She's so good,* Daphne thought.

Before Skylar could respond, out of nowhere KC bolted ahead of the group.

"Oh sweet potato, what is she doing *now?*" Skylar asked.

"She's like a superhero," Doug said with a wistful smile as he watched KC go.

Daphne laughed. "She *is* like a superhero. Can you believe she pulled out the Running Man and the Robot on the dance floor?"

Doug kept smiling. "I get happy just thinking about that. I love how she doesn't care about looking like an idiot. Not that she's an idiot, of course. You know what I mean, right?" He scratched the back of his head. "Oh hell, that came out wrong. Did that make me sound like an asshole?"

"You *are* an asshole," Scott said.

Clay laughed. "Takes one to know one."

Skylar patted Doug on the arm. "No worries, I totally get what you're saying. Now let's catch her before she tries to swim to Florida." She quickened her pace, as did Doug and Scott, leaving Clay and Daphne trailing behind.

Daphne waved good-bye at them. "No more running for me. I've had enough exercise for today."

Clay laughed. "You're putting your foot down, are you? Just saying no?"

She smiled up at him. "I guess I am. Not really by choice, though. Sad as it sounds, I'm just too tired. Maybe I should go to California and follow KC around for a few weeks. That would whip me into shape."

"Where do you live now?"

"Columbus. About as far from the beach as it gets. I guess that's not really true, but it's far enough. What about you?"

"I'm in New York, but plenty of my buddies from business school work in Chicago, so let me know if you ever need me to pick you up a purple sweatshirt. Or maybe a purple license plate holder? I know you Wildcats love your purple."

She smiled. "Thanks, I'll remember that. Oh my gosh, look! KC's doing one of her best moves!" She pointed about fifty feet ahead of them.

KC, who had finally stopped running, now had stretched her arms straight over her head. She remained that way for a moment, then proceeded to bend backward until her hands reached the sand. Skylar, Doug, and Scott stood a few feet away, buckled over in laughter.

"Is she really doing a *backbend*?" Clay squinted down the beach.

Daphne clasped her hands together and smiled. "I knew it was only a matter of time before she pulled that one out of her pocket. I'm surprised it took this long, to be honest. After I found out she'd been doing shots, I figured we'd see a backbend right on the dance floor."

"I take it you've seen her do this before?"

Daphne pushed a loose strand of hair away from her eyes. "Oh yes, many times. In college that was her go-to party trick, or one of

174

them, at least. I'm sure it doesn't surprise you that she had multiple party tricks."

He chuckled. "No, I can't say that it does."

"I can't believe she can still contort her body that way. Doesn't it look painful?"

Clay made a strained face and put his hands on his lower back. "I think I'd end up in traction if I attempted a stunt like that."

Daphne put her hands on her lower back too. "You and me both. The girl has superhuman DNA, that's the only way to explain it. Either that or she's been lacing her oatmeal with steroids all these years."

Clay chuckled again. "I doubt that. Her voice is way too high." He glanced at his watch. "Hey, it's after midnight, so it's officially tomorrow. May I be the first to wish you a very happy birthday?"

She covered her face with her hands. "Oh my gosh, I can't believe I'm forty." *But it feels kind of good to say that out loud.*

He put his hand on top of her head. "Come on, you look great for *any* age, and you know it."

She removed her hands and smiled. "You're just saying that to be nice." *But I'm thrilled you said it.*

He gestured toward the multiple thatched-roof bars and restaurants peppering the beach. "I respectfully beg to differ. Come have a birthday drink with me?"

"Now?" *Weren't we just talking about being tired and going to sleep?*

"Why not? The Pirate's Cove is right over there. We had a few drinks there our first night on the island. It's a fun little spot."

"What about them?" Daphne pointed down the beach. KC was up and running again, barely a dot on the horizon now. Skylar, Doug, and Scott were trailing behind, a trio of silhouettes in the darkness.

"They're all adults—they'll find their way back. Come on, Daphne, it's your *birthday.*"

She pressed her palms together and stared briefly into the moonlight. She hated to ditch her friends, but then again, KC wouldn't last much longer anyway, and given the obvious chemistry between Scott and Skylar, it was probably only a matter of time before they wanted to be alone together. And besides, wasn't that part of the reason Daphne had come to St. Mirika in the first place? To focus on herself, for once? To stop being locked in the past? To let go of her expectations about what life *should* be like and finally start . . . *living it? No more vanilla!*

Clay was nice and smart and funny. And very good-looking. And he was asking to buy her a birthday drink. On the beach. Just the two of them. Maybe it meant nothing, but what did that matter? She tried to squash the internal chatter. *Stop worrying so much! Just have fun! Take a chance for once!*

"Daphne? You there?" Clay waved a hand in front of her face. "What do you say? Can I buy you a drink to ring in your birthday?"

She hesitated for just a moment, then smiled. "Okay, sure, why not?"

"That's the spirit. Let's go."

They walked up the sand to the Pirate's Cove. A small bamboo roof covered a handful of round wooden tables surrounding a sliver of a dance floor. A string of red lights encircled the rows of intermittent bamboo poles on either side that served loosely as a fence. The place was barely a quarter the size of the Castaway, and Daphne was immediately drawn to its cozy charm.

"What's your poison, pirate?" Clay asked her as they approached the tiny bar.

She held up her palms. "I have no idea. What kind of poison do pirates drink on their birthdays?"

He picked up a laminated list of drink specials and studied the options. "Hmm. How about a Treasure Chest? Or a Booty Drop?"

She gave him a look. "There's really a drink called *Booty Drop?*"

He pointed to the menu. "Swear to God. I couldn't make up something that bad."

She smiled. "Okay then, I'll try a Booty Drop. Why not, right?"

"Do you want to know what's in it?"

"Not really. I prefer not to know, actually." *I'm scared to know, actually.*

He arched his eyebrows. "Going in blind, are we now? Are you always this adventurous?"

She smiled. "Not really. Maybe." *I want to be. I used to be.*

"I like your attitude. Why don't you grab one of those high tables, and I'll order the drinks."

"Sounds good." *I'm liking my attitude too.*

She climbed onto a wooden stool and observed her surroundings. The place was about half-full and hummed with conversation, but it felt downright subdued compared to the mayhem they'd just experienced. The demographic here was also noticeably older than that of the Castaway, and Daphne felt like she'd left—make that *escaped from*—a college fraternity party to join an adult cocktail party. Civilized, calm, and pleasant. She loved it. *This is much more my style.*

As if on cue, soft island-style music began playing in the background. Daphne smiled, and for the first time wondered *why* she'd been so fixated on turning forty. Yes, it was a big milestone, but the earth was still rotating. She was also pretty sure the sun was going to come up in a few hours. Maybe she'd let this birthday take on too much symbolism? Maybe it was time to stop being so afraid of starting over?

Clay approached with their drinks. He took a seat and handed her a glass, then raised his to hers. "Happy birthday, Daphne White. Here's to a long and happy life."

She clinked her glass against his. "Thank you, Clay Hanson." *Clay Handsome.*

Without realizing it, Daphne found herself studying him as they each sipped their drink.

"What?" he finally said, touching his cheeks and chin. "Do I have something on my face?"

She laughed and shook her head. "No."

"Then what?"

She took a deep breath. *Just say it.*

"To be honest, I didn't expect to be ringing in my birthday with the likes of you."

Clay narrowed his eyes. "The likes of me? Am I that unappealing?"

She blushed. "I'm sorry, that came out wrong. It's just that . . ." She looked down.

"Do you think there's a warrant out for my arrest or something?"

She laughed and regained eye contact. "I highly doubt the police are on your heels. What I was trying to say is that . . ." *Do it!*

She took another deep breath, then continued. "What I was trying to say is that I haven't been out for a drink with anyone since my ex-husband and I split up. Not that this is a *date* or anything, but I'm just feeling a little out of my comfort zone even being here. I'm sorry, I'm rambling."

"When did you get divorced?"

"We separated over two years ago, but the divorce wasn't final until recently."

"Do you have kids?"

"A daughter, she's fifteen."

"For real? You look way too young to have a fifteen-year-old daughter."

She laughed and pushed a strand of hair out of her eyes. "Tell that to her."

"You haven't been on a date in more than two years?"

She blushed and cast her eyes downward. "No."

He finished his drink and set the glass on the table. "Then let's call this a date."

"What?" She looked up at him.

"You heard me. I'm a man, you're a woman, we're having a drink, *on the beach in St. Mirika*, I might add." He gestured to himself and then to her, then pointed toward the ocean. "I say we label this a date."

She felt her cheeks flush and stared at the table again, too flustered—and thrilled—to respond. *Is this really happening?*

Before she could say anything, the unmistakable roar of thunder shook the Pirate's Cove. They both looked out at the ocean, then up at the sky.

"It's going to pour," Clay said. "Happens all the time here."

Daphne gazed wistfully toward the water again. "So I've heard."

"Do you like rain?"

She tapped her fingertips on the table. "I didn't used to, but the rain here is different. It's so warm, and soothing. I find it . . . enchanting."

"Your hands are enchanting," he said. "Very elegant."

Caught off guard by the non sequitur, she stopped tapping and looked at her fingers, suddenly self-conscious. "Thank you," she said softly.

"And for the record, I wasn't just saying all that to be nice," he said.

She slowly looked up at him. "You weren't just saying what?" She practically whispered the words.

"When I said that you look great for any age, or that you look way too young to have a fifteen-year-old."

She felt her cheeks turn a deeper shade of pink. Acknowledging her age was one thing. *Discussing* it was another.

"Am I making you uncomfortable, Daphne White?"

"A little. Maybe we can change the subject?"

He put a hand over hers. "Sure. How about we talk about how I was serious when I said we should call this a date?"

She swallowed and felt her insides stir at the touch of his skin on hers. *Oh my gosh. This is really happening.*

He began to move his thumb over her hand. "Does it make you nervous that I find you attractive? You seem nervous."

She swallowed and pulled her hand away from his to pick up her glass. "A little."

He chuckled. "You're totally nervous right now. It's cute."

She took a sip of her drink. "So . . . what happened to the girl?"

"What girl?"

"The blonde one you were with at the Castaway?" *The pretty one hanging off you like a necklace?*

He shrugged. "She was nice enough, but not for me."

Daphne sipped her drink again. "Is that so?"

"That is so. Plus, if you hadn't noticed, I've had my eye on someone else tonight."

She gave him a playful look. "Hmm. Interesting." *He likes me!*

He stared at her. "Yes, interesting. I know you're older than I am, Daphne, but if it's not obvious by now, I don't care about age. To be honest, I like you *because* you're older. It makes you different." He began to stroke her forearm with his fingers, and she felt a flurry of tiny sparks flashing throughout her body.

He kept stroking her arm. "That younger woman tonight? I'd be lying if I said I didn't find her attractive, but with you . . . let's just say there's something appealing about dealing with . . . a more sophisticated buyer."

She laughed. "So I'm a harder sell?" *If you only knew how unsophisticated I feel right now.*

"In a way, yes. Now dance with me." He set down his drink and reached for her hand, then pulled her onto the tiny dance floor. He put his hands around her lower back, and together they began to sway to the reggae music. Just one other pair shared the space, a married couple Daphne guessed to be in their fifties. They gave Daphne and Clay a friendly smile before returning their attention to each other.

"The way you carry yourself is elegant, like a ballerina," Clay said. "I noticed that right away when I saw you on the beach yesterday."

"I used to take dance classes when I was younger," she said.

He pulled her closer to him. "I can tell. It's sexy."

She looked up at him. "So you like a challenge? Is that what this is about?"

He tucked a free strand of hair behind her ear, then returned his hand behind her lower back. "Let's stop overanalyzing it, okay? I find you attractive, period."

She smiled. "Really?"

"Yes. From the moment I saw you, I was interested, and that's only grown as I've gotten to know you a little bit. You're pretty, and you're fun to talk to, but I don't want to talk right now." He pulled her even closer, then leaned down and gently touched his lips against hers. She was too surprised to resist, not that she wanted to. As she'd just admitted to him, she hadn't kissed anyone in years. Her body responded accordingly. *Please do that again.*

The tiny sparks she'd felt had been one thing, but the heat that was now buzzing inside made her a bit dizzy. His lips were warm and soft, and her body instinctively pushed against his.

"You're so beautiful," he whispered into her ear.

You smell so good. She inhaled deeply to breathe in his scent. She was entranced by it, and she wanted to drink it in.

"Mmm . . . so hot." He nuzzled her neck, then kissed her shoulder before moving back to her lips.

They kissed for a bit longer, then Clay began to caress the back of her neck with his hand. She caught her breath. *Oh my God that feels so good.*

Suddenly aware of what was happening in a very public place, she opened her eyes and glanced around to see if anyone was watching them. The older couple was gone now, and as far as she could tell, no one else there was even looking in their direction, which helped make her a bit less self-conscious. The alcohol also served to dim the glow of self-awareness. She tried to remember the last time she'd behaved like this in public, much less on a dance floor, but her memory didn't reach that far back.

Her mind was also too distracted at the moment to focus on anything besides how good his hands felt on her, how good his lips felt on her. *Please kiss me again.*

"I love your body," he murmured. "And your posture. I thought maybe you were a yoga instructor."

She laughed. "Definitely not."

"Well, whatever you're doing, it's working."

She smiled but didn't respond to the compliment. If he only knew how her muscles already ached. She really needed to start exercising more often, especially now that she knew guys like Clay Hanson were paying attention.

Just then they heard another roar, followed by the crashing din of raindrops hitting the roof.

"There it is," Clay said as he looked up. "Don't you just love that sound?"

Daphne closed her eyes and nodded. "It's beautiful."

He leaned down and spoke softly into her ear again. "*You're beautiful.*"

"I could listen to the rain all night," she said, her eyes still closed. *I could stay like this all night.*

"Can I spend it with you?"

She pulled away from him and opened her eyes. "What?" Had he read her mind?

He gave her a suggestive smile and pulled her back toward him. "You heard me."

She did her best not to giggle like a teenager, but she couldn't help herself. "Is this how it works now? I've been out of the loop for a while."

"You tell me." He began caressing her shoulder, then lightly ran his fingers up and down her arm.

She closed her eyes again, so glad she'd worn a sundress, savoring the touch of his hands on her skin. She pressed her cheek against his firm chest, listening to the drumming of the rain on the thatched ceiling above them.

They swayed like that for few minutes before he spoke again. "Please take me home with you," he whispered into her ear.

The question sent a sizzle down her spine. The familiar yet unfamiliar sensation of attraction, mixed with anticipation, stirring something warm inside her. *I forgot what this feels like.*

Their bodies pressed together, they continued to slow dance. The rain poured around them in sheets, nearly drowning out the soft sound of the music.

After a few moments, she spoke quietly in his chest. "Okay." *Come home with me. Make me feel alive again.*

He lifted her chin with his fingertips and smiled down at her. "Is that a yes?"

She glanced out at the beach. Her friends were long gone by now, and for the first time she wondered if any part of the group's separation had been intentional. If it had been, she was grateful to whoever had orchestrated it. She turned her eyes back to Clay and felt her lips turn up at the corners. Then she nodded ever so faintly. "That's a yes."

. . .

When Clay and Daphne reached her beach house, soaking wet from their walk home in the rain, all the lights were off save for a small one on the back deck. The inside was still and quiet. Daphne peered in the window, then turned toward Clay and put a finger over her lips.

Clay eyed her with suspicion. "Do you want me to be quiet so we don't wake them, or so they don't know I'm here?"

Daphne tried not to giggle but couldn't help herself. "Both. Will you take those off?" She pointed to his flip-flops before awkwardly removing her own. "I think you got me a little tipsy."

He arched an eyebrow. "So you're saying I'm taking advantage of you?"

She reached for the door handle. "Only if you want to." *Please take advantage of me.*

He laughed and scratched the back of his head. "I'm not sure how to take that. That's hardly a glowing invitation."

"Any invitation is better than no invitation, am I right?" She quietly opened the glass door and stepped inside the dark house.

"Touché," he said as he followed her.

"Oh my gosh, it's dark in here," Daphne whispered.

He put a hand on her lower back and kept his deep voice hushed as well. "I like dark. Lead the way to the bedroom so I can get you out of that wet dress."

"Scared I might catch cold, are you?" She reached behind her and took his hand, then carefully led him through the living room toward the hall, tiptoeing across the tile floors. *I can't believe I'm doing this. I'm so glad I'm doing this.*

"I feel like we're sneaking into your parents' house," he said. "If we get caught, are you going to be grounded?"

Daphne giggled again. "Shh." She couldn't remember the last time she'd *giggled.* She also couldn't remember the last time she'd tiptoed in the dark while holding hands with a man she barely knew. *This is so much fun.*

When they reached the kitchen, she noticed two empty bottles of wine on the counter—and two used goblets in the sink. She pointed to them and was about to say something when Clay pulled her toward him and kissed her deeply, stroking her hair as he did so. When they finally broke apart, he gently touched her cheek.

"I've wanted to do that since I first saw you," he whispered.

She smiled up at him but didn't say anything, trying to catch her breath. Her mind, at the moment, was consumed by a single thought. *Please do it again.*

"You had to know that," he said.

"I wasn't sure." *I hoped, but I didn't know.*

He put a hand over his heart. "You're killing me."

She put her hand over his. "That's a criticism of *me,* not of you. I'm sort of out of practice at this, if you couldn't tell."

He slipped his hands around her lower back, then leaned down and kissed her bare shoulder. "Maybe that's why I'm so attracted to you."

She smiled up at him. "You find it attractive that I can't even tell when a guy's flirting with me?" *I find that sort of . . . pathetic.*

He grazed her forehead with his fingertips. "I find you attractive because you don't try too hard. A lot of women my age . . . they try too hard."

She cast her eyes downward. A vision of Janine from earlier suddenly flashed before her. *I used to be like that. I don't want to be like that ever again.*

She knew now that by default women Janine's age were beautiful and attractive. They didn't *have* to try. *Youth really is wasted on the young.*

"You smell so good." He nuzzled her neck. "What perfume are you wearing?"

She shook her head. "I'm not. Must be my shampoo, or maybe the body lotion I put on? I just grabbed whatever was in the bathroom."

He stroked her cheek again. "*Another* example of not trying too hard. It's what makes you so sexy." He lightly tugged at the strap of her sundress. "I think this is sexy too. Simple, yet beautiful."

She glanced downward. "You like it?"

He put his finger on her chin and gently lifted it. "Very much. However, as nice as it looks on you, I think it would look much nicer crumpled up next to the bed."

She laughed, then quickly covered her mouth and lowered her voice. "That's a pretty good line, I'll give you that. Did you get it from the same guy who gave you the tequila jokes?"

"I actually came up with it all on my own, so take that as a compliment. Now can we please go make out?"

Daphne smiled and put a finger to her lips, then gestured for him to follow her down the hall. As silently as was possible for a man his size, Clay tiptoed behind her. A sliver of light shone underneath the door to KC's room. Skylar's room, located at the far end, was completely dark. When they arrived in front of her room, Daphne reached for the doorknob, but Clay stopped her before she touched it. He turned her shoulders, then gently pressed her back up against the door.

"You're so sexy, Daphne."

Before she could respond, he leaned down and moved his lips softly along her neck and shoulder. "You're driving me crazy," he whispered.

Again she felt intoxicated by his scent, by the tingling sensation of his mouth against her skin, by the seductive sound of his breathing. *The feeling is mutual.*

After a few moments he lifted his head, stared intensely into her eyes without speaking, then quietly opened the door and pulled her inside.

Chapter Nine

When Daphne woke up, the first thing she saw in the soft morning light was Fred. The gecko. Perched on the ceiling directly above her. She smiled at him. *Hi, Fred. Can you see me?* She was about to stretch her arms over her head, then caught her breath as the memory of the night before hit her. Along with the realization that she wasn't wearing pajamas. *Oh my gosh.* She slowly turned her head to the right. Clay lay on his back, sound asleep, breathing deeply. She bit her lip. *Oh my gosh. What do I do now?* She shut her eyes tight, then opened them and looked back up at the ceiling, trying not to laugh. *Fred, tell me what to do!*

She lay there frozen, literally paralyzed with uncertainty over what to do at that exact moment, not to mention how to act when Clay woke up. It had been more than fifteen years since she'd spent the night with anyone other than Brian. And while she'd had her share of make-out sessions before she got married, she'd never *slept* with a man so quickly before. Was there a next-morning protocol she was supposed to follow? She didn't know it back then, and she certainly didn't know it now. *Does this mean I'm slutty? Or am I kind of cool?* She smiled to herself. What she *did* know was that she'd enjoyed herself the night before. A lot. Clay had made sure of that.

She flushed at the memory and glanced up at Fred again. *My green friend, today I will consider myself cool.*

She hadn't expected to sleep with Clay. When she agreed to bring him back to the beach house, she thought they'd continue what they'd begun at the Pirate's Cove, make out a little bit, nothing all *that* serious. But things changed once he closed the bedroom door. At first she'd been nervous to be alone with him, but her anxiety didn't last long. The intensity with which he'd kissed her lips, neck, and shoulders; the compliments he'd breathed into her ears; the gentle way he'd caressed her skin: one by one her inhibitions began to slip away, and then it just . . . happened.

She'd relished every minute of it, especially the way he'd wrapped his strong arms around her and grazed the top of her head with his lips as they finally settled in to get some sleep.

"You're beautiful," he'd whispered before drifting off.

She closed her eyes, the hint of a smile still on her face. *I slept with Clay Handsome.*

Just as she began to replay the steamy highlights in her head, she felt a tingling in her throat, followed by an uncontrollable need to cough. *No! Not now!*

She reached her hand to her neck and squeezed gently, as if that might somehow prevent the inevitable. She knew what was coming, but she didn't want to wake him up. She wasn't ready to face him, not yet. She willed the sensation to go away, but it only grew more intense, and soon her eyes started watering. She thought about trying to exit the bed without making much commotion, but now it was too late. She sat up and grabbed the pillow, then coughed into it.

She gently let go of the pillow and looked at Clay again, then slowly removed the comforter from her chest and—as quietly as she could—got out of bed. She desperately wanted to brush her teeth, check her face, and put something on! She choked back a laugh at the sight of her and Clay's clothes—still damp—lying in a heap on the floor. She scooped them up, tiptoed into the bathroom and gently closed the door, then carefully hung them over the shower railing, remembering the lusty rush with which they'd been removed, and was delighted to realize she wasn't the least bit disturbed by the mess. *Apparently we had more important things to do.*

She pulled her nightie off the hook on the door, then quickly slipped it over her head. *That's better.* As she reached for her toothbrush, she evaluated her appearance in the mirror. Besides a tiny smudge of mascara under one eye, her face looked pretty good, or at least as good as it could after only a few hours of sleep—and more than a few rum punches. She carefully removed the mascara with a Q-tip, then pulled her hair back into a ponytail and splashed cold water over her cheeks and forehead, hoping the noise of the running faucet wouldn't wake Clay—and simultaneously wondering if there was any chance he'd sleep through the sound of a flushing toilet.

She chuckled to herself at the absurdity—and unfamiliarity—of her behavior. She'd been married for more than a dozen years, yet here she was, acting like someone half her age. For not the first time this trip, she felt as if she'd gone back in time.

When she was ready to reenter the bedroom, she reached for the door, took a deep breath, and mentally prepared herself to see Clay sitting up in bed, wide awake. Or worse, gone. *Please don't be gone.*

She felt a shudder of dread at the thought that he might have taken off once she left the room. Seeing him after their intimate night together would be awkward, of course, but returning to an empty bedroom? That would be much worse. She hesitated. *He wouldn't do that, would he?*

Holding her breath, she gently nudged the door open with what she hoped was a relaxed look on her face, or at least a seminormal expression, given all the thoughts running around in her head. Assuming Clay was still there, she had no idea what she was going to say to him. While half her brain was still reliving the feel of his lips on her skin, the other half reminded her that she'd just slept with a complete stranger. Her eyes immediately darted to the bed. Clay was sound asleep on his back, still breathing deeply. She exhaled. *Thank God.*

She quietly walked toward the dresser and picked up her phone to see if there were any messages from Emma, but the screen was blank. She set it back down, then turned around and carefully approached the bed, watching Clay's chest rise and fall softly with his breath. Suddenly a strange thought occurred to her, one that caught her by surprise and—momentarily, at least—trumped her anxiety about having just slept with a man she barely knew. *I'm so glad you're not Brian.*

Before she could ponder the significance of that thought, Clay slowly opened his eyes. He furrowed his brow as if registering his surroundings, then slowly turned his head and made eye contact with her. She gave him a shaky smile and waved. "Good morning."

He yawned and smiled back. "Good morning to you too. And happy birthday."

She put a hand over her mouth. "Oh my gosh, I totally forgot today is my birthday." *What a way to ring it in.*

"I'm that good?" He sat up and patted himself on the back. "Well done, Clay."

She laughed, grateful for the break in tension. "Glad to hear you're not lacking in the self-confidence department." Then again, he had no reason to. She blushed at the memory of how he'd made her feel, how attentive he'd been to her desires.

"What time is it?" he asked.

She glanced at the clock on the nightstand, then crossed her arms in front of her and leaned her weight on one hip. "Just after eight." *Is he planning to leave?*

"I wonder how your buddy KC's feeling today," he said.

"Not great, I imagine. If she's even awake, that is."

"That was quite a gymnastics expo she put on there."

"Yep." Daphne had no idea what to do next, so she just stood there in front of the bed, her arms crossed. *Should I climb back in bed? Would he want me to do that?*

She didn't see any obvious signs of regret in his eyes, but then again, she was hardly an expert at reading the facial expressions of men, especially ones waking up naked in a virtual stranger's bed. *Should I bring up last night?*

Her mind raced for something, anything, to say, but she came up with nothing, so she remained silent, again wishing she had a guidebook for appropriate post-one-night-stand behavior. *Don't make this awkward.*

Clay glanced up at the ceiling. "Nice gecko. We have one in our house too."

"I named him Fred," Daphne blurted, then immediately regretted having done so. Talking to a gecko was odd enough. Naming him was worse. But *telling* anyone about it? That bordered on peculiar, with *peculiar* being a generous euphemism for *weird*.

Clay chuckled. "Nice. I named ours Gordon."

Daphne let out a tiny gasp. "You're joking. You named a gecko too?"

"Not joking. Isn't Gordon the perfect name for a gecko? Doug wanted to call him Mervyn, but I won the house vote."

"Gordon is clever, better than Fred. I'll give you that. But Mervyn is pretty good too. My neighbors in Columbus have a dog named Mervyn, and it always makes me laugh to greet him." She smiled at the thought. *Hi, Mervyn.*

He laughed, and she felt the tension between them soften a bit more. *What was I so freaked out about? Just go with it.*

She decided to climb back in bed with him, but the moment she took a step forward, he sat up and pulled the duvet cover to one side. "I'd better get going," he said, swinging his legs onto the tile floor.

She froze. "Oh yes, of course." She felt the awkwardness come rushing back and pointed to the bathroom. "Your clothes are hanging in there. Just to warn you, they're still a bit damp."

.   .   .

While Clay was in the bathroom, Daphne quietly poked her head outside her bedroom door and peeked down the hall toward the kitchen. *Why am I so embarrassed?* She wondered why it bothered her that her friends would soon know that Clay had spent the night. Unless KC had been the one drinking wine with Skylar, which Daphne highly doubted, Scott had probably slept over too. *Stop worrying. They'll be proud of you. So should you.* She glanced back at the shut bathroom door and sighed. She knew what was really bothering her. *Couldn't he have* pretended *he wanted me to crawl back in bed with him? Even for just a few minutes?*

Yes, Skylar and KC would be happy that she'd spent the night with Clay, but there was no getting around how quickly he'd jumped out of bed and said he had to "get going." No matter what her age, no woman wanted to hear those words from a man she's just slept with for the first time. She winced. *What if I was terrible?*

She took a deep breath, then stepped into the hall and quietly closed her bedroom door behind her. As she padded toward the kitchen, she braced herself for the inevitable encounter with her friends, but the spacious room was empty, the lights off, and the living room equally still. She turned around and looked back down the hall. Both Skylar's and KC's doors were closed. Maybe they were still sleeping? If Daphne had had as much to drink as KC, she'd be in a coma for at least half the day, but KC's body operated on a different level. It wouldn't surprise Daphne if KC were already out for a run.

Skylar, on the other hand, was more of a wild card. How late she—and Scott?—would sleep was anyone's guess.

She decided to make some coffee and go sit out on the deck. She reached into the cupboard for a mug, and as she stood in front of the machine watching the liquid drip into the cup, she heard footsteps behind her. She turned around and saw Clay standing there, fully dressed, albeit in clothes that were decidedly more rumpled than when he'd worn them just a few hours earlier.

"Want some coffee?" Daphne pointed to the fancy machine. She hoped it wasn't superobvious how uncomfortable she felt, but there was no getting around the reality of her mood.

Clay shook his head. "Thanks, but I'm not much of a coffee drinker. I was thinking about hitting the smoothie stand."

"Did I hear someone mention the sweet nectar that is *coffee?*"

Daphne looked to her right and caught her breath at the man she saw strolling into the kitchen . . . and wearing nothing but a pair of striped boxer shorts.

"Doug, hi," she said in a near whisper.

"Mornin', Daphne. Hey, Clay." He yawned and scratched his cheek.

Daphne felt her blood run cold. *No!* Doug knew how drunk KC had been last night. *How could he take advantage of her like that?* She quickly turned toward the coffeemaker, unable to look Doug in the eye, furious at him, at herself, at all of them. *I shouldn't have left them alone. How could Skylar have let KC do that? She didn't know what she was doing. We should have protected her.*

"Daphne?"

It was Clay speaking to her now, but she still couldn't bring herself to turn around.

"Yes?" she said in a strained voice.

"Doug and I are going to sit on the deck for a few minutes before I take off, okay?"

"Sure, no problem. I'll bring his coffee out when it's ready. You sure you don't want anything?" she called over her shoulder, trying to keep her speech steady.

"Water would be great, or juice if you have it."

"Okay, got it." Acting on autopilot, she fumbled around for a second mug and a juice glass, then awkwardly pressed the button on the coffee machine. She opened the fridge and removed a carton of orange juice, then filled up a glass for Clay before brewing another cup of coffee. Her mind continued to race. *What should I do? How could this have happened?*

When the second cup of coffee was ready, she set all three drinks on a tray with cream and sugar fixings and two spoons, then carefully walked toward the deck, with the tray visibly trembling. She prepared herself for how to address Doug. *Don't be rude to him. He's not the married one here.*

When she stepped outside and looked toward him and Clay, she nearly dropped the tray. KC was on the deck too. She was dressed in workout gear and leaning against the railing, stretching her quads one at a time by pulling her heels up against her backside. Doug and Clay were seated at the teak picnic table.

"There's the birthday girl!" KC stopped stretching, then bounced over to Daphne and took the tray from her. She set it down on the table, then gave Daphne a huge hug. "*Happy birthday*, my friend!"

Daphne hugged her back, bewildered by her positive mood given the circumstances. "Thanks. Um, did you already work out?"

KC let go of her and nodded. "Yes, ma'am. Had to sweat out all those cocktails. My body's not used to alcohol cruising through the bloodstream like kids on a slip-and-slide."

"How do you feel?"

KC adjusted her baseball cap. "I feel fine *now*, but I'm not gonna lie. When I woke up at six o'clock, I wasn't feeling so hot. But Doug made me drink a *ton* of water before I went to bed, so that helped a lot." She blew him a kiss. "Thanks, pal. I owe you one."

"No problem. After the show you put on last night, I felt I owed you a little TLC." He picked up the coffee mug and took a sip, then lifted it toward Daphne. Thanks for the tasty cup of joe, it's exactly what I need right now."

Daphne smiled as much as she could manage. "You're welcome. All I did was push a button."

"Well, you did a damn fine job," Doug said.

"You also poured a mean glass of juice," Clay said.

"Thanks." Daphne smiled at him too and tried her best to hide how rattled she was by the entire situation. Didn't anyone else feel horribly awkward right now? Or was a casual *morning-after* scene like this par for the course for single people? Or was the correct word *unattached* people? *Unmarried* people? She'd been out of the game for so long, she didn't even know the current nomenclature. Then again, KC wasn't any of those things, and she seemed completely comfortable at the moment. *What is going on? Why are they acting so normal?* She felt as if she were watching a movie in a foreign language—with no subtitles.

"Is one of those for me? I feel like I've just risen from the grave."

Daphne whirled around. Skylar emerged from the house wearing a short robe and slippers, her long auburn locks pulled up into a haphazard bun that somehow looked simultaneously messy and chic.

"Hi, Skylar," Daphne said, then pointed at the tray. "You can have mine if you want." Right now all she wanted to do was go inside and escape this weirdness . . . and maybe go back to bed. Or back to Ohio.

"On your *birthday*? Don't even think about it." She wrapped her arms around Daphne and squeezed her tight. "Happy birthday, sweets. I love you lots." Then she added as a whisper into Daphne's ear, "Good for you, by the way. He's dreamy."

"I'm so confused right now," Daphne whispered back.

Doug stood and held up his mug. "Take mine, Skylar. You like cream and sugar?"

"Right now I like anything that has caffeine in it." She walked up to Doug, and Daphne's jaw dropped at what happened next.

"Thanks, babe." Skylar stood on her tiptoes and gave Doug a quick kiss on the cheek before taking the mug and sitting down on a bench. "Mmm, come to Mama," she cooed to the dark liquid.

Daphne stood there, her mouth still slightly agape. *Huh?* She hoped her expression hadn't telegraphed her bafflement, but she highly doubted it. *Skylar and Doug? What?*

KC, who still didn't seem the slightest bit perturbed, proceeded to stretch out her calves against the railing of the deck. "Hey, Skylar, how would you feel about postponing our spa day?"

"Please tell me you're joking," Skylar said without looking up from her coffee. "Why in God's name would we do that?"

KC jutted her chin toward Doug. "Because my bestie here just invited us to join him and his buddies on a catamaran!"

Daphne stiffened. What did Clay think about this invitation? More importantly, what did *she* think about the invitation? Until now she'd assumed Clay would be gone with the juice in his glass.

Skylar arched an eyebrow. "A catamaran? Tell me more."

KC pointed to Doug. "He'll fill you in. I'm going to pop in the house for some water. Anybody else need anything?"

Maybe an explanation of what the heck is going on? Daphne asked with her eyes, but KC didn't seem to notice. While she was immensely relieved to know that KC hadn't cheated on Max, she was still trying to process that Skylar and Doug had ended up together. And where was Scott? What had happened to him? *Where are the subtitles?!*

Doug pointed toward the ocean. "We chartered a big one, includes drinks, lunch, the works. You're more than welcome to join us, we have plenty of room."

Skylar sipped her coffee. "Okay, let's do it. As long as I'm *above* the water, I'm good."

"Sounds like you're more of a land person?" Clay asked her.

"I'm a prefer-not-to-drown person," she said as she gestured toward Daphne. "Ms. Thesaurus over there would know the correct word choice."

Doug and Clay looked at Daphne, and she felt her face flush.

She swallowed before responding. "I . . . I think the adjective she's looking for is *hydrophobic*," she said without smiling. She was too off-kilter to even fake a smile at this point.

"See? Beautiful *and* smart," Skylar said, and Daphne shot her a thankful look. Even in adulthood, there was a fine line between feeling smart and feeling like a nerd. And right now she needed a confidence boost.

KC returned with a tray of waters and proceeded to pass the glasses around. "What do *you* think, birthday girl? It's your special day, so it's up to you."

Daphne cautiously turned toward Clay in search of an answer in his eyes, but he wasn't looking in her direction. She took a deep breath and prepared to say no, but when she spoke, she heard her voice saying the words, "Okay, sure." *Why not? How often do I get invited on a catamaran?*

KC pumped her fist. "Awesome! I'm totally going snorkeling, if that's an option." She swung her head toward Doug. "Is that an option?"

Doug nodded. "Definitely. We'll cruise up to a cove on the north shore of the island, go swimming there and have lunch, then circle back down here. It's going to be a blast."

"Then it's settled," Skylar stood up, clapped her hands, and headed toward the house. "We'll do the spa thing tomorrow. Let me go arrange it. What time do we have to leave? I need to make a couple work calls first."

Doug looked at his watch. "We leave at ten sharp and return at four. The boat is picking us up in front of the beach house. Meet us there?"

"Deal." Skylar made her way toward the glass door to the living room. "I hate to drink and run, my friends, but I'm doing it anyway."

KC jumped up and followed her. "I need to call Max. He's going to be so jealous!"

Doug followed them inside to retrieve the rest of his things, leaving Daphne and Clay alone on the deck.

"Should be a fun day," Clay said. "I've heard that cove is off the charts."

Daphne looked at the deck floor, acutely aware of his chosen words, or lack of flirtatious undertones therein. She also couldn't ignore the physical distance between them. "Definitely. I've never been on a catamaran," she said.

He stood up and gestured down the beach. "I guess I should go home and get in line for a shower. Will you tell Doug I'll see him back at the house?"

"Will do. See you soon."

He gave her a quick kiss good-bye, but she knew it felt forced—for both of them. As she watched him climb down the steps of the deck to the beach, she briefly wondered if last night had been a mistake. But only briefly. *It wasn't a mistake. It was fun. Don't take it so seriously. Just be yourself. Be yourself and enjoy.*

She remembered the early morning ride to the airport just a couple days ago, when she'd been so worried about what her friends would think of her, of who she had become. Now after such a brief time on St. Mirika, away from Columbus, she no longer felt like that tormented woman in the car. *Who am I now?* Was this a new version of her old self? Or someone else entirely? She turned toward the ocean and stared out at the horizon.

Whoever Daphne White was becoming, or *returning to*, she was glad to have her here.

Chapter Ten

Doug left a few minutes later. Daphne waved good-bye and calmly waited until he'd walked down the steps of the deck onto the beach, then quietly closed the French doors, turned around, and looked at her friends.

"Well?" Skylar called from her desk.

Daphne pressed her hands against her cheeks. "I totally slept with him!"

"I *knew* it!" KC yelled from a stool at the kitchen island. "Nice work!"

"Am I a slut now? Or should I be proud of myself?" Daphne half laughed, half whispered. "I'm not sure which way to go."

Skylar placed her headset on the desk and held up a finger. "Give me five seconds to finish this e-mail . . . okay . . . sending . . . done!" She set down the headset, then stood up and walked toward Daphne, her arms extended. "I'm so proud of you, *dahling*. I knew you could break that dry spell. And God no, you're hardly a slut. Anyone who would suggest otherwise is a complete idiot."

"Agreed," KC said with a firm nod. "You were due for a little horizontal tango."

Daphne laughed, then took Skylar's hands and pulled her down with her so that they were both seated on the plush couch. "What about *you*? Did you really hook up with Doug?"

Skylar shook her head. "Oh God *no*. He took one of the empty bedrooms. We were pretty drunk after we broke out the good stuff, so he decided to crash here." She pointed to the empty bottles on the counter.

"What happened to Scott?" Daphne asked. "The last I saw, he was putting on a full-court press."

Skylar shrugged. "After that drama at the Castaway, I kind of lost interest. Then Doug mentioned that he has a girlfriend, so I unsubscribed for good. Scott's a hottie, but I don't play that game, even on vacation."

Daphne pointed at KC. "And *you*, little lady, nearly gave me a heart attack."

KC put a hand on her chest. "Me? Why? What did I do?"

"Because I thought Scott was with Skylar last night. So when I saw Doug cruising around in his underwear this morning, I thought *you* had hooked up with him."

KC cracked up. "Yeah, right. Can you imagine? Max would have loved that."

Skylar shrugged. "I told him to put on some clothes."

"You have no idea how freaked out I was," Daphne said. "Thank God it was all a misunderstanding."

"Anyhow, back to you and Clay," Skylar said. "How was it?"

Daphne blushed. "Um, good, I guess."

"How good?"

Daphne smiled and looked down. *It was amazing.*

"Don't be shy now," Skylar said. "Was it one-sided? We're too old for one-sided sex."

"Amen!" KC called from her barstool.

Daphne laughed. "No, it wasn't one-sided. To be honest, he was quite concerned about making sure I, um, enjoyed myself." She felt a shiver run through her at the memory.

Skylar snapped her fingers. "Yet another benefit of being older. Men know we won't put up with sexual selfishness like we did in our twenties. Remember those days? Good riddance."

"That's quite a tongue twister," KC called. "*Sexual selfishness. I can picture the protests now. Stop the sexual selfishness!*" She pumped a fist in the air.

Daphne smiled at KC, then looked back at Skylar. "It was kind of awkward this morning, though." *A lot awkward, actually.* "I had no idea how to act, or what to say, literally no idea. I kind of just froze up."

"It's always awkward the next morning," Skylar said. "I wouldn't sweat it. I'm superproud of you."

"*So* proud of you!" KC lifted her water glass in the air. "Daphne got some!"

Daphne frowned. "I kind of wish Doug hadn't invited us on the catamaran trip. I didn't want to say no, but I don't think Clay was too thrilled about that. I kind of got the feeling that he would have preferred to leave things as a 'one and done,' you know?"

"I wouldn't overthink it one way or the other," Skylar said. "You're never going to see him again after this week anyway, so I say just relax and try to have fun. Plus, there will be enough people on the boat to provide a buffer if things get a little weird. Big picture, you bedded a hot guy, and you get to go on a catamaran on your birthday."

"A win-win!" KC called.

"You sound like my neighbor, Carol. That's one of her favorite expressions," Daphne said.

"Your old-lady neighbor uses the expression 'bedded a hot guy'?" Skylar asked.

"Sweet! Sounds like we need to visit Columbus," KC said.

Daphne laughed. "I mean she likes the expression 'win-win.'"

KC made a lasso motion with her arm. "I think we should focus on the bedded-a-hot-guy part of this conversation. That bar was overflowing with girls in their twenties, but look where Clay woke up this morning. Yes, that would be *here*. You totally roped him in. I love it!"

Daphne blushed, but she could feel the hint of a smile on her face. "Actually, he kind of roped *me* in. It was after midnight, so he said he wanted to buy me a birthday drink."

"Handsome *and* chivalrous. I love that too!" KC said. Then she turned to Skylar and pretended to cast a fishing line. "And *you*, turning down Scott like that after you'd successfully reeled him in. That was an impressive display of skill *and* willpower. You were both on fire last night!"

Skylar stood up and pulled the tie out of her bun, letting her hair fall loose around her shoulders. "Reeling him in wasn't all that hard, actually. Getting a man interested is all about how you carry yourself. Janine is a perfect example of that. She's a beautiful girl, but the poor thing had desperation written all over her. Guys just aren't attracted to that. That's why so many of them like older women."

"I wish I had your confidence," Daphne said. "I woke up feeling good about last night, but then I half expected Clay to sneak out when I was in the bathroom."

Skylar shook her head. "But he didn't, right? You can't think like that."

"Agreed, negative energy only leads to negative energy." KC jumped off her stool and walked toward them. "The end story is that the birthday girl here had a holiday tryst with a younger man, how exciting!"

"A *hot* younger man, don't forget that critical adjective," Skylar said.

KC nodded. "Indeed. Well done, Daphne."

"Aren't you glad I dragged you to the Castaway?" Skylar said to them both. "I told you we'd have a blast."

"Understatement of the year," KC said. "Although I'm not gonna lie. I could do without the headache right now."

"Do you *ever* lie?" Daphne asked.

KC laughed. "Good point."

. . .

"There they are, my favorite neighbors." Doug waved from the deck as the trio approached the bachelors' beach house.

"Hey, everyone." KC trotted up the stairs and gave a quick wave to the group. "Long time no see."

A small cheer erupted. "MVP!" someone yelled from the back, and KC took a little bow.

At the sight of all the guys milling around the deck, Daphne's nerves reappeared. Where was Clay? She stopped walking until Skylar nudged her in the back.

"Confidence, confidence," Skylar whispered. Then she interlaced her arm with Daphne's and led her up the stairs. "Gentlemen," she said with a cool nod. "It's nice to see you again. Scott, looking quite dapper, as always."

"Morning, Skylar," Scott mumbled.

Daphne noticed that Skylar didn't seem the least bit fazed that Scott, if not the other guys, probably knew that Doug had spent the night with her, however platonically. Or maybe they didn't know? Did men talk about that sort of thing with their friends the way women did? That line of thought made her wonder if the guys knew where Clay had spent the night. It was all Daphne could do to keep from breaking out into a cold sweat at the idea. Her brain turned with a question she was afraid to know the answer to. *Does everyone here know I slept with him?*

Being more adventurous was one thing. Publicizing a one-night stand was another.

She quickly scanned the rest of the deck for Clay but didn't see him. She did, however, spot three younger women huddled in a corner. She immediately recognized one of them as Janine from the night before. Next to her were two blondes, one of whom had been dancing with Scott when Janine left the Castaway. The other didn't look familiar.

Janine made eye contact with Daphne and gave her a quick wave hello.

Daphne smiled and waved back. *What are they doing here?*

Just then Clay emerged from the house, his eyes scanning the deck. When he noticed Daphne, he turned and walked straight toward her, which both thrilled and terrified her.

"Hey, Daphne, long time no see." He held out a bottle of water. "Can I interest you in some water? I heard you got some exercise last night."

Relieved that he'd made the effort to break the ice, she laughed and took the bottle, then lowered her voice. "Do you think we could keep that on the down low? I hate to broadcast it to the world."

He pretended to look hurt. "I will do my best *not* to take that personally. But you're the birthday girl, so I'll defer to your wishes."

"Much appreciated." She felt her face flush and put the cold water bottle against her cheek, not sure if it was the heat or the memory of what they'd done last night that was causing her temperature to rise.

"Who invited the sorority girls?" Skylar appeared at Daphne's side.

"I was wondering the same thing," Daphne said.

"Scott invited them," Clay said. "They showed up this morning." He gestured toward the house. "I'm going to go grab my backpack. See you on the boat?"

"Sounds good," Daphne said. *What was I worried about? He's not acting weird at all. This is going to be fine.*

Once Clay was out of earshot, Skylar lowered her voice and leaned in close to Daphne. "Drama alert on sorority row, three o'clock. This could get ugly."

Daphne stole another peek at the young women. All three of them were wearing makeup and heels and had their hair down. *Who wears makeup and heels at the beach? Who wears their hair down on a boat?*

"I wonder why Scott invited them?" she whispered to Skylar.

"Why wouldn't he? They're young and nice to look at, and he loves the attention. Plus, he's probably miffed that he ended up alone last night when he easily could have hooked up with one of them. It's textbook game playing for him to have all of us here. Reminds me a bit of my younger self, to be honest."

Daphne put her arm around Skylar. "I love how forthright you are."

Skylar shrugged. "No point in sugarcoating things. All that does is make you fat."

Daphne glanced back at the young women. "So his game is *literally* to put you all in the same boat."

Skylar laughed. "You and your words."

"Hey, people, the catamaran's here! Let's get a move on!" Doug hopped up on the railing and yelled to the group, "Don't forget your swimsuit and shades. Wilson, don't forget your tampons. They have everything else on deck."

"Suck it, Bates!" A stocky man Daphne assumed to be Wilson yelled back.

KC bounded toward Daphne and Skylar. "I'm so excited! I've been on a sailboat before, but never a catamaran."

"Are my favorite neighbors ready to go?" Doug pointed down at them from the railing.

Daphne started rummaging through her oversized tote to check her inventory. "Let's see . . . sunscreen, bug repellent, hat, salty snacks, sugary snacks, energy bars, water, hand lotion, tissues, hand sanitizer, sewing kit, tin of safety pins, mini-first-aid kit, and two tampons just in case of an emergency, although I guess *Wilson* over there has that covered." She looked up at Doug and smiled. "I think we're good."

Skylar peered into the canvas bag. "Good lord, you're in serious mom mode. Do you have a minivan in there too?"

Daphne slung the tote bag over her shoulder. "What can I say? I like to be prepared. Is that bad?"

KC shook her head. "Not at all. It's cute. Very endearing."

Daphne lowered her voice and glanced around the crowded deck. "You think everyone here would freak if they knew I had a teenage daughter?"

"Maybe. The sorority girls probably would. But who cares? *You're* the one who woke up with the hot guy in your bed," Skylar said.

"Shh!" Daphne said.

"It's the truth," Skylar said with a shrug. "Why not own it?"

Daphne thought about it for a moment, then smiled. "You're right, I *did* wake up this morning with a hot guy in my bed. Thank you for reminding me of that." A tiny victory bell rang in a far corner of her brain.

Skylar bowed her head. "You're welcome."

KC pointed at the tote bag. "Can I have one of those energy bars?"

• • •

The catamaran was quite large, so despite the size of their group, once everyone was on board it felt spacious and not crowded at all. At least in Daphne's opinion. Skylar had traveled on many a fancy yacht, so once again *perspective* became the operative word.

After they got moving, three crew members appeared on deck, each holding a tray of rum punches, which were gone in a blink and quickly replaced by a fresh round. The crew also turned on the stereo to play reggae at a decibel that managed to strike the perfect balance between soft and jarring. Again, that was just in Daphne's opinion. She had a sneaking feeling that the younger members of the group might have preferred an uptick in the volume. She remembered those days of ear-ringing dance music, and while she had never been much of a fan, it certainly didn't bother her then as much as it did now.

KC held up her plastic cup for a toast. "Ladies, this is already my favorite day of the trip."

Skylar poked her in the arm. "Who are you, and what have you done with KC?"

"Huh?" KC said.

Skylar pointed to KC's cup. "It's ten thirty in the morning. Even *I* can't drink alcohol at ten thirty in the morning, and I'm a professional."

KC grinned. "When in Rome, right?"

Daphne hunted in her tote bag for a bottle of water. "I think I'll wait until noon to canvas that territory again."

Just then Clay and Doug wandered around from the opposite side of the catamaran, followed by Janine and one of her friends. Both women were barefoot now, the bemused captain having informed them that heels were most certainly not allowed on board.

They were also holding their hair behind them, trying unsuccessfully to keep it from flying in their faces.

Daphne reached for her tote. "Do you need ponytail holders? I think I have some extras in here."

"I want a bag of tricks too," Doug said. "That thing's like a damn Costco."

"Do you have any Rollerblades in there?" Clay peered at the bag. "Or maybe a croquet set?"

Daphne laughed. "Don't be knocking my tote bag. You know if we end up on a deserted island, I'm the one everyone's going to be making an alliance with."

Janine gave Daphne a grateful smile. "I'd love a hair tie, thanks so much."

"Thanks," her friend said with a shy smile of her own. Daphne didn't recognize her, so she wasn't the one who had been flirting with Scott the night before. She glanced around the boat and wondered if that girl was talking to Scott now. Scott was clearly all about talking to pretty women, despite the one he apparently had waiting for him at home.

Daphne handed them each a hair tie. "What's your name? I'm Daphne," she said to Janine's friend. She also introduced the others.

"Becca." The young woman set her drink down and pulled her long locks into a ponytail.

"We hear you're on spring break?" KC said.

Janine nodded. "From Florida State."

"What are you studying?" Skylar asked them.

Becca tucked a few remaining strands of hair behind her ear. "I'm a communications major with a minor in psychology. I'm thinking about applying to law school." The words sounded rehearsed, as if she were trying to impress a potential summer employer rather than engage in casual conversation.

Janine also answered somewhat robotically. "I'm majoring in sociology. I think I might want to be a teacher." She glanced downward as she spoke, essentially addressing the deck floor and not a group of actual people.

Skylar gave Daphne a look, and it was clear what she was thinking. Despite their outward appearance—sexy sundresses and lots of makeup—now that their hair was pulled away from their faces, Janine and Becca looked almost childlike, an impression punctuated by their obvious discomfort in answering such innocuous questions.

"I have a niece who wants to be a teacher too," Skylar said. "She's only fourteen, though, so who knows how long that will last? Last year she wanted to be an astronaut. My sister and her husband are convinced she'll end up a general because she's always telling everyone what to do."

Everyone laughed, yet Daphne couldn't help but realize that Skylar's niece, not to mention her own daughter, were closer in age to these young women than she and her friends were. Daphne had already begun to dread the day when Emma would straddle that delicate line between adolescence and adulthood. Watching her daughter navigate the rocky waters of high school was difficult enough. She wasn't ready for what was to come after that.

After a few more minutes of somewhat stilted small talk, Janine and Becca headed down below to use the restroom. As soon as they were gone, Clay spoke.

"Does anyone else feel old right now?" he said in a hushed voice.

Skylar pushed her sunglasses on top of her head. "No kidding. My niece is more articulate than those two, and she's in eighth grade."

KC laughed. "Be nice now. They're trying so hard to fit in. They've probably never socialized with actual *adults* before."

"Hanson! Bates! Come hither, my henchmen!"

211

Everyone turned their heads. Perry, the groom, was standing at the front of the catamaran, holding up a drink with one hand, waving Clay and Doug toward him with the other.

"Sorry, ladies, duty calls," Doug said.

Skylar held out her arm to let them pass. "By all means, it's tough work being a bridesmaid."

"We'll catch up with you later," Clay said. He smiled as he walked away, but he didn't specifically make eye contact with Daphne.

"Sure," Daphne said. She wasn't sure if she believed him, but she was thrilled to realize that she didn't really care all that much. She had other things on her mind. *It's a gorgeous day. It's my birthday. I'm aboard a fancy catamaran in the Caribbean Sea—with my best friends in the world right next to me.* However the day was unfolding, Daphne was feeling carefree, something just a few days ago she didn't think possible.

· · ·

A few minutes after four o'clock, the catamaran pulled up in front of the guys' beach house, about a hundred yards out from shore.

"Do we *have* to get off?" KC frowned at the small motorboat approaching to ferry them back to land. "I kind of want to stay put."

Daphne raised her hand. "I second that motion."

"Raising a hand is KC's move," Skylar said. "Could you be more original? Come on, ladies, time is a wasting. We've got to shower and get dolled up for Daphne's birthday evening." She gave both Daphne and KC a gentle shove from behind. Not enough to topple them into the ocean, but enough to let them know she'd had enough of the water.

Daphne looked over her shoulder at Skylar as she climbed into the motorboat. "Let me guess, you have a work call before dinner?"

"Perhaps," Skylar said with a shrug.

"It never ends," KC said as she took a seat in the boat.

For Daphne, the day had been glorious. When they'd reached the cove at the north end of the island, most everyone on board had donned a snorkel and dived into the water, which because of the cove formation appeared even greener than the water by their houses, if that was even possible. As promised, the crew expertly led the swimmers to a small group of turtles. After some prodding by KC, Daphne had reached down and gently grazed one with her fingertips.

Janine and her friends had also joined in the fun, albeit reluctantly, and once back on board all three of them quickly disappeared into the bathroom and reemerged shortly thereafter with their faces freshly painted. They were nice girls, but at the end of the day that's what they were . . . *girls*. Scott had spent the early part of the trip chatting them up, but by the afternoon it was clear that even his interest level had waned.

Skylar carefully climbed into the small boat behind Daphne and KC, who were already seated, then pointed toward the shore. "Ladies, a fabulous evening awaits!"

"Are gentlemen invited?"

Daphne looked up and saw Clay looking down from the railing at them. She hadn't spent much time with him on the catamaran, so she was taken off guard by his question. Not that she didn't want to see more of him. Of course she did. But for her birthday dinner? Would Skylar and KC be okay with that? Would it be weird? Should they invite Doug then too? *What does the guidebook say I should do?* She didn't mean to hesitate as her mind jumped about, but she did. A little too long.

"Daphne, say something to him," Skylar finally whispered.

Clay held up a hand. "You know what? On second thought, I don't want to intrude on a birthday celebration. Consider the question withdrawn, your honor."

"I'm sorry, you just caught me a little off guard." Daphne quickly glanced at her friends. "And Skylar already made reservations."

"What about the Castaway?" Skylar whispered. "Maybe we could meet up with him and the guys there later?"

"The Castaway *again*?" KC looked less than thrilled. "I emptied that tank last night."

Daphne gave Skylar a *What should we do?* look, and Skylar responded with one that said *your call.*

The boat started pulling away from the catamaran, so Daphne knew she had to say something. She looked back up at Clay as they pulled away. "Maybe we'll run into you at the Castaway later?"

He nodded. "That works. Have fun at dinner."

She waved good-bye. "Thanks!"

"Bye, Clay!" KC waved to him too. "Say good-bye to my bestie!" Scott and Doug were down below settling the bill with the crew.

The motorboat roared to life, and as it ferried the women back to shore, Daphne frowned and looked at her friends. "That was really awkward."

Skylar leaned over and put her hand on Daphne's thigh. "You did fine. Don't stress."

"Do you *want* to see him again?" KC asked.

Daphne sighed. "I'm not sure. I guess I do, or *did*, but I wasn't getting much of a vibe from him today, so I was kind of thrown off just there."

"That's better than being thrown off the catamaran," KC said.

Daphne laughed. "True."

A few minutes later the boat pulled up to shore, and Daphne carefully climbed out, followed by Skylar. KC was the last to exit, but there was nothing careful about her descent. She leaped into the knee-deep water, then shrieked out in pain upon landing.

"Ouch!"

Daphne and Skylar, who had already reached the beach, immediately turned around to see what had happened.

"Are you okay?" Daphne called out.

"I think I just got stung by a jellyfish!"

Daphne and Skylar began to rush back into the water to help, but KC held up an arm to keep them at bay. "Stop. I don't want it to get you too!" She hopped on one leg toward the shore, then collapsed onto the sand. Her right thigh was red, blistered, and swollen. "Oh my holy hell, this hurts."

Daphne kneeled next to her and took a good look. "That's a jellyfish sting all right. Looks like it got you pretty bad."

KC made a strained face. "Holy frick, this hurts more than when I tore ligaments in my ankle."

Daphne held out her palm. "Grab my hand. You're going to be fine, just try to stay calm, okay? Don't worry, we'll take care of you." She spoke in a soothing voice and began to examine KC's leg. "First we need to get the stinger . . . Okay, here it is. Now don't move, I'm going to get a pair of tweezers." She dug around inside her tote bag for her first-aid kit, then pulled out a tiny pink sleeve containing the tweezers.

"Such a mom," KC said with a grimace. "Who carries around tweezers?"

"I do sometimes," Skylar said. "But for my *eyebrows*, not for treating jellyfish-attack victims."

Daphne carefully removed the stinger, then slid the tweezers back into the sleeve. "I wish I had some vinegar."

KC laughed weakly. "If you did, I would be worried about you. Maybe *you* should have bought that candy striper dress. How do you know so much about jellyfish stings anyway?"

Daphne paused to think. "I saw a documentary about them once."

KC and Skylar exchanged a glance.

"Are you thinking what I'm thinking?" Skylar asked her.

"That episode of *Friends*?" KC said.

Skylar nodded.

KC put a hand on Daphne's arm. "Are you planning to have someone pee on me?"

"Not it." Skylar took a step backward. "Get Doug to do it. God knows he drank enough rum punch today to donate some urine to his *bestie*."

"Is Doug going to have to pee on me?" KC asked Daphne.

Daphne grabbed a fistful of sand and began to rub it over KC's thigh. "Not to worry, no urination necessary. If I remember correctly, this should do the trick." She scooped up some saltwater with her hands and washed it off several times, then reached into her tote bag, pulled out a pink silk scarf, and tied it around KC's upper leg. "The sand should remove any other tentacle stingers, and this pressure will help stop the venom from spreading."

KC looked at her. "Venom? That doesn't sound good."

Daphne shook her head. "It's just a toxin. Your leg will be itchy and sore for a while, but you'll be fine. They were clear about that in the documentary. This is actually quite common."

"Will I be able to play in my tournament next weekend?" KC asked.

"I don't think they mentioned soccer," Daphne said with a smile.

"Did they mention that KC is insane?" Skylar said.

Daphne laughed, and both she and Skylar looked at KC, expecting a witty comeback, but she didn't make one.

"Are you feeling okay?" Daphne asked her.

"I'm . . . having a little trouble breathing," KC said, her face now a bit pale.

Daphne put a hand on KC's shoulder. "Okay, they definitely mentioned that in the documentary. It probably means you're having an allergic reaction to the sting, so we'll need to get you to the hospital. But I don't want you to worry, because you're going to be fine, okay? You're going to be fine." She looked up at Skylar, who was still standing a couple feet away. "Can you go flag a cab while I work on this a bit more?"

"We have a car we can use, it's in our garage," Skylar said. "I'll go get it, will meet you right there, okay?" She pointed to the street behind the sand dune near Clay and Doug's place, then turned and ran toward the beach house.

Once Skylar was gone, Daphne turned back toward KC. "This is nothing to be concerned about, okay? I know I'm not a doctor, but I totally remember that documentary."

KC smiled, but she looked a bit frightened now. "I thought I was only allergic to beets," she said in a near whisper.

Daphne put her hand on KC's arm and gave it a gentle squeeze. "Do you trust me?"

KC nodded her head. "I trust you. And yes, I realize that we just quoted Leo and Kate in *Titanic*."

• • •

"Skylar, seriously, will you stop tailgating those poor people? You're going to kill us all, assuming this stupid jellyfish venom doesn't do me in first," KC called from the backseat. "Damn this hurts," she added.

"You're hardly dying if you still have the energy to mock me," Skylar said.

"Worst. Driver. Ever," KC groaned.

Daphne turned around from the passenger seat and gave KC a nod of solidarity. "For the record, I'm glad it's not just me. I'm fearing for my life up here."

"Did you hear that Skylar? You are the worst driver I've ever seen, and that's saying a lot for someone who has been in a car with teenage boys behind the wheel," KC said.

Skylar rolled her eyes in the rearview mirror. "I live in New York City, okay? I don't drive much. Plus, I'm trying to save your life, if you hadn't noticed."

"At least keep your eyes on the road, can you please do that?" Daphne looked at Skylar and pressed her palms together in prayer.

"Were you this bad of a driver in college?" KC asked. "I must have blocked it out."

"Trying to save your life," Skylar repeated.

"You should have let Daphne drive," KC said. "The world would be a safer place with you in the passenger seat."

"There it is!" Skylar pointed to the sign for the hospital, then jerked the car to the right and screeched through the entrance at nearly full speed.

"God help us." Daphne closed her eyes.

"I heard that," Skylar said.

"I hope God heard it too," KC said.

. . .

After the nurse took KC inside, Daphne and Skylar settled into the small waiting room, which was nearly empty.

"I hope this means we won't be here that long," Skylar said. "A crowded waiting room is never a good sign."

Daphne pointed at the door leading to the examination area. "Depends on how many doctors are here, or if there's a pressing emergency ahead of you. I took Emma in once for a broken arm, and we were there for seven hours."

"I wonder how pressing an allergic reaction to a jellyfish sting is." Skylar pulled out her phone. "I'm going to look it up."

Daphne stood up to peruse the magazine choice in a rack hanging on the wall. "Jeez, this is slim pickings. Some of these are older than Emma."

Skylar didn't look up from her phone. "I'll stick with WebMD, thank you very much. Oh, bite me."

Daphne turned around. "What's wrong?"

"I missed an important call. They moved up the time, but I didn't see the e-mail because we were on the catamaran."

"Is that bad?"

Skylar stood up and reached for her purse. "It's bad. I need to get back to the house right away. Take the keys, I'll hop in a cab. I'm sorry about this, but if I want to keep from getting fired, it looks like I'm not going to be able to make your birthday dinner."

Daphne gestured toward the door through which KC had disappeared. "No worries, I've had enough birthday excitement this trip to last me until next year. Plus, something tells me you're not the only one who's not going to make dinner."

Skylar's eyes followed. "Poor thing. I wonder how long she'll be down?"

"If it were a normal person, probably a few days or a week. But given that it's KC, she'll probably be out running on the beach before you and I are even awake tomorrow morning."

•   •   •

Daphne rushed toward KC the moment she saw her emerge from the hall with a nurse—and with a noticeable limp. "How are you feeling?" she asked.

KC smiled weakly. "You were totally right. Apparently I'm allergic to jellyfish. Who knew?"

Daphne put a hand on KC's cheek. "Are you in pain? Can I get you anything?"

"She's going to be fine," the nurse said. "Sore and itchy for a few days, but fine."

"More than anything I was worried about missing the tournament next weekend, but they said I should be able to play. Yeah!" KC half pumped her fist, then looked around the waiting room. "Where's Skylar?"

Daphne held up the keys. "Something came up at work, so she went back to the house to make a call. The good news is she took a cab, so she won't be driving us home."

"Oh thank heavens," KC said. "I can't take any more Formula One action today."

Daphne pointed to KC's leg. "So Skylar's most likely out for tonight, and you should probably rest that thing. I'm thinking we cancel dinner, get some takeout, and go home and relax."

"For your birthday? Are you sure?" KC asked.

"Trust me, I'm sure. After all this activity, chilling on the couch for an evening sounds glorious."

"What about meeting up with Clay?"

"That wasn't set in stone, was it? I think a night in with friends is just what the doctor ordered for both of us. And to be honest, I can't think of a better way to spend my birthday."

Chapter Eleven

After a quiet evening at the beach house, Daphne awoke early the next morning feeling rested, refreshed . . . and *happy*. She looked up at the ceiling and smiled. *I'm happy.* For a few moments she stared at the wooden fan spinning above her, marveling at how silent it was. Fred the gecko was perched on the ceiling again, but not in his usual spot. This time he was closer to the sliding glass doors leading to the deck.

"Hi, little guy. You mixing things up today? It's good to mix things up once in a while." *Just not every night.* While it would have been fun to see Clay again, she'd enjoyed the uneventful time in with her friends.

She tossed back the duvet cover and wiggled her feet into a pair of slippers, then walked over to the dresser to check her phone for a message from Emma. Not expecting one, she was delighted to see her daughter's name on the display.

Hi Mom, reception is really bad here so just got your last text. I'm having a great time! Hope your birthday was fun. See you in a couple days.

She typed a quick reply, then set the phone down and smiled, joyful that her daughter was having so much fun. Joyful that *she* was having so much fun. She couldn't put her finger on exactly what it was, but something about today felt . . . *new. She* felt new. Was it because she was forty now? Or because she was no longer so *afraid* of being forty . . . and unattached . . . and without a litany of bylines to her name, much less a Pulitzer?

Maybe turning the page to a new decade, a new phase of her life, a new *outlook* on her life, was exactly what she needed? A blank slate? A fresh start? Or maybe it was a soothing, healing mixture of all of that, like the rain. She couldn't put her finger on it exactly, but she didn't need to. *St. Mirika really is a magical place,* she thought.

• • •

When Daphne ambled into the kitchen a few minutes later, Skylar was sitting at the desk in the living room, quietly sipping coffee and staring at her laptop screen, her headset resting around her shoulders.

"Hey, sweets, how'd you sleep?" She pushed her reading glasses on top of her head.

Daphne yawned. "Like a corpse. I haven't slept that well in years."

Skylar chuckled. "I'm not surprised. You had quite a night to recover from."

Daphne reached for a ceramic mug and set it under the cof-feemaker. "An accurate statement. So how's your morning going so far? Any new fires to put out?"

"How did you know? I wouldn't be surprised if I have to head straight back to the airport the morning after I get home."

"Do you want to talk about it? Maybe vent a little?"

Skylar gave her a weary smile. "You're a dear to ask, but trust me, right now I want to do anything but talk about my job. I just want to try and enjoy the time we have left here."

"Remind me again why we made the trip so short?" Daphne asked.

Skylar gave Daphne a gentle tap on the shoulder on her way to brew a fresh cup of coffee. "How quickly they forget."

Daphne nodded slowly. "Okay, I'll take that." *She'd* been the one reluctant to leave home for longer than a few days—and only if it coincided with Emma's spring break. At the time it had seemed so important, so pressing, but now it just seemed . . . foolish.

"It would have been harder for me to get away for much longer anyway, so don't feel bad," Skylar said. "Hopefully the next trip can be longer."

I hope so too, Daphne thought.

Skylar gestured outside. "Should we go sit on the deck?"

Daphne glanced down the hall. "Is KC still sleeping? Or is she out running a marathon?"

"I haven't seen her, and I've been up for about an hour. I bet she's still down for the count, especially with that sting in her leg. Even the Energizer Bunny needs to take it easy once in a while."

"Want to walk to Bananarama and get a smoothie after we finish our coffee? We can bring one back for her," Daphne said.

Skylar held up her mug. "You don't have to ask me twice."

· · ·

It wasn't even eight o'clock, but the air was already warm and sticky when Daphne and Skylar reached the smoothie hut. And they weren't the only early birds there. As they waited on a nearby bench for the pleasant owner to slide open the window, Daphne found herself surveying the surrounding tables in search of other familiar faces. After just a few days on St. Mirika, she already felt like a member of a community, however small, however ephemeral.

She also felt a little twinge of sadness at the realization that it would be ending very soon.

"I love how calm it is here at this time of day." She watched the clear green waves gently roll up against the empty beach. "Going to the bars and stuff has been fun, but I prefer this so much more. It's just so . . . peaceful."

Skylar glanced up at the cloudy sky. "It's going to pour buckets soon, can you feel it?"

Daphne held out her arms and tilted her head back, eyes closed. "I can't wait. The rain here is so purifying, don't you think?"

Skylar patted her cheeks. "That reminds me, I think I'm getting a purifying facial at the spa today."

Daphne opened her eyes. "I know this might sound a little New Agey, but there's something about the rain on this island, about *everything* on this island, actually, that's helped me learn to embrace life again. Then again, it could just be that I've been hanging around you and KC."

Skylar laughed. "Whatever works, right? I'm all for anything that gets your juices going. Some of the people at my company are so dead inside, it's sad."

"Dead inside how?"

"Hang on a sec." Skylar stood up. Bananarama was officially open, and she was about to become the first customer of the day. She ordered three smoothies, then turned to Daphne. "Depends on the person, but a lot of them are in bad marriages, yet another reason why I'm not sure I'll ever go down that route. Some of them are clearly in the wrong profession, but they feel trapped because they have financial obligations and can't afford to start over. I guess the common thread is that somewhere along the way they got on the wrong path and don't know how to get off it, and as a result they dry up inside."

The smiling owner handed Skylar two smoothies, plus one in a bag for KC, and she and Daphne began the walk home. After a few minutes of silence, Daphne took a deep breath and looked at Skylar. "I became one of those people," she said quietly.

"Was it really that bad with Brian?"

Daphne nodded. "Toward the end, yes. I didn't mean for it to happen. I just . . . became numb inside. I think it was some sort of coping mechanism."

Skylar sipped her smoothie. "Coping mechanism for your marriage? Or for what you gave up for it?"

"For all of it, probably. It helped me, I don't know . . . *manage*. It sounds so cliché, but it was easier to focus on fixing physical things, like remodeling the kitchen or getting the house painted, than to address what really needed fixing . . . our relationship." That evasion seemed glaringly obvious to Daphne now, but for years she just hadn't seen it. Or hadn't wanted to see it.

Skylar stopped walking and put a hand on Daphne's shoulder. "You know what I think?"

Daphne waited for her to continue.

"I think you still have a ways to go, but you've started to become *Daphne* again on this trip,"

Daphne felt a tear form in the corner of her eye. "Really?" *I think so too.*

Skylar squeezed her shoulder. "Without a doubt, and it makes me really happy. You had a one-night stand with a hot guy in his *twenties*, for God's sake! If that isn't living, I'm not sure what is."

Daphne hugged her tight. "Thank you, Skylar," she whispered.

Skylar hugged her back. "You'll get there, don't worry."

They began walking along the beach in a comfortable silence, both of them staring out at the water. All of a sudden Skylar grabbed Daphne's arm and cocked her head toward the sand dune.

"Speak of the devil." They were approaching Clay and Doug's place. The back deck was empty, a handful of empty beer bottles strewn about. "I wonder how late those guys were out last night?" Daphne said.

"A lot later than we were, that's for sure."

"You think they met other women?"

Skylar shrugged as they passed by. "Scott, probably. Clay, possibly. Doug, unlikely. Hey, speaking of women, there's our favorite one." She pointed ahead to their own beach house. KC was sitting on the deck, a steaming mug of coffee in one hand.

"Hey, Wonder Woman, how are you feeling today?" Skylar asked as they climbed the steps.

KC grinned. "*Way* better than yesterday, that's for sure. Leg is still pretty sore, though. I didn't sleep that well once whatever they gave me at the hospital wore off."

"You should have taken more painkillers before you went to bed," Skylar said.

KC held her hands up as if to protect her face. "Those things scare me. I've seen too many horror stories about regular people falling under the spell of addiction after a routine injury."

Skylar rolled her eyes and handed KC the paper bag with the smoothie inside. "*Falling under the spell of addiction?* Who talks like that? Methinks someone's been watching a little too much TV."

"Maybe," KC said as she opened the bag. "But I don't want to take any chances. Thanks for this, by the way. Yummy."

Daphne eyed her with suspicion. "Are you taking it easy like the doctor told you to, or did you just run like fifteen miles?"

KC sipped her coffee and smiled. "I promise you both, the only exercise I've gotten today is lifting this tasty beverage to my lips. I figured a day or two off won't kill me."

Skylar coughed and sat down next to her. "A *day or two*. I have no trouble going a month or two without exercise. Then again, that's probably why you can still shop in the juniors' department and I cannot."

KC pinched Skylar's side. "I bet you'd have trouble going a month or two without working. You can't even go an *hour* or two. There are all kinds of addictions, my friend."

Skylar shrugged. "I tried taking the day off yesterday, and I almost got myself fired."

"Was it really that bad?" Daphne asked.

Skylar took a drink of her smoothie. "I might be exaggerating just slightly. Okay, more than slightly. I wasn't in danger of losing my job at that exact moment. However, our company *was* in danger of losing a major account, which for someone in my position is usually the first step on the road to unemployment. So it was pretty serious."

"But it's okay now?" KC asked.

Skylar finished her smoothie and gestured inside. "Yes. *However*, unfortunately I do need to make a couple calls before we head to the spa. Can you two be ready to leave by ten?"

"What about the monkey forest?" KC said.

"If we want to see the monkeys, it will have to be on the way back. We're lucky they could accommodate us at all after we canceled at the last minute yesterday. So does ten o'clock work?"

KC stood up. "It's perfect. I'm going to call Max and fill him in on my little . . . incident."

Daphne pointed to the beach. "I think I'm going to read on the beach for a while."

"Sounds good to me," KC said. "I'm kind of liking this quiet evening, early morning thing. I had fun the other night, but my liver can't take that kind of abuse too often. Hey, what about those cliffs on the other side of the island? Doug said the views are amazing. Maybe we can do that tomorrow?"

"Let's do it," Skylar said.

Daphne flinched at the thought of how high the cliffs would be.

"I can't believe we leave the day after tomorrow," KC said. "On our next trip let's stay a little longer, okay?"

"Okay." Daphne smiled, then exchanged a knowing look with Skylar. Next trip would be longer, and it wouldn't take ten years to happen. Both of them would make sure of that.

.   .   .

An hour or so later Daphne checked her watch and realized it was time to head back to the house. She closed her book and tossed it into her tote bag, then stood up and began shaking out her beach towel.

"Hey there, stranger."

She turned around, a bit startled by the sound of a man's voice. *His* voice.

"Clay, hi."

He was wearing navy-blue board shorts and running shoes, no shirt. Beads of sweat dotted his forehead and chest.

"You look tired," she said as she folded the beach towel. "Long run? Or long night?"

He laughed. "Both, I guess."

She smiled and adjusted her bag over her shoulder. "That's the way to do it, right?"

"I guess so." He hesitated for a moment, then spoke again. "How was the birthday night out? Did you get into trouble?"

"KC did. She got into a tussle with a jellyfish and lost. That's why we didn't make it to the Castaway."

"A jellyfish? Are you serious?"

Daphne pointed down the beach. "Right when we got off the catamaran."

"Is she okay?"

"She's sore, but she'll be fine. We were a little scared when she started having an allergic reaction, but not as scared as when Skylar drove us to the hospital."

He raised an eyebrow. "Huh?"

Daphne tucked the towel into her bag. "Just be glad you'll never have to ride in a car with Skylar."

"So noted. When are you headed back to the States?"

"The day after tomorrow. What about you?"

"Tomorrow. I can't say I'm looking forward to it." He wiped the sweat from his brow. "I'll be daydreaming about this place from my office, that's for sure."

She sighed and gazed up at the sky. "I hear you. I wish I could stay here forever."

"What do you have planned before you go?"

She regained eye contact with him, the anxiety she'd felt when they'd first met now a distant memory. "We're finally doing the spa thing today, and maybe the monkey forest. KC wants to check out those cliffs you and Doug were talking about, so we'll probably do that tomorrow."

"And tonight?"

"Just dinner." She considered asking him what his plans were but decided not to. *This is the perfect way to say good-bye.*

Before he could speak again, she looked up at the house. "I should probably get going so I'm not too late. I'm already pushing it as it is, and you know how Skylar can be."

She knew she was being a bit abrupt given their history, but drawing out their farewell seemed pointless, and verbalizing what she was really thinking just didn't seem appropriate. She wanted him to know that she appreciated what he'd done for her, how grateful she was for their encounter—however fleeting—for jolting her out of the emotional trance she'd been in for much too long. For making her feel young again. Attractive again. *Alive* again. But she had no idea how to convey any of that without sounding like she'd overanalyzed what to him was probably nothing more than a holiday fling. So instead she said nothing.

After a noticeable silence, Clay spoke. "Well, if I don't see you again, enjoy the rest of your trip."

"You too. It was really nice meeting you." She gave him a hug and kiss on the cheek, then turned and started walking toward the house. As she made footprints in the sand, she wondered if one day, far down the road perhaps, he'd realize the impact their night together had on her.

"Hey, Daphne?" Clay called after her.

She stopped and turned around. "Yes?"

He saluted. "Give my regards to Fred, will you?"

She laughed and returned the salute. "Will do."

$$\bullet \quad \bullet \quad \bullet$$

"I'm officially a new person. I may even have to change my name." KC wiggled her arms as they left the spa a few hours later. She turned around and gave an enthusiastic thumbs-up to the sign on the front door. "Well done, Paradise Spa at the Four Seasons. My grateful muscles and I will miss you."

Skylar poked KC in the shoulder. "See? Lying around for a few hours isn't the worst thing in the world."

"I just hope my arms aren't too wobbly to cuddle a monkey," KC said.

Skylar rolled her eyes as she opened the car door. "Trust me, you won't be cuddling any monkeys."

"A girl can dream, right?" KC said as she climbed inside.

Daphne pressed her palms against her cheeks. "My massage was good, but the cucumber revitalizing facial was *amazing*. My skin feels so soft right now." She looked at Skylar. "I could get used to your lifestyle. I mean, the nonwork side of it. The other side would eat me alive."

"You've been the head of the PTA how many times? Trust me, you could handle it," Skylar said.

"I bet you ran a tight ship at that PTA," KC said to Daphne. "You were crazy organized in college, and we've all seen your tote bag."

Daphne blushed. "Maybe."

"Hey, speaking of your *mom* persona, have you been in touch with Emma?" KC asked.

"Not much, the reception is terrible there."

"You doing okay with that?" KC asked.

Daphne smiled. "Actually, *yes*. Once I realized it was out of my hands, it sort of freed me up to focus on other things this week."

"You mean . . . like *yourself?*" Skylar said as she pulled onto the road. "God forbid any mother should do *that*."

Daphne smiled. "You know what I mean. It's hard to separate the two sometimes."

"I hear ya," KC said. "No matter where I am, Josh and Jared are always in the back of my head."

"I can't imagine having to worry about that all the time," Skylar said. "I'm not averse to dating a man who has kids, but I don't know how well I'd handle being a stepmother."

"I think you'd make a fantastic stepmother," KC said. "Especially to girls. You'd be such a great role model, outside of the driving thing, of course. Do you see how tightly I'm gripping this door handle right now? That's the fear of death, my friend."

"Zip it," Skylar said.

Daphne turned around and grimaced at KC in the backseat. "For the record, I'm holding on just as tight."

"You zip it too," Skylar said. "Anyhow, I think any woman who is doing whatever it is that makes *her* happy is a great role model.

Whether it's having a corporate job or being a stay-at-home mom, the important thing is to show kids that it's up to them to choose the life *they* want. Take Daphne here. We all know she could have crushed it professionally, but she chose to dedicate herself to raising Emma, which I think is commendable."

Daphne gave Skylar a grateful look, then cleared her throat. "Actually, I think I'm going to look into some new adventures when I get home."

"Adventures? I like the sound of that. What did you have in mind?" KC asked.

"For starters, I was thinking about signing up for a dance class, just so I could have a hobby of my own, something outside of Emma's world. Plus, being around *you* all week has inspired me to get in better shape."

"I love that idea," KC said. "I love inspiring people!"

Daphne smiled at her. "I also think it's time to dip my toe back into journalism so I can use the part of my brain that I've neglected for too long. I know the industry has changed dramatically since I learned the ropes in school, but I'm kind of excited about learning something new."

"Ready to pop that suburban bubble, are we?" Skylar said.

"*Pop* might be an overstatement, but while I love being a mom, part of me has known for a long time that I need more than that in my life. It took this trip for me to come to terms with it, and to realize that it's okay to want more for *myself* while still loving my daughter to pieces."

"Of course it's okay," KC said. "You have to love yourself too."

"Maybe you should try one of my business ideas," Skylar said.

Daphne looked at her. "You think I should start my own company? What do I know about starting a business?"

Skylar shrugged. "What does anyone know about anything before they try it? You're smart, you could totally do it. *Plus*, I could use some stock options in a hot new venture. I still want to hire my traveling stylist someday."

Daphne laughed. "I think I'll start with submitting an article to a magazine, but I'll keep that in mind. So is anyone up for a walk on the beach before dinner?"

. . .

Early that evening, the three friends were taking a stroll along the shore when the skies erupted for the second time that day. The first downpour had been while they were at the monkey forest after the spa, much to the delight of KC. The rain had briefly cleared the park of the fair-weathered, leaving her free to attract the monkeys with the enormous batch of bananas she'd purchased at the entrance. She'd already set the wallpaper on her phone to a picture Daphne had taken of her, featuring a plump monkey perched on one shoulder, the trademark KC grin on her face.

"I love this rain." Daphne tilted her head back and held her arms open wide. "It's so refreshing."

"Not as refreshing as a rum punch would be right now. Anyone up for cocktails on the beach after dinner?" Skylar said.

"I wonder if Clay and the guys will be at the Castaway tonight," Daphne said. "I ran into him earlier today."

Skylar raised her eyebrows. "Is that so? Interesting that you chose to keep that little nugget of information to yourself."

"We didn't talk for that long." Daphne looked at KC and pointed to her leg. "I told him about your little voyage to the emergency room."

"Did you two talk about getting together again?" Skylar asked.

Daphne glanced back in the direction of the house where Clay was staying. "I decided not to go there. I think I just want to spend as much time with you two as I can before we have to return to reality."

Skylar held up a hand. "I fail to see how you can't do both. It's not like peg leg here or I have plans to sleep in your bed tonight." She gestured to KC, then to herself.

Daphne laughed. "You know what I mean."

"We could always drop by the Castaway later to see if he's there," KC said. "There's no harm in that."

"If I were you, I'd listen to peg leg," Skylar said. "I say you knock it out of the park or go down swinging." She pointed to KC's thigh. "How's the peg feeling, by the way?"

"Okay, not great. I think it will feel better after a couple cocktails."

Skylar rubbed her hands together. "*Now* we're talking. Maybe we should head back to the house for a predinner drink?"

"Sounds good to me," KC said.

The three of them turned around and began walking toward the beach house. After a few minutes KC squinted at two figures in the distance. "Is that Harry and Eleanor? I can't see that far."

Daphne nodded. "I think so."

As they approached the couple, Daphne and KC waved hello. Harry and Eleanor both returned the greeting, but Daphne immediately sensed a difference in their energy—and Harry's appearance. His skin was notably pale, almost ashen, and he was moving quite slowly. But he met them with a warm smile. "There they are. The prettiest ladies on the island, after my wife, of course."

"Ahoy mates," KC said. "This is our friend Skylar, also known as the third Musketeer."

"It's lovely to meet you, dear." Eleanor seemed distracted, but she took Skylar's hand in hers. "Is this your first visit to St. Mirika?"

Skylar nodded. "It's also my first tropical vacation with my best girlfriends in tow, so it's been my favorite."

"Yesterday was Daphne's birthday," KC said.

Harry smiled at Daphne. "Happy belated birthday, kiddo. You don't look a day over twenty-five to me."

"Thank you, Harry. Are you . . . feeling all right?" She didn't mean to pry, but she couldn't pretend she hadn't noticed his condition.

"I've been better," he said.

"What have you darlings been up to since we met you?" Eleanor asked.

Skylar pointed at KC. "That one got herself stung by a jellyfish."

Harry chuckled. "Is that so?"

KC frowned. "Little sucker got me pretty bad."

"She ended up in the hospital," Daphne said. "It turns out she's allergic."

"First beets, and now jellyfish. Who knew?" KC said.

Eleanor interlaced her arm with Harry's. "Big H here was in the hospital earlier today too."

Daphne and her friends all looked at him, his pallid tone suddenly taking on more significance. "Oh my gosh. Are you okay?" Daphne asked.

He smiled and shook his head. "Unfortunately, no. It's my ticker."

"He's on his second," Eleanor said, the shadow in her eyes growing a bit darker.

Wide-eyed, Daphne asked, "You had a heart transplant?"

Harry nodded. "We were hopeful this one would stick, but it doesn't look like that's in the cards."

"We're not giving up, though," Eleanor said. "I'm never giving up."

"She's more optimistic than I am," Harry said. "Always has been, that's one of the reasons I love her."

"I'm so sorry," Daphne whispered.

A hush enveloped the group. Daphne was too stunned to say anything else, and Skylar and KC were equally taken aback. *Harry's dying?*

Eleanor stroked Harry's cheek with her hand, then turned toward Daphne and her friends. "Thanks, love. If there's one thing I'd tell young people like you three dolls, it's just enjoy every day while you can, especially every *birthday*, and don't waste time fussing over things that don't mean squat."

Harry took Eleanor's hand and kissed it. "Well said, my love. Enjoy the party while you can still dance, that's my motto."

Daphne stared at the wise couple standing before her. *He's really dying?*

Eleanor wrapped her arm tightly around her husband's, then carefully looked at the three friends, giving them each a warm smile as she did so. "We'd better get back to the house. It was such a pleasure running into you again. Happy belated birthday, Daphne! Enjoy the continued celebration, and be sure to soak up every minute you have left here, promise?"

Daphne, KC, and Skylar all nodded like schoolchildren. They knew Eleanor was no longer talking about St. Mirika.

Harry gave them a wave as he and Eleanor slowly ambled away. "Have a drink for me to toast this glorious sunset."

. . .

"I can't believe he's that sick," KC said on the slow walk back to the beach house. "When we met on the beach the other day, he was so . . . *sprightly*."

"He still is, at least on the inside," Skylar said. "He knows what's important in life. They both do."

"I want to be like that when I'm that age," Daphne said. "Actually, what am I saying? I want to be like that *now*."

"We should all be like that," Skylar said.

KC pinched both their waists. "Does that mean you're up for a workout tomorrow morning? You know what they say—a healthy body makes for a healthy soul. I should probably take it easy, however."

"Maybe. It depends on how late I stay up tonight," Daphne said.

Skylar looked at her. "You have plans we don't know about?"

Daphne bit her lip. "Maybe."

Skylar narrowed her eyes. "Would these *plans* involve a certain Clay Handsome?"

Daphne smiled slightly. "I was thinking it was best to close that book, but seeing Harry like that just now is kind of making me look at things in a different way. Maybe it wouldn't be such a terrible thing if I ran into Clay one last time, right?"

"Of course it wouldn't be," Skylar said.

"Definitely not," KC said.

"You think we should stop by the Castaway later?" Daphne asked them. "Just to check it out? He might not even be there, though."

"But he *might* be," Skylar said. "I say it's worth a flyby."

KC pretended to maneuver the controls of an airplane. "I don't think I have another wild night in me, but I'm happy to play wingman."

Daphne blushed. "I haven't heard the term *wingman* in a long time."

Skylar put a hand on Daphne's shoulder. "I never thought I'd say this to *you*, but maybe it's time you refreshed your vocabulary. Now, let's go get some dinner. I'm starving."

Chapter Twelve

That evening they had just left the restaurant and were strolling down the sidewalk on Main Street when Skylar froze in her tracks.

"What is it?" Daphne asked, coming to a halt beside her.

"It's my phone. Damn it." Skylar reached into her purse and fished out the vibrating device, then frowned at the text message on the screen. "I knew it."

"Another work emergency?" KC said.

Skylar began walking again. "Yes. I'm sorry, ladies. No Castaway for me tonight. I need to go back to the house for an important call."

"Does it ever stop?" Daphne asked. At the beginning of the week she'd assumed the endless conference calls were related to one particular emergency that needed attention, but now she realized Skylar's job required her to hop continuously from one crisis to the next, with no end in sight and the weight—and heat—of each fire resting firmly on her shoulders.

Skylar tossed the phone back into her purse. "I don't *think* it used to be this bad, but I might just be saying that. I'm so used to it now that I don't realize how all-consuming it is until I'm around people who live relatively normal lives."

"You have spent a lot of this week on the phone," KC said.

Skylar sighed. "I know. I love my job and the lifestyle it allows me to lead, but in moments like this, when I'm supposed to be on *vacation*, I can't help but ask myself if I've traded too much in return. I know that sounds cliché, but it's kind of true."

"How would you change things if you could?" Daphne asked.

Skylar hesitated for a moment before responding.

"I don't know exactly," she finally said. "I've had an amazing career, but I've never been in a committed, serious relationship. Not that it's ever been something I've really coveted, but meeting Eleanor and Harry tonight made me wonder if one day I'm going to regret that, if when I'm their age, I'm going to wish I had someone by my side until the very end, you know?"

Daphne and KC nodded, sensing Skylar wasn't done.

She continued. "I don't necessarily think that having a demanding job and a serious relationship are mutually exclusive, but sometimes I can't help but think that maybe in my case they are, if somehow I've stopped myself from finding the right man without even realizing it. Not that my goal has ever been to get married, but I guess on some base level we all want to love someone . . . and feel loved in return, right?"

Daphne looked at Skylar, her fair skin slightly sun-kissed, her auburn locks flowing down her back, not a strand out of place. Dressed in a silky turquoise halter top and flowy island-chic white pants, she was the picture of success, yet this was the first time Daphne had ever heard her express an ounce of misgiving over the price she'd paid for it. *No one's life is perfect. Not even Skylar's.* Before she realized what she was doing, she walked over to Skylar and hugged her tight.

"Whoa, are you okay?" Skylar asked. "Where is this coming from?"

"I would never unsubscribe from you," Daphne said. "I just think it's about time I told you that."

. . .

When they reached the Castaway, Skylar bade Daphne and KC good-bye, then hurried down the beach back to the house.

KC pointed toward the bar. "Okay champ, you ready? Let's do this for Harry!"

Daphne laughed. "I get the sentiment, but that sounded kind of creepy." They began walking toward the deck entrance. Despite her determination to be casual and just have fun, as they ascended the steps, she felt her nerves begin to jitter. *Do I really want to do this?*

"Maybe this is a mistake," she called to KC over her shoulder. The steel drum band was playing again, and the dance floor was filled with bobbing heads.

"Just keep moving," KC yelled back. "Dance while you still can, remember?"

They climbed the steps and joined the scene, which looked exactly the same as it had the night they'd been there. Couples snuggling in the lounge chairs, friends bopping together in groups in the center of the room, revelers doing shots at the bar. The stage and the play unfolding upon it remained essentially unchanged, except for the characters flowing in and out like a gentle breeze.

"I think I had enough of this place the other night," KC said. "I'm getting a hangover just remembering my hangover."

Daphne gave her a hopeful look. "So we can go back to the house? I'd much rather relax on the couch than face this scene right now."

KC shook her head. "We have to at least do a run-through to see if he's here. You'll kick yourself if we don't. Besides, Skylar's probably going to be at her desk for a while, so it's better if we give her some space."

Daphne nodded. She knew KC was right: she *would* kick herself if she bailed out now. "Okay."

Beginning at the outdoor bar where KC had downed her tequila shots, they slowly began to survey the landscape for any sign of Clay or his friends. They didn't spot them anywhere on the deck, so KC put her hand on Daphne's back and nudged her inside. The area in front of the long bar was packed, but Daphne immediately noticed a tall man at the far end near the street entrance. His face was obstructed, but she could see the back of his head.

"I think that's Scott," she said to KC.

"Nice." KC snapped her fingers. "Houston, we have contact."

They squeezed their way through the crowd until they reached the area where Scott was standing. KC stood on her tiptoes and tapped him on the shoulder. "Hey, you!" she said with a grin.

He turned around and looked down, a surprised expression on his face. "Oh hi, KC. Hey, Daphne." He gestured toward the young redhead sitting next to him. "This is Ashley."

KC smiled at Ashley, then looked back up at Scott. "Are Clay and Doug here?"

Daphne's eyes darted around the bar. *Is he here?* She recognized a couple other guys from their crew milling about, but not the one she really wanted to see.

Scott jutted his chin toward the back deck area. "They're with their lady friends."

"Their *lady friends*?" KC said.

Daphne felt like she'd been kicked in the stomach. *This was a bad idea.*

Scott pointed back toward the deck. "Last I saw they were dancing. You didn't see them on your way in?"

"No," KC said.

Scott shrugged. "Maybe they took off." He turned back toward Ashley and began to play with her hair as she giggled. Empty shot glasses sat on the bar before them. Daphne wondered what Scott's girlfriend back home was doing right now. Then again, maybe Scott's girlfriend was running her fingers through someone else's hair too. Who was she to judge their relationship from the outside?

"Okay, thanks, Scott. It was nice meeting you, Ashley." KC smiled again, then pulled Daphne by the arm back into the crowd. "You want to keep looking?" she asked her.

Daphne laughed and shook her head. "After *that* revelation? Definitely not. Can we go home now? I miss my slippers."

"You sure you don't want to give it one more shot?"

"Give *what* one more shot? You heard Scott, he's with someone else."

"So? That doesn't mean anything."

Daphne sighed. "Okay, let's walk out the back way. If we see him, we see him. If we don't, at least I tried. Does that work for you?"

KC grinned. "That's the spirit. Harry would be proud."

They made their way back outside, and while KC scanned the crowd, Daphne countered her unease by replaying the conversation she'd had earlier with Clay in her head. *He likes you. He'll be glad to see you, regardless. Don't overanalyze it.*

"There's my bestie!" KC suddenly yelled. "He's on the dance floor macking on some girl. I'm so proud of him!"

"Do you see Clay?" Her eyes followed KC's.

KC peered through the crowd. "Affirmative. He's with a girl too, but they're not swapping spit."

Daphne laughed and looked at KC sideways. "I can't remember the last time I heard the terms *macking* and *swapping spit*."

KC caught her breath and reached for Daphne's hand. "He sees us. I think he's coming over here."

Daphne scanned the dance floor, then gave KC's hand a squeeze as she spotted Clay emerging from the crowd, a bit disheveled, but not overtly intoxicated like Scott.

"Hey, Daphne, KC. I'm surprised to see you here."

Daphne let go of KC's hand and quickly peered around him to see if a pretty young thing trailed behind him, but he appeared to be alone. "Surprised in a good way, I hope," she said, thrilled to hear the words come out somewhat flirtatiously.

"Of course," he said with a grin. "Always."

"I see my bestie's having a little fun out there." KC pointed over Clay's shoulder.

"He is indeed," Clay said. "And it's about time, if you ask me."

"Good for him. Who shouldn't have a little fun on vacation, right?" Daphne said. This time she made—and held—eye contact with Clay. *Another small victory!*

Just then an attractive brunette appeared out of nowhere and grabbed Clay's arm. "There you are. You disappeared on me." She stood on her tiptoes and gave him a sloppy kiss. "I'm going to the little girls' room. Wait for me here?" Without acknowledging Daphne and KC, she wobbled away on her stiletto heels, leaving the two of them standing there with Clay.

Daphne hesitated for a moment. *Don't give up so easily. You can do this.* She took a deep breath and focused her eyes on Clay. "I see we have a little problem," she said with just the hint of a smile on her lips.

Clay kept the eye contact but didn't speak, and Daphne held her breath. After a pause that was just long enough to be noticeable, his lips slowly curled upward. "Not one we can't take care of."

Daphne felt the squeeze of KC's hand on her torso in a subtle gesture of celebration. Then KC yawned and slowly took a step backward. "My pals, it's been fun, but I think I'm going to get a head start on that walk home. Give Doug a hug good-bye for me, will you, Clay? I assume you'll make sure my girl Daphne gets home safely?"

"You know I will," he said. "Sleep tight."

She gave him the thumbs-up sign, then turned and trotted toward the back exit.

Best wingman ever, Daphne thought as she watched her disappear down the steps.

"So . . ." Clay said after KC was gone.

"So . . ." Daphne said with a bat of her eyelashes.

They stood there smiling at each other for a moment, then Daphne nodded her head toward the restroom. "About your friend there . . ."

"She'll be fine." Taking a step forward, he slipped a hand around the small of Daphne's back, and her insides did a little flip-flop. "Besides, you and I have some unfinished business to attend to," he added.

Daphne looked up at him, a suggestive expression on her face. "Is that so?"

He nodded. "It is so. Especially after you ditched me like that."

"You mean last night?"

"Last night and yesterday morning too. Three times in a row would be a little tough on the old ego, even though I'm not that old."

She furrowed her brow. "How did I ditch you yesterday morning?"

He smiled and scratched the back of his head. "You're joking, right?"

"Are you messing with me?"

"Not messing with you."

"Are you drunk?" she asked.

"Have I been drinking? Yes. Am I drunk? No."

"Daphne!" Doug emerged from the crowd and enveloped Daphne in a bear hug. "Is KC here?"

Daphne pointed toward the water. "You just missed her. She said to give you a hug good-bye."

"Coolest girl ever," Doug said wistfully.

Clay elbowed him. "It was never gonna happen, dude. Where's your dance partner?"

"She's getting us some more drinks. I need to drain the weasel." He gestured toward the men's room.

Daphne laughed. "Nice euphemism."

As Doug sauntered away, Clay took Daphne's hand. "Let's get out of here." He quickly pulled her through the crowd toward the back exit, then down the steps to the beach. He didn't let go of her hand until they were nearly at the shore.

Daphne glanced back at the Castaway. "What about that girl?"

"What about her?"

"Shouldn't you at least say good-bye? You can't just ditch her."

He smiled. "Why, because ditching isn't nice?"

"I told you, I didn't ditch you. At least in the morning, I mean." What was he talking about? She'd told him about their trip to the emergency room.

He raised an eyebrow, crossed his arms, and took a few steps back from her. "I beg to differ. If I recall, when I woke up in your bed, you were standing *like this* as far away from me as possible, without actually leaving the room, which made it pretty clear you weren't about to get back into bed until I vacated the premises."

She felt her cheeks blush. That was partially true.

"But . . ."

He kept smiling. "But what?"

"I did that because . . . because I thought you had coyote arm," she said softly.

He laughed. "Did you just say *coyote arm?*"

245

She swallowed. "You know, when a guy wakes up after a night out and realizes a girl is sleeping on top of his arm? He feels like a trapped coyote and would rather chew off his own limb than—"

He held up his hand. "I'm familiar with the term. But how do *you* know it?"

She shrugged. "I was in college once. I heard stuff."

He took a step closer and put a hand on her shoulder. "Daphne, I did *not* have coyote arm. I had an incredible time with you, for real."

She stared at the sand without replying.

He chuckled. "And I thought you did too, until you started acting like I have the plague. You should have seen the look of terror in your eyes when you came out of the bathroom."

She gave him a sheepish look. "That bad?"

"Worse, like you'd never been afraid of anything more than the idea of being anywhere near me again. You should have heard the heckling I got from the guys on the catamaran. It was pretty clear where I'd just spent the night, but it was also pretty clear you were no longer interested."

She looked down again. "I'm sorry. I didn't mean to do that. When I saw you in my bed, I was . . . pensive."

"I assume that's a fancy word for . . ."

"I'm sorry. I mean I was kind of thinking."

"About what?"

"To be honest, I was thinking how you weren't my ex-husband."

He laughed. "I'm not sure how to take that."

"I mean I was thinking that I was *glad* it was you there and not him. I mean that it was good for me to have gotten over that hump, so to speak."

"Hmm. Interesting word choice."

She smiled. "You know what I mean. Plus, I guess I was . . . nervous."

He reached for her chin and lifted her head. "I make you nervous?"

She nodded. "A little. I know I'm older than you, but I'm kind of a late bloomer in a lot of ways."

He stroked her cheek with his thumb. "You're sexy when you're nervous. Has anyone ever told you that?"

She gave him a tiny smile. "I'm learning a lot about myself on this trip."

"Oh yeah? Like what?"

She sighed. "You'll think I'm silly."

He cocked his head toward the Castaway. "The scene in *there* is silly. Having a conversation with you on this beautiful beach? Not silly."

She took a deep breath before speaking. "Before I came here, I thought I'd screwed up my chance to be happy in life, but now I'm learning that you don't get just one chance, that in a way life is *always* just beginning, that no matter how old we are it's still in *front* of us, every day until the end, so it's important to look forward and not backward all the time."

"That sounds like a lesson everyone could learn."

"I'm also realizing that regardless of where I am, or how I got here, if I don't do what I can to enjoy my life *now*, one day I may wake up and wonder where it all went."

Clay didn't respond right away, and she looked up at the sky, which was quickly becoming covered in dark clouds. *It's so magical here. I'm so glad I came.*

A cracking sound broke the silence. Then the rain came pouring down. Hard.

Clay laughed and glanced around. "How's that for dramatic timing? Think a director's going to appear out of nowhere and yell *cut?*"

Daphne smiled. "I wouldn't be surprised. I love the rain here. It makes everything feel brand-new. Sometimes we all need a fresh start, right?"

"Indeed." He glanced up into the downpour, then back at her. "So . . . speaking of fresh starts, I feel like I got off on the wrong foot with Fred. Would you mind if I came over and tried again? I'd hate to leave St. Mirika knowing I didn't do everything in my power to make a good impression."

She wiped a few raindrops from her eyes, then smiled up at him. "I think . . . I think that could be arranged."

He slipped his hands around her lower back and pulled her close. "Good."

Chapter Thirteen

Daphne strolled into the kitchen the next morning, her step a bit lighter from her encounter with Clay. Again she'd been the one to wake up first, but this time around she didn't fret about how to act once they were both awake or about how the elusive hookup guide said she should behave. She'd simply leaned over and kissed him on the cheek, then snuggled up next to him and promptly fallen back asleep for another hour until they'd both woken up for good. Now he was probably on his way to the airport, and tomorrow she would be on her way back to Ohio. Back to a future that didn't look so bleak anymore. One that looked quite sunny, in fact. She closed her eyes and smiled to herself. *Thank you, Clay Handsome. Thank you, St. Mirika.*

She didn't see KC or Skylar and wondered if they were still asleep. She knew she'd agreed to another beach workout before they left the island, but she secretly hoped KC was already out on a long run so that she'd be off the hook this morning. Her body had finally stopped hurting from the first boot camp, and she wasn't looking forward to the soreness returning anytime soon. Then again, she *was* looking forward to getting in better shape.

She set an empty mug under the coffeemaker, pressed the button, and watched the black liquid drip into the cup. Soon she'd be standing in her own kitchen, back to sipping coffee from her favorite pink mug. Chipped or not, she was never letting that precious cup go. She smiled at the thought of seeing her daughter.

"Morning, sweets." Skylar walked down the hall wearing her silk bathrobe, her hair wrapped in a towel. "Are you the only one up?"

Daphne turned around. "I'm not sure. Maybe KC's already out on a run?" She looked at the French doors, which were ajar.

Skylar tilted her head toward Daphne's bedroom, then lowered her voice. "I wasn't talking about KC."

Daphne blushed as she doctored her coffee with cream and sugar. "Oh."

Skylar reached for a mug. "Is he still here?"

Daphne gave her a teasing smile. "What makes you think he was here at all?"

Skylar laughed as she set her mug under the coffeemaker. "That would be the writing on your face, babe. It says *I hooked up with a hot guy last night.*"

Daphne giggled too. "He left a little while ago. Had to go home and pack."

"Look at you, all grown up with your first vacation fling under your belt. Welcome to the fun side of being single, my friend."

"Good morning." Skylar and Daphne turned around as KC appeared from the hall, dressed in workout gear, but lacking her typical morning cheer.

Skylar narrowed her eyes. "Who are you, and what have you done with KC?"

KC frowned. "I spoke to Max before I went to bed last night . . ."

They stared at her, waiting for her to continue.

She closed her eyes for a moment, then opened them, a pained look on her face. "Josh's girlfriend is pregnant."

"Oh sugar." Skylar covered her mouth with her hand.

KC sighed, her shoulders slumping. "I can't believe it."

Daphne walked over to her. "That's not a terrible thing, right? Didn't you say they're already living together?"

KC shook her head. "That's Jared. Josh is still in college."

Daphne caught her breath. "Oh."

"He's only nineteen. Oh man, what a mess." KC pressed her hands against her cheeks and walked over to the couch.

"Is she going to keep it?" Skylar asked.

KC nodded and plopped onto the couch. "Looks like I'm going to be a forty-year-old grandmother."

"You'll be the hottest grandma in town, that's for sure," Skylar said.

"Are they going to drop out of school?" Daphne asked.

KC sighed. "Max said they're not, but to make that possible, I think there's a good chance they'll end up moving in with us."

"That's crazy," Daphne whispered.

KC nodded. "Now *that*, my articulate friend, is a major understatement."

"So you may be raising a real baby soon?" Daphne said, remembering how at the airport KC had referred to her cats as babies. *Was that really just a few days ago?*

KC sat there for a moment, then pressed her hands against her thighs and stood up, now wearing a weary smile. "I think that's a definite possibility. Either of you want to join me in a beach run to kick off our last full day here? There's nothing I can do about this disaster right now, so I might as well try to enjoy the time we have left in paradise."

Skylar pointed to the towel on her head. "Sorry, I just showered. I will watch you from the deck, however. Now that you're nearly a *grandmother*, I want to make sure you don't overexert yourself and get injured."

"Don't think you're not coming to the baby shower." KC stuck out her tongue at Skylar, then looked at Daphne. "What about you?"

"You really feel like exercising?" Daphne said. "If I got news like that, I think I'd head straight to bed with a bag of Oreos."

"Now you're talking," Skylar said. "That's a workout I can get on board with."

"God knows I could use a good sweat right now," KC said. "I was also thinking that since it's our last day . . . maybe we could finally check out those cliffs we keep hearing about? Seems more fitting than ever right now, don't you think?"

Daphne paused for a moment, then picked up her coffee and smiled. "I do. Count me in for both the workout and the cliffs."

.   .   .

"Oh my gosh, they're gorgeous." Skylar gazed up at the cliffs as she shut the car door.

Daphne's eyes followed to the soaring rock structures, which were covered in bright green moss and even higher than she'd feared. A wide staircase snaked up the biggest one, which was then linked to an adjacent and equally tall yet narrower rock by a small suspension bridge.

"Are we supposed to *climb* that?" she asked, her voice a bit unsteady.

"Looks like it," Skylar said

Daphne cleared her throat. "I was under the impression that we'd be looking over cliffs, not climbing to the top of them."

KC pointed to the bridge. "Now *that* looks fun."

Daphne was of a different opinion. As if climbing to the top of the main rock wasn't going to be terrifying enough, to her the thought of also crossing a shaky wooden bridge was quite the opposite of *fun*.

"This doesn't scare you two *at all*?" she asked her friends.

"I'm more scared by the idea of a bad haircut than climbing some rock," Skylar said with a shrug.

KC pointed to the parking lot, then to Skylar. "I'm more scared by the thought of getting back inside *that* car with *her* behind the wheel."

"You're more than welcome to walk home, Grandma," Skylar said.

Daphne swallowed and felt a few beads of sweat forming on her brow. She reached into her tote bag for a pack of tissues, then pressed one against her forehead. *You can do this. Just don't look down.*

KC pointed to a small thatched hut at the edge of the dusty parking lot. "I think that's where we buy the tickets."

The three of them walked over to the booth and got in line behind a white-haired couple who made Daphne think of Harry and Eleanor. She wondered what they were doing right now, and how Harry was feeling. Skylar and KC kept chatting, but Daphne's mind began to wander, so she didn't partake in their conversation. As she stood a couple feet behind her friends, lost in her own thoughts, two men got in line.

"Damn that's steep," Daphne heard one of them say. KC and Skylar were still engrossed in conversation, so Daphne inadvertently began to eavesdrop on the men.

"I jumped off a rock formation like that once, in Greece, right after college," the other man said. "Seems like a lifetime ago."

"College *was* a lifetime ago," the first man said. "We're getting up there, man."

Daphne casually turned around and gave them each a discreet once-over. Both men were tall and appeared to be in their midforties, or perhaps a bit older. One was wearing a dark red base-ball hat that said "Texas A&M" on the front. He was also sporting a platinum band on the ring finger of his left hand. The second man wasn't wearing a hat or a wedding band. Both men were reasonably handsome, yet there was an aura around the one with the bare ring finger that suggested he was feeling a bit uncomfortable in his own skin. Maybe he was afraid of heights too? The thought, however projected, helped soothe her jittery nerves. *At least I'm not the only one less than thrilled right now.*

"Scary how fast the years go by, isn't it?" she said to them with a smile—and an easiness that surprised her. "I've decided to embrace the life-begins-at-forty mentality." *I don't care if you know how old I am. Age doesn't mean squat.*

The man in the baseball hat nudged his friend. "He's recently divorced. If that isn't beginning a new life, I don't know what is."

Daphne looked at the man's friend. "I'm sorry to hear that. How long has it been?"

"It was official the first of the month. This trip is sort of our celebration, sad as that sounds," he said.

His friend patted him on the back. "You're better off without her. You know that."

Daphne held up her bare left hand. "Welcome to the club."

The divorced man gave her a weary smile. "Thanks, if that's even the right word. It's definitely not a club I ever thought I'd join, that's for sure."

She smiled. "Trust me, neither did I. Do you have kids?"

He nodded. "Two teenage boys."

"How are they taking it?"

"I think they're okay with the divorce, but they're not big fans of having to go back and forth between two houses all the time. It makes me feel kind of guilty for causing such upheaval in their lives when they didn't do anything to deserve it."

Daphne adjusted the strap of her tote bag over her shoulder. "You know what? You can't beat yourself up about it. I have a teenage daughter, and for a long time I felt guilty, like I'd failed for not being the picture-perfect mother." She pointed her thumb behind her. "My wise girlfriends here have helped me begin to let go of that destructive mentality—finally—and realize that being divorced and being a good parent aren't necessarily mutually exclusive. Emma knows her dad and I both love her, and that's what really matters."

"See? Kids are resilient," his friend said, then looked at Daphne. "They'll come around, right?"

"Your boys will get used to it," she said to the divorced man with a nod. "And eventually, you will too."

"You willing to put money on that?" He laughed a bit awkwardly. He was clearly doing his best to put on a good face, but the tired look in his eyes showed how much was going on beneath the surface. Daphne knew that look all too well. She'd seen it countless times in the mirror.

Surprising herself yet again, she put a hand on his arm and gave it a gentle squeeze. "It gets better. I promise." Then she lowered her voice and leaned toward both men. "There were days when I didn't want to get out of bed, and that is a sad thing when you're the only one in it."

The divorced man laughed. "I wish I had your attitude," he said. "You're so confident. And insightful too."

Daphne laughed too. "Confident and insightful? Those are two adjectives I don't often hear to describe myself, but thank you for the compliment."

Just then KC turned around and put her hands on her hips. "I feel like I'm missing a good conversation here. Am I missing a good conversation here?" Skylar was now at the ticket window.

"Depends on whom you ask," Daphne said. "I think it's pretty interesting, but my new friends here might beg to differ."

The guy in the hat gave the thumbs-up sign. "We were just talking about being in bed, which in my opinion is always a topic worthy of discussion."

"I concur with your opinion," Daphne said with a firm nod.

"So you're one of the wise friends?" the divorced man asked KC.

"I'm KC." She grinned and held out her hand. "I'm not sure how *wise* I am, but I just found out that I'm going to be a grandmother in a few months. Does that count for anything?" She pointed to the guy in the baseball cap. "I dig your hat, by the way. Go, Aggies!"

He chuckled. "I'm Phil. And I find it hard to believe you're going to be a grandmother."

"*Step*grandmother," Daphne said. "She wasn't having babies in high school or anything."

"True, true," KC said, then turned to the divorced man. "And you are . . . ?"

"I'm Derek," he said.

"He's recently divorced too," Daphne said to KC. "I was telling him that there's light at the end of the tunnel."

KC nodded and slipped her arm around Daphne's waist. "There definitely is. My pal Daphne here is living proof of that."

"Your name's Daphne?" Derek said to her. "That's unusual. And very pretty."

She smiled brightly. "Thank you." *I think so too.*

"Suits her, doesn't it?" KC said to the men. "Makes me think of a bright bouquet of daffodils."

"You ladies ready to rock these rocks?" Skylar said from behind them.

Daphne looked up at Derek and Phil. "You two want to climb with us?"

"We'd love to," Derek said.

She introduced them to Skylar, then pointed toward the bottom of the stone staircase. "Meet us at the entrance?"

Phil gave the thumbs-up sign again. "Sounds good."

The three women turned and walked away, and as soon as they were out of earshot, KC pinched Daphne's waist. "Did you hear what just happened back there?"

"What do you mean?"

"That entire conversation! You were totally your old self again. Charming, witty, not insecure in the least. It was great!"

"I was?"

KC laughed. "You didn't notice?"

"I guess not."

"Well it was fun to watch, that's for sure. It's good to have you back."

Daphne gave her a warm smile that said, *Thanks for bringing me back.*

"That Derek guy's kind of sexy." Skylar glanced back toward the ticket booth. "What's his deal? I didn't see a wedding ring."

"Recently divorced," Daphne said. "They're here on a guys' trip to, shall we say, *commemorate* it, if you will."

"Talk about a euphemism," KC said, then quickly looked at Daphne. "Did I use *euphemism* right?"

Daphne nodded and patted the top of KC's baseball hat. "Well done."

"Hmm . . . recently divorced." Skylar raised an eyebrow at Daphne. "Maybe you could soothe those wounds a little bit this evening? What man doesn't enjoy the company of an empathetic woman?"

Daphne rolled her eyes. "Yeah, right."

Skylar shrugged. "I'm just saying, there's nothing wrong with a little TLC. And as we've already witnessed this week, it's not like you're averse to a little roll in the hay with an attractive stranger. Why stop at one when you could double your pleasure, double your fun?" She elbowed Daphne.

"Stop it." Daphne laughed and elbowed Skylar back as they reached the base of the stone steps.

"Speaking of attractive strangers, two are rapidly approaching at six o'clock, so you might want to shut your traps," KC whispered.

Daphne craned her neck back at the towering rock formation. "Wow, that is *steep*."

"Wow, that is *steep*," Phil said from behind them.

KC turned around. "Is there a parrot out here?"

Daphne made a sheepish face. "Is anyone else having second thoughts about this?"

"Too late to back out now," Skylar said as she handed their tickets to the uniformed man standing by the roped-off entrance. "Everyone ready?" There were a handful of people on the observation deck at the very top, but the zigzagging path to reach it was clear.

Daphne walked over to Derek and put her hand on his arm again. "This can't be any harder than what we've already been through, right?" She was speaking to comfort herself now, not him.

He looked at her for a moment, then smiled just slightly. "That sounds like something only club members can understand."

She smiled back. "*Exactly.*"

The five of them began ascending the steps, which were framed by a rope attached to the rocky walkway with spikes set at intervals all the way to the top. The path snaked left and right, and as they climbed, Daphne kept her eyes focused on the step directly in front of her, too afraid to look anywhere else. Her breathing and heart rate began to increase, and she willed herself to remain calm. *Keep moving. You're going to be fine. You can do this.*

"Damn, this is high!" Skylar called from the front of the group. "Whose idea was this, anyway?"

"Do you think anyone has ever fallen into the ocean from here?" Phil called from the very back.

"Don't be an asshole, Phil," Derek said with a laugh. He was a few steps ahead of Phil. The easy banter between them reminded Daphne of the chatter she'd heard during the flag football game on the beach.

"Humor is a good tool for diffusing tension," Phil yelled. "I learned that at some boondoggle sales training in Vegas."

"I wish I were in Vegas right now," Skylar yelled back. "I should have an enormous guitar-shaped margarita in my hand instead of a rope that looks older than dirt and may snap at any moment, after which I will plummet to my death and probably drag all of you down with me."

Now Daphne laughed too. Apparently Phil had a point. *This isn't nearly as bad as I'd feared.*

They were about two-thirds of the way to the top when KC, who was directly in front of Daphne and had been uncharacteristically quiet the entire climb, stopped moving.

"Did you drop something?" Daphne said.

KC didn't respond.

Daphne gently reached for KC's lower back. "Hey, are you okay?"

"I can't do it," KC whispered.

Daphne climbed up next to her and saw that KC's face was ashen. She was shaking.

"KC, honey, what's wrong?" Daphne asked.

KC shook her head. "I can't . . . move."

Daphne was puzzled. "Are you scared?" KC was never scared.

Slowly the shake turned into a nod, and KC shut her eyes tight. "I've never been up this high. I think I'm going to pass out."

"Is everything okay up there?" Derek was now just two steps behind them.

Daphne nodded. "Yes, we're fine." She put her hand on KC's head and smoothed her hair, then lowered her voice. "You're a strong woman, and you're going to do this, okay? We're going to do this together."

KC's speech was stuttered, her breath short. "I've . . . never . . . felt . . . anything . . . like . . . this." She briefly opened her eyes, then squeezed them shut again.

Daphne kept the tone of her voice soft. "I'm not going anywhere, okay? You're fine. We're almost to the top. You just need to take a deep breath, hold on to the railing, and move one foot, then the other. Can you do that for me?"

KC shook her head. "I can't move."

Daphne put a hand on KC's shoulder. "KC, listen to me. You can do this. You *know* you can do this. Just open your eyes for me, okay?"

Slowly, very slowly, KC opened her eyes. She looked terrified.

Daphne squeezed KC's shoulder. "Good, good. Now keep your gaze on the step directly in front of you. You don't need to look anywhere else. Can you do that?"

KC nodded and stared at the step in front of her.

Daphne spoke calmly. "Good, good. Now just move one foot to the next step. Just like this, okay? There's plenty of room for both of us on this step, so just do as I do."

Daphne took a step up, and KC slowly followed.

"That's perfect. Now do the same with the other foot, can you do that?"

"I'm so embarrassed," KC whispered.

"Don't be. You're doing great. Just keep moving like this, okay?" Daphne took another step up the cliff, then waited for KC to do the same. Derek and Phil followed behind in a respectful silence. Everyone knew this was no time for heckling. After several minutes Daphne glanced up to the top of the rock formation and saw Skylar peering down at them from the observation deck.

Her voice still gentle and relaxed, Daphne coaxed KC to the top. "That's it, that's it . . . See KC? You're doing great . . . We're almost there . . . Just keep your eyes in front of you . . . That's it, keep going . . . just a few more steps. See? You did it!"

Daphne took a final step to the fenced-in platform at the top of the steps, then reached for KC's hand and pulled her up alongside her. KC immediately wrapped her in a hug and squeezed her tight.

"Thank you, Daphne," she said. "Thank you so much."

Daphne stroked her friend's ponytail. "Oh honey, you don't have to thank me."

Skylar approached them as they finished their embrace, her hands on her hips. "You okay there, babe?"

KC nodded and pressed a palm against her forehead. "I am now. I had no idea I was so afraid of heights. I think that was the most scared I've been in my entire life."

"Looks like Superwoman found her kryptonite," Skylar said.

KC smiled weakly. "I guess I did."

"Look on the bright side: if you can do that, you can *definitely* be a grandmother," Skylar said. "Am I right?"

KC laughed, the tension visibly disappearing from her face. "I think you're probably right."

Skylar pointed to the suspension bridge leading to the second rock formation. "You ready for that, or you want to stop here? It's totally up to you."

KC looked at Daphne. "Will you help me get across?"

Daphne put an arm around her. "It would be my pleasure. How about we take a little break first?"

KC smiled. "Sounds good; thanks, Daphne."

Skylar, KC, and Phil wandered to the other side of the platform to take some photos before crossing the bridge. Daphne sat down on a bench and reached into her tote bag for a bottle of water. After a moment Derek walked over and sat down next to her.

"This is quite a view," he said, turning his head in a panoramic sweep.

She sipped her water. "Isn't it? I can't believe I'm up here right now, to be honest."

"Why not?"

She laughed. "Because I'm terrified of heights."

"Is that a joke I'm not getting?" He looked perplexed.

She smiled and shook her head. "Not joking. *Terrified.*"

"Well, you sure fooled me. You didn't look afraid of anything back there. You were really great with your friend. She was having a rough time of it."

Daphne took another sip of water. "I guess my motherly instinct kicked in. It has a tendency to do that."

"Then you're clearly a very good mother, despite your marital status. I heard from a wise woman once that being divorced and being a good parent aren't mutually exclusive."

She laughed, then looked him in the eye. "Thank you. I'm not sure what grade my daughter would give me, but I think I'm doing a decent job." *A fine job, actually.*

"I have a feeling she knows she's got it pretty good. We'll see if my boys figure that out about me at some point."

Daphne glanced in the direction of her friends, then back at Derek. "Skylar likes to say that despite their parents' best efforts to shape them, kids pretty much come with their bags packed. But she doesn't have kids of her own. Do you agree with that theory? Sometimes I wonder about the whole nature/nurture thing."

Derek pointed to the sky. "When my boys are *angels*, I like to believe it's due to nurture." Then he pointed downward. "But when they're *devils*, I cast the blame squarely on nature."

Daphne held up her water bottle. "Cheers to that strategy."

A soft wind began to blow, and she pushed a loose strand of hair behind her ears. "My ex is getting remarried soon," she said softly.

Derek hesitated a moment before responding. "Did he . . . leave you for her?"

Daphne shook her head. "Thankfully, no. Is that what happened to you?"

He nodded slowly. "I never even saw it coming, but the more I think about it, the more I realize that was part of the problem, if that makes any sense."

She leaned over and gave him a friendly nudge with her shoulder. "Believe me, I understand more than you can possibly imagine. I know I sound like a broken record, but things will get better for you. And for your boys too."

"You really think so?"

"I know so. Of course it hurts, but at some point you just have to let go of it. If I've learned anything about getting divorced, it's that it has defined me for too long because I've let it define me for too long. Feeling like a failure, feeling like I should have done things differently, feeling like it's my fault that life didn't turn out the way I thought it would—buying into the idea that being divorced is like having a disease. But I've finally begun to realize that none of that is true, and the only thing obsessing about it has done is keep me mired in the past—and miserable. So if I have any advice to offer to you or anyone else whose marriage has ended, for whatever reason, it's to learn from my mistake and have a shorter mourning period so that you can move on with your life."

"I think that's easier said than done."

She pushed another strand of hair out of her eyes. "Maybe, but it's worth thinking about. And being on this magical island will certainly help, it's nourishing for the soul. When did you get here?"

"Late last night. This is the first thing we've seen."

She smiled and looked up at the sky. "Give it a few days. And wait for the rain."

·   ·   ·

"I never thought I'd hear the following words come out of my mouth, but I need a stiff drink," KC said once they were safely back at the bottom of the cliff.

Skylar laughed and gestured to the dusty parking lot. "I can help with that. Ladies, shall we proceed to the car?"

"Another phrase I never expected to say to *you*, but yes, please drive me away now," KC said.

KC and Skylar bade good-bye to Derek and Phil, then made their way across the lot, arm in arm. Daphne hung back for a minute.

"Thanks again for your insight on the whole divorce thing," Derek said to Daphne as Phil went to retrieve their rental car. "You've really helped me see my situation from a different perspective."

Daphne adjusted her bag over her shoulder. "Oh gosh, it was my pleasure. Not that I've got it all figured out by any stretch of the imagination, but I'm definitely in a much better place than I used to be, so if my experience can help others in the least, I'm all for it."

"Well, as one of the *others*, I appreciate your wisdom. Maybe you should start an actual club for divorced parents, although it might be hard for me to make many meetings, given that I live in Chicago."

She laughed. "Now that's an idea. It might be the blind leading the blind, but at least we'd all be jumping off the cliff together, right? But maybe you're onto something. In college I had all these grandiose plans of being a journalist that never materialized, so maybe I could write a blog for divorcées? The first post would, of course, be about the magical healing properties of St. Mirika." *As well as the magical healing properties of a good old-fashioned fling.*

She was joking, but then a thought struck her. *Maybe I shouldn't be joking?*

He pointed to himself. "I'd subscribe to that blog in a heartbeat, so if you get something together, let me know."

"Will do." She glanced again at the parking lot. Skylar and KC were in the idling car.

It was time to say good-bye, and they both knew it.

Instead, Derek changed the subject.

"Where are you staying?" he asked. He stood just a hair closer to Daphne than was necessary. Something was different now.

"In a beach house on the other side of the island. What about you?"

"We're at the Four Seasons."

She felt her eyes brighten. "We went there yesterday for spa treatments! It's beautiful. Nothing like a massage to melt away the tension." She maintained eye contact as she spoke. *This man is attracted to me. And I'm going to enjoy it.*

Derek swallowed. "So, are there any other things you suggest Phil and I do while we're here?"

She patted her stomach. "Be sure to check out Bananarama on the beach if you like smoothies. Delicious."

"Bananarama. Like the band?"

She nodded. "I just adored them back in the day. Oh and speaking of music, you might want to check out the Castaway if you like to dance. The crowd skews a little young, but it's fun nonetheless, at least for a night." *Yes, I'm forty and I'm not afraid to go out dancing. Just not every night.*

She glanced again in the direction of the car, and Derek cleared his throat. "Do you have plans tonight? I'd love to buy you a drink, if you're up for it, that is," he said. He was clearly flustered, which she found endearing.

She smiled at him. "It makes perfect sense. And I'd love to, but we leave tomorrow, so I think we're going to make it a girls' night."

He reached for his wallet and pulled out a business card, then handed it to her. "Does life ever bring you to Chicago?"

She studied the card, then slipped it into her tote bag. "A week ago I would have said no to that question."

He chuckled. "Is that a yes then?"

She gave him a quick kiss on the cheek, then turned to go. "To be perfectly honest, I'm not sure what it is, but I'm looking forward to finding out."

Chapter Fourteen

"Well aren't *you* the picture of rest and relaxation. You look absolutely revitalized!" Carol greeted Daphne with a smile at the curb outside baggage claim. She moved her enormous umbrella to one side and gave Daphne a quick hug before reaching for her suitcase. "Can you believe this downpour? It's been coming down in buckets nonstop for days!"

"It rained in St. Mirika too, but only in little bursts," Daphne said, already missing the feel of the warm drops on her skin.

Once they were safely buckled inside the SUV, Carol pulled away from the curb, then glanced at Daphne. "Looks like you got a little color on that fair complexion of yours, it suits you. So, how did it go? Was it everything you hoped it would be?"

Daphne sighed and leaned back into the leather seat. "I don't even know how to answer that question."

Carol laughed. "I hope that's a good thing."

Daphne smiled. "It is. I missed Emma, of course, but it was so nice to get away. I had no idea how much I needed that."

"Let me guess. Being with your old pals brought out another side of you?"

Daphne nodded. "I hadn't realized how much I'd changed until I was with people who reminded me of what I was like *before* I got married. I used to be afraid to even think about peeling those layers back, but now that I've started to do it, I'm finally beginning to feel like my old self again, and it feels good."

Carol reached over and gave Daphne's knee a squeeze. "Sounds like you watered those plants with some of that island rain."

Daphne stared ahead for a moment, her eyes picturing the first downpour she experienced on St. Mirika, before remembering what Carol had said just a few days earlier—although it seemed like much longer than that. "I guess I did. We promised to get together at least once a year, even if it's just for a weekend. We already decided that our next trip is going to be to Vegas."

"Good for you." Carol held the steering wheel with one hand and increased the speed of the windshield wipers. "Holy moly, it is *really* coming down today."

Daphne turned her head to the right and gazed out into the storm. Then she smiled. *I used to hate the rain.*

. . .

"Still up for Jeni's?" Carol asked as she pulled to a stop in front of Daphne's house. "I'd still love to treat you to a belated birthday scoop, despite this awful weather."

"It's not *so* bad. Emma's not due home for a few hours, so let me unpack and take care of a few things, and then I'll come over. Would that work?" She opened the door and stepped onto the wet sidewalk.

Carol shifted the gear into park and held up her palms. "I'm all yours."

"Great. See you soon." Daphne was just about to shut the passenger-side door when a thought occurred to her. She turned and poked her head back inside the car. "Hey, Carol? Where's a place to get a good smoothie around here?"

"A smoothie? I have no idea."

Daphne pursed her lips. "That's what I thought. Okay, see you in a bit." She shut the door and hurried up the manicured walkway into the house. The rain was coming down even harder now, and she was already feeling the chilly air creep underneath her coat. Once inside she turned on the lights and rolled her suitcase into the foyer. The house was quiet and still and clean, but it didn't feel so empty anymore. She glanced around and saw it the way Skylar and KC would. Tastefully decorated. Charming. Welcoming and warm.

Daphne hadn't thought of her house that way in a long time, but she was seeing it with different eyes now. It wasn't just a house. It was a home. It was *her* home. And Emma's. *My life isn't empty.*

She stood there for a few moments, the memories of her time on St. Mirika floating around in her head; then she turned and walked into the kitchen to get some water. She reached into the cabinet and pulled down a glass, the clatter of the rain against the windowsill nearly drowning out the sound of the faucet. She took a long sip, then set the glass on the counter and reached into the drying rack for her favorite pink mug. She held it for a moment, then kissed it and gently placed it back inside the cupboard. Then she turned and looked at the refrigerator, scanning Emma's activity schedule.

This weekend was a volleyball tournament. Brian and Alyssa would most likely be there.

Daphne braced herself, expecting to feel a pang somewhere deep inside at the thought of seeing them together. But it didn't happen. She felt no pang. No heartache. No regret. Instead, she felt calm . . . hopeful . . . free. She closed her eyes and sighed. *I'm free.*

She'd finally stopped focusing on the past. She was only just beginning to figure out the future, but that was okay with her. It was more than okay.

She finished the water and set the empty glass in the sink, then reached into her tote bag and pulled out the business card Clay had set on her dresser yesterday morning before dashing out the door to pack. She flipped it over and smiled at the note he'd scrawled on the back: *My door's always open for you, Daphne White. For Fred too.*

She skipped into her bedroom, gave the card a quick kiss, then carefully tucked it into the top drawer of her dresser. She gently closed the drawer, then left her bedroom and strolled into the kitchen. She knew she'd probably never see Clay again, but that didn't matter. It didn't matter at all.

When she reached the refrigerator, she pulled out another business card from her bag, this one from Derek Donovan, strategic consultant, in Chicago. She smiled at the name for a moment, then slid Emma's schedule a few inches to one side before securing the card with a magnet. She probably wouldn't see Derek again either, but then again, maybe she would. *Maybe I will.*

Her future was wide open, and it was all up to her. She smiled. It was time to get ice cream with Carol and celebrate.

She wouldn't be ordering vanilla.

Acknowledgments

People often ask me if I have the plot figured out before I begin writing a novel. It's a great question, but one to which I don't have a stock answer. The truth is, sometimes I do, and sometimes I don't. Actually, that's not quite accurate. I've never had an *entire* plot figured out ahead of time, but for some of my books I wrote from a general outline without straying too far outside the lines, and with others I began with a vision of the first and last scenes, then figured out the rest as I went. When I started writing *Wait for the Rain*, however, I didn't have an outline. I didn't have a beginning. Or an end. I didn't have anything! All I had was the general idea of three friends reuniting to celebrate a milestone birthday. How that evolved into *Wait for the Rain*, I'm still not sure, but now that I think about it, maybe that's the whole point of the story.

For this book I had the pleasure of working with Danielle Marshall and Charlotte Herscher for the first time, and it was indeed a pleasure. I once read somewhere that editors are part business manager/part therapist, and as the KC character would say, "I'm not gonna lie"—it's pretty true. Ladies, thank you both for your insight, guidance, patience, and passion! I also would like to thank my longtime editor Christina Henry de Tessan, whom I simply adore. I hope you know how much you've helped me grow as a writer.

My high school pal Tami May McMillan gets yet another shout-out for her support and input throughout the entire gestation of this book, as does my mommy dearest, the master proofreader. I'm lucky you two haven't figured out that I should be paying you for all your help . . .

I'd also like to acknowledge a handful of friends who unwittingly contributed to this story just by being themselves. When readers tell me they enjoy how realistic my books are, I always say it's because I like to include funny or interesting things the people in my own life say and do. This time around I have the following to thank for the inspiration/material: Debbie Bolzan, Kat and Mike Burn, Kristi Candau, Amy Clarfeld Lavin, Chris Conroy (who also took the headshot on my bio page—thanks, Conroy!), Deb Custodio, Lynette Ecklund, Annie Flaig, Natalie Gonzalez, Siobhan Jones, Lea (Eaglette) Knop, Anna Krause, Jen Livingstone, Peggy (Turtle!) Prendergast, Lea Redmond, Jen Moscow Rittmaster, Carrie Jean Schmidt, Brett Sharkey, Michele Murnane Sharkey, Trudi Sharpsteen, Gene Sky, Jamie Strait, Steve Summer, Hilary Teper, and Ithti Toy Ulit. If any of you read this book and your contribution doesn't jump out at you, let me know, and I'll refresh your memory. I bet some of you don't even realize how witty you are, but I certainly do.

And to the team at Lake Union Publishing: In addition to Danielle Marshall, it's been a joy working with Terry Goodman, Thom Kephart, Jessica Poore, Susan Stockman, and Gabriella (Gabe) Van den Heuvel. Writing can be a lonely profession sometimes, so thanks for making me feel like part of the gang!

About the Author

A former PR executive who abandoned a successful career to pursue a more fulfilling life, Maria Murnane is the bestselling author of *Cassidy Lane, Katwalk, Perfect on Paper, It's a Waverly Life, Honey on Your Mind,* and *Chocolate for Two,* which garnered a starred review in *Publishers Weekly.* Originally from California, she now lives in Brooklyn. Learn more at www.mariamurnane.com.